ENGLISH GRAMMAR

This new edition of Downing and Locke's award-winning text-book has been thoroughly revised and rewritten by Angela Downing to offer an integrated account of structure, meaning and function in relation to context. Also used as a reference book, it provides the linguistic basis for courses and projects on translation, contrastive linguistics, stylistics, reading and discourse studies. It is accessible and reader-friendly throughout.

Key features include:

- Chapters divided into modules of class-length materials
- Each new concept clearly explained and highlighted
- Authentic texts from a wide range of sources, both spoken and written, to illustrate grammatical usage
- Clear chapter and module summaries enabling efficient class preparation and student revision
- Exercises and topics for individual study
- Answer key for analytical exercises
- Comprehensive index
- Select bibliography
- Suggestions for further reading

This up-to-date, descriptive grammar is a complete course for first degree and post-graduate students of English, and is particularly suitable for those whose native language is not English.

Angela Downing is Professor Emeritus in the Department of English Language and Linguistics (English Philology I) at the Universidad Complutense, Madrid.

The late **Philip Locke** taught at the Institute of Modern Languages and Translation at the Universidad Complutense, Madrid.

ENGLISH GRAMMAR

A University Course
Second edition

Angela Downing and Philip Locke

Routledge
Taylor & Francis Group

LONDON AND NEW YORK

First published 1992
by Prentice Hall International (UK) Ltd

Routledge edition published 2002 by Routledge

This second edition published 2006
by Routledge
2 Park Square, Milton Park, Abingdon, Oxon OX14 4RN

Simultaneously published in the USA and Canada
by Routledge
270 Madison Ave, New York, NY 10016

Routledge is an imprint of the Taylor & Francis Group

© 2006 Angela Downing and Philip Locke

Designed and typeset in Amasis and Futura
by Keystroke, Jacaranda Lodge, Wolverhampton
Printed and bound in Great Britain
by TJ International Ltd, Padstow, Cornwall

British Library Cataloguing in Publication Data
A catalogue record for this book is available from the British Library

Library of Congress Cataloging in Publication Data
A catalog record for this book has been requested

ISBN10: 0–415–28787–1   ISBN13: 9–78–0–415–28787–6 (pbk)
ISBN10: 0–415–28786–3   ISBN13: 9–78–0–415–28786–9 (hbk)

This book is for:

Enrique

and to the memory of Philip Locke

CONTENTS

FOREWORD

It is now 13 years since the publication of Angela Downing and Philip Locke's *A University Course in English Grammar*, which broke new ground by offering to advanced students of English a comprehensive course, based on Halliday's Systemic Functional Grammar. It went beyond the merely structural, to present an integrated account of structure and function, which gives students the information they need in order to link the grammar of English to the overall structure of discourse and to the contexts in which it is produced.

Ever since its publication, the book has been used in many countries in South America, the Middle East and Europe, including of course Spain, to whose tertiary education systems both authors devoted the majority of their working lives. Downing and Locke's grammar, while clearly rooted in Hallidayan linguistics, also responds to a number of other influences, including the grammars of Quirk and his colleagues. However, it also made its own important contribution to our knowledge and understanding of many points of English grammar, and has been widely cited by scholars working within functional linguistics.

Sadly, Philip Locke died in 2003, but he would, I am sure, have been very proud of this new edition of the work, which still bears his name and has been retitled as *English Grammar: A University Course*. The new version of the grammar embodies three themes evident in Angela Downing's research work over the last decade or so, themes which reflect the directions in which functional linguistics has moved in the late twentieth century and the beginning of the twenty-first.

First, the linking of grammar to the structure and functioning of discourse, already evident in the first edition, has been taken still further, giving students an even better grasp of aspects of text production in which even advanced foreign learners of English are often rather weak.

Second, the account of English grammar offers benefits from the recognition that discourse is not a static product, but a constantly changing, negotiated process: as interaction proceeds, interlocutors build up and modify mental representations of their addresses, the context and the discourse itself. This perspective on language leads to the integration, within this new version of the grammar, of ideas from cognitive linguistics.

Finally, although the first edition of the grammar drew on a wide range of sources to show language in use, the new edition makes considerable use of examples from the large corpora now available for searching by computer (notably the 100-million-word British National Corpus), as well as other textual materials collected by Angela Downing.

The result is that the grammar is attractively illustrated by authentic text samples from many registers of English, ranging from very informal conversation through to more formal productions.

This new version of the Downing and Locke grammar will serve not only as a course book for new generations of advanced students of English, but also as a reference source for students, teachers and researchers looking for a detailed treatment of English grammar which integrates structural, functional and cognitive perspectives into a coherent and satisfying whole.

Christopher Butler
Honorary Professor
University of Wales Swansea

PREFACE TO THE SECOND EDITION

The structure of this book remains essentially the same as that of the first edition. The most obvious difference is the collapsing of chapters 11 and 12 into one (adjectival and adverbial groups), leaving 12 (prepositions and the prepositional phrase) as the final chapter. Following the welcome feedback from reviewers and consultants, there has also been some rearrangement of the material: in particular, the section on negation has been brought forward to Chapter 1, and the syntax of prepositional and phrasal verbs is made more explicit in Chapter 2. Chapter 5 has also been rearranged, in order to clarify the correspondences between clause types and their speech act functions.

Some of the modules have been considerably rewritten, in order to accomodate the description of certain elements that had not been dealt with. Still others were partly rewritten in order to incorporate certain insights and research findings published since 1990 or, if earlier, not included in the first edition. The motion event analysis in Chapter 8 is one of these, and the semantics of prepositions in Chapter 12 is another. A few analytical changes have been made, notably the re-analysis of those features that were grouped together under the function labelled 'predicator complement'. This re-analysis has been made possible by a clearer specification of the criteria adopted for the classification of clause constituents.

A considerable number of new textual illustrations have been incorporated, replacing some of the previous ones. Also introduced are sections on further reading and a select bibliography.

Our debts to our predecessors in writing this second revised edition are clearly now more numerous and greater than before. In addition to the wealth of information and accurate detail of the various grammars by Randolph Quirk, Sydney Greenbaum, Geoffrey Leech and Jan Svartvik, we now have the new dimensions provided by the *Longman Grammar of Spoken and Written English* (Douglas Biber, Stig Johansson, Geoffrey Leech, Susan Conrad and Edward Finegan) and the *Cambridge Grammar of the English Language* (Rodney Huddleston and Geoffrey K. Pullum, together with their collaborators). Their inspiration will be evident in many of the chapters in this book. The insights of Michael Halliday were influential in the first edition and they are still present, but once again with certain modifications that Halliday may not agree with, modifications made in order to suit the rather different learning objectives of many of our readers. Unfortunately, the third edition of *An Introduction to Functional Grammar* became available only after the relevant chapters of this book had been completed.

Reference to individual publications cannot be made in this paragraph, but all works consulted are reflected in the select bibliography and many in the sections on further reading.

Among the many consultants, friends and colleagues who have made helpful comments on the previous edition, I would especially like to thank Andrei Stoevsky (University of Sofia), who made detailed comments on every chapter, and Chris Butler (University of Wales Swansea) who has given invaluable assistance and advice through two editions of this book. Also much appreciated were the many useful comments made by Mike Hannay and Lachlan Mackenzie (Free University, Amsterdam), Ana Hansen (Universidad Nacional de Cuyo, Mendoza), Mohsen Ghadessy (University of Brunei), Martin Wynne (University of Oxford), Belinda Maia (University of Oporto), Marta Carretero and Elena Martínez Caro (Universidad Complutense, Madrid), Amaya Mendikoetxea, Rachel Whittaker and Laura Hidalgo (Universidad Autónoma, Madrid) and Carmina Gregori (University of Valencia). I remember with gratitude Emilio Lorenzo Criado, of the Real Academia Española, who encouraged us to start in the first place. I am indebted to Bruce Fraser (University of Boston) for some excellent suggestions on the presentation of the materials, and to Geoff Thompson (University of Liverpool) for the best real-life spontaneous utterance of multiple left-detachment. The responsibility for any failings in the text lies with the authors, but any improvement and credit there may be I gratefully share with them.

I am grateful to Lou Burnard for permission to use examples from the British National Corpus and to Antonio Moreno Ortiz for the use of the BNC Indexer; also to Miguel Treviño and Enrique Hidalgo for preparing the diagrams. I also want to thank my students and the many tutors and students who have contacted me by e-mail from Saudi Arabia, Iraq, China and other places to request information, to ask questions or make comments on particular points of grammar. Thanks also to Jean Smears for allowing a personal letter of hers to be published as an illustrative text, and to John Hollyman for spontaneous conversations recorded with some of his students at the University of Bristol.

I especially wish to thank Louisa Semlyen of Routledge for her unfailing patience, support and confidence in me throughout this revision. I am grateful to our publisher, Routledge, for technical and expert assistance. My thanks go to Katherine Davey, Production Editor at Routledge, Maggie Lindsey-Jones of Keystroke and Ruth Jeavons for taking care of the book's progress up to publication; also to Ben Hulme-Cross of Routledge for his work on the design of the text. Thanks are due to Isobel Fletcher de Téllez for reading through the whole of the manuscript of the second edition and making some useful suggestions. To Gerard M-F Hill I want to express my thanks for his patience and my appreciation of his energy, thoroughness and good judgement as copy-editor and indexer in preparing the script for publication.

Finally, I wish to thank my daughters Laura, Alicia and Raquel, my twin sons Enrique and Eduardo, and my grandchildren Natalia, Daniel, Jorge, Martina and Pablo, for the joy and fun they bring to everything. Without their presence the writing of this second edition would have taken place in a very different setting.

I am writing now in my own name for, sadly, Philip Locke was not able to accompany me on the venture of this second edition. To him I dedicate this edition and to my husband Enrique Hidalgo, without whose support, resilience and belief in mountains as therapy this second edition would not have been completed.

Angela Downing
Madrid, July 2005

ACKNOWLEDGEMENTS

All the material in this book appears with the permission of those who hold the copyright. The authors and publishers thank the following for their permission to reproduce extracts of the copyright material:

Smart Publications (www.smart-publications.com) for 'Health and Wellness Update'; Dennis Publishing Ltd for the following publications from *The Week*: 'In Rushdie's Shadow', 9 July 2003; 'How to Survive a Columbian Kidnapping' and 'What the Scientists are Saying ... Fire Threat to Apes', both 8 March 2003; 'The Week' by Jeremy O'Grady, 8 November 2003; 'A Robot for Granny', 27 December 2003; 'The Archers: What Happened Last Week', 22 March 2003; 'A Purple Polar Bear ...', 26 July 2003; 'The "Lost" Van Gogh', 22 November, 2003; 'The Main Stories ... It Wasn't All Bad', 31 January 2004; The Telegraph Group Ltd for 'Breaking and Entering: How British Burglars Pick Their Victims', appearing in *The Telegraph*, 2003; BBC Enterprises for *The Complete Yes Prime Minister*, edited by Jonathan Lynn and Antony Jay; Blackwell Ltd for 'Oxford Today', volume 1, number 3, pp. 37 and 58 appearing in *Oxford Today* and reprinted with permission of the Chancellor and Scholars of Oxford University; The Bodley Head for *Don't Fall Off The Mountain*, Shirley Maclaine and *Zen and the Art of Motorcycle Maintenance*, Robert Pirsig; Cambridge University Press for *The Universe Around Us*, James Jeans; Casarotto Company Ltd for extracts from J. G. Ballard; Chatto and Windus for *Just Between Ourselves*, Alan Ayckbourn; Curtis Brown London Ltd for permission to reproduce *Doctor on the Boil*, Copyright Richard Gordon 1973; David Higham Associates for *Akenfield*, Ronald Blythe, and *The Spy Who Came In From The Cold*, John le Carré; Hamish Hamilton Ltd for *The New Confessions*, William Boyd; Hamish Hamilton Ltd and Houghton Mifflin Company for *The Long Goodbye*, Raymond Chandler; Harcourt Brace Jovanovich Ltd for *North to the Orient*, Copyright 1935 and renewed 1963 by Anne Morrow Lindbergh; Harper Collins Publishers for *Beat Jet Lag*, Kathleen Mayes; Harrap Publishing Group Ltd for *The Boundaries of Science*, Magnus Pike; Hogarth Press and Random Century Group for *Mrs Dalloway*, Virginia Woolf; Laurence Pollinger Ltd and the Estate of Frieda Lawrence Ravagli for *The Lost Girl*, D. H. Lawrence; Longman Group UK for *Advanced Conversational English*, Crystal and Davy, and *Metals and Alloys*, H. Moore; The MacDonald Group for Futura Publications' *Lightning in May*, Gordon Parker; Martin Secker & Warburg Ltd and Octopus Publishing Group Library for *The British Museum is Falling Down* and *How Far Can You Go*, David Lodge, and *The Wedding Jug from Twenty Stories*, Philip Smith; Methuen and Octopus Publishing Group Library for *Find Me* in *Plays by Women: Volume 2*, Olwyn Wymark; Oxford University Press for *Varieties of Spoken English*, Dickinson and Mackin; Peters Fraser & Dunlop for *Brideshead Revisited*, Evelyn Waugh; Penguin Books for *Artists Talking: Five artists talk to Anthony Schooling*, in the Success with English: Outlook series ed. G. Broughton. *Billy Phelan's Greatest Game*, Copyright 1975 by William Kennedy, used by permission of Viking Penguin, a division of Penguin Books USA Inc.; Penguin Books and The British Museum Press for *The Innocent Anthropologist*, Nigel Barley; The Society of Authors on behalf of the Bernard Shaw Estate for *A Sunday on the Surrey Hills*, G. B. Shaw; Thames & Hudson Ltd for *Recollections and Reflections*, Bruno Bettelheim; Copyright 1990 The Time Inc. Magazine Company, reprinted by permission 'Education: doing bad and feeling good', Charles Krauthammer, 5 February 1990; Copyright 1986 Time Warner Inc., reprinted by permission, 'Turning brown, red and green', 15 December 1986; Victor Gollancz Ltd for *The Citadel*, A. J. Cronin; Virago Press for *Nothing Sacred*, Angela Carter; William Heinemann Ltd and David Higham Associates for *The Heart of the Matter*, Copyright 1948 Verdant SA, Graham Greene; William Heinemann Ltd and The Octopus Publishing Group Library for *The Godfather*, Mario Puzo; William Heinemann Ltd for *Making a New Science*, James Gleick.

Every effort has been made to trace and acknowledge ownership of copyright. The publishers will be glad to make suitable arrangements with any copyright holders whom it has not been possible to contact.

INTRODUCTION

AIMS OF THE COURSE

This book has been written primarily for undergraduate and graduate students of English as a foreign or second language. It is also addressed to tutors and others interested in applying a broadly functional approach to language teaching in higher education. It assumes an intermediate standard of knowledge and practical handling of the language and, from this point of departure, seeks to fulfil the following aims:

1   to further students' knowledge of English through exploration and analysis;
2   to help students acquire a global vision of English, rather than concentrate on unrelated areas;
3   to see a grammar as providing a means of understanding the relation of form to meaning, and meaning to function, in context;
4   to provide a basic terminology which, within this framework, will enable students to make these relationships explicit.

While not pretending to be exhaustive, which would be impossible, its wide coverage and functional approach have been found appropriate not only in first-degree courses but also in postgraduate courses and as a background resource for courses, publications and work on translation, stylistics, reading projects and discourse studies.

A FUNCTIONAL APPROACH TO GRAMMAR

We distinguish several ways in which grammar is functional. In the first place, adopting a broadly systemic-functional view, we base our approach on the assumption that all languages fulfil two higher-level or meta-functions in our lives. One is to express our interpretation of the world as we experience it (sometimes called the 'ideational' or the 'representational' function); the other is to interact with others in order to bring about changes in the environment (the 'interpersonal' function). The organisation of the message in such a way as to enable representation and interaction to cohere represents a third (the 'textual' meta-function), and this, too, is given its place in a functional grammar.

In the second place, the regular patterns of different kinds that can be distinguished reflect the uses which a language serves. For instance, the structural patterns known as 'declarative', 'interrogative' and 'imperative' serve the purposes of expressing a multitude of types of social behaviour. In this area we draw on the pragmatic concepts of speech act, politeness, relevance and inference to explain how speakers use and interpret linguistic forms and sequences in English within cultural settings.

When we come to describe the more detailed mechanisms of English, we also make use of the notion of 'function' to describe syntactic categories such as Subjects and Objects, semantic roles such as Agent and informational categories such as Theme and Rheme, Given and New. These different types of function constitute autonomous dimensions of analysis, so that there is no one-to-one relationship between them. Rather, we shall find that they can conflate together in different ways, the choice of one or other being largely determined by such factors as context, both situational and linguistic, particularly what has gone before in the message, by the speaker–hearer relationship and by speakers' communicative purposes.

Third, this type of grammar is functional in that each linguistic element is seen not in isolation but in relation to others, since it has potential to realise different functions. Structural patterns are seen as configurations of functions, whether of participants and processes, of modifiers and head of, for instance, a noun, or of Subject, verb and Complements, among others. These in turn are realised in a variety of ways according to the communicative effect desired. Speakers and writers are free, within the resources a particular language displays, to choose those patterns which best carry out their communicative purposes at every stage of their interaction with other speakers and readers.

With these considerations in mind, the present book has been designed to place meaning firmly within the grammar and, by stressing the meaningful functions of grammatical forms and structures, to offer a description of the grammatical phenomena of English in use, both in speech and writing. This book, we hope, may serve as a foundation for further study in specific areas or as a resource for the designing of other materials for specific purposes.

PRESENTATION OF CONTENT

The grammatical content of the course is presented in three blocks:

- a first chapter giving a bird's-eye view of the whole course and defining the basic concepts and terms used in it;
- seven chapters describing clausal and sentence patterns, together with their corresponding elements of structure, from syntactic, semantic, textual and communicative-pragmatic points of view; and
- five chapters dealing similarly with nominal, verbal, adjectival, adverbial and prepositional groups and phrases.

In each case the aim is that of describing each pattern or structural element in use, rather than that of entering in depth into any particular theory. Chapter titles attempt to reflect, as far as possible, the communicative viewpoints from which the description is made.

The chapters are divided into 'modules' (sixty in all), each one being conceived as a teaching and learning unit with appropriate exercises and activities grouped at the end of each chapter.

Each module begins with a summary, which presents the main matters of interest. It is designed to assist both tutor and students in class preparation and to offer a review for study purposes.

Exemplification

Many of the one-line examples which illustrate each grammatical point have been drawn or derived from actual utterances observed by the authors. Some of these have been shortened or simplified in order to illustrate a grammatical point with maximum clarity. A further selection of examples is taken from the British National Corpus and other acknowledged sources. These have not been modified.

In addition we have made regular use of short excerpts of connected speech and writing from a wide variety of authentic sources. Our intention here is to illustrate the natural use of the features being described.

Exercises and activities

Each of the sixty modules which make up the course is accompanied by a varying number of practice exercises and activities. Some involve the observation and identification of syntactic elements and their semantic functions, or of the relations between them; others call for the manipulation or completion of sentences in various meaningful ways; grammatical topics are sometimes proposed for discussion between pairs or groups of students; mini-projects are suggested for individual research by students based on their own reading, experiences and materials gathered outside the class; topics are proposed for the writing of original letters, short articles, narratives, descriptions and dialogues for social purposes.

Some exercises involve the interpretation of meanings and intentions which are to be inferred from the use of particular forms and structures within certain contexts. The different areas of grammar lend themselves to a wide variety of practical linguistic activities limited only by the time factor. Those proposed here can be selected, adapted, amplified or omitted, according to need.

Answers are provided at the end of the book for those analytical exercises which have a single solution. There are many activities, however, that have no solution of this kind, such as discussions and explanations of grammatical topics. Activities involving the interpretation of meanings or those whose solution is variable are either not keyed at all or are accompanied by a suggested solution, since it is felt that they are more appropriately left to classroom discussion.

It is the opinion of the authors that university study should not attend solely to the attainment of certain practical end-results. Its value lies to a great extent in the thinking that goes on in the process of ensuring the results, not only in the results themselves. It is rather in the performance of a task that the learning takes place. The premature reference to a key negates the whole purpose of the tasks and should be resisted at all costs.

SUGGESTIONS FOR USING THE BOOK

First of all, it must be pointed out that the chapters which comprise this book can be used selectively, either singly or in blocks. In starting with the clause, our aim has been to provide a global frame, both syntactic and semantic, into which the lower-ranking units of nominal, verbal and other groups naturally fit, as can be seen in Chapter 2. It is perfectly possible, however, to reverse this order, starting with the verbal or nominal groups and using the subsequent chapters as a course on grammar 'below the clause', if this is found more convenient. Morphological information is provided in each of these chapters.

Similarly, chapters 2 and 3 together provide an introduction to functional syntax, while chapters 5 and 7 address basic semantic roles, and tense, aspect and modality, respectively. Other chapters, such as 10, 11 and 12, contain extensive sections on the semantics of the unit under discussion. Chapter 4 deals with the clause as a vehicle for interaction through language, and 6 with the grammatical resources used in information packaging. Related areas and topics are 'signposted' by cross-references.

When this book is used as a basis for classroom teaching of English language at universities, it may be treated as a resource book by approaching it in the following way:

- First, *either:* by presenting the 'Summary' outlined at the beginning of each module and amplifying it according to the time allotted, with reference to appropriate parts of the module; *or:* by taking an illustrative text as a starting-point, and drawing out the meanings, forms and functions dealt with in the module.
- Then, the complete module can be read by the students out of class and any suggested exercises prepared. Some may be assigned to different students and discussed collectively. Others may more usefully be prepared by all members of the class. Alternatively, for assessment purposes, students may be allowed to build up a dossier of exercises of their own choice. Certain exercises can be done collectively and orally in class, without previous preparation. Students should be encouraged to bring in selections of their own texts, whether self-authored or collected from specific genres, for presentation and discussion within a group.
- A further session may be devoted to clarification of points raised as a result of students' reading and of carrying out the exercises.

Whether the book is studied with or without guidance, access to the grammatical terms and topics treated in it is facilitated in four ways:

1 by the initial list of chapter and module headings;
2 by the section and subsection headings listed at the beginning of each chapter;
3 by the alphabetical list of items, terms and topics given in the general Index at the end of the book.
4 by the abundant cross-references which facilitate the linking of one area to another. Reference is made to the number and section of the module in which an item is explained.

TABLE OF NOTATIONAL SYMBOLS

CLASSES OF UNITS

cl	clause
fin.cl	finite clause
non-fin.cl	non-finite clause
-ing cl	*-ing* participial clause
-en cl	past participial clause
inf. cl	infinitive clause
to-inf. cl	*to*-infinitive clause
wh-cl	*wh*-clause
NG	nominal group
AdjG	adjectival group
AdvG	adverbial group
PP	prepositional phrase
VG	verbal group
n	noun
pron	pronoun
adj	adjective
adv	adverb
conj	conjunction
prep	preposition
v	verb (as word class)
v-*ing*	present participle
v *to*-inf	*to*-infinitive
v-*en*	past participle

SYNTACTIC FUNCTIONS AND ELEMENTS OF STRUCTURE

S	subject
P	predicator
O	object
Od	direct object
Oi	indirect object
Op	prepositional object
Ob	oblique object
C	Complement
Cs	Complement of the subject
Co	Complement of the object
C_{loc}	Locative/ Goal Complement
A	adjunct
F	finite
h	head
m	modifier (pre- and post-modifier)
d	determiner
e	epithet
clas.	classifier
c	complement (of noun, adjective, adverb and preposition)
o	operator
x	auxiliary verb
v	lexical verb, main verb

SEMANTIC FUNCTIONS

Ag	Agent
Aff	Affected
Rec	Recipient
Ben	Beneficiary

UNIT BOUNDARIES

				complex sentence
			clause
		group

Tonicity

//	end of tone unit
/	rising tone
\	falling tone
∧	rising-falling tone
v	falling-rising tone
CAPITAL	letters are used to indicate the peak of information focus in the tone unit

Pauses from brief to long

.   – –– –––

OTHER SYMBOLS

*	unacceptable or ungrammatical form
(?)	doubtfully acceptable
( )	optional element
/	alternative form
+	coordination, addition
×	dependency
[ ]	embedded unit
†	keyed exercise
1, 2, etc.	superscript marking item in extract
BNC	British National Corpus
BrE	British English
AmE	American English
vs	versus

British National Corpus

Examples from the British National Corpus cite their source by a 3-letter code and sentence number. Most of the source texts are copyright and may not be cited or re-disseminated except as part of the Corpus. Full details of every source and the BNC project itself can be found on its website (http://www.natcorp.ox.ac.uk/), which is searchable.

BASIC CONCEPTS   CHAPTER 1

LANGUAGE AND MEANING   *MODULE 1*

A functional grammar aims to match forms to function and meaning in context. This module introduces the three strands of meaning that form the basis of a functional interpretation of grammar: the representational, the interpersonal and the textual.

Each of these strands is encoded in the clause (or simple sentence) as a type of structure. The three structures are mapped onto one another, illustrating how the three types of meaning combine in one linguistic expression.

1.1 COMMUNICATIVE ACTS

Let us start from the basic concept that language is for communication. Here is part of a recorded conversation taken from a sociological project of the University of Bristol. The speakers are Janice, a girl who runs a youth club and disco in an English town, and Chris, one of the boys in the club, who is 19 and works in a shop. In the dialogue, we can distinguish various types of communicative act, or **speech act**, by which people communicate with each other: making statements, asking questions, giving directives with the aim of getting the hearer to carry out some action, making an offer or promise, thanking or expressing an exclamation.

Offer	J:	If you like, I'll come into your shop tomorrow and get some more model aeroplane kits.
Reminder	C:	O.K. Don't forget to bring the bill with you this time.
Promise	J:	I won't.
Question		Do you enjoy working there?
Statements	C:	It's all right, I suppose. Gets a bit boring. It'll do for a while.
Statement	J:	I would have thought you were good at selling things.
Statement	C:	I don't know what to do really. I've had other jobs. My Dad keeps on at me to go into his business. He keeps offering me better wages,
Exclamation		but the last thing to do is to work for him!
Question	J:	Why?
Echo question	C:	Why? You don't know my old man! I
Exclamations		wouldn't work for him! He always
Statement		wanted me to, but we don't get on. . . .

Question		D'you think it's possible to get me on a part-time Youth Leadership Course?
Offer/Promise	J:	I'll ring up tomorrow, Chris, and find out for you.
Thanking	C:	Thanks a lot.

In a communicative exchange such as this, between two speakers, the kind of meaning encoded as questions, statements, offers, reminders and thanks is **interpersonal** meaning. Asking and stating are basic communicative acts. The thing asked for or stated may be something linguistic – such as information or an opinion (*Do you enjoy working there? It's all right, I suppose*) – or it may be something non-linguistic, some type of goods and services, such as handing over the aeroplane kits.

This non-linguistic exchange may be verbalised – by, for instance, *Here you are* – but it need not be. Typically, however, when goods and services are exchanged, verbal interaction takes place too; for instance, asking a favour (*Do you think it's possible to get me on a part-time Youth Leadership Course?*) or giving a promise (*I'll ring up tomorrow, Chris, and find out for you*) are carried out verbally.

The grammatical forms that encode two basic types of interpersonal communication are illustrated in section 1.3.2. The whole area is dealt with more fully in Chapter 5.

1.2 THE CONTENT OF COMMUNICATION

Every speech act, whether spoken or written, takes place in a social context. A telephone conversation, writing a letter, buying a newspaper, giving or attending a lecture, are all contexts within which the different speech acts are carried out. Such contexts have to do with our own or someone else's experience of life and the world at large, that is, the doings and happenings in which we are involved or which affect us.

Any happening or state in real life, or in an imaginary world of the mind, can be expressed through language as a **situation** or **state of affairs**. Used in this way, the terms 'situation' or 'state of affairs ' do not refer directly to an extra-linguistic reality that exists in the real world, but rather to the speaker's conceptualisation of it. The components of this conceptualisation of reality are **semantic roles** or **functions** and may be described in very general terms as follows:

1 **processes**: that is, actions, events, states, types of behaviour;
2 **participants**: that is, entities of all kinds, not only human, but inanimate, concrete and abstract, that are involved in the processes;
3 **attributes**: that is, qualities and characteristics of the participants;
4 **circumstances**: that is, any kind of contingent fact or subsidiary situation which is associated with the process or the main situation.

The following example from the text shows one possible configuration of certain semantic roles:

I	'll come	into your shop	tomorrow
participant	process	circumstance	circumstance

The kind of meaning expressed by these elements of semantic structure is **representational** meaning, or meaning that has to do with the content of the message. The various types of process, participants, attributes and circumstances are outlined in the following sections and described more fully in Chapter 4.

1.3 THREE WAYS OF INTERPRETING CLAUSE STRUCTURE

The clause or simple sentence is the basic unit that embodies our construal of representational meaning and interpersonal meaning. The clause is also the unit whose elements can be reordered in certain ways to facilitate the creation of **textual** meaning. The textual resources of the clause, such as the active–passive alternative, enable the representational strand and the interpersonal strand of meaning to cohere as a message, not simply as a sentence in isolation, but in relation to what precedes it in the discourse.

Each type of meaning is encoded by its own structures; the three types of structure combine to produce one single realisation in words.

To summarise, the three kinds of meaning derive from the consideration of a clause as: (a) the linguistic representation of our experience of the world; (b) a communicative exchange between persons; (c) an organised message or text. We now turn to the three types of structure that implement these meanings.

1.3.1 The clause as representation: transitivity structures

The representational meaning of the clause is encoded through the transitivity structures, whose elements of structure or functions include: Agent, Recipient, Affected, Process, Attribute and Circumstance, as described in Chapter 4. Some of these make up the semantic structure of the following example:

Janice	will give	Chris	the bill	tomorrow
Agent	Process (action)	Recipient	Affected	Circumstance (time)

With a process of 'doing' such as the action of giving, the Agent is that participant which carries out the action referred to by the verb; the Recipient is that participant who receives the 'goods' or 'information' encoded as the Affected. Circumstances attending the process are classified as locative, temporal, conditional, concessive, causal, resultant, etc.

1.3.2 The clause as exchange: mood structures

When a speaker interacts with others to exchange information, or to influence their behaviour and get things done, she adopts for herself a certain role, such as 'questioner' and, in doing so, assigns a complementary role, such as 'informant', to her addressee. Unless the conversation is very one-sided, the roles of 'questioner' and 'informant' tend to alternate between the interlocutors engaged in a conversation, as can be seen in the exchange of speech roles between Chris and Janice in the text on page 3.

The clause is the major grammatical unit used by speakers to ask questions, make statements and issue directives. The exchange of information is typically carried out by the indicative mood or **clause type**, as opposed to directives, which are typically expressed by the imperative mood. Within the indicative, making a statement is associated characteristically with the declarative, and asking a question with the interrogative. More exactly, it is one part of these structures – consisting of the Subject and the Finite element – that in English carries the syntactic burden of the exchange. The rest of the clause remains unchanged.

In a declarative clause, the Subject precedes the Finite.

Declarative

Janice	will	give	Chris	the bill	tomorrow
Subject	Finite operator	Predicator	Indirect Object	Direct Object	Adjunct

Interrogative

Will	Janice	give	Chris	the bill	tomorrow?
Finite operator	Subject	Predicator	Indirect Object	Direct Object	Adjunct

In the interrogative structure, the positions of Finite operator and Subject are reversed, the Predicator and the rest of the clause remaining the same. The Finite is that element which relates the content of the clause to the speech event. It does this by specifying a time reference, through tense, or by expressing an attitude of the speaker, through modality. Also associated with finiteness, although less explicitly in many cases in English, are person and number. The Finite element is realised in the examples above by the modal auxiliary *will* (see 3.1.1 and 23.3 for the interrogative). Clause types and the meanings they convey are treated in Chapter 5.

1.3.3 The clause as message: thematic structures

Here, the speaker organises the informational content of the clause so as to establish whatever point of departure is desired for the message. This is called the Theme, which in English coincides with the initial element or elements of the clause. The rest of the clause is the Rheme:

Janice	will	give	Chris	the bill	tomorrow
Theme	Rheme				

The Theme may coincide with one of the participants, as in this example, or it may 'set the scene' by coinciding with an initial expression of time, place, etc. These possibilities are illustrated in 1.3.4. and treated more fully in Chapter 6.

1.3.4 Combining the three types of structure

The three types of structure we have briefly introduced are examined more closely in Chapters 4, 5 and 6. Here, they are mapped simultaneously on to the example clause, in order to show the tripartate nature and analysis of English clauses from a functional point of view. Predicator, Indirect and Direct Objects, and Adjunct are included as **syntactic functions**, which correspond to the semantic roles. We examine the syntactic functions more closely in Chapter 2.

	Janice	will give	Chris	the bill	tomorrow
Experiential	Agent	Process	Recipient	Affected	Circumstance
Interpersonal	Subject	Finite + Predicator	Indirect Object	Direct Object	Adjunct
Textual	Theme	Rheme			

In a typical active declarative clause such as this, Agent, Subject and Theme coincide and are realised in one wording, in this case *Janice*. But in natural language use, a situation can be expressed in different ways, in which the order of clause elements can vary, since different elements of structure can be moved to initial position. Our present example admits at least the following possible variants:

1 Chris   will be given the bill (by Janice) tomorrow.
2 The bill   will be given to Chris tomorrow (by Janice).
3 Tomorrow, Chris will be given the bill (by Janice).

It can be seen that the three types of structural elements do not coincide (vertically) in the same way as they do in the typical active declarative clause. For example: Theme now coincides with Recipient in 1, with Affected in 2, and with Circumstance in 3; Agent no longer coincides with Theme or with Subject in any of the variants. The configurations for 1 are illustrated below.

Chris	will be given	the bill	by Janice	tomorrow
Recipient	Process	Affected	Agent	Circumstance
Subject	Finite + Predicator	Direct Object	Adjunct	Adjunct
Theme	Rheme			

The motivation for this and the other variants is not to be sought in the clause in isolation, but in its relationship to that part of the discourse at which it is located. The speaker organises the content of the clause in order to achieve the best effect for their communicative purpose. This involves establishing the point of departure of the clausal message – that is, the Theme – in relation to what has gone before. This choice conditions to a large extent the way the clausal message will develop and how the speaker or writer will lead the hearer or reader to identify that constituent which is presented as New information, usually at the end of the clause.

By choosing variant 1, for example, *Chris* becomes the point of departure, while *tomorrow* is still in final position, with the Agent, *Janice*, nearing final position. By using the passive, instead of the active voice, the Agent can be omitted altogether, leaving the Affected, *the bill*, nearer final position. Finally, if we bring the circumstantial element of time, *tomorrow*, to initial position as Theme, as in 3, this element will serve as a frame for the whole event. By means of such reorganisations of the clausal message, the content of the clause can be made to relate to the rest of the discourse and to the communicative context in which it is produced. It is for this reason that the active–passive choice, which determines the constituent of the clause that will be Subject, is related to choice of Theme and the 'packaging' or distribution of information.

The textual motivations outlined in the previous paragraph, and the syntactic strategies that serve to produce different kinds of clausal message, are discussed in Chapter 6.

We will now look at the full range of grammatical units in a hierarchy where the clause is central. We will then look briefly at the unit above the clause, the 'complex sentence', and the units immediately below the clause, the 'groups'.

LINGUISTIC FORMS AND SYNTACTIC FUNCTIONS

2.1 SYNTACTIC CATEGORIES AND RELATIONSHIPS

In this module we shall outline the basic syntactic concepts on which our structural analysis is based. These include the structural **units** which can be arranged by **rank**, **the classes** into which these units can be divided, and the **elements** of which they are composed. We shall also consider the ways units of one rank are related to those above or below them. This is explained on pages 19 and 20, and in chapters 2 and 3.

2.2 TESTING FOR CONSTITUENTS

Before attempting to see how a stretch of language can be broken down into units, it is useful to be able to reinforce our intuitions as to where boundaries lie. This can be done by applying certain tests in order to identify whether a particular sequence of words is functioning as a constituent of a higher unit or not.

For instance, the following sequence, which constitutes a grammatical clause or simple sentence, is ambiguous:

Muriel saw the man in the service station

Two interpretations are possible, according to how the units that make up the clause are grouped into constituents, expressed graphically as follows:

1 ‖ Muriel │ saw │ the man in the service station ‖

2 ‖ Muriel │ saw │ the man ‖ in the service station ‖

In version **1**, the prepositional phrase *in the service station* forms part of the constituent whose head-word is *man* (*the man in the service station*) and tells us something about the man; whereas in version **2** the same prepositional phrase functions separately as a constituent of the clause and tells us where Muriel saw the man.

Evidence for this analysis can be sought by such operations as (a) coordination, (b) *wh*-questions, (c) clefting, (d) passivisation and (e) fronting. Tests (b) to (e) involve moving the stretch of language around and observing its syntactic behaviour. Testing by coordination involves adding a conjoin that realises the same function; only stretches of language that realise the same function can be conjoined:

(a) It can be seen that different types of conjoin are required according to the function of *in the service station*:

    (i)   Muriel saw *the man in the service station* and *the woman in the shop*.
    (ii)   Muriel saw the man *in the service station* and *in the shop*.

(b) The *wh*-question form and the appropriate response will be different for the two versions:

    (i)   *Who* did Muriel see? – The *man in the service station*.
    (ii)   *Where* did Muriel see the man? – In *the service station*.

(c) Clefting by means of *it* + *that*-clause highlights a clause constituent (see 30.2) and thus yields two different results:

    (i)   It was *the man in the service station* that Muriel saw.
    (ii)   It was *in the service station* that Muriel saw the man.

Wh-clefting (see 30.2) gives the same result:

    (i)   The one Muriel saw was the *man in the service station*.
    (ii)   Where Muriel saw the man was *in the service station*.

The form *the one* (*that . . .*) is used in this construction since English does not admit *who* in this context (**Who Muriel saw *was* the *man in the service station*).

(d) Passivisation (see 4.2.3 and 30.3) likewise keeps together those units or bits of language that form a constituent. The passive counterpart of an active clause usually contains a form of *be* and a past participle:

    (i)   *The man in the service station* was seen by Muriel.
    (ii)   The man was seen by Muriel *in the service station*.

(e) A constituent can sometimes be fronted, that is, brought to initial position:

    (i)   *The man in the service station* Muriel saw.
    (ii)   *In the service station* Muriel saw the man.

It is not always the case that a sequence responds equally well to all five types of test. Certain types of unit may resist one or more of these operations: for instance, frequency adverbs such as *often* and *usually*, and modal adverbs like *probably*, resist clefting (**It's often / usually / probably that Muriel saw the man in the service station*), resulting in a sentence that is ungrammatical. Unlike some languages, in English the finite verbal element of a clause normally resists fronting (**Saw Muriel the man in the service station*). Nevertheless, if two or more of the operations can be carried out satisfactorily, we can be reasonably sure that the sequence in question is a constituent of a larger unit.

We now turn to the description of units, their classes and the relationship holding between them.

2.3 UNITS AND RANK OF UNITS

The moving-around of bits of language, as carried out in 2.2, suggests that language is not a series of words strung together like beads on a string. Language is patterned, that is, certain regularities can be distinguished throughout every linguistic manifestation in discourse. A **unit** will be defined as any sequence that constitutes a semantic whole and which has a recognised pattern that is repeated regularly in speech and writing. For instance, the previous sentence is a unit containing other units such as *a recognised pattern* and *in speech and writing*. Sequences such as *defined as any* and *repeated regularly in*, which also occur in the same sentence, do not constitute units since they have no semantic whole and no syntactic pattern. The following sequence, which comments on the effects of a nuclear accident, constitutes one syntactic unit which is composed of further units:

> The effects of the accident are very serious.

In English, it is useful to recognise four structural units which can be arranged in a relationship of componence on what is called a **rank-scale**:

Unit	Boundary marker	Example
Clause:	‖	‖ the effects of the accident are very serious ‖
Group:	|	| the effects of the accident | are | very serious |
Word:	a space	the effects of the accident are very serious
Morpheme:	+	{EFFECT} + {PLURAL}, realised by the morphs *effect* and *-s*

For the initial stages of analysis it may be helpful to mark off the boundaries of each unit by a symbol, such as those adopted in the example. The symbol for 'clause boundary' is a double vertical line ‖, that for 'group boundary' is a single vertical line\|, and that for 'word boundary' is simply a space, as is conventionally used in the written language. The independent clause is the equivalent of the traditional 'simple sentence'. Combinations of clauses, the boundaries symbolised by ‖\|, are illustrated in 2.4.1 and treated more fully in Chapter 7.

The relationship between the units is, in principle, as follows. Looking downwards, each unit **consists of** one or more units of the rank below it. Thus, a clause consists of one or more groups, a group consists of one or more words and a word consists of one or more morphemes. For instance, *Wait*! consists of one clause, which consists of one group, which consists of one word, which consists of one morpheme. More exactly, we shall say that the elements of structure of each unit are realised by units of the rank below.

Looking upwards, each unit fulfils a function in the unit above it. However, as we shall see in 3.6.3 and in later chapters, units may be 'embedded' within other units, such as the clause *who live in the north* within the nominal group *people who live in the north*. Similarly, the prepositional phrase *of the accident* is embedded in the nominal group *the effects of the accident*.

We shall be concerned in this book mainly with two units: clause and group. The structure and constituents of these units will be described in later sections, together with their functions and meanings.

2.4 CLASSES OF UNITS

At each rank of linguistic unit mentioned in 2.3, there are various classes of unit.

2.4.1 Classes of clauses

A. Finite and non-finite clauses

At the rank of 'clause', a first distinction to be made is that between **finite and non-finite** clauses. As clauses have as their central element the verbal group, their status as finite or non-finite depends on the form of the verb chosen. Finite verbs, and therefore also finite clauses, are marked for either tense or modality, but not both. Their function is to relate the verb to the speech event. **Tensed** forms distinguish the present tense (*lock, locks*) from the past tense (*locked*) in regular verbs and many irregular verbs also, as in *eat, ate; go, went*. This distinction is not made on all irregular verbs, for example *shut*, which has the same form for the present and past tenses. Person and number are marked only on the third person singular of the present tense (*locks, shuts*) – except for the verb *be*, which has further forms (see 3.1.1).

Tense is carried not only by lexical verbs but also by the finite operators. Modality is marked by the modal verbs, which also function as operators (see 3.1.1). If the speaker wishes to express tense or modality, together with person and number, a 'finite' form of the verb is chosen, therefore, such as *is, eats, locked, went, will stay* and the clause is then called a **finite clause (fin.cl)**. For example, in the following paragraph all the verbs – and therefore all the clauses (marked [1], [2] etc.) – are finite:

|||I *had* a farm in Africa, at the foot of the Ngong hills.|||[1] |||The Equator *runs* across these highlands a hundred miles to the north,||[2] and the farm *lay* at an altitude of over six thousand feet.[3]||| In the daytime you *felt* that you *had got* high up, near to the sun,[4]|| but the early mornings and evenings *were* limpid and restful,[5]|| and the nights *were* cold.[6]|||

(Karen Blixen, *Out of Africa*)

If the verb-form does not signal either tense or modality, the verb and the clause are classified as **non-finite (V-non-fin; non-fin.cl)**. The non-finite verb forms are:

- the **infinitive** (inf.) (*be, eat, lock, go*) sometimes called the 'bare' infinitive;
- the **to-infinitive** (*to*-inf);
- the participial **-*ing*** form (*-ing*) (*being, eating, locking, going*); and
- the past participial form, symbolised in this book as **-*en*** (*been, eaten, locked, gone*).

These forms are said to be **non-tensed**. Non-finite clauses are illustrated by the following examples:

1	They want *to hire a caravan*.	*to*-infinitive clause
2	Tim helped her *carry her bags upstairs*.	bare infinitive clause
3	We found Ann *sitting in the garden*.	*-ing* participial clause
4	The invitations were sent *written by hand*.	*-en* participial clause

Most of these non-finite verb forms occur in the following passage from A. J. Cronin's *The Citadel*. (Note that the same form serves for both the finite and non-finite status of many English verbs; *locked* and *shut*, for instance, each function both as a tensed (past) form and as a non-finite *-en* participle.)

> Three men, *cramped*[1] together on their bellies in a dead end, were doing their best to *revive*[2] another man who lay in a huddled attitude, his body *slewed*[3] sideways, one shoulder *pointing*[4] backwards, *lost*,[5] seemingly, in the mass of rock behind him.
>
> [1]non-finite, *-en*; [2]non-finite, *to*-infinitive; [3]non-finite, *-en*; [4]non-finite, *-ing*; [5]non-finite, *-en*.

B Independent and dependent clauses

A further necessary distinction to be made is that between **independent and dependent** clauses. An independent clause (indep.cl) is complete in itself, that is, it does not form part of a larger structure, whereas a dependent clause (dep.cl) is typically related to an independent clause. This is illustrated in the following sentence:

They locked up the house (**indep.cl**), before they went on holiday (**dep.cl**).

All grammatically independent clauses are finite. Dependent clauses may be finite or non-finite. In the previous example, the finite dependent clause *before they went on holiday* can be replaced by a non-finite clause *before going on holiday*. The dependent status of non-finite clauses is signalled by the form itself.

Only independent clauses have the variations in clause structure that make for the different clause types: declarative, interrogative, imperative and exclamative (see Module 23):

Jack's flat is in Hammersmith.   (declarative)
Is his address 20 Finchley Road?   (interrogative)
Give me Jack's telephone number.   (imperative)
What a large apartment *he has*!   (exclamative)

Dependent clauses, even when finite, do not have these possibilities.

C. Finite dependent clauses

Seven kinds of finite dependent clause are illustrated in this section, along with three important sub-types of the nominal clause.

The subordinate status of a finite dependent clause is normally signalled by means of subordinating conjunctions ('subordinators') such as *when, if, before, as soon as* in **circumstantial clauses**, as in **1** below (see also 35.2), or by 'relativisers' such as *which, that* in **relative clauses** as in **2** (see 49.3):

1 *As soon as she got home*, Ann switched on the television.
2 Paul took one of the red apples *that his wife had bought that morning*.

Nominal clauses fulfil the functions of Subject, Object and Complement in clause structure. In a sentence such as *He saw that the bottles were empty*, the clause [*that the bottles were empty*] is **embedded** as a constituent (in this case as Object) of the **superordinate** clause *he saw x*. The part without the embedded clause is sometimes called the **matrix** clause.

The main types of nominal clause are the ***that*-clause 3**, the ***wh*-nominal relative clause 4** and the dependent ***wh*-interrogative clause 4** and **5**. The **dependent exclamative 6** is a further type of *wh*-clause:

3 He saw *that the bottles were empty*.   (*that*-clause)
4 *What I don't understand is why you have come here.*   (nominal relative clause + dependent *wh*-interrogative)
5 I'll ask *where the nearest Underground station is*.   (dependent *wh*-interrogative)
6 She said *how comfortable it was*.   (dependent exclamative clause)

Embedded clauses are discussed and illustrated in chapters 2 and 3.

Comparative clauses occur following the comparative forms of adjectives and adverbs. The comparative clause, introduced by *than*, provides the basis of comparison:

7 The results are much better *than we expected*.

Supplementive units are not integrated into the main clause, as embedded units are, but add supplementary information. They are subordinate but not embedded. They are set off from the main clause by commas, or by a dash, and have their own intonation contour. Here is an example of a supplementive non-finite *-en* clause:

Built of cypress, brick and glass, the house exhibits many of the significant contributions that Wright made to contemporary architecture.

In spoken discourse, and in written texts that imitate spoken language, such as fictional dialogue, we can often come across supplementives that are freestanding, despite their subordinate form, as in the following italicised example (see also chapters 5, 7 and 10):

The large size doesn't seem to be available. *Which is a pity*.

Not only clauses, but other units can have the status of 'supplementives' (see 49.2).

A subsidiary type of clause is the **verbless** clause. This is a clause which lacks a verb and often a subject also. The omitted verb is typically a form of *be* and is recoverable from the situational or linguistic context, as in:

Book your tickets well in advance, *whenever possible.* (= whenever it is possible)

(See also Chapter 5.) The following extract from Elaine Morgan's, *The Descent of Woman* illustrates this type very well:

> Man, apes and monkeys can all be observed to cry out *when in pain*, flush *when enraged*, yawn *when tired*, glare *when defiant*, grin *when tickled*, tremble *when afraid*, embrace *when affectionate*, bare their teeth *when hostile*, raise their eyebrows *when surprised*, and turn their heads away *when offended*.

We shall also classify as verbless clauses many irregular constructions such as the following:

Wh-questions without a finite verb:	Why not sell your car and get a new one?
Adjuncts with the force of a command, sometimes with a vocative:	Hands off! Into the shelter, everybody!
Ellipted interrogative and exclamative clauses:	Sure? (Are you sure?) Fantastic! (That/It is fantastic)
Proverbs of the type:	*Out of sight, out of mind.*

Finally, we shall call **abbreviated clauses** those such as *can you? I won't, has she?* which consist of the Subject + Finite operator alone, with the rest of the clause ellipted because it is known. These clauses typically occur as responses in conversational exchanges and as tags (see 22.4), but can also express such speech acts as reprimand (*Must you?*), given an appropriate social context.

2.4.2 Classes of groups

Groups are classified according to the class of the word operating as the main or 'head' element. Headed by a noun, an adjective, an adverb and a verb respectively, we can identify the following classes:

Nominal Groups	(NG)	*films*,	wonderful *films* by Fellini
Verbal Groups	(VG)	*return*,	will *return*
Adjectival Groups	(AdjG)	*good*,	quite *good* at languages
Adverbial Groups	(AdvG)	*fluently*,	very *fluently* indeed

Units such as these centre round one main element, which prototypically cannot be omitted. Furthermore, the main element can replace the whole structure: *films, return, good* and *fluently* can have the same syntactic functions as the whole group of which each is head, or, in the case of *return*, as lexical verb. By contrast, the unit formed by a preposition and its complement, such as *on the floor*, is rather different. The preposition can't function alone as a unit. Both elements are obligatory. This unit will therefore be called the 'Prepositional Phrase' (PP).

2.4.3 Classes of words

Words are classified grammatically according to the traditional terminology, which includes **noun, verb, adjective, adverb, preposition, pronoun, article** and **conjunction**. These 'parts of speech' are divided into two main classes, the open and the closed. The open classes are those that freely admit new members into the vocabulary. They comprise noun, verb, adjective and adverb. The closed classes (preposition, pronoun and article) do not easily admit new members. Prepositions have gradually expanded their membership somewhat by admitting participles such as *including, concerning*, but the remaining classes are very resistant to the introduction of new items. This has been noticeable in recent years when attempts have been made to find gender-neutral pronouns.

2.4.4 Classes of morphemes

Words are made up of morphemes. We shall consider the morpheme to be an abstract category that has either a lexical or a grammatical meaning. We have already indicated in 2.3 that a word such as *effects* can be considered as formed from the lexical morpheme {EFFECT} + the {PLURAL} morpheme. These abstract categories are realised by **morphs** such as *effect* and *-s* or /ifekt/ and /s/, the actual segments of written and spoken language, respectively.

Since the study of words and morphemes takes us out of syntax, and into morphology and phonology, the scope of this book does not allow for further treatment of these units.

2.5 THE CONCEPT OF UNIT STRUCTURE

The term 'structure' refers to the relationships that exist between the small units that make up a larger unit. For example, the basic components of a table are a flat board and four long thin pieces of wood or metal, but these elements do not constitute a structure until they are related to each other as a horizontal top supported at the corners by four vertical legs. In this way, each 'element' is given its position and its 'function', which together we may call the 'grammar' of all those members of the general class of objects called 'table'.

Everything in our lives has structure. A house may be built of bricks, but its structure consists of rooms having different formal, functional and distributional characteristics. Tables, chairs, cars, all objects are composed of functionally related 'formal items'; and the same applies to activities such as speeches, plays, concerts and football matches. It is natural that languages, which are the spoken and written representation of our experience of all these things, are also manifested in structured forms. Linguistic structures are described in terms of the semantic functions of their various elements and the syntactic forms and relationships which express them.

We have seen in 1.3.1 a brief preview of the main semantic elements of the clause, together with some of the possible configurations produced by the combinations of these elements. Groups, whose function it is to express the things, processes, qualities and circumstances of our experience, also have semantic elements and structures. These are different for each type of group and are treated in the relevant chapter on each of these classes of unit. Here we shall briefly present the syntactic elements of all ranks of unit.

2.5.1 Syntactic elements of clauses

Clauses have the greatest number of syntactic elements or functions of all classes of unit. The criteria for their identification, the syntactic features and the realisations of each are discussed in Chapter 2. Here we simply list and exemplify the clause elements within common clause structures. The type of structure used in order to express a 'situation' or 'state of affairs' depends to a great extent on the verb chosen. Verb complementation types are treated in Chapter 3.

Subject (S)	*Jupiter* is the largest planet.	SPCs
Predicator (P)	The election campaign *has ended*.	SP
Direct Object (Od)	Ted has bought *a new motorbike*.	SPOd
Indirect Object (Oi)	They sent *their friends postcards*.	SPOiOd
Prepositional Object (Op)	You must allow *for price increases*.	SPOp
Subject Complement (Cs)	He is *powerless to make any changes*.	SPCs
Object Complement (Co)	We consider the situation *alarming*.	SPOdCo
Locative/Goal Complement (C_{loc})	We flew to *Moscow*.	SPC_{loc}
Circumstantial Adjunct (A)	The news reached us *on Tuesday*.	SPOdA
Stance Adjunct (A)	*Unfortunately*, we could not reach York in time.	ASPOdA
Connective Adjunct (A)	*However*, other friends were present.	ASPCs

It will be seen that for interrogative and negative clauses we use an additional function, the Finite (see 3.1 and 23.3).

2.5.2 Syntactic elements of groups

Nominal groups, adjectival groups and adverbial groups are composed of three primary elements or functions: a head **(h)** preceded by a pre-modifier **(m)** and followed by a post-modifier **(m)**. This last element is sometimes called a 'qualifier'. In the chapters devoted to these groups we also distinguish '**complement**' **(c)** as a special type of post-head element. Complements of nouns and adjectives are introduced by a preposition or by a *that*-clause which is controlled by the head-word of the group. For example, the adjective *good* controls a complement introduced by *at*: *good at chess*. The noun *belief* controls a *that*-clause: *the belief that he is always right*. In the case of **nominal groups**, we also distinguish between 'modifiers', which describe or classify the head, and 'determiners' **(d)**, which specify it in terms of definiteness, quantity, possessiveness, etc. Thus, we give the determiner and the pre- and post-modifiers equal syntactic status as primary elements of nominal groups (see 45.2). The following are examples of these group structures:

> NG: dmhm: those | beautiful | paintings | by Goya
> AdjG: mhc: extremely | difficult | to translate
> AdvG: mhm: very | carefully | indeed

In **Verbal Groups**, the lexical verb is regarded as the main element **(v)**, which either functions alone, whether in finite or non-finite form, as in the example ***Walking*** *along the street, I **met** a friend of mine*, or is preceded by auxiliaries **(x)**, as in *will go or has been reading*. The first auxiliary (or the auxiliary, if there is only one) is called the 'finite operator' **(o)**. It is the element that contributes information about tense, modality, number and person, and so helps to make the VG finite and fully 'operative'. It is also the element that operates in the syntactic structure to make the clause interrogative and/ or negative (see 3.1), and to make elliptted responses:

> *Have you* been driving for many years? – Yes, I *have*.

> *Do* you enjoy driving? – Yes, I *do*.

In the more complex verbal groups, each element is telescoped into the following one (see 38.7):

> v: plays
> ov: has | played   [*have* + *-en*]
> oxv: will | be | playing   [*will* + [*be* + *-ing*]]
> oxxv: must | have | been | played   [*must* + [*have* + *-en*] [*be* + *-en*]]

The lexical verb is sometimes followed by an adverbial particle (symbolised by '**p**') as in *ring up, break out, take over*. Many such combinations form integrated semantic units which are idiomatic. Although the particle frequently forms an integral part of the meaning of the lexical verb, and in fact can often be replaced by a simple verb *form* (*ring up* = *telephone; break out* = *escape, erupt*), transitive combinations can be discontinuous as in *I'll ring you up, They've taken it over.*

However, most particles are not otherwise moveable (see the constituency tests in 2.2); we can't say *Up I'll ring you or *Out broke an epidemic. The only exception is in 'free combinations'where the particle has a directional meaning, and in such cases we classify them as directional complements with special uses: *Down came the rain and up went the umbrellas.* However, grammars differ in this respect. The syntax of phrasal verbs and other multi-word combinations is discussed in 6.4 and the semantics (in terms of Source, Path and Goal) in 40.2.

In **Prepositional Phrases (PP)** there are two obligatory elements: the prepositional head (**h**) and the complement (**c**). There is also an optional modifier (**m**), which is typically realised by an adverb of degree (e.g. *right, quite*). The structure of PPs is illustrated as follows:

mhc: right | across | the road

         quite | out of | practice

Prepositional phrases appear as realisations of many functions throughout this book. The structure and grammatical functions of the prepositional phrase are treated in Chapter 12, together with prepositional meanings, which are described in terms of locative, metaphorical and abstract uses.

2.5.3 Componence, realisation and function

Any structure can be considered to be composed of elements which form a configuration of 'functions', whether semantic functions such as Agent-Process-Affected or syntactic functions such as the clause configuration Subject-Predicator-Direct Object or the modifier-head-modifier structure of the nominal group.

Each of these functions is in turn realised by a unit which is itself, at least potentially, a configuration of functions, and these in turn are realised by others until the final stage is reached and abstract categories such as subject, head, modifier, etc., are finally realised by the segments of the spoken or written language. The 'structural tree' on page 20 diagrams this model of analysis at the three unit ranks of clause, group and word, to illustrate the clause *The bus strike will affect many people tomorrow*:

An important property of language is the fact that there is no one-to-one correspondence between the class of unit and its function. While it is true that certain classes of unit *typically* realise certain functions, Nominal Groups at Subject and Object functions, for instance, it is nevertheless also true that many classes of unit can fulfil many different functions, and different functions are realised by many different classes of unit. For instance, the NG *next time* can fulfil the following clause functions, among others:

Subject: *Next time* will be better.
Adjunct: I'll know better *next time.*
Direct Object: We'll enjoy *next time.*

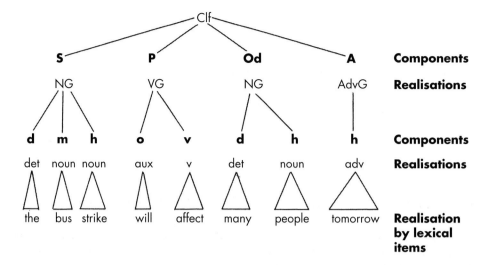

	S	P	Od	A	**Components**
	NG	VG	NG	AdvG	**Realisations**

The nearest to a one-to-one relationship in the grammar is that between the process and the verbal group that realises it.

This many-to-many relationship is fundamental for understanding the relationship of the grammar of English to discourse. By this it is not implied that discourse (or even a text) is a kind of super-sentence, a grammatical unit that is simply 'larger' than a sentence and with the same kind of relationship holding between its parts as that which holds between grammatical units. A piece of discourse is quite different in kind from a grammatical unit. Rather than grammatical, it is a pragmatic-semantic unit of whatever length, spoken or written, and which forms a unified whole, with respect both to its internal properties and to the social context in which it is produced.

To take a minimal instance, a pragmatic act such as 'leavetaking' may be realised by a modalised declarative clause (*I'll be seeing you*) or by the formulaic expression *Goodbye*, among others. Typically, a discourse is made up of various types of pragmatic acts, which in turn are realised semantically and syntactically. In this book, although we start from the grammar rather than from the text, the relationship between the two is of primary interest.

NEGATION AND EXPANSION   *MODULE 3*

3.1 NEGATIVE AND INTERROGATIVE CLAUSE STRUCTURES

Negating and questioning are basic human needs, which are encoded grammatically by negation and by the interrogative, respectively. English is unlike many other languages in using a **finite operator** to form negative and interrogative clause structures.

The verb's corresponding negative forms normally have *n't* added to the positive forms. The following are irregular: *can't* (from *cannot*), *shan't* (from *shall not*), *won't* (from *will not*). *May not* is not usually abbreviated to *mayn't*. When *n't* follows a consonant – as in *didn't*, *wouldn't* – it is pronounced as a separate syllable. The inflectional *n't* forms are used in spoken English and in informal written styles that imitate speech, such as fictional dialogue. The full form *not* is used in formal written styles and for emphasis – as in *The play was not a success*, rather than *The play wasn't a success*.

3.1.1 The finite operator

The **operator** is a **verb**, of one of the following types: primary, modal or *do*, as explained below.

primary:	positive: *am, is, are, was, were, have, has, had* negative: *am not* (*aren't* in negative-interrogative), *isn't, aren't, wasn't, weren't, haven't, hasn't, hadn't*
modal:	positive: *can, could, will, would, shall, should, may, might, ought* negative: *can't, couldn't, won't, wouldn't, shan't, shouldn't, may not, mightn't, oughtn't*
the 'do' operator:	positive: *does, do, did* negative; *doesn't, don't, didn't*

We also mention here the **lexical-auxiliaries** based on the primary verbs *be* (*be about to, be sure to, be going to*, etc.) and *have* (*have to, have got to*), which are discussed in 37.3. The primary verb functions as a normal operator in these combinations.

Less commonly in use are the semi-modals **dare** and **need**, which as modals are used in negative and interrogative clauses, and admit the abbreviated forms *daren't* and *needn't*, respectively. (*Dare* you go? I *daren't* go. *How dare* you speak to me like that? *Need* I go? You *needn't* go).

Dare can be used with *will, should* and *would*, a possibility that is not open to modals in general: Nobody *will dare* vote against the proposal; I *wouldn't dare* take a space-trip even if I were offered one.

Dare and *need* also behave like full lexical verbs requiring the *do*-operator: *I didn't dare go. I didn't need to go. Didn't you dare go? Didn't you need to go? Didn't dare* is more common now than *dared not* (He *dared not* say a word, He *didn't dare say* a word).

3.2 CLAUSAL NEGATION

In clauses, negation is usually made with the particle *not*, by negating the finite operator (*is not, cannot/isn't, can't*, etc.), or a non-finite verb in a dependent clause (*not wishing to disturb them*). **Amn't* is not used in Standard English for the first person singular; instead *I'm not* (declarative) and *Aren't I* (interrogative) are used. If no other auxiliary is present, a form of *do* (*do, does, did*) is brought in as operator. Compare the following positive and negative declarative clauses:

That man *is* the Secretary.	That man *is not/isn't* the Secretary.
He *took* the car.	He *didn't take* the car.
Ed always *does* the dishes.	Ed *doesn't* always *do* the dishes.

The last example here illustrates the use of *does* both as a lexical verb and as operator.

Don't is the regular negative form used in second person imperatives: *Don't be late*!

Some operators admit an alternative type of abbreviation with the subject in negative clauses. This occurs usually only with a pronoun. Both types are used in spoken English:

They aren't ready.	They're not ready.
She isn't coming with us.	She's not coming with us.
He hasn't finished.	He's not finished.
We haven't got enough.	We've not got enough.

3.2.1 Interrogative clauses

These invert the operator with the subject of the clause:

Positive-interrogative	*Negative-interrogative*
Is that man the Secretary?	Isn't that man the Secretary?
Did he take the car?	Didn't he take the car?
Does Ed always do the dishes?	Doesn't Ed always do the dishes?

There are two types of interrogative clause. One is the **yes/no type**, illustrated here, which simply asks for an answer in terms of *yes* or *no*. The other is the **wh-type**, which asks for the information represented by the *wh*-word *what? who? where?* and so on. The inversion of subject–operator is the same as for the *yes/no* type, except when *who* functions as subject:

> *Who came* to see you? When *can you* come to see us?
> What *does* Ed *do*? When *did* you *see* him last?

3.3 *NO*-NEGATION VS *NOT*-NEGATION + *ANY*

Another way of negating a clause is by using a non-verbal 'nuclear' negative word such as *nobody, nothing, no* or *never*. When we need a negative element as subject, a nuclear form is necessary: *Nobody* came after all, *Nothing* was said, *No money* was found (see below, and also Chapter 10). Nuclear negative words are also common in existential clauses: *There's nothing to worry about*.

In many cases a similar idea can be expressed by using either *no*-negation or *not*-negation + *any*:

> Have you *any* money? I have*n't any* money.
> I have *no* money.
>
> Do you know *anyone* called Stern? I don't know *anyone* called Stern.
> I know *no-one* called Stern.

In questions, either alternative is possible even when the negative item is subject, as opposed to the single possible structure in negative declarative clauses. Compare:

> Declarative negative: *Nobody* has called this afternoon.
> Interrogative negative: Has *nobody* called this afternoon?
> Has*n't anybody* called this afternoon?

When both are possible, the *no*-form tends to be more emphatic or more suited to writing or formal spoken English. A very emphatic negative meaning is conveyed in spoken English also by, for example, *She's no friend of mine. He's no actor*.

3.4 *ANY* AND OTHER NON-ASSERTIVE WORDS

Unlike many languages, Standard English does not favour cumulative negation, that is a 'not' negative together with one or more nuclear negatives in one clause, such as *We're **not** going **nowhere***, although this is a feature of some dialects. Instead the first negative item is followed throughout the rest of the clause by one or more non-assertive items such as *any*, as in:

> We're *not* going *anywhere* with *any* of our friends.
> I did*n't* say *anything* about it to *anyone*.

It is important to remember that the '*any*' words in English (*any, anyone, anybody, anything, anywhere*) are not in themselves negative. In order to be used in a negative clause they must be preceded by *not* or a negative word; they must be within the 'scope of negation' (see 3.5). So instead of *Nobody came*, it is not acceptable to say **Anybody came* or **Anybody didn't come*. These are ungrammatical and meaningless, hence the deliberate oddity of e.e. cummings' poem 'Anyone lived in a little how town'.

The *any* words (together with *ever* and *yet*, among others) are what we call 'non-assertive' items, as opposed to *some* and its compounds, which are 'assertive'. Assertive forms have **factual meanings** and typically occur in positive declarative clauses. Non-assertive words such as *any* are associated with **non-factual meanings** in the sense of **non-fulfilment** or **potentiality**, which is a feature of negative, interrogative, conditional and comparative clauses, and semi-negative words such as *without* and *hardly*, among others. It is, in fact, the general non-factual meaning, rather than any particular structure which provides the context for non-assertive items to be used:

> We have *some* very good coffee.   (declarative, factual)
> This coffee is better *than any I have ever tasted*.   (comparative, non-factual)
> If you want *any* more coffee, you must make it yourself.   (conditional, non-factual)
> Did you say *anything*?   (interrogative, non-factual)
> Did*n't* you go *anywhere* interesting?   (interrogative-negative, non-factual)
> Without *any* delay.
> *Hardly* anyone knew his name.

Stressed *any* is used in positive declarative clauses, and has a non-factual meaning (= it doesn't matter which/who); see also 47.1.

> Choose *any* of the questions in section one.
> *Anybody* with a bit of sense would have refused to go.
> *Any* house is better than *no* house.

Here is a summary of assertive and non-assertive items:

	Assertive	**Non-assertive**
Determiners/pronouns	some	any
	someone	anyone
	somebody	anybody
	something	anything
Adverbs	somewhere	anywhere
	sometimes	ever
	already	yet
	still	any more/any longer
	a lot	much

Biased *yes/no* questions with *some* and *any* words are explained in 26.4.

3.5 THE SCOPE OF NEGATION

By the scope of negation we mean the semantic influence that a negative word has on the rest of the clause that follows it. Typically, all that follows the negative form to the end of the clause will be non-assertive and within the scope of negation. Thus, in *Some people don't have any sense of humour*, *some* is outside the scope of negation, whereas *any* is inside it.

As the non-assertive forms are not in themselves negative, they cannot initiate the scope of negation by standing in initial position in the place of a nuclear negative form. Assertive forms such as *some* and its compounds can occur after a negative word, but they must necessarily stand outside the scope of negation. Compare the difference in meaning between the two following clauses:

> **1**   He didn't reply to any of my letters.
> **2**   He didn't reply to some of my letters.

The non-assertive form *any* in clause **1** expresses the scope of negation as extending to the end of the clause. *None of the letters received a reply*. Example **2**, on the other hand, implies that some letters received a reply, while others didn't. *Some* must be interpreted as outside the scope of negation.

The scope of negation is closely related to the function of Adjuncts in the clause. Compare the difference in meaning between examples **3** and **4** below, in which the manner Adjunct *clearly* is within the scope of negation in **3**, whereas the attitudinal sentence Adjunct *clearly* in **4** is outside it:

> **3**   She didn't explain the problem *clearly*.
> **4**   She *clearly* didn't explain the problem.

The scope of negation can also explain the occasional occurrence of two negative words in the same clause as in *You can't NOT go*. Here each negative item has its own scope.

3.6 LOCAL NEGATION

Our discussion so far has centred on clausal negation. Groups, words and non-finite clauses can be negated by *not*, without the entire finite clause being negated:

> She was admitted into hospital *not long ago*.
> *Not* realising the danger, she walked in the dark towards the edge of the cliff.
> Try *not to get too tired* playing tennis.
> She would prefer *not to go on a Mediterranean cruise* for a holiday.

Negative declaratives typically express a negative statement, but they can also be used to ask tactful questions, as in the following extract from a detective story. The person questioned replies mostly with straight negative statements, adding in[2] the expression of polite regret *I'm afraid*, but in[8] she avoids total commitment:

'You don't know the actual name of the firm or association that employed her?'[1]
'No, I don't,[2] I'm afraid.'
'Did she ever mention relatives?'
'No. I gather she was a widow and had lost her husband many years ago. A bit of an invalid he'd been, but she never talked much about him.'[3]
'She didn't mention where she came from[4] – what part of the country?'
'I don't think she was a Londoner.[5] Came from somewhere up north, I should say.'
'You didn't feel there was anything – well, mysterious about her?'[6]
Lejeune felt a doubt as he spoke. If she was a suggestible woman – but Mrs. Coppins did not take advantage of the opportunity offered to her.[7]
'Well I can't really say[8] that I did. Certainly not from anything she ever said.[9] The only thing that perhaps might have made me wonder was her suitcase. Good quality it was, but not new.'

(Agatha Christie, *The Pale Horse*)

[1]question; [2]negative statement; [3]negative statement; [4]question; [5]transferred negation; [6]question; [7]negative statement; [8]hedge; [9]negative statement.

Transferred negation consists in displacing the negative element from its logical place in the reported clause to negate the verb in the main clause. So in 5, instead of *I think she wasn't a Londoner*, we have *I don't think she was a Londoner*.

3.7 EXPANDING LINGUISTIC UNITS

Each of the linguistic units outlined in section 2 has been illustrated by single occurrences of that unit, for instance, one Nominal Group functioning at Subject or Direct Object, one modifier of an adjective or an adverb. Quite frequently our everyday communication requires no more. But units can be expanded to enable the speaker or writer to add further information which is, nevertheless, contained within the chosen structure at any point in the discourse. Here we simply exemplify **coordination, subordination and embedding** of various classes of elements, with the reminder that most elements of structure can be realised more than once, recursively.

3.7.1 Coordination

The following are examples of **coordination** of various classes of elements:

morphemes in a word:	*pro-* and *anti-* abortionists
heads of nominal groups:	*books, papers* and *magazines*
modifier in a NG:	a *beautiful* and *astonishing* sight
modifier in an AdjG:	He says he is *really* and *truly* sorry for what happened.
adjuncts in a clause:	You can put in the application *now* or *in a month's time* or else *next year*.

| **independent clauses:** | She *got dressed quickly, had breakfast* and *went out* to work |
| **dependent clauses:** | I will take a holiday *when the course is over* and *if I pass the exam* and also *provided I can afford it.* |

The following short extract illustrates coordinated units:

> Over the next decade, automation and the mechanisation of production[1] will improve and transform[2] farming, industrial plants and service industries[3] and also make our leisure time more productive, creative and interesting.[4]
>
> [1]coordinated groups (NG + NG); [2]coordinated main verbs); [3]coordinated groups (NG + NG + NG); [4]coordinated adjectives (adj. + adj. + adj.).

If the various conjoined clauses share the same subject or the same operator, these elements are regularly ellipted because they are recoverable (see 29.3), and are implicit in subsequent conjoined clauses. This occurs in the above example where the sequence *automation and the mechanisation of production* is ellipted, as is *will*, before the predicator *make*.

Ellipsis similarly occurs in group structures, as in the above example, where in one interpretation of [4], the modifier *more* is ellipted before *creative* and *interesting*.

3.7.2 Subordination

Similarly, the following are examples of **subordination** of various classes of elements:

modifier in a NG:	A very lovable, (*if rather dirty*), small boy.
Cs in a clause:	He is *quite brilliant* (*though totally unreliable*).
adjuncts in a clause:	We arrived (*late* (*though not too late*)) for the wedding.
dependent clauses:	I'll let you borrow the CDs (*as soon as I've finished*) [*provided you bring them back* [*when I need them*]].

In this complex sentence, the fourth clause *when I need them* is dependent on the third clause *provided you bring them back*; these together form a block which is dependent on the block formed by the first (independent) clause *I'll let you borrow the CDs* and its dependent clause *as soon as I've finished*.

'Sentence' is the term traditionally used to denote the highest grammatical unit on a scale of rank. While not rejecting this term, we shall prefer, however, to use the term 'clause' to refer to one independent unit. This applies also to a superordinate clause with embedded clauses in one or more functions, as illustrated in the next section. We keep the traditional term 'compound sentence' for units of two or more coordinated clauses, while the equally traditional term 'complex sentence' applies to units containing dependent clauses or dependent and conjoined clauses, as we have seen in some of the examples above. We shall say that in a complex sentence any number of clauses can be involved. These questions are further illustrated in Chapter 7 under the heading 'Clause combining'.

3.7.3 Embedding

A third way of expanding the content and the structure of a linguistic unit is by **embedding**, a kind of subordination by which a clause functions as a constituent of another clause or of a group. This is a pervasive phenomenon in both spoken and written English and is found in elements such as the following, where the embedded clause is enclosed in square brackets:

clause at S:	[*That he left so abruptly*] doesn't surprise me.
clause at Od:	I don't know [*why he left so abruptly*].
clause at c in a PP:	I'm pleased about [*Jane winning a prize*].
clause at m in NG	Thanks for the card [*you sent me*].
clause at A:	[*After they had signed the contract*] they went off to celebrate.
group in group	[[[*Tom's*] sister's] husband's] mother
	the box [*on top of the cupboard* [*in my bedroom*]]

EXERCISES ON CHAPTER 1
Basic concepts

Module 1

1   †For each of the following clauses say whether a participant or a circumstance has been chosen as Theme (the first constituent in the clause):

   (1)   Main Street is usually crowded on late shopping nights.
   (2)   The girls armed with hockey-sticks chased the burglar.
   (3)   Quite by accident I came across a very rare postage-stamp.
   (4)   Away in the distance you can see Mount Kilimanjaro.
   (5)   What I am going to tell you must not be repeated.

2   †In each of the following clauses say whether the Subject, the Direct Object or the Adjunct has been chosen as Theme:

   (1)   About fifty or sixty thousand years ago, there lived on earth a creature similar to man.
   (2)   Skulls and bones of this extinct species of man were found at Neanderthal.
   (3)   Where the first true men originated we do not know.
   (4)   These newcomers eventually drove the Neanderthalers out of existence.
   (5)   In Asia or Africa there may be still undiscovered deposits of earlier and richer human remains.

Module 2

3 †Look at the clauses below and apply the tests outlined in Module 2.2 to answer the questions following them:

(1) The little boy in the red jersey is making a sand castle on the beach.
    (a) Is *the little boy* a constituent of the clause?
    (b) Is *on the beach* a constituent?
    (c) Is *in the red jersey* a constituent?
    (d) Is *castle* a constituent?

(2) Tom happened to take the road to the factory by mistake.
    (a) Is *the road* a constituent?
    (b) Is *to the factory* a constituent?
    (c) Is *by mistake* a constituent?
    (d) Is *happened* a constituent?

4 †Identify each of the uncontextualised clauses listed below as (a) independent; (b) dependent finite; (c) dependent non-finite; (d) abbreviated; (e) verbless. Punctuation and capitals have been omitted.

(1) the complacency of the present government amazes me
(2) although presumed dead
(3) not being a tele-viewer myself
(4) as I am the principal at a large boarding-school for girls
(5) her future husband she met on a course for playleaders
(6) I certainly will
(7) while on vacation in Bali
(8) because he is over-qualified for this job
(9) just when he was starting to get himself organised
(10) we'll probably get only a fraction of the factory's worth

5 †Say to which class of group each of the following belongs:

(1) the anti-terrorist laws
(2) not quite hot enough
(3) within three quarters of an hour
(4) pretty soon
(5) aren't playing
(6) wide awake
(7) his departure from Moscow
(8) in spite of the bad weather

Module 3

6 †Read the text below from *Time*, and then answer the questions which follow:

> 'DOES SHE[1] or doesn't she?'[2] The fashionable answer nowadays is always a louder and louder yes.[3] From Manhattan to Los Angeles a sunburst of bold, exotic, and decidedly unnatural colors, is streaking, squiggling and dotting across the hairstyles of the nation's trendy younger set,[4] and even making inroads among more mature professionals.[5] The startling palette of reds and blues, golds and silvers, greens and purples comes from inexpensive temporary hair-coloring products[6] that are easily applied at home[7] and almost as easily showered away.[8] Confrontational coloration, once a shocking British and American punk emblem,[9] is now celebrated as the sleek plumage of the up-and-coming yuppie generation.[10]

(1) Say which of the numbered clauses are (a) finite independent; (b) finite embedded; (c) abbreviated; (d) verbless.

(2) Which of the numbered clauses are in a coordinating relationship?

(3) Which of these clauses have ellipted elements?

(4) Identify as many recursive elements as you can in the text. Do you consider the choice of recursive elements to have any special importance in this article?

7 †Make the following sentences (a) negative and (b) interrogative-negative:

(1) It will be difficult to find a nice present for Henry.

(2) Sheila has something to tell you.

(3) Someone has left a bag on a seat in the park.

(4) He knows someone who lives in Glasgow.

(5) It is worth going to see some of those pictures.

8 †Fill in the blanks with an appropriate non-assertive item. Say why such an item is needed in this context:

(1) That's a pretty kitten you have there. Have you got . . . . more like it?

(2) She hardly . . . . complains about . . . . he does.

(3) I honestly don't think I could recommend . . . . within ten miles of the coast.

(4) I don't remember seeing . . . . talking to Milly.

9   †Account for the acceptability of the forms without an asterisk and the unacceptability of the forms marked by an asterisk (*) in each of the following sets:

(1)   (a)   He has never spoken to anyone here.
       (b)   He hasn't ever spoken to anyone here.
       (c)   *He has ever spoken to anyone here.
(2)   (a)   Nobody was able to work out the puzzle.
       (b)   There wasn't anybody able to work out the puzzle.
       (c)   *Anybody was able to work out the puzzle.

THE SKELETON OF THE MESSAGE *CHAPTER 2*

Introduction to clause structure

SYNTACTIC ELEMENTS AND STRUCTURES OF THE CLAUSE

SUMMARY

1   The independent clause (or simple sentence) has two basic constituents: subject and predicate. The Subject (S) encodes the primary participant in the clause.

2   The predicate may consist simply of the Predicator (P), realised by a verb, or of a Predicator followed by one or more central constituents. These central elements, the Object (O) and the Complement (C) are, together with the Subject and the Predicator, the major functional categories of the clause.

3   More specifically, we distinguish two main types of Object: Direct (Od) and Indirect (Oi) and two main types of Complement (Subject Complement (Cs) and Object Complement (Co). A subsidiary type of Object is the Prepositional Object (Op). A further type of Complement is the circumstantial Complement, the most frequent being the Locative/Goal type (C_{loc}).

4   In addition, the clause may contain a number of Adjuncts (A). These are usually syntactically able to be omitted. Those of the largest class, the circumstantial Adjuncts, are the most integrated in the clause. Somewhat separated from clause structure by a pause or a comma, stance Adjuncts express a speaker's or writer's attitude, while connective Adjuncts link clauses or parts of clauses, and paragraphs.

5   Objects and Complements are determined by verb type and are limited in number in any one clause. Adjuncts are not limited in number.

6   On the simplest level, the central functional categories of the independent clause are: S, P, O and C, with A usually optional.

4.1 SUBJECT, PREDICATOR, OBJECT, COMPLEMENT, ADJUNCT

4.1.1 Subject and Predicator

Traditionally, the single independent clause (or simple sentence) is divided into two main parts, **subject** and **predicate**. Semantically and communicatively, the **Subject** encodes the main participant (*the plane/ Tom*) in the situation represented by the clause and has the highest claim to the status of **topic**. The predicate can consist entirely of the **Predicator**, realised by a verbal group, as in **1** below, or the Predicator together with one or more other elements, as in **2**:

	Subject	**Predicator**	
1	The plane	landed	
2	Tom	disappeared	suddenly after the concert

It is the predicator that determines the number and type of these other elements. Syntactically, the **Subject (S)** and the **Predicator (P)** are the two main functional categories. For the purpose of analysing and creating discourse it is helpful to see how the predicate is made up, since this tends to be the most informative part of the clause. A first distinction can be made between elements that are essential and elements that are usually optional. This can be seen by comparing 1 and 2.

The two clause elements in **1**, the Subject (*the plane*) and the Predicator realised by the verb *landed* are essential constituents. In **2** on the other hand, the predicate contains, as well as the predicator (*disappeared*), two elements, *suddenly* and *after the concert*, which are not essential for the completion of the clause. Although they are to a certain extent integrated in the clause, they can be omitted without affecting the acceptability of the clause. Such elements will be called **Adjuncts** (A).

4.1.2 Object and Complement

In other cases the predicate consists of the Predicator followed by one or more central constituents that complete the meaning. The two main functional categories which occur in post-verbal position are the **Object** (O) as in **3** and the **Complement** (C) as in **4**:

	S	P	O
3	The students	carried	backpacks
4	Jo	is	a student
	S	P	C

Without these, each of the above clauses would be incomplete both semantically and syntactically: [*The students carried] and [*Jo is], respectively. There are two main types of Object, the **Direct Object (Od)** as in **5**, and the **Indirect Object (Oi)** as in **6**, the indirect object preceding the direct object.

	S	P	Oi	Od
5	All the men	wore		dark suits
6	Tom	sent	me	an email

Semantically, the objects encode the key participants in the event other than the subject: *dark suits, an email* (Od) and *me* (Oi) in these examples. Note that participants include not only human referents, but inanimate things and abstractions (see Chapter 4).

Complements encode constituents that, semantically, are not participants but are nevertheless normally required both syntactically and semantically.

There are two main types of Complement, the **Complement of the Subject (Cs)** (Subject Complement) as in **7a** and **8a**, and the **Complement of the Object** (Object Complement) **(Co)**, as in **7b** and **8b**:

	S	P	Cs		S	P	Od	Co
7a	That map	was	*useful*	**7b**	We	found	that map	*useful*
8a	Ken Brown	is	*President*	**8b**	They	made	Ken Brown	*President*

The Subject Complement and Object Complement do not encode a different kind of participant. Rather, they characterise or identify the Subject or the Object, respectively.

The basic clause structures formed by configurations of these functions are as follows:

S-P   S-P-O   S-P-O-O   S-P-C   S-P-Od-Co   S-P-O-C

4.1.3 The Adjunct

We will recognise three main classes of Adjunct:

- **Circumstantial Adjuncts**, which provide the setting for the situation expressed in the clause, as regards place, time and manner, among others: The new liner 'Queen Elizabeth II' sails *tomorrow from Southampton*.
- **Stance Adjuncts**, which express the speaker's attitude to or evaluation of the content of the clause: *Obviously*, he'll rely on you even more now.
- **Connective Adjuncts**, which link two clauses, or parts of clauses, signalling the semantic relation holding between them: The hotel was rather noisy. *On the other hand*, it wasn't expensive (contrast).

4.2 CRITERIA FOR THE CLASSIFICATION OF CLAUSE ELEMENTS

The criteria adopted for the classification of clause functions are four: determination by the verb, position, ability to become the subject and realisations of these functions.

4.2.1 Determination by the verb

The number and type of objects and complements that can occur in a clause are determined by the verb according to its potential – described in chapters 3 and 5 as its 'valency'. We say that a certain verb predicts an object or a complement. *Eat*, for example, predicts an object that expresses the thing eaten. One sense of *carry* predicts an object that refers to the thing carried (They carried *backpacks*). *Disappear*, however, does not predict or admit an object (*He disapppeared *the money*). Determination is related to verb class.

Transitive verbs usually require one or more objects. They occur in type SPO (*carry*), type S-P-Oi-Od (*send*), and type S-P-O-C (*find*) in one of its uses.

Intransitive verbs such as *disappear* occur in type S-P. They do not admit an object, but certain intransitive verbs predict a complement of space or time, as will be explained shortly.

More exactly, we should talk about transitive or intransitive **uses** of certain verbs, as a great many verbs can be used in English both transitively and intransitively (see Chapter 3). *Land* is transitive in *The pilot landed the plane safely*, but intransitive in *The plane landed. Carry* is transitive in *They carried backpacks*, but it has an intransitive use in *His voice carries well* (= 'projects').

A **locative element** is required by a few transitive verbs such as *put* and *place* (*Put* the handkerchiefs *in the drawer, Place* the dish *in the microwave*). Without this locative element, the clause is syntactically and semantically incomplete (**Put the dish*). It therefore has the status of a central clause element. A locative element is also predicted by many intransitive verbs of motion such as *come, go, fly, drive*, which can predict such meanings as Direction (flying *south*) and Goal, which marks an end-point (go to *Rome*). Both types will be represented here as Locative/Goal Complements subsumed under the abbreviation (C_{loc}). However, it is also possible to use these verbs without a locative, as in for example *Are you coming? Don't go! I'll drive*. (*Drive* in fact predicts an object or a locative or both, as in *I'll drive you to the station*.)

From these we can see that prediction is less strong than requirement. An expression of manner is required with one sense of *treat* (*they treated the prisoners badly*) and with the intransitive verb *behave* (*she has been behaving strangely lately*). The verb *last* predicts an expression of extent in time (*the concert lasted three hours*); however, sometimes the lack of duration can be inferred as in *Their love didn't last*. When predicted or required by the verb, elements such as place or time are analysed as circumstantial Complements, the equivalent of obligatory adverbials in some grammars. A cognitive-semantic view in terms of Source, Path and Goal, following verbs of motion, is given in chapters 8 and 12.

Copular verbs, a type of intransitive, require a Subject Complement. Only verbs capable of being used as copulas can be used in this way. So, for instance, *be* and *feel* as in *I am cold, I feel cold* can be used as copulas in English but *touch* cannot (**I touch cold*).

Besides predicting an attribute, verbs of being such as *be, remain, stay* predict being in a location. Their Complements are then analysed as locative (C$_{loc}$).

The following examples illustrate the parallel between attributes as Subject and Object Complements and the Locative/Goal types. Evidently there are many other verbs which function in only one of these patterns:

Attributive	**Locative/Goal**
He stayed *calm*	He stayed *in bed*
She went *pale*	She went *to work*
He drives me *mad*	He drives me *to the airport*
A bicycle will get you *fit*	A bicycle will get you *to work*

By contrast, adjuncts are not determined by any particular type of verb. *Suddenly*, for instance, can be used with intransitive verbs like *disappear* and transitive verbs like *carry*. Moreover, adjuncts differ from subjects and objects in that there is no limit to the number of adjuncts that can be included in a clause.

4.2.2 Position

Objects occur immediately after the verb, with the indirect object before the direct object when both are present (The bomb killed *a policeman* (Od); He sent *me* (Oi) *an email* (Od)). Complements also occur after the verb or after an object. Adjuncts occupy different positions according to type, and are often moveable within the clause.

4.2.3 Ability to become the subject

Objects can normally become the subject in a passive clause, since the system of voice allows different semantic roles to be associated with Subject and Object functions (*The bomb killed the policeman/ The policeman was killed by the bomb; I sent her an email/ She was sent an email*).

However, passivisation with 'promotion' to subject is not a watertight criterion for the identification of object functions. It can be too exclusive and too inclusive. Passivisation excludes from object status NGs following verbs such as *fit*, which otherwise fulfil the criteria for objects (see 6.1.1).

Conversely, passivisation can promote to subject NGs that are certainly not objects. Such is the case in the well-known example *This bed was slept in by Queen Victoria*, derived from the active *Queen Victoria slept in this bed*, in which *this bed* is part of a prepositional phrase (PP) functioning as a locative Complement, not as an object. A prepositional phrase has within it a nominal group, however, which increasingly in present-day English is able to become subject in a corresponding passive clause. Examples of this kind, such as *The flowerbeds have been trampled on* occur when the subject referent is visibly affected by the action, as is the case here, or acquires some importance, as in the case of the bed slept in by Queen Victoria.

4.2.4 Realisations of these functions

As participants, Objects are typically realised by NGs and answer questions with *what?* who? or which? as in *What did they carry?* in response to example **3** in 4.1.2.

Subject and Object Complements can be realised by Adjective groups (AdjG) (*useful*), as in 7a and 7b, or by a NG (*a student*), as in 8a and 8b.

Circumstantial Adjuncts are realised by PPs (drive *on the right*) or AdvGs (drive *slowly*) and sometimes NGs (I'll see you *next week*). They generally answer questions with *where? when? how? why?* as in *Where does he work?* or *How did it happen?*

4.3 BASIC SYNTACTIC STRUCTURES OF THE CLAUSE

Clausal elements or functions enter into varied relationships with each other to express different types of proposition concerning different states of affairs. These are exemplified as follows, and are treated further in Chapter 3.

S-P	Tom | disappeared
S-P-Od	We | hired | a car
S-P-Oi-Od	I | have sent | them | an invitation
S-P-Cs	My brother | is | a physiotherapist
S-P-A	He | works | in London
S-P-Od-Co	They | appointed | James | First Secretary
S-P-Od-C$_{loc}$	I | put | the dish | in the microwave

The following extract illustrates some of the possible configurations of clause elements (where + stands for a coordinating element):

At the hotel | I | paid | the driver | and gave |
    A   S   P   Oi   +   P

him | a tip. || The car | was | powdered with dust. ||
Oi Od   S   P   Cs

I | rubbed | the rod-case | through the dust. ||
S   P   Od   A

It | seemed | the last thing that connected me with
S   P   Cs

Spain and the fiesta. || The driver | put | the car |

                                            S   P   Od

in gear | and | went | down the street. || I | watched

C_{loc} +   P C_{loc} S   P

it turn off to take the road to Spain. || I | went |

Od   S   P

into the hotel | and | they | gave | me || a room. ||

C_{loc} +   S   P   Oi   Od

It | was | the same room I had slept in when Bill and

S   P   Cs

Cohn and I were in Bayonne. || That | seemed | a very long time ago. ||

                                     S   P   Cs

Ernest Hemingway, *Fiesta (The Sun Also Rises)*

In the remaining sections of this chapter we shall describe the syntactic features of each clausal function and the principal realisations of each, together with any relevant discourse characteristics. Reference will be made to the semantic roles associated with these elements, but these are dealt with more fully in Chapter 4.

Clause functions such as Subject and Predicator are capitalised when first introduced. Later mentions are usually in lower case, with the exception of Complement as a clause function, which is always capitalised, in order to distinguish it from the complement of a noun, adjective or preposition.

4.4 REALISATIONS OF THE ELEMENTS

It is important to remember that, with the exception of the predicator function, there is no one-to-one correspondence between class of unit and syntactic function in English. So, whereas the predicator is always realised by a verbal group, the other functions display a considerable range of possible realisations by different classes of group and clause. It is true that most functions are typically realised by a certain class of unit (for example, subjects and objects by NGs), but the versatility of the language is such that almost any group or clause can realise these functions. As we analyse texts, or create our own, we must be aware that each function can be realised by different classes of unit, and each class of unit can perform various functions.

In the following pages, the realisations of each clause element are arranged in order of typicality. We sometimes use the more exact word '**prototypical**' for something that shows most of the characteristics of its type and is therefore a good example of the type or function, and '**non-prototypical**' for something that is a less good example. A nominal group, for example, is a prototypical realisation of the subject function, whereas a prepositional group is non-prototypical in subject function. When the element is realised by the head-word of a group, the realisation is normally regarded as a group unit.

SUBJECT AND PREDICATOR   *MODULE 5*

SUMMARY

1   The Subject is the syntactic function identified by the features of position, concord, pronominalisation and reflection in question tags. Semantically, almost all participant roles can be associated with the subject. Cognitively, it is that element which has the highest claim to function as Topic in a specific clause in context. Syntactically, it is prototypically realised by a NG, but can also be realised by a wide variety of groups and clauses.

2   The Predicator is the syntactic function that determines the number and type of Objects and Complements in a clause. It is identified syntactically by position and concord. It is associated with a number of semantic domains.

5.1 THE SUBJECT (S)

5.1.1 Semantic, cognitive and syntactic features

A. Semantic and cognitive features

The Subject is that functional category of the clause of which something is predicated. The prototypical subject represents the primary participant in the clause and has the strongest claim to the cognitive status of Topic – who or what the clausal message is primarily about (see 28.4). This means that in basic clauses (that is: finite, active, declarative clauses) of 'doing', the subject aligns with the semantic function of Agent, the one who carries out the action. If there is an agent in the event expressed by such a clause, that element will be the subject.

However, the subject can be associated with almost every type of participant role. The following examples illustrate some of the possible roles aligned with the subject:

Jones kicked the ball into the net.   (Agent)
The ball was kicked into the net.   (Affected in a passive clause)
Tom saw a snake near the river.   (Experiencer in a mental process) (see 17.1)
The secretary has been given some chocolates.   (Recipient in a passive clause)

Semantic roles are treated in Chapter 4, Topic and Theme in Chapter 6.

B. Syntactic features

The **Subject** is that syntactic function which, in English, must be present in declarative and interrogative clauses, but is not required in the imperative. In discourse, when two or more conjoined clauses have the same subject, all but the first are regularly ellipted.

He came in, sat down and took out a cigarette.

A clear and easy criterion is the **question tag**. The Subject is that element which is picked up in a question tag (see 23.8) and referred to anaphorically by a pronoun:

Your brother is a ski instructor, isn't *he*?
Susie won't mind waiting a moment, will *she*?

The Subject is placed **before the finite verb** in declarative clauses, and in *wh*-interrogative clauses where the *wh*-element is Subject (see 23.6):

Unfortunately, *everyone* left early.
Who came in late last night?

It is placed **after the finite operator** (the first element of the VG, 2.5.2) in *yes/no* interrogative clauses, and in *wh*-interrogative clauses in which the *wh*-element is not Subject (see 23.6):

Are *you* pleased with the result?
Did *everyone* leave early?
What film did *you* see last night?   (*What film* is Object)
When did *Sylvia* get back?   (*When* is Adjunct)

When **pronouns** are used, the pronominal forms – *I, he, she, we* and *they* – are used to realise subject function, in contrast to the objective forms *me, him, her, us* and *them*, which are used for Objects. *You* and *it* are the same for both. Possessive forms may stand as subject:

Yours was rather difficult to read.
Jennifer's got lost in the post.

Subjects determine the **concord** of number (singular or plural) and person with the verb. Concord is manifested only in those verb forms that show inflectional contrast:

The librarian/ he/ she/ has checked the book.
The librarians/ I/ you/ we/ they have checked the book.
Where is *my credit card*? Where *are my credit cards*?

With verb forms that show **no number or person contrast** – such as *had*, in *the money had all been spent* – we can apply the criterion of paradigmatic contrast with a present form such as *has* (*the money has all been spent*).

When the Subject is realised by a collective noun, concord depends on how the referent is visualised by the speaker:

The committee is sitting late.   (seen as a whole)
The committee have decided to award extra grants.   (seen as a number of members)

Subjects determine number, person and gender **concord with the Subject Complement**, and of reflexive pronouns at Cs, Oi and Od:

Jean and Bill are *my friends.*
She cut *herself* (Od) on a piece of broken glass.
Why don't you give *yourself* (Oi) a treat?

5.1.2 Realisations of the Subject

Subjects can be realised by various classes of groups and clauses:

A. Nominal Groups – *That man is crazy*

Nominal groups are the most prototypical realisation of subject, as they refer basically to persons and things. They can range from simple heads (see 45.3.1) to the full complexity of NG structures (see 50.1):

Cocaine can damage the heart as well as the brain.
The precise number of heart attacks from using cocaine is not known.
It is alarming.

B. Dummy it – *It's hot*

This is a non-referential or semantically empty use of the pronoun *it*, which occurs in expressions of time, weather and distance, such as:

It's nearly three o'clock.
It's raining.
It is six hundred kilometres from Madrid to Barcelona.

Syntactically, English requires the presence of a subject even in such situations, in order to distinguish between declaratives and interrogatives:

Is it raining? How far is *it* from here to Barcelona?

There is no plural concord with a NG complement, as would occur in Spanish counterparts, for example: *Son las tres. Son seiscientos kilómetros a Barcelona.*

C. Unstressed there – *There's plenty of time*

Unstressed *there* (see 19.3; 30.4) fulfils several of the syntactic criteria for subject: position, inversion with auxiliaries and repetition in tag phrases; but unlike normal subjects it cannot be replaced by a pronoun. Concord, when made, is with the following NG:

> There *was only one fine day last week*, wasn't there?
> There *were only two fine days last week*, weren't there?

Concord with the following NG is made in writing, but not always in informal spoken English with the present tense of *be*, and is never made when the NG is a series of proper names:

> How many are coming? Well, *there's Andrew and Silvia, and Jo and Pete.*
> *There *are* Andrew and Silvia and Jo and Pete.

Because of the lack of concord and pronominalisation, unstressed *there* can be considered as a subject 'place-holder' or 'syntactic filler', rather than a full subject, since the unit following the verb is clearly the notional subject. For its function as a presentative device, see 30.4.

The following comment on Monte Carlo by J. G. Ballard in *The Week* illustrates some of the syntactic features and realisations of the Subject (see exercise).

> Have *you* ever been to Monte Carlo?[1] *It's* totally dedicated to expensive shopping.[2] *You* go to these gallerias and walk past a great temple to ultra-expensive watches, then another to ultra-expensive clothes.[3] *It's* quite incredible[4] – *you* see the future of the human race there.[5] *There* is a particularly big galleria, which never has anyone inside it.[6] *It's* five or six floors of cool, scented air, with no one in it.[7] *I* thought to myself – is *this* supposed to be heaven?[8] And *I* realised that, no, *it's* not heaven[9] *It's* The Future.[10]

D. Prepositional phrase and Adverbial group as subject – *Now is the time*

These function only marginally as subject and usually specify meanings of time or place, but instrumental meanings and idiomatic manner uses can also occur.

> Will *up in the front* suit you? (PP of place)
> *Before midday* would be convenient. (PP of time)
> *By plane* costs more than by train. (PP of means)

Just here would be an ideal place for a picnic.   (AdvG of place)
Slowly/gently does it!   (AdvG of manner)

E. Adjectival head – *the poor*

The Adjectival Group as such does not function as subject. However, certain adjectives – preceded by a definite determiner, normally the definite article, and which represent either (a) conventionally recognised classes of people, as in *The handicapped* are given special facilities in public places, or (b) abstractions – can function as heads of (non-prototypical) NGs (see 51.5). The latter type is illustrated in this extract from a book blurb:

> This novel plunges the reader into a universe in which *the comic, the tragic, the real* and *the imagined* dissolve into one another.

F. Embedded clauses (see 3.6.3)

Clauses can realise every element or function of clause structure except the predicator. Cognitively, this means that we as speakers encode, as the main elements of clauses, not only persons and things but facts, abstractions and situations. Both finite and non-finite clauses are available for embedding but not every clause function is realised by all types of clause. The main types were outlined in Chapter 1. Here five of the relevant one(s) are referred to when describing the realisations of subject, objects and complements.

There are two main types of embedded finite clause: **that-clauses** and **wh-clauses**, the latter being either indirect interrogative clauses or nominal relative clauses. They are illustrated in the following examples, where they all realise the subject element.

> *That he failed his driving test* surprised everybody.   (*that*-clause)
> *Why the library was closed for months* was not explained.   (*wh*-interrogative)
> *What he said* shocked me.   (*wh*-nominal relative clause)

That-clauses at subject are used only in formal styles in English. In everyday use they are more acceptable if they are preceded by *the fact*. The *that*-clause thus becomes complement of a NG functioning as subject:

> *The fact that he failed his driving test* surprised everybody.   (NG)

A more common alternative is to **extrapose** the subject *that*-clause, as in *It surprised everybody that he failed his driving test*, explained in G. below.

Wh-interrogative clauses express indirect questions. They do not take the inversion characteristic of ordinary interrogatives, however; so, for instance, **Why was the library closed for months was not explained* is not acceptable.

Nominal relative clauses also have a *wh*- element, but they express entities and can be paraphrased by 'that which' or 'the thing(s) which' as in:

> *What he said* pleased me = 'that which'/the things which *he said pleased me*.

Non-finite clauses at Subject are of two main types, depending on the VG they contain: **to-infinitive**, which can be introduced by a *wh*-word, and **-*ing* clauses**. (The third non-finite clause type, the *-en* clause, is not used in this way.) The 'bare' infinitive is marginally used:

> *To take such a risk* was rather foolish.   (*to*-inf. clause)
> *Where to leave the dog* is the problem.   (*wh*- + to-inf. clause)
> *Having to go back for the tickets* was a nuisance.   (*-ing* clause)
> *Move the car* was what we did.   (bare infinitive clause)

To-infinitive and *-ing* clauses at subject can have their own subject; bare infinitive clauses cannot. A *to*-infinitive clause with its own subject is introduced by *for*:

> *For everyone to escape* was impossible.   (*For* + S + *to*-inf.)
> *Sam having to go back for the tickets* was a nuisance.   (S + *ing*-cl.)

The pronominal subject of an *-ing* clause can be in the possessive or the objective case. The objective form is the less formal:

> *Him / his having to go back for the tickets* was a nuisance.

G. Anticipatory it + extraposed subject – It was silly to say that

Subjects such as *that he failed to pass the driving test* and *for everyone to escape* sound awkward and top-heavy, especially in spoken English. The derived structure with 'anticipatory *it*' is now generally preferred, as it is much easier to encode and the pronoun *it* is the 'lightest' possible subject filler:

> *It* surprised everybody *that he failed his driving test.*
> *It* was impossible *for everyone to escape.*

Here the *that*-clause or the *to*-infinitive clause is extraposed (see 30.5), that is, placed after the Od (*everybody*) or Cs (*impossible*). The initial subject position is filled by the pronoun *it*. Extraposition is commonly used in both speech and writing, especially when the subject is long and heavy, and is better placed at the end of the sentence, in accordance with the informational and stylistic principle of 'end-weight' (see 30.3.2).

Extraposed subjects frequently occur as the complement of a noun or adjective in SPCs structures, as in the following illustrations:

> It's *easy to forget your keys. (To forget your keys is easy)*
> It's *a pity* (that) you are leaving the firm. *(That you are leaving the firm is a pity)*
> It is *time* he stopped fooling around.

Notice that, for the apparently extraposed clause that follows *It is (high) time*, there is no corresponding pattern with the clause in initial position (**That he stopped fooling around is high time*).

Likewise, the clause following *it* + *verbs* of seeming (*seem, appear*) and happening (*happen, turn out*), is obligatorily extraposed:

> It seems that you were right after all. (*That you were right after all seems.)
> It so happened that the driver lost control. (*That the driver lost control happened.)

Pronouns account for a high percentage of subjects in the spoken language, as can be seen in the following recorded dialogue about the mini-skirt. Several other types of subject are also illustrated in the main and embedded clauses of this text, including two different functions of *it*:

Q. What about the mini-skirt itself? What was the origin of that?

A. That[1] started in the East End of London. *Mary Quant*[2] picked it up and then *a lot of other designers*[3] did too. *I*[4] think again *it*[5] was reaction against the long skirts of the 1950s. *It*[6] was smart to get much, much shorter. *I*[7] think that, partly, *it*[8] was fun to shock your father and older people, but *it*[9] was also a genuinely felt fashion, as *we*[10] can see by the fact that it spread nearly all over the world. *I*[11] think *it*[12] is a lovely look, long leggy girls. *The fact that fat legs are seen, too,*[13] is just bad luck. But *I*[14] still don't think that *the mini-skirt*[15] is going to disappear for some time. *I*[16] think *girls*[17] just love the feeling.

[1]demonstrative pronoun; [2]proper noun; [3]NG; [4]pronoun; [5]pronoun: [6]anticipatory it + to-infinitive; [7]pronoun; [8]anticipatory it + to-infinitive; [9]pronoun; [10]pronoun; [11]pronoun; [12]anticipatory it + NG; [13]*the fact* + *that*-clause; [14]pronoun; [15]NG; [16]pronoun; [17]NG

(Janey Ironside in *Artists Talking: Five artists talk to Anthony Schooling*)

5.2 THE PREDICATOR (P)

We use the term Predicator for the clause element present in all major types of clause, including the imperative clause (in which the subject is not usually present in English).

The predicator is the clause function that largely determines the remaining structure of the clause, by virtue of being intransitive, transitive or copular.

As seen in 4.1, the predicator may constitute the whole of the predicate, as in *The plane landed*, or part of it, as in *The plane landed on the runway*.

The predicator is identified by position in relation to the subject.

The predicator function is realised by both finite (e.g. *waits*) and non-finite (*waiting*) lexical and primary verbs.

Functionally, finiteness is often carried by an auxiliary verb – such as *is, was* – to specify tense (past/present) and voice (*be* + *-en*), and is then followed by the predicator (is making, was made). For the Finite–Subject relation in interrogative structures, see Chapter 5.

Semantically, the predicator encodes the following main types of 'process':

- material processes of 'doing' with verbs such as *make, catch, go*;
- mental processes of 'experiencing', with cognitive verbs of perception (e.g. *see*), cognition (*know*), affectivity (*like*) and desideration (*hope*); and
- relational processes of 'being' with verbs such as *be* and *belong*.

These, and certain subsidiary types, are discussed in Chapter 4.

Phrasal verbs and prepositional verbs are discussed in this chapter (as clause element) and in Chapter 8 (as regards meaning).

The following passage about the Valley of the Kings shows the Predicator function in both finite and non-finite clauses (see exercise):

It [the Valley of the Kings] lies about six hundred kilometres south of Cairo, the present-day capital of Egypt, near the Nile.[1] Across the river is the city of Luxor,[2] once called Thebes and one of the greatest capitals of the ancient world.[3] This dusty, dried-up river valley is the most magnificent burial ground in the world.[4] During the second millennium B.C., Egyptian workers quarried a series of tombs beneath this valley,[5] decorating them with mysterious predictions of the underworld[6] and filling them with treasures.[7] There, with infinite care and artistry, they laid out the mummified and bejewelled bodies of their rulers[8] and surrounded them with their belongings,[9] making the valley one of the greatest sacred sites in history.[10]

(Gerald O'Farrell, *The Tutankamun Deception*)

DIRECT, INDIRECT AND PREPOSITIONAL OBJECTS

SUMMARY

1   The Direct Object (Od) and Indirect Object (Oi) are central syntactic functions which encode participants in transitive clauses, and are identified by the following features:

2   *Position.* In clauses with one Object, The Direct Object follows the verb (She wanted to borrow *a video*). When there are two Objects, the Direct Object follows the Indirect Object (So I lent *her* (Oi) *one* (Od)).

3   *Paraphrase.* The Oi usually has an alternative prepositional paraphrase (I lent one *to her*), with the status of a Prepositional Object, but the Od has not.

4   *Pronominalisation.* Since objects encode participants, they can be realised by objective case pronouns (*me, him, her, us, them*).

5   *'Promotion' to subject in a passive clause.* Both direct and indirect objects usually have the potential of being subject in a corresponding passive clause (He sent *them a fax. The fax* (S) was sent. *They* (S) were sent *a fax*).

6   *Semantic roles.* The indirect object is associated with the Recipient and Beneficiary roles, the direct object with the Affected, among others.

7   *Realisations.* Both Objects are realised typically by Nominal Groups expressing entities; less typically by other classes of unit.

6.1 THE DIRECT OBJECT (Od)

6.1.1 Syntactic and semantic features

After the subject and the predicator, the direct object is the most central of all clause constituents. It is characterised by the following features:

- It occurs only in transitive clauses with transitive verbs such as *hit, buy, send*.
- It is placed immediately after the predicator, but follows an indirect object, if there is one –

> I have sent *the invitations* (Od).
> I have sent *everyone* (Oi) *an invitation* (Od).

- It is typically realised by a NG, as in *I saw the burglar* (NG), but may also be realised by embedded clauses, as in *I saw what he did* (cl.).
- It can generally be 'promoted' to become subject in a corresponding passive clause –

> *The invitations* (S) have been sent. (corresponding to the Od in *I have sent the invitations*)

- Direct objects can be tested for, by questions beginning with *Who(m)? What? Which? How much/ many?* and by *wh*-clefts.

> What did you send?
> What I sent were the invitations   (*wh*-cleft)

- Semantically, a prototypical direct object occurs in a high-transitivity situation (see 21.4) – that is, in a process of 'doing' in which the referent's state or location is affected in some way, as in the first example below.

However the Od is associated with a wide variety of semantic roles in which 'affected-ness' is not a feature, and with many types of verbs (see Chapter 4), some of which are illustrated in the following examples:

> He headed *the ball* into the net.   (Affected)
> The burglars used *an acetylene lamp* to break open the safe.   (Instrument)
> I felt *a sudden pain in my arm*.   (Phenomenon: i.e. that which is experienced)
> He gave the door *a push*.   (Range: i.e. the nominalised extension of the verb; see
> 20.2)
> He swam *the Channel*.   (Affected locative)

The highly non-prototypical Range Ods (20.2) include *have a rest/ smoke/ drink; take a sip/ nap, give a kick/nudge, do a dance,* and many others. The NG in these cases is a deverbal noun (i.e. derived from a verb) which follows a verb that is 'light' in semantic content such as *have*. Such combinations are very common.

The Channel in *swim the Channel* is a direct object, whereas in *swim across the Channel* it is the NG complement of a prepositional phrase functioning as Adjunct. The difference is that the Od version is more integrated within the clause, and perhaps for this reason appears to present the event as more of an achievement. The same difference is present in *climb Everest* and *ride a horse* vs *climb up Everest* and *ride on a horse*, respectively. The achievement is clearly completed in the former case, but leaves open the possibility of incompletion in the latter. Speech act deverbal nouns such as *promise* and *warning* are commonly used as Ods, in some cases following a light verb (*make*), in others a specific verb (*issue*):

> He made a promise
> He issued a warning

6.1.2 Realisations of the Direct Object

The Direct Object can be realised by groups and by clauses. There are five main possibilities:

A. Nominal Group   *We hired a caravan*

The typical realisation of the Direct Object function is the nominal group, ranging from a pronoun **1** or proper name to full NGs **2**. In fact, as new entities are often introduced into the discourse in object position, the principle of end-weight (see 30.3.2) can make for the frequent occurrence of longer and more complex NGs at Direct Object in certain registers as in **3**:

1 I don't understand *it*.
2 Have you read *that new novel I lent you*?
3 Forest fires are threatening *the world's remaining population of orang-utangs*.

A small number of common verbs take **untypical direct objects**. They include verbs such as *have* (They have *two cars*), *cost* (it cost *ten pounds*), *lack* (She lacks *confidence*), *resemble* (She resembles *her elder sister*), *fit* (Do these shoes fit *you*?), *suit* (That colour doesn't suit *me*), *weigh* (The suitcase weighs *twenty kilos*), *contain* (That box contains *explosives*) and *measure* (It measures *two metres by three*.) All these answer questions with *What? Who? How much/how many*?, as is usual with Ods. These verbs don't passivise, but their Ods pass the *wh-cleft* test: *What she lacks is confidence*.

B. Anticipatory it – *I find it strange that she left*

The semantically empty pronoun *it* is necessary as an 'anticipatory Direct Object' in SPOdCo structures in which the Od is realised by a finite or non-finite clause:

S	P	(Od)	Co	Od
I	find	it	strange	*that he refuses to come.*
She	might consider	it	insulting	*for you to leave now.*
You	must find	it	flattering	*having so many fans.*

C. Prepositional Phrase – The boss prefers before 10 for the meeting

Prepositional phrases of time or place can marginally realise direct object:

> I would prefer *before noon* for a meeting.
> Don't choose *by a swamp* for a picnic.

D. Finite clause – You know (that) I'm right

The two types of finite clause found at subject can also function as a less prototypical Direct Object: nominal *that*-clauses, *that* often being omitted in informal styles, and *wh*-clauses (see Chapter 3).

> They fear *that there may be no survivors.*   (nominal *that*-clause)
> No-one knows *where he lives.* (*wh*-clause)
> You can eat *whatever you like.* (*wh*-nominal clause)

Both *that*-clauses and *wh*-clauses at Od can sometimes become subject in a passive clause and then extraposed:

> It is feared *that there may be no survivors.*   (extraposed cl.)
> It is not known *where he lives.*

However, passivisation is not a unique criterion for assigning object status. A more reliable test is the *wh*-cleft paraphrase, as seen above. We can apply this to the following example with *wonder*, which rejects passivisation but fulfils the *wh*-cleft test:

> I wonder *whether they know the truth.*
> *Whether they know the truth is wondered.
> *What I wonder* is whether they know the truth.

E. Non-finite clause – They enjoy travelling by train

Non-finite clauses realising Direct Object function are of two types: infinitive clauses with or without *to*, and *-ing* clauses.

> Many Londoners prefer *to travel by train.*
> Many Londoners prefer *travelling by train.*

We analyse such clauses as embedded at Od on the strength of the following criteria:

- The non-finite clause can be replaced by a NG (*prefer the train*) or by *it/that* (*prefer it*).
- The non-finite clause can be made the focus of a *wh*-cleft sentence (*What many Londoners prefer is to travel/ travelling by train*).

However, not all non-finites pass these tests. We do not analyse as embedded clauses at direct object 'phased' verbal groups with certain types of catenatives, as in *He failed to appear, I tried to speak* (see 39.2). Although superficially similar, they do not fulfil the above criteria. Taking *He failed to appear*, we can't say **He failed it*, nor make a corresponding cleft **What he failed was to appear*. In both cases it would be necessary to add *to do*; *What he failed to do was appear*, which confirms the phased nature of such VGs. As a full lexical verb, as in *fail the exam, fail* does of course fulfil these criteria.

Many embedded clauses at direct object occur with an explicit subject of their own; otherwise, the implicit subject is the same as that of the main clause:

(i)   *to*-infinitive clause –

The villagers want *to leave immediately*.   (implicit subject [*they*])
The villagers want *the soldiers to leave immediately*.   (explicit subject *the soldiers*)

(ii)   *-ing* clause –

Do you mind *waiting a few minutes*?   (with implicit subject)
Do you mind *me/my waiting a few minutes*?   (with explicit subject in objective or possessive case)

(iii)   *to*-infinitive or *-ing* clause –

He hates *telling lies*.   (implicit subject)
He hates *people telling lies*.   (explicit subject)
He hates *for people to tell lies*.   (*for* + explicit subject + to-inf) (AmE)

Again, non-finite clauses are very non-prototypical direct objects. They represent situations, not entities, and do not easily passivise. However, many can become the focus in a *wh*-cleft: What he hates is *people telling lies/ for people to tell lies*.

The following news item, 'Fire Threat to Apes' from *The Week*, illustrates some of the realisations of subject and object functions (see exercise 2, p. 77).

> *Coal fires raging deep underground in the forests of Borneo* could threaten *the world's remaining populations of wild orang-utans.*[1] *Scientists* fear *that the blazes may trigger another devastating cycle of forest fires,*[2] *reducing the apes' habitat to the point of extinction.*[3] *Scientists* have identified *150 fires in the region*[4] – but suspect *the total number could exceed 3,000.*[5] *Coalfield fires expert Dr. Alfred Whitehouse* described *the devastation caused by underground fires he witnessed in the Kutai national park.*[6] *"The orang-utans* are driven into smaller and smaller areas of forest,"* he said.[7] "*It* was tragic.[8] *I* was in a mining area[9] and *there* were three orang-utans hanging to the last standing tree.[10]

6.2 THE INDIRECT OBJECT (Oi)

6.2.1 Syntactic and semantic features

The indirect object occurs only with verbs which can take two objects such as *give, send*. Its position in clause structure is between the verb and the direct object: I sent *them* a fax.

It is typically realised by a NG, but occasionally by a *wh*-nominal clause. As a pronoun, it is in the objective case.

The indirect object is associated with two semantic roles, Recipient (the one who receives the goods or information), and the Beneficiary or 'intended recipient'. The differences between the two are reflected in the syntax.

Recipient Oi	Beneficiary Oi
She has lent *me* a few CDs.	I'll buy *you* a drink.
The doctor gave *the injured man* oxygen.	He got *us* the tickets.
Sammy Karanja is teaching *the students* maths.	She left *him* a note.

In passive counterparts the Recipient **Oi** corresponds to the subject. By contrast, most Beneficiary Objects do not easily become subject in a passive clause, although this restriction is not absolute, at least for some speakers:

Recipient as Subject	Beneficiary as Subject
I have been lent a few CDs.	*You'll be bought a drink.
The injured man was given oxygen.	*We were got the tickets.
The students are being taught maths by Sammy Karanja.	He was left a note.

Both Recipient and Beneficary **Oi** have an optional prepositional paraphrase, which functions as a Prepositional Object. For the Recipient, the preposition is *to*, for the Beneficiary it is *for*. The prepositional form is often used to bring the **Oi** into focus, particularly when it is longer than the **Od**:

The doctor gave oxygen *to the injured man*.	I'll buy drinks *for you all*.
She lent a few CDs *to her next-door neighbour*.	He got the tickets *for us all*.
He is teaching maths *to the first-year students*.	She left a note *for her husband*.

The Oi can generally be left unexpressed without affecting the grammaticality of the clause:

The doctor gave oxygen.   I'll buy the drinks.
He doesn't like lending his CDs.   He got the tickets.
Sammy Karanja is teaching maths.   She left a note.

With some verbs (*show, tell, teach*, etc.) the Od may be unexpressed:

Who told *you* (the answer)?
Perhaps you could show *me* (how to do it.)
He's teaching *immigrant children* (maths).

6.2.2 Realisations of the Indirect Object

Both Recipient and Beneficiary Indirect Objects are typically realised by NGs, and less typically by *wh*-nominal relative clauses, which occur more usually as a prepositional alternative:

The clerk handed *him* the envelope.   (Recip./NG)
You can lend the dictionary *to whoever needs it*.   (Recip./nom. relative cl.)
Phil has booked *all his friends tickets* for the show.   (Ben/NG)

More marginally, a Recipient Oi can be realised by a non-finite *-ing* clause or a PP, but these options are not open to a Beneficiary Oi, which always refers to an entity:

I'm giving *reading magazines* less importance lately.   (*-ing* cl)
Let's give *before lunch-time* priority.   (PP)

6.3 PREPOSITIONAL VERBS AND THE PREPOSITIONAL OBJECT (Op)

A subsidiary type of Object is that which is mediated by a preposition. We will call this the Prepositional Object (Op) – Oblique Object is another term – as in:

Jo looked after my cat.
You can rely on Jane in an emergency.
The other kids all laughed at Amy when she got her face dirty.

These examples all have in common the following characteristics:

- The NG following the preposition encodes a participant in the clause structure.
- The preposition is associated with a particular verb, often called a prepositional verb. Idiomatic prepositional verbs have separate lexical entries in dictionaries.
- Without the preposition, the clause would either be ungrammatical (*look my cat, *count Jane, *laughed Amy) or, in some cases, have a different meaning altogether, as in *see to the baggage* (attend to it) as opposed to *see the baggage*.

- The preposition can't be replaced by another preposition without changing the meaning (*look after the cat, look for the cat, look at the cat*).

6.3.1 Types of verb + preposition combinations

There are three main types of prepositional verb, as illustrated by the previous examples.

Type A (look + after)

This combination functions as a lexical unit in which the verb + the preposition together have a different meaning from their separate words. 'Look after' has nothing to do with looking, nor with the usual meaning of 'after' in relation to space or time. Other verbs of this type are exemplified here:

I came across some old photos (find)   She takes after her mother (resemble)
How did you come by that job (obtain)   We took to each other at once (like)
Sandy has come into a fortune (inherit)   I've gone off yogurt (lose the liking for)

Type B (rely + on)

This is a less idiomatic combination whose meaning is sometimes, though not always, transparent. Verbs in this group – *account for* (explain), *refer to, tamper with* (interfere with) – are not used without their specific preposition:

How do you account for the lack of interest in the European elections?
Someone has been tampering with the scanner.

Type C (laugh + at)

The verb + preposition represents a special use, usually with a distinctive meaning, of a verb which otherwise can function without the preposition (for example, *Everyone laughed*; *Don't laugh*). Other verbs include *look* (*at*), *believe* (*in*), *count* (*on*), *hear* (*of*), *wait* (*for*), *hope* (*for*).

look at the sky   hear of a good offer
wait for the bus   hope for a rise in salary

6.3.2 Syntactic behaviour of prepositional verbs

Applying some of the constituency tests (see 2.2), we find the following:

Type A

The verb + preposition behave syntactically as one unit, whereas the PP 'after the cat' does not, as regards fronting, focus of a cleft, *wh*-question and adverb insertion:

	Acceptable	Unacceptable
Fronting:	My cat Jo looked after.	*After my cat Jo looked.
Focus of a cleft:	It's my cat (that) Jo looked after.	*It's after my cat (that) Jo looked.
Wh-question:	Whose cat did Jo look after?	*After whose cat did Jo look?
Adverb insertion:	Jo looked after my cat carefully.	?Jo looked carefully after my cat.

Type B

The PP can function as an independent unit, although the effect is marked and very formal. In spoken English the preposition preferably stays close to the verb:

	Formal	Informal
Fronting:	On Jane you can rely.	Jane you can rely on.
Focus of a cleft:	It's on Jane (that) you can rely.	It's Jane you can rely on.
Wh-question:	On whom can you rely?	Who can you rely on?
Adverb insertion:	You can rely totally on Jane.	Who can you totally rely on?

Type C

Syntactically, the PP functions in the same way as Type B. However, the formal variant is at odds with the type of verb that usually falls into this group.

	Formal	Informal
Fronting:	At Amy the kids laughed.	Amy the kids laughed at.
Focus of a cleft:	It was at Amy that they laughed.	It was Amy they laughed at.
Wh-question:	At whom did the kids laugh?	Who did the kids laugh at?

6.3.3 Stranding the preposition

When the preposition stays close to its verb, as occurs in the examples on the right, we say that it is **stranded**, that is, displaced from its position in a PP. The verb and the preposition stay together, with the stress usually on the verb. Stranding of prepositions occurs, not only in the structures illustrated, but also with prepositional verbs used in passive clauses, as we'll see in a moment, and in **relative clauses**, as in the following:

Non-stranded preposition	Stranded preposition
*The cat after which Jo looked . . .	The cat that Jo looked after . . .
The person on whom you can rely . . .	The person you can rely on . . .
The girl at whom the kids laughed . . .	The girl the kids laughed at . . .

Taking all these tests together, it is clear that in idiomatic Type A combinations, the preposition always stays close to the verb, that is, it is always stranded. In Type B and Type C, the whole prepositional phrase can stay together as a unit, although this is a marked option in spoken English. The non-stranded form, when it occurs, is reserved for highly formal contexts and formal text types, such as academic prose. But even in highly formal contexts the stranded form is usually preferred in spoken English, as the following quotation illustrates. The speaker is the US Secretary of State, Colin Powell, addressing the United Nations Council in February 2003:

> **What we need is not more inspections. What we need is not more immediate access. What we need is immediate full unconditional cooperation by Irak. To this day we have not seen the level of cooperation that was expected, *looked for, hoped for*.**

6.3.4 The prepositional passive

The previous quotation also illustrates stranding in the prepositional passive (was looked for, hoped for). In many combinations, although not in all, the NG complement of a PP can become subject in a passive clause. The preposition is obligatorily stranded:

My cat was looked after	*After my cat was looked
Jane can be relied on	*On Jane can be relied
Amy was laughed at	*At Amy was laughed

6.3.5 Realisations of the Prepositional Object

Experientially, the unit following the preposition is seen as a participant in the situation, for the reasons previously discussed. NGs are the typical realisations of the Op, but nominal clauses and non-finite -*ing* clauses also occur:

He almost ran over *a rabbit* on a country road last night.   (NG)
I strongly object to *what you are insinuating*.   (nominal clause)
He believes in *getting things done as quickly as possible*.   (*-ing* cl.)

It is clear that verbs which control prepositions do not constitute a homogeneous class. There are various degrees of integration, ranging from the relatively loosely integrated such as *smile* (*at*) and *wait* (*for*), where the verb can function without a preposition, to those which bond with the preposition to form a new lexical unit (*look after, take to*). The latter are given separate entries in dictionaries and, in those dictionaries which provide grammatical information, are given different analyses. The PP following Type 3 verbs such as *smile* and *wait* is often classified as Adjunct or as prepositional Complement (PPC). According to use in context, one analysis may be more suitable than another.

In this book we use the term prepositional Object for the NG complement of a preposition which can refer to a participant, distinguishing this function from that of the circumstantial PP functioning as C_{loc} or as Adjunct. Compare, for example, *We waited for the bus* with *We waited at the bus-stop*, where *at the bus-stop* is Adjunct. The distinction is not absolute, however, as we saw in the example *This bed was slept in by Queen Victoria.* Cognitive factors of attention and salience intervene to allow some of the NGs in circumstantial PPs to become subjects, as in *this house hasn't been lived in.*

6.4 PHRASAL VERBS: THE VERB + PARTICLE COMBINATION

Phrasal verbs consist of a lexical verb + an adverbial 'particle' (p). They can be intransitive (without an Object: *get up*) or transitive (taking a Direct Object: *switch it off*).

Phrasal prepositional verbs consist of a lexical verb + a particle + a preposition (*put up with*). They function like idiomatic prepositional verbs.

6.4.1 Syntactic features

Phrasal verbs are combinations of a lexical verb and an adverbial particle (**p**) (*get up, switch on/off, take back, sit down*). They may be intransitive, with no object, as in **1** or transitive (with a direct object) as in **2** and **3**:

1   What time do you usually *get up* in the morning?
2a She *switched off* the light.   **2b** She *switched* the light *off.*
3   She *switched **it** off.*

With a noun as Object, the particle in most cases may either precede or follow the object as in **2**. But if the Object is a pronoun, the particle is placed after it, as in **3**.

The motivation for this choice has to do with the distribution of information. We focus on the new information by placing it last. So in **2a** the new information is the light; while in **2b** and **3** it is the switching off (see Chapter 6). Pronouns do not usually represent new information and are placed before the particle.

This choice of emphasing either the noun or the particle is not possible with a synonymous one-word verb. Compare:

They *cancelled* the wedding. (focus on *wedding*)
They *called off* the wedding. (focus on *wedding*)
They *called* the wedding *off*. (focus on *off*)

Some verb + particle combinations can be used both transitively and intransitively, e.g. *blow up* (= explode), *break down* (= reduce to pieces). In some cases the transitive and intransitive clauses form an ergative pair (see 15.1) with a causative meaning in the transitive:

Terrorists have *blown up* the power station. (transitive)
The power station has *blown up*. (intransitive)

while in others the meaning is related by metaphorical extension:

They *broke down* the door to rescue the child. (transitive)
Her health *broke down* under the strain. (intransitive)
The car has *broken down*. (= stop working) (intransitive)

6. 4. 2 Differences between phrasal verbs and prepositional verbs

We explain here differences of position, stress and adverb insertion in the clause, illustrating them with the phrasal verb *break up* and the prepositional verb *break with*, as in *He broke up the party* (phrasal verb) and *He broke with his girl-friend* (prepositional verb).

A pronoun follows a preposition but precedes the particle of a phrasal verb (as elsewhere, the asterisk indicates an ungrammatical sequence):

He broke with *her*.   He broke *it up*.
*He broke *her* with.   *He broke *up it*.

The particle in phrasal verbs is stressed, especially when in final position in the clause, whereas a preposition is normally unstressed. In prepositional verbs the stress normally falls on the verb (capitals indicate the stressed syllable; see also 29.2):

He broke it UP.   He has BROken with her.
Which party did he break UP?   Which girl has he BROken with?

As seen in 6.3.2. Type B, an adverb can sometimes be placed between a verb and its following preposition. Phrasal verbs do not normally admit an adverb between the verb and the particle:

*He broke *completely up* the party.   He broke *completely* with his girl-friend.

In idiomatic phrasal verbs the particle is usually analysed as part of the verb (*peter out*. There is no separate verb '*peter*') In 'free' combinations in which the adverb particle is directional, this is analysed as Complement, as in *The rain came down*. The adverbial particle can be fronted (*Down came the rain*) for rhetorical purposes, and this mobility is a feature of Complements and Adjuncts. With non-directional meanings, the adverbial particle is inseparable from the verb, and can't be fronted (*The car broke down*, **Down broke the car*).

The semantics of phrasal verbs is described in Chapter 8.

6.4.3 Phrasal-prepositional verbs

Phrasal-prepositional verbs consist of a lexical verb followed by an adverbial particle and a preposition, in that order: *run up against, do away with*. They are particularly characteristic of informal English, and new combinations are constantly being coined. Phrasal-prepositional verbs function like prepositional verbs, taking a prepositional object in the clause:

> We *ran up against* difficulties.   (=encounter)
> They have *done away with* free school meals.   (=abolish)

Finally, it is important to realise that many verbs, whether single- or multi-word, can be followed by a PP functioning as a circumstantial Complement in the clause, as in They went *into the garden*. They express meanings of place, direction, time or means. They are generally questioned by *Where, when* or *how* (*Where did they go (to)? How did you come?*) as opposed to *What? Who?* as is usual with Objects.

Multi-word verb	Prepositional Object		PP as Adjunct or Comp.
I'll call on	Dr. Jones	I'll call	on Friday
They looked into	the matter	They looked	into the cave
She came by	a fortune	She came	by bus
I'll stand by	my word	I'll stand	by the window
We put up with	the noise	We put up	at a hotel
They played on	our sympathy	They played	on their home ground

Furthermore, there is a parallel between intransitive phrasals like *walk down* and single verbs of movement followed by a directional Complement (*walk down the stairs*). In many cases, it is possible to analyse the former as the elliptical version of the latter, especially when the situation is known.

These alternatives also allow us to specify direction as Path + Ground or as Path alone. (These notions are explained in Module 40.) Compare:

> He   walked   down the stairs.   He   walked   down.
> S   P   C (Path + Ground)   S   P   C (Path)

In this passage from *Three Men in a Boat*, the three friends decide to have a picnic (see exercise 6 on p. 78):

When George *drew out*[1] a tin of pineapple from the bottom of the hamper and rolled it into the middle of the boat, we felt that life was worth living after all. We are very fond of pineapple, all three of us. We *looked at the picture*[2] on the tin; we *thought of the juice.*[3] We *smiled at one another,*[4] and Harris got a spoon ready.

Then we *looked for something to open the tin with.*[5] We *turned out*[6] everything in the hamper. *We turned out*[7] the bags. We *pulled up*[8] the boards at the bottom of the boat. We *took everything out*[9] on to the bank and shook it. There was no tin-opener to be found.

Then Harris tried to open the tin with a pocket-knife, and broke the knife and cut himself badly; and George tried a pair of scissors, and the scissors *flew up*[10] and nearly *put his eye out.*[11] While they were dressing their wounds, I tried to make a hole in the tin with the spiky end of the boat pole, and the pole slipped and jerked *me out*[12] between the boat and the bank into two feet of muddy water, and the tin *rolled over*[13] and broke a tea-cup.

SUBJECT AND OBJECT COMPLEMENTS

SUMMARY

1   There are two main types of Complement: that which complements the Subject (Cs) and that which complements the Object (Co). The Subject Complement completes the predicate after a copular verb by specifying an Attribute of the Subject or its identity. No passivisation is possible. The Subject Complement can be realised by AdjGs, by definite and indefinite NGs, and by clauses.

2   The Object Complement (Co) completes the predicate with an AdjG or a NG following a direct object. The Direct Object, but not the Complement, can become subject in a passive clause. The Co is realised by AdjGs, definite and indefinite NGs and clauses.

3   When the Cs is a pronoun, use is divided between the subjective and the objective case. The Co pronoun is always objective.

7.1 THE COMPLEMENT OF THE SUBJECT (Cs)

7.1.1 Syntactic and semantic features

The Subject Complement is the obligatory constituent which follows a copular verb and which cannot be made subject in a passive clause:

> Who's there? *It's me/It's I.*
> She became *a tennis champion* at a very early age.
> Feel *free to ask questions!*

The Subject Complement does not represent a new participant, as an Object does, but completes the predicate by adding information about the subject referent. For this reason the Subject Complement differs from the Object in that it can be realised not only by a nominal group but also by an adjectival group (Adj.G), as illustrated in the previous examples.

The objective case (*me*) is now in general use (*It's me*) except in the most formal registers, in which the subjective form (*it's I*) or (*I am he/she*) are heard, especially in AmE.

As well as *be* and *seem*, a wide range of verbs can be used to link the subject to its Complement; these add meanings of transition (*become, get, go, grow, turn*) and of perception (*sound, smell, look*) among others, and are discussed in modules 12 and 17. The constituent following such verbs will be considered Subject Complement if the verb can be replaced by *be* and can't stand alone, without a change of meaning:

> I know it *sounds stupid*, but . . . (= *is stupid*)   cf. *I know it *sounds.*
> That *looks nice*.   (= is nice)   cf. *That *looks.*

More problematic is the constituent following other verbs that could be used intransitively with the same meaning, as in:

> Saint Etheldreda was born *a Saxon princess*. (she was born)
> He returned *a broken man*. (he returned)
> He died *young*. (he died)

We shall consider such constituents as Complements on the strength of the possible paraphrase containing *be* (*When he returned he was a broken man; When he died he was young*).

There is, typically, number agreement between the subject and its Complement, and gender agreement with a reflexive pronoun at complement, as in Janet isn't *herself today*. There are, however, several common exceptions to number agreement:

> Joan and Lionel make *a good* couple.
> My neighbour's cats are *a nuisance/a joy*.
> Are these socks wool? No, they're *cotton*.
> The twins are *the same height*.

Complements of the type *a good couple* in *Joan and Lionel make a good couple* are explicable on semantic grounds, *couple* being inherently plural in meaning. Semantic criteria may also be invoked to explain the use of *a nuisance/a joy* in *My neighbour's cats are a nuisance/a joy*, since abstractions such as these are equally applicable to singular or plural subjects.

A third type, exemplified by expressions such as *wool, cotton, rather an odd colour, the same height/length/shape*, etc., can all be paraphrased by a PP with *of* (*of wool, of rather an odd colour, of the same height*, etc.), which formerly had greater currency. They all express qualities of the subject, and in present-day English the NG form without a preposition is the more common.

Copular verbs predict meanings of being something, describing or identifying the subject referent. The Subject Complement completes the predicate by providing information about the subject with regard to its Attributes or its identity. The identifying type is typically reversible, the attributive is not:

The concert was *marvellous.* (attributive)   *Marvellous was the concert.
The concert was *a great success.* (attributive)   *A great success was the concert.
The orchestra was *the London Philharmonic.*   (The London Philharmonic was
   (identifying)   the orchestra.)

When *be* is followed by an expression of location in space or time (*in the garden, at 10 o'clock*), this Complement is analysed as locative (see 4.2.1; 9.2). Sometimes a circumstantial expression (e.g. *out of work*) is semantically equivalent to an attributive one (e.g. *unemployed*).

7.1.2 Realisations of the Subject Complement

Attributive subject complements are realised by AdjGs and NGs. Identifying Subject Complements can be realised by NGs and by clauses.

A. Attributive Complements (S-P-Cs) – She was ambitious

AdjG	She is *twenty-two years old.*
NG	Sam is *a very lucky man.*
As + NG	His research was recognised *as a great contribution to science.*
	The Rolling Stones' concert was acclaimed *as the event of the season.*

B. Identifying Complements (S-P-Cs) – Her name was Bettina

NG	Sierra Leone is *one of the world's biggest producers of diamonds.*
Fin. *that*-cl.	Ken's belief is that *things can't get any worse.*
Nominal relative cl.	He has become *what he always wanted to be.*
Non-fin. bare inf.cl.	The only thing I did was *tell him to go away.*
Non-fin. *to-inf.* -S	My advice is *to withdraw.*
+ *for* + S	The best plan is *for you to go by train.*
Non-fin. *-ing* cl -S	What I don't enjoy is *standing in* queues.
+S	What most people prefer is *others doing / for others to do the work.*

Note that NGs and AdjGs can occur as attributive or identifying Subject Complements, in passive clauses derived from S-P-Od-Co structures:

You are regarded *as a friend of the family*   (We regard you *as a friend of the family*)
The gates were left *open* all night   (Someone left the gates *open* all night)

Some realisations of Subject Complements are illustrated in the following passage from a university magazine, *Oxford Today*, in which a graduate, Steve Baker, characterises the early stages of his career:

New College, poorest of the rich colleges, dullest of the clever colleges and so far down the river that we had to row on the Thames *is the place where I grew up*.[1] I loved it then and I love it now. But for me real life started in investment banking. It was called *merchant banking*[2] but was just *as fashionable then to pretentious young squirts as it is now*.[3]. The pay on the other hand was *something else*.[4] Everyone apart from me seemed to have a private income. Worse still, they all had private shoots and invited the chairman. No shoot, no promotion. No promotion, no pay. No pay, no shoot. It was *circular*[5] and it was vicious.[6] Then there were the social duties. Clients tended to be *rich, foreign and important*.[7] We squirts were the *entertainment*[8] when their offspring hit town. Unfortunately, one of them was, to me, *quite beautiful*.[9] I stumbled, flailed around a bit and fell. It was *ridiculous*.[10] I still drove my bubble car, she owned the bank that owned the factory. It could not last. It didn't.

[1]NG (ident.); [2]NG (attrib); [3]AdjG (attrib.); [4]NG (attrib.); [5]AdjG (attrib.); [6]AdiG (attrib); [7]AdjG (attrib.); [8]NG (ident.); [9]AdjG (attrib.); [10]AdjG (attrib.)

7.2 THE COMPLEMENT OF THE OBJECT (Co)

7.2.1 Syntactic and semantic features

The Object Complement is the constituent that completes the predicate when certain verbs such as *find, make* and *appoint* lead us to specify some characteristic of the Direct Object (see also Module 11). The Co is normally placed immediately after the direct object:

> You (S) are making (P) me (Od) *angry* (Co).
> You (S) aren't going to like (P) me (Od) *angry* (Co).

There is typically number agreement between the Direct Object and the nominal group realising the Object Complement, as in: *Circumstances* (S) *have made* (P) *the brothers* (Od) *enemies* (Co). But there are occasional exceptions – expressions of size, shape, colour, height, etc. – which are to be explained in the same way as those seen in 7.1.1:

> You haven't made the sleeves *the same length*.

The Object Complement can characterise the direct object by a qualitative attribute or by a substantive attribute expressing the name or status of the object referent.

Police found the suspects *unwilling to cooperate.* (qualitative)
They have elected Ken *captain of the golf club.* (substantive)
The burglars left the house *in a mess.* (circumstantial)

Sometimes a Co realised by a prepositional phrase (The burglars left the house *in a mess*) is similar in meaning to an adjectival complement (The burglars left the house *untidy*). We can distinguish its status as Complement from the superficially similar realisation by an optional Adjunct (*in five minutes* in *The burglars left the house in five minutes*) by the intensive relationship linking the Od and its complement. This can be tested by paraphrase with *be* (The house was *in a mess*; *The house was *in five minutes*). The two meanings are dependent on the related meanings of *leave*: 'leave something in a state' and 'go away from', respectively.

7.2.2 Realisations of the Object Complement

Attributive Object Complements can be realised by:

AdjG	A sleeping pill will rapidly make you *drowsy.*
NG	His friends consider him *a genius.*
Finite nominal cl.	Dye your hair *whatever colour you like.*
Non-finite *-en* cl.	The authorities had the demonstrators *placed under house arrest.*

Nominal Co elements are sometimes introduced by the prepositions *as* or *for*, and are then analysed as 'oblique' Object Complements. That is, the relationship between the NG and the verb is not direct, but mediated by a preposition. Some verbs require this; with others such as *consider* it is optional:

as + NG	Party members regard him *as the best candidate.*
for + NG	Do you take me *for a complete idiot?*

ADJUNCTS (A)

SUMMARY

1 Adjuncts (A) are optional elements of a situation expressed by a clause. There are three main types according to their function.

2 Circumstantial Adjuncts provide information concerning time, place, manner, means etc. These are treated more fully in Module 20.

3 Stance adjuncts provide an attitudinal comment by the speaker on the content of the clause or sentence. There are three classes of stance adjuncts: epistemic, evidential and evaluative.

4 Connective adjuncts are not elements of structures, but connectors of structures. They signal how the speaker intends the semantic connections to be made between one part of the discourse and another. In discourse studies, many connective adjuncts are analysed as discourse markers.

5 Adjuncts are realised by groups and clauses, according to type and function.

8.1 SYNTACTIC AND SEMANTIC FEATURES

In contrast with the more central clausal constituents, which are realised only once in a clause – there is one subject/direct and indirect object/predicator/subject or object complement per clause – it is common to find a number of adjuncts in a single clause. The following illustration has five circumstantial adjuncts, which in this clause are all optional: they can be omitted without affecting the grammaticality of the clause. The bracketed items are adjuncts:

(If at all possible) I'll see you (tomorrow) (after the show) (with Pete and Susan) (outside the main entrance).

Adjuncts can be added to any of the basic clause structures:

SP(A)	The bells rang *all day long.*
SPOd (A)	Tom hired a car *at Doncaster.*
SPOp(A)	You must allow for delays in *holiday periods.*
SPOiOd(A)	He sends me flowers *through Interflora.*
SPCs(A)	The weather is rather unpredictable *in these parts.*
SPOdCo(A)	They elected her Miss Universe *in Miami.*

Whereas the more central elements of clause structure typically have fixed places in the clause, many adjuncts are characterised by their flexibility as regards position:

Hastily she hid the letter.
She *hastily* hid the letter.
She hid the letter *hastily.*

While the great majority can occur at the end of the clause, they also occur frequently in initial and medial positions, these being determined to a great extent by semantic and pragmatic considerations (see 55.2).

Semantically, adjuncts represent circumstances, specifications and comments of many different types which are attendant on the verb or the whole clause. A further characteristic of adjuncts is the tendency of different types of meanings to be expressed by different adjuncts in a single clause, not as coordinated realisations of a single adjunctive element, but as separate, multiple adjuncts:

Surprisingly (stance), she *almost* (degree) forgot to set the alarm clock *last night* (time).

8.2 MAIN CLASSES OF ADJUNCTS

Adjuncts (A) are grouped into three main classes according to their function in the clause: **circumstantial adjuncts** (8.2.1), **stance adjuncts** (8.2.5) and **connective adjuncts** (8.2.7).

A fourth group consists of **operator-related adjuncts**. Certain single adverbs and adverbial groups which can function as adjuncts of **usuality** (*usually*), **frequency** (*sometimes, never*), **degree** (*just*), **modality** (*probably*) and **aspectuality** (*still, yet, already*), among others, relate closely to the verb. These tend to be placed near the finite operator (*We have just finished; she is probably waiting*). They are discussed in Chapter 11, together with the distribution, position and function of adverbs.

8.2.1 Circumstantial Adjuncts

Circumstantial adjuncts provide experiential details about the action or state described by the verb, and answer such questions as *where? when? how? why?* and occasionally *what?* as in *What do you want it for? What did he die of?* Of all the types of adjunct, the circumstantials are the ones most similar to clause constituents: like subject and object they may be made the focus of a cleft. So in the example *Tom bought a new car last month*, we may highlight each element except the verb, including the adjunct of time. Other types of circumstantial adjunct don't pass this test, however:

It was *last month* that Tom bought a new car.   (adjunct)
It was *a new car* that Tom bought last month.   (object)
It was *Tom* who bought a new car last month.   (subject)
*It was probably/*usually/*surprisingly/*still that Tom bought a new car last month.

8.2.2 Realisations of the Circumstantial Adjunct: Summary

Circumstantial adjuncts are realised by a wide variety of units:

She called me *yesterday*.	Adverb
She called me *too late*.	AdvG
She called me *from the office*.	PP
She called me *this morning*.	NG
She called me *while I was out*.	Finite clause
She called *to tell me the news*.	Non-fin. *to*-inf.cl
She called me, *using her mobile*.	Non-fin.-*ing* cl.
She called me, *scared out of her wits*.	Non-fin.-*en* cl.
Afraid to leave the house, she called me.	Verbless clause

While non-finite -*ing*, -*en* and verbless clauses undoubtedly give background information, syntactically it is more problematic to analyse them as adjuncts. They are more loosely integrated into the clause and can't be made the focus of a cleft (*It was *scared out of her* wits that she called me) as can other circumstantials, including *to*-infinitive clauses (It was *to tell me the news* that she called me).

Units that are set off from the main clause by a comma or a pause are called **supplementives** (see also Chapter 10 for various types of supplementive). The -*ing* and -*en* types, as well as verbless clauses such as *afraid to leave the house* fall into this category. Semantically, they may be understood as reduced clauses of means or reason with an adjunctive function. Here, *Afraid to leave the house* not only lacks a main verb and a subject but is related to the predicate. (*She was afraid to leave the house.*) Such 'detached predicatives' are used in written genres, where they economically add information, typically in initial position as part of Theme (see 28.10 and 51.5).

8.2.3 Circumstantials functioning as central clause elements

As explained in 4.1, certain verbs predict a circumstantial element, without which the clause is incomplete syntactically and semantically. They then have the status of a Complement, and are summarised again here:

- **Location in place or time**, after a verb of position such as *be, stay, live, lie*, etc., as in: We live *in troubled times*, The farm is situated *in a valley*.
- **Extent in time or place** with verbs such as *take*, as in The journey takes *several days*, or *last*, as in The performance lasts *(for) three hours*, in which the preposition is optional. In discourse, the time duration may be omitted if it is understood, as in *Their love didn't last*, meaning 'didn't last a long time'.

- **Direction and Goal** after verbs of movement such as *go, come* or of movement + manner such as *fly*, as in We flew *south* (Direction), We flew *to New York* (Goal).
- **Source** in She tiptoed *out of the bedroom*, We flew *from London*.
- **Manner** with *behave*, as in, She is behaving *rather strangely*. Also with one sense of the transitive verb *treat*, as in: They treated the prisoners *badly*.

8.2.4 Circumstantials and their ordering in discourse

There is a strong tendency to add circumstantial information, even when it is not strictly required by syntactic or semantic criteria for a single clause, one reason being that it is often crucial to the development of the discourse. So, rather than saying *Tom disappeared*, we might add an optional circumstantial such as *among the crowd, into the Underground* or *below the surface of the lake*.

Even more clearly, the conditional clause adjunct – as in *If you don't learn*, you're not much good as a teacher – is necessary for a full understanding of the speaker's intended meaning. Without it, the message is very different. Conversely, with verbs such as *leave, arrive* and *go*, Source, Goal and Location adjuncts are omitted if they are contextually understood (*haven't they left/arrived/gone yet?*). The semantic classification of circumstantial elements is described in Module 20.

When a number of circumstantials cluster at the end of a clause, they tend to be placed in certain semantic orderings, such as Source-Extent-Path-Goal. This is partly illustrated in this slightly adapted sentence from the text below, taken from a report entitled 'How to survive a Colombian kidnapping', in *The Week*. We can see that 'Source' does not figure, while 'Purpose' does.

I slithered	a few yards	down the steep bank	to the stream	for a wash
	Extent	direction (Path)	(Goal)	Purpose

When I was not playing games with Tom, I started to make up nicknames for our guards. One morning I slithered down the steep bank to the stream for a wash, accompanied by one of the female guards. I was in desperate need of a shave and my washing companion kindly lent me her mirror. I removed the whiskers with my final blunt razor and looked up to see if she approved. She was standing there in a striking combination of lacy red knickers and bra, offset by Wellington boots, an AK-47 and a surly stare. I could make out a large lovebite on her right breast. God! I thought, I've landed myself on the set of a Russ Meyer movie: *Bras and Guns*. As I stood there awkwardly, uncertain as to where to look, her boyfriend appeared at the top of the bank. He was dressed smartly in an American woodland leaf uniform and carried an AK-47. How he kept his uniform so clean and pressed was a mystery. In the top of his boot I noticed a pink comb and pink-backed mirror. He pulled them out and began to do his hair. From that point on the couple were known as Mr and Mrs Comb.

8.2.5 Stance Adjuncts

These express the speaker's evaluation or comment on the content of the message, or the viewpoint adopted. Syntactically, they often remain somewhat separate from the clause, since their message refers to the whole of the clause or sentence. For this reason, they are usually found before the clause or after it, as in the first two examples below. But they can also be placed parenthetically or between commas, within a clause or sentence, as in the last two:

Naturally, he spoke to me when he saw me.
He spoke to me when he saw me, *naturally*.
He *naturally* spoke to me when he saw me.
He spoke to me, *naturally*, when he saw me.

Textually, stance adjuncts are of three main kinds: **epistemic**, **evidential** and **evaluative** (see also 28.12, as Theme).

A. Epistemic stance adjuncts – *Do you believe me? Of course I do*

These express the speaker's opinion regarding the validity of the content, commenting on the certainty, doubt, possibility and obviousness of the proposition:

Undoubtedly, he is the finest pianist alive today.
Obviously, he'll rely on you even more now.

B. Evidential adjuncts – *Apparently, the picture is a fake*

These signal the source of knowledge or information. Sources range from the speaker's own experience or belief (*In my view/ In my experience*) to the beliefs or accounts of others (*According to . . . In the words of . . .* and finally hearsay – *supposedly, apparently*):

According to the weather forecast, there's a hurricane on the way.

C. Evaluative adjuncts – *Amazingly, he won a gold medal*

These are attitudinal, reflecting the subjective or objective attitude of the speaker towards the content and sometimes also towards the addressee:

Surely you can make up your own mind!
Broadly speaking, the Health Service is satisfactory.   (objective)
Unfortunately, our team didn't win.   (subjective)

D. Style and domain adjuncts

Two further types of stance adjunct are Style and Domain adjuncts. Style adjuncts are the speaker's comment on the way s/he is speaking (honestly, frankly, confidentially).

Domain adjuncts signal from what viewpoint the message is orientated (technologically, legally, saleswise, etc.):

> *Quite frankly*, it seems to me a lot of bullshit.
> *Medically*, the project has little to recommend it.

8.2.6 Realisations of the Stance Adjunct: summary

Stance adjuncts can be realised by adverbs, prepositional phrases, finite and non-finite clauses:

Adverbs:	surely, obviously, frankly, honestly, confidentially, hopefully, probably
PPs:	in fact, in reality, at a rough guess, by any chance, of course
Non-fin cl:	to be honest, to tell the truth, strictly speaking
Fin. cl:	if I may be frank with you . . .; don't take this personally, but . . .

8.2.7 Connective Adjuncts

These tell us how the speaker or writer understands the semantic connection between two utterances, or parts of an utterance, while indicating the semantic relationship holding between them: The hotel was rather noisy. *On the other hand*, it wasn't expensive (contrast). They are not therefore elements of structure, but connectors of structure:

Between groups:	Lord Shaftesbury was a persuasive speaker and *furthermore* a great pioneer of social reform.
Between clauses:	The students are on strike; *nevertheless*, the examinations will not be cancelled.
Between sentences:	He has been undergoing treatment for asthma since he was a boy. *Consequently*, he never went in for sports.
Between paragraphs:	*In addition to all this . . .*
	First of all . . .
	In conclusion . . .

That is to say, such connectors occur at some boundary established at a significant point in the organisation of the text. They have a textual function.

Semantically, many different types of connection can be expressed. Here, we shall briefly exemplify four main types (see also chapters 6 and 7):

additive:	besides, in the same way, what's more, moreover, plus (AmE), as well, also
contrast:	instead, on the contrary, on the other hand, nevertheless, rather, yet
causal:	for, because, so, therefore, then, in that case, consequently, thus
temporal:	first, then, next, after that, finally, at once

8.2.8 Realisations of the Connective Adjunct: summary

Adverbs: nevertheless, moreover, first, therefore, next, now namely, accordingly, consequently, alternatively
PPs: in other words, by the way, on top of that
AdjGs: last of all, better still
AdvGs: more accurately
Fin. cl: that is to say, what is more
Non-fin.cl: to sum up, to cap it all

In daily life, turns in conversation are often initiated by a common institutionalised connective adjunct, such as *Well . . ., Now . . ., Oh . . ., So . . ., Right . . .*, functioning as **discourse markers**. Their role is double: they mark a new speaker's turn in the conversation, and at the same time they mark the management of information, as well as the speaker's attitude to the message. *Well* has a variety of meanings, signalled by intonation, ranging from decision to deliberation. *Oh* is a surprisal, indicating that the information received is contrary to expectations, or that the speaker is adjusting to the new information or perception. *I mean, you see* and *you know* regulate shared and unshared knowledge. *Look* and *Hey* are attention signals, while *yes, yeah, no* and *nope* are responses that can occur together with other markers. Here are some examples of discourse markers in spoken English:

Oh my coffee's gone cold!	[BNC KCU]
It was dreadful! That shop.	Oh, that's supposed to be a good shop! [BNC KST]
I've lost my keys!	Well, what do you expect? You never put them away.

The semantic and textual functions of circumstantial, stance and connective adjuncts are described and illustrated in chapters 6 and 7, and – as realised by adverbs – in Chapter 11.

Several of these markers, as well as stance and connective adjuncts, occur in the following extract from Alan Ayckbourn's play *Just Between Ourselves*, in which Neil comes to Dennis's house to inspect a car for sale.

Dennis: It's the pilot light, you see. It's in a cross draught. It's very badly sited, that stove. They should never have put it there. I'm planning to move it. *Right, now.*[1] You've come about the car, haven't you?

Neil: That's right.

Dennis: *Well,*[2] there she is. Have a look for yourself. That's the one.

Neil: Ah.

Dennis: *Now*[3] I'll tell you a little bit about it, shall I? Bit of history. *Number one,*[4] it's not my car. It's the wife's. *However,*[5] *now*[6] before you say ah-ah – woman driver, she's been very careful with it. Never had a single accident in it, touch wood.

Well[7], I mean[8] look[9], you can see hardly a scratch on it. Considering the age[10]. To be perfectly honest[11], just between ourselves[12], she's a better driver than me – when she puts her mind to it. I mean[13], look[14] considering it's what now – seven – nearly eight years old.[15] Just look for yourself at that body work.

Neil: *Yes, Yes[16]*.

[1]marker/connective; [2]connective; [3]connective; [4]connective; [5]connective; [6]connective; [7]marker; [8]marker, [9]attention signal; [10]stance; [11]stance; [12]marker; [13]stance; [14]attention signal; [15]stance; [16]response signal.

FURTHER READING

Biber et al. (1999); Fawcett (2000); Greenbaum and Quirk (1990); Halliday (1994); Huddleston and Pullum (2002); Quirk et al. (1985); Schiffrin (1987); Thompson (2002); *Surely* as a stance marker: Downing (2001); Downing (2005).

EXERCISES ON CHAPTER 2
The skeleton of the message: Introduction to clause structure

Module 4

1   †Bracket the non-essential constituent(s) in each of the following clauses

    (1)   Many of the houses must have disappeared since my father's day,
    (2)   I explained briefly to Mrs Davies that there was a power cut.
    (3)   It seemed a good idea at the time.
    (4)   The war lasted more than forty years.
    (5)   I felt my face turn red.
    (6)   Somebody snatched my bag in the park.
    (7)   Before the fall of the Berlin Wall, spying practically dominated the political life of that capital.
    (8)   I'll just put something in the microwave.
    (9)   The telephone began to ring insistently at six o'clock on a cold November day.
    (10)   Arsenal became League champions for the fifth time on Monday.

Module 5

1   †Check the criteria for identifying Subject. Then read the text about Monte Carlo in 5.1.2 (p. 45). Which of the criteria for Subject are clearly fulfilled? Which do not occur at all? Add some question tags and note the pronominal forms that occur.

2 †Identify the constituent that realises Subject function in each of the following clauses:

(1) The use of caves for smuggling is as old as the hills.
(2) There were about half a dozen men seated in the bar.
(3) The light of a torch flickered.
(4) What the critics failed to understand is that his art was not sacrificed to popularity.
(5) The list of people who she says helped her is long.
(6) It was my great good fortune to meet him before he died.
(7) Run like mad was what we did.
(8) It makes sense to tell the neighbours you are going away on holiday.
(9) It is sometimes argued that there is no real progress.
(10) Reading in a poor light is bad for your eyes.

3 †Extrapose the Subject in the following clauses. Start with 'It . . .:

(1) That Pam is seeking a divorce surprised us.
(2) To leave without saying goodbye was bad manners, really.
(3) Who she goes out with doesn't interest me.
(4) For such a man to succeed in the world of politics requires a lot of nerve.
(5) That recognising syntactic categories at first sight is not easy is obvious.

4 Read the passage on the Valley of the Kings in 5.2 (p. 49). Underline the words that realise the Predicator function and say which are finite and which non-finite.

Module 6

1a †Identify the constituent which functions as Direct Object in each of the following clauses, and the class of unit which realises this function.

(1) I've lived most of my life in the country.
(2) He banged the door shut as he went out.
(3) He pointed out that foreign doctors were not permitted to practise in that country.
(4) The negotiations have achieved very little.
(5) She lacks discretion.
(6) A team of divers have discovered what they believe to be sunken treasure.
(7) He considers it unlikely that the money will be refunded
(8) One doubts that many will survive the long trek over the mountains.
(9) You might ask what is the use of all this.
(10) He shovelled a ton of gravel into the back garden.

1b Discuss these realisations from the point of view of their prototypicality as Od.

2 Turn to the text 'Fire Threat to Apes' at the end of 6.1.2 (p. 54), where you will find the Subjects and Direct Objects in italics.

a †Identify them by S and O respectively, and state the type of realisation in each case.

b. †Comment on the relative length and 'heaviness' of the units. Which are heavier in general – those of S or O? What is the subject in [5]? Is the Subject of [8] a dummy or, if not, what is it referring to?

3 †Which of the following clauses contain a constituent that functions as Recipient Indirect Object, and which contain a Beneficiary Indirect Object? Apply the passivisation and prepositional tests to distinguish between the two:

(1) They did not give the leaders time to establish contact.
(2) Why should I write him his French essays?
(3) I am going to get myself another coffee.
(4) Can I get you girls anything?
(5) He is offering us a chance in a million.
(6) Can you give me a lift as far as the station?
(7) You owe me 7 Euros for that pair of tights from the Sock Shop.
(8) She has bought her boy-friend a butterfly pillow to use on long flights.

4 †Applying the criteria discussed in 6.4, identify the phrasal verbs, prepositional verbs and phrasal-prepositional verbs in the following clauses:

(1) Does it put you off to enter a room and find everyone staring at you?
(2) They don't approve of what we are doing.
(3) Is that the time? I'd better get back.
(4) A burglar could not easily break into this house.
(5) So he didn't turn up after all at McDonald's?
(6) His work-mates are always getting at him, he says.
(7) Things don't always come up to our expectations.
(8) This is our stop. We get off here.

5a †Sort the following examples according to whether they contain Op or Adjunct:

a. She ran through the film script. c. You can see through the trees
b. She ran through the streets. d. You can see through his excuses.

5b †Why is *Up large bills she ran ungrammatical while *Up the stairs she ran* is acceptable?

5c †*She decided on the bus* is ambiguous. Explain the two readings, adding material if necessary.

5d †For the following sequences provide an ellipted version consisting of verb + adverb:

He rode out of the courtyard. They jumped over the fence.
We swam across the lake. Get into the car, all of you!

6 Read again the passage from *Three Men in a Boat* in section 6.4.3 (p. 63). Identify the italicised sequences. Say whether the verb + adverb combinations are transitive or intransitive. Try to find one-word lexical equivalents for these. Do they give the same flavour and informality as the phrasal verbs? Discuss possible alternative analyses for 2, 3 and 4.

Module 7

1 †Identify the types of Complement (Subject, Object) in each of the following clauses and state the class of unit which realises each of these.

(1) Acting is not very hard. The most important things are to be able to laugh and to cry (Glenda Jackson in *The Times*).
(2) They must prove themselves fit for the task.
(3) Spying on firms has become a multi-million pound industry.
(4) What will they call the baby?
(5) Life is a series of accidents. That's what he thinks.
(6) He made his films accessible to a wide public.
(7) The weather has turned unexpectedly cold.
(8) Video-games keep them happy for hours.
(9) She looked utterly miserable.
(10) Sweden has made it illegal for parents to smack their children.

2a †The following short text on bike riding illustrates Complements. Underline the part of each numbered unit which realises an obligatory Complement and state whether it is Cs, Co, Locative/Goal or any other type:

> Cyclists are not only healthy[1] – they are smart.[2] Bike riding is one of the most efficient ways of getting about.[3] When comparing the energy expended with speed and distance covered, even the rustiest two-wheeler outstrips the hummingbird, the cheetah and the jumbo jet.
>
> There are an estimated 14 million bikes in Britain – with 5 million of them gathering dust in garages. A pity, because bicycles are so versatile as transport or for simple pleasure.[4]
>
> While getting you to work,[5] a bicycle also gets you fit.[6] For every half an hour's pedalling, a 150lb person burns up 300 calories. The heart and back leg muscles are strengthened – all while sitting down. Because the bodyweight is supported, cycling is effective exercise.[7]

2b Write a paragraph in which you argue against the supposed benefits of cycling.

Module 8

1 †Distinguish between the different types of Adjunct (circumstantial, stance and connectives) in the clauses below:

(1) He was chairman of the English Tourist Board for five years.
(2) First, we booked the seats, then we went for dinner, and after that we took a taxi to the theatre.
(3) The soldier allegedly crawled under the barbed wire to reach the arms depot.

(4)   Hopefully, student admissions will continue to rise.

(5)   Shaped like a spiral staircase, the 'double helix' of DNA continues to transform our understanding of the story of life.

2   †Analyse the constituents following the verb *find* in these two clauses:

(1)   The police found the gang's hide-out without much difficulty.

(2)   The police found the gang's hide-out more elaborately equipped with technology than they had expected.

3   †In the following extract from Kathleen Mayes' *Beat Jet Lag*, mark each constituent of the clauses with I. Then give (a) the function, *and* (b) the class of unit which realises the function:

> The sun never sets on the tourist empire. But travel pictures, business contracts and sports programmes don't tell the full story: getting there may be no fun at all. Aircraft perform flawlessly, but what happens to passengers, flight crews and cabin staff? Jet lag. A mass phenomenon, almost as universal as the common cold.

THE DEVELOPMENT OF
THE MESSAGE

Complementation of the verb

CHAPTER 3

INTRODUCTION: MAJOR COMPLEMENTATION PATTERNS AND VALENCY

Complementation of the verb refers to the syntactic patterns made up by configurations of the clause elements that we examined individually in the previous chapter. Each pattern contains a Subject and a Predicator. The number and type of other elements in each pattern is determined by the verb, as we saw in Chapter 2. Complementation of the verb is a very rich and complex area of English grammar.

The aim here is to outline as simply as possible the main choices open to speakers from the standpoint of the verb. Choices are, however, balanced by requirements. Certain verbs in English may not admit a pattern, or a realisation of a pattern, that is perfectly normal in another language.

There are three main types of complementation: intransitive, copular and transitive. The transitive has three sub-types.

Type of complementation	Structural pattern	Illustration
Intransitive	S-P	Ted laughed
Copular	S-P-C	The idea is crazy
Transitive		
Monotransitive	S-P-O	He bought a video
Ditransitive	S-P-O-O	He gave Jo the video
Complex-transitive	S-P-O-C	I find the idea crazy

The number of verbs in common use in English is very large, especially in certain constructions, such as the monotransitive. In addition, many verbs – especially those of general meaning, such as *get, turn* and *make* – admit more than one type of complementation, each of which reflects a different type of situation. *Make*, for instance, can enter into all but intransitive patterns:

I'll make some tea.	SPOd
I'll make you a pizza.	SPOiOd
He made the coffee too strong.	SPOdCo
They make a good couple.	SPCs
It makes for good relations.	SPOp

The potential number of participants, including the subject – that is, the number of 'places' in the clause that the verb controls – is sometimes referred to as its **semantic valency**. Different classes of verbs have different semantic valencies. The verb *eat*, for example, is a two-place verb: it has a semantic valency of two, because in any event of eating there must be an eater and a thing eaten. There are one-place verbs, which have a subject only, belonging in principle to the SP pattern. Two-place verbs have a subject and one other element, as in the SPC and SPO patterns. Three-place verbs have a subject and two other elements as in the SPOO and SPOC patterns. Syntactic valency refs to the number of nominal elements present in any given clause that have a direct grammatical relation to the verb. In *The lions ate away at their prey*, there is one nominal element, as *their prey* does not have a direct grammatical relation to the verb. Syntactic valency often corresponds to its semantic valency, but not always. Weather verbs such as *rain* and *snow*, for instance, have no semantic participant and so have a semantic valency of zero. As finite clauses in English require a subject, however, dummy *it* is used with such verbs, giving a syntactic valency of 1. Valency is reduced when one or more elements are omitted in use. For instance, *eat* has a semantic valency of 2 as in *He ate an orange*; the valency is reduced to 1 in *What time do you eat here?*

INTRANSITIVE AND COPULAR PATTERNS

SUMMARY

1   Where there is no complementation the verb is said to be **intransitive**. The structure is S-P. Some verbs are always intransitive (*arrive, snow, blink, vanish*). Others represent intransitive uses of basically transitive verbs (*eat, drive, read*).

2   Some intransitive verbs, particularly those of position (*live, lie*) or movement (*go, walk*), usually require a Locative or Goal Complement, respectively.

3   Locative Adjuncts are commonly present but not necessarily required after many verbs such as *work, arrive, retire* and *stop*. Locative and other circumstantial information is often pragmatically inferred in discourse.

4   The S-P-Cs pattern contains a copular verb that links the subject to a Complement encoding what the subject is or becomes. The most typical copula is *be*. Other verbs used as copulas in English provide additional meaning to the mere linking. This may be sensory (*look, feel, smell, sound, taste*) or refer to a process of becoming (*become, get, go, grow, turn*). The notion of 'being' also includes being in a place, expressed by a circumstantial locative Complement, as we saw in 8.2.3.

9.1 SUBJECT – PREDICATOR

This pattern contains a one-place verb such as *sneeze*, which has a subject but no complement. We distinguish the following types of intransitive verb:

*   verbs of **behaviour** which is typically involuntary or semi-voluntary: *laugh, smile, cry, blink, blush, cough, sneeze, sigh, tremble, yawn; wait, stay; die, collapse, faint, fall,* (They all *laughed*, someone *yawned*, one soldier *fainted*.)
*   verbs of **weather**: *rain, snow* (It's *raining*. It's *snowing*. The sun *rose*.)
*   verbs of **occurrence**: *appear, disappear, go, come, arrive, depart, vanish, fade, happen*:

Has everyone *arrived*?

Hopes of avoiding war are now *fading*.

- **idiomatic intransitive phrasal verbs** such as *crop up* as in *a problem has cropped up*, where there is no verb 'crop' of the same meaning (see 6.4.2). By contrast, with free combinations of verb + particle used literally as in *the bird flew away*, the particle is analysed as a directional Complement (6.4.2 and 9.2). Opinions differ in this respect, however, some preferring Adjunct in the case of free combinations.

Note that some of these 'pure intransitives' can also function in other structures, as we shall see later on.

9.2. SUBJECT–PREDICATOR–LOCATIVE COMPLEMENT (C_{loc})

Other intransitives of the following types typically require a Complement of place, direction or destination to complete their meaning. Location in space is extended to include location in time (see also 10.8 for certain transitive verbs with similar requirements):

- Location in place or time: *be, stand, live, lie, remain*
- Movement + manner of movement: *walk, run, stroll, crawl, fly*

> The National Theatre stands *near the river*.
> The amusement park is *just over there*
> She is lying *in a hammock*.
> Lunch was *at one o'clock*.
> We walked *home*.
> The soldier crawled *under the wire fence*.

We can compare this verb *lie*, meaning to be in a prone position, with *lie*, a 'pure' intransitive, meaning to tell lies: *He is lying in a hammock* vs *He is lying*.

We can also contrast uses of the same verb, such as *run*, which can occur either as a pure intransitive in the answer to How *does Tom keep fit? – He runs*, or with a Goal Complement in *He runs to the bus-stop every morning* (see 8.2.3).

Note that, for brevity, the term C_{loc} is used to encompass both Locative and Goal meanings.

9.2.1 Pragmatic inference of circumstantial meanings

Similarly, other verbs of position, such as *wait* and *stay*, and verbs of movement such as *go, leave, come* and *walk* can either function as pure intransitives or be followed by a Locative/Goal Complement. The choice depends to a great extent on whether there is sufficient support from the context to sustain the intransitive. For example, if a contrast is being made – as in *Do you want to leave or would you rather stay?* – the intransitive verb alone is sufficient, because the location is pragmatically inferred as being the place where the addressee is. Similarly, in *You can either take the bus or walk*, the destination is obviously known from the context, and a suitable reply would be 'I'll walk'.

However, if the location or destination are not inferrable, a locative or Goal Complement becomes necessary as in *We went home*. Without the specification 'home', the verb would carry insufficient semantic 'weight' and informativeness to complete the predicate.

Complements are more tightly integrated than Adjuncts, the tightest being the Subject and Object complements following copular verbs (see 9.4; 10.7).

9.3 SUBJECT – PREDICATOR – ADJUNCT

With other verbs such as *work, arrive, retire, stop* a circumstantial Adjunct is commonly added, but it is not a requirement because the verb has sufficient weight in itself. This may be for cultural reasons, for example, *work* being interpreted as 'have a job' (**1b** below), *retire* as 'retire from employment' (**3b**), or because of the aspectual meanings conferred by the perfect (**3b**, **4b**) and progressive (**2b**) aspects, which lend 'weight' to the verb (see 43.3). Compare:

S-P-A		S-P	
1a	Tom works in London.	**1b**	Does his sister Priscilla work?
2a	We arrived late.	**2b**	The guests are arriving.
3a	He retired last year.	**3b**	He has retired.
4a	We stopped at the Equator.	**4b**	The clock has stopped.

The following extract from a war correspondent's records illustrates similar choices:

Real travelling, of course, is done the hard way. Planes merely *get* you to the general area;[1] to *penetrate* to the difficult places[2] you *have to go* by four-wheel drive or by horse or by boat. Or you *can walk*.[3]

It is the expeditions that *stand out*[4] most in the memory: *being driven*[5] across the North African desert by bedouin who relied on the sky and the look of the sand dunes rather than instruments, and who *arrived*[6] at precisely the right place at precisely the time they had promised; or *heading*[7] out from Yekaterinburg, the former Sverdlovsk, to visit Boris Yeltsin's home village of Butka, on a morning so cold that the road was a slick ribbon of ice and the driver *had to peer*[8] through the strip of clarity two inches thick on the windscreen; or leaving the Ugandan capital Kampala *to drive*[9] into Rwanda, *stopping*[10] at the Equator to take photographs of ourselves, and shredding three tyres along the way; or hiring a marvellously colourful bus which drove us to the nastiest and most frightening of the Peruvian drugs towns in relative safety, because it never occurred to the drug dealers or their allies, the military, that we would *arrive*[11] in this fashion.

(John Simpson, *It's a Mad World, My Masters*) (see exercise, p. 117).

9.4 SUBJECT – PREDICATOR – COMPLEMENT OF THE SUBJECT

Copular verbs link the subject with a complement which characterises or identifies the subject referent:

> A couch potato (S) is (P) someone who lies watching television all day (Cs).
> This new game (S) is (P) incredibly simple and endlessly gripping (Cs).

The most prototypical copular verb is *be*, which can be followed by a wide range of adjectives and NGs. Others, such as *remain, keep, taste, smell, sound, fall, feel, come, grow* and *turn*, are followed by a more limited range of adjectives which are often specific to a particular verb, as illustrated below.

9.4.1 Verbs of being and becoming

Verbs of being are stative and introduce current or existing attributes:

> The reason *is* simple.
> Lloyd George *was* a man of principle but he *was* also intensely pragmatic.
> We have to *remain* optimistic about the future.
> *Will* you keep still!

Verbs of becoming are dynamic and introduce resulting attributes. In addition, *grow* suggests gradual change, while *go* is used to indicate drastic changes:

> Her latest novel has *become* a best-seller.
> We began to *grow* uneasy when the skin-diver didn't appear.
> His face *went* white.

An adjective functioning as Cs may have its own *to*-infinitive clause complement (*we are anxious to hear from you; glad to hear the good news*). The various meanings expressed by such complements are explained in 53.1.2. Here are some typical combinations of verb + adjective, current and resulting:

Current	*Resulting*
be careful	become dangerous
seem annoyed	get stressed
look cheerful	turn nasty
sound familiar	prove unsatisfactory
smell spicy	go wild

9.4.2 Other linking verbs

A small number of verbs that are normally used without a complement (*fall, come, run*) can function as copulas with specific adjectives as Cs:

The child *fell flat* on its face.
The soldiers all *fell asleep/ fell ill.*
The label has *come unstuck.*

As *be* predicts not only being something but being somewhere, it can also link the subject to a circumstance, usually of position, place or time. The Complement is then identified as C_{loc}, as described in 4.2 and 9.2.

The following extract from an interview in the *Sunday Times Magazine* gives an idea of how the verb and its complements contribute to the expression of interpersonal relations in a text. The young person interviewed is Kirsty Ackland, the daughter of an actor. The structures she chooses help to express the meanings she wants to convey. When she describes herself or another person she uses copular complementation. When she describes the interaction between herself and her actor father, or between herself and her school-friends, she uses ditransitive complementation.

Until *I was about* 13,[1] when *I became terribly shy,*[2] *I was absolutely desperate to be an actress.*[3] My sister Sammy and *I would beg Dad to*[4] *let us go to drama school*[5] but there was no way he would *allow it*[6] until we'd been educated. I went *to Putney High School.*[7] *I was the only one in the family*[8] who didn't *get a scholarship.*[9] *Dad turned up*[10] for parents' evenings and things like that but *he never helped*[11] with the homework. I used to *help him.*[12] *I loved hearing his lines.*[13] But I *never told anyone*[14] *I was the daughter of an actor.*[15] Most of the fathers of the girls at school *were 'something in the City'* and I pretended *Dad was an interior decorator.*[16]

[1]copular (state); [2]copular (becoming); [3]copular (state); [4]ditransitive + Od + *let* + inf.clause; [5]ditransitive vb + Od +clause; [6]monotransitive + situation; [7]intransitive + C_{loc}; [8]copular, state, identifying; [9]monotransitive + thing; [10]intransitive; [11]transitive (Od unexpressed); [12]monotransitive + Od; [13]monotransitive + situation; [14]ditransitive; [15]copular (state); [16]object (*that*)-clause of fact

TRANSITIVE PATTERNS *MODULE 10*

SUMMARY

1 **Monotransitive** patterns contain a two place verb (*carry, say*) and have one Object. The Object is a Direct Object or a Prepositional Object. Objects, like Subjects, most typically represent an entity (a person or thing), less typically a fact or a situation within the main situation. Entities are typically realised by group structures, facts and situations by clauses. We will postpone the discussion of clausal realisations to Module 11.

2 **Ditransitive** patterns contain a three-place verb (*give, offer, rob, blame*). Semantically, they express situations in which three participants are involved, encoded syntactically as the subject and the two objects. There are two main patterns.

3 One pattern contains a verb such as *give, send, owe*, which takes two Objects, Indirect and Direct, sequenced in that order (*give Jo a copy*), each of which can potentially become subject in a passive clause.

4 The second pattern, with verbs such as *remind* and *rob*, takes a Direct Object followed by a Prepositional Object whose preposition is controlled by the verb (*It reminds me of Italy*). Only the Direct Object can become subject in a passive clause.

5 The **complex-transitive** pattern has one Object and one Complement, after verbs such as *appoint, name* and *find*.

10.1 SUBJECT – PREDICATOR – DIRECT OBJECT

Verbs which take a direct object are very numerous and of different semantic types (***carry*** the luggage, ***know*** the answer, ***feel*** the heat of the flames, ***enjoy*** the film, ***want*** a copy). The semantic types are described in Chapter 4.

I (S)	ate (P)	*a toasted cheese sandwich* (Od) [for lunch today A]
She	was wearing	*one of her father's extra-large T-shirts.*
They	don't watch	*kids' TV programmes.*
We	must put away	*all this stuff.*

10.2 VERBS USED TRANSITIVELY AND INTRANSITIVELY

Many verbs in English are used both transitively and intransitively with the same meaning. They include several types:

1 **Verbs with an implied Object**, such as *smoke (cigarettes), drive (a car), park (a car), drink (alcohol), save (money), wave (one's hand)*, as in *Do you smoke? He doesn't drive.* Such intransitive uses can be considered as instances of valency reduction, that is the normal valency of two of these verbs is reduced to one. As these reductions are based on cultural schemas and tend to have an implication of habituality, they are not extended to other object referents such as *wave a flag, drink milk*. With certain verbs such as *read, write, eat* and *teach* the deleted direct object is not specific, and is perhaps unknown, as in *He teaches and she writes.*

> *Drinking* and *driving* don't match.
> It is impossible to *park* in the city centre.
> They are *saving* to buy a house.
> He *waved* to us from the bridge.

2 **Causatives with an intransitive counterpart**, constituting an **ergative pair** (see Chapter 4):

> He opened the door. (SPOd)   The door opened. (SP)
> The camera clicked.   She clicked the camera.

3 **Verbs with a reflexive meaning**:

> He shaved (himself), She dressed (herself).

4 **Verbs with a reciprocal meaning**:

> Tom and Jo met at a concert. (met each other)

10.3 SUBJECT – PREDICATOR – PREPOSITIONAL OBJECT

Verbs which take a Prepositional Object are: prepositional verbs such as *see + to, deal + with* (*see to the plane tickets, deal with an emergency*), phrasal prepositional verbs such as *run out of* (*run out of petrol*), and multi-word combinations that end in a preposition, such as *get rid of* (*get rid of old newspapers*). The criteria for distinguishing these verbs from phrasal verbs are discussed in Chapter 2.

Here is a short list of some common verbs followed by a preposition. Certain verbs, such as *think* and *hear*, control more than one preposition with a slight difference of meaning.

Common verbs that can be followed by a preposition

for	on	to	at	with	in	of	after
account	bank	admit	aim	deal	believe	dispose	look
allow	call	consent	get	reason	confide	think	take
hope	count	keep	hint			hear	
long	rely	refer	look				
look		resort					

> The Prime Minister (S) can't account (P) for the loss of votes(Op).
> We're banking on everyone's support for the rally.
> He would never resort to cheating.
> What are you hinting at?

10.4 SUBJECT – PREDICATOR – INDIRECT OBJECT – DIRECT OBJECT

There are two main types of ditransitive complementation: the basic type, in which an Indirect Object is followed by a Direct Object, illustrated here, and another, in which a Direct Object is followed by a prepositional Object. The first is discussed now, the second in 10.5.

10.4.1 Verbs of transfer (*give, lend*) and intended transfer (*buy, get*)

Types: I gave her a present   I got her a present

This is the basic ditransitive pattern. Three-place verbs like *give* have a subject and two Objects, representing the transfer of goods or information from one person to another. They also include speech act verbs such as 'offer' and 'promise'. Here are some more verbs like *give*:

hand	lend	offer	owe	pass	promise	read	send	show	teach	throw	write

> He showed *the policeman* his driving licence. (He showed his driving licence *to the policeman*.)

We are offering *our clients* a unique opportunity. (. . . *to our clients*)
She owes *several people* large sums of money. (. . . *to several people*)

As the examples show, the indirect Object has a prepositional counterpart, the *give* type with *to*, the *get* type with *for* (*I gave a present to her. I got/bought a present for her*). The PP functions as a prepositional object.

Verbs of intended transfer carry out a service for someone, or even a disservice, as in *They set him a trap/They set a trap for him*. Other verbs like *get* and *buy* include the following:

---

book   bring   build   buy   cash   cut   fetch   find   leave   spare   keep   make   pour
save

Book *me* a sleeper on the night train. (. . . a sleeper *for me*)
Will you call *me* a taxi, please? (. . . a taxi for me)
He got *us* a very good discount. (. . . a good discount *for us*)

With the 'give' type, two passives are usually possible:

Active: I gave Jo a copy.
Passive 1:   Jo was given a copy.   (Oi in active clause → S in passive clause)
Passive 2:   A copy was given to Jo.   (Od in active clause → S in passive clause)
              ?A copy was given Jo.   (? Indicates divided acceptability)

The 'first passive' brings the Recipient participant to subject (*Jo*). The 'second passive' brings the thing given to subject, followed by the Recipient as prepositional object (*to Jo*). The non-prepositional form *A copy was given Jo*, is considered ungrammatical by many speakers, but is accepted by others. Two orderings whose equivalents are acceptable in certain languages but which are ungrammatical in English are the following: **To Jo was given a copy* and **To Jo it was given a copy*.

The difference between the two valid passive forms is a question of information packaging (see 29.1). They are useful alternatives when the active subject is not known or is not important in the discourse, as can be seen in the following extract from an article in *Time* magazine under the heading 'Education: doing bad and feeling good':

A standardized math test was given to 13-year-olds in six countries last year. Koreans did the best, Americans did the worst, coming in behind Spain, Britain, Ireland and Canada. *Now the bad news. Besides being shown triangles and equations, the kids were shown the statement 'I am good at mathematics'.* Koreans came last in this category. Only 23% answered yes. Americans were No. 1, with an impressive 68% in agreement.

> American students may not know their math, but they have evidently absorbed the lessons of the newly fashionable self-esteem curriculum wherein *kids are taught to feel good about themselves* . . . Judging by the international math test, . . . kids already feel exceedingly good about doing bad.

Note that certain ditransitive verbs such as *send* are often used with a directional meaning encoded as Goal Complement (C_{loc}): They sent their children *to boarding-school*. There is no non-prepositional counterpart of a Goal Complement as there is with *send* + Oi + Od: Compare: *They sent me a postcard* with **They sent boarding-school their children.* The latter is ungrammatical.

10.4.2 Less prototypical three-place verbs

There is a good deal of variation in ditransitive verbs. Not all verbs display the alternative structures of those listed in 10.4.1. Here are just a few of the most common variants:

Type: explain + NG + Prepositional Object   He explained the problem to us

Typical verbs are: *announce, confess, deliver, mention, return* and *say*. There is no corresponding structure with the Oi in its usual place: **He explained us the problem.* That is, these verbs take only the oblique, that is, prepositional object as a second object.

> What did she *say to* you?
> I never *mentioned* your name *to* anyone.

Type: wish + NG + NG   We wish you luck

Other verbs: *allow, cost, wish, refuse* and 'light' uses of *give* (see 20.2).
  These verbs have no prepositional counterpart with *to*. Note that the starred counterparts on the right are ungrammatical. *Ask something of someone* is sometimes possible, however.

They allow everyone a ten-minute break.	*They allow a ten-minute break to everyone.
He gave the door a push.	*He gave a push to the door.
Let's ask someone the way.	*Let's ask the way to someone.

Many three-place verbs allow valency reduction from 3 to 2 when there is contextual support, as in *He called a taxi, he got a discount, they blamed me, let's ask the way.*

10.5 SUBJECT – PREDICATOR – DIRECT OBJECT – PREPOSITIONAL OBJECT

Although predicted by the verb, the Op in this ditransitive pattern (e.g. *It reminds me of you*) is further away from the verb and less object-like than when the Prepositional Object is the only object in a clause. The NG (*you*) can't be made subject in a passive clause. However, like other Objects, it encodes a participant that can be questioned by *who* **1**, *what* **2** placed either before the preposition or, more usually, stranded (see 6.3.3). It can also occur in a *wh*-cleft **3**:

    1   *Who* does it remind you of? (Of whom does it remind you?)
    2   *What* are you thanking me for? (For what are you thanking me?)
    3   What it reminds me of is Italy.

In discourse, this element may be omitted when its referent is understood, as in *They blamed me* (for something already mentioned). The Direct Object is usually a person and the Op may be an entity or an event.

    Some of the verbs taking this construction are listed here according to preposition. Remember that a NG is placed between the verb and the preposition.

Some verbs taking Prepositional Object as well as Direct Object

for	from	of	to	with	on
blame	prevent	accuse	introduce	charge	blame
thank	protect	convince		compare	compliment
		deprive	help	supply	congratulate
		rob	sentence		

S	P	Od	Op
This sunblock	will protect	your skin	from *the sun's rays.*
They	robbed	her	of *her watch and jewels.*
They	charged	him	with *assault.*
I	congratulated	Janet	on *her success.*

Only the direct object constituent can become subject in the passive clause:

    Your skin will be protected from the sun's rays.
    She was robbed of her watch and jewels.
    He was charged with assault.
    Janet was congratulated on her success.

Blame, a three-place verb, admits two alternative constructions with different prepositions, which reflect the way the event is viewed in each case. The more central of the two participants is placed first, as Od. In one version this is *Jane*; in the other *the accident.*

blame someone (Od) for something (Op)   *He blamed Jane for the accident*
blame something (Od) on someone (Op)   *He blamed the accident on Jane.*

There are thus two passives – *Jane was blamed for the accident, The accident was blamed on Jane* – which centre respectively on 'Jane' and on 'the accident'.

Likewise, the NG following the preposition can be questioned by *who* or *what* (*What was Jane blamed for? Who was the accident blamed on?*).

Other verbs that present a similar variation are *supply, load and drain*:

We supply the school with paper (Op).   We supply paper(Od) to the school (Op)
They loaded the cart with hay.   They loaded hay on to the cart. (C_{loc})
They drained the pool of water.   They drained water from the pool. (C_{loc})

With *load* and *drain* the cognitive representation is rather different with each alternative. With the receptacle *the cart* and *the pool* as object, there is a notion of totality: the cart is completely full of hay, the pool completely drained of water. By contrast, with *hay* and *water* as object, there is an impression of partialness: some hay is loaded, some water is drained. If the definite article is used (*the hay, the water*), the implication is of totality.

10.6 FRAME, PERSPECTIVE AND ATTENTION

The cognitive notion of **frame** allows us to conceptualise a situation from different **perspectives**. For instance, Fillmore's 'commercial event' frame for [BUY] includes a reference to four other variables, namely to a BUYER, a SELLER, GOODS and MONEY. A syntactic pattern formulated from the perspective of the BUYER could be as follows:

Tom bought some old CDs from Phil for twenty euros.

In this sentence all four variables of the BUY frame are encoded linguistically, each filling a different syntactic function: the BUYER (Tom) as subject, the GOODS (the CDs) as direct object, the SELLER (Phil) as the first adjunct and the MONEY (for twenty euros) as the second adjunct. This distribution of syntactic functions is the syntactic perspective, which here is largely controlled by the choice of the verb BUY.

Within the same frame, it would be easy to take a different perspective by choosing another related verb such as SELL, CHARGE or PAY. The verb *sell* perspectivises SELLER and GOODS as subject and object, *charge* also perspectivises the SELLER as subject but the BUYER as object, and *pay* perspectivises the BUYER and MONEY, with the SELLER as optional indirect object.

Phil sold some old CDs to Tom for twenty euros.
Phil charged Tom twenty euros for some of his old CDs.
Tom paid Phil twenty euros for some old CDs.

The notion of perspective draws on the cognitive ability to direct one's **attention**. To a large degree, we conceptualise events in different ways according to what attracts our attention. As language users, we use the verb *buy* when describing a commercial event in order to draw attention to the BUYER and the GOODS, functioning as subject and object respectively. We use the verb *sell* to focus attention on the SELLER and the GOODS. By means of the frame we can even call up cognitive categories that had no prominence and were not expressed (though they were implied) in the frame itself, for instance SPEND and COST. These can be externalised in sentences such as the following:

Tom spent twenty euros on some old CDs
The old CDs cost Tom twenty euros.

For complementation by clauses see modules 11 and 12.

10.7 SUBJECT – PREDICATOR – DIRECT OBJECT – OBJECT COMPLEMENT

SUMMARY

1 Three-place verbs with one Object and one Complement of the Object are called complex transitive. The Direct Object typically represents a person or thing, and the Object Complement adds information about this referent in the form of an attribute: *I found the house **empty**, He got his shoes **wet**.*

2 The attribute is either current (as with *find*) or resulting (as with *get*).

3 The participant encoded as direct object can typically be made subject in a corresponding passive clause.

10.7.1 Current and Resulting Attributes – He got his shoes wet

This three-place pattern is essentially an S-P-Od pattern with an attributive Object Complement added. As attribute the complement specifies the state or status of the Od referent in relation to the situation described by the verb. The attribute may be 'current', contemporaneous with the verb (*He keeps the garden beautiful*), or the result of the action denoted by the verb (*They elected her Vice-President*).

Verbs that take a current attribute after the object are stative, and include:

- verbs of causing to remain in a certain state such as *hold* and *keep*
- verbs such as *believe, consider, think, find, imagine, presume, hold*

- verbs such as *want, like* and *prefer*

> Keep your hands *steady*!
> I imagined him *much older*.
> Do you want the roast chicken *hot or cold*?

Verbs that take resulting attributes represent processes of doing, and include *bake, drive (mad), get, leave, make, paint, turn, wipe* as well as verbs of declaring, such as *appoint, elect, call, name, declare, report* and *certify*, which confer an official status.

With AdjG Complement:

> It wipes the windscreen *dry*.
> That barking dog is driving me *mad*.
> The heat has turned the milk *sour*.
> Get your priorities *right*!
> They presumed her *dead*.

With NG Complement:

> They elected her *Vice-President*.
> They appointed him *Manager*.

The direct object referent in complex transitive structures can be made subject in a passive clause, which then has a S-P-Cs structure. In fact, with some verbs the passive is more common than the active, particularly when the Agent is unexpressed, as in *she was presumed dead; he is reported missing; he was certified insane*.

With some verbs, the attribute is not essential to make a grammatical clause (*It wipes the windscreen*). This is because many verbs enter into more than one structure: *wipe* can function in a monotransitive structure (*wipe the windscreen*) or in a complex transitive structure (*wipe the windscreen dry*). Other examples which, without the complement, also fit the monotransitive structure include *You've cut your hair (short); we got the books (cheap)*.

A further type of attribute is that of **respect**. This is expressed by *as* + NG when introduced by such verbs as *regard, refer to, write off, acclaim*:

> Churchill referred to him *as an outstanding leader*.
> Fans acclaimed the Rolling Stones' concert *as the event of the season*.

As a consequence of the multi-functionality of many verbs, examples can be invented in which one type of unit such as a NG can realise two different types of constituent:

He called her an angel.	S-P-Od-Co
He called her a taxi.	S-P-Oi-Od
I'll make you First Secretary.	S-P-Od-Co
I'll make you an omelette.	S-P-Oi-Od

10.8 SUBJECT – PREDICATOR – DIRECT OBJECT – LOCATIVE COMPLEMENT

Verbs such as *put, place, stand, lead* occur with a Locative/Goal Complement:

> I put the dish *in the microwave.*
> Stand the lamp *near the desk.*
> The track led us *to a farm.*

Many other verbs such as *talk, take, bring* and *show* can be used in this way, while *keep* and *hold* can function with both Attributes and in Locative/Goal patterns.

> I didn't want to go, but she talked me *into it.* (C_{loc})
> Keep your hands *on the wheel!* (C_{loc})   Keep your hands *steady!* (Co)
> Hold your head *up!* (C_{loc})   We hold you *responsible.* (Co)

COMPLEMENTATION BY FINITE CLAUSES

SUMMARY

1   All clausal complements are determined by the verb. Many verbs admit more than one type of complementation.

2   *That*-clauses form the largest group of finite clause complements and are controlled by transitive verbs. They are classed according to communicative function and meanings, which include facts, perceptions, reports and proposals.

3   *Wh*-clause complements are of three types: a) indirect *wh*-interrogatives, b) *wh*-nominal clauses and c) indirect exclamatives. They occur after verbs such as a) *ask, inquire* b) *advise, show, teach, tell*, and c) *say, tell, believe* respectively.

4   Clausal complements can be considered non-prototypical realisations of clause constituents. In these sections, however, we concentrate mainly on the patterns.

We saw in Chapter 2 that most elements of clause structure can be realised by a subordinate clause functioning as Subject, or Object, or as Complement of either the Subject or the Object. Such clauses are then said to be **embedded**, as in: The doctor knows *that you are waiting*.

The whole clause (*the doctor knows that you are waiting*) in which the subordinate clause is embedded is called the **superordinate** clause, while *the doctor knows* is the matrix clause. The embedded clause, introduced by a complementiser (subordinator), functions as a non-prototypical direct object.

The complementiser *that* has little semantic value and functions as introducer of an embedded clause. By contrast, a *wh*-word has meaning and functions as a constituent of the embedded clause, as in *The doctor knows what you need*.

The main verb is said to determine or control the dependent clause. Adjectives and nouns can also control clausal complements, as in *We are **glad** (that) you came after all* (here in a SPCs structure) and *He has the **conviction** that he is a great actor* (SPOd) respectively, and these will be discussed in the relevant chapters. Here, the clauses will

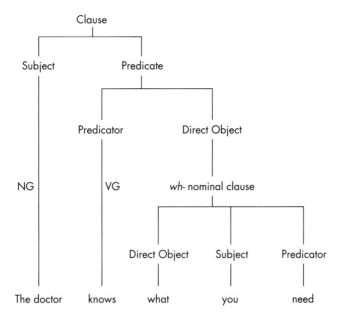

Main clause and embedded nominal *wh*-clause

be discussed as realising Object and Complement functions (Cs and Co). Clauses fulfilling subject function were described in 5.1.2.

The four main types of dependent complement clause are: ***that*-clauses**, ***wh*-clauses**, ***to*-infinitive clauses** and **-*ing* clauses**. They are distinguished by their complementiser (subordinator) such as *that* or a *wh*-word, and by their own structure. They are shown here complementing monotransitive verbs.

Clause as complement with monotransitive verbs

finite that-clause:	He believes that *he's right.*
finite *wh*-clause:	He asked *what I meant.*
	He believed *what I told him.*
	I said *how nice it was.*
non-finite to-infinitive clause:	
without dep.cl subject	He wants *to stay.*
with dep.cl. subject	He wants us all *to stay.*
non-finite -ing clause:	
without dep. cl. subject	He doesn't like *driving in fog*
with dep. cl. subject	He doesn't like *her driving in fog*

That-clauses and *wh*-clauses are finite, having a subject and tense-modality features, while *to*-infinitive and *-ing* clauses are non-finite, and lack these distinctions. All of these types can be used to complement verbs and adjectives. Less versatile are the 'bare' infinitive (*He helped me* **carry** *the bags*) and the *-en* participle clause, which occurs in the complex-transitive structure (*I heard two shots* **fired**). Non-finite complementation is discussed in Module 12.

11.1 MEANINGS AND PATTERNS OF *THAT*-CLAUSE COMPLEMENTS

A *that*-clause complement can be used to express factual or non-factual information which is reported, known, believed or perceived; it can be used to make proposals and suggestions and to describe situations that produce an emotive effect on the subject. The choice of verb combines with the meaning to determine the structural pattern.

11.1.1 Verb + *that*-clause – I think it's beautiful

Facts, beliefs, doubts, perceptions – I believe you are right

These meanings are expressed by a *that*-clause containing an indicative. This represents an indirect statement and follows verbs of certain types:

- Verbs of cognition – knowing, doubting, perceiving – such as *think, know, believe, imagine, see, doubt*; with *doubt, don't know*, the subordinator is *if* or *whether*.

  We know *that you have lived abroad for some time.*
  He could see *that she was not at all happy.*
  I doubt/I don't know *if/whether we'll get there before dark.*

- Verbs of expectation – *expect, hope, suppose* and *wish* – which refer to potential situations rather than facts, frequently take a modal auxiliary in the indicative *that*-clause.

  I expect (that) *you would like something to drink after your journey.*
  I suppose (that) he *must have lost his way.*

For omission of complementiser *that*, see 11.2.

Reports – Jo says she is ill

Reports encode things that people have said. They are introduced by verbs of communicating, such as *say, announce, answer, explain, mean, mention, report*, and performatives such as *admit* and *confess*. Reports are treated in Chapter 7 under 'indirect speech'.

  The Minister answered *that he didn't know.*
  You never mentioned *that you were married.*

Many of these verbs (but not *answer*) can take an optional prepositional object with *to*. This makes them appear ditransitive; however, an indirect object can't be added in its usual place after the verb, as occurs in ditransitive clauses. Such verbs are therefore neither typical monotransitive nor typical ditransitive verbs:

> Let me explain the situation (to you).   *Let me explain you the situation.
> You never mentioned (to me) that   *You never mentioned me that you
>   you were married.   were married.

In the systemic-functional approach, verbs such as *think* and *say* are said to 'project' a dependent, but not embedded, clause as a locution or as an idea, respectively. Locutions and ideas do not linguistically express the cognitive representation of reality as do verbs of seeing or doing, for example. Rather, they express 'a representation of a representation'.

Proposals – *The party suggests he call/should call an election*

Verbs such as *propose, suggest, recommend* and *demand* aim at getting someone to do something. The meaning in the complement clause is therefore potential, for which many European languages require a subjunctive. English has traditionally two possibilities: an uninflected subjunctive (e.g. *be*), common in AmE, or *should* + *infinitive*, common in BrE. Both are illustrated in **1** and **2**. The same choices are open before an *it* + *adj* construction. Illustrated here is a formal use:

> It is right *that this House debate this issue and pass judgement.* (PM Tony Blair in the House of Commons, 18 March 2003)

A third choice, adopted by some speakers, is the indicative, as illustrated in a news report **3**:

> **1**   He demands *that she pay/ should pay him back.*
> **2**   The chairman proposed *that a vote be taken/ should be taken.*
> **3**   They demand *that he apologises to the Iraqi people.*

(For complementation by *to*-infinitive clause, see 12.2.)

11.1.2 Dropping or retaining the complementiser *that*

We can drop or retain the complementiser (or subordinator) *that* without affecting the meaning of the clause. However, certain factors appear to favour one choice or the other.

Omission of *that* is favoured by the following factors:

(a) when *think* or *say* is the main verb – I *think* it's nice, Tim *says* it's easy
(b) when the subject refers to the same entity in the main clause and in the *that*-clause, as in **Tim** *promised* **he**'d do it

(c) when there is a pronoun rather than a noun head in the *that*-clause (*I think **I**'ll have a cola, She knew **he** would* do it)

It has also been suggested that *I think* and *I know*, for example, are not main clauses at all, but are better analysed as epistemic, evidential or evaluative parentheticals, while what is traditionally classed as the complement clause in fact carries the main proposition. This view is based on two pieces of evidence: the verb + its subject can be placed parenthetically after the clause – *I'll have a cola, I think; He'll do it, I know* – and the tag-question relates to the complement clause, not to the main clause – *I think she'll have a cola, won't she?* (not **don't I?*).

Retaining *that* after a verb is favoured by:

(d) coordinated *that*-clauses: Many people *believe that big is best and that war is right.*
(e) passive voice in the main clause: *It is believed that peace is in sight.*
(f) a NG or PP (or clause containing a NG) placed between the main clause and the *that*-clause: Can you prove *to the commission* that the effects are not harmful?

Overall, *that* is omitted most in informal spoken registers, which is where the 'abc' factors tend to cluster, while the subordinator is retained most in formal written registers, which are characterised by the 'def' factors. These are not strict divisions, however, as even formal registers nowadays are often a mix of the formal and the less formal. The following short extracts from *The Peacemakers* and *Girls Out Late*, respectively, illustrate the tendencies:

> **People have often assumed that, because Lloyd George opposed the Boer War, he was not an imperialist.[1] On the contrary, he had always taken great pride in the empire but he had never thought it was being run properly.[2]**
>
> **She said she thought he was a stupid little creep.[3]** (see exercise 2 on p. 118)

***That*-clauses** do not follow **prepositions** in English and consequently cannot realise the Op function. Instead, one of three solutions is adopted: a) the preposition (e.g. *on*) is omitted; b) the preposition is retained and is followed by anticipatory *it*, or c) *the fact* can be inserted before a *that*-clause with a factual meaning:

a.   He insists that we all go.
b.   He insists on it that we all go.
c.   You must allow for the fact that they are handicapped.

11.1.3 Verb + NG + *that*-clause – I told you I'd be late

Many verbs of communicating (*tell, inform*), verbs of causing someone to think or believe or know something (*convince, persuade, remind, teach*), and the performative verbs *promise* and *warn*, can take a *that*-clause after the direct object:

He finally *convinced the jury that he was telling the truth*.
Experience *has taught them that a back-up copy is essential*.

11.2 *SAY* AND *TELL*

Note that *say* and *tell* have different complementation patterns:

- *Say* is monotransitive, controlling a direct object (*Say that number again; He said he was sorry*), while *tell* is ditransitive, with two objects (*Tell me your name, tell me you love me*).
- *Say* can take an added oblique object (*What did you say **to him**?*), but not an indirect object (**What did you say **him**?*).
- Quoted speech may realise the object of *say*, but not that of *tell* (*Jill said 'Hello'*, but not **Jill told me 'Hello'*).

See also 36.5.

Recursive embedding is when a series of clauses is embedded, each within the previous one: *I reminded him he'd said he'd find out about the flight schedules*. Here, the *that*-clause direct object of *remind*, which comprises the remainder of the sentence, (*he'd said he'd find out about the flight schedules*) contains a further embedded *that*-clause *he'd find out*, which has a PP (*about the flight schedules*) as complement.

11.3 MEANINGS AND PATTERNS OF *WH*-CLAUSE COMPLEMENTS

Wh-clause complements are usually either embedded **interrogative clauses** or **nominal relative clauses**. The first express doubt or lack of knowledge, while the second contain factual information. A third type, with a *to*-infinitive complement, is a **non-finite variant** of types 1 and 2. A fourth type, the **indirect exclamative**, is similar to the ordinary exclamative and has an intervening NG after verbs such as *tell*, but not after *say*.

There are two main patterns, which are controlled by specific verbs. Pattern 1 has simply a *wh*-complement. Pattern 2 has an intervening NG (a Recipient). Certain verbs such as *ask* can function in both patterns. A third type, with a *to*-infinitive complement, is a variant on types 1 and 2 and is very common, especially in spoken English.

11.3.1 Indirect interrogatives

V + *wh*-clause – Ask where the station is

The verbs *ask, wonder, doubt, enquire, don't know* control indirect interrogatives. The subordinator *if* is often used as an alternative to *whether* in indirect questions where the answer is either *yes* or *no*:

We asked *what we should do/what to do.*
The tourist enquired *why the museum was closed.*
Pat wondered *whether/if her friends would recognise her.*

As indirect interrogatives contain an embedded question, it is important to remember that subject–operator inversion does not normally occur in embedded questions, unlike the obligatory inversion found in most independent interrogatives. Compare:

independent interrogative	**dependent interrogative**
Where is the dining-car?	Let's enquire *where the dining-car is.*
	Not *Let's enquire where is the dining-car.

11.3.2 Nominal relatives

V + NG + *wh*-clauses – Give them what they want

These verbs – common ones include *advise, give, show, teach* and *tell* – can control nominal relative clause complements, which represent factual information and can be distinguished by replacing the *wh*-word by a more general word, such as 'the thing(s)/ person(s) that', and in some cases by a non-finite complement clause:

He told me *what I already knew.* (the things which I already knew)
Tom will show you *where you can send it/the place* where you can send it/*where to send it.*
The instructor taught *the dancers how they should breathe/the way* they should breathe/*how to breathe.*

As these examples illustrate, some verbs can convey a similar meaning by a non-finite complement.

11.3.3 Non-finite variants

V + NG + *wh* + *to*-infinitive clause – Ask (him) how to do it

This combination provides a shorter variant of 11.3.1 and 11.3.2, with verbs such as *ask, know, show, tell, teach* and *wonder*. The NG recipient is obligatory with *tell, show* and *teach*, optional with *ask*, and not used at all with *know* and *wonder*.

We didn't know **where to go**. (indirect interrogative)
Tom told us **what** to do. (nominal relative)

Ambiguity can sometimes occur with *wh*-complements, as in *He asked me what I knew*, which can be analysed as an indirect interrogative (compare with the direct form *What do you know?*) or as a nominal relative (*the things I knew*) – the latter, for example, in the context of reporting on an examination.

11.3.4 Indirect exclamatives

V + (NG) + *what* **+ NG or** *how* **+ AdjG –** I said how nice it was

The embedded **exclamative** is introduced by either *how* (+ *adjective*) or *what* (+ NG) after two types of verbs: verbs of communicating such as *say* and *tell*, and mental verbs such as *believe* and *think*. Like ordinary exclamatives, it has an emotive quality (see 24.1):

> You'll never believe *what a good time we had.*
> I told her *how sorry I was.*

COMPLEMENTATION BY NON-FINITE CLAUSES

MODULE 12

SUMMARY

1   Non-finite clauses are more loosely integrated into the superordinate clause than are finite clauses. Only the *to*-infinitive complements of certain verbs such as *want, like* and *prefer* and the *-ing* complements of *like, hate* among others, can be treated as (non-prototypical) object constituents.

2   A series of non-finite clauses can be analysed as a chain-like structure of embedded non-finite complements.

3   *To*-infinitive clauses tend to evoke potential situations, whereas *-ing* clauses are factual and bare infinitive clauses evoke an event in which the end-point is included.

4   Participial *-en* clauses function as Object Complements after four types of verb.

12.1 CATENATIVE COMPLEMENTS

A **catenative verb** is a verb that controls a non-finite complement. 'Catenative' means 'chaining' and reflects the way that the verb can link recursively with other catenatives to form a chain, as in:

We decided to try to rent a house near the sea.

Here there is a chain of three verbs: *decide, try* and *rent*, with *to try to rent a house near the sea* functioning as the catenative complement of *decide*, and *to rent a house near the sea* functioning as the catenative complement of *try*.

We can add further catenative verbs to produce an even longer chain of four catenatives, two of which, *persuade* and *help*, have a NG object. The final verb *rent* is not a catenative:

We decided to try to persuade Bill to help us rent a house near the sea.

i	*decide*	to try to persuade Bill to help us rent a house near the sea.
ii	*try*	to persuade Bill to help us rent a house near the sea.
iii	*persuade*	Bill to help us rent a house near the sea.
iv	*help*	us rent a house near the sea.

Further catenatives appear in the following section. A special type of catenative construction – as in *He failed to appear* – is discussed in 39.4. Not all catenatives behave in the same way. Only the complements of a few catenatives such as *want*, *like* and *prefer* can be analysed as (untypical) objects. Others cannot (see also 6.1.2E).

12.2 MEANINGS EXPRESSED BY *TO*-INFINITIVE CLAUSES

12.2.1 Type 1: V + *to*-infinitive – I want to go

These three groups of verbs take *to*-infinitive clause complements:

(a) *Want, wish, intend, arrange*
(b) *like, love, prefer, can't bear, hate*
(c) *promise, agree, learn, forget, decide*

The *to*-infinitive clause in Type 1 has no explicit subject, the implied subject being that of the main clause. Semantically this is clear. If I want to go, the going is to be done by me. For the (c) group of speech-act verbs, there is an equivalent *that*-clause complement with the same meaning, but this alternative is not available to the (a) and (b) groups of desiderative and affective verbs:

1   The boss wants to see us immediately. (no *that*-clause counterpart in **1**, **2** and **3**)
2   I have arranged to go to London tomorrow.
3   I would have preferred to invent something which helps people. A lawnmower, for example. (Mikhail Kalashnikov, inventor of the AK47 assault rifle, in *The Times*)
4   I *promise to ring* you later. (compare: I promise *that I will ring* you later)
5   They *agreed to wait* a bit longer. (compare: they agreed *that they would wait* a bit longer)

To-infinitive clauses tend to evoke a situation that is potential. Cognitively, the infinitive reflects an event, with *to* symbolically reflecting the movement towards the event. For this reason the controlling verb typically 'looks forward' to the moment when the event begins.

12.2.2 Type 2: V + NG + *to*-infinitive clause with subject
– He wants us to go

The 'want' verbs include: *want, like, love, prefer, can't bear, dislike, hate, wish, arrange.*

> The people want the troops to leave.
> And her mother did not like her to be out for too long. (BNC GOB 1660)
> I only want us to be together. (GWH 1130)
> I have arranged for the students to go to London tomorrow.

The 'want' type verbs of **1a** and **1b** in the previous section can also take a *to*-infinitive clause that has an explicit subject. Semantically, what the people want, what her mother did not like are situations, not persons or things. For this reason, the non-finite clause, together with its subject, is analysed as a single unit which can be considered an untypical direct object. This can be tested by (a) replacement by a pronoun (Her mother did not like *that*), (b) coordination (*and she herself did not like it either*), and (c) clefting: the non-finite clause and its subject can become the focus of a *wh*-cleft (*What her mother did not like was for her to be out too long*).

Furthermore, although these subjects of *to*-infinitive clauses are in the objective case (*us, her*) they can't be analysed as objects of the main verb. The complete clause does not entail *The people want the troops* or *Her mother did not like her*. Nor can they become subject in a passive clause: **The troops were wanted to go*, **She was not liked to be out too long*. In this respect, verbs like *want* contrast with those of Type 3 (in the next section) such as *ask*, *advise* and *expect*, in which the NG does represent a separate clause element.

Note the use of *for* as a subordinator, introducing the non-finite clause with its subject (*for the students to go to London tomorrow*) after the main verb *arrange*. In AmE this use of *for* is extended to other verbs such as *want* and *prefer*.

Finally, we can test *want*-type verbs with a *What* question: *What do you want?* rather than a *Who* question: *Who do you want?* The object of my wanting is (for) us to be together.

12.2.3 Type 3: V + NG + *to*-infinitive
– We asked the taxi-driver to stop

The verbs in this type are speech-act verbs: *advise, allow, ask, beg, expect, invite, tell, persuade, urge.* The NG is both the object of the main verb and the implicit subject of the embedded *to*-infinitive clause. This NG behaves as if it were the object of the finite verb and can become subject in a passive clause. This divisibility of the NG is an important feature of ditransitive and most complex transitive complements. As with other verbs of this type, passives are common.

> They persuaded *us to stay.*   *We were persuaded* to stay.
> A television campaign is advising   *Teenagers are being advised* to keep off
> *teenagers to keep off drugs.*   drugs.

Semantically, we persuade, advise and invite someone, not a whole situation. Consequently, a test question will be with *Who* (Who did they persuade?). The *to*-infinitive expresses the course of action to be taken.

For these reasons, the NG referent following verbs like *advise* or *ask* must be human, or at least animate. This is not the case with verbs like *want*. Compare:

> The Browns want their house to be painted.
> *They advised/persuaded their house to be painted.

Note that, when a *to*-infinitive clause is ellipted (see 29.5), *to* remains (*They invited us to stay and we agreed to*).

Factual verbs such as *believe, consider, know, report, suppose* also take NG + *to*-infinitive as a 'raised object' alternative to a *that*-clause complement (see also 37.4). Passive forms are common in formal styles:

> People consider that he is a great actor.
> People consider him to be a great actor.
> He is considered (to be) a great actor.

12.3 MEANINGS EXPRESSED BY BARE INFINITIVE CLAUSES

12.3.1 Type 4: V + NG + bare infinitive – We let them go

Typical verbs are: *let, have, make; see, hear, feel; help*.

Bare-infinitive clauses evoke an event in which an end-point is included, as in *we let them go, we saw them go*. Relatively few verbs occur in this pattern. They include three verbs of coercion, illustrated below, a few verbs of perception and the verb *help*.

> Don't let *anxiety spoil your life*.
> They made *the prisoners stand for hours*.
> I'll have *my secretary make you a reservation*.

Syntactically, we analyse the non-finite clause of the *make* type as an object complement, complementing the direct object. Notice the parallel between: She *made* them *angry*/ She *made* them *sit down*.

Analysis of the NG + bare-infinitive complement of perceptual verbs illustrated below is more problematic. Is the NG the object of the matrix clause or the subject of the non-finite clause? Does the NG + bare infinitive refer to a whole situation, as with *want*?

> I saw someone enter the shop late at night.
> She felt something hard hit her on the head.

While the 'whole situation' view appears to be semantically acceptable, 'I saw someone enter the shop' entails 'I saw someone', this entailment not being the case with the *want* type. Syntactically, the NG is the object of the matrix clause and is also the subject of the bare-infinitive clause.

Some of the clauses of coercion and perception (but not with causative *have*, or with *feel*) can be passivised, with the NG as subject and the bare infinitive replaced by a *to*-infinitive, as in: *The prisoners* were made to stand for hours, *Someone* was seen to enter the shop. *Let* is usually replaced by *allow* (*They were allowed to go*). In this respect we find the same divisibility of the NG as occurs with the 'ask' type.

It is notoriously difficult to pin down the difference in meaning between *help* + bare infinitive and *help* + *to*-infinitive. One analysis sees the bare infinitive as direct or active involvement in bringing about the action expressed by the infinitive, as in: *I'll help you carry your luggage upstairs.* With *help* + *to*, by contrast, the event is seen to be the consequence of the helping, and often means 'contribute to' rather than active involvement by the helper, as in *Acupuncture can help people to give up smoking.*

12.4 MEANINGS EXPRESSED BY *-ING* CLAUSES

12.4.1 Type 5: V + *-ing* clause – I like listening to music

This type of clause uses the verbs: *like, love, avoid, dislike, hate, enjoy, miss, resent, risk, can't, help.*

Non-finite *-ing* clauses as complements tend to express factual meanings. Syntactically they function as non-prototypical direct objects, following the criteria adopted for analysing *to*-infinitive clauses as objects in 12.2, Type 2.

> They disliked *living in a big city.*
> I avoid *travelling in the rush hour.*

12.4.2 Type 6: V + NG + *-ing* clause – I saw them waiting

See, hear, feel, smell, find, leave, catch, discover, come across, keep
The subject of the *-ing* clause is also the object of the superordinate clause. It can become subject in a passive clause.

> They caught *him stealing from the till.*   He was caught stealing from the till.
> She found the *child sleeping peacefully.*   The child was found sleeping peacefully.

With verbs of perception we can often make a distinction between a completed action, expressed by the bare infinitive, and an uncompleted action or action in progress, expressed by an *-ing* clause. Compare: *We watched the house burn down* and *We watched the house burning.*

Note that verbs of *starting, stopping* and *continuing* among others, when followed by either *to*-infinitive or *-ing* clauses, are analysed in this book not as lexical verbs followed by a complement, but as 'phased' or concatenated verbal groups that express aspectual meanings such as ingressive, egressive and continuative (see 39.2), as in *He started smoking at the age of fifteen.*

Verbs of retrospection such as *regret, remember* and *forget* (but not *recall*, which takes only *-ing*) mark a difference of time reference in relation to the main verb. With a *to*-infinitive clause, the action expressed is seen as *following* the mental process of remembering or forgetting, whereas an -*ing* form marks the action as *previous* to the mental process:

I remembered *to turn off the gas.*	(I remembered that I had to turn off the gas and I did.)
I remembered *turning off the gas.*	(I remembered that I had turned off the gas.)
I forgot *to turn off the gas.*	(I forgot that I had to turn off the gas and didn't turn it off.)
I regret *telling/having told you the bad news.*	(I am sorry that I told you the bad news.)
I regret *to tell you there is some bad news.*	(I am sorry to have to tell you bad news.)

Regret + *to*-infinitive is always followed by a verb of communication – *say, tell, announce, inform* – used with present time reference. Both the regretting and the telling occur at the moment of speaking, whereas *regret* + -*ing* has no such limitation (She regretted *going out without an umbrella*).

12.4.3 Potential and factual meanings contrasted: *to*-infinitive and -*ing* clauses

Because the *to*-infinitive looks forward to the event, it tends to be used when a specific occasion is referred to, often of a future or hypothetical kind, as in *I would like* to *go to Paris*. An -*ing* clause, by contrast, expressing factual meanings, as in *I like going to Paris*, entails that I have been to Paris, whereas *I would like to go to Paris* does not.

Emotive verbs such as *like, love, hate* and *prefer* (but not *enjoy, detest* and *dislike*, which admit only -*ing* clauses) can establish this distinction clearly.

I like *listening to music.*	I'd like *to buy a good stereo.*
Most people hate *standing in queues.*	Most car-owners would hate *to be without a car.*

For many speakers, however, the *to*-infinitive is a valid alternative in the expression of factual meanings, especially with a notion of habit: *I like to cook for my friends*.

12.5 PAST PARTICIPIAL CLAUSES

12.5.1 Type 7: V + NG + -*en* clause – We'll get it mended

These are S-P-Od-Co structures with a past participial complement. They are controlled by four types of verb:

- the causative verbs *get* and *have* – We'll have some repairs *done to the house*,
- volitional verbs: *want, like, prefer* – The boss wants *these records updated*;

- verbs of perception: *see, hear, feel* – I felt *my arm grasped from behind*; and
- verbs of finding and leaving – Airport officials have found an unidentified bag *abandoned in the coffee-shop*.

Some of the variety of two-complement patterns is illustrated in this extract from the *National Enquirer*.

Sniffing food for about 30 seconds before you eat it *can help you lose weight*[1] says an expert in weight loss.

'*You're in fact tricking the brain into thinking*[2] that you've already eaten, explains Dr. Alan Hirsch, 'so you don't eat as much.'

In a study, Dr. Hirsch *had 20 people sniff their food*[3] before eating it – and the results were amazing. 'We found that they each lost between 10 and 12 pounds over a three-month period.'

So if you have an urge for a candy bar, *hold it up to your nose*[4] for 30 seconds, then *put it away*.[5] Usually you'll be able to resist the urge to eat it!

[1]*help* + Od + infinitive clause (potential action); [2]*trick* + Od + prep. + *-ing* clause (metaphorical Goal); [3]causative *have* + Od + infinitive clause (action); [4]*hold* + Od + two Loc/Goal Complements; [5]*put* + Od + Loc/Goal Comp.

SUMMARY OF MAJOR VERB COMPLEMENTATION PATTERNS

1   No complement patterns with intransitive verbs

V only ('pure' intransitive)	The post *has arrived*.
V + implied object	That dog *bites*.
V (reciprocal meaning)	They *met* at a party.
V + obligatory locative	She lives *in Tokyo*.

2   One-complement patterns with copular verbs

V + AdjG	The game is *very simple*.
V + NG	This road is *the M40*.

3   One-complement patterns with monotransitive verbs

V + NG	That dog bit *me*.
V + prep + NG	I'll see *to the sandwiches*.

Finite clause

V + finite *that*-clause	He believes *that he is right*.
V + finite *wh*-clause	

(indirect interrog.)	She asked *what I meant.*
(nominal relative)	He believed *what I told him.*
(indirect exclamative)	I said *how sorry I was.*

Non-finite clause

V + non-finite *to*-infinitive clause
| With implicit subject | He wants *to stay.* |
| With explicit subject | He wants *us all to stay.* |

V + non-finite *-ing* clause
| With implicit subject | They like *staying out late.* |
| With explicit subject | She doesn't like *them staying out late.* |

4 Two-complement patterns with ditransitive verbs

| V + NG NG | I gave *Jo a copy.* |
| V + NG + prep + NG | We reminded *her of the time.* |

Finite clause

V + NG + *that*-clause	He assured *her that he cared.*
V + NG + *wh*-interrog. clause	She asked *me where the library was.*
V + NG + nominal *wh* clause	He told *me what I needed to know.*

Non-finite clause

| V + NG + *to*-inf clause | She told *us to sit down.* |

5 Two-complement patterns with complex-transitive verbs

V + NG + AdjG	I found *it useful.*
V + NG + NG	They consider *him a genius.*
V + NG + as + NG	They denounced *the bill as unconstitutional.*
V + NG + obligatory locative	Put *the dish in the microwave.*

Non-finite clause

V + NG + *to*-infinitive clause	They believe *him to be a genius.*
V + NG + bare inf clause	He made *them stand up.*
V + NG + bare infinitive	She saw *two men enter the shop.*
V + NG + *-ing* clause	He kept *us waiting.*
V + NG + *-en* clause	I heard *two shots fired.*

Complementation patterns are illustrated in this summary of a well-known radio serial, published in *The Week*:

> ## The Archers: what happened last week
>
> Alistair asks David if he will join him in The Three Peaks Challenge[1] [climbing Ben Nevis, Scafell and Snowdon in 24 hours]. Oliver asks Caroline to marry him.[2] [Caroline says no], but suggests they live together at Grange Farm.[3] Oliver is delighted. Dross is in trouble now that both Fallon and Ash have left. Kenton teases David and Alistair about the mountain challenge[4] and suggests the Ambridge Three Peaks instead.[5] They jump at the idea.[6] [Tom's love life is a source of gossip.] Most people think he is going out with Fallon to get at Kirsty.[7] Matt Crawford tells David he's found another bit of land.[8] [Kenton is being driven mad living with his parents] and asks David, Kathy and even Elizabeth if he can stay with them.[9] [They all say no.] Jill tells Kenton that Daphne's Café is going to need a manager[10] and suggests he has a word with Jack.[11] Kenton begs Jack to give him the job of managing the café.[12]

FURTHER READING

Biber et al. (1999); Duffley (1992); Greenbaum and Quirk (1990); Huddleston and Pullum (2002); Levin (1993); Quirk et al. (1985); Thompson (2002); Ungerer and Schmid (1997); on the infinitive: Duffley (1992); on frames: Fillmore (1982); on valency: Payne (1977); on *that*-clauses: Thompson (2002).

EXERCISES ON CHAPTER 3
The development of the message: Complementation of the verb

Module 9

1   †With the help of a monolingual dictionary, say whether the verbs in the examples below are (a) exclusively intransitive or (b) can be used either transitively or intransitively:

   (1)   Women today *are achieving* in many professions which were previously open only to men.
   (2)   The two planes *collided* in mid-flight.
   (3)   He *has exhibited* in all the major art galleries over the last five years.
   (4)   You *must be joking*!
   (5)   Most of our students *baby-sit* two or three evenings a week.
   (6)   Pete doesn't *adapt* easily to new situations.
   (7)   My brother-in-law *ghost-writes for* at least two politicians.

(8)   The little bird *quivered in* my hands.
(9)   He thinks he can take me in, but I know when he's *bluffing*.
(10)   Those couples who have no children of their own are often eager to *adopt*.

2   †Of the verbs which could be used transitively in exercise 1, which ones can be considered to have an Object unexpressed (a) by social convention, (b) with reflexive meaning, (c) with reciprocal meaning?

3   †Suggest the underlying semantic valency of the verb *pay*.

4   Turn to the text by John Simpson in 9.3 (p. 87). Underline those expressions in the text that you consider to be loc/manner/goal Complements. Discuss why they appear to be obligatory; hasn't the verb sufficient semantic weight without them? Discuss those cases in which an Adjunct is not present because it is inferrable from the context.

Module 10

1   †(a) Choose the most appropriate prepositional verb from the list in 10.3 to fill the gap in each of the sentences below. Then (b) put each sentence into the passive:

(1)   You can't . . . . Cecil, he has such fixed ideas.
(2)   It is not easy to . . . . old broken furniture.
(3)   They will . . . . the Minister of Defence to explain the charges of negligence.
(4)   The target they are . . . . is too high.
(5)   You should . . . . your schedule if you hope to deliver the goods on the agreed date.

2   Explain the semantic difference between 'She wrote a letter to her brother' and 'she wrote a letter for her brother'.

3   With the help of a good dictionary, work out the complementation patterns, and the meanings of *leave*. Give examples.

Module 11

1   †Combine the following pairs of clauses so that the first clause can be analysed as an embedded constituent of the superordinate clause. Add or omit whatever is necessary. The first is done for you:

(1)   He has lived abroad for several years. I gather that from what he says.

       From what he says, I gather (that) he has lived abroad for several years.

(2)   Have we enough petrol to reach Barcelona? I doubt it.
(3)   Is there an emergency kit in the building? Who knows?
(4)   Where is the nearest Metro station? I asked.
(5)   You keep the keys. We have all agreed on that.

(6)　Some of the documents are missing. The Under-Secretary can't account for it.
(7)　Why doesn't he look in the safe? I suggest that.
(8)　We have just heard that. The spokesman confirmed it.
(9)　He has been under great strain lately. We must allow for that.
(10)　These letters must be posted today. Will you see to it please?

2　†Read again section 11.1.2 on dropping or keeping the *that* complementiser. Identify which factors make for the retention or omission of the subordinator *that* in each *that*-clause in the examples that follow the explanation on p. 104.

3　†Give a reason for the omission or retention of *that* before the embedded clauses in:

(a)　In a friendly way Wilson had also suggested that Koo travel to France on the same boat as the Americans. (*The Peacemakers*)

(b)　I said I thought she was still crazy about him. (*Girls Out Late*)

4　†Analyse the following in terms of recursive embedding:
He says he's really sorry he said he'd take someone else to the dance.

5　†Say which of the italicised clauses in the examples below are nominal relative clauses, which are indirect interrogative clauses and which are embedded exclamatives:

(1)　He asked *where I had been all afternoon*.
(2)　The spokesman announced *what we had all been hoping to hear*.
(3)　You've no idea *how cold it was in Granada at Easter*.
(4)　They don't know *who sprayed the graffiti on the Faculty walls*.
(5)　I said *what a pity it was they couldn't be with us*.
(6)　He's sure to fall in with *whatever you suggest*.

6　†Explain why the following constructions are ungrammatical:

(a)　*They suggested to start at 8.00.
(b)　*She explained me the difference between the two constructions.

Module 12

1　Answer the following questions using *to*-infinitive clauses or *-ing* clauses to express situations within the main situation – at least to start off with!

(1)　What do you particularly dislike doing on Monday mornings?
(2)　Is there anything you regret not doing?
(3)　If people go off on holiday without locking up the house, what do they risk?
(4)　What things do you feel you can't afford?
(5)　What kind of thing would you absolutely refuse to do?
(6)　Is there any kind of situation that you miss when you are away from home?

2 Analyse the following catenative chain:

They want to try to get all their neighbours to refuse to sign the petition.

Now try to construct a catenative chain using a series of *to*-infinitive clauses beginning as follows: I hope to . . .

3 Answer the questions below and note the complementation patterns you use:

(1) What kind of thing would you find it impossible to promise someone to do?
(2) Would you rather owe someone money or a favour, or have money or a favour owed to you?
(3) What would you advise an overweight friend to eat?
(4) How would you encourage an oversensitive person to react?
(5) How would you help someone to be assertive without being aggressive?
(6) What would you recommend a bored housewife to do?

4 †Write out the complementation pattern of each of the following. The first is done for you:

(1) He never allowed Thomas to drive the jeep in his absence.

   v + NG + to-inf.

(2) The shopkeeper asked me what I wanted.
(3) His powerful imagination makes him quite different from the others.
(4) Keep your shoulders straight.
(5) He left her sitting on the bridge.
(6) They like their next-door neighbours to come in for a drink occasionally.
(7) I would prefer Mike to drive you to the station.

5 Read again 'The Archers: what happened last week' (p. 116). Underline the main verb and write out the complementation pattern it determines in each numbered clause. Ignore the clauses in brackets. For example, sentence (i) is as follows: V+NG+*wh*-cl (*if* = *whether*).

6 If you are giving an opinion in English about a person, a place, a thing, an event, etc., from a rather subjective point of view, you will find yourself using monotransitive structures with *that*-clause complements (*I think she is rather silly*), complex transitive complementation (*Oh, I found her good fun*) and copular complementation (*He seems rather too full of himself*). Discuss among a group of friends a person, place or event known to you all. Tape your conversation (try to forget you are being recorded!) and then analyse what you have said. Note the constructions you have not used.

7 With the help of a good dictionary, work out the various complementation patterns that the following verbs can control: *prefer* and *drive*.

CONCEPTUALISING PATTERNS OF EXPERIENCE

CHAPTER 4

Processes, participants, circumstances

CONCEPTUALISING EXPERIENCES EXPRESSED AS SITUATION TYPES

SUMMARY

1   Semantically, a clause represents a pattern of experience, conceptualised as a situation type.

2   Situation types comprise three main types: material, mental and relational. There are also three subsidiary types: behavioural, verbal and existential.

3   Each situation type consists of the following:

   • The process: the central part of the situation, realised by a verb. Process types include those of doing, happening, experiencing, being and existing.
   • Participant roles: these symbolically represent the persons, things and abstract entities involved in the process.
   • Attributes: the elements which characterise, identify or locate the participant.
   • Circumstances: those of time, place, manner, condition, etc. attendant on the situation.

4   The type of process determines the nature and number of the participants. Certain inherent participants can remain unactualised when understood in the context.

5   The valency of the verb specifies the number of inherent participants of any process, and by reduction indicates the result of unactualising one or more participants. This type of analysis runs parallel to the traditional transitive–intransitive analysis.

13.1 PROCESSES, PARTICIPANTS, CIRCUMSTANCES

In this chapter we look at the clause as a grammatical means of encoding patterns of experience. A fundamental property of language is that it enables us to conceptualise and describe our experience, whether of the actions and events, people and things of the external world, or of the internal world of our thoughts, feelings and perceptions. This is done through transitivity, contemplated in a broad sense, which encompasses not only the verb but the semantic configuration of situation types.

The clause is, here too then, the most significant grammatical unit. It is the unit that enables us to organise the wealth of our experience, both semantically and syntactically, into a manageable number of representational patterns or schemas. Our personal 'construals' of each individual situation are then selected from these patterns. In describing an event, for instance, we might say that it just happened, or that it was caused by someone's deliberate intervention, or that it is unusual, or that we feel sad about it, among other possible construals. In this chapter we will be talking about patterns of 'doing', 'happening', 'experiencing' and 'being' as the main types, together with a small number of subsidiary types.

As language-users, we are interested in events and especially in the human participants involved and the qualities we ascribe to them, what they do, say and feel, their possessions and the circumstances in which the event takes place. The semantic schema for a situation, therefore, consists potentially of the following components:

- the process (a technical term for the action (e.g. hit, run), state (e.g. have) or change of state (e.g. melt, freeze) involved.
- the participant(s) involved in the process (basically, who or what is doing what to whom);
- the attributes ascribed to participants; and
- the circumstances attendant on the process, in terms of time, place, manner, and so on.

13.1.1 The process

There is no satisfactory general term to cover that central part of a situation, the part which is typically realised by the verb and which can be an action, a state, a meteorological phenomenon, a process of sensing, saying or simply existing. Following Halliday, we here use the term 'process' for all these types. We can also analyse them as dynamic processes and stative processes.

Dynamic and stative processes

Dynamic situations and processes involve something that occurs or happens; they can be tested for by means of the question 'What happened?' **Stative** situations and processes are conceived of as durative over time, and as existing rather than happening, so it doesn't make sense to ask 'What happened?' in such cases. Generally, dynamic processes easily occur in the progressive (*Pete is going away*) and the imperative (*Go away, Pete!*), whereas most stative processes don't usually accept the progressive or the imperative (**Pete is seeming kind. *Hear a noise!*). See also 43.5.

13.1.2 The participant roles (semantic functions) involved in the situation

In classifying situations into schemas, we filter out the wealth of detail that we find in our personal experiences, to focus on the salient participant(s) that belong to different types of situation. These are usually just one or two, at the most three. When one of the participants is human, it is typically assigned the primary role (Agent/Subject) in the semantic and syntactic constructions. This is a consequence of our anthropocentric orientation in conceptualising events.

While human participants occupy a prime place among the semantic roles, the term 'participant' does not refer exclusively to persons or animals, but includes things and abstractions. A participant can be the one who carries out the action or the one who is affected by it; it can be the one who experiences something by seeing or feeling; it can be a person or thing that simply exists. The terminology used to identfy participant roles may be less familiar to you than the corresponding syntactic terms. As we go on, you will find that labels are useful in semantics, just as in syntax, in order to talk about concepts. We will try to keep them as simple and transparent as possible.

The **Attributes ascribed to entities** either identify or characterise the entity, or state its location in space or time. They are realised syntactically by the intensive Complements (Complement of the Subject and Complement of the Object).

13.1.3 The circumstantial roles associated with the process

These include the well-known circumstances of time, place, manner and condition, as well as a few others. They are typically optional in the semantic structure, just as their adjunctive counterparts are in the syntactic structure. Circumstances can, however, be inherent to the situation: for instance, location is obligatory with certain senses of 'be', as in *the ice-cream's **over there***, and with 'put' in its sense of 'placing' as in *let's put it **in the freezer*** (see 4.2.1; 10.8).

Fred	bought	a new shirt	in Oxford Street	yesterday
Participant	Process	Participant	Circumstance	Circumstance

At the present time	the state of the economy	is	critical
Circumstance	Participant	Process	Attribute

We have now outlined the framework that will serve to carry the different configurations of semantic functions that go to make up semantic structures. It is not the case, however, that any particular configuration is inherently given in nature. There are various ways of conceptualising a situation, according to our needs of the moment and what the lexico-grammatical resources of a language permit.

For instance, on the day planned for a river picnic we may look out of the window and say *it's cloudy*, specifying simply a state (*is*) and an Attribute (*cloudy*); alternatively, that *the sky is cloudy*, adding a participant (*the sky*) for the Attribute. More ominously, someone might say *the clouds are gathering*, in which the situation is represented as a dynamic happening rather than as a state, with a participant (*clouds*) and a dynamic process (*are gathering*), leaving implicit the circumstance of place (*in the sky*). Or we may say nothing at all about the clouds, but instead interpret what we see by saying *I think it's going to rain*.

There is no one-to-one correlation between semantic structures and syntactic structures; rather, the semantic categories cut across the syntactic ones, although with some correlation. Semantic structures and syntactic structures do not, therefore, always coincide; rather, they overlap. In both cases, however, it is the process, expressed by the verb, that determines the choice of participants in the semantic structure and of syntactic elements in the syntactic structure. In Chapter 3 the possible syntactic combinations are discussed from the point of view of verb complementation and verb type. In this chapter we shall start from the semantics; at the same time we shall try to relate the choice of semantic roles to their syntactic realisations.

One obvious problem in the identification of participants and processes is the vastness and variety of the physical world, and the difficulty involved in reducing this variety to a few prototypical semantic roles and processes. All we can attempt to do is to specify the paradigm cases, and indicate where more detailed specification would be necessary in order to account semantically for the varied shades of our experience.

13.2 TYPES OF PROCESS

There are three main types of process:

(a) Material processes are processes of 'doing' (e.g. *kick, run, eat, give*) or 'happening' (e.g. *fall, melt, collapse, slip*).
(b) Mental processes, or processes of 'experiencing' or 'sensing' (e.g. *see, hear, feel, know, like, want, regret*).
(c) Relational processes, or processes of 'being' (e.g. *be, seem*) or 'becoming' (e.g. *become, turn*), in which a participant is characterised, or identified, or situated circumstantially.

There are also three subsidiary processes: behavioural, verbal and existential. We shall see, as we go on, that the presence or absence of volition and energy are important factors in distinguishing between processes.

13.3 INHERENT PARTICIPANTS AND ACTUALISED PARTICIPANTS

Most processes are accompanied by one or more inherent participants; the nature of the process determines how many and what kind of participants are involved. The material process represented by the verb *fall* for instance, has only one participant, whereas *kick* typically requires two: one participant is the Agent who carries out the action, and must be 'animate' and typically 'human'; the other is the participant affected by the action of kicking, and is not required to be human, or even animate.

In the example *Ted kicked the ball* both the inherent participants are **actualised** as *Ted* and *the ball*. If we say *Ted kicked hard*, however, only one participant, the Agent, is actualised. The second participant, the one affected by the action, is **unactualised but understood**. In everyday uses of English, speakers frequently find it convenient not to actualise certain inherent participants. *Give*, for instance, is typically a three-participant process as in *Mary gave the Red Cross a donation*. Only two participants are actualised, however, in *Mary gave a donation* and only one in *Mary gave generously*.

Certain participants are omitted in this way when they are conventionally understood from the context of culture or context of situation, for example:

Do you drive?   (a car)
Have you eaten yet?   (lunch/dinner)
Shall I pour?   (the tea/coffee)
Our team is winning   (the match/race)
I can't see from here   (the screen, the time . . .)

The participant is not specific in *electricity can kill, remarks like that can hurt, elephants never forget, Enjoy!* and is perhaps not even known to the speaker in *he teaches, she writes*. Processes such as *meet* and *kiss* can be understood as having implicit reciprocity in, for instance, *your sister and I have never met* (each other).

Some processes have typically no participants; for example, statements about the weather, time and distance such as *it's snowing, it's half past eleven, it's a long walk to the beach*. In these the pronoun *it* is merely a surface form required to realise the obligatory Subject element. It has no corresponding semantic function.

Traditionally, the term **intransitive** has been used to refer to verbs that express one-participant processes such as *fall* or no-participant processes such as *rain*, whose action does not extend to any Object. The term **transitive** has been used to refer to verbs and clauses in which the process is extended to one or more Objects. Following this convention, *give* is transitive in *Mary gave a donation* but intransitive in *Give generously!*

Similarly, the **semantic** analysis into actualised and unactualised participants is paralleled by the **syntactic** analysis of verbs such as *drive, eat* etc. as being either **transitive** (taking an Object) or **intransitive** (with no Object).

In this book we shall use 'transitive' and 'intransitive' as syntactic terms, while referring semantically to one-, two- or three-participant processes, with 'actualised' or 'unactualised' inherent participants.

The number of participants (including the subject) involved in a process can also be referred to as its **valency**. A process with one participant is said to be **monovalent** – as in *the ice melted*. A process with two participants is **bivalent** – as in *the postman rides a motorcycle*; a process with three participants is **trivalent** – as in *Mary gave the Red Cross a donation*. The valency is reduced from three to two, or from two to one when participants are not actualised, as in the examples above (see also Chapter 3, Introduction).

To sum up, processes such as *eat* and *see* each have two inherent participants (the one who eats or sees, and the one that is eaten or seen). But in our previously listed examples only one is actualised. The items in brackets represent the conventionally understood second participant. As regards valency, in each case the normal valency of two is reduced to one. As regards transitivity, each of the verbs is potentially transitive, but as the second participant is unactualised, the use is intransitive.

MATERIAL PROCESSES OF DOING AND HAPPENING

SUMMARY

1   The first main category of processes, material processes, includes several kinds: 'doing', 'happening', 'causing' and 'transferring'. Typically, the action of 'doing' is carried out by a volitional, controlling human participant: the Agent. A non-controlling inanimate agent is called Force, for instance an earthquake.

2   In processes of doing, the action either extends no further than the Agent itself, as in *she resigned*, or it extends to another participant, the Affected (*the ball* in *Pelé kicked the ball*). A special type of 'doing' is the process of transfer, in which an Agent transfers an Affected participant to a Recipient or is intended for a Beneficiary (*give someone a present, make someone a cake*, respectively).

3   In involuntary processes of happening, the Affected undergoes the happening (*the roof fell in, the old man collapsed*).

4   The order of elements in the semantic structures is iconic, that is, the linguistic ordering of the event reflects our conceptualisation of the event.

14.1   AGENT AND AFFECTED IN VOLUNTARY PROCESSES OF 'DOING'

Material processes express an action or activity which is typically carried out by a 'doer' or Agent. By 'Agent' we mean an entity having energy, volition and intention that is capable of initiating and controlling the action, usually to bring about some change of location or properties in itself or others. Agents are typically human.

A. Agentive Subject of a voluntary process of 'doing' – They all left

A voluntary one-participant process can be carried out by an Agent as Subject operating on itself:

Agent	Process
The Prime Minister	resigned
We	sat down

One-participant voluntary material processes answer the question **What did X do?** (What did the Prime Minister do? The Prime Minister *resigned*.) To test for Agent, we can ask the question **Who resigned**? (The Prime Minister did).

B. Affected participant in a voluntary process of 'doing' – *Ted hit Bill*

With action processes such as resigning and sitting down, the action does not extend to another participant. With others, such as hitting and carrying, it does. The second participant is someone or something affected by the action denoted by the verb in an active clause, as a result of the energy flow. This participant is called the **Affected** (other terms in use for this participant are **Patient** and **Goal**).

Agent	Process	Affected
Ted	hit	Bill
Pelé	kicked	the ball
The porter	is carrying	our baggage

For those material processes that have two participants, an Agent and an Affected, it also makes sense to ask the question What did Ted do? (He *hit Bill*), and to identify the Affected by the question 'Who(m) did Bill hit?'

C. Affected Subject in a passive clause – *Bill was hit by Ted*

Consequently, if the process extends to an Affected participant, the representation can be made in two forms, either active, in which Agent conflates with Subject, as above, or passive, in which Affected conflates with Subject:

Affected	Material process	Agent
Bill	was hit	by Ted
The ball	was kicked	by Pelé
Our baggage	is being carried	by the porter

A further kind of material process is illustrated in *Fiona made a cake* and *Dave wrote a letter*. Neither the cake nor the letter existed before the process of making or writing, so they cannot be classed as 'Affecteds'. Rather, they are created as a result of the process, and can be called 'Effected participants'. However, no syntactic distinction is made between Affected and Effected participants; the distinction is purely semantic.

14.2 FORCE

The notion of **agency** is a complex one, which includes such features as animacy, intention, motivation, responsibility and the use of one's own energy to initiate or control a process. In central instances, all these features will be present. In non-central instances, one or more of these features may be absent. If we say, for example, that *the horse splashed us with mud as it passed* we do not imply that the horse did so deliberately. We do not attribute intentionality or responsibility or motivation to the horse in this situation. We might call it an 'unwitting Agent'.

The higher animals, and especially pets, are often treated grammatically as if they were humans. Nevertheless, rather than devise a different term for every subtype of agency we will make just one further distinction: that between animate and inanimate Agents. This is useful in order to account for such natural phenomena as earthquakes, lightning, electricity, avalanches, the wind, tides and floods, which may affect humans and their possessions. They are inanimate, and their power or energy cannot therefore be intentional. They can instigate a process but not control it. This non-controlling entity we call **Force**; it will include such psychological states as anxiety, fear or joy.

Force	Process	Affected
The volcano	erupted	
Lightning	struck	the oak tree
An earthquake	destroyed	most of the city
Anxiety	can ruin	your health

In the following description, the subjects in italics realise the role of Force and most of the verbs encode material processes:

> *The cold* crept in from the corners of the shanty, closer and closer to the stove. *Icy-cold breezes* sucked and fluttered the curtains around the beds. *The little shanty* quivered in the storm. But *the steamy smell of boiling beans* was good and *it* seemed to make the air warmer.
>
> (Laura Ingalls Wilder, *The Long Winter*)

14.3 AFFECTED SUBJECT OF INVOLUNTARY PROCESSES OF 'HAPPENING'

Not all material processes involve a voluntary action carried out by an Agent. In situations expressed as *Jordan slipped on the ice, the roof collapsed, the children have grown, the vase fell off the shelf*, the participant, even when animate, is neither controlling nor initiating the action. This is proved by the inappropriateness of the question 'What did

X do?' and of the *wh*-cleft test (**What the children did was grow*). Rather, we should ask 'What happened to X?' The participant on which the action centres in such cases is, then, Affected. It is found in involuntary transitional processes such as *grow* and *melt*, which represent the passage from one state to another, and in involuntary actions and events such as *fall*, *slip* and *collapse*, which may have an animate or an inanimate participant.

Affected Subject	Involuntary process	Circumstance
Jordan	slipped	on the ice
The children	have grown	
The roof	collapsed	
The vase	fell	off the shelf

In the following passage almost all the clauses are intransitive: the Subject participant varies from Agentive (voluntary) to Affected (involuntary animate, or inanimate).

Encounter between an Indian father and his son

So I raced out of my room,[1] with my fingers in my ears, to *scream*[2] till *the roof fell* [3]*down* about their ears.

But *the radio* suddenly *went off*,[4] *the door to my parents' room* suddenly *opened*[5] and *my father appeared*,[6] bathed and shaven, *his white 'dhoti' blazing*,[7] *his white shirt crackling*,[8] *his patent leather pumps glittering*.[9] *He stopped*[10] in the doorway and *I stopped*[11] on the balls of my feet and *wavered*.[12]

(Anita Desai, *Games at Twilight*)

[1]Agentive Subject; [2]implicit Agentive Subject; [3]Affected inanimate Subject; [4]Affected inanimate Subject; [5]Affected inanimate Subject; [6]Agentive Subject; [7]Affected inanimate Subject; [8]Affected inanimate Subject; [9]Affected inanimate Subject; [10]Agentive Subject; [11]Agentive Subject; [12]animate diminished volition

---

The high number of one-participant processes in this text helps to make us participate in the boy's apprehension. Inanimate objects (*radio, door, roof, 'dhoti', shirt, pumps*) appear to take on a life of their own, able to carry out actions which to him are potentially violent and threatening (*fall down, blaze, crackle, glitter*). Potentially threatening, too, are his father's actions, in this context. They are not extended to any other entity; he simply *appears* and *stops*. But the foreboding is there. The boy's actions are not directed towards anything except escape (*race out*). But this initial volition weakens, becomes semi-voluntary (*scream*) and is almost lost in the final intransitive (*wavers*).

CAUSATIVE PROCESSES   *MODULE 15*

SUMMARY

1   In causative material processes some external Agent or Force causes something to happen. In the paradigm case, a responsible, purposeful human Agent directly causes an Affected to undergo the action named by the verb. The Affected, not the Agent, is the inherent participant that undergoes the process, as in *I rang the bell*.

2   When the Affected object of a transitive-causative clause is the same as the Affected subject of the corresponding intransitive clause, we have an 'ergative pair'.

3   A 'pseudo-intransitive' expresses the facility of a participant to undergo a process: *Glass breaks easily*.

15.1 CAUSATIVE MATERIAL PROCESSES AND ERGATIVE PAIRS

The prototypical pattern of direct causation is quite complex. A controlling, purposeful, responsible Agent directs its energy towards something or someone (the Affected), so that this undergoes the action named by the verb, with a consequent change of state. The following example illustrate this **transitive-causative** structure.

Initiating Agent	Process	Affected
Paul	opened	the door
Pat	boiled	the water
I	rang	the bell

From this perspective, the action of boiling, ringing, etc. is initiated by a controlling Agent or a Force participant: *The sun melted the ice*.

The Affected is, however, the essential participant, the one primarily involved in the action. It is the door that opens, the water that boils and the bell that rings.

If we conceptualise the situation from a different angle, in which no Agent initiator is present, we encode the process as 'happening' of its own accord. An Agent can't be added. This is the **anti-causative** structure.

Affected	Process
The door	opened
The water	boiled
The bell	rang

When the Affected object of a transitive clause (e.g. *the bell*) is the same as the Affected subject of an intransitive clause, we have an **ergative alternation** or **ergative pair**, as in *I rang **the bell*** (transitive) and ***the bell*** *rang* (intransitive). This key participant in both cases is sometimes called the Medium. Ergative systems in many languages are ordinarily characterised by morphological case marking, the subject of the intransitive clause and the object of the transitive clause being marked in the same way, while the Agentive subject is marked differently. This is not the case with English which instead marks both the subject of an intransitive clause and that of a transitive clause as nominative, and the object of the transitive as accusative. We can see this in the two meanings of *leave*: ***he** left* (*went away*, intrans.), ***he** left **them*** (*abandon*, trans.).

Nevertheless, the term 'ergative' has been extended to English on the basis of the semantic association between S (intrans.) and O (trans.) in alternations illustrated by *boil, ring*, etc. The semantic similarity between these two is one of change of state.

The test for recognising an ergative pair is that the causative-transitive, two-participant structure must always allow for the corresponding one-participant, anti-causative structure. Compare the previous examples (e.g. *he opened the door/the door opened*) with the following, in which the first, although transitive, is not causative. There is no intransitive counterpart, and consequently, no ergative pair:

Pelé kicked the ball.   *The ball kicked

Ergative pairs account for many of the most commonly used verbs in English, some of which are listed below, with examples:

burn	I've burned the toast. The toast has burned.
break	The wind broke the branches. The branches broke.
burst	She burst the balloon. The balloon burst.
close	He closed his eyes. His eyes closed.
cook	I'm cooking the rice. The rice is cooking.
fade	The sun has faded the carpet. The carpet has faded.
freeze	The low temperature has frozen the milk. The milk has frozen.

melt	The heat has melted the ice. The ice has melted.
run	Tim is running the bathwater. The bathwater is running.
stretch	I stretched the elastic. The elastic stretched.
tighten	He tightened the rope. The rope tightened.
wave	Someone waved a flag. A flag waved.

Within this alternation – described here as an 'ergative pair' – there is a set of basically intransitive volitional activities (*walk, jump, march*) in which the second participant is involved either willingly or unwillingly. The control exerted by the Agent predominates in the causative-transitive:

He *walked* the dogs in the park.	The dogs *walked*.
He *jumped* the horse over the fence	The horse *jumped* over the fence.
The sergeant *marched* the soldiers.	The soldiers *marched*.

It is also possible to have an additional agent and an additional causative verb in the transitive clauses of ergative pairs; for example, *The child got his sister to ring the bell, Mary made Peter boil the water.*

15.2 ANALYTICAL CAUSATIVES WITH A RESULTING ATTRIBUTE

One final type of causative we will consider is the analytical type, based on combinations with verbs such as *make* and *turn*. In these an Agent brings about a change of state in the Affected participant. The resulting state is expressed by an Attribute (Complement of the Object in a syntactic analysis).

Agent	Process	Affected	Resulting Attribute
They	are making	the road	wider and safer.
This machine	will make	your tasks	simple.
The heat	has turned	the milk	sour.
Pat	had	her face	lifted.

The resulting change of state in the Affected participant is sometimes part of the meaning of a morphologically related causative verb: *widen* is the equivalent of *make wide* and *simplify* means *make simple*. With such verbs there are alternative SPOd causative structures: *They are widening the road; This machine will simplify your tasks.* For other adjectives such as *safe* there is no corresponding causative verb. Certain dynamic verbs such as *turn* can be used in specific causative senses in English. *Have* introduces a passive sense, expressed by a participle (cause to be *-en*).

Analytical causatives and causative-transitives are illustrated in the following text:

> The cold wind *made the horses eager to go.*[1] They *pricked their ears* forward and back[2] and *tossed their heads*,[3] *jingling the bits*[4] and pretending to shy at their own shadows. They *stretched their noses* forward,[5] pulling on the bits and prancing to go faster.
>
> (Laura Ingalls Wilder, *The Long Winter*)
>
> [1]causing a change of state (*eager*) in the Affected participant (*horses*); [2]causing the Affected (*their ears*) to undergo an action (*prick . . . forward and back*); [3]causing the Affected (*their heads*) to undergo an action (*toss*); [4]causing the Affected (*the bits*) to undergo an action (*jingle*); [5]causing the Affected (*their noses*) to undergo an action (*stretch . . .*).

Clauses 2, 3, 4 and 5 contain verbs used causatively and could have an anti-causative counterpart:

Their ears pricked forward and back
Their heads tossed
The bits jingled
Their noses stretched forward

In clause 1 *the cold wind* is the inanimate causer, which initiates the action. In the remaining clauses *they* (the horses) are the causative Agent, setting in motion parts of themselves or their harness. By choosing the two-participant, rather than the one-participant structure, the author is able to present the horses as lively, eager beings.

15.3 PSEUDO-INTRANSITIVES

A further type of Affected Subject occurs with certain processes (*break, read, translate, wash, tan, fasten, lock*) which are intrinsically transitive, but in this construction are construed as intransitive, with an Affected subject.

Glass breaks easily.
This box doesn't shut/close/lock/fasten properly.
Colloquial language translates badly.
Some synthetic fibres won't wash. Usually they dry-clean.
Fair skin doesn't tan quickly, it turns red.

Pseudo-intransitives differ from other intransitives in the following ways:

* They express a general property or propensity of the entity to undergo (or not undergo) the process in question. Compare *glass breaks easily* with *the glass broke*, which refers to a specific event.
* Pseudo-intransitives tend to occur in the present tense.

- The verb is accompanied by negation, or a modal (often *will/won't*), or an adverb such as *easily, well*, any of which specify the propensity or otherwise of the thing to undergo the process.
- A cause is implied but an Agent can't be added in a *by*-phrase.
- There is no corresponding transitive construction, either active or passive, that exactly expresses the same meaning as these intransitives. To say, for instance, *colloquial language is translated badly* is to make a statement about translators' supposed lack of skill, rather than about a property of colloquial language. The difficulty of even paraphrasing this pattern shows how specific and useful it is.

For the similarity of intransitive subjects and transitive objects as conveyors of new information, see Chapter 6. These are the roles in which new information is over-whelmingly expressed.

See 30.3 for passive counterparts of active structures and 30.3.3 for the *get*-passive. These, like copular counterparts, are not identical in meaning to the structures discussed here, but demonstrate some of the many ways of conceptualising an event.

Ed broke the glass	active
The glass was broken (by Ed)	*be*-passive
The glass got broken	*get*-passive
The glass was already broken	copular (state)
The glass broke	(anti-causative)
Glass breaks easily	(pseudo-intransitive)

PROCESSES OF TRANSFER   *MODULE 16*

SUMMARY

1   There are three participants in the processes of transfer: Agent, Affected and Recipient or Beneficiary.

2   The Recipient is a central participant in three-participant processes such as *give*. It encodes the one who receives the transferred material.

3   The Beneficiary is the optional, non-central participant in three-participant processes such as *fetch*. It represents the one for whom some service is done.

16.1   RECIPIENT AND BENEFICIARY IN PROCESSES OF TRANSFER

With processes that encode transfer – such as *give, send, lend, charge, pay, offer* and *owe* – the action expressed by the verb extends not only to the Affected but to a third inherent participant, the **Recipient**, as in:

> Ed gave *the cat* a bit of tuna.
> Bill's father has lent *us* his car.
> Have you paid *the taxi-driver* the right amount?

The **Recipient** is the one who usually receives the 'goods', permission or information. (With *owe* there is a 'moral' Recipient who has not yet received anything.) The **Beneficiary**, by contrast is the optional, not inherent, participant for whom some service is done. This often amounts to being the intended recipient. However, it is not necessarily the same as receiving the goods. I can bake you a cake, but perhaps you don't want it.

This difference is reflected in English in the syntax of verbs such as *fetch, get, make, buy, order* and many verbs of preparation such as *cook, bake* and *mix*, which can be replaced by *make*. These can represent services done for people rather than actions to people.

Nurse, could you fetch *me* a glass of water?
Yes, but soon I'll *bring* you your orange juice. I'll get *you* something to read, too.

Semantically, both Recipient and Beneficiary are typically animate and human, while syntactically both are realised as indirect object (see 6.2.1). Occasionally an inanimate Recipient occurs as in: 'We'll give *the unemployment question* priority.' An inanimate Beneficiary is possible but unlikely: ?I've bought the computer a new mouse.

The two syntactic tests for distinguishing Recipient from Beneficiary, namely passivisation and the prepositional counterpart, are discussed in 6.2.1 and 10.4.1.

Recipient and Beneficiary can occur together in the same clause, as in the following example, which illustrates the difference between the one who is given the goods (*me*) and the intended recipient (*my daughter*): She gave *me* a present for *my daughter*.

Both Recipient and Beneficiary may be involved in processes of an unbeneficial nature such as *they sent him a letter-bomb*, in which *him* is Recipient; and *they set him a trap* in which *him* is Beneficiary.

16.2 SUMMARY OF MATERIAL PROCESS TYPES

Example	Participant(s)	Type
The Prime Minister resigned	Agent	doing (intrans.)
Ed kicked the ball	Agent + Affected	doing (trans.)
The volcano erupted	Force	doing (intrans.)
The dog died	Affected	happening (intrans.)
Ed broke the glass	Agent initiator + Aff/Medium	causative-trans.
The glass broke	Affected/Medium	anti-causative
Glass breaks easily	Affected	pseudo-intrans.
The glass was broken (by Ed)	Affected (+ optional Agent)	passive
The glass got broken	Affected	*get*-passive
They made the road wider	Ag. + Aff + Attribute	analytical causative
Ed gave the cat a bit of tuna	Ag. + Rec + Aff	transfer (trans.)

CONCEPTUALISING WHAT WE THINK, PERCEIVE AND FEEL   *MODULE 17*

SUMMARY

1   Mental processes comprise processes of perception (*see, hear, feel*), of cognition (*know, understand, believe*) and of affection and desideration (*like, fear; want, wish*).

2   There is always a conscious participant, the **Experiencer**, who perceives, knows, likes, etc. There is usually a second participant, the **Phenomenon** – that which is perceived, known, liked or wanted.

17.1 MENTAL PROCESSES

Not all situations that we wish to express linguistically centre on doings and happenings. Mental processes are those through which we organise our mental contact with the world. There are four main types: **cognition**, such as *know, understand, believe, doubt, remember* and *forget*; **perception**, encoded by verbs such as *see, notice, hear, feel* and *taste*; **affectivity**, such as *like, love, admire, miss* and *hate*; **desideration** such as *hope, want, desire* and *wish*. Some of these are illustrated in the following invented sequence:

> Tom *saw* a ball in the tall grass. He *knew* it wasn't his, but he *wanted* to get it. He didn't *realise* there were lots of nettles among the grass. He soon *felt* his hands stinging. He *wished* he had *noticed* the nettles.

With mental processes it makes no sense, as it does with material processes, to talk about who is doing what to whom. In, for example, *Jill liked the present*, Jill is not doing anything, and the gift is not affected in any way. We can't apply the 'doing to' test to processes of liking and disliking, asking for instance 'What did Jill do to the present?' In many cases, a better test is to question the Experiencer's reaction to something. It is therefore inappropriate to call Jill an Agent and *the present* the Affected. Rather, we need two more semantic roles:

Jill	liked	the present
Experiencer	Process	Phenomenon

The **Experiencer** (or **Senser**) is the participant who sees, feels, thinks, likes, etc., and is typically human, but may also be an animal or even a personified inanimate object (*The rider heard a noise*, *the horse sensed danger, your car knows what it needs*). The use of a non-conscious entity as Experiencer in a mental process is often exploited for commercial ends, as in this last example.

The second participant in a mental process, that which is perceived, known, liked, etc., is called the **Phenomenon**. Mental processes are typically stative and non-volitional. When they occur in the present tense they typically take the simple, rather than the progressive, form. Compare this feature with material process verbs, for which the more usual, 'unmarked' form for expressing a happening in the present is the progressive. Another feature of stative verbs is that they do not easily occur in the imperative (*Know thyself* is a famous exception).

> *Jill is liking the present   *Like the present, Jill!   (mental)
> Bill is mending the bicycle.   Mend the bicycle, Bill!   (material)

Mental processes can sometimes be expressed with the Phenomenon filling the Subject slot and the Experiencer as Object, although not necessarily by means of the same verb. This means that we have two possible construals of the mental experience: in the one case, the human participant reacts to a phenomenon, as in **1** and **2**, while in the other the phenomenon activates the attention of the experiencer, as in **3** and **4**. Reversibility is helped by the fact that the passive is possible with many mental processes:

Experiencer	Process	Phenomenon
1 I	don't understand	his motives
2 Most people	are horrified	by the increase in violence
Phenomenon	**Process**	**Experiencer**
3 His motives	elude	me
4 The increase in violence	horrifies	most people

Similarly, English has the verb *please*, which is used occasionally in this way: *I don't think her choice pleased her mother* (BNC G31639). More often '*pleased*' is used as an adjective, as in *he was very pleased with himself*, which adjusts to the predominant pattern by which human subjects are preferred to non-human ones. '*Pleased*' also tends to be equivalent to '*satisfied*' or polite '*willing*' as in *University officers will be pleased to advise anyone . . .* (BNC G31 871), which is quite different affectively from '*like*'.

In all the examples so far, the Phenomenon has been a single entity, expressed as a nominal group as the Object of the verb. But it can also be a fact, a process or a whole situation, realised by a clause (see 11.1), as in the following examples:

We	knew	that it would be difficult
Nobody	saw	the train go off the rails
I	fancy	going for a swim

17.2 COGNITIVE PROCESSES: KNOWING, THINKING AND BELIEVING

Cognitive processes are encoded by such stative verbs as *believe, doubt, guess, know, recognise, think, forget, mean, remember, understand*. A selection of examples is given below. *Feel* is also regularly used as an equivalent of 'believe'. Most verbs of cognition have as their Phenomenon a wide range of things apprehended, including human, inanimate and abstract entities encoded as nominal groups (a) and (b). Facts, beliefs, doubts, perceptions and expectations are encoded as finite *that*-clauses (c) and (f), finite *wh*-clauses (e), or non-finite clauses (d), as discussed in modules 11 and 12.

Experiencer	Cognitive process	Phenomenon	
I	don't know	anyone of that name (entity)	(a)
Everybody	remembered	his face (entity)	(b)
Susan	felt	that the first idea was the best (fact)	(c)
She	has forgotten	to leave us a key (situation)	(d)
Nobody	realised	that it was too late (situation)	(e)
Beryl	thought	that you were ill (belief)	(f)

Many cognitive processes allow the Phenomenon to be unexpressed when this is 'Given information' (see 29.2), for example *I don't know, Jill doesn't understand, Nobody will remember.*

In the following short extract, the author has chosen processes of cognition, perception, affection and one behavioural to reflect the mental make-up of a meteorologist whose work contributed to chaos theory:

> Lorenz *enjoyed*[1] weather – by no means a prerequisite for a research meteorologist. He *savored*[2] its changeability. He *appreciated*[3] the patterns that come and go in the atmosphere, families of eddies and cyclones, always obeying mathematical rules, yet never repeating themselves. When he *looked*[4] at clouds he *thought*[5] he *saw*[6] a kind of structure in them. Once he had *feared*[7] that studying the science of weather would be like prying a jack-in-the-box apart with a screwdriver. Now he *wondered*[8] whether science would be able to penetrate the magic at all. Weather had a flavor that could not be expressed by talking about averages.
>
> (James Gleick, *Chaos, Making a New Science*)
>
> [1]affection; [2]perception; [3]cognition; [4]behavioural; [5]cognition; [6]perception; [7]affection; [8]cognition

17.3 PERCEPTION PROCESSES: SEEING, HEARING AND FEELING

As expressed by the non-volitional senses of *see* and *hear* in English, perception is an involuntary state, which does not depend upon the agency of the perceiver, who in fact **receives** the visual and auditory sensations non-volitionally. However, as the term Recipient has been adopted for the one who receives goods and information in three-participant processes, we will keep to the terms **Experiencer** or Senser. In the following illustrations you will notice that *can* is used when expressing non-volitional perception at the moment of speaking. This use replaces the present progressive, which is ungrammatical in such cases (**I am smelling gas*).

> Tom *saw* a snake.   *Can* you *taste* the lemon in the sauce?
> I *can feel* a draught.   I *can smell* gas.
> We *heard* a noise.

The verbs *see* and *feel* are often used in English as conceptual metaphors for the cognitive processes of understanding and believing, respectively, as in *You do see my point, don't you? – No, I don't see what you mean. I feel we should talk this over further.* In addition, *see* has a number of dynamic uses, such as *See for yourself!* with the meaning of 'verify', and *see someone off*, meaning 'accompany someone to the station, airport', among many others. The progressive can be used with these (see 43.5).

Corresponding to non-volitional *see* and *hear*, English has the dynamic volitional verbs *look, watch* and *listen*, among others. These are classed as **behavioural** processes.

The perception processes of 'feeling, 'smelling' and 'tasting' each make use of one verb (*feel, smell* and *taste*) to encode three different ways of experiencing these sensations: one stative and non-volitional (*I can smell gas*), a second dynamic and volitional (*Just smell these roses!*) and the third as a relational process (*This fish smells bad*). In languages other than English, these differences may be lexicalised as different verbs.

In processes of seeing, hearing and feeling, English allows the Phenomenon to represent a situation that is either completed (*I saw her cross the road*) or not completed (*I saw her crossing the road*) (see 12.4).

17.4 AFFECTIVE AND DESIDERATIVE PROCESSES: LIKING AND WANTING

17.4.1 Affective processes: loving and hating

Under affectivity process we include those positive and negative reactions expressed by such verbs as *like, love, please, delight, dislike, hate* and *detest*. Common desiderative verbs are *want* and *wish*.

> We both *love* dancing.
> I *detest* hypocrisy.
> The ballet performance *delighted* the public.
> Do you *want* a cup of coffee?

The Phenomenon in affectivity processes can be expressed by a nominal group which represents an entity, or by a clause representing an event or a situation. The situation is represented as actual or habitual by means of an *-ing* clause, while a *to*-infinitive clause will be interpreted as potential. For this reason, the latter is used in hypothetical meanings. Some verbs admit only one or other of the forms. Other verbs such as *like, love* and *hate* admit either (see also 12.4), and illustrate this semantic distinction in the following examples:

-ing clause	*to*-infinitive clause
They enjoy *walking in the woods*.	They love to *walk in the woods*.
She likes *visiting her friends*.	She would like *to visit Janet*.
I hate *having a tooth out*.	I would hate *to have my teeth out*.

17.4.2 Desiderative processes: wanting and wishing

These are expressed by such verbs as *want, desire* and *wish*. The Phenomenon role of *want* and *desire* can be expressed as either a thing or a situation, encoded by a nominal group or a *to*-infinitive clause, respectively; with *wish* only the situation meaning is possible. Both *desire* and *wish* can be used as very formal variants to *want*, and consequently occur in quite different registers and styles.

Do you *want* anything else? (thing)
Do you *desire* anything further this evening, sir? (thing)
If you *want* to stay overnight, just say so. (situation)
If you *wish* to remain in the college, you must comply with the regulations. (situation)
If you *desire* to receive any further assistance, please ring the bell (situation)

Wishing, however, can also express in the Phenomenon role a longing for an event or state that is counter to reality. This notion of unreality is expressed by a simple Past tense (or the Past subjunctive *were* if the verb is *be*) or a Past Perfect. These Past tenses have the effect of 'distancing' the event from speech time. *Wish* takes modal *would* + infinitive to refer to future time. The complementiser *that* is normally omitted (see 11.1):

present-time reference   I wish Ted *were* here with us.
past-time reference   I wish Ted *had been* here with us.
future-time reference   I wish Ted *would come* soon.

RELATIONAL PROCESSES OF BEING AND BECOMING

SUMMARY

1   The third main category of processes, relational processes, expresses the notion of being, in a wide sense. In English there are two main patterns of 'being': the **Attributive**, as in *Tom is a pilot*, and the **Identifying**, as in *Fred is the doorman*.

2   The participant in the Attributive structure is the *Carrier*, the entity to which is ascribed an **Attribute**. The relations are of three kinds: **attributive**: *Tom is keen, Tom is a pilot*; **circumstantial**: *The bus stop is over there*; **possessive**: *That car is mine*. In possessive structures the participants are known as the **Possessor** and the **Possessed**.

3   The identifying pattern is reversible: it identifies one entity in terms of another. These are the **Identified** and the **Identifier** as in *Fred is the doorman/The doorman is Fred*. A different analysis assigns **Value** to the more general role (*the doorman*) and **Token** to the one that fills that role (*Fred*).

4   The process itself is encoded by linking verbs (mainly *be* and *have*) whose function is to carry tense and to relate the Carrier to its Attribute, the Identified to its Identifier and the Possessor to the Possessed. Others like *lack* and *feel* encode additional meanings.

18.1   TYPES OF BEING

Relational processes express the concept of being in a broad sense. They answer the questions 'Who or what, where/when or whose is some entity, or What is some entity like?' In other words, relational processes cover various ways of being: being something, being in some place/at some time, or in a relation of possession, as illustrated here:

1	Mont Blanc	is	a (high) mountain. (an instance of a type)
2	Mont Blanc	is	popular with climbers. (attribution)
3	Mont Blanc	is	the highest mountain in Europe. (identification)

4 Mont Blanc	is	in the Alps. (circumstance: location)
5 Those gloves	are	yours. (possession)

There are two main patterns, the attributive as in 1, 2, 4 and 5 and the identifying, as in 3. We shall take a look at each in turn.

18.2 THE ATTRIBUTIVE PATTERN

There is one participant, the Carrier, which represents an entity. Ascribed to the Carrier is an Attribute, which characterises the entity in some way. Here are some examples:

Carrier	Process	Attribute
Their eldest son	was	a musician
The unemployment figures	are	alarming
Sports equipment	is	on the third floor

In the examples seen so far, the Attribute characterises the entity in the following ways: as an instantiation of a class of entities (*a mountain, a musician*) or a subclass (that of high mountains, as in (1); by a quality (*popular with climbers, alarming*); by a location (*in the Alps, on the third floor*); or as a type of possession (*yours*) (see also 18.4).

There is an intensive relationship between the Carrier and its Attribute. That is to say, the Carrier *is* in some way the Attribute. The Attribute is not a participant in the situation, and when realised by a nominal group the NG is non-referential; it can't become the Subject in a clause. Attributive clauses are non-reversible in the sense that they don't allow a Subject–Complement switch. They allow thematic fronting (see 28.7) as in . . . *and a fine musician he was too*, but *a fine musician* is still the Attribute, and *he* the Subject.

The process itself, when encoded by *be*, carries little meaning apart from that of tense (past time as in *was*; present as in *is, are*). Its function is to link the Carrier to the Attribute. However, the process can be expressed either as a state or as a transition. With stative verbs such as *be, keep, remain, seem* and verbs of sensing, such as *look* (= 'seem'), the Attribute is seen as existing at the same time as the process described by the verb and is sometimes called the **current Attribute**.

With dynamic verbs of transition such as *become, get, turn, grow, run*, the Attribute exists as the result of the process and can be called the **resulting Attribute**. Compare *The weather is cold* with *The weather has turned cold*.

Current Attribute	Resulting Attribute
We kept quiet	We fell silent
He remained captain for years	He became captain
Your sister looks tired	She gets tired easily
The public are weary of strikes	The public has grown weary of strikes

There is a wide variety of verbs in English to express both states and transitions (see 9.4). As states, the most common verbs of perception such as *look, feel, sound, smell* and *taste* keep their experiential meaning in relational clauses. An Experiencer participant (e.g. *to me*) can be optionally added to this semantic structure:

feel	The surface feels too rough (to me)
feel as if	My fingers feel as if they were dropping off with the cold
look	Does this solution look right? (to you)
look like	[What's that insect?] It looks like a dragonfly (to me)
sound	His name sounds familiar (to me)
smell	That fish smells bad (to me)
taste	This soup tastes of vinegar (to me)

The verb *feel* can function in two types of semantic structure: with an Experiencer/ Carrier (*I feel hot; she felt ill*), or with a neutral Carrier (*the surface feels rather rough*). In expressions referring to the weather, such as *it is hot/cold/sunny/windy/frosty/cloudy/ foggy*, there is no Carrier and much of the meaning is expressed by the Attribute.

18.3 CIRCUMSTANTIAL RELATIONAL PROCESSES

These are processes of being in which the circumstantial element is essential to the situation, not peripheral to it (see also 9.2). The circumstance is encoded as Attribute in the following examples and stands in an intensive relationship with the Carrier:

Location in space:	The museum is *round the corner.*
Location in time:	Our next meeting will be *on June 10.*
Means:	Entrance to the exhibition is *by invitation.*
Agent:	This symphony is *by Mahler.*
Beneficiary:	These flowers are *for you.*
Metaphorical meanings:	He's *off alcohol.* Everyone's *into yoga* nowadays.

The circumstance is encoded by the verb in *The film script **concerns** (= is about) a pyschopath who kidnaps a girl, The desert **stretches** as far as the eye can see, The carpet **measures** three metres by two, The performance **lasted** three hours.*

Examples such as *Tomorrow is Monday; Yesterday was July 1st* are reversible and can be considered as identifying circumstantial processes.

18.4 POSSESSIVE RELATIONAL PROCESSES

The category of possession covers a wide number of subtypes, of which the most prototypical are perhaps part-whole (as in *your left foot*), ownership (as in *our house*) and kinship relations (such as *Jane's sister*). Other less central types include unowned possession (as in *the dog's basket*), a mental quality (*her sense of humour*), a physical quality (*his strength*), occupancy (*his office*) and an association with another person (*my friends and colleagues*). All these types and others are grammaticalised at the level of the clause in possessive relational processes. A relatively small number of verbs occur, principally *be, have, own* and *possess*. The two participants involved are the **Possessor** and the **Possessed**. The notion of possession is expressed either by the Attribute, as in *That computer is mine*, or by the process itself, as in *I have a new computer*.

A. Possession as Attribute

In this, the verb is *be* and the Attribute/Possessor is encoded by a possessive pronoun (*mine, yours, his, hers, ours, theirs*) or by an *'s* phrase such as *John's* in *The green Peugeot is John's*. The sequence is similar with *belong*, although it is then the verb that conveys the notion of possession:

The *be/belong* possessive structure

Possessed/Carrier	Process	Possessor/Attribute
These keys	are	my brother's
This glove	isn't	mine
This mansion	belongs	to a millionaire

B. Possession as process

English has several verbs to express possession. With *be, have, own, possess* and the more colloquial *have got*, the Carrier is the Possessor and the Attribute is the Possessed.

Also included in the category of 'possessing' are the notions of not possessing (*lack, need*), of being worthy to possess (*deserve*), and the abstract relations of inclusion, exclusion and containment:

Verbs of possession in the Possessor–Possessed structure

Possessor/Carrier	Process	Possessed/Attribute
The baby	has	blue eyes
His uncle	owns	a yacht
I	don't possess	a gun
He	lacks	confidence
Plants	need	water
You	deserve	a prize
The price	includes	postage
The price	excludes	breakfast
That can	contains	petrol

Relational processes are extremely common in all uses of English. The following extract is based on an interview with a young farmer who breeds pigs. He describes them, not by what they do, but as they are; this view is reflected in the large number of Attributes.

Pigs are *different*.[1] A pig is *more of an individual*,[2] *more human*[3] and in many ways a *strangely likeable character*.[4] Pigs have *strong personalities*[5] and it is easy to get *fond of them*.[6] I am always getting fond of pigs and feel a bit *conscience-stricken*[7] when I have to put them inside for their whole lives. Pigs are *very clean animals*[8] but, like us, they are all *different*;[9] some will need *cleaning out*[10] after half a day and some will be *neat and tidy*[11] after three days. Some pigs are always *in a mess*[12] and won't care. Pigs are *very interesting people*[13] and can leave quite a gap when they go off to the bacon factory.

(Ronald Blythe, *Akenfield*)

18.5 THE IDENTIFYING PATTERN

The participant roles in an identifying relationship are known as **Identified** and **Identifier**. Identification means that one participant, the Identified, is identified in terms of the other (the Identifier), in a relation of symbolic correlates. The Identifier is the one that fills the *wh-* element in a *wh-*question corresponding to the identifying clause:

(a) [*What/Which is Mont Blanc?*]
Mont Blanc (Identified) is the highest mountain in Europe (Identifier).

(b) [*Which is your father-in-law?* Looking at a photograph]
My father-in-law (Identified) is the one in the middle (Identifier).

Identifying processes are reversible. The previous illustrations can be turned around, with the Identified/Identifying roles now represented by the opposite constituent:

(c) [*What/Which is the highest mountain in Europe?*]
The highest mountain in Europe (Identified) is Mont Blanc (Identifier).

(d) [*Who/Which is the one in the middle?*]
The one in the middle (Identified) is my father-in-law (Identifier).

The difference between the two sequences lies in which element we want to identify; for instance, do we want to identify Mont Blanc or do we want to identify the highest mountain in Europe? In a discourse context this is a matter of presumed knowledge. Question (a) presumes that the listener has heard of Mont Blanc but doesn't know its ranking among mountains. The answer could be 'Mont Blanc (Identified) is **the highest mountain in Europe** (Identifier)', in which the highlighted part represents tonic prominence and the new information. Question (c) presumes that our listener knows there are high mountains in Europe, but not which one is the highest, receiving the answer 'The highest mountain in Europe (Identified) is **Mont Blanc** (Identifier)'. Alternatively, in answer to the same question *Which is the highest mountain in Europe?* we could say '**Mont Blanc** (Identifier) is the highest mountain in Europe (Identified)'.

In spoken discourse it is the Identifier that typically receives the tonic prominence that is associated with new information, whether this is placed at the end (the usual position) or at the beginning of the clause. In each sequence, then, one half is typically something or someone whose existence is already known (the Identified), whereas the Identifier presents information as unknown or new to the listener. (These notions are explained more fully in Module 29 on information packaging.)

Reversibility in Identifying clauses		
Identified		*Identifier*
Mont Blanc	is	**the highest mountain in Europe.**
My father-in-law	is	**the one in the middle.**
Identifier		*Identified*
Mont Blanc	is	the highest mountain in Europe.
My father-in-law	is	the one in the middle.

A further concept complementary to Identifying processes is that of 'representation' or 'roles filled'. One participant, the **Token**, is the entity that 'represents' or 'fills the role of' the other, the **Value**, as in:

Token/Identified		*Value/Identifier*
My father-in-law	is (= fulfils the role of)	the club's Secretary
Negotiation	is (= represents)	the key to resolving the dispute

Here the question is 'Which role (Value) does my father-in-law/ negotiation (Token) fulfil or represent?' However, we can put the question the other way round: 'Which is the role of Club Secretary played by?/ the key to resolving the dispute fulfilled by?' We have a different conflation of Identified/ Identifier with Token/ Value:

Value/Identified		*Token/Identifier*
The club's Secretary	is (fulfilled by)	my father-in-law
The key to resolving the dispute	is (represented by)	negotiation

The two sets of roles are different in kind. Identified and Identifier depend for their interpretation on the point in discourse in which they occur: the Identified is the one which has already been introduced, and the Identifier identifies it in a new way. Token and Value assignation depends, by contrast, on the intrinsic semantic properties of the two ways of referring to the entity. Whichever is the more generalisable is the Value, while the Token is the specific representation of the Value. In a particular text, the Value points to particular cultural values and organisation, such as the importance of negotiation in resolving disputes, and granting denominations to people who fill certain functions in society. The following passage, *Colours in Rugs across Cultures*, illustrates such correspondences:

> The meaning of individual colours varies from culture to culture. In Muslim countries, green – the colour of Mohammed's coat – is sacred and is very rarely used as a predominant colour, but it forms an important part of the dyer's palette in non-Muslim cultures, particularly in China; here, the sacred colour is yellow, in which the Emperor traditionally dressed. White represents grief to the Chinese, Indians and Persians. Blue symbolises heaven in Persia, and power and authority in Mongolia. Orange is synonymous with piety and devotion in Muslim countries, while red, the most universal rug colour, is widely accepted as a sign of wealth and rejoicing.
>
> (BNC EXO 393–398)

Finally, the difference between the Attributive and the Identifying patterns is reflected in the syntax in three ways: Only the identifying type is reversible (cf. *A high mountain is Mont Blanc*); only the characterising type can be realised by an adjective (*The unemployment figures are alarming*); and Nominal groups that realise characterising Attributes are usually indefinite (*a musician*), while NGs that realise identifying Attributes are usually definite (*the club Secretary*).

Certain relational processes of possession can be analysed by the Identifying pattern, and are reversible if suitably contextualised as identifying people's possessions. For example, sandwiches: *Yours is the ham-and-cheese; Tim's is the egg-and-lettuce and mine is the tomato-and-tuna*. Similarly, circumstantial Attributes can be reversed when explaining the layout of an area: *Across the road, past the fountain is the Prado Museum. On your left is the Ritz Hotel. Further back is the Real Academia*.

PROCESSES OF SAYING, BEHAVING AND EXISTING

SUMMARY

1   Processes of saying and communicating are verbal processes. The participant who communicates is the Sayer, and is typically human, while what is communicated is the 'Said' and may be a reported statement, a reported question or a reported directive (order, request, etc.). A Recipient, the addressee, is required with *tell*, and a Target may also be present in some verbal processes.

2   Behavioural processes are half-way between material and mental processes, in that they have features of each. They include involuntary processes (*cough*) and volitional processes (*watch, stare, listen*).

3   Existential processes, rather than stating that things simply exist, tend to specify the quantification and/or the location of something: *There are bits of paper everywhere.* The single participant is the Existent, which may be an entity or an event.

19.1   VERBAL PROCESSES

Verbal processes are processes of 'saying' or 'communicating' and are encoded by such verbs as *say, tell, repeat, ask, answer* and *report*. They have one participant which is typically human, but not necessarily so (**the Sayer**) and a second essential participant, which is what is said or asked or reported (the **Said**). A **Recipient** is required with *tell* and may be present as an oblique form (e.g. *to me*) with other verbal processes:

Sayer	Verbal process	Recipient	Said
She	had to say		her name twice
That clock	says		five past ten
The police officer	repeated		the question
Jill	told	him	what she knew
Our correspondent	reports		renewed fighting on the frontier

The Sayer can be anything which puts out a communicative signal (*that clock, Jill, our correspondent*). What is said is realised by a nominal group or a nominal *what*-clause (*what she knew*). As these examples show, verbal processes are intermediate between material and mental processes. From one point of view, communicating is a form of 'doing', and in fact the Sayer is usually agentive or made to appear agentive, as in the case of the clock. Like material processes, verbal processes readily admit the imperative (*Say it again!*) and the progressive (*What is he saying?*).

On the other hand, the action of communicating is close to cognitive processes such as thinking. Verbs of saying, telling and others can be followed by a clause that represents either the exact words said (direct report) or a reported version of the meaning (indirect report). Many speech-act verbs can function in this way, to report statements, questions, warnings, advice and other speech acts:

She	said:	'I won't be late' (quoted statement or promise)
She	said	she wouldn't be late (reported statement or promise)
She	said:	'Don't go to see that film' (quoted directive: advice)
She	told	us	not to go to see that film (reported directive: advice)

These alternative encodings are described more fully in Chapter 7. For the syntactic-semantic differences between *say* and *tell* in English, see 11.2.

When however, the message is encapsulated as a speech act by means of a nominal – such as 'apology', 'warning', 'greeting', 'thanks' and many others – it is treated as a participant in the verbal process. The verb then may express the manner of saying:

The airport authorities issued an apology
Someone shouted a warning
Retired cop vows revenge (press headline)

Wish in *I wish you a merry Christmas* is clearly both mental and verbal. *Talk* and *chat* are verbal processes, which have an implicit reciprocal meaning (*They talked/ chatted [to each other]*). *Talk* has no second participant except in the expressions *talk sense/ nonsense*. *Speak* is not implicitly reciprocal and can take a Range participant; see 20.1 (*She speaks Spanish. He speaks five languages*).

Besides the Sayer and the Said, a further participant, the Target, encodes the person or thing at which the message is directed, as in:

Everyone is acclaiming *the new musical* as the event of the year.

19.2 BEHAVIOURAL PROCESSES

A borderline area between mental processes and material processes is represented by **behavioural** processes such as *cough, sneeze, yawn, blink, laugh* and *sigh*, which are usually one-participant. They are considered as typically involuntary; but it may be that there is a very slight agency involved. They can be deliberate, too, as in *he coughed discreetly, he yawned rudely*, in which the adjunct of manner implies volition. Acting excepted, most volitional adjuncts could not be used with *die, collapse* and *grow*, which are typically lacking in agency and volition.

We have already seen that mental processes such as *see* and *hear* have behavioural counterparts (*watch* and *listen*, respectively), which are dynamic and volitional, and have agentive Subjects, while *see, taste* and *feel* have both non-volitional and volitional senses. Similarly, *think* (in the sense of *ponder*) and *enjoy* can be used dynamically:

> What are you thinking about?
> I am enjoying the play enormously.
> Enjoy!

19.3 EXISTENTIAL PROCESSES

Existential processes are processes of existing or happening. The basic structure consists of unstressed *there* + *be* + a NG (*There's a man at the door; there was a loud bang*). *There* is not a participant as it has no semantic content, although it fulfils both a syntactic function as Subject (see 5.1.2) and a textual function as 'presentative' element (see 30.4). The single participant is the **Existent**, which may refer to a countable entity (*There's* **a good film** *on at the Scala*), an uncountable entity (*There's* **roast lamb** *for lunch*) or an event (*There was* **an explosion**).

Semantically, existential processes state not simply the existence of something, but more usually expand the Existent in some way:

* by adding a quantitative measure and/or the location of the Existent:

    > I went for a walk in the woods. It was all right, *there were lots of people there.*
    >
    > BNC GUK 2339–2400
    >
    > There were *all sorts of practical problems.*

* with quantification and an Attribute characterising the Existent:

There	are	*some* people	*blank.*
There	were	*few* people	*in favour.*

* with quantification and expansion of the Existent by the addition of clauses:

There	are	few people who realise the danger.
There	's	nothing to be done about it.

The process in existential clauses is expressed by the following verbs:

* most typically by *be*;
* certain intransitive verbs expressing positional states (*stand, lie, stretch, hang and remain*);
* a few intransitive dynamic verbs of 'occurring', 'coming into view' or 'arrival on the scene' (*occur, follow, appear, emerge, loom*) (cf. 30.4.3).
    These are illustrated below:

    > There remain many problems.
    > There followed a long interval.
    > There emerged from the cave a huge brown bear.

Existential *there* may be omitted when a locative or directional Adjunct is in initial position:

> Below the castle (there) stretches a vast plain.
> Out of the mist (there) loomed a strange shape.

Without 'there' such clauses are very close semantically to reversed circumstantial clauses. However, the addition of a tag question – with *there*, not a personal pronoun (*Close to the beach stands a hotel, doesn't there? *doesn't it?*) – suggests that they are in fact existentials.

The following extract from D. H. Lawrence's story *The Lost Girl* illustrates existentials:

She looked at the room. There was a wooden settle in front of the hearth, stretching its back to the room.[1] There *was* a little table under a square, recessed window,[2] on whose sloping ledge *were* newspapers, scattered letters, nails and a hammer.[3] On the table *were* dried beans and two maize cobs.[4] In the corner *were* shelves,[5] with two chipped enamel plates, and a small table underneath, on which *stood* a bucket of water and a dipper.[6] Then there *was* a wooden chest, two little chairs and a litter of faggots, cane, vine-twigs, bare maize hubs, oak-twigs filling the corner by the hearth.[7]

EXPRESSING ATTENDANT CIRCUMSTANCES

MODULE 20

SUMMARY

The circumstantial element in English covers a great variety of meanings, of which the most common are those related to place and time, manner, contingency, accompaniment, modality, degree, role, matter and evidence. They are described from the point of view of their syntactic function in 8.1 and also as group structures in 57.

20.1 PLACE, TIME AND OTHER CIRCUMSTANCES

There are many parallel expressions of place and time, in many cases introduced by the same preposition (see also Module 59):

	Place	Time
location	at home, in the park, on the desk	at 5 o'clock, in May, years ago, on Tuesday
source	from the library, from Ed	from January
path	the plane flew over the hills, through the clouds	They stayed over the weekend
direction	towards the south	towards midnight
goal	to Canada	to June
	[we went] home	
extent	for several miles	for several years
extent + goal	as far as Granada	until 10 o'clock, by Tuesday
relative	here, there, nearby, in front, behind us	now, then, recently, before/ after dinner
distributive	at intervals, every 100 yards, here and there	at intervals, every so often, now and then, off and on

Locative, goal and directional meanings are questioned by *where?* (the preposition *to* is not used in questions other than the verbless *Where to?*); source meanings by *where . . . from?* and for time, *since when?* extent by *how far? how long?* and distribution by *how often?*

A. Manner

The notion of manner (*How?*) is extended to include the notions of means (*By what means?*, instrumentality (*What with?*) and comparison (*What like?*):

Manner	how?	Don't do it *that way;* do it *gently.*
Means	how?	It's cheaper *by bus.*
Comparison	what . . . like?	Snow lay *like a blanket* on the ground.
Instrument	what . . . with?	You can stick the pieces together *with glue.*
		They levelled the site *with a bulldozer.*

B. Instrument

This is the tool or means, generally inanimate, used by a controlling Agent to carry out the process. It is strongly associated with the preposition *with*: *Write with a pen.*

With some verbs the notion of Instrument is incorporated into the process itself. In this way, *bulldoze* can be used as a material process: the builders *bulldozed* the site. Other examples include:

He *elbowed* his way through the crowd. (by using his elbows)
Figo *headed* the ball into the goal. (by using his head)
They *levered* the rock into position. (by using a lever)

C. Contingency

The circumstantial element of contingency covers such meanings as cause, purpose, reason, concession and behalf:

Cause	what cause?	The child took the pen *out of envy.*
		They are dying *of hunger.*
Purpose	what . . . for?	He is studying *for a degree.*
		The team is training *to win.*
Reason	why?	We stayed in *on account of the rain.*
		He stopped *because he was tired.*
Concession	despite what conditions?	*In spite of the delay,* we reached the concert hall in time.
Behalf	who/what for?	Give up smoking *for the sake of your health.*
		I'll speak to the Director *on your behalf.*
Condition	under what conditions?	Send a telegram, *if necessary.*

D. Accompaniment

Accompaniment expresses a joint participation in the process, involving either the notion of 'togetherness' or that of 'additionality'. Each of these can be either positive or negative:

togetherness	positive	Tom came *with his friend/with a new haircut.*
togetherness	negative	Tom came *without his friend/without the car.*
additionality	positive	Tom came *as well as Paul.*
additionality	negative	Tom came *instead of Paul.*

E. Modality

Modality expresses the notions of possibility, probability and certainty (see 44.1):

possibility	His new novel will *possibly* come out next month.
probability	It will *probably* be well received.
certainty	It will *certainly* cause a lot of controversy.

F. Degree

Circumstantial expressions of degree either emphasise or attenuate the process:

emphasis	I *completely* forgot to bring my passport.
attenuation	You can *hardly* expect me to believe that.

G. Role

Role answers the question *What as?* or *In what capacity?*

capacity	I'm speaking to you *as a friend.*
	As *an actor* he's not outstanding, but *as a dancer* he's brilliant.

H. Matter

This element adds the notion of 'with reference to . . .' and is realised by a wide variety of simple and complex prepositions, including those circumstantial complements that follow certain verbs such as *deprive, rob* and *help oneself* (see 7.3.1 and 10.3.2):

We have been talking *about* her wedding.
Is there any news *of* the missing seamen?
With regard to your order of July 17 . . .
As for that, I don't believe a word of it.
You shouldn't deprive yourself *of* vitamins.
Help yourself *to* wine.

I. Evidence

Relates to the source of information in verbal processes and is expressed by *as x says*, or *according to x*:

As the saying goes, no news is good news.
According to the weatherman, there will be heavy snowstorms this weekend.

Some of the numerous types of circumstance available are illustrated in the following extract from John Le Carré, *The Spy Who Came In from the Cold*. This type of fiction tends to contain very detailed references to the circumstances accompanying each episode:

He'd noticed it first *during the Riemick case,*[1] *early last year.*[2] Karl had sent a message; he'd got something special for him and was making one of his rare visits *to Western Germany;*[3] some legal conference *at Karlsruhe.*[4] Leamas had managed to get an air passage *to Cologne,*[5] and picked up a car *at the airport.*[6] It was *still*[7] *quite early in the morning*[8] and he'd hoped to miss most of the autobahn traffic *to Karlsruhe*[9] but the heavy lorries were already[10] on the move. He drove seventy kilometres *in half an hour,*[11] weaving between the traffic, taking risks *to beat the clock,*[12] when a small car, a Fiat *probably,*[13] nosed its way out *into the fast lane*[14] *forty yards ahead of him.*[15] Leamas stamped on the brake, turning his headlights full on and sounding his horn, and *by the grace of God*[16] he missed it; missed it *by the fraction of a second.*[17]

[1]extent: time; [2]location: time; [3]goal: space; [4]location: space; [5]goal: space; [6]location: space; [7]relative: time; [8]location: time; [9]goal: space; [10]relative; [11]extent: time; [12]purpose; [13]modality; [14]direction: space; [15]location: space; [16]cause; [17]degree.

20.2 RANGE

Rather than a circumstance, Range is a participant: the nominal concept that is implied by the process as its scope or range: *song* in *sing a song, games* in *play games, race* in *run a race*. Some, such as *song*, are derived from a related verb; others such as *game* are not.

Perhaps the most common type of Range element today are the deverbal nominals which complement lexically 'light' verbs such as *have* and *give*:

> ***Have*** *an argument, a chat, a drink, a fight, a rest, a quarrel, a smoke, a taste, an experience*
> ***Give*** *a push, a kick, a nudge, a smile, a laugh, a kiss; a presentation, a lecture*
> ***Take*** *a sip, a bath, a nap, a photograph, a shower, a walk*
> ***Do*** *a dance, a handstand, a left/ right turn, a sketch, a translation, some work, some cleaning, some painting*

Ask *a question*

Make *a choice, a comment, a contribution, a mistake, a payment, a reduction, a suggestion*

Using this type of range participant (*a kick, a push*, etc.) with a 'light' verb entails the meaning of the nominal as verb. In other words, if you take a sip of the juice, you sip the juice. If we have a chat, we chat. In some cases, such as *make an effort*, there is no corresponding verb. One reason for the popularity of this construction today is the potential that the noun has for being modified in various ways. It would be difficult to express by a verb, even with the help of adverbs, the meanings of specificness, quantification and quality present in *she took a long, relaxing hot bath, they played two strenuous games of tennis, I had such a strange experience yesterday.*

As a result of modification, the nominal is longer and heavier than the verb which precedes it. This allows us to build up our message to a climax (see 6.1.2d). Furthermore, the Range nominal can initiate a *wh*-cleft structure more easily than a verb can (see 30.2) as in *A good rest is what you need.*

CONCEPTUALISING EXPERIENCES FROM A DIFFERENT ANGLE

Nominalisation and grammatical metaphor

SUMMARY

1   The semantic structures described so far reflect the basic semantic-syntactic correspondences we use when encoding situations. They reflect the typical way of saying things. Agents carry out actions that affect other participants, Experiencers perceive Phenomena. Furthermore, processes have been realised by verbs, entities by nouns, and Attributes by (for instance) adjectives and possessives. These are the basic realisations which are found in the language of children and in much everyday spoken English. But any state of affairs can be conceptualised and expressed in more than one way. A more nominalised version encodes actions and states as nouns, which involves a complete restructuring of the clause. This has been called 'grammatical metaphor'. Its most obvious characteristic is nominalisation.

2   Thus, a process can be realised as an entity: *government spending* is one example. Similar transferred functions occur with attributes and circumstances. These alternative realisations of the semantic roles involve further adjustments in the correspondences between semantic roles and syntactic functions in the clause.

3   Grammatical metaphor is a feature of much written English and of spoken English in professional registers.

4   The 'transitivity hypothesis' offers an alternative view, in which transitivity is a matter of gradation from high to low.

21.1 BASIC REALISATIONS AND METAPHORICAL REALISATIONS

Situations and events can be conceptualised and expressed linguistically in two major ways. More transparent, because they are closer to the speaker's experience, are the basic transitivity patterns that we have examined so far throughout this chapter. In these semantic structures the processes, participants and circumstances are encoded by their typical clause functions, with agency and chronological sequencing made explicit. That is, in active clauses, the inherent participants such as Agent, Affected, Experiencer and Carrier are realised by NGs, processes are realised by VGs and circumstantials by PPs and by AdvGs. This correspondence between the semantics and the syntax of English structures is indeed the typical one, but it is by no means the only one.

We have to beware of assuming that a one-to-one correspondence exists between any semantic function and any syntactic function. We have to beware of assuming that entities such as people and things are necessarily expressed by nouns, that actions are necessarily expressed by verbs and that qualities are necessarily expressed by adjectives. Except in the language of children and in very basic English, our linguistic representation of reality tends to be more complex. Any situation can be expressed in more than one way; the first or typical realisation may be called the 'iconic' one, in which the form mirrors the meaning; any others are the 'metaphorical'. The two forms may be illustrated by an example.

Suppose that I wish to tell you that my friends and I walked in the evening along the river as far as Henley. In the 'typical' or 'iconic' version, I first select the process type from the options 'material', 'mental' and 'relational' processes. A process of 'doing' fits the conceptualised situation best, and more specifically, a process of motion which includes manner. Among possible types of motion I select a material process *walk*. To accompany a process such as *walk* used intransitively, I then select an Agent, or 'doer' of the action, and a number of circumstantial elements, of time, place and direction as a setting, to give the following semantic structure and its lexico-grammatical realisation:

Agent	Material process	Time circ.	Place circ.	Goal circ.
NG	VG	PP	PP	PP
We	walked	in the evening	along the river	to Henley

This is not the only way of expressing this situation. Instead, I could have said *Our evening walk along the river took us to Henley*. In this 'metaphorical' interpretation the semantic functions are 'transferred' in relation to the syntactic functions. The material process *walk* has now become Agent, and the circumstances of time (*in the evening*) and place (*along the river*) have become classifier and post-modifier, respectively, of the new Agent realised at subject (*evening walk along the river*). The original Agent *we* is now divided into two; one part functions as possessor of the Subject entity (*our evening walk along the river*), the other as Affected (*us*) of a new material process expressed by the verb *took*. Only the Goal circumstance *to Henley* is realised in the same way in both interpretations:

Agent	Material process	Affected	Goal
NG	VG	NG	PP
Our evening walk along the river	took	us	to Henley

This second interpretation is a very simple instance of 'grammatical metaphor' or alternative realisations of semantic functions, and is a phenomenon which occurs all the time, in different degrees, in adult language, especially in certain written genres.

Even in everyday spoken language it sometimes happens that the metaphorical form has become the normal way of expressing a certain meaning. We have seen that the Range element (see 20.1) *drink/chat/rest* in *have a drink/chat/rest* is the one that expresses the process, while the syntactic function of Predicator is now realised by the 'light' verb *have*. These are simple types of transferred semantic functions which have been incorporated into everyday language. Now compare the ordinary correspondences in example **a** below with the nominalised version of **b**:

Agent/Subject	Material process	Place/Adv	Comparison/Adv
a. People in all countries	are [now] travelling	abroad	much more than they used to.
Abstract Subject	**Relational process**	**Time/Adv**	**Abstraction**
b. Foreign travel	is	everywhere	on the increase.

In **a** we have a process of 'doing' (*are travelling*), with an Agent/Subject and three circumstances (*now, abroad* and *much more than they used to*). In **b**, by contrast, the process is relational with *be*, the human Agent has disppeared, and instead we have an abstract subject based on the verb 'travel' (*foreign travel*), followed by two circumstances. Apart from these differences, we note that the two meanings are not quite equivalent. The notion of 'all countries' is replaced by the less explicit 'everywhere', that of 'abroad' is replaced by 'foreign', while the notions expressed by 'now' and 'used to' are not encoded at all, but remain implicit.

More importantly, the two versions represent two different cognitive mappings of a situation on to different semantic and syntactic structures. The event is 'perspectivised' differently in each case, with attention centred in the second on the salient abstraction 'foreign travel', rather than on persons.

21.2 NOMINALISATION AS A FEATURE OF GRAMMATICAL METAPHOR

It is clear that a choice of transferred realisations such as these has as one result the loss of human agency, which is usually replaced by an abstraction related to the original Agent (*government spending, foreign travel*). A second result is an increase in lexical density: Nominal groups become long and heavy. For this reason, nominalisation is the form of grammatical metaphor most consistently recognised under different labels. It distances us from the event, raising the representation of a situation to a higher level of abstraction. Once objectified and depersonalised in this way, the event or abstraction is conceptualised as if it had temporal persistence, instead of the transience associated with a verb.

At the same time, nominalisations are more versatile than verbs. The noun 'explosion' from 'explode' can carry out all the functions realised by nominals, such as a Subject or Direct Object (*The explosion occurred at 6 a.m.; leaking gas caused an explosion*). With this new status as a referent, a nominalisation can give the impression that what it expresses is a recognised piece of information, whose validity is beyond dispute. Compare the following **a** extract from a news item with the non-nominalised **b** version:

> **a.** *Government spending* showed *positive growth* in the last quarter in contrast to *its sharp fall* in the previous one.
> **b.** *The government spent much more* in the last quarter than was planned, whereas *it spent considerably less* in the previous one.

As soon as we examine samples of more formal English – that used in specialised fields such as the natural sciences, the social sciences, politics, administration and business, finance and technology – we find a great number of such nominalisations. These tend to be abstract nouns derived from verbs and other parts of speech, which can encode quite complex meanings.

Lexical metaphor can occur together with grammatical metaphor, as illustrated by 'growth' and 'fall', so common in texts on economics. Here, grammar borders on lexis, and different languages have different means of visualising one semantic function as if it were another. Here we can do no more than briefly outline some of the transfers of semantic functions. In the following sections, metaphorical forms are given first, with a basic corresponding meaning suggested in the right-hand column.

21.2.1 Process realised as entity

This is by far the most common type of grammatical metaphor. Many are institution-alised nominalisations, such as the following:

	Nominalised form	**Basic form**
a.	Without the slightest *hesitation*.	Without *hesitating* at all.
b.	Take a deep *breath*.	*Breathe* deeply.
c.	There was a sudden *burst of laughter*.	X *burst out laughing* suddenly.
d.	The *exploration and mapping of the world* went on.	X continued to *explore and map* the world.

Many others, however, represent a more original view of reality on the part of the speaker or writer, as in example **e**:

e.	*His conception of the drama* has a very modern *ring*.	He conceives of the drama in a way that *sounds* very modern to us.

21.2.2 Attribute realised as entity

An Attribute can be realised as an entity by means of an abstract noun. The forms may be morphologically related: *bigness–big* as in example *a* and *usefulness–useful* in *b*. The remaining parts of the sentence may have different correspondences, which are not in a one-to-one relationship with the forms of the nominalised version.

a. *Bigness* is paid for, in part, by *fewness*, and *a decline in competition*.

If firms are very *big*, they will be *fewer* and will have less need to compete.

b. The *usefulness* of this machinery is dwindling.

This machinery is becoming less *useful*.

21.2.3 Circumstance as entity

A common shift is to have a temporal circumstance functioning as a locative Subject. This involves a new verb, such as 'find', 'witness' and 'see' in these examples:

a. *August 12* found the travellers in Rome.

The travellers were/arrived in Rome *on August 12*.

b. *The last decade* has witnessed an unprecedented rise in agricultural technology.

During the last decade agricultural technology has increased as never before.

c. *The seventeenth century* saw the development of systematic scientific publication.

In the seventeenth century scientific works began to be published systematically.

As these new processes are transitive, typically taking an Object, further nominalisations are to be expected, such as *rise (or increase) in agricultural technology*, instead of *increase* as a verb. In many cases, such as **c** it is difficult to 'unpack' the metaphorical encoding completely into a simpler form. The two forms of expression are the result of different cognitive encodings.

21.2.4 Dependent situation as entity

A whole state of affairs, which in its congruent form would be realised as a subordinate clause, can be visualised as an entity and expressed by a nominal:

Fears of disruption to oil supplies from the Gulf helped push crude oil prices up dramatically.

Because people feared that oil would not be supplied as usual from the Gulf, the price of crude oil rose dramatically.

We can observe that, in many cases of nominalisation, normal human Agents and Experiencers are absent, replaced by abstractions that are in some way related to them ('fears', 'laughter') and may be more emotionally charged. In other cases, those where a temporal entity 'witnesses' the event, the human Agent may not be recoverable at all, as in *b* and *c* above.

These few examples may serve to show that in English grammatical metaphor is a very powerful option in the presenting of information. It reconceptualises an event as a participant, with the consequent restructuring of the rest of the clause, which influences the way the information is perceived. It presents a different cognitive mapping from that of the 'congruent' or iconic correspondence between syntax and semantics that is found in basic English. In institutionalised settings, the concept of grammatical metaphor goes a long way towards explaining professional jargons such as journalese and officialese as written forms. Others, such as the language of business management, use nominalisation in spoken as well as written English (see p. 166 for summary of processes, participants and circumstances).

21.3 HIGH AND LOW TRANSITIVITY

A different approach to transitivity, which has not been discussed in this chapter for reasons of space, is the 'transitivity hypothesis'. This views transitivity in discourse as a matter of gradation, dependent on various factors. A verb such as *kick*, for example, fulfils all the criteria for high transitivity in a clause with an expressed object such as *Ted kicked the ball*. It refers to an action (B) in which two participants (A)are involved, Agent and Object; it is telic (having an end-point) (C) and is punctual (D). With a human subject it is volitional (E) and agentive, while the object will be totally affected (I) and individuated (J). The clause is also affirmative (F) and declarative, realis, not hypothetical (irrealis) (G). By contrast, with a verb such as *see* as in *Ted saw the accident*, most of the criteria point to low transitivity, while the verb *wish* as in *I wish you were here* includes even irrealis (G) in its complement as a feature of low transitivity. *Susan left* is interpreted as an example of reduced transitivity. Although it has only one participant, it rates higher than some two-participant clauses, as it fulfils B, C, D, E, F, G and H.

	high transitivity	low transitivity
A. PARTICIPANTS	2 or more participants	1 participant
B. KINESIS	action	non-action
C. ASPECT	telic (end-point)	atelic (no end-point)
D. PUNCTUALITY	punctual	non-punctual
E. VOLITIONALITY	volitional	non-volitional
F. AFFIRMATION	affirmative	negative
G. MODE	realis	irrealis
H. AGENCY	Agent high in potency	Agent low in potency
I. AFFECTEDNESS OF O	Object totally affected	Object not affected
J. INDIVIDUATION OF O	Object highly individuated	Object non-individuated

21.4 SUMMARY OF PROCESSES, PARTICIPANTS AND CIRCUMSTANCES

Process		Example	Participant	Attribute	Circumstance
	1	The Prime Minister resigned	Agent		
	2	Ted kicked the ball into the net	Agent + Affected		Locative/Goal
	3	Lightning struck the oak tree	Force + Affected		
	4	Jordan slipped on the ice	Affected		Locative
	5	Pat boiled the water	Agent + Affected		
	6	The water boiled	Affected		
	7	They're making the road wider.	Agent + Affected	Resulting	
Material	8	Glass breaks easily	Agent + unactualised Affected		Manner
	9	Do you drive?	Affected		
	10	I gave the cat some tuna.	Agent + Rec. + Affected		
	11	Will you fetch me a newspaper?	Agent + Ben. + Affected		
Behavioural	12	Tom watched the snake.	Experiencer (volitional) + Phenom.		
	13	Tom saw the snake.	Experiencer (non-volitional) + Phenom.		
	14	Tom knows the answer.	Experiencer + Phenom.		
Mental	15	We were pleased by the news.	Rec. Experiencer + Phenom.		Degree
	16	The news pleased us very much.	Phenom. + Rec. Experiencer		
	17	I wish you were here.	Experiencer + Phenom. (unreal)		
	18	Tom is generous.	Carrier	Characterising	
	19	Tom is the secretary.	Carrier/Token Identified	Value/Identifying	
	20	The film lasted three hours.	Carrier	Circumstantial	
	21	Those gloves aren't mine.	Possessed	Possessor	
Verbal	22	I didn't say that.	Sayer + Said		
	23	Mary told me a secret.	Sayer + Rec. + Said		
Existential	24	There's a notice on the door.	Existent		Locative
	25	There are some pages blank.	Existent	Current	

FURTHER READING

Halliday (1994); Thompson (1996); on relational processes, Davidse (1992), Davidse (1996) and Davidse (2000); on Token and Value, Toolan (1992) (together with works cited above); on types of 'being' and 'possessing', Langacker (1991). On grammatical metaphor and nominalisation: Chafe (1994); Downing (2000); Eggins (1994); Halliday (1994); Martin (1992). On object omission, pseudo-intransitives, ergatives, Kilby (1984), Martínez Vázquez (1998), Payne (1997). On valency, Payne (1997). On verb classes and alternations, Levin (1993). On 'take a sip' etc., Round (1998). On the 'transitivity hypothesis', Hopper and Thompson (1980).

EXERCISES ON CHAPTER 4
Expressing patterns of experience: Processes, participants, circumstances

Modules 13 and 14

1 †Identify each process in the following examples as a process of 'doing' (material), a process of 'experiencing' (mental) or a process of 'being' (relational):

    (1)   This country exports raw materials.
    (2)   I prefer ballet to opera.
    (3)   The abbey is now a ruin.
    (4)   Do you know the author's name?
    (5)   The wounded soldier staggered down the road.
    (6)   The weather has turned warm. The days are becoming longer.

2 †Work out for each of the examples below:

- the number of inherent participants (the verb's semantic valency)
- the number of actualised participants in this use
- whether the verb's valency is reduced in this use

    1a) She teaches 12-year-olds maths.   2) This dog bites.
    1b) She teaches maths.
    1c) She teaches.   3) Cats purr.

3 †Say whether *it* in each of the following clauses refers to a participant or is merely a Subject-filler:

    (1)   *It* rained heavily last night.
    (2)   I can lend you ten pounds. Will *it* be enough?
    (3)   Her baby is due next month and she knows *it* is a girl.
    (4)   Where's your bicycle? *It's* in the garage.
    (5)   *It's* our first wedding anniversary today.

4 †Fill in the blank space with a suitable Force participant:

  (1) As we left the hotel,. . . . . .was blowing off the sea.
  (2) Huge . . . . crashed onto the beach and broke against the rocks.
  (3) Several bathers were caught by the incoming . . . . and had to be rescued by the coastguard patrol.
  (4) Further inland, a usually tranquil . . . . broke its banks and flooded the surrounding fields.
  (5) In the mountains above the village, campers were surprised by a sudden . . . . which threatened to engulf their tents.

5 Write a short paragraph on 'A forest fire', using Force participants and material processes.

6 †Say whether the italicised nominal group is an Agentive Subject or an Affected Subject:

  (1) *Beatrice* writes black-humour comedies for television.
  (2) *The little bird* died of cold.
  (3) *Angry housewives* attacked the striking dustmen with umbrellas.
  (4) *Three shop-assistants* were sacked by their employer.
  (5) *Many buildings* collapsed during the earthquake.

7 †Identify the italicised participant as Affected or Effected:

  (1) He paints *surrealist portraits of his friends*.
  (2) Don't pick *the flowers*!
  (3) In their youth they wrote *pop-songs* and made *fortunes*.
  (4) They carve *these figures* out of wood.
  (5) Engineers are installing *a telephone booth*.

Module 15

1 †Say which of the following clauses are causative and write underneath these the corresponding intransitive constructions where appropriate.

  (1) The stress of high office ages most Prime Ministers prematurely.

      . . . .

  (2) Smoking can damage your health.

      . . . .

  (3) Swarms of locusts darkened the sky.

      . . . .

  (4) They sprayed the crops with insecticide.

      . . . .

  (5) Pain and worry wrinkled his brow.

      . . . .

(6)   The photographer clicked the camera.

. . . .

(7)   The truck tipped a load of sand onto the road.

. . . .

(8)   This year the company has doubled its sales.

. . . .

2   †Say whether the participant in the following one-participant situations is acting (Agent), is acted upon (Affected) or whether the propensity of the participant to undergo the action is being expressed.

(1)   This kind of material creases easily.
(2)   The car broke down.
(3)   Glass recycles well.
(4)   Two of the deputies arrived late.
(5)   He ruled with an iron hand.
(6)   This cream whips up in an instant.
(7)   Peaches won't ripen in this climate.

3   †Explain the difference in meaning, in terms of participants and processes, and the types of relations we have examined, between the following representations:

(a)   Sarah is cooking the rice.
(b)   Sarah is cooking.
(c)   The rice is cooking.
(d)   Sarah cooks beautifully.
(e)   Rice cooks easily.
(f)   Why would you not expect to hear normally 'Sarah cooks easily'?

4   †Comment on the italicised processes in the following quotation from Shakespeare's *Antony and Cleopatra* (Act 2, Scene 2, l.224):

> Age cannot *wither* her, nor custom *stale*
> Her infinite variety: other women *cloy*
> The appetites they *feed*, but she *makes* hungry
> Where most she *satisfies*.

5   Imagine you are a copy-writer for a well-known cosmetic firm. You are told to write a brochure for a new range of cosmetics. Include in your description causative verbs such as *soften, whiten, lighten, lessen, tighten, freshen, refresh, cleanse, smooth, moisturise* and/or SPOdCo structures containing *make* or *leave* and an Attribute.

6   With the help of a good dictionary, draw up a list of verbs that can be used in ergative pairs and compare them with their equivalents in another language.

Module 16

1 †Identify the italicised participant as Recipient or Beneficiary:

    (1)   Don't forget to send *us* a postcard.
    (2)   *My brother-in-law* has been offered a job analysing mud for an oil company.
    (3)   Can I get *you* something to eat?
    (4)   I think Sammy would like you to buy *him* an ice-cream.
    (5)   How much do we owe *your parents* for the tickets?

Module 17

1 †Identify each of the processes in the main clauses of the following sentences as one of perception, cognition or affectivity. Say whether the Phenomenon is an entity, a fact or a situation:

    (1)   He recognised a group of fellow Americans by their accent.
    (2)   Yesterday I saw a mouse in the supermarket.
    (3)   The miner knew he wouldn't see the light of day again for many hours.
    (4)   Most people hate going to the dentist.
    (5)   Did you watch the World Cup Final on television?
    (6)   He wondered whether he had heard correctly.
    (7)   He could hardly believe that what had happened to him was true.
    (8)   With a cold like this I can't taste what I'm eating.

2 †Write an alternative construction for each of the following clauses so that Experiencer is made to coincide with Subject, as in (b) below:

    (a)   The news delighted us.
    (b)   We were delighted with the news.

    (1)   Neither of the proposals pleased the members of the commission.

        . . . .

    (2)   His presence of mind amazed us.

        . . . .

    (3)   The dramatic increase of crime in the cities is alarming the government.

        . . . .

    (4)   The fact that she seems unable to lose weight worries her.

        . . . .

    (5)   Will the fact that you forgot to phone annoy your wife?

        . . . .

Module 18

1a †Identify the types of 'being' and the participants in the following relational processes 1–8.

1b †Assign Token and Value to the participants in 7 and 8.

> (1) The dormouse is a small rodent related to the mouse.
> (2) The dormouse is famous for its drowsiness and long winter sleep.
> (3) The Dormouse is one of the characters in *Alice in Wonderland*.
> (4) I felt quite nervous all through the interview.
> (5) I haven't any change, I'm afraid.
> (6) The concert will be in the sports stadium at nine o'clock.
> (7) Food is the supreme national symbol.
> (8) What we call civilisation or culture represents only a fraction of human history. [BNC HRM 433]

2 †Add a suitable Attribute or circumstance to each of the following clauses and say whether it is current or resulting:

> (1) After wandering around in circles for more than an hour, we ended up . . . .
> (2) Keep your money . . . . in this special travelling wallet.
> (3) Growing coffee proved to be more . . . . than they had expected.
> (4) Stand . . . . . . while I bandage your hand.
> (5) Feel . . . . to do as you like.

3 Below are two opposite opinions on the effects of television on viewers: (a) the opinion of an art specialist, and (b) that of a psychologist. Elaborate on one of these opinions, expressing your opinion of television programmes by at least a proportion of relational clauses:

> (a) Watching television easily becomes a compulsive and addictive occupation, unlike watching ballet or looking at pictures.
> (b) Our children are neither bored nor stultified; all of us need to dream the same daydream until we have had our fill of it . . . and the more frustrating reality is for us, the greater is our need.

Module 19

1 †Complete each of the following sentences containing verbal processes and say whether the result is a reported statement, a reported question or a reported directive:

> (1) Mounted policemen urged the crowd . . . .
> (2) This notice says . . . .
> (3) The usher at the House of Commons explained . . . .
> (4) Let's enquire at the information desk . . . .
> (5) I have asked the nightwatchman . . . .
> (6) You'd better not tell the children . . . .
> (7) A voice over the loudspeaker announced . . . .
> (8) Recent reports from the north confirm . . . .

2a Add a suitable Existent to each of the following existential clauses and say whether your Existent represents a countable entity, a non-countable entity or an event:

(1) There appeared on the horizon . . . .
(2) There was . . . . . . .and all the lights went out.
(3) There's . . . . . . .in the next village, where you can get quite a good meal.
(4) On the floor there lay . . . .
(5) Just opposite the cinema there's . . . . . .you can send an email from there.
(6) There's no . . . . . . .to lose; the taxi will be here in five minutes.

2b †In which of the clauses in 2 could *there* be omitted and why?

3 †Look at *The Lost Girl* text on p. 154 and identify which Existents are introduced by existential *there* and which are not. How are these others introduced? What appears to be the main conditioning factor? Is quantification important for distinguishing the two types?

4 Add expansions of three types (locative, attributive, clausal) to each of the following existentials:

(1) There was a plane . . . . . .
(2) There were a few members . . . .
(3) There's nothing . . . .

5 Study the text in 18.4 (p. 148) and then write a paragraph describing one of the following:

(1) The house of a friend who collects objects from all over the world.
(2) A carnival.

Use existential clauses with different types of expansion and omit *there* sometimes.

Module 20

1 †Identify the italicised circumstantial element in each of the following:

(1) Trains to Lancing run *every twenty minutes in off-peak periods*.
(2) It's supposed to be quicker by *first-class mail*.
(3) *In spite of the forecast for storms*, they set off in a rowing-boat to cross the lake.
(4) Someone may have done it *out of spite*.
(5) Payments must be made *by the end of the month*.
(6) The horse show was cancelled *on account of the epidemic*.
(7) *As a do-it-yourself decorator*, I'm not the most enterprising.
(8) *As for the dog*, he'll have to go to a kennels *for a month*.

2 †Say which of the following italicised items is Instrument, which is Means and which Range:

(1) They blocked the road *with dustbins*.
(2) We crossed *the Channel* by ferry.

(3) Rita and Pam had *a fierce quarrel*.
(4) She managed to open the suitcase *with a hairpin*.
(5) They lead *a quiet life*.

Module 21

1 †Give a possible basic form for each of the following sentences. Comment on the semantico-syntactic changes involved in the nominalised form here. Provide a translation into another language of the 'metaphorical' (i.e. more nominalised) form, if possible.

   (1) We had a long chat.
   (2) Bombing continued throughout the night.
   (3) Canada saw the launch of a 50-day election campaign last weekend.
   (4) His obvious intelligence and exceptional oratory won him [Franz Josef Strauss] a place in Konrad Adenauer's 1951 cabinet as minister without portfolio.
   (5) The release came after rising expectations in Washington throughout the day that Professor Steen, aged 48, would be the hostage to be freed.

2 Revision exercises: turn to the extract of an interview with Kirsty Ackland on p. 89.

   (1) On some paper, make out separate columns to fill in each type of process, such as mental processes of perception, cognition and affectivity. Make a column for problematic processes.
   (2) Go through the text again, assigning each process with its participants to a column, Include ellipted participants when these are clearly understood. List the circumstantials. Make a numerical or statistical count of the number of instances of each type of process. List them in order of frequency.
   (3) Which type of process is the most frequent? Do you find this surprising? Which aspects of her life is Kirsty most concerned with? What do you think this tells us about the speaker? Would a dialogue in which you took part, on the same subject, be similar?
   (4) Read the article on the transitivity hypothesis (in Hopper and Thompson 1980) and try to apply the criteria to some of the examples in exercise 21.1.

3 Do you find that instances of grammatical metaphor and nominalisation in the sentences tend to be high rather than low, or conversely, low rather than high in transitivity? Can you explain the reasons for your conclusion? (You may want to check up first on the aspectual distinctions discussed in 42.2.)

INTERACTION BETWEEN SPEAKER AND HEARER

CHAPTER 5

Linking speech acts and grammar

SPEECH ACTS AND CLAUSE TYPES

SUMMARY

1   Speech acts are the acts we perform through words. Certain general types of speech act are basic to everyday interaction; these are statements, questions, exclamations and directives, the latter covering orders, requests and instructions among others.

2   Each of these basic speech acts is associated in the grammar with a type of clause: the declarative is typically used to encode a statement, the interrogative a question, the imperative a directive and the exclamative an exclamation. These are the direct correspondences between form and function that we refer to as direct speech acts.

3   Indirect correspondences are also common in English. Thus declaratives, as well as encoding statements, can be used to ask questions, utter exclamations and issue directives, in addition to other speech acts such as promising and warning. In such cases the form is used to convey an 'illocutionary force', or intended meaning, that is different from its basic one. *You're staying here, then*? has the form of a declarative – but, with appropriate intonation, the force is that of a question, as is indicated by the punctuation. The relationship between clause type and force is therefore not one-to-one but many-to-many.

4   Even more indirectly, the words we use do not always express the full illocutionary force of our intended speech act. For example, *It's cold in here* might be intended, and interpreted, as a request to turn up the heating. Hearers use inference to recover the intended meaning at specific points in a conversation, based on assumptions of cooperativeness, truth, relevance and cultural knowledge.

22.1 THE BASIC CORRESPONDENCES

When we speak or write to each other, we perform acts through words, such as thanking and promising. These are 'speech acts'. Certain general types of speech act are very basic, in that most, if not all, languages have ways of representing them by means of the grammar. These are **statements, questions, exclamations** and **directives**.

These basic speech acts are encoded in the grammar in the system of clause types or moods, as shown in the diagram below. The indicative is the grammatical category typically used for the exchange of information, in contrast to the imperative, which grammaticalises our acting on others to get things done by requesting, ordering and so on. The exclamative grammaticalises the expression of emotion.

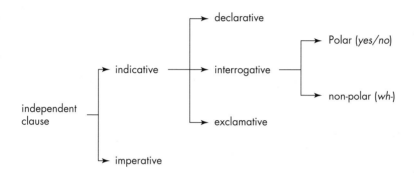

Interrogative clauses can be either polar (*yes/no* interrogatives) or non-polar (*wh*-interrogatives). These are discussed in Module 23.

The basic correspondences between clause types and speech acts are summarised as follows:

Clause type	Basic speech act	Example
Declarative	making a statement	You are careful.
Interrogative (*yes/no*)	asking a question	Are you careful?
Interrogative (*wh*-)	asking a question	How careful are you?
Exclamative	making an exclamation	How careful you are!
Imperative	issuing a directive	Be careful!

The traditional term 'command' is nowadays applicable only in contexts of great inequality and power such as the military. The term **directive** is used instead in everyday environments, to cover such acts as requests, prohibitions and instructions, as well as orders and commands.

22.2 DIRECT AND INDIRECT SPEECH ACTS: WHAT THE UTTERANCE 'COUNTS AS'

It is important to separate the concepts of statement, question and directive, which are semantic-pragmatic categories of meaning in use, from the grammatical categories of declarative, interrogative and imperative, which are typically associated with them. When a clause type is used to carry out the speech act typically associated with it, it is considered to be a **direct speech act**. Thus, in a direct speech act the declarative is said to have the **illocutionary force** of a statement, an interrogative has the force of a question, an imperative has the force of a directive, and an exclamative has the force of an exclamation. The force is the speaker's 'intended meaning' at that particular point in the discourse. The table above shows this basic or typical correspondence between the two sets of categories; and in the following invented dialogue based on an advertisement, each clause type in the independent clauses realises its typical speech act:

> Is that you Brad?[1] Simon here.
> Hi, Simon.
> Did the board reach a conclusion?[2]
> They've decided to launch the product,[3] if the terms are right.
> How do ours compare?[4]
> Very well. But are you sure you can put up the necessary capital?[5]
> We've got a massive loan from the Bank of England.[6]
> In that case, let's go.[7]
> Have we got the deal, then?[8]
> You've got it.[9]
> Fantastic. How soon do you expect to be able to sign?[10]
>
> [1]interrog./question; [2]interrog./question; [3]declar./statement; [4]interrog./question; [5]interrog./question; [6]declar./statement; [7]imper./directive; [8]interrog./question; [9]declar./statement; [10]interrog./question

In interpersonal interaction, however, the relationship is frequently more complex – and more flexible. Every clause type can carry out different speech acts. When a clause type has any other but its typical force, we consider it an **indirect speech act**. That is, it 'counts as' an act different from its typical correspondence.

We can rewrite one of the executives' utterances so that the correspondence between gramatical form and its function is no longer direct:

So *we've got* the deal, then?   (declarative which 'counts' as a question)

Looking at it the other way round, our new version of this utterance still 'counts as' a question, as in the original text, even though it's expressed by a different clause type. Even more indirectly, the words we use do not always express the full meaning of our intended act, as we can see in the following familiar situational dialogue:

A. The door-bell's ringing.
B. I'm in the bath.
A. Okay, I'll go.

A's first utterance is to be interpreted as a directive to B: 'Answer the door'. B's utterance counts as a statement explaining why she can't answer the door ('I'm in the bath'), at the same time implying that A should answer the door. A's second utterance shows that he has inferred the implied request and will comply with it. Notice that neither participant has made specific reference to answering the door.

In this chapter we will be more concerned with the first type of indirect correspondence, the relationship between grammatical form and pragmatic meaning. In interpersonal interaction, however, especially in conversation, the second type – 'not saying exactly what you mean' and expecting the addressee to infer your meaning – is also extremely common in English.

The motivation for using indirect speech acts is often that of tact, politeness or simply economy of effort. Assuming that speakers are cooperative and make their utterances relevant, hearers use inference in order to recover the intended meaning. For instance, a colleague's question on leaving the office *Have you come by car today?* may lead the addressee to infer that the colleague is politely requesting to be given a lift. Inference is also based on cultural knowledge, for example, that people who have cars often give lifts to those who don't.

In inferring the speaker's meaning, the situational context is all-important, as is the relationship between speaker and hearer. In different situations, or at different points in a conversation, any one utterance may take on a different pragmatic force. If an explosion has just been heard in the car-park, *Have you come by car today*? will suggest a very different intended meaning, perhaps that of a warning, or a suggestion to go and see what has happened. As in other areas of the grammar, a form can fulfil more than one function, and a function can be fulfilled by more than one form.

It is not always possible to make a clear-cut distinction between one type of indirect speech act and another. *Sit over here by me* may be a request or an invitation, or a combination of the two. Similarly, Simon's response *We've got a massive loan from the Bank of England* is at once a statement and an assurance in answer to Brad's somewhat anxious question. This indeterminacy of pragmatic meaning is not, in general, a disadvantage, as it allows the interlocutors in a situation to negotiate the outcome of any one utterance as they go along.

THE DECLARATIVE AND INTERROGATIVE CLAUSE TYPES

MODULE 23

SUMMARY

1   Syntactically, the five clause types are distinguished in English by the presence or absence of Subject and the ordering of Subject (S) and a finite verb (F). The rest of the clause remains the same. The Finite is realised by a primary verb (*am, is, are, was, were, has, had*), a modal verb (*can, must,* etc.) or a tensed lexical verb (*sells, sold,* etc.), and is the first or only element of the verbal group.

2   The declarative is the basic clause type, with Subject-Finite ordering (***It is*** *ready,* ***I can*** *swim,* ***Ice melts***). Interrogative and negative clauses in English require a finite operator. The primary verbs *be* and *have*, and the modal verbs (*can, will,* etc.) function as finite operators, carrying inversion (***Is it*** *ready?* ***Can you*** swim?), polarity (the positive–negative distinction) – as in ***It is*** *ready* vs ***It isn't*** *ready* – and emphasis (*I* ***am*** *ready*). If there is no primary or modal verb in the clause, a form of *do* is used as operator (***Does*** *she smoke? She* ***doesn't*** *smoke*).

3   Interrogative structures in English are of two main types: *yes/no* (polar) and *wh-* (non-polar), the latter with a preceding *wh-*element. Both have Finite-Subject ordering except when *Who* is Subject (*Who said that?*). A subtype, the alternative interrogative, consists of two polar interrogatives joined by *or* (*Do you want it or don't you?*). The *wh-* words ending in – *ever* act as intensifiers (*Whatever do you mean?*), as do more colloquial items (*What the devil . . .*).

4   Echo questions repeat all or part of a previous speaker's utterance (*We leave at 5 a.m. – 5a.m?*). Double interrogatives consist of one interrogative embedded within another (*Do you know what time it is?*), the answer being pragmatically determined.

5   Abbreviated clauses (*I can't, Is it?*) are independent ellipted clauses based on Subject–operator and operator – Subject patterns. They are commonly used as short interactive responses after questions, statements, exclamations and directives.

6 Question tags are also abbreviated *yes/no* interrogatives. They are not independent, but appended to a main clause. There are two types, reversed and constant, distinguished by polarity, appendibility and, in part, intonation. Invariant tags include *right, okay* and – for some speakers – *innit*, the latter often socially stigmatised. Like other ellipted forms, tags are an important interactive device in spoken English.

23.1 CLAUSE TYPES AND THE MOOD ELEMENT: SUBJECT-FINITE VARIATION

In English, the declarative, interrogative and imperative moods of a clause are distinguished syntactically by variation in one part of the clause, called the mood element, while the rest of the predicate, sometimes called the residue, remains unchanged. The elements of structure which together form the mood element are Subject (S) and Finite (F). Variation consists in the presence or absence of Subject and the ordering of the two elements, as summarised in the table below. These different syntactic variations are referred to as 'clause types':

Clause type	Order	Example
Declarative	Subject-Finite	Jane sings.
Interrogative (yes/no)	Finite + Subject	Does Jane sing?
Interrogative (wh-)	wh + Finite + Subject	What does Jane sing?
Exclamative	wh + Subject + Finite	How well Jane sings!
Imperative	no subject, base form of verb	Sing!

23.2 THE DECLARATIVE CLAUSE TYPE

The **declarative** is the basic clause type, with Subject-Finite ordering, as in:

	Subject	Finite	Predicator		
1	*We*	*are*	meeting	again tomorrow.	[BNC AON 1644]
2	*You*	*might*	need	a holiday.	[BNC AYP 47]

The Finite, meaning specified for tense or modality, is always the first or only element of a verbal group (see also chapters 1 and 8). It is realised by either a **verbal operator** (*is, can, has*, etc.), as in 1 and 2, or a **tensed** (past or present) form of the lexical verb, as in 4 and 5. The primary verbs function both as operators 1 and as main verbs 3:

Subject	Finite/Predicator	
3 We	*are*	late again.
4 *She*	*arrives*	tomorrow.
5 *They*	*sell*	fish and chips here.

More exactly, in positive declarative clauses, Finite and Predicator fuse in the present and past tensed forms of lexical verbs and of *be* and *have* when used as main verbs. The operator is always realised by a verb: primary, modal or *do*, as explained and illustrated in 3.1.

The Finite element relates the proposition to a point of reference: either a time reference, by tense, or the speaker's judgement by means of modality, as discussed in chapters 8 and 9.

23.3 INTERROGATIVE CLAUSES, NEGATION AND THE *DO*-OPERATOR

In **interrogative clauses**, the Finite verb precedes the Subject, the rest remaining the same.

Finite	Subject	Predicator	
Are	*we*	meeting	again tomorrow?
Do	*you*	need	a holiday?
Does	*she*	expect	us soon?
Did	*they*	emigrate	to Australia after all?

When no operator is already available in the clause, a form of *do* (*do, does, did*) is brought in as a dummy operator. That is, it has no semantic value but simply fulfils the syntactic requirement of 'finite operator' (see 3.1.1), as illustrated in the last three examples. The functions of the operators that interest us here are, first, that they signal by position that the clause is interrogative, and second, they carry **polarity**, that is, they are either **positive** or **negative**. This positive–negative contrast is an essential semantic feature associated with finiteness. In order to be affirmed or denied, a proposition has to be either positive or negative.

Negation, as we saw in 3.2, is usually expressed by the negative particle *not*, which follows the operator or is joined to it as *n't*. Note that the negative interrogative with 1st person singular 'I' is not **amn't* but *aren't* in Standard English. Other exceptions include *can't*, *won't* and *shan't*. (Operators also function in question tags, both positive and negative, as illustrated here and discussed with further examples shortly. See also Chapter 8.)

Subject	Finite	Predicator		
I	*won't*	be going	home for lunch.	[BNC KNY 251]
It	*doesn't*	seem	right, does it?	[BNC FUL 178]
You	*don't*	sell	bibles, do you?	[BNC C86 2553]

Negative-interrogative forms (see also Chapter 1) are illustrated as follows:

Finite	Subject	Predicator	
Won't	you	be going	home for lunch?
Don't	you	sell	bibles?

The *do* forms can be used to add emphasis with lexical verbs in the declarative:

Subject	Finite	Predicator		
They	**do**	sell	them	
You	**do**	know	about that, don't you?	[BNC H9W 1033]

Interrogative clauses typically occur in interpersonal situations, and their direct speech-act function or force is to ask for information. There are two main types of interrogative, the **yes/no** type and the **wh**-type. The examples we have seen so far are of the *yes/no* type.

23.4 *YES/NO* INTERROGATIVES AND THEIR RESPONSES

In the *yes/no* type it is only the polarity that is in question. The speaker asks for confirmation or denial of the clause content, to be expressed by *yes* or *no*. Such minimal replies often sound rather curt, however:

> A. Do you sell fish fingers?
> B. No.
> A. At all? You don't?   [BNC KBC 717–721]
> (B's first response overlaps with A's question; B's reply might be):
> B. You can get them from the supermarket.

A feature of spoken English is the use of ellipted responses such as *Yes, it is, No, we don't, I can't, has he?* based on the Subject-operator (declarative) and operator-Subject (interrogative) patterns. These are independent **abbreviated clauses**. They are used in response to questions, statements, exclamations and directives. They show more interest and involvement than a mere *Yes* or *No*, and even more than mere silence! In conversation they keep the talk alive by passing the turn from one speaker to another:

> A. Always drunk isn't he?
> B. He's a sweet old man though.
> A. *Is he?*
> B. Gets me nice birthday presents.
> A. *Does he?*
> B. Mm.   [BNC 3503–3507]

Another way of responding is by an **echo question**. This repeats part, or sometimes all, of an immediately preceding utterance by another speaker. The motivation for using echoes is that the hearer did not comprehend, found difficult to believe, or did not hear properly what had been said:

I'm going to sell my golf clubs.   Sell them?
What did you say to him?   What did I say to him?

In interactive situations, in fact, a wide range of responses occurs, as speakers often express greater or less certainty about the proposition:

Have you got any stamps?
No, I don't think I have, in fact I know I haven't.   [BNC KCX 3771–3772]

In the following extract from Harold Pinter's *Applicant* an eager applicant for a job is asked a great many unexpected questions by the interviewer Miss Piffs. All her questions are of the *yes/no* type, yet few are in fact answered by *yes* or *no*. The applicant Lamb shows his perplexity and surprise by responding in a variety of ways:

Piffs:	*Would you* say you were an excitable person?	[1]
Lamb:	Not – unduly, no. Of course, I –	[2]
Piffs:	*Would you* say you were a moody person?	[3]
Lamb:	Moody? No, I wouldn't say I was moody – well, sometimes occasionally I –	[4]
Piffs:	*Do you* ever get fits of depression?	[5]
Lamb:	Well, I wouldn't call them depression exactly.	[6]
Piffs:	*Do you* often do things you regret in the morning?	[7]
Lamb:	Regret? Things I regret? Well, it depends what you mean by often, really – I mean when you say often –	[8]
Piffs:	*Are you* often puzzled by women?	[9]
Lamb:	Women?	[10]
Piffs:	Men.	[11]
Lamb:	Men? Well, I was just going to answer the question about women –	[12]
Piffs:	*Do you* often feel puzzled?	[13]
Lamb:	Puzzled?	[14]
Piffs:	By women.	[15]
Lamb:	Women?	[16]
Piffs:	Men.	[17]
Lamb:	Oh now, just a minute I . . . Do you want separate answers or a joint answer?	[18]

23.5 ALTERNATIVE INTERROGATIVES

Alternative interrogatives also start with an operator, like the *yes/no* type, but *yes* or *no* is no longer an appropriate answer. Instead, one of the two alternatives presented in the question is expected to be chosen, but again, variants are possible, as shown in B's answers:

> A. Do you study for enjoyment or to advance your career?   [BNC BNA 1630]
> B. – For enjoyment
>   – To advance my career
>   – Both

23.6 *WH*-INTERROGATIVES

Wh-interrogatives contain an element of missing information which is embodied in the *wh*-word. What the speaker is seeking in this type of interrogative is the identity of that element. The rest is presupposed, that is, taken as given. For instance, *What do you want?* presupposes that you want something. The *wh*-word can fill a syntactic function of the clause or be part of a group or phrase.

Wh-word	Finite	Subject		Syntactic function
What	do	you	want?	(Od)
What	is	it	for?	(complement of a prep.)
Who(m)	have	they	appointed?	(Od)
Who	can	it	be?	(Cs)
Whose dog	is	it?		(determinative in NG)
When	shall	we	go?	(A)
How	did	it	happen?	(A)
How old	is	she?		(Cs)
How long	have	you	known him?	(A)
Why	would	I	do that?	(A)
Where	have	you most	enjoyed working?	(A) [BNC BNA 28496]

There is one exception to the Finite-Subject order in *wh*-interrogative clauses. This is when the *wh*-element itself functions as subject or as part of a NG at subject:

Subject	F/P		
Who	told	you that?	
Which glass	got	broken?	(determinative in NG)

The functional motivation for the ordering of interrogatives in English is that whatever is questioned comes first. If it is the polarity that is questioned, the finite operator comes first. If it is the identity of an unknown element, a *wh*-element comes first, followed by the Finite-Subject ordering. If the unknown element is the Subject, that (in the form of a *wh*-element), comes first.

This means that, basically, the entire interrogative system in English has Finite-Subject ordering, except when the Subject's identity is itself questioned.

Note that, in some languages, interrogative inversion is that of the Subject and the whole verbal group, as in Spanish *¿Ha llegado Pedro?* We must be aware that this variation is ungrammatical in English (**Has arrived Peter?*), except with primary verbs (*be* and *have*) in simple tenses. Compare: *Has Peter a bicycle?* is possible, but **Has had Peter lunch?* is ungrammatical. Furthermore, certain languages rely on intonation to express a question, using only the declarative form. This is also possible in English (see 26.4) but it does not regularly replace the use of the interrogative structures.

The following dialogue between two friends illustrates declarative clauses and the two main interrogative types. Finite elements are italicised:

> So what *did* you do at the weekend, Janet?
> Well, Jeff and I *went* off to Whitby to visit our in-laws. We *took* the dog with us and we all *ended up* having a walk along the beach.
> *Can* you walk right along the cliffs to Robin Hood's Bay?
> I *think* you probably *could* do, but it's quite dangerous. You *can* get through occasionally when the tide's out, but it *doesn't* stay out for very long and you *can* get caught.
>
> (authors' data)

The *wh*-interrogative words sometimes combine with the word *-ever*, which acts as an intensifier expressing the surprise, perplexity or disbelief of the speaker. *Why ever* is often spelt as two words, the other items as either one or two:

> Whoever would believe such a story?
> Wherever did you hear that?
> Why ever didn't he let us know he was coming?

Besides the *-ever* combinations, *wh*-interrogative words can be intensified informally by certain lexical items which include *on earth, in the world*, and other more marked colloquialisms including semi-taboo words, such as *the devil, the hell*.

> *Why on earth* didn't you get in touch?
> Ellie! *Where the hell* have you been?   (*Girls Out Late*)

See 3.1 and 26.3 for negative-interrogatives.

23.7 DOUBLE INTERROGATIVES: QUESTIONS WITHIN QUESTIONS

A *wh*-interrogative can be embedded as a constituent of a polar interrogative, in which case the *wh*-interrogative has the order of a declarative clause, as in *Do you know what time it is?* rather than **Do you know what time is it?* (see also Chapter 3). There are two questions involved in this case: (a) the polarity of the main clause, in this example whether the addressee knows the answer to the *wh*-question; and (b) the content embodied in the *wh*-element. The intention of the speaker, together with the context, will 'weight' one or other in importance. For example, if the addressee is slowly packing a suitcase to catch a train shortly, (a) 'knowing the time' is likely to be more important. On the other hand, if the speaker's watch has stopped, (b) 'the time is x' is likely to be of greater interest to the speaker. The force is different too. In (a) *Do you know what time it is?* has the force of a polite reminder, while in (b) it will be interpreted as a request.

23.8 QUESTION TAGS

Question tags are not independent clauses, but they do require a response, and are highly interactive. Structurally, tags are abbreviated *yes/no* interrogatives consisting of an operator (either positive or negative) and a pronoun, which repeats the subject or substitutes for it. Question tags are attached to one of the following clause types:

a declarative clause:	It was quiet in there, *wasn't it?*
an exclamative clause:	How quiet it was in there, *wasn't it?*
an imperative clause:	Be quiet for a moment, *will you?*

Of these, the declarative is by far the most common. The tag is usually placed at the end **1–5**, but sometimes in the middle **6**:

1 Ben is in South Africa, *isn't he?*
2 He isn't with Gordon, *is he?*
3 You live in Hammersmith, *don't you*?
4 You don't live in Chelsea, *do you*?
5 It doesn't really matter, *does it*?
6 It's easy, *isn't it*, to get into the habit?

23.9 FEATURES OF THE MAIN TYPES OF TAG

There are two main types of declarative mood tag, distinguished by polarity sequence. Type 1 tag has opposite polarity to that of the main clause. That is, if the main clause is positive, the tag is negative, and vice versa, as in the examples so far.

There is either **rising** or **falling intonation** on the tag. A rising tone on the tag indicates doubt, and so the meaning is 'Am I right?' If however the intonation is falling, it expresses greater certainty, so that the meaning of the tag is more like 'I'm asking you to confirm this' and simply seeks agreement.

The **Type 2 tag** has constant polarity, that is, the same as the main clause. It occurs mostly in combinations of positive declarative clauses with positive tags. Type 2 tags typically have a rising tone on the tag, and the statement is often preceded by a discourse marker, such as *Oh, So* or *Well now*, which indicates that the speaker is expressing a conclusion or inference drawn from the situation or from what has been said before. The effect is often emotive and can either express an agreeable surprise or else sound pejorative, depending on the implication.

> *Oh*, so you're the new assistant, *are you?*
> *Oh* so that's what she said, *is it?*
> *Well now*, this is the Norman chapel, *is it?*
> You found the address, *did you?*

The following extract, from James Saunders' play *Over the Wall*, parodies a doctor's questioning of a patient, who is not allowed time to reply:

> Falling hair, loss of weight, gain of weight, tenseness, got a drink problem *have you*, smoking too much, hallucinations, palpitations, eructations, on drugs *are you*, can you read the top line, overdoing it at work perhaps, worrying about the work, about the spouse, about where to go for your holiday, about the mortgage, about the value of the pound, about the political situation, about your old mother, about the kids, kids playing up *are they*, not doing well at school, got a drink problem *have they*, smoking, on drugs *are they*, suffering from loss of weight, falling hair, got any worries *have you?*
>
> Yes!

In both types of question tag, the pronoun in the tag is co-referential with the subject, and the operator, not the pronoun, carries the tonic stress.

There is a third, less common but very useful variant, illustrated by the following example:

> Ooh! I love squirrels, don't **you**?   [BNC KBW 12683–12684]

Here the pronouns are not co-referential. The sentence subject is invariably *I* and that of the tag, *you*. It is *you*, not the operator, that carries the tonic stress, marking a contrast with the 1st person, the speaker. The tag invites the addressee to agree or disagree with the speaker's opinion.

When an embedded clause that encodes the main propositional content of the sentence is introduced by a clausal fragment such as *I think* or *I suppose* expressing epistemic stance, the tag refers to the embedded clause, not to the clausal fragment (see also 36.2). The stance expression can be placed parenthetically:

> *I think* he left before lunch, *didn't he?* (not **don't I?*)
>   (He left, *I think*, before lunch, didn't he?)

I suppose you'd prefer a cold drink, *wouldn't you?* (not **don't I?*)
(You'd prefer a cold drink, *I suppose*, wouldn't you?)

Indefinite human singular pronouns take *they* in the tag:

Everybody seemed to enjoy themselves, didn't *they?*
Nobody will agree to that, will *they?*
Somebody should be told, shouldn't *they?*

The discourse function of tags following declaratives is to seek confirmation or agreement with the previous statement and to keep the conversation going. Tags are questions and so require an answer. They enable the speaker to elicit a response from the hearer, where a tagless declarative or imperative would not necessarily achieve this end. Together with abbreviated clauses and fragments as short responses, tags provide the main structural-functional devices for furthering speaker-hearer involvement.

With certain speech act functions, such as good wishes and warnings, a question tag is not used. Instead, other forms such as the following are used, in which the adverbs do not have their normal ideational value:

See you later, *then!*   Have a good journey, *then!*
That plate is hot, *mind*   Look out, there!   Come on, *now!*

23.10 INVARIANT QUESTION TAGS

Invariant tags are those such as *Right?* **1** and *okay?*, which are not derived from the structure of the main clause. A form which is spreading rapidly is *innit*. This was originally derived from *isn't it*, and is used in popular, non-standard speech as a tag appended to a declarative **2**, **3**. In the vernacular it is also used as a negative interrogative main verb and a question tag, in the same sentence **4**. Furthermore, in some communities it is becoming a generalised tag used in environments other than those containing the operator *is* **5**. In this respect, *innit* is like *right* and *okay*, although less generally accepted than they are.

1   Getting over a cold, *right?*   [BNC KBF 13393]
2   It's a nice pattern *innit?*   [BNC KB8 7338]
3   Oh it's cold *innit?*   [BNC KE3 8928]
4   Ah *innit* lovely *innit?*   [BNC KBE 9639]
5   You know our life story *innit?*   [BNC KCS 1718]

Like other tags, *innit?* seeks confirmation or agreement from the addressee. *Right* and *okay*, however, also function (like *all right*) as responses indicating agreement or compliance **6**, and also as discourse markers to call attention and initiate an action **7**:

6   . . . whenever you want to read there, you can do that.
        Okay right right.   [BNC KCV 0941–0942]
7   *Right*, er, let's have a look then   [BNC KB3 1867]

THE EXCLAMATIVE AND IMPERATIVE CLAUSE TYPES

SUMMARY

1   Exclamative clauses open with a *wh-* element *what* or *how*, followed by a NG or adjective/adverb, respectively. Like the declarative, they have Subject-Finite ordering. Exclamative *what* is a determinative (*What a mess!*), while *how* functions as a degree adverb (*How strange it was!*), unlike pronominal *what* and manner adverb *how* in *wh-* interrogatives (*What is it? How is she?*). They are used to make exclamative statements.

2   The imperative consists of the base form of the verb alone, without modals, tense or aspect (*Stop!*). This can be preceded by the negative form *don't* or emphatic *do*. There is no overt subject, but a 2nd person subject (stressed *you*) can be added, usually for purposes of contrast with another person (**You** *sit down and I'll stand*). *Somebody, everybody, nobody* can also be used and, like *you*, refer to the addressee(s). These, and other forms, can also be used as vocatives. A polite clause tag is *will you? Let's* is the imperative particle used for a 1st person imperative, typically suggesting a joint action. It is to be distinguished from the lexical verb *let*, from which it derived. The unmarked function of imperatives is to issue a directive.

3   Reduced clauses are extremely common in spoken English and fulfil an important interactive function. They include abbreviated clauses (basically S-F or F-S in structure) that function independently, question tags, verbless clauses of various degrees of ellipsis, echoes, and freestanding subordinate clauses (*which it does*). In this module we refer mainly to the typical speech act associated with each clause type.

4   The subjunctive is not a clause type but a verb form. It remains outside the system of clause types and has a very limited use in British English, rather more in American English.

24.1 THE EXCLAMATIVE

The exclamative clause type starts with a *wh-* word, either the determinative *what*, followed by a nominal group or the degree adverb *how* and an adjective, adverb or statement:

Wh- element

What a shock	they'll have!	
What a mess	we've got ourselves into!	[BNC G0J 4081]
What a lot of interference	there is! [on the telephone]	
How dark	it is!	
How	it snowed!	

Exclamatives have the Subject-Finite ordering that is characteristic of the declarative, and the element following the *wh-* word is a clause constituent which has been brought to the front of the clause. For these reasons exclamative clauses are sometimes considered as an emotive element superimposed on the declarative rather than as a distinct mood.

The declarative clauses corresponding to these examples are as follows:

They'll have a shock.
We've got ourselves into a mess.
It is dark.
It snowed.

How-exclamative clauses sound somewhat theatrical nowadays, especially when followed by an adverb (*How well he played!*). More commonly heard than clausal exclamatives in everyday spoken English are abbreviated noun-headed or adjective-headed forms:

What a mess!	What a surprise!	What a nightmare!
What a player!	What very sad news!	How exciting!
Oh great!	Big deal!	Fantastic! (see also 25.2)

Embedded (or indirect) exclamatives occur regularly in both spoken and written English. We refer to them in 11.3.4 under *wh-* complements, and simply illustrate them here:

You wouldn't believe *how badly the prisoners were treated.*

24.2 THE IMPERATIVE

The most striking feature of an imperative clause is that it requires no overt Subject in English. In this it differs sharply from the other clause types:

Be careful!
Come on! *Hurry* up!

The subject is pragmatically understood to be the addressee, and this is confirmed by the presence of a reflexive pronoun (*yourself, yourselves*) **1**, a question tag (*will you*) **2** or by a vocative (*you, you people, you guys*, used to address women as well as men) **3**, **6**. Stressed *you* positioned immediately before the imperative is usually interpreted as subject, and is typically used to mark a contrast with the speaker or a 3rd person **4**. Subject and vocative are less distinct when realised by *someone* **7**, *everyone*, or a NG such as *passengers on flight IB580 to Vigo* **8** preceding the verb. They could be either subject or vocative, or even merge. Both are optional and both refer to the addressees, representing either all or a sub-set of those persons present in the speech situation. When placed in final position **1**, a pronoun or NG would normally be considered a vocative.

1 Help *yourselves, everyone*!
2 *Be* quiet, *will you*!
3 Shut up, *you two*!
4 *You* stay here and I'll get the tickets.
5 Hey, *Helena*, calm down!   [BNC KCE 1507]
6 Come on, *you guys*, the shops will be shutting soon.   (*Girls Out Late*)
7 *Someone* call an ambulance!
8 *Passengers on flight number IB580 to Vigo* please proceed to gate number 17.

Vocatives are able to occupy various positions, typically final **3**, but also medial **6** and initial, often preceded by an attention-getter **5**. Common vocatives are first names, *Johnny, Pat*, kinship names *Mum/Mom, Grandad*, endearments *darling, love, honey, pet*, pronoun *you* + noun *you guys*, surnames and titles, *Mr Roberts*, and (now less common) honorifics *madam, sir*. Vocatives fulfil important interpersonal functions in getting someone's attention, singling out one individual among a group and maintaining relationships, either of a close or friendly nature or, less commonly nowadays, marking distance and respect.

As these examples illustrate, imperatives typically encode directives, which range from orders **2**, **3** to encouragement **6**, urgent request **7**, invitation **1** and instructions **8** (see also 27.1).

The following exchange between two women friends was overheard on the London Underground when a seat became vacant. Two functions of *you* occur; as subject of an imperative and as vocative after an imperative:

A$_1$ Sit down!
B$_2$ No, you sit down!
A$_3$ You're the one with the feet.
B$_4$ So are you. You sit down!
A$_5$ Sit down with the feet, you!

You in B$_2$ and B$_4$ subject of imperative. *You* in A$_5$ vocative after an imperative.

24.2.1 The verb in the imperative

Another important structural feature of the imperative is that it uses the base form of the verb, with no modals or tense-aspect forms. This is shown by the use of *be* in *Be careful!* (not *are (being) careful*, *can be careful*). The grammatical status of the base form as a non-finite is somewhat problematic, however. It does not share functions with other non-finite verb forms; rather, the imperative has more in common, functionally, with finites than with the non-finites. Like interrogatives, it relates the speaker to the hearer and to the here-and-now, typically in face-to-face interaction.

Because the base form is indistinguishable from some declarative forms, there is potentially structural ambiguity between an imperative with a *you*-subject and a declarative. This is disambiguated only in speech, by stress on the imperative subject:

A. How do we get tickets for this show?
B. *You* go and stand in the queue. (unstressed, declarative, use of 'generic' *you* = 'one')
A. What shall we do, then?
B. **You** go and stand in the queue while **I** park the car. (stressed, imperative)

There is, however, a distinction between declarative and imperative when the verb is *be*, as in role-taking. This is because *be* has retained different forms for person and tense (*am, is, are*). Compare:

You *be* the doctor and I'll be the nurse. (imperative)
You're the doctor and I'm the nurse. (declarative)

The declarative 3rd person singular finite form *-s* avoids ambiguity with a 3rd person subject imperative. Note however that *please* always points to a directive meaning:

Imperative	Declarative
Everybody sit down, please!	Everybody sits down.
Nobody say a word!	Nobody says a word.

If the Subject is plural, the verb form is the same in both types, but intonation, pause, gesture and common sense serve to clarify the meaning in a specific context.

Ticket-holders (pause) come this way!

Ticket-holders come this way.

Those in agreement (pause) raise their hands!

Those in agreement raise their hands.

24.2.2 Negative and emphatic imperatives

Don't (placed before a subject) and *do* are used to negate or emphasise 2nd person imperatives, respectively. (To some speakers, *do* sounds rather old-fashioned now.)

Negative & emphasis	Subject	Base/Predicator	
	You	be	careful, now!
Don't		be	silly!
Don't	you	speak	to me like that!
Do		keep	still, Pat!

24.2.3 *Let's* and *Let us*

Another feature of the imperative in English is the use of *let's* to form a 1st person plural imperative with the implicit Subject *we*. Its typical use is to suggest or urge a collaborative action that includes both speaker and addressee(s). It is also used, however, as a disguised order by speakers in authority, as in the third example. The tag question used with 1st person imperatives is *Shall we?*

> Let's take a few photos, shall we?
> Let's go home, shall we?
> Let's have some silence now!

Let's is historically derived from *let us* and in very formal settings, including church services, the unabbreviated form is heard:

> Let us pray.
> Let us consider the possible alternatives.

It may be that *let's* is beginning to function as an unanalysed pragmatic particle, as in non-standard *let's you and I do it*. The negative form of *let's* is *let's not*, although *don't let's* is also heard

> *Let's not* waste any more time.   [BNC AMB 799]
> Oh, *don't let's* talk about it, Len.   [BNC GVT 2492]

Let's is not to be confused with the normal imperative of the lexical verb *let* meaning *permit, allow*, as in:

> *Let* me do it!   *Let* me help you.

As an illustration of the differences between the particle *let* and lexical *let* (= *allow*), compare:

> *Let's go* and see that new film!   (particle *let*)
> Please *let us go* and see that new film.   (lexical *let*)

Let's go! (*let* as particle)	Let us go! (lexical verb *let*)
us = I + you	*us = me + other(s)*
Pronoun *us* reduced to *'s*	Pronoun *us* not reduced
No subject pronoun can be added	2nd person subject *you* can be added: *You* let us go!
The tag is *shall we?*	The tag is *will you?* / *can't you?*
The verb is not ellipted	Phrasal verb is ellipted with verbs of direction: *Let us in/out* (= *come/go in/out*)

Obviously, both uses of *let* can occur in the same clause, as in *Let's let them in now*. The pragmatic particle *let* can also introduce a wish (the optative mood) as in *Let there be light* and is used only in formal registers (for inclusive and exclusive *we/us*, see 45.7.1).

24.3 VERBLESS AND FREESTANDING SUBORDINATE CLAUSES

Spoken English and genres which imitate it are rich in ellipsis and reduced forms in general. We have already seen examples of abbreviated clauses, echo questions and tags.

Verbless clauses

We use the term 'verbless clause' to cover elliptical clauses which lack one or more structural elements: Subject and Finite verb **1, 2, 3, 5**, Finite verb **4**. They therefore lack the alternative orderings characteristic of abbreviated clauses. Some can take question tags, however, with either rising or falling intonation. Without a tag, intonation indicates the force of a statement, question or exclamation.

 1   (He is) in New York, isn't he? (question)
 2   What a waste of time, (it was) wasn't it! (exclamation)
 3   (This is) Simon here. (self-identifying statement on the phone)
 4   (Are) you ready? (question)
 5   (It's) fantastic! (exclamation)

In conversational exchanges in English, certain *wh-* questions without a finite verb play a part as initiators and responses. They can have the force of an invitation (*How about some lunch?*), an encouraging suggestion (*Why not* give it another try?), an inquiry (*How come* Sheila's not with you?)

Freestanding subordinate clauses

These also are characteristic of ongoing conversation. Two very common types are the sentential relative clause introduced by *which* **1** and clauses of reason introduced by *because* or *cos* **2** (see 35.3). The interesting feature is that they are not attached to a previous clause, but are freestanding, both intonationally and as regards punctuation. Functionally, they reinforce or give the reason for making the previous utterance:

1 and, he said, well with the coal fire and all that, he said, it'll, it'll get dirty
  Mm *which it will*, won't it? [BNC KE6 10518–10519]
2a *Because you're worth it.* (Closing utterance in L'Oréal hair care advertisements.)
2b Did you see King Lear when it was on on the television? *Cos I taped that as well.*
  [BNC KDM 3696–3697]

24.4 THE SUBJUNCTIVE IN ENGLISH

In English, mood has to do with clause types rather than verb inflection. It leaves the subjunctive somewhat isolated, since this is not a clause type, but a verb form which in present-day British English plays a very marginal role, although it is rather more common in American English.

As regards the expression of non-factual meaning, the subjunctive has also lost ground. In independent clauses the subjunctive can express a wish, but only in fossilised stereotyped expressions like *Long live the Queen! So be it, Heaven be praised! Far be it from me to doubt your word.* Even in subordinate clauses, a clearly identifiable present subjunctive is limited to the uninflected VG occurring with a 3rd person singular subject in *that*-clause complements of certain verbs and adjectives, as in: *It is right that this House **debate** this issue.* In less formal contexts the indicative or *should* + infinitive are now used by many speakers. (We recommend that he **gets/should get** a visa.)

A past subjunctive can be identified only in the form *were* in the 1st and 3rd persons singular of *be* (*If I* were *you . . . If he were to return alive . . .*) in subordinate clauses of condition and concession, where it is still very current. Most non-factual notions, such as the expression of doubt and hypothesis, are conveyed in English by other grammatical means, principally *any* and its compounds and the modal auxiliaries, especially *should, could, may* and *might* (see Module 44).

One area in which an indicative–subjunctive contrast is made is in a certain type of *if* clause, as in:

If he *was* here I didn't see him.   (indicative)
If he *were* here I would surely see him.   (subjunctive)

Only the second *if* clause is truly conditional. The first, meaning 'if it is true that he was here', is rhetorical condition in that his being here is not a condition for my seeing him. This is also referred to as pragmatic conjunction (see 35.3).

INDIRECT SPEECH ACTS, CLAUSE TYPES AND DISCOURSE FUNCTIONS

SUMMARY

While examining the structure of clause types, we have mainly illustrated them with their unmarked correspondences, but these are not the only ones. All language in use carries out acts, and this is what distinguishes an utterance from a sentence. A sentence is a grammatical object, but when it gets used in context what we have is an utterance. The meaning of an utterance depends on what it is being used to do – what kind of speech act is being performed.

In this section we shall start with the speech act and see how the clause types can carry out different intended meanings from their basic ones.

1   All language performs acts, but there is no one-to-one correspondence between clause type and speech-act function. Here we look at some of the indirect correspondences, together with other discourse functions.

2   Certain verbs such as *promise, advise* and *warn*, when used in the declarative, are potentially explicit performatives, that is they can carry out the act they name. This is the case with a 1st person subject and the present tense (*I promise*).

3   Exclamations can be made, with appropriate intonation, by all clause types, as well as by verbless clauses reduced to a nominal group or an adjective.

25.1 PERFORMATIVES AND THE DECLARATIVE

We have seen that making a statement is the basic function of the declarative. A statement describes a state of affairs in the world and has a truth value, which can be confirmed, questioned or denied (*She is at home; Is she at home? She is not at home*). Stating something is performing the verbal act of stating. The declarative is unique among clause types, however, in its ability to carry out certain acts by naming them. These are **explicit performatives**.

With certain verbs – such as *promise, advise* and *warn* – a declarative carries out the speech act it names. Such declaratives usually address the hearer directly, as in:

1 I *promise* I'll be careful.   [BNC B3J 1436]
2 We *advise* you to book early to avoid disappointment.   [BNC AMW 1335]
3 If you insist on staying, I *warn* you, you'll get no help   [BNC H94 724]
    from me.
4 And we have a very good selection of Indian restaurants: [BNC HDT 49]
    I *recommend* the Kashmir.

That is, the speaker carries out the act of promising, advising, warning and recommending, respectively. Declaratives such as these don't have truth value. It makes no sense to ask if they are true or false. Instead, we can ask if they work as performatives. With a 1st-person speaker and present tense, as in *I promise I'll be careful*, the performative is explicit and the speaker is fully accountable as the doer of the speech act.

As long as the underlying Subject is the speaker or the writer, the passive forms **5**, **6**, or an active form with an impersonal NG Subject **7**, have the same effect:

5 *You are advised* to book early to avoid disappointment.
6 *Passengers are requested* to have their boarding cards ready.
7 *Liverpool Airport apologise* for any inconvenience caused to the public during
    building works.

Performatives become less explicit when modalised (with *can* or *must*), when introduced by *let, want, I'm afraid* or when nominalised. They still count as performatives, however:

8 I *can offer* you beer, whisky, gin, coke . . .
9 *Let me thank* you once more for your collaboration.
10 *My apologies* for cross-postings. (for sending a repeated email message)
11 I *must* beg you not to tell anyone about this.
12 I *am afraid I have to* request you to move to another seat.
13 I *wanna* thank you all. God bless you. (President George W. Bush to the
    American people in the aftermath of 11 September 2001)

These 'hedged', that is, indirect, forms are felt to be still performing the act named by the verb. In addition, they are more polite than direct forms because they avoid invoking power and status. Hearers may perceive them to be more sincere, as is also the case with the informal use of *wanna* instead of *want to* in the President's thanks.

Other verbs that can be used as explicit performatives include: *agree, apologise, beg, bet, congratulate, declare, guarantee, offer, object, warn, wish* and many others.

With pronouns other than *I/we*, or with past tense or perfect aspect, such verbs do not carry out the act they name; instead, they are statements which report a speech act:

I offered them beer, whisky, gin, cola . . .
They have requested passengers to have their boarding cards ready.

You might wonder why we don't use performatives all the time, if they are so efficient. One reason is that not all verbs are potentially performative. For instance, we can't threaten someone in English by saying 'I threaten you', nor hint by saying 'I hint that you are wrong'. These acts have to be done indirectly.

A second reason is that explicit performatives sometimes appear to invoke authority or status. The power factor is most obvious in 'ritual performatives' such as:

Then I *declare* the meeting closed. [BNC GUD618]

I *name* this ship Aurora. (Authorised person at launching of
  the ship) [BNC 9W787]

Negative declaratives typically express a negative statement, which may have the force of a rejection **1**. Negating an explicit performative can have the effect of greatly attenuating the force, as in **2**, though this is not the case with passives **5**. Negative declaratives can also express a polite question **3**, an exclamation **4** or a prohibition **5**:

1 I don't need any more calendars, thank you.
2 I don't promise you that I'll convince him.
3 Bill hasn't said anything about the weekend?
4 I never heard such rubbish!
5 Smoking is not allowed in here

With some performatives such as *advise*, what we have is **transferred negation**. The negative particle *not* is transferred from its logical place in the dependent clause to the main clause (see 3.6 for other verbs, such as *think*, which behave this way):

I don't advise you to buy those shares (= I advise you not to buy those shares).

Certain verbs such as *promise* and *bet* are sometimes used performatively to carry out a different act from the one they name. Basically, *promise* carries out acts which benefit the addressee, while *bet* is used to lay a wager. But, in the examples that follow, this is not the case: *promise* is being used to threaten the addressee while *bet* informally expresses strong probability:

Now get out of bed and don't you dare make a sound. One sound and you won't
  make another, I *promise* you. [BNC FSG 2608–2609]

I bet they have their problems, like us. [BNC H94 862]

25.2 EXCLAMATIONS

Appropriate intonation can be imposed on any type of unit, including a single word, to express an exclamation (*Splendid!*).

With appropriate intonation, all the clause types can be used to make exclamations: the exclamative structure **1**, **2**; an interrogative **3**, **4**; a declarative **5**, **6**; an imperative **7**; a verbless clause **8**, **9**; a nominal group **10**:

| *Using the exclamative structure*: | **1** | What an idiot he is! |
| | **2** | How tall you've grown! |

Using an interrogative	**3**	Isn't it a lovely day!
	4	Would you believe it! (expressing disbelief)
Using a declarative	**5**	You must be joking!
	6	You can't be serious!
Using an imperative	**7**	Fancy meeting you here!
Using a verbless clause	**8**	What an idiot!
	9	Amazing! Rubbish!
Using a nominal group	**10**	The trouble I've had with Jamie!

Interrogative exclamations, unlike basic exclamatives, call for agreement or disagreement from the hearer: A. *Isn't it a lovely day!* B. *Yes, it is.*

Such, so and other intensifying items such as *terribly* also confer exclamative force on a declarative:

He's such a bore!   It's so tiring!
It's terribly hot!   It was extraordinarily beautiful!

QUESTIONS, CLAUSE TYPES AND DISCOURSE FUNCTIONS

SUMMARY

Questions typically seek information from the hearer that the speaker does not know. Responding to different motivations are questions functioning as preliminaries, rhetorical questions and leading questions of various types. The latter include interrogatives that are biased according to the kind of answer the speaker expects, towards a neutral, positive or negative assumption. These are marked by non-assertive forms (*any*), assertive forms (*some*) and negative forms (*no, not any*), respectively. Positive assumptions allow for positive forms, with *some* even in negative questions. Other leading questions consist of tentative declaratives with conducive markers and appropriate intonation, sometimes called 'queclaratives'. Ellipted verbless clauses rely heavily for interpretation on intonation and their position in the exchange.

The most basic intention in asking questions is to get information that we believe the addressee knows. It is not the only one, however. We here refer to two others.

26.1 RHETORICAL QUESTIONS

Do you expect me to wait here all day?
What could I say?
Why bother?

Rhetorical questions are used to make a comment or an exclamation. A response is not expected.

26.2 QUESTIONS AS PRELIMINARIES

In interpersonal interaction the *yes/no* interrogative is sometimes used as a preliminary to something else. That is, the question is not so much seeking information as serving as a preliminary to an expansion of the speaker's topic **1** or a veiled request **2**:

1 A. Have you read this book?

    B. No, no.

    A. It's about a plane that crashes in the Andes and no-one comes to their rescue
       ...

2 A. Are you going to the hospital this morning?

    B. No.

    A. Well if you do it'll give us a chance to find out whether he's coming home
       today or tomorrow.   [BNC KP1 36–38]

This function of *yes/no* questions would appear to be the basis of advertisements which use this type of interrogative in their text in imitation of speech patterns. Using a problem–solution schema, the following ad poses a series of problems or worries as questions, which are answered by a diagnosis in a clause of another type:

> **Do you need coffee and colas to keep you going throughout the day?**
> **Do you feel run-down and stressed, and struggle to keep up with life's daily**
> **demands?**
> **Are you exhausted for several days after a hike or work-out at the gym?**
> **Is the "war on terrorism" making you feel worried, tired or depressed?**
> **You may be suffering from adrenalin disease.**
>
>   **(Smart Publications)**

26.3 *SOME, ANY* AND NEGATIVE FORMS IN BIASED QUESTIONS

The questions expressed by *yes/no* interrogatives are often biased according to the kind of answer the speaker expects, and are based on neutral, positive or negative assumptions.

    If the speaker has a neutral assumption about the answer, **non-assertive** forms (*any, anybody, ever, yet*, etc. (see 3.3)) will be added to a positive interrogative:

> Do you know *anyone* in Westminster?
> Is the bank open *yet*?

With a positive assumption, **assertive** forms (see 3.3) – *some, somebody, always, already, too*, etc. – are added to the positive interrogative:

> Do you know *someone in* Westminster?
> Is the bank open *already?*

Negative-interrogative *yes/no* questions are based on conflicting attitudes. The speaker had originally expected that the answer would be or should be positive, but new evidence suggests that it will be negative. This conflict produces a feeling of surprise, disbelief or disappointment. If the addressee is directly involved, the biased question can imply a reproach. In this type of question, nuclear **negative** forms (see 3.2) – *no, nobody, no-one, never*, etc. – can be added to a positive interrogative:

Is there *no* butter?	(There should be some butter, but it seems there isn't.)
Do you know *no-one* in Westminster?	(You ought to know someone, but it seems you don't.)

Alternatively, **non-assertive** forms can be added to a negative interrogative:

Isn't there *any* butter *anywhere*?
Don't you know *anyone* in Westminster?

Assertive forms can be added to a negative interrogative to reflect a positive bias despite an originally negative assumption:

Isn't there *some* butter *somewhere?*	(It seems there isn't, but I expect there is.)
Don't you know *someone* in Westminster?	(It appears that you don't, but I think you must know someone.)

With offers, it seems more polite in English to assume a positive outcome, namely that the offer will be accepted. For this reason, the *some* forms are normal in such cases:

Would you like *some* more coffee?	[BNC KPV 2948]
Do you want *something* – a soft drink – before you go?	[BNC KCA 952]

Negation by nuclear negative elements – as opposed to negation by the negative particle *not* – is explained in Chapter 1 (section 3.3), together with assertive and non-assertive items (see 3.4).

26.4 BIASED DECLARATIVES WITH ATTITUDINAL MARKERS

Speakers also use declaratives to seek confirmation of their assumptions in a tactful way. Most simply, the declarative is accompanied by appropriate intonation: *You are seeing her? You don't mind if I stay?* They are, in fact, leading questions and for this reason have been called **queclaratives**. Frequently, certain items function as **markers** to 'draw out' the desired information by reinforcing the speaker's assumption:

* epistemic verbs with 1st person subject (*I suppose, believe, guess, bet, assume*)
* hearsay verbs with 1st person subject (*I understand, I'm told, I hear*)
* adverbs used as inferential connectives (*so, then*)
* attitudinal adjuncts of assurance or assumption (*of course, no doubt*)
* attitudinal adjunct of challenge or assumption (*surely*)
* a displaced *wh-* element (*who, what, where*, etc. in final position)

Examples are:

I suppose you've heard the news?	(epistemic verb)
I understand you're leaving your job?	(hearsay verb)
I hear you've been offered a new post?	(hearsay verb)
She wasn't invited to the wedding, *then*?	(inferential connective)
So there's nothing we can do?	(inferential connective)
She knows all about it, *of course*?	(attitudinal adjunct)
But *surely* you can just defrost it in the microwave?	(attitudinal adjunct)
So you took the documents to *which Ministerial office?* And you left them *where*?	(displaced *wh*-element)

More indirectly still, speakers can hint that information should be provided by *You were about to say . . .?*

The position of the declarative in the conversational sequence and the reply that follows can also help us to see how these markers function. For instance, an interviewer in a chat show might press a participant to admit that she had left her husband and child, which she denies:

Interviewer:	So you've reported, basically, that you walked out?
Young woman:	No, I didn't walk out.

Ellipted *yes/no questions* (a type of verbless clause) are extremely common in spoken English. With these, it is even more important than usual to use appropriate intonation.

For example, if you are pouring coffee for someone, you might offer sugar and milk by saying simply *Sugar? Milk?* with a rising tone. A falling tone would be inferred as a statement, 'Here is the sugar, here is the milk', but wouldn't necessarily be interpreted as an offer.

DIRECTIVES: GETTING PEOPLE TO CARRY OUT ACTIONS

SUMMARY

1   The clearest way of trying to get someone to do something is by an imperative. Strong impositions that invoke power and status are not socially acceptable in English in many everyday situations, even when accompanied by *please*. Orders are usually avoided and are preferably made indirectly as requests by using other clause types. Question tags either soften or heighten the force of the directive; with imperatives, tags tend to sound familiar.

2   Modalisation is another resource for producing directives. With modalised declaratives the effect is usually stronger and more formal, while modalised interrogatives tend to sound more polite. In contexts of urgency (*Help! Stop!*) the imperative can be used, as in others in which the hearer's welfare is referred to (*Sleep well! Have fun!*).

3   Besides directing other people to do things, the speaker can commit him/herself to carrying out an act. Performative uses of *promise* and modal *will* with a declarative do precisely this. The particle *let's* is used to make suggestions for actions, usually to be carried out jointly with the addressee. It can also function, however, as a disguised order or request.

27.1   DIRECTIVES AND THE IMPERATIVE

Although the basic speech act associated with imperative clauses is commonly held to be that of expressing a command, the imperative is used more frequently in English for less mandatory purposes. It can imply attitudes and intentions that are not actually formulated in the clause, and which can only be interpreted through a knowledge of the background context and of the relationships that exist between the persons involved.

   In fact, the difference between commands and other directives such as requests, invitations and advice is, as we have already seen, not clear-cut. It depends on such factors as the relative authority of the speaker towards the addressee and whether the addressee is given the option of complying or not with the directive: in the case of a command there is no option, whereas with a request there is.

Other factors include which of the two interlocutors is judged to benefit from the fulfilment of the action: a piece of advice benefits the addressee, whereas a request benefits the speaker. Good wishes (*Get well soon!*) rarely refer to agentive acts (see 14.1) and so aren't directives.

Politeness is also a major factor. The more the action is likely to benefit the addressee, the more socially acceptable an imperative will be. Otherwise, an imperative is likely to sound curt or demanding in English.

Consider the following cost–benefit scale on which the imperative is kept constant. The utterances at the lower end of the scale sound more polite than those at the top, even though there are no specific markers of politeness present:

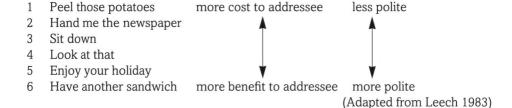

1   Peel those potatoes   more cost to addressee   less polite
2   Hand me the newspaper
3   Sit down
4   Look at that
5   Enjoy your holiday
6   Have another sandwich   more benefit to addressee   more polite
                                            (Adapted from Leech 1983)

Other factors override politeness, however, such as emergency (*Help!*) or attention-seeking in conversation *(Look, what I meant was . . .)*; the imperative can also be used when the speaker and hearer are carrying out a joint task (*Pass me the spanner*), when the hearer's interests are put first (*Don't worry! Cheer up! Take care!*), and even as a discourse initiator or topic introducer (*Guess who I saw this morning at the bank*).

The speech-act force of imperatives has, therefore, to be worked out by the addressee from the logical meaning of the sentence combined with the inferences made on the basis of context and the speaker–hearer relationship. Isolated examples can simply illustrate some typical interpretations:

Get out of here!	command
Keep off the grass.	prohibition
Please close the window!	request
Don't tell me you've passed your driving test!	disbelief
Do that again and you'll be sorry.	condition of threat
Pass your exams and we'll buy you a bike.	condition of promise
Don't forget your umbrella!	reminder
Mind the step!/ Be careful with that hot plate!	warning
Feel free to take as many leaflets as you like.	permission
Just listen to this!	showing interest/involvement
Try one of these!	offer
Let's go jogging!	suggestion
Come on now, don't cry!/ Go on, have a go!	encouragement
Sleep well! Have a safe journey!	good wishes
Suppose he doesn't answer.	considering a possible happening

Think nothing of it.	rejecting thanks
[Some people make easy profit.] *Take* drug handlers.	illustrative example of a claim

27.2 THE DISCOURSE FUNCTION OF *LET'S* IMPERATIVES

Imperatives (especially with *let's*) can fulfil a textual function in regulating the conversational flow, in many cases to the advantage of the more powerful speaker:

Let's get started	a call to attention
Let's start by . . .	management of the topic
Let's see/let me see	hesitation marker, to avoid silence and keep the floor
Let's just stick to the main concern	disallowing an interruption/topic management
More people read magazines than, *let's say*, historical treatises.	giving a possible example

27.3 POLITENESS IN DIRECTIVES

After an imperative, a modal tag acts as an intensifier, either softening or heightening the insistence of the directive. *Will you*? and *could you*? convey a high degree of optionality while *can't you*? questions the hearer's apparent inability to do something, conveying impatience and low optionality. The more optional the act appears to be, the more polite is the request.

Intonation and the words used can make even *will you* less polite, however; *Shut up* and *Drop dead* don't become polite by adding *will you*. Rising intonation is typically polite and persuasive, failing intonation more insistent.

Check this for me, will you?	polite, anticipates willingness
Sign this for me, would you?	polite, anticipates willingness
Keep this for me, can you?	familiar, anticipates willingness
Hold this for me, could you?	less familiar, anticipates willingness
Keep quiet, can't you?	insistent, anticipates unwillingness

These examples are characteristic of contexts of familiarity. With the exception of *can't*, they question and anticipate the addressee's willingness to carry out the action, and are polite but familiar, expressing solidarity. The negative imperative tag *will you?* is also familiar as in *Don't be late, will you?*, while the invariable tag *mind* is more insistent: *Don't be late, mind!*

Where there is no relationship of closeness between the speakers, these forms may sound over-familiar. In such cases most modalised interrogatives are safer without tags.

27.4 MODALISED INTERROGATIVES AS POLITE DIRECTIVES

The directive force is overlaid onto the interrogative. Such directives are more polite precisely because as interrogatives they appear to give the addressee the option of refusing, as in the following examples:

1 Can you close the door?
2 Will you close the door?
3 Could you close the door?
4 Would you close the door?
5 Won't you close the door?
6 Can't you close the door?
7 Must you leave the door open?
8 Do you mind closing the door?

The modals in **3** and **4** *Could you?* and *Would you?* are most polite because by the use of oblique ('past') forms they create conceptual distance between themselves and the speech act. Furthermore, distance correlates with less social involvement. The speaker conveys the impression that closing the door is of no great personal benefit; this gives the hearer a wider margin for possible refusal. As in the imperative tag, *can't* **6** is not polite as a request. *Won't* **5** is not polite either, as it appears to question the hearer's unwillingness to carry out the rather trivial act of closing the door. Such unwillingness to carry out simple actions that obviously need doing also violates cultural conventions of cooperation. By contrast, *won't you?* as an offer or invitation (*make yourself at home, won't you*) is polite because it expresses warmth and generosity, and presumes that the act benefits the addressee. *Must* **7** is ironical, implying that the hearer has an insurmountable urge to leave the door open.

Responding to directives

Requests are sometimes responded to by a standard phrase: A. *Do you mind closing the door?* B. *Not at all/Certainly/Sure*. Of these, *not at all* responds to the sentence meaning of *Do you mind?*, whereas *certainly* and *sure* clearly respond to the pragmatic meaning of 'request' rather than to the sentence meaning, since they are not to be taken as *certainly/sure I mind closing the door*. Offers can be accepted by *Yes, please* or *Thanks*, and refused by *No, thanks*. *Thank you* alone is not interpreted as a refusal in English. Suggestions are responded to in many different ways such as *okay, I might, it's an idea*.

27.5 DECLARATIVES AS DIRECTIVES

A declarative which contains a modal auxiliary (e.g. *can, shall, will, may, might, must, ought, should*) and refers to an action to be carried out by the addressee can be used with the force of a directive. They are usually quite strong, invoking authority:

You *will* report to Head Office tomorrow.   (command)
Dogs *must* be kept on a lead.   (strong obligation)

You *may/can* leave now. (permission)
Surely you can take your own decisions! (exclamative-directive)

A 1st person declarative with a modal can have the effect of committing the speaker to a course of action:

I'*ll* meet you at the entrance at about nine.
I *must* rush off now to my aerobics class.

Note that the modals also express meanings of prediction (*will, shall*), logical necessity (*must*), possibility (*may, might*) and reasonable inference (*should, ought*) – see 44.3. These meanings are almost always clearly distinguishable from the directive meanings, as in:

There *will* be time for a few questions. (prediction)
It *must* be almost half-past nine. (logical necessity/deduction)

27.6 INDIRECTNESS, IMPOLITENESS AND CONFRONTATION

Indirectness is part of everyday interaction in spoken English. It is important to learn to handle and interpret the conventional politeness forms and the force each carries, as these serve to construct and negotiate meanings and actions which lead to a satisfactory outcome for both or all the participants.

This does not mean that speakers are invariably polite to each other. Far from it. Mutual insults among some communities represent a form of solidarity. In many other contexts, competitiveness or a desire to score off the adversary lead quickly to confrontational attitudes and acrimonious exchanges. Indirectness and implicit meanings are common in such cases also, as is illustrated in the following extract from Ian Rankin's novel *Set in Darkness*.

Detective Inspector Linford is sitting in his BMW in the only spare bay belonging to a large office block in Edinburgh. Another car approaches and stops, its driver sounding the horn and gesturing:

'That's my space you're in, so *if you wouldn't mind.......?*'.[1]
Linford looked around. '*I don't see any signs.*'[2]
    '*This is staff parking.*'[3] A glance at a wristwatch. '*And I'm late for a meeting.*'[4]
Linford looked towards where another driver was getting into his car. '*Space there for you.*'[5]
    '*You deaf or what?*'[6] Angry face, jaw jutting and tensed. A man looking for a fight.
    Linford was just about ready. '*So you'd rather argue with me than get to your meeting?*'[7] He looked towards where another car was leaving. '*Nice spot over there.*'[8]

> 'That's Harley. He takes his lunch hour at the gym. I'll be in the meeting when he gets back, and that's his space.'[9] 'Which is why you move your junk heap.'[10]
>
> 'This from a man who drives a Sierra Cosworth.'[11]
>
> 'Wrong answer.'[12] The man yanked Linford's door open.
>
> 'The assault charge is going to look bloody good on your CV.'[13]
>
> 'You'll have fun trying to make a complaint through broken teeth.'[14]
>
> 'And you'll be in the cells for assaulting a police officer.'[15]
>
> The man stopped, his jaw retreating a fraction. His Adam's apple was prominent when he swallowed. Linford took the opportunity to reach into his jacket, showing his warrant card.
>
> 'So now you know who I am.'[16] Linford said, 'But I didn't catch your name . . .?'[17]
>
> 'Look. I'm sorry.'[18] The man had turned from fire to sun, his grin trying for embarrassed apology. 'I didn't mean to . . .'[19] (see exercise)

You will see that the numbered sentences of the fictional dialogue are either declaratives or interrogatives, although some of the clauses are verbless. Notice how the two speakers overlay the basic force of question and assertion with other more implicit forces such as **explanation, reason, warning, threat, apology, challenge, provocation, suggestion, excuse**. It is these indirect meanings that are inferred and which interest us here.

Linguists have long debated on how we successfully interpret such indirect speech acts and how we distinguish between different degrees of politeness. One cognitive explanation is that such meanings are represented in the form of 'illocutionary scenarios', that is, organised structures of our generic knowledge. Such scenarios are abstracted in our minds from a number of stereotyped situations in everyday life within a particular culture. For English, though not necessarily for other languages, the indirect way of making a request is, as we have seen, to question the addressee's capability (*can you?*) or willingness (*will you?*) to carry out the act. As capability and willingness are necessary conditions for doing the act, such questionings **stand for** the whole speech act of requesting, by a process of metonymy – the part standing for the whole. In activating a scenario for strong directives, however, the cost-benefit and power factors have also to be taken into account.

27.7 CLAUSE TYPES AND ILLOCUTIONARY FORCE: SUMMARY TABLE

This table illustrates some of the more conventional correspondences between mood types and their illocutionary force. Many speech acts can also be expressed by units both larger and smaller than the clauses, as well as by non-linguistic means such as gestures.

Clause type	Illocutionary force	Example

DECLARATIVE	Statement
	Explicit performative
	Hedged performative
	Biased question
	Question (displaced *wh-*)
	
	Exclamation
	
	Directives:
	
	    order
	    request
	
	    prelude to request
	    advice
	    warning
	    offer
		We are ready to go.
		I beg you to reconsider your decision.
		We wish to thank you for all your help.
		So you went out with her?
		You took the documents to which
		    ministry?
		It was so hot!
		
		Papers are to be in by April 15.
		I wonder if you would lend me your car.
		I suppose you haven't got any change
		    on you.
		I'm terribly sorry but, could you . . .?
		I'd sell if I were you.
		That plate's hot!
		You must try one of these.

EXCLAMATIVE	exclamation	What an angel you've been!

INTERROGATIVE	question
	rhetorical question
	    rebuke
	exclamation
	    rebuke
	
	Directives:
	
	    order
	    request
	    suggestion/advice
	    offer/invitation
		Who is that man over there?
		Who will believe that story.
		    How could you be so careless?
		Isn't it wonderful!
		    How dare you speak to her like that!
		
		Will you please be quiet!
		Could you lend me a pen . . .?
		Why don't you see a doctor?
		Won't you sit down?

IMPERATIVE:	Directives:
	
	    order
	    request
	    offer
	    warning
	    instructions
	    disbelief
		
		Shut up!
		Save some for me!
		Have a drink!
		Mind your head!
		Twist off.
		Don't tell me you've passed!

27.7.1 Clause combinations

Combinations of clauses can be used in English to express a polite request. The greater the imposition on the hearer, the longer the combination is likely to be, and it may be preceded by an apology:

I'm terribly sorry to bother you. I wonder if you could possibly write me a testimonial. If it's not too inconvenient, perhaps you could let me have it back by tomorrow.

Clauses without subject or finite verb

How about a swim?   *Wh*-questions as suggestion
Why not start again?
Why all this fuss?   verbless *Why*-questions as inquiry
What to do in case of fire   *Wh-to*-inf. clauses as directive headings
How to boost your self-esteem

Subordinate clauses

To think what we might have missed!   *to*-infinitive clauses as exclamations
Not to worry!   or as friendly advice
If only I had taken his advice!   *if only* clauses, indicating regret
What if we all go for a swim?   *Wh-if*-clauses as suggestions

Groups and words with speech act force

Straight ahead!
Down with war!
Careful!
Silence!
Scalpel!

FURTHER READING

For clause types, distribution and conversational grammar: Biber et al. (1999). The mood element and interpersonal interaction, Halliday (1994). Direct and indirect speech acts, Searle (1975), Thomas (1996), Grundy (1995). Performative(ness), Austin (1962), Thomas (1995). Politeness and the cost-benefit scale, Leech (1983), Brown and Levinson (1987). Queclaratives, Geluykens (1987), Downing (2005); *Surely* as a stance marker, Downing (2001); 'I think', Thompson (2002), Kärkkäinen (2003); Cooperativeness and inferencing, Grice (1975). Types and functions of questions, Taylor (1989), Weber (1993). Intonation in ellipted questions, Gumperz (1982). Discourse functions of the imperative, De Clerck (2002). Metonymy, Panther and Thornburg (1998), Pérez Hernández and Ruiz de Mendoza (2002).

EXERCISES ON CHAPTER 5

Interaction between speaker and hearer

Module 22

†The following text is an email advertisement for computer software. It has no punctuation. Mark the clause boundaries by punctuation and identify the clause types, giving reasons for your analysis. Now suggest what type of speech acts are being performed.

In business and personal life
Paper is the communication medium & storage device
Documents fill the space
Communication takes time
Corrections are inevitable
Clarifications are unavoidable
Inaccuracy costs money
Mistakes cause losses and lost opportunites
Efforts may be fruitless
Results may be unattained

Technology rises to the occasion
The software solution is available
For your daily private and business use
[EDIFACT Prime takes you beyond the edge]
Breakthroughs are your tools
Perfection and harmony is your lifestyle
Exchange the routine for simplicity and speed

Module 23

1 †In the following extract from a news item by Jeremy O'Grady in *The Week*, identify at least one occurrence of each of the following: a positive declarative, a declarative with a word ending in *-ever*, a *wh*-interrogative, a declarative with a modal operator, an exclamative, an imperative. What element goes with the interrogative and what is its function? Do you think these clause types show their usual speech act correspondences?

> I'm all in favour of the free market in theory,[1] but what a disappointment it often proves to be in practice.[2] Take plumbers.[3] In economic theory, London should be awash with them, the demand for their services being so high and the costs of entry to their trade so relatively low.[4] So where the hell are they when you want one?[5] Or take the principle of consumer service.[6] In theory you'd expect the market to acknowledge that 'the consumer always knows best'.[7] In practice, whenever one complains about shoddy service, one is dismissed as an idiot.[8]

2 †Underline the Subject and Finite elements in each of the following clauses. Then (a) make the declarative clauses negative; (b) convert the negative declaratives into *yes/no* negative interrogatives (main clause only); (c) underline the Subject and new Finite elements:

(1) I am going to be the last one to hear about it.
(2) Nadine's mum bought enough blue denim to make two skirts.
(3) He tells everyone his life history every time he meets them.
(4) Sheila knew where the keys were all the time.
(5) Bill took on a great deal of responsibility in his previous job.

3 †Imagine you are helping at an optician's. Below are the replies to a questionnaire, but the questions are missing. You have to provide them. 1, 2, 3, 6, 8 and 10 are *wh*-questions; 4, 5, 7 and 9 are *yes/ no* questions

(1) My name is Pat O'Connor.
(2) My address is 31 St Gerard's Avenue, Birmingham.
(3) I was born in Ireland in 1980.
(4) Yes, I am using eye drops.
(5) No, my eyes don't smart.
(6) Not often. I take just aspirin occasionally.
(7) No, I don't. I wear contact lenses.
(8) I've been wearing them for a year.
(9) Yes, I'm allergic to certain things – pollens, for example.
(10) I started to have visual problems two days ago.

4 †If both abbreviated clauses and tags are based structurally on Subject-Finite variation, in what way do they differ? Look again at the dialogue on page 183 and identify the instance(s) of each. For greater clarity replace B[3]'s *Mm* by an abbreviated clause. Clue: Consider subject-operator alternation and the position of the utterances in the exchange.

5 †Read this extract of a fictional dialogue between Nadine and Ellie and then answer the questions:

N.	Why have you gone pink, Ellie?	[1]
E.	Oh God, I haven't, have I?	[2]
N.	Shocking pink. What is it?	[3]
E.	Nothing.	[4]
		(Girls Out Late)

(a) What kind of interrogatives does Nadine use in speaking to Ellie in 1 and 3?
(b) What does Nadine want to know?
(c) Does she get this information in reply in 2 and 4?
(d) What kinds of units does Ellie use in reply in 2 and 4?

6 †Provide abbreviated clauses as (a) confirming and (b) disconfirming responses to each of the following questions:

    (1)   It doesn't seem to matter who you are.
    (2)   You have two children, haven't you, Charles?
    (3)   Will you be going to the concert this evening?
    (4)   Let's find a seat.

7 †Add (a) a reversed polarity tag to each of the following clauses, when possible; (b) a constant polarity tag when possible:

    (1)   This wallet is yours.
    (2)   You've got a new bicycle.
    (3)   Susie likes doing crossword puzzles.
    (4)   Don't be late.
    (5)   Be careful!
    (6)   Your father used to work for the City Council.
    (7)   Some of these shops overcharge terribly.
    (8)   So he fell on his hand and broke it.

8 Discussion: What functions do tags fulfil in interpersonal interaction?

9 Practise saying the tags in the following examples: (a) with rising intonation, and (b) with falling intonation. In your reading aloud, you should aim to get in (a) the meaning of 'Am I right?' and in (b) 'Please confirm this'.

    (1)   He approved of the plan, didn't he?
    (2)   He didn't approve of the plan, did he?
    (3)   We'll have enough money, won't we?
    (4)   We won't have enough money, will we?

Module 24

1 †Decide whether the italicised item is a subject, a vocative or either. Give reasons.

    (1)   Keep still, *Edward*, there's a good boy.
    (2)   *Somebody* pass me the insect repellent, quick! Thank you, *dear*. Now *you* take some.
    (3)   *Everybody* lift at the same time! Right, up she goes, *everybody!*
    (4)   Do shut up, *Helen*, you're making a fool of yourself.
    (5)   *You all* wait here, that will be best. I'll be back in a moment.
    (6)   *You* just leave him alone, do you hear?

2 †The following extracts are from Al Gore's concession speech at the conclusion of the 2000 US presidential campaign, after he had lost the election. For each extract, say whether *let* is (a) a 2nd person imperative of the verb *let* (=*allow*), (b) the pragmatic particle *let* introducing a wish (the optative), or (c) the same particle in its function of suggesting an action to be carried out by speaker and addressee (a 1st person plural imperative). Say which type is not represented and suggest a reason for its absence:

(1)   Let there be no doubt, while I strongly disagree with the court's decision, I accept it.
(2)   Let me say how grateful I am to all those who've supported me.
(3)   And I say to our fellow members of the world community: Let no-one see this contest as a sign of American weakness.

Module 25

1   †Say which of the verbs in the following clauses perform the act they name and which don't:

(1)   I *admit* I was to blame.
(2)   I *appeal* to you as an honorary Roman to nip over here in your Popemobile and put an end to this wanton destruction.   [BNC CA6 5953]
(3)   I *demand* to be paid for the hours I put in, whether your cousin passes her exams or not.   [BNC JXT 454]
(4)   Neil and I *argue* about football all the time.   [BNC CA6 5953]
(5)   I'll *say* goodnight and I *apologise* for disturbing you so late.   [BNC HWP 3355]
(6)   No really I *insist*. Please, after you!   [BNC HNS 113]
(7)   The bed in the room next to you is perfectly adequate for me, I *promise*.
                                                                        [BNC JYC 454]
(8)   Much as I love the works of J.R.R. Tolkien, I *refuse* to call any dog Bilbo Baggins, so Bill he has become.   [BNC EWB 372]
(9)   I *bet* you didn't sit on the sofa with him holding hands   [BNC BMS 3669]
(10) Referring to an elusive particle that is crucial to standard theories of physics, Stephen Hawking is said to have placed a wager with Professor Gordon Kane, saying, 'I'll *bet* you $100 it has not been discovered'.

Module 26

1   †Identify the clause type and suggest the possible **force** each utterance has:

(1)   Is there any coffee?
(2)   Coffee?
(3)   Could you tell me the way to the nearest Tube station, please?
(4)   What could I say?
(5)   She didn't leave a message, then?
(6)   Wasn't it exciting!
(7)   Where would we be without tin openers?
(8)   Are you going to the Post Office? Yes. Then could you get me some stamps?
(9)   He is aware of the risk, of course?
(10) So it wasn't you who rang just now? No. I wonder who it was.

2 †(a) Provide whichever biasing element seems most suitable in the following questions (that is, neutral, positive or negative, realised by *any, some, not . . . any/no* or their compounds, respectively). (b) Answer the questions, using a suitable orientational element.

(1) Have you . . . copies of The Times and the Guardian?
(2) Could you get me . . . orange juice, please?
(3) So there isn't . . . we can do? (3b) So there is . . . we can do?
(4) Did you meet . . . interesting at the party?
(5) Do you know . . . nice to stay for a quiet holiday near the coast?
(6) Would you like . . . more cake?

Module 27

1 Provide a context for the following indirect speech acts. For instance No. 1 could be a father speaking to a son or daughter. If the correspondence were direct, the question would be asking for information, expecting an answer such as 'No, I won't'. This is clearly not the case. The correspondence is indirect, equivalent to 'Don't leave your bicycle outside in the rain!' That is, a directive.

(1) Will you never learn not to leave your bicycle outside in the rain?
(2) How many times do I have to tell you not to eat crisps on the sofa!
(3) Surely you could try to drive more slowly.

2 †If someone says to you 'Have you change of a pound?' and you say 'Yes' without bringing out the change, you are reacting to the structural meaning of the interrogative, but not to the pragmatic meaning, the force of 'request'. Such a response can be uncooperative or impolite. Suggest (i) an uncooperative and (ii) a cooperative response for the following utterances:

(a) Would you mind signing this petition in favour of genetically modified crops?
(b) Do you know the way to the Victoria and Albert Museum?

However, the power factor may skew the reply. The following exchange occurred in a film:

Lord Longhorn to his butler: Do you mind taking this book back to the library? (*handing over the book*)
Butler: Yes sir (*taking book and leaving*).

(c) What is the butler responding to? Is it polite? Why does he say yes rather than no?
(d) And what would the butler say if he were responding to the structural meaning of 'Do you mind . . .?'

3 Discussion

If the unmarked illocutionary force of the imperative is that of a directive, why is the imperative mood so often replaced by another mood structure in interpersonal interaction in English? In what circumstances and with what kinds of speech act is the imperative socially acceptable?

4   †(a) Suggest what illocutionary force would conventionally be assigned to each of these utterances. Final punctuation is omitted. (b) Identify the clause type of each, specifying those which are performatives.

(1)   I order you not to smoke in the dining-room.
(2)   Do not smoke in the dining-room.
(3)   Members will refrain from smoking in the dining-room.
(4)   No smoking in the dining-room.
(5)   Smoking is not allowed in the dining-room.
(6)   Would you mind not smoking in the dining-room?
(7)   Members are requested not to smoke in the dining-room.
(8)   Thank you for not smoking in the dining-room.

5   †The background of the following dialogue is a psychiatric hospital, where Jean and Edward have brought their daughter. For each numbered stretch of the text, identify the clause type (including ellipted ones). Discuss the possible force of each:

clause type	act	
(1) _____	_____	Nurse: Who sent you in here?[1]
(2) _____	_____	Edward: The porter at reception.[2]
(3) _____	_____	Jean: We've been waiting nearly half an hour.[3]
(4) _____	_____	Nurse: I'm sorry.[4]
(5) _____	_____	We're very understaffed today.[5]
(6) _____	_____	It's the bank holiday.[6]
(7) _____	_____	Edward. Yes.[7]
(8) _____	_____	Nurse: He should have sent you straight to Admissions.[8]
(9) _____	_____	If you'll just come this way.[9]

(Olwen Wymark, *Find Me*, in *Plays by Women*, vol. 2)

6   †Directives: Suggest a specific directive force for each of the following questions:

(1)   Must you make so much noise?
(2)   Can you pass me that hammer?

(3) Would you mind signing here?
(4) Will you have some more icecream?
(5) Why don't you help yourself?
(6) Why don't you apply for that job?

7 In pairs, take turns to carry out a series of directives, with the aim of getting your hearer to do something, first by means of a direct directive, and then by means of an indirect directive. Notice how your hearer reacts in each case. Remember that the greater the imposition on the hearer and the greater the social distance which separates speaker and hearer, the more polite, i.e. indirect, the speaker will have to be. But remember too that people are not always polite, especially if they get angry.

(1) You need a testimonial from your tutor in order to apply for a grant at a foreign university. The letter must reach the university in no more than a fortnight.
(2) Someone has repeatedly been scrawling graffiti on the wall of your house. One day you unexpectedly catch him/her in the act. You decide to complain.
(3) You are at the annual staff party and inadvertently spill black coffee onto the General Manager's clothes. You have to apologise.

8 †Turn to the extract from Ian Rankin on pages 209–10 and suggest the force conveyed or inferred by each numbered sentence. Bear in mind such forces as **explanation, reason, threat, apology, challenge, provocation, insult, suggestion, excuse**. Now consider the following questions:

(1) How many different speech acts have you identified in the dialogue of this text?
(2) List them, giving the identification number.
(3) Which types of speech act occur most frequently?
(4) Which speech acts are expressed by the man, and which by Linford?
(5) From this analysis, what inferences do you draw about the attitudes of the man and Linford and of how the encounter develops?

ORGANISING THE MESSAGE   *CHAPTER 6*

Thematic and information structures of the clause

THEME: THE POINT OF DEPARTURE OF THE MESSAGE

SUMMARY

1   Theme is an element of the thematic structure of a clause, of which the other element is Rheme. It is therefore a different category from the syntactic Subject and from the discourse category of Topic – what the message is about – although these three often coincide in one wording.

2   It is convenient to think of Topics as organised hierarchically according to their level of operation: a global topic is what the whole text or discourse is about, an episode topic represents what a shorter, but integrated, stretch of talk or writing is about. Local topics are the main referents that persist throughout a stretch of text by means of anaphora, establishing a participant frame or referent chain. They are the topics most clearly related to grammatical categories. English makes use of certain devices to introduce new referents, potential topics, into the discourse and to maintain topic continuity.

3   Theme is identified as the first clause constituent and communicatively is the point of departure of the message. When Theme conflates with Topic and Subject it can be called topical Theme. When Theme is realised by a temporal or spatial Adjunct it is a circumstantial Theme, which sets up a time-space frame within which the participant chain develops. More marked Themes such as fronted Complement and Object have a local textual function, such as initiating a change of direction by means of contrast. Relating Theme to grammar, Theme is unmarked when it coincides with the expected element, such as Subject in a declarative clause. When some other element is brought to initial position it is a marked Theme, and carries some additional significance in the discourse. Objects, Complements and Adjuncts can be thematised or fronted. Whole clauses can be thematised in complex sentences.

4   Other items which tend to be placed at the beginning of the clause may be considered to be part of the Theme. These include connective Adjuncts such as *however*, stance Adjuncts such as *personally*, vocatives (*Doctor!*) and discourse markers such as *Well*. In this way we can talk of 'multiple Themes'. They are not, however, topics. A subordinate clause in initial position may be considered as Theme of a clause complex.

Our attention in the two previous chapters has centred on two kinds of meaning: **experiential meaning**, which is encoded in the grammar in terms of participants, processes and circumstances, and **interpersonal meaning**, as encoded by the mood structures. We now turn to a third type of meaning, which helps us to organise and relate individual sentences and utterances within our discourse. This is **textual meaning**. We will be considering three important dimensions of textual meaning which have a place in English grammar and contribute to discourse coherence: first, the **Theme–Rheme** textual structure and its relation to **Topic**; second, the **order of constituents** in the clause and how the normal order may be altered to achieve different textual effects; and third, the **distribution and focus of information**, which makes an essential contribution to coherence and understandability in spoken and written English.

INTRODUCTION

To start, consider the following versions of the same piece of information about a coach tour:

1   We'll reach Toledo, but not Seville, before noon
2   Before noon we'll reach Toledo but not Seville.
3   Toledo, but not Seville, we'll reach before noon.

All three utterances have the same **experiential** meaning: the content is the same. All three would normally be used to make a statement, and so they are **interpersonally** equivalent too. The difference between **1**, **2** and **3** lies in the **textual** component of meaning: the information is the same, but the message is arranged or 'packaged' in different ways, and the different forms highlight different aspects of the message. More specifically, the element which occupies first position in the clause is different in the three examples: in **1** it is *we*, in **2** it is *before noon* and in **3** it is *Toledo*. This element is the Theme of the clause. Since first position is salient, what to put in it is an important choice, particularly in connected discourse.

28.1 THEME AND RHEME

Theme and Rheme are the two components which together make up the organisational construct that is the thematic structure of the clause. The Theme comes first and is identified as the first constituent in the clause. What follows is the Rheme.

Looking at the clause as a unit of communication, we can say that Theme is the clause constituent which, whatever its syntactic function, is selected to be the point of departure of the clause as message. What goes in initial position is important for both speaker and hearer. It represents the angle from which the message is projected and sets up a frame which holds at least to the end of the clause. For the speaker, the communicative choice associated with Theme is 'What notion shall I take as my starting-point in this clause? Shall I start by saying where we are going? Or shall I start with the 'time-frame' – *before noon*? Or with the places we'll visit?' From whichever point of departure we choose, the rest of the clause must proceed. For the hearer or reader Theme acts as a signal, creating expectations and laying the foundation for the hearer's mental representation of how the message will unfold. Given these cognitive and communicative functions, it is not surprising that the element in initial position is so important.

While the Theme lays the basis of the message, the Rheme says something in relation to it. Typically, important new information is presented in the Rheme. Let's diagram this thematic structure on to our previous examples:

	Theme	Rheme
1	We	'll reach Toledo, but not Seville, before noon.
2	Before noon	we'll reach Toledo but not Seville.
3	Toledo, but not Seville	we'll reach before noon.

28.2 UNMARKED THEME AND MARKED THEME IN DECLARATIVE CLAUSES

In selecting Theme, speakers must choose between a neutral order of clause constituents or a marked order. The order of clause elements in **1** has the Subject as Theme. This is the neutral, **unmarked** choice in a declarative clause, used when there is no good reason to depart from the usual. Any other constituent but the Subject will be **marked**, and signals an additional meaning. In the case of **2** the Theme is a circumstance of time, syntactically an Adjunct, and is marked. However, it does not strike us as very unusual. This is because adjuncts of time can occupy several positions in the clause. Theme **3** is an Object participant whose normal position is after the verb. Objects are not so mobile and sound highly marked in English when brought to initial position. Marked constituent orders always signal some additional meaning and have to be motivated. Thematised Objects tend to express a contrast with something said or expected by the hearer. By specifying *Toledo but not Seville* as the Object, the speaker refers explicitly to a contrary expectation and justifies the thematised element. We will return shortly to the most frequent types of marked Theme. For the moment, you can 'feel' that certain elements sound more striking than others when in initial position.

From these considerations, it is clear that the Theme of a clause represents a choice, both as the absolute point of departure of a discourse and also that of each subsequent clause and of each paragraph. It gives us the choice of taking as point of departure one or other participant in the situation described, or something else, such as a circumstance. It can serve to link up with what has gone before in the discourse and it helps to push the message forward. Because sentences do not normally occur in isolation, and previous sentences and utterances condition later ones, not all thematic choices will be equally appropriate from the point of view of creating a coherent whole.

28.3 THEME IN NON-DECLARATIVE CLAUSES

All the examples seen so far are of declarative clauses. In these the unmarked Theme is Subject. Non-declarative clauses, that is, interrogatives and imperatives, have unmarked Themes derived from their respective clause type, as illustrated in the examples below.

In examples, **4** to **7**, the starting-point of the clause is the expected one, which announces the clause-type. Theme is marked when any other but the expected one is placed in initial position, as in examples **8** to **10**. Marked Themes in non-declarative clauses are relatively uncommon.

Unmarked Themes

4	*Are we* going to Toledo?	Operator + subject in *yes/no* interrogative
5	*When* will we get there?	*Wh*-word in *wh*-interrogative
6	*Have* your tickets ready!	Base form of verb in 2nd person (imperative)
7	*Let's* go for a swim instead.	*Let's* in 1st person (imperative)

Marked Themes

8	*We* are going where?	Non *wh*-subject in a *wh*-interrogative
9	*Do* hurry up, all of you!	Emphatic *do* in an imperative
10	*You* keep quiet!	Subject in an imperative

In *yes/no* interrogatives in English, unmarked Theme is the Finite operator (see 3.1), together with the Subject, as in **4**. In *wh*-interrogatives, the Theme is the *wh*-word as in **5**. In 2nd person imperative clauses, unmarked Theme is the verb, as in **6**, and *let's* in first person imperatives, as in **7**. Any other order is marked. When the *wh*-element is displaced, as in **8**, the element that remains as Theme (*we*) is marked for a *wh*-interrogative. Emphatic *do*, as in **9**, and the Subject *you*, as in **10**, are marked Themes in the imperative.

28.4 TOPIC, THEME AND SUBJECT

Topic is a discourse category which corresponds to 'what the text, or part of the text, is about'. A whole book, chapter, essay or lecture can have a topic, for instance, 'car maintenance' or 'the English novel in the 20th century'. A topic which coherently organises a whole piece of language can be called a **global topic**. (More exactly, of course, it is speakers and writers who have topics and do the organising of the text.) On an intermediate level, **paragraphs** or sections in writing and '**episodes**' in talk each have their own topics. In writing, these will typically be organised under the 'umbrella' of the global topic, but they display an internal coherence of their own. Finally, utterances and sentences have topics which contribute to the episode and help to build up the discourse as a whole. We call these **local topics**.

All three levels of topic are integrated in normal texts and discourses. Local topics are usually the only ones that have a direct grammatical realisation. They are associated with the main referential entities represented in speakers' sentences and utterances, which to be coherent will have to relate in some way to the higher levels of topicality of the discourse as a whole. Sentence and utterance topics are the most relevant to the study of grammar, because this is one area in which discourse interfaces with a 'pragmatic grammar'. In a functional grammar of English, we are interested in seeing how the category of mainly local topic interacts with Subject and with Theme.

28.5 COGNITIVE FEATURES OF THE TOPIC

A number of cognitive features have been associated with major topic entities. First, the topic entity is inherent to the event described and it initiates the action.

Second, the topic entity is typically high on what is called the **empathy hierarchy**. This has to do with what attracts our empathy. It starts from the speaker, since we all empathise most with ourselves, and continues as follows:

Speaker > hearer > human > animal > physical object > abstract entity

After the speaker, the hearer – as co-participant in a conversation – can be important, and is included with the speaker in the inclusive use of 'we', as in **1**. But in many discourses a 3rd-person topic is even more common, in that we frequently talk and write about people, creatures and things distinct from the speaker and hearer. Abstract entities come last in the empathy hierarchy.

A third feature is definiteness. This is a subjective factor since it depends on whether speakers and hearers have established empathy with the topic. When contact has been established, the topic is easily accessible and is definite.

Fourth, the topic is the most salient participant on the scene of discourse.

From the point of view of cognitive salience, all these features are closely associated with the Subject function in English. The prototypical Subject referent is inherent to the event described in the clause; it fulfils the semantic function of Agent, if there is an Agent, and initiates the action. It is typically human and definite and is the main participant at any one point on the scene of discourse as represented in a particular clause or utterance. Subject and Topic are therefore closely related in English. (It must be pointed out that this does not imply that all Subjects have these characteristics.)

These features are not, however, necessarily associated with Theme. Theme and Topic are quite different types of category. Topics are what a text, section or clause is **about**, and Topic is always conceptualised as an entity or a nominalisation (Module 21). Theme, on the other hand, is what the speaker or writer chooses as the point of departure for the message in any one clause or sentence. It may be an entity, a circumstance or an attribute. Only entities initiate referential chains. Let's look now at the main types of themes, starting from the most central.

28.6 TOPIC AND SUBJECT AS THEME

Themes which conflate with Subject are participants in the transitivity structures and typically refer to persons, creatures and things. As such, they are the most likely candidates to fulfil the discourse role of Topic or 'topical Theme' at clause level. They are typically presented by the speaker as identifiable or at least accessible to the hearer and are usually encoded by full nominal groups or proper names when introduced for the first time. Important Theme-Topic-Subject referents set up **referent chains** which can transcend clausal boundaries, maintaining **topic continuity** as long as the speaker or writer wishes. This is an important test for 'aboutness'. Many referents enter the discourse, but only a few are selected to be major topics.

We can track the referent chain, which can also be seen as an **identity chain**, of a major referent as it is repeated across several clauses by an anaphoric pronoun, by an alternative NG or by repetition of the name or proper noun. Such is the case in the extract about the American artist Andy Warhol from a leaflet at the Tate Modern in London. Andy Warhol is one of the painters whose pictures figure in the exhibition. Visitors are establishing contact with him through his pictures and through the following description:

> *Andy Warhol* (1962), called the 'Pope of Pop', cleverly fashioned his use of popular culture into a highly distinctive style. Working from his New York studio, called The Factory, he adopted mechanical processes of reproduction like stencilling and silkscreen printing to produce serial images taken from the media, as in *Twenty-Five Coloured Marilyns* (1962). *Warhol* wanted to dissolve the distinctions between 'high art', the kind you go to a museum to see, and 'low art', the kind used in advertisements. Yet he was capable of many shades of irony, and [*zero anaphor*] produced some of the icons of American art, including *Ambulance Disaster*.

The 'referent chain' of this paragraph can be shown graphically as follows: *Andy Warhol* (Subject, proper name) – *he* (Subject pron.) – *Warhol* (Subject, surname) – *he* (Subject pron.) – zero (anaphora in which the subject pronoun is omitted in coordinated clauses).

Indefinite, and therefore unidentified, but specific referents as Subject Themes are also found in English, however. We might start up a conversation by saying *A man I met in Beirut once told me a good story*. At this point in the discourse we haven't established contact with either the man or the story, and for this reason both are presented as indefinite. Similarly, news items in the press often present an indefinite (but specific) Subject Theme such as 'an amateur yachtsman' in the text below, which can set up an identity chain whose referent is identified only in the second clause. (The NG Theme in the headline is indefinite too, with the indefinite article '*a*' omitted, as is usual in journalese.)

> **Fogbound sailor was yards from shore**
>
> *An amateur yachtsman* has spent four days fearing that *he* was in the middle of the North Sea, unaware that *he* was 100 yards from shore.
>   *Allan McKeand, a retired industrial chemist from Skipton, North Yorkshire*, ran into fog off the North East coastal town of Redcar on Monday.

28.7 INTRODUCING NEW POTENTIAL TOPICS INTO THE DISCOURSE

New referents have to be introduced into the discourse in order to be discussed. Some languages have specific morphological markers to indicate that something is being presented as a potential new Topic. English has no such morphological devices, but there are still ways of presenting new referents into the discourse. These include the following:

1   The subject of an intransitive clause (including copular clauses) can present or identify a new entity. Such is the case in the italicised NG that identifies the fogbound sailor in the second of the two paragraphs in the news item. When spoken, extra pitch and stress (see 29.1) help the hearer to make contact with the new referent.
2   When the Subject is known, the direct object often introduces a new entity: *I saw **a most extraordinary person** in the park this afternoon*. It has been estimated that between them the subject of an intransitive verb and the object of a transitive verb account for the majority of new entities introduced in spoken discourse.
3   Unstressed *there* with *be* – or a presentative verb such as *appear*, which has the same effect – can introduce a new referent, as in *There was **a good programme** on television last night* (see 30.4).
4   A statement can explicitly inform the hearer what the Topic is going to be, as in *Today I want to talk to you about **genetic engineering***.
5   Inversion of a copular clause can introduce a new Topic, as in *Worst of all was **the lack of fresh water*** (see 28.9).

It must be emphasised that not every entity introduced into the discourse is maintained as a major topic with its own identity chain. Many do not survive the first mention, such is the volume of incoming detail to be processed mentally. In conversation, establishing a discourse topic is eminently collaborative, and some new entities may not be considered newsworthy enough to survive.

28.8 CIRCUMSTANTIAL ADJUNCTS AS THEMES

Among the marked Themes, Circumstantial Adjuncts – particularly those of time and place – are the least unusual. Comparing the examples below, we can say that the circumstantials in *London last year* have been transferred from their normal position in the Rheme to initial position; that is, they have been **thematised** or 'fronted'.

Theme	Rheme
We	did a lot of sightseeing *in London last year.*
In London last year,	we did a lot of sightseeing.

The function of such circumstantials is to set the necessary temporal and/or spatial coordinates of the text world within which the participants move, establishing a **time-frame** or **place-frame** for the rest of the message. Such frames or settings can hold over wide spans of discourse, until a different frame is set up. The exhibition leaflet in which Warhol figures has many such temporal spans, as it describes the chronological progression of modern art.

> **The break between European and American art**
>
> **In the first decades of the twentieth century** Paris was the centre of modern art. Picasso, Braque and Matisse all worked there; Cubism was born there. The first part of this exhibition describes the dialogue that took place between Europe and America that gave rise to American modernism . . .
>
> **By the early 1940s** young American artists made the conscious decision to disconnect the line to Europe. They wanted to provoke and shock, to be the standard-bearers of the avant-garde in a specifically American way. This radical group of artists launched the revolutionary movement called Abstract Expressionsim that by 1950 had successfully invented a new contemporary art vocabulary. And, **for the first time in the history of Western art**, the centre of the artistic avant-garde shifted away from Europe to America.

Initial circumstantials of time constitute a useful device for structuring lengthy stretches of text on a chronological basis. Time and place adjuncts do not initiate cohesive chains, however, although they can be referred to anaphorically in subsequent clauses by the adverbs *there* and *then*, respectively: *We went to the theatre there, too, and it was then that I learned some Cockney slang.* Locations such as *Paris*, when Subject, can set up topical chains and can also be followed by co-referential *there*, as in the text.

There is competition between subject and adjunct Themes for initial position. If chronological sequencing is adopted as a method of development of the text, as in this extract, temporal Themes are chosen to mark crucial points, while the topic (*Paris, young American artists*) takes second position, although it is Subject. The topical participant chain of the young American artists is built up within the time-span created by the Theme. Temporal adjuncts which are not thematic, such as *by 1950*, are backgrounded by their position within a topical chain. Nevertheless they can signal important temporal landmarks such as turning points, shifts and the end of a previous time-span as in the case of *by 1950*. While circumstantial Themes are important in mapping the surface development, it is the topic referents, (participant Themes when initial), however, which structure the cognitive development of the text as a whole, in terms of its global topic.

28.9 OBJECTS AND COMPLEMENTS AS THEMES

Apart from contrast, another motivation for thematising direct objects is that of retrospective linking to something in the previous sentence or context:

> *Moussaka* you ordered, and *moussaka* you've got.
> Janet asked me to bring her some tea from London. *This* I did.

When **subject complements** are thematised they tend to occur as evaluative comments made spontaneously in context, often in response to another speaker. In each case, there is retrospective linking. **Identifying clauses**, such as *The music was the best of all*, are reversible. When reversed, as in the second example, they look both backwards and forwards, linking to something just said, but also marking a shift to something new.

[How did the meeting go?] – *A complete waste of time* it was (Subject Complement. The unmarked order: *It was a complete waste of time.*)
[Was the festival a success?] Not bad. *The best was the music.* (reversed identifying clause from *The music was the best.*)
Fantastic I call it! (Object Complement. Unmarked order: *I call it fantastic.*)

28.10 LESS COMMON THEMATISATIONS IN THE DECLARATIVE CLAUSE

28.10.1 Negative adverbs

When we place negative adverbs such as **never** in initial position, we seem to be responding to a communicative human need to foreground and emphasise the negation. But while *Never!* can be used as a one-word full negative response in conversation, thematised negative constituents are much less easy to use in English than in some other languages. This is because they trigger the inversion of an existing auxiliary (or *do*-operator) with the subject. Furthermore, thematised negatives have an emphatic, marked effect, as can be seen from the following famous utterance made by Winston Churchill after the Battle of Britain in the Second World War. The second, more recent quotation, was made as a comment on television about the IRA's apology in 2002 for the loss of life of non-combatants over three decades.

Never in the field of human conflict was so much owed by so many to so few.
Never before has the IRA acknowledged the loss of life in its 30-year paramilitary campaign.

In everyday use such a rhetorical effect may be undesirable, and it is best to reserve fronted negative elements for emphatic statements or directives. With the imperative, there is no inversion, as the base form of the verb is used: *Never say 'never again'!* Certain dependent clauses of condition are likewise fronted: *Should you wish to change your mind*, please let us know. The negative adjuncts *never* and *under no circumstances*, fronted seminegatives such as *hardly, scarcely* and *only* + an adverb of time all have a marked effect when fronted. Their unmarked position before the main verb avoids this problem (*I have never seen . . . You must under no circumstances leave . . .*).

The positive and negative elements most commonly thematised in everyday spoken English are *so* and *neither* or *nor* as substitute words (see 29.6). They behave like initial negatives, provoking operator-subject ordering, but they have no rhetorical effect.

All my friends passed the driving-test and **so** *did I.*
Never *have I* seen such a mess!
Under no circumstances *must medicines* be left within reach of children.
Only then *did I* realise what he really meant.

28.10.2 Negative Objects

These produce the same inversion, but are much less common. Negative subjects do not produce inversion. Compare: **Not a thing** *could the patient remember*, where *not a thing* is Object, with **Nobody** *could remember a thing*, where *nobody* is Subject.

28.10.3 Adverbs followed by verbs of motion

Initial adverbs such as *up, down, in* and deictics such as *here, there* and *then* are commonly used with verbs of motion such as *come, go, run.* In short spoken utterances they accompany or signal actions, such as *In you get*! (helping someone into a car) or *There/ Here you go*! (handing something to someone). There is no inversion when the subject is a pronoun. With a full nominal group, however, the verb and the subject invert: *Down came* **the rain** *and up went* **the umbrellas**: *There goes* **my last dollar**! *Here comes* **the bus**. In certain types of written texts such as historical narrative in tourist brochures, this structure can be used to mark a new stage in the narrative, and in such cases usually initiates a new paragraph, as in:

Then came the Norman Conquest.

Only simple tenses are used in this structure, not the progressive or perfect combinations.
    Thematised verbs rarely occur in the declarative clause in English. When they do, it is the non-finite part that is thematised:

([He told me to run,) so] *run I did.* (Unmarked order: *He told me to run, so I did run.*)

In the media non-finite and finite forms are sometimes fronted, together with the rest of the clause:

Coming up to the stage now is this year's winner of the Oscar . . .
Snapped back the 18-year-old princess: 'No comment'.

28.10.4 Detached predicatives

These are units headed by a noun, an adjective or a participle. They are closely tied to the subject but, instead of occupying a position after the verb, they are fronted, and have the status of supplementives, with an adjunctive function:

A Saxon princess, she was born at Exning near Newmarket around AD 630, the daughter of Anna, King of the East Angles.

These fronted phrases are common in such genres as fiction, history, advertising and tourism, where they provide an economical means of packing information around a main topic entity, without holding up the narrative. When thematic, they are retrospective, linking up with the immediately preceding text. When they are placed after the subject, they add extra details about the topic entity as in *the daughter of Anna, King of the East Angles*.

28.11 DETACHED THEMES: ABSOLUTE THEME, DISLOCATIONS AND DOUBLE THEMES

28.11.1 Absolute Theme

The Themes analysed so far all have a place within the syntax and semantics of the clause. This is not the only type, however. Across the world's languages, a very basic way of presenting a 'newsworthy' piece of information is by means of a **detached** lexical NG standing outside the clause. This 'Chinese-style topic' is always a definite NG or proper name which does not function as a constituent of the clause which follows it. The construction, here called Absolute Theme, is common in the spoken registers of many European languages, as illustrated by the following sentence, from Spanish:

Los Beatles, sin *Sgt. Pepper* no tendríamos ni la mitad de la música pop de ahora.

(*The Beatles*) (without *Sgt. Pepper*) (we wouldn't have) (even half the pop music [we have] now)

The Theme *The Beatles* is completely detached, with no grammatical relations connecting it to the second part of the message. Nevertheless, it provides a pragmatic frame by which the connection is made inferentially, based on contextual knowledge.

Absolute Themes in English occur sometimes in spontaneous talk; they do not occur normally in written text. Here are two instances, both from news interviews on television. The first is in the context of a public appeal in a police inquiry, the second during the anthrax alarm in the aftermath of 11 September 2001. In both, the Absolute Theme provides a personal frame to the utterance.

Now *Manchester United*, their players have been holding up a banner.
The woman who died in New York, that's obviously affecting her colleagues who work in the hospital.

28.11.2 Dislocations

Dislocations are different from Absolute Themes in that the 'dislocated' element is a constituent of the clause, frequently subject (as in the examples below), and is repeated by a co-referential pronoun (*it* and *those* respectively here) in its normal position within the clause. The connection is therefore encoded grammatically, not established inferentially. The first two illustrate what are usually known as **left-dislocations**. The last one is a **right-dislocation**.

> *That letter*, was *it* from Bruce?   (corresponding to: Was that letter from
> Bruce?)
>
> And *those flood waters* that affected the Czech Republic, *those* are the ones that are
> sweeping towards Germany?
>
> Is *it* new, *that top* – No, I bought it   (Non-dislocated form: Is that top new?)
> last year.

One explanation sometimes given of left-dislocation is that the speaker presents the main person or thing s/he wishes to talk about (*that letter, those flood waters that affected the Czech Republic*) without having worked out the structure to be used. A more positive view, cognitively and communicatively, is that by 'detaching' the salient referent and putting it first, the speaker side-steps grammatical complexity, presenting a 'topic–comment' structure that is more easily grasped than the normal one. Interrogatives and relatives are complex structures in English, and it is in these cases that we can find left-dislocation.

Right-dislocations are more problematic to analyse as Themes, as they are not initial, but instead are placed after the clause as a full NG, (*that top*) whose referent had been previously introduced as a pronoun (*it*). The traditional view is that the final nominal is an afterthought, which again, implies a construction failure on the part of the speaker. A cognitive-functional explanation, however, suggests a motivation for this structure, namely, that of making explicit a referent (*that top*) which was accessible to the speaker in the context, but perhaps not so obvious to the hearer, or not in the speaker's mind at the moment.

Affectivity may provide a different kind of motivation, as in the next two examples. In the first the referent was an escaped pig, called McQueen; the second a relative of the speaker. In the third, a deictic pronoun *this* refers to the immediate context:

> And *he* not only flew over the fence, *he* could swim, *that pig*.   (news report)
> *He's* a cool dude, *Sam*.   (author's data)
> *It's* a nice place, *this*.

28.11.3 Double detached Themes

Two detached Themes may occur together, the first an Absolute, the second a left-dislocation. The relationship between them must be pragmatically relevant.

1 And *Ben, his sister*, she has disabling osteo-arthritis.
2 And *this consultant*, what I like about *him* is that *he* doesn't pass everyone on to his underlings; *he* attends to you himself.
3 *The white house opposite, the woman who lives there, her dog, he's* had to be put down.

In **2** there is a *wh*-cleft, *what I like about him* (see 30.2), which is not detached. Both of these combinations are heard in spoken English, but rarely find their way into the written language. In **3** there are three detached nominal groups, the last of which, *her dog*, is picked up by the pronoun *he*. The function of multiple detachments is to 'anchor' the final referent to other related referents, which are presumed to be accessible to the hearer.

28.12 NON-EXPERIENTIAL THEMES

The Theme of an utterance is essentially a constituent of the transitivity structures. It is possible to allow for a number of non-experiential Themes, which precede the experiential Theme. These can be grouped into two main kinds: **interpersonal** Themes and **textual** Themes.

Interpersonal Themes

These include three main subtypes. **Continuative Themes** (or discourse markers), such as *Oh, well, Ah, please* (see 8.2.8), have various functions as markers of attention, response, request, state of knowledge, surprise and hesitation, among others. Overall, they signal acknowledgements by speakers and transitions from one speaker to another or a move to another point in spoken discourse. Examples are:

> Now who wants to come to the castle? – *Oh, actually* I have to do some shopping. *Well*, we'll see you later, then.

Another group of interpersonal Themes, **Adjuncts of stance**, include three main sub-types: **epistemic**, (*certainly*), **evidential** (*apparently*) and **evaluative** (*surely, surprisingly*) **1**. Further sub-types include style adjuncts, such as *frankly, honestly*, and domain adjuncts, such as *legally, technologically, consumerwise* **2**, which limit the domain of reference of the rest of the sentence. All are discussed and illustrated in Section 8.2.5.

A third type is made up of **vocatives**, such as *Doctor! Mum!*, and **appellatives** – *ladies and gentlemen* – which address people by name or by role or status **3**.

> **1** *Surely* you could find yourself a job somewhere? *Honestly*, I've tried.
> **2** *Technologically*, though, the new model hasn't been a success.
> **3** *Ladies and gentlemen*, please take your seats. The coach will depart in five minutes.

Textual Themes

Textual Themes include a variety of connectors or **connective adjuncts** such as *however, besides, therefore, now, first, then* (non-temporal) *next* and *anyway*. These connect the clause to the previous part of the text by indicating relations such as addition, concession, reason, consequence, and so on (see 8.2.7 and 8.2.8).

> I don't feel like playing tennis. *Besides*, it's starting to rain.

All these different types of element can be considered as being part of the Theme, as long as they are placed before the experiential theme (Subject, Circumstantial, Object or Complement). Most of them can function in other positions in the clause, and so represent a real choice when used thematically. Coordinators such as *and, but* and *or*, conjunctions such as *when* and relative pronouns such as *who, which, that* are inherently thematic and do not have alternative placements. For this reason, they will not be taken into account in our analyses.

Non-defining relatives, however, because they are analysed as supplementives (see 2.4.1, 49.2), may be considered as having Themes and Rhemes in their own right, as in the following sentence, which may be analysed as two Theme–Rheme units as follows:

> Ladies and gentlemen, this afternoon we are going to visit the cathedral, which was built in 1241 not long after the last of the great wars.

Ladies and gentlemen, this afternoon	we are going to visit the cathedral
Theme	**Rheme**

which	was built in 1241 not long after the great wars.
Theme	**Rheme**

By including the many different classes of items within the Theme category, it is possible to claim that the three macro-functions of language, the experiential, the interpersonal and the textual, can be represented by items within the Theme. Here is an examples of **Multiple Themes**.

Well	now,	Mrs Jones,	what	can I do for you?
Continuative	Connective	Vocative	Experiential	
Interpersonal	Textual	Interpersonal	Experiential	
Theme				**Rheme**

28.13 CLAUSES AS THEMES

Time and place are not the only types of circumstance that can be thematised: other types of situational frame can be established. Consider just three of the many meanings of *as*, illustrated in the following sentences: **a** *As a gardening tool*, it's not much use (role); **b** *As children under five, they get in free* (status); **c** *As children, we used to roll our eyes whenever grandfather told us the same old story yet again* (time).

The time Adjunct in **c** *As children . . .* could be reworded as **d** *When we were children*. This fact enables us to see a similarity of function between circumstances realised as

Adjuncts, as in **a, b** and **c**, and circumstances expressed as subordinate clauses as in **d**. We can say that in a unit composed of two or more clauses, the first clause acts as Theme to the rest.

Coordinated clauses joined by 'and' reflect the chronological order of the events described. The first clause is therefore the natural temporal and factual starting-point of the sequence. For this reason not all coordinate clauses are coherently reversible:

> The lone rider got on his horse and rode into the sunset.
> *The lone rider rode into the sunset and got on his horse.

Even when the clauses are reversible, the resultant meanings are likely to be different; for, as well as chronological sequence, other meanings such as cause and effect are implied:

> He bought an oil-tanker and made a fortune. (i.e. his fortune resulted from his buying the tanker)
> He made a fortune and bought an oil-tanker. (i.e. he bought the tanker with his fortune)

Subordinate clauses impose no obligation to maintain chronological sequencing. However, an initial subordinate clause takes as starting-point the meaning it encodes, such as reason **1**, simultaneity **2** and condition **3**:

1 *As you weren't at home*, I left a message on your answer-phone.
2 *As she stepped off the kerb*, a cyclist crashed into her.
3 *If you don't like it*, you can probably change it for something else.

Such Themes set up meaningful frames within which the rest of the clause develops, as is illustrated in the following short extract from Alan Ayckbourn's *Just Between Ourselves*:

> I haven't got time, mother, to start putting things in tins. *If I want a nail*, there's a nail. I bang it in and that's that. *If I can't find a nail* I use a screw. *And if I can't find a screw*, I don't bother.

Such initial clauses also set up expectations, which obviously does not happen when the subordinate clause is final. For instance, compare the next two examples. Each contains a **non-finite to-infinitive clause of purpose** in initial and final position, respectively:

4 *To cure stress*, try a Jacuzzi whirlpool bath.
5 He braked hard *to avoid hitting the cyclist*.

The initial purpose clause in **4** not only sets up a purpose frame, but also names the goal to be achieved. For this reason, the *to*-infinitive clause here emphasises a sense of premeditated purpose, which is much less explicit in **5**, where the purpose clause is in final position.

The two remaining types of non-finite clause, the **participial -*ing* clause** and the **-*en* clause**, are closely tied to the main participant in the discourse and are discussed in Chapter 7. The -*ing* clause **6** is active in meaning and expresses an action or state dependent upon the main situation. The -*en* clause **7** is passive in meaning and is retrospective, summing up a previous situation:

> **6** *Taking advantage of his present popularity*, the Prime Minister called an election.
> **7** *Thwarted in the west*, Stalin turned east.

It is useful to remember that speakers adjust their choice of Theme to the context, 'attending first to the most urgent task'. When the tourist guide starts with 'Ladies and gentlemen', for instance, s/he is doing just that: attracting the hearers' attention before giving them the information they need. **Context** is understood here to include potentially:

- the situational context in which the participants interact, including the place, the time and the participants themselves;
- the texual context, or 'co-text', which covers the previous spoken or written discourse; and
- cognitive features such as the participants' knowledge, beliefs and assumptions, in so far as these are relevant at any particular point in the discourse.

THE DISTRIBUTION AND FOCUS OF INFORMATION

SUMMARY

1 In order to be understood, messages are divided into chunks called **information units**, which are represented in speech by **tone units**. These do not correspond to any one grammatical category, since the speaker is free to break up the message as desired into units which are smaller or larger than a clause.

2 Each tone unit contains a **tonic syllable**, which represents the highest point of the **focus of information**. Information focus extends to the syntactic unit in which the tonic occurs.

3 The tone unit in English signals the distribution of information into Given and New. Each information unit contains an obligatory New element and, optionally, a Given element, the unmarked order being Given–New. The Given is the information that the speaker presents as recoverable by the hearer; the New is the information that is presented as not recoverable by the hearer. The whole tone unit may contain New information, for instance at the start of a conversational exchange.

4 The devices of **ellipsis** and **substitution** are used to avoid repeating information that is recoverable.

5 Unmarked focus falls on the last non-anaphoric lexical item of the information unit. If the intonation nucleus is made to fall on some other item, it is marked and unequivocally represents New information. This is **marked focus**. Its function is to contrast one item with another or to add emotive colouring to the utterance. Focus can coincide with marked Theme and is a cohesive device in texts.

29.1 THE INFORMATION UNIT

Speakers divide their messages into chunks called **information units**. In the spoken language these are not represented directly by any one type of grammatical unit, although there are certain correlations. Rather, they are signalled **prosodically**, by means of the intonation system of the language. Information units are therefore defined in terms of the spoken language and how speakers organise it. Readers of a written text, however, interpret what they read by mentally assigning information units to the text, helped by punctuation and the grammar.

The prosodic unit that represents a unit of spoken information is the **tone unit**. A tone unit consists potentially of a series of stressed and unstressed syllables, and always contains one syllable, the **tonic**, which is singled out by **tonic prominence**. That is, it carries the main pitch movement (for instance, falling, rising, falling and then rising, rising and then falling), a jump, up or down, in pitch and possibly extra stress and added duration. Its function is to mark the **focus of information**. Or rather, it signals the nucleus or highest point of the unit which is informationally in focus, as in the example below (the capitals represent the tonic syllable):

He's arriving on THURSday.

If this utterance were used to convey information, it is likely that there would be a jump in pitch up to THURS and that this syllable would have a pitch fall on it. In this example, the tone unit coincides with a clause. But speakers can choose to make tone units longer **1** or shorter **2** than a clause, depending on how much of the information they want to make prominent. (The symbol // indicates the end of a tone unit.) Short answers, questions and commands can consist of a single prominent syllable, such as YES! WHY? or DON'T! If a speaker wishes to make the message highly informative and emphatic, each lexical word may be treated as an information unit, with as many tonics as there are words, as in **2** (where the tonic syllable in *immediately* is *ME*):

1   I think it's a great pity she didn't GET the job //
2   COME // HERE // IMMEDIATELY //

Speakers shorten or lengthen tone units in response to their communicative needs. This response is emotive rather than deliberate, and is therefore less likely to be controlled than, for instance, the choice of a lexical item. Variation in the length of tone units also depends on several factors, some cultural, others personal. According to one cognitive view, the intonation unit or tone group represents the limited amount of information that our consciousness can focus on at any one time. This has led to the 'one chunk per clause principle' or 'one new idea constraint', in conversation at least. For spoken English a short independent clause with few content words represents the typical information unit.

Other grammatical units which may correspond to tone groups include various kinds of adjunct, especially when initial (*in the late nineteen thirties, better still, unfortunately*); a dependent clause (*although it wasn't your fault*); a main clause with an embedded clause (*I thought we were leaving*), coordinated predicates with the same Subject (*he's seen the pictures and likes them*) and possibly NG Subjects (*all the lonely people*). The following are examples of utterances consisting of two tone units:

// in the late nineteen THIRTIES // he went to HOLLYWOOD //
// better STILL // send an E-mail //

The following transcription illustrates how one speaker organises an episode into tone units of varying length, with overlapping units (in brackets) by speaker B. The dots and dashes (. -) represent progressively longer pauses. The speakers have been talking about football grounds in Britain, many of them quite old.

Of course // the CONTINENTALS I suppose // they came in LATE // and they . build them – (B: PROPERLY //) you know// this MILAN ground // . there's a famous one THERE . ÍSN'T there? // . (B: erm) you know// they were saying how SUPERB they were // . But the one in SPAIN // was the BEST // – (B: of course //) I thought it was in MADRID // – was it Real MADRID// they were fan (b: they're all erm . . .) oh they were FANTASTIC // it showed the PHOTOGRAPHS of them // . people sitting there in the hot SUN // you know // smoking CIGARS// and it showed the crowds . EMPTYING // – (B: they had a practice – erm) EXIT //// (B: YEAH //) and about . thirty seconds LATER // or a minute later they were CLEAR //

29.2 GIVEN AND NEW INFORMATION

The distribution of 'Given' and 'New' information is to a great extent the motivation for the information unit. Each information unit contains an obligatory 'New' element, which is associated with the tonic of the tone unit, the focus of information. There can also be optional 'Given' elements of information, which are associated with the rest of the tone unit. Rather than a clear-cut distinction between 'Given' and 'New', however, there is a gradation of givenness and newness. This is compatible with the notion of communicative dynamism, by which the message typically progresses from low to high information value (see 29.3).

The **Given element** is concerned with information that the speaker presents as recoverable by the hearer, either from the linguistic co-text, that is, what has been said before, or because it can be taken as 'known' from the context of situation or the context of culture. The **New element** is concerned with whatever information the speaker presents as not recoverable by the hearer. The following exchange illustrates the possible relationship of Given and New to information focus:

A. What's new then?
B. Well, Jim's bought *a new CAR* //, Norma's getting a *DIVORCE* // and Jamie's got *CHICKEN-POX* //, but apart from that . . .

In each tone unit, the tonic syllable, identified here by capitals, represents the culmination of the New information. The syntactic unit in which the tonic occurs (*a new CAR, a DIVORCE, CHICKEN-POX*) is in each case 'in focus'. The referents of the proper names *Jim, Norma* and *Jamie* are treated as identifiable and Given, or at least accessible, in the discourse situation (that is the function of proper names) and there is a gradation from Given to New, with the verbs *bought, getting* and *got* marking the transition:

Jim's	bought	a new CAR
Norma's	getting	a DIVORCE
Jamie's	got	CHICKEN-POX
Given - - - - - - - - - - - - - New		

29.3 UNMARKED FOCUS AND MARKED FOCUS

In normal, unemphatic discourse, it is customary to start our message from what we think our hearer knows and progress to what s/he does not know. In other words, the unmarked distribution starts with the Given and progresses towards the New. This is often called the principle of **end-focus**.

The neutral position for information focus is therefore towards the end of the information unit. In grammatical terms, this usually means that **unmarked (end-)focus** falls on the last non-anaphoric lexical item or name in the clause, as in the above exchange. Items which occur after the tonic can be taken as Given and are always unstressed, like *about it* here:

> Pete's just   COMPLAINED   about it.
> Given - - - - New - - - - - - - - - Given

Here, the words after *complained* are both grammatical rather than lexical words: that is, they have a largely grammatical meaning. Pronouns such as *it* always refer to something known, unless they are contrastive and therefore marked (see below). In the following example, the second use of WANT is anaphoric (the notion of 'wanting' occurs in the question), and is therefore not marked. Instead, DON'T is marked:

> A. Don't you WANT it then?   B. No, I DON'T want it.

When the focus of information is placed on the last non-anaphoric lexical item in the clause, almost the whole clause may be New or just one part of it. For example, *Jane dropped the COFFEE-POT* could be intended to mean that it was just the coffee-pot and not something else that Jane dropped; or the whole unit could contain new information. The amount of New material can be verified by formulating questions. In answer to the first, only the coffee-pot would be New and the rest Given (and probably ellipted in speech; see 29.3), while in answer to the second, the whole unit would represent new information:

> What did Jane drop?   [Jane dropped]   the COFFEE-POT
>   New - - - - - - - - - - - -
> What happened?   Jane dropped the COFFEE-POT
>   - - - - - - - - - - - - New - - - - - - - - - - - -

Marked focus occurs when the tonic is placed on any other syllable than the tonic syllable of the last non-anaphoric lexical item. Marked focus is used for the purpose of **contrasting** one item with another, as in **1** and **2**, or to add an **emotive overlay**, as in **3**:

> **1**   SHE didn't make the phone call, ROBERT did.
> **2**   The kids didn't SIT on the sofa, they JUMPED on it.
> **3**   I'm SO THIRSTY!

The first would be used in a context in which the speaker assumes that the hearer knows they are talking about someone making a phone call ('make the phone call' is Given information). As contrastive focus treats the focused element as New information, both *she* and *Robert* are treated as New, even though both must be identifiable in the context.

Focus can fall on other, non-lexical items such as pronouns, prepositions and auxiliaries, again with an implied contrast or correction. The following examples illustrate some of the possibilities of marked focus. When auxiliaries receive focus it is meanings such as those of polarity contrast (i.e. positive/ negative) or tense which are presented as New or important information:

MY brother sold his motorbike.	[not someone else's brother]
Put the dog's bowl UNDER the table.	[not ON the table]
[Wait for me!] I AM waiting for you.	[corrects first speaker's assumption that x is not waiting]
[Don't forget to return the video!] I HAVE returned the video.	[corrects the assumption that the video has not been returned.]
[Why didn't you tell the truth?] I DID tell the truth.	[corrects the assumption that x did not tell the truth]

Whether for emotive reasons or for the purpose of emphasising or contrasting, it can happen that a single tone group contains more than one nucleus. The fall-plus-rise or the rise-plus-fall tones often accompany focusing of this kind.

//It was QUITE exciting REALLY.//
//I DO wish you'd shut UP.//

The following advertisement illustrates the possibility speakers have of assigning focus to practically any item. Some of these utterances could be interpreted as contrastive, others simply as emphatic.

DO you know what kind of a day I've had?
  Do YOU know what kind of a day I've had?
    Do you KNOW what kind of a day I've had?
      Do you know WHAT kind of a day I've had?
        Do you know what KIND of a day I've had?
          Do you know what kind of a DAY I've had?
            Do you know what kind of a day I'VE had?
              Do you know what kind of a day I've HAD?
Well, DO you?

29.4 EVENT UTTERANCES

Event utterances are usually short and typically intransitive. They provide an interesting exception to the principle of end-focus, in that a NG Subject receives the tonic stress. The reason for this is that the whole event is in Focus, and there is no presupposition (assumption) such as 'something is bleeding', 'something has gone out', 'someone is coming':

> My NOSE is bleeding!
> The LIGHT's gone out!
> [I won't be able to go away this weekend.] My PARENTS are coming.

Event sentences are extremely common in conversation. They often occur 'out of the blue', that is, unrelated to what was previously said, as surprisals or interruptions of an ongoing discourse topic. This is not always the case however. In the third example, the event utterance is incorporated into the dialogue as a reason for not going away this weekend. In languages with flexible constituent order, this type of message would probably be conveyed by inversion of S–P. In English, inversion is not an option here; instead, stress and intonation patterns are used.

29.5 ELLIPSIS

By means of **ellipsis** we leave out those elements of the clause that are recoverable. As a result we highlight the new information and our discourse gains in cohesion and coherence. Information can be recovered from the linguistic co-text or from the social context. Ellipsis of the first type is **textual** and of the second **situational**.

29.5.1 Textual ellipsis

Textual ellipsis occurs when two consecutive clauses have elements in common. The two clauses may form part of the same utterance by one speaker **1**, or they may be distributed between two speakers, as in **2**. The words in common are omitted in the second clause. In English the remaining part often ends with an auxiliary or a pronoun. (In the examples, ellipted material is recovered in italics.)

> **1** I'm sure he would help you, if he could (*help you*).
> **2** Shall we go for a swim? – Yes, let's (*go for a swim*).
> **3** Why can't he just send a message? And for that matter, why can't *YOU*? (*just send a message*)

Catenative verbs which take *to*-infinitive clauses such as *want, mean* (= *intend*), *used to* and *like* obligatorily retain the *to*, with the rest of the clause ellipted, as in **4**. *Wh*- complement clauses and questions can be ellipted, leaving the *wh*-element as in **5**:

> **4** A fine mess you've made of things. – I didn't *mean to* (*make a fine mess of things*).
> **5** Why can't he find you a comfortable job? – He will (*find me a comfortable job*), but I don't know when (*he'll find me a comfortable job.*)

These examples illustrate final ellipsis. Medial ellipsis is featured in **6** and **7**, while **8** illustrates initial ellipsis, where ellipsis of the pronoun is an alternative analysis to zero anaphora.

6 What time does this party of Robin's start? He said [*it starts at*] six-to-eight.
7 Shirley wore jeans and Tina (*wore*) a miniskirt.
8 They got on the bus and (*they*) sat down in the front seat behind the driver.

29.5.2 Situational ellipsis

In conversation and writing that imitates speech, unstressed pronouns and other functional items are frequently ellipted, as they are recoverable from the interactional context.

Can't hear a word	(Subject *I* ellipted)
See you soon	(*I'll* ellipted)
Like a drink?	(*Would you* ellipted)
Any news?	(*Is there* ellipted)

Situational ellipsis is also the organising factor in 'block language', which includes newspaper headlines, telegrams and other announcements. We soon reach a point, however, both in textual and situational ellipsis at which the exact material ellipted is no longer recoverable. In such cases the concept of ellipsis is strictly not applicable, as in:

To let. For hire. For sale. Vacancies. Bed and Breakfast. No parking.

29.6 SUBSTITUTION

Substitution likewise avoids the repetition of recoverable information; but while ellipsis leaves a structural slot empty, substitution replaces it by a 'filler' word. Consequently, the exact words which have been ellipted are not recoverable. A commonly used clausal substitute is *do so*, as in **1** below. This is not acceptable, however, where the verb is not agentive (for instance, *know, like*) and in such cases ellipsis is used, as in **2**:

1 You can hire a self-drive car, but I wouldn't advise you to *do so*. (hire a self-drive car)
2 Some people like mangoes, others don't. (**don't do so*).

So substitutes for clause complements after verbs such as *say, hope, think, expect, be afraid, suppose* and *believe*. *Not* is the negative substitute with *hope, be afraid* and *suppose*:

Is it going to rain tomorrow? The weather man *says so* (i.e. that it is going to rain).
I *hope not*. (i.e. that it's not going to rain).

So can also be used as an alternative to an auxiliary + *too* to substitute positively, just as *neither* alternates with auxiliary + *either* to substitute negatively:

This hair-dryer makes an awful noise. *So does* mine. / Mine *does* too. / Mine too.
I wouldn't like to live in this climate. *Neither/ Nor* would we. / We *wouldn't either*.

Ellipsis and substitution in nominal groups

In nominal ellipsis we replace the head element by pronouns such as *these, any, each, all, both, either, neither, none* (*I'll take these, There aren't any left*); possessives such as *John's*, and numeratives such as *the first, the next three*. These are discussed in modules 46 and 47. Nominal substitution makes use of *one/ones (I prefer the dark one(s)) this, that* and the pronouns *(an)other* (see 45.7.4):

THE INTERPLAY OF THEME–RHEME AND GIVEN–NEW

SUMMARY

1   From the point of view of communicative effect, the important positions in the clause are the **initial** position and the **final** position. We have examined separately the two structures involved, which are mapped on to each other: the **Theme–Rheme** thematic structure and the **Given–New** information structure. We now turn to the interplay between the two. We start by going beyond the clause to look at **thematic progression** in a paragraph.

2   We then turn to a few of the major resources used in English for shifting information either to the beginning of the clause or to the end. We have already seen **thematisation** (thematic fronting), which brings an element to initial position. We shall next examine the much more common device of **clefting**, which places an element to be focused near the front of the clause.

3   Equally important are the resources for shifting information towards the end of the clause where it receives **end-focus** without being marked. The function of the **passive** voice, of the existential **sentence** and of **extraposition** is in part just this. At the same time, a different Theme is selected. Speakers and writers of English make great use of all these devices to achieve coherence and liveliness in their speech and writing.

4   The highlighting of newsworthiness is not the only motivation of information flow. Pragmatic motivations of an interpersonal kind, such as politeness, may be the influencing factor in the selection and ordering of clausal elements, in particular the order of clauses in complex sentences.

30.1   THEMATIC PROGRESSION

The unmarked correlation between Given–New and Theme–Rheme is for Given to coincide with the Theme, and New information with some part of the Rheme. Going beyond the clause, a consistent progression from Given to New will help the reader's understanding of the text. Three basic types of thematic progression are identified: **simple linear**, **continuous** and **derived**.

30.1.1 Simple linear progression

In this type, something introduced as new information in the Rheme of the first clause is taken up to be the Theme of the second. The wording need not be identical.

> *She* has a huge team of people working for her.[1] *Some of them* have been with her for years.[2]

In this example, Theme 1 is *she*, while a *huge team of people* is the focused part of Rheme 1. A semantic sub-set, *some of them*, then becomes the Theme of the second clause. We can present it graphically as follows:

Clause 1   Theme 1 + Rheme 1

Clause 2   Theme 2 + Rheme 2

                                             Adapted from Daneš 1974)

30.1.2 Continuous progression (constant Theme)

In this type, the same Theme, *Mum*, is maintained across a series of coordinated clauses, each with its own Rheme:

> *Mum* was always a hard worker[1] and (*zero*) had plenty of drive[2] but, in a small way, *she* was also proving to be quite a successful business woman.[3]

This type of progression can be diagrammed as follows. Note that the same Theme is maintained in the second clause by 'zero anaphora', which could be replaced by the corresponding pronoun *she*.

> *Mum* (T1) was always a hard worker[1] (R1) and (*she*)(T1) had plenty of drive(R2),[2] but, in a small way, *she*(T1) was also proving to be quite a successful business woman (R3).[3]

Clause 1   Theme 1 + Rheme 1
Clause 2   Theme 1 + Rheme 2
Clause 3   Theme 1 + Rheme 3

In the illustrations of these two first types of thematic progression, we find that the progression is made on the basis of topic referent chains. The following news item *The 'lost' Van Gogh* uses both simple linear progression and constant Theme (see exercise at end of chapter):

When *Vincent Van Gogh* left his home in the Dutch village of Nuenen in 1895,[1] having had a blazing row with the parish priest over his use of female models,[2] *he* left hundreds of his early pictures behind in his mother's keeping.[3] Soon after, *his mother*, too, left the village for the nearby town of Breda.[4] *She* packed all her belongings, including a chest containing her son's works, onto a cart,[5] and then left the chest in storage with a family friend.[6] *The friend*, a local merchant, threw many of the pictures away[7] and sold others off the back of his cart for about five cents a-piece.[8]

30.1.3 Derived Themes

In this third type, the different themes of a number of Theme–Rheme structures all relate to a 'hypertheme' or 'global topic'. The following text comes from Aldous Huxley's *The Doors of Perception*, in which he describes research on the drug mescalin. The Hypertheme is stated in the first sentence.

Mescalin research has been going on sporadically ever since the days of Lewin and Havelock Ellis. *Chemists* have not merely isolated the alkaloid; *they* have learned how to synthesize it, so that the supply no longer depends on the sparse and intermittent crop of a desert cactus. *Alienists* have dosed themselves with mescalin in the hope thereby of coming to a better, first-hand understanding of their patients' mental processes. Working unfortunately upon too few subjects within too narrow a range of circumstances, *psychologists* have observed and catalogued some of the drug's more striking effects. *Neurologists and physiologists* have found out something about the mechanisms of its action upon the central nervous system. And *at least one professional philosopher* has taken mescalin for the light it may throw on such ancient, unsolved riddles as the place of mind in nature and the relationship between the brain and consciousness.

The Hypertheme is mescalin research. From this, the passage develops in terms of the classes of researchers (the Themes, derived from the Hypertheme) and what they did (the Rhemes) (see diagram opposite)..

A fourth type of progression has a **split rheme**, which is a combination of types **1** and **2**. This can be illustrated by the following text, which is about some photographs of Saddam Hussein:

I had two particular favourites: in one he sported a green eyeshade and carried a tennis racket; in the other he wore a university gown and had a mortar-board on his head.

Clause 1   I had two particular favourites
Clauses 2–3 In one he sported a green eyeshade and carried a tennis racket

Clauses 4–5 In the other he wore a university gown and a mortar-board on his head

This can be expressed graphically

Clause 1   T1 – R1. The Rheme implies two items, A and B:
Clauses 2–3   In one (A) _____ (T2 _____ R2)
Clauses 4–5   In the other (B) _____ (T2″ _____ R2″)

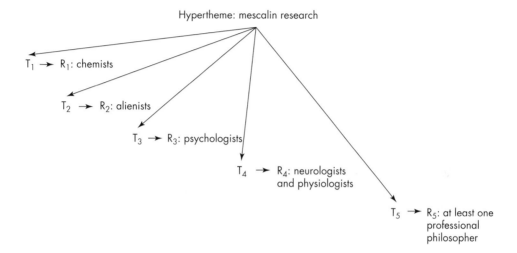

30.2 CLEFTING: *IT*-CLEFTS AND *WH*-CLEFTS

In clefting, we re-organise the content of a single clause into two related parts. The effect of the resulting structures is to focus on one element, the New, which always follows a form of the verb *be*. There are two kinds of cleft: the **it-cleft** and the **wh-cleft**. Here is an example of each. Compare these with the plain version: *They need money*.

It's MONEY (that) they need   (*it*-cleft)
What they <u>need</u> is MONEY   (*wh*-cleft)

Both types of cleft have MONEY in strong focus; the *it*-cleft brings the focus (marked by tonic stress) near the front of the first unit; the *wh*-cleft has the focus at the end of the second unit. There is a lesser stress, here underlined, on *need*, the last word of the unit containing Given or **presupposed** information. Presupposed information is that which is assumed by the speaker, without being asserted. Here what is assumed is 'they need something'.

If spoken, then, the devices of intonational prominence and syntactic structure reinforce each other to single out *money* in these examples. Let's look first at the **it-cleft**. This consists of the pronoun *it*, + a form of the verb *be*, + the strongly focused item + a clause starting with a relative pronoun such as *who*, *that* or *which*:

It was *last TUESDAY* that I met Richard (compare: I met Richard last TUESDAY)
It was *the WOMEN* that did the bartering. It was *the WOMEN* that actually got
    enough to feed the family.   BNC F7L 174
Who must register for VAT? It's *the PERSON*, not *the BUSINESS, who is registered
    for* VAT.   BNC FAU 761–762

In such examples, *it* is a dummy element with no other function but to provide a subject
for the verb *be*. The item in focus can be a noun group, a prepositional group, a pronoun
or a clause.

30.2.1 Discourse functions of the *it*-cleft

The main function of the *it*-cleft is to mark **contrastive focus**. The contrast is very
often implicit, as in *Tuesday* (not another day), *the women*, not *the men*; but the contrast
may be made explicit, as in *It's the person, not the business*, who is registered for VAT.

A different, non-contrastive use, is illustrated in the following sentence from Huxley's
work:

1   *It was in 1886* that the German pharmacologist, Louis Lewin, published the first
    systematic study of the cactus, to which his own name was subsequently given.

The function here is not to contrast 1886 with a different date. Rather, the function of
such clefts, which often highlight expressions of time or place, is to signal the beginning
of an episode in discourse. It may be the very beginning of the text, as in **1**, or an oral
announcement, **2**; otherwise, the cleft may signal a shift to a new episode **3**:

2   It is with great pleasure that I announce the name of this year's winner . . .
3   It was only years later that I realised what he meant.

30.2.2 Discourse functions of the *wh*-cleft

1   What we want is **WATney's**

This was a famous advertising slogan, at one time, for Watney's beer. It is clearly much
more emphatic than the plain version **2** and even more than the *it*-cleft **3**.

2   We want WATney's
3   It's Watney's (that) we want.

In both types of cleft there is presupposed information: in this case, that we
want something. But while the *it*-cleft **3** suggests contrast (Watney's, not Heineken, for
instance), the *wh*-cleft **1** suggests exclusiveness at the point in the discourse when it is
used. (It's ONLY Watney's we want, and no other). The *wh*-cleft consists of a *wh*-word,
of which by far the most common is *what*, followed by a clause containing Given
or presupposed information, then a form of *be*, followed by the New information:

//What we want// (it is presupposed: that we want something) is   Watney's//
Given   New

This structure is also sometimes called a **thematic equative**, since it is of the form
'X = Y'.

30.2.3 Variants of the *wh*-cleft

The one(s) who/that acts as replacement for the now ungrammatical *who*-cleft:

> *The one who* told me the news was Lizzy herself. (*Who told me the news was Lizzy
> herself)

All (that) is used instead of *all what. '*That*' is usually omitted.

> *All* you need is love.

Reversed *wh*-clefts have the main focus at the beginning of the first unit, not at the
end after *be*, as in regular *wh*-clefts. Some combinations (*that's what/why/how/the way*)
are stereotyped, as are *the thing is/the problem is*, which can also be included here:

> All you need is LOVE. (regular *wh*-cleft)
> LOVE is all you need. (reversed *wh*- cleft)
>
> What you should do is *THIS*. (regular *wh*-cleft)
> *THIS* is what you should do. (reversed *wh*-cleft)
>
> *That's what* I told you.
> *That's why* we came.

The effect is to put the new information as end-focus, but to indicate its selectively New
status very clearly. The exclusiveness inherent in an element focused in this way allows
the *wh*-cleft to be used for two important discourse purposes: (a) to introduce a new
topic (in the New part), as in **1**; and (b) to correct a previous statement or assumption,
as in **2**.

> **1**   What I don't understand is why they don't have a secretary in that place.
> **2**   What he did was take the money and run.

The *Wh*-cleft identifies a particular element exclusively. In this it differs from the basic
clause structure and from the ordinary cleft. Compare:

> We all need a holiday.   (neutral: no doubt we need other things too)
> It's a holiday we all need.   (implied contrast with something else)
> What we all need is a holiday.   (the only thing focused on)

Wh-clefts are always reversible, and this property distinguishes them from *wh*-embedded clauses which are not clefts. Compare the following:

> *What he said* was that he didn't like the play. (*wh*-cleft)
> *What he said* was very interesting. (nominal relative clause)

The first is a *wh*-cleft, corresponding to the plain version *He said that he didn't like the play*. The next is NOT a *wh*-cleft. There is no equivalent to the form **He said very interesting*. Another way to test this is to try for reversibility. The first is reversible, the second is not:

> That he didn't like the play was what he said.
> *Very interesting was what he said.

Certain stereotyped *wh*-clefts (which are not all reversible) such as *What happened was . . ., What I mean is . . .* and *The thing is . . .* are also used for a variety of purposes such as pre-signals to certain speech acts, such as giving an excuse or an explanation:

> *What happened was* that I missed the last train.
> *The thing is*, we have tickets for a concert that evening.
> *What I mean is* we should all try to convince him.

30.3 THE ACTIVE–PASSIVE ALTERNATIVE

In describing situations which involve two participants, it is usually possible to take one or other participant as Subject and Theme/Topic. This is done in English by means of the active–passive voice alternative:

> *The President* has released the prisoners. (active voice)
> *The prisoners* have been released [by the President]. (passive voice)

In the active construction, the Agent is mapped on to Subject and Theme/Topic, while the Affected is in final position and receives normal, unmarked end-focus:

The President	has released	the prisoners.
Agent		Affected
Subject		Direct Object
Theme/Topic	_____	Rheme _____
		Unmarked end-focus

In the passive construction these correspondences are reversed. The Affected is now promoted to Subject and provides the point of departure, while the Agent is demoted from its privileged position as Subject and is usually omitted. If present, it occupies final position and receives normal end-focus:

The prisoners	have been released	[by the President]
Affected		Agent
Subject		Adjunct
Theme/ Topic	_____	Rheme _____
		[optional end-focused element]

We can see that the active–passive alternative allows speakers and writers to exploit the two main positions in the clause, the beginning and the end. In each case, a single clause can be arranged so that important new information is placed in end-position, while already known information is placed at the beginning. What is new and important and what is known is of course estimated by the speaker, and is dependent on the context and the estimated state of knowledge at that point in the discourse.

30.3.1 Promoting one participant, demoting another

From the point of view of the textual organisation of what the speaker wants to say, it follows that any of three possibilities may condition the choice between active and passive:

1. An element which is not Agent is desired as Theme/Subject/Topic.
2. The Agent is New information, so will be placed last.
3. The Agent is not New and is silenced. Some other element is New and is placed last.

It is not simply a change of position that is involved in the re-structuring of the passive clause. It is also a question of topic promotion and demotion. In the active clause, the Agent–Subject has the discourse role of Topic. That is, it is the most important participant of the discourse at the point when the clause is produced. In the passive clause, the Agent ceases to be Subject/ Topic. Another participant (usually the Affected) takes on the roles of both Subject and Topic. The Recipient (see 6.2.1) can also become Subject in a passive clause, as in *The boy was given a mountain bike for his birthday*.

The demotion of one participant and the promotion of another are two sides of the same coin. If we demote the Agent (or Experiencer, or Sayer), then a different participant (Affected, Recipient) is automatically promoted to Subject. It is clear, therefore, that, first, the passive is not a type of fronting or thematisation; second, it does not produce a marked Theme, but a different unmarked Theme; and third, the type of Theme involved is a participant Theme, which in this book we call Topic. Circumstantial Themes and textual Themes are optional additions to the core clause and play no part in restructuring the clause as passive.

We now turn to the discourse motivations that involve the choice of passive. Basically, these are: to cut out unnecessary Given information; to manoeuvre important information into end position; to establish smooth connections between clauses, making for good information flow. These motivations work together in connected discourse. Choices of passive against active are not open, but are conditioned in each individual case by the immediate contextual environment.

30.3.2 Choosing to be informative

Using the passive gives us the choice of *not* stating who carried out the action. This is an important factor, because in the active clause this information can't be omitted. What conditions our choice, then, between a passive without an agent and one in which we keep the Agent in a *by*-phrase at the end? The answer is: informativeness. If the Agent is new important information, keep it. If not, omit it. Look at this extract from Stephen Hawking writing about black holes, in which there is an example of each type:

> Although the concept of what we call a black hole goes back more than two hundred years, the name black hole *was introduced* only in 1967 *by the American physicist John Wheeler*. It was a stroke of genius: the name ensured that black holes entered the mythology of science fiction. It also stimulated scientific research by providing a definite name for something that previously had not had a satisfactory title. The importance in science of a good name *should not be underestimated*.

In this passage, Hawking gives credit to the originator of the term *black hole*, with the full name of the physicist encoded as an Agent *by*-phrase. The second passive has no Agent because it is generic and implied (by *anyone working in science*).

An additional motivation for the use of a passive with an Agent *by*-phrase occurs when the Agent is long. By putting it at the end we follow the principle of end-weight ('shortest first, longest last') as in the following examples, in which the Agent is 'weightier' than the passive Subject:

The front seats were filled *by members of the families of the victims.*
The goal was scored *by Raúl, the player with most goals to his credit this season.*

It is clear that **end-focus, end-weight** and **informativeness** are closely linked. New participants introduced onto the scene of discourse need to be described and defined in more detail than known ones. They are, consequently 'heavy' and are better placed at the end, whereas the subject in a passive clause tends to be 'light' (*the front seats, the goal*), pronouns being the lightest.

Instead of an Agent, an event or a force of nature may occur in final position, as in the examples below, while *Scotland's railway network* and *the house* will be considered important enough to become subject:

Scotland's railway network has been paralysed *by the one-day strike.*
The house was struck *by lightning.*

30.3.3 Passives without an Agent

We have seen that uninformative Agents are silenced in discourse. More exactly, this may happen because the Agent is implied by the nature of the verb, but is unknown **1**; anaphorically predictable **2**; predictable by general knowledge **3**; universal or general **4**; irrelevant at this point in the discourse **5**; deliberately silenced in order to avoid giving or taking blame or responsibility **6** or to maintain privacy **7**; finally, recoverable as the author of the text. Authorial 'I' is preferably not mentioned in formal writing **8**:

1 My car has been stolen.
2 When he won his gold medal he gave a huge party. Everyone was invited. [by him]
3 The heart transplant was carried out successfully. [by one or more surgeons]
4 It is hoped that war can be avoided. [Everyone has this hope]
5 Ten thousand soldiers will be needed to operate the emergency service.
6 The documents have been shredded and the fax hasn't been sent.
7 It was given to me as a present. [speaker doesn't want to reveal the Agent]
8 This point will be dealt with in a later chapter.

When the Agent *by*-phrase is omitted in a passive clause, some other element necessarily receives end-focus. This may be a verb **9**, an Adjunct **10**, or a Complement **11**. For a verb to be focused, it must contain the main New information and the Agent must be dispensable.

9 *Is* this seat *taken*?
10 Nothing has been heard of him *for months*.
11 The letters had been sent *unstamped*.

30.3.4 Making smooth transitions

Look at the following examples. Version **A** is based on a real occurrence:

A. Ann: Where did you get *that wallet*?
        Jo: *It* was given to me by   my *GIRL-friend*.
               Given............................ New

In this exchange *that wallet* is introduced at the end of the first clause and is picked up as subject pronoun in the second. Here we have again the simple linear Theme–Rheme pattern, but in this case it is the choice of the passive that enables the speaker to maintain topic continuity, as well as unmarked end-focus. Now look at version **B**:

B. Ann: Where did you get *that wallet*?
        Jo: My GIRL-friend   gave it to me.
               New................................ Given

In this version, instead of initiating a topic chain headed by *that wallet*, a new participant (my GIRL-friend) is introduced, as subject, necessarily with heavy stress (marked focus). This compensates for the lack of topic continuity, since in English stress patterns override the usual Given–New pattern, producing instead a New–Given pattern.

It is not necessarily the passive which serves to maintain topic continuity, however. Compare the versions **b.** and **c.** in each of the following sets of clauses. In each case **c.** rather than **b.** preserves the continuity better with **a.**, whether by means of the passive

(**1** and **2**) or the active (**3**). Moreover, **2b** violates the 'animacy' and 'empathy' hierarchies, which give priority to human referents. All are grammatically acceptable, however.

1a. The Prime Minister stepped off the plane.
1b. Journalists immediately surrounded her.
1c. She was immediately surrounded by journalists.

2a. The Prime Minister stepped off the plane.
2b. The wind immediately buffeted her.
2c. She was immediately buffeted by the wind.

3a. The Prime Minister stepped off the plane.
3b. All the journalists were immediately greeted by her.
3c. She immediately greeted all the journalists.

30.3.5 The *get*-passive

The *get*-passive is used much more in speech than in writing and has an informal flavour, the reverse of the *be*-passive. Here are some examples from conversation:

Poor fellow, he *got knocked down* in a road accident.
She *got bitten* by a new bug of some sort in France.
I *got attacked* by a fan at a football match.
He *got promoted*, the lucky devil!

The *get*-passive grammaticalises affective meaning, and so potentially reflects speakers' **involvement**, whereas the *be*-passive is more objective. The use of the *get*-passive is therefore an option. Speakers' interest centres on the *get*-passive subject and what happens to it, while with the *be*-passive interest centres on the event. Involvement of the subject referent is also implied by the *get*-passive, in that the subject is partly responsible for the significant result, whether this is beneficial or adverse. The *be*-passive, by contrast, is neutral. Compare:

a. She *got* (herself) *promoted.*   **b.** She *was promoted.*
a. I *got stung* by a wasp.   **b.** I *was stung* by a wasp.

The action undergone by the subject of the *get*-passive is more often adverse than beneficial. In fact, all the adverse and violent things that can happen to a person or thing are expressible by the *get*-passive: *get arrested, abused, fined, fired, beaten up, burgled, kidnapped, killed, mugged, raped, sacked, shot, vandalised* and many more. The subject referent is either unlucky or has made an error of judgement (being at the wrong place at the wrong time) when bad events are described. On happier occasions, such as getting invited or promoted, there is often an implication that the subject referent has contrived to be promoted, invited and so on, or was lucky, being at the right place at the right time. Here is another extract from Hawking's *Black Holes and Baby Universes*, with an example of each type of passive. He is discussing the idea that:

> if one could pass through a black hole, one might re-emerge anywhere in the universe. Quite how to choose your destination is not clear: you might set out for a holiday in Virgo and end up in the Crab Nebula.
>
> I'm sorry to disappoint prospective galactic tourists, but this scenario doesn't work: if you jump into a black hole, *you will get torn apart and crushed out of existence.* However, there is a sense in which the particles that make up your body will carry on into another universe. I don't know if it would be much consolation to *someone being made into spaghetti* in a black hole to know that his particles might survive.

30.4 THE PRESENTATIVE FUNCTION OF EXISTENTIAL CLAUSES

There are several reasons for thinking that existential *there* has acquired a new role:

- We saw in 19.3 the structure of the existential clause (unstressed *there* + a form of *be* + a NG), as in *There was a fight.* The semantic role of Existent is associated with the NG, which occupies the position after the verb and is, experientially, the notional subject.
- Unstressed *there*, however, fulfils most of the syntactic requirements for subject, as seen in 5.1.1, including its use in the tag: *There's a café just round the corner, isn't there?*
- Plural concord is not always maintained in spoken English, as for example: *There's some chocolate chip cookies out there* if you want some.
- Existential *there* can occur with the stressed adverb of place *there* in the same clause, as in *There's plenty more over there.*

These facts support the view that existential *there* (and especially *there's*) has lost its original locative meaning and is on the way to becoming a kind of introductory particle. An alternative view is that its locative and deictic meaning is not entirely lost: rather, *there* points to the upcoming noun.

Unstressed *there* is a presentative device in discourse. *There* points to the New information conveyed by the noun group placed at the end of the clause, where it carries end-weight and end-focus. In the basic types, the reverse order is not allowed, as we can see in the examples below. In these, a verb of very low communicative dynamism, *be*, placed in final position and preceded by an indefinite subject, violates the Given–New progression. The result is an ungrammatical clause in most cases. The corresponding existential clauses in 1–4 here are therefore **basic existentials**: they have no corresponding plain clause.

1 *Hundreds of millions of stars are.   There are hundreds of millions of stars.
2 *Plenty of time is.   There is plenty of time.
3 *A storm was last night.   There was a storm last night.

4	*Seven of us are in the family.	There are seven of us in the family.
5	?A man is at the door.	There's a man at the door.

30.4.1 Derived existentials

These are existentials that have a corresponding plain clause, based on a 'weightier' verb than *be*. In the following examples, the verb of the plain clause (*bark, hijack*) appears in the post-modifier position of the existential NG:

Existential clause	**Plain clause**
There's a dog barking outside.	A dog is barking outside.
There was another plane hijacked yesterday.	Another plane was hijacked yesterday.

Semantically, the location and/or the quantification of the NG referent are important (see 19.3) because such features may well be the most informative part of the utterance. When we say, for instance, *there's no milk*, it is not the non-existence of milk that we are predicating, but rather the fact that there is no quantity of milk available at the moment of speaking. The spatial location is implicit. 'Existence', then, has to be understood in a very broad sense.

30.4.2 Short existentials

Short existentials, many containing a negative word specifying no quantity or number such as *no, none, nobody/ no-one* and *nothing*, are common in everyday English, as in the following examples:

1. There's no problem.
2. There's no point staying on then, is there?
3. There's nothing wrong, nothing at all.
4. There's nothing on television.
5. There's no-one around today.
6. There's none left.

One of the functions of negation is to deny something previously said or implied, and this may be the motivation for some utterances in context (**3** and **6**, for instance). But speech acts such as reassurance (**1** and **3**) may be the motive for the denial. Positive declarative existentials may provide factual information (**8**) or, when they refer to the future, may be interpreted as predictions (**7**) or assurances (**9**):

7. I think this is a long-term battle. *There will be battles.* (George W. Bush, remarks to the employees of the Pentagon, 17 September 2001)
8. There *have been* heavy snowfalls in the north.
9. There *is bound to be* another opportunity.

30.4.3 Extended existentials

These occur as the result of expansions of the noun group (see 19.3). Common expansions include -*ing* clauses, which present an entity in action **1** or in a state **2**. Certain postposed adjectives can express a temporary state **3**, **4**. Passives and comparatives are also common, especially with the constructions *there's nothing better/worse than . . .* in **5** and **6** respectively:

1 There are hundreds of people *clamouring for food.*
2 There is a box *containing dynamite* in the corner.
3 There was plenty of food *available.*
4 There are not many shops *open* at this hour.
5 There were several civilians *killed in a terrorist attack yesterday.*
6 There's nothing worse than being stuck in a traffic jam when you're late for an appointment. (comparative clause)

The function of these expansions is to establish the relevance and coherence of the new referent at the point when it is introduced into the discourse.

In formal English and in fiction, verbs of **appearing** and **emerging** lend themselves naturally to the presentation of New information (see 19.3) as in *Fossil records suggest that there emerged a fern resistant to this disease.* However, existence or appearance should not always be taken in a literal sense, but rather in relation to the discourse: it is appearance on the scene of discourse, or cognitive awareness, that counts. Because of this, even a verb like *disappear* may, in an appropriate context, function as a presentative, as in the first sentence of the novel by H. P. Lovecraft, *The Strange Case of Charles Dexter Ward*:

> From an asylum for the insane near Providence, Rhode Island, *there* recently *disappeared* an exceedingly singular person.

From this it becomes clear that the notions 'bringing something into cognitive awareness' or 'onto the scene of discourse' are the key to the discourse function of *there*-structures. In this sense we can also apply the traditional term 'existential': once introduced, the new referent is 'present' in the discourse, and can be taken up and developed as a topic.

30.4.4 *There*-structures as states of affairs

A *there*-structure is commonly used in English to express events, happenings and states of affairs in a schematic way, without the intervention of participants. Frequently, the noun is a nominalisation of a verbal process (see 21.2):

1 There was *a fight.*
2 There was *an abrupt knock at the door.*

3 There has been *unprecedented industrial expansion*.
4 There was *a sudden feeling of panic*.
5 There is still *bribery*, there is *still corruption*. No doubt there always will be.

There-constructions with nominalisations have the effect of silencing the Agent of the action. We don't know who knocked at the door, who panicked, who bribes whom, who fought whom. The occurrence is the only important part of the message.

While the NG is typically indefinite, even definite NGs – which represent referents that are already accessible – can be introduced by a *there*-construction. This typically occurs when listing names of people or things **1**, or when moving on to a new related topic **2**:

1 Who's coming to the barbecue? Well, there's Silvia and Pete, and Megan . . .
2 (Describing a nation and its peoples) And then there are the poor.

This is how a woman described her new portable sauna bath, introducing each part by means of a *there*-construction:

There's *an oval mat you put down on the floor*,[1] then *there's the box which holds the heating element*,[2] with a wooden seat on it – I put a towel on top, otherwise it gets too hot – then *there are the sides which are soft and which you zip up*.[3] It all packs away neatly afterwards.

[1]indefinite NG; [2]definite NG; [3]definite NG

30.5 EXTRAPOSITION OF CLAUSES

Certain types of long subject clauses are usually avoided in English because they violate the end-weight principle, and sound awkward (see p. 47). **Finite *that*-clauses, *wh*-nominal clauses** and ***to*-infinitive clauses** can all be shifted to the end of the sentence and replaced by 'anticipatory *it*' in subject position. The resulting structure is called **extraposition**.

Clause as Subject	**Extraposed clause**
That the banks are closed on Saturday is a nuisance.	*It*'s a nuisance *that the banks are closed on Saturday*.
What they are proposing to do is horrifying.	*It*'s horrifying *what they are proposing to do*.
To interfere would be unwise.	*It* would be unwise *to interfere*.

Extraposed clauses are much preferred in English to the non-extraposed, as they sound much less awkward. The reason for this is that they satisfy the principles of end-weight and end-focus, thus 'packaging' the information in a way that is easier to process. For extraposed direct object clauses see 6.1.2d.

Extraposition is often used to express an opinion or to argue one's case. An evaluative word, such as *a nuisance, horrifying, unwise* comes in the middle, carrying a certain amount of stress. The main focus falls at the end of the sentence, reversing the distribution of information in the non-extraposed clause.

Normal *-ing* clauses as subject are not perceived to be awkward, and there is less motivation to extrapose them. When they are extraposed, they are usually short and do not necessarily carry the main focus. For this reason they give the impression of being additions to the main clause, rather than extraposed subjects:

Having you with us has been a PLEASURE.	*It's* been a PLEASURE, *having you with us.*
Seeing all the family again was NICE.	*It* was NICE *seeing all the family again.*

Unlike some languages, English does not normally allow extraposed NGs: **It was amazing his insolence* is not possible – though, as a right dislocation (see 28.11) with appropriate intonation, it is possible to have *It was amazing, his insolence*, where a pause or a comma signals the dislocated NG. A few extraposed NGs do occur, however, and these contain expressions of quantity or extent, as follows:

> It's unbelievable *the lengths some people are prepared to go to.*
> It surprises me *the amount of work he can get through.*

Obligatory extraposition after *seem, appear, happen, look as if* – after the expressions *it's high time, it's a pity, it's no use*, and the passive of *say, hope* and *intend* – is illustrated in 5.1.2.

Certain constructions do not admit extraposition. One of these is the *wh*-cleft with a clause as subject, as in *What we should do next is the main problem.* (**It is the main problem what we should do next.*) Another case is multiple embedding, as in *That he failed his driving test the seventh time demonstrates that he lacks confidence.* Here the first *that*-clause cannot be extraposed over the second (**It demonstrates that he lacks confidence that he failed his driving test for the seventh time*).

30.5.1 Raised elements as new Themes

A person or thing mentioned in the extraposed clause, as direct object or even as part of the adjunct, can sometimes be brought forward ('raised') to stand as Theme. The result is a new subject Theme which is a person or thing (see also 37.4):

> To cook *rice* is easy – It is easy to cook *rice* – *Rice* is easy to cook.
> To live with *Bill* is difficult – It is difficult to live with *Bill* – *Bill* is difficult to live with.
> To teach *her* is a pleasure – It is a pleasure to teach *her* – *She* is a pleasure to teach.

Only certain adjectives and nouns permit the final raising stage. They express an evaluative attitude to the situation, most commonly regarding the ease or difficulty involved. Interestingly, the new Subject/Theme appears to be made responsible for the situation.

30.6 POSTPONEMENT

Units can be made discontinuous when we want to avoid the awkwardness of having long, heavy units to the left of the main verb, especially when this is 'light'. Postmodifiers in NGs **1**, appositive reflexive pronouns **2** and clauses of comparison **3** can all occur:

1 [?*The time when no-one will write by hand any more* will come]
      The time will come *when no-one will write by hand any more.*
2 [You yourself did it]
      You did it *yourself.*
3 [?*More people than used to twenty years ago* are buying a second car]
      More people are buying a second car *than used to twenty years ago.*

30.6.1 Postponement with ditransitive verbs

We saw in 10.2 that certain ditransitive verbs – such as *give, deny, grant, lend, owe, show* among others – allow two alternative structures:

We've given the children bicycles. (SPOiOd)
We've given bicycles to the children. (SPOdOb)

This alternative allows us to place end-focus either on the Recipient (*the children*) or on the other participant, without using the passive. This way of adjusting the clause, to get the end-focus where we want it, is especially useful when one of the participants is Given information, often realised by a pronoun; this will normally be placed in medial position:

We've given *them* bicycles.
We've given *them* to the children.

The oblique object (*to the children*) must be distinguished from a Goal Complement, which has no alternative position. Compare:

I've sent the telegram *to the club's treasurer.* (oblique object)
      I've sent the club's treasurer the telegram.
I've sent the telegram to *his home.* (Loc/Goal Complement)
      *I've sent his home the telegram.

If we wish to combine destination and Recipient in the same clause, we replace the preposition *to* by *at:*

I've sent the telegram to the club's treasurer at his home.

Two-complement verbs which do not admit postponement of a Recipient are explained in 10.3.

FURTHER READING

On Theme and Rheme, Halliday (1994); on information structure, Chafe (1994), Fries (1981), Downing (1991), Halliday (1994), Thompson (1996), Jiménez Juliá (2000); on thematic progression, Daneš (1974); on functional sentence perspective, Daneš (1974), Firbas (1992); on topicality and coherence, Downing (2002), Downing (2004), Givón (2001); Goutsos (1996); on dislocations and existentials, Givón (1993), Biber et al. (1999), Huddleston and Pullum (2002); on Absolute Theme, Matthiessen (1995); for an overall view of relevant theories, Gómez-González (2000); on discourse markers, Schiffrin (1987), Jucker and Ziv (1998); on negation in discourse, Hidalgo-Downing (2000). On clefting, Collins (1991). On detachments and left/right dislocations, Lambrecht (1994), Downing (1997); on postponement with ditransitive verbs, Collins (1995). On cohesion, Halliday and Hasan (1976). On the *get*-passive, Downing (1996).

EXERCISES ON CHAPTER 6

Thematic and information structures of the clause

Module 28

1   †Underline the Theme in each of the following examples and say whether it is marked or unmarked. If marked, say which clause constituent has been thematised (fronted) in each case:

   (1)   Paul telephoned an antique dealer in Brussels.
   (2)   Abruptly they were cut off.
   (3)   Is he a friend of yours?
   (4)   Celebrating her victory today is downhill ski champion Marina Kiehl of Germany.
   (5)   Freezing cold it was.
   (6)   Meet me at eight at the Café de Paris.
   (7)   In the American soft-drinks industry, plastic bottles are extensively used.
   (8)   For months, all had been quiet in the Holy Wars.
   (9)   Crazy I call it.
   (10)   Never again will I fly with that airline.

2   †Thematise one constituent of the second clause so that it links up with the first clause:

   (1)   He asked me for paper, glue, sticky tape and clips. I bought him all of these.
   (2)   I swim thirty lengths a day for fun. You call it fun!
   (3)   He told us the history of the place. We already knew most of it.
   (4)   I can't remember what post Biggins occupies in the Government.   He is Government spokesman.
   (5)   I thought I would never get there but I did get there.

3 †The following extract is the beginning of a story by James Joyce.

> *Mrs Mooney* was a butcher's daughter. *She* was a woman who was quite able to keep things to *herself*: a determined woman. *She* had married her father's foreman, and opened a butcher's shop near Spring Gardens. But as soon as his father-in-law was dead *Mr Mooney* began to go to the devil. *He* drank, plundered the till, ran headlong into debt. It was no use making *him* take the pledge: *he* was sure to break out again a few days after. By fighting *his wife* in the presence of customers and by buying bad meat *he* ruined his business. One night *he* went for *his wife* with the cleaver, and *she* had to sleep in a neighbour's house.
> After that, *they* lived apart.

(1) First, identify the topic entities. Next, see how each is introduced. That is, which of the syntactic devices listed in 28.7 as topic introducers is used by the author to introduce Mrs Mooney and then her husband? Is Mr Mooney identified at his first mention? By what means are these topics maintained?

(2) Check in which cases Topic coincides with (a) Subject; (b) Theme.

(4) What does '*that*' refer to in the last line?

4 Each of the clauses below contains an experiential element as Theme. Add as many non-experiential Themes as you can from the types given in 28.12 (continuatives, adjuncts of various types, vocatives and appellatives), to make up suitable multiple Themes e.g:

Those flowers are ready to be thrown away.
But honestly, Mary, judging by the look of them, those flowers are ready to be thrown away.

(1) Violence in schools is an issue requiring urgent attention.
(2) Bad manners among motorists mean danger to others.
(3) What would you like for your birthday?

Module 29

1 In the extract from a conversation below, B tells how Susie looks for the money left by the tooth fairy under her pillow in exchange for her tooth, but her parents have forgotten to leave the money. Practise reading this text aloud, then tape your reading and compare it with that of a native speaker.

The prosodic features indicated are as follows:
//   tone unit boundary
| first prominent syllable of the tone unit ('onset')
↑   the next syllable is stressed and also steps up in pitch

-
- -   } pauses, from brief to long
- - -

Capitals are used to indicate the nucleus.

B | ANYway // - | Susie SAID // - that . there were | no such things as FAIRies // ELVES // ↑ this that and the ↑ Other // – WELL // . The | night she ↑ PUT // her tooth under the PIL | ow // we for | got to put the ↑ MOney there // and take it a ↑ WAY // we for | got all aBOUT it // (A laughs) so she got | UP in the MORning // – my | TOOTH'S all gone // and there's | no Money // | Dave said well / there you ↑ ARE you SEE // | YOU said | you didn't be | LIEVE in FAIRies // so | how can you ex'pect the ↑ fairies to come and ↑ SEE you if // - - | OH // but I | DO believe in FAIRies // (D laughs) you | KNOW // | | really DO // (A laughs) so | Dave said well – ↑ try Again toNIGHT // - -

(adapted from D. Crystal and D. Davy,
Advanced Conversational English)

2   †Read the following exchange aloud, trying to identify the intonation nucleus of each tone unit:

   A.   What did she say?
   B.   I don't know. I didn't hear her.
   A.   Didn't you hear anything?
   B.   No, I've told you, I was in the other room.
   A.   I don't think you care about Leslie.
   B.   I do care.
   A.   Why don't you talk to her then?
   B.   I'm always talking to her.

   (1)   Write in capitals the syllable which contains the nucleus of each tone unit.
   (2)   Which of the units have unmarked focus and which have marked focus? Justify your identification of each in terms of Given and New information, including emphasis and contrastive polarity.

3   Read aloud each clause of the advertisement on p. 242 (section 29.3) and discuss whether, as an utterance, each element in focus expresses an implied contrast, or is simply emphatic.

4   †The following extract is from the play by Giles Cooper, *Everything in the Garden*. In pairs, reproduce it from memory and then act it out, marking the intonation nuclei clearly. Then, look at the discussion question below.

Jenny: Do you want an egg?
Bernard: Are you having one?
Jenny: Do you want one?
Bernard: If you're having one, I will, otherwise no.
Jenny: You are a lazy devil!
Bernard: No. It's just that I don't want an egg enough to start everything going towards cooking it, but if you were going to do one for yourself, well, I'd want it enough for that.
Jenny: I don't think I'll have one.
Bernard: I'll do you one if you like.

Jenny: You do want one?
Bernard: No, I don't. I'll just do you one. You ought to eat.

What do you consider to be the principal communicative purposes of the marked focuses in this text?

5 †Complete each of the sentences below using elliptical or substitution forms. Some have more than one possible form.

(1) If YOU can't do it, I very much doubt whether I . . .
(2) I told you I'd given it back and I . . .
(3) They arranged to come and put in a new water-heater, but they . . . yet
(4) Peter asked the girls if they would like to go for a sail and they said Yes, they . . .
(5) Ed has the ambition to do some script-writing, but he really doesn't know . . .
(6) Sue's children usually want to spend a long time on the swings, but today they . . .
(7) He told me to turn down the next side-street and I . . .
(8) And it was a one-way street? – Yes, I'm afraid . . .

6 The following exchange, from an interview, contains an ellipted reply:

(a) A. You don't think genetically modified crops is the way to go?
    B. Definitely not.

The reply in the next exchange, also from an interview, contains no ellipsis at all:

(b) A. Did you take a bribe?
    B. I did not take a bribe, I would never take a bribe and it is absolutely out of the question that there was any bribe.

(c) Both ellipsis and substitution are economical. Can you suggest any conditions in which it might be better not to ellipt? And others in which ellipsis might be a discourse necessity?

(d) Comment on the use of ellipsis and substitution in ads, both written and spoken (for instance, on television and radio), as in *Ashamed of your mobile?*

Module 30

1 †Turn to the text *The 'lost' Van Gogh* on p. 248. Identify the thematic progression type used to link each clause to the next in the paragraph.

2 †Change the information structure of each of the following clauses into one *it*-cleft and, when possible, two *wh*-cleft structures:

(1) Experts are working on the recycling of plastic.
(2) Smoking can cause fatal diseases.

(3)   Last thing at night I unwind by reading and listening to the radio.

(4)   The computer industry is fighting against viruses.

(5)   Shortly after I got home I realised I had lost my purse.

3   †The following extract is the opening paragraph of a short story, 'Lord Mountdrago' by Somerset Maugham, in *The World Over: The Collected Stories*, vol. 2:

> **Dr. Audlin was a psycho-analyst.[1] He had adopted the profession by accident and practised it with misgiving.[2] When the war broke out he had not been long qualified and was getting experience at various hospitals;[3] he offered his services to the authorities and after a time was sent out to France.[4] It was then he discovered his singular gift.[5]**

(1)   Identify the single cleft sentence in the paragraph and say which element is focused.

(2)   What is the discourse function of this type of cleft?

4   †Decide whether option (b) or option (c) provides better topic continuity with (a). With which option could (a) be coordinated using *and* or *but* and a zero anaphor?

(1)   (a)   They stepped out of the coach.
        (b)   The owner of the hotel greeted them.
        (c)   They were greeted by the owner of the hotel.

(2)   (a)   Edith chose a piece of chocolate cake.
        (b)   She took it to her table together with an iced drink.
        (c)   It was taken to her table together with an iced drink.

(3)   (a)   James had planned to take the plane to Vancouver.
        (b)   An air-traffic controllers' strike delayed it.
        (c)   It was delayed by an air-traffic controllers' strike.

(4)   (a)   She stood on the solitary beach.
        (b)   She let the wind ruffle her hair.
        (c)   The wind was allowed to ruffle her hair.

5   †(a)For each of the sentences below, write the corresponding passive form, if passivisation is possible.

(1)   They founded the first kindergarten in the United States in 1856 in Watertown, Wisconsin.

        . . . .

(2)   That legacy has traditionally benefited Milwaukee residents.

        . . . .

(3) People have taken four-year-old kindergarten as much for granted as summer breezes off Lake Michigan.

. . . .

(4) Now there is a severe budget crunch. Milwaukee Public School officials have proposed the unthinkable: eliminating four-year-old kindergarten.

. . . .

(5) 'Are we to raise property taxes or are we to keep four-year-old kindergarten? These are the choices we may have to make,' said a school board member.

. . . .

(6) Gov. O'Keefe's new budget has produced the dilemma.

. . . .

(7) The budget reduces the proportion of the state's share of education costs and imposes cost controls on local district spending.

. . . .

(b) You now have a number of active–passive alternatives. Note that (2) does not passivise, but that the verb 'benefit' allows different postponed alternatives.

Now make the sentences into a text, choosing the active or passive alternative in each case, according to which you find more cohesive. Add conjunctions and conjunctive expressions wherever these help to clarify the logical connections.

6 Read the extract below from Raymond Chandler's *The Long Goodbye*, noting the use of presentative 'there':

> There are blondes and blondes and it is almost a joke nowadays. All blondes have their points, except perhaps the metallic ones who are as blonde as a Zulu under the bleach and as to disposition as soft as a sidewalk. There is the small cute blonde who cheeps and twitters, and the big statuesque blonde who straight-arms you with an ice-blue glare. There is the blonde who gives you the up-from-under look and smells lovely and shimmers and hangs on your arm and is always very, very tired when you take her home. She makes that helpless gesture and has that god-damned headache and you would like to slug her except that you are glad you found out about the headache before you invested too much time and money and hope in her. Because the headache will always be there, a weapon that never wears out and is as deadly as the bravo's rapier or Lucrezia's poison vial. There is the soft and willing and alcoholic blonde who doesn't care what she wears as long as it's mink or where she goes as long as it is the Starlight Roof and there is plenty of dry champagne. There is the small perky blonde who is a little pale and wants to pay her own way and is full of sunshine and common sense and knows judo from the ground up and can toss a truck driver over her shoulder without missing more than one sentence

out of the editorial in the 'Saturday Review'. There is the pale, pale blonde with anaemia of some non-fatal but incurable type. She is very languid and very shadowy and she speaks softly out of nowhere and you can't lay a finger on her because in the first place you don't want to and in the second place she is reading 'The Waste Land' or Dante in the original, or Kafka or Kierkegaard or studying Provençal. She adores music and when the New York Philharmonic is playing she can tell you which one of the six bass viols came in a quarter of a beat too late. I hear Toscanini can also. That makes two of them. And lastly there is the gorgeous show piece who will outlast three kingpin racketeers and then marry a couple of millionaires at a million a head and end up with a pale rose villa at Cap d'Antibes, an Alfa Romeo town car complete with pilot and co-pilot, and a stable of shop-worn aristocrats, all of whom she will treat with the affectionate absentmindedness of an elderly duke saying goodnight to his butler. The dream across the way was none of these, not even of that kind of world. She was unclassifiable.

From the use of the 'there' construction in this text, can you argue for the view that the existential structure expresses existence? Or is it a presentative or a cognitive device?

EXPANDING THE MESSAGE   *CHAPTER 7*

Clause combinations

CLAUSE COMBINING *MODULE 31*

SUMMARY

1   The term 'sentence' is widely used to refer to quite different types of unit. Grammatically, it is the highest unit and consists of one independent clause, or two or more related clauses. Orthographically and rhetorically, it is that unit which starts with a capital letter and ends with a full stop, question mark or exclamation mark.

2   'Complex sentence' is the term we shall use to refer to a unit consisting minimally of two clauses of equal status, or two clauses of unequal status. Coordinated clauses and those in an appositional relationship have equal status. Dependent clauses have an unequal status with respect to a main clause. Clauses embedded as Adjuncts are constituents of the superordinate clause in which they are embedded.

3   In everyday uses of English, coordination and dependency typically interrelate in various patterns that contribute to produce flexible and dynamic discourse.

4   Clause combinations reflect the cognitive organisation of our experience into what is presented as more salient and foregrounded, and what is less salient and backgrounded.

31.1 THE COMPLEX SENTENCE

The highest grammatical unit is traditionally called the **sentence**. Three possible types of sentence are usually distinguished:

- The simple sentence consists basically of one independent clause, as in *Sam bought the tickets*. The independent clause is the unit we consider primary, in that it comprises minimal grammatical completeness and unity.
- The compound sentence consists basically of two independent clauses, linked in a relationship of coordination, as in *Sam bought the tickets and Sue parked the car*.

- The complex sentence consists basically of one independent clause and one dependent clause, linked in a relationship of dependency, as in *Sam bought the tickets, while Sue parked the car.*

In connected discourse, however, the combinations may be more complex and variable than this simple outline suggests. Coordination and subordination of clauses do not necessarily occur unrelatedly, each in combination with a main clause, as illustrated in the compound and complex sentence above. More often they interrelate. Numerous combinations are possible. Here are two examples. In **1**, a combination of clauses occurs in a report about the dangers of walking on hills:

> **1** However, hillwalking is largely safe(1) but there are risks(2) and we have to educate people about these risks(3) if we are going to improve safety(4).
> [BNC CHK 1798]

After the connective adjunct *however*, two coordinated clauses (1 and 2) are followed by a unit consisting of a third coordinated clause (3) in which a subordinate conditional clause is embedded (4) as adjunct. This clause 'if we are going to improve safety' could alternatively be placed after 'and' but not at the beginning of the whole complex sentence. In these examples the + sign indicates coordination, the × sign subordination. Round brackets enclose independent clauses, square brackets enclose subordinate clauses,

> (hillwalking is largely safe) + (but there are risks) + (and we have to educate people about these risks) × [*if* we are going to improve safety]
> Adjunct

Example 2 comes from a news item and illustrates a different pattern: one independent clause with two subordinate clauses successively embedded as adjuncts:

> **2** A boy saved the lives of his brother and two sisters yesterday(1) when fire broke out(2) while they were at home alone(3). [BNC AHX 185]

The three clauses are organised in a hierarchical relationship. An independent clause (1) encodes the main content – a boy saved the lives of his brother and two sisters yesterday. Two subordinate clauses (2 and 3) encode the circumstances of time, when fire broke out, while they were alone in their home. The first of these circumstantial clauses functions as A in the independent clause, the second as A in the previous subordinate clause. This is a case of double, or 'layered' embedding:

> (A boy saved the lives of his brother and two sisters yesterday)
> ×   [when fire broke out
>   Adjunct
>   ×   [while they were at home alone.]]
>   Adjunct

Adopting a broader application of the term, we will say that a **complex sentence** can consist of any number of clauses of different types and in different combinations.

31.2 THE SENTENCE AS AN ORTHOGRAPHIC AND RHETORICAL UNIT

The structural criteria outlined in the preceding section are not the only criteria which have intervened in the traditional and widely accepted concept (or concepts) of 'sentence'. For most native speakers of English, a sentence is something that starts with a capital letter and ends with a full stop (AmE 'period'), a question mark or an exclamation mark. It is, then, a category associated primarily with the written language and can be described as an orthographical and rhetorical unit.

31.2.1 Clausal and non-clausal material

We have already seen (Chapter 5) how units of lower rank than an independent clause, such as nominal and adjectival groups, as well as incomplete clauses, appear in plays, stories and advertisements between a capital letter and a full stop, functioning independently as orthographic and rhetorical sentences. Such is the case with the italicised expressions in the following examples:

The large size is unavailable.	*Which is a pity.* (freestanding subordinate clause)
[A. We've got the deal.]	B. *Fantastic!* (adjective-headed exclamation)
You deaf or what?	(verbless clause)
A. Have you seen the satellites, erm, you know, our satellite places?	B. *Oh those, no, no.* (non-clausal) [BNC KBB 2402–2405]

The following advertisement from *Newsweek* uses full stops and a dash to reflect tone units, as described in Chapter 6. Here, units 2, 3 and 4 could be combined to form one sentence, just as when analysing spontaneous speech, we can attempt to make a distinction between clausal units and non-clausal material. As a structural unit the clause is easier to identify, because of its own internal structure, as described in chapters 2 and 3.

> With Fax the possibilities are endless.[1]
> It can send a document anywhere in the States within minutes.[2]
> Including drawings, diagrams – even musical notes.[3]
> Exactly as it's written.[4]
> Fax.[5] Worth making a song and dance about.[6]
>
> [1]independent clause; [2]independent clause; [3]PP or non-finite -*ing* clause; [4]dependent clause of manner; [5]NG; [6]verbless clause

In this advert, only [1] and [2] are structurally independent clauses. Punctuation serves to reinforce the presentation of each rhetorical unit as if it were independent, as would be done equally clearly if the text were read aloud.

To summarise, if we take the complex sentence as the highest structural unit, we can say that, structurally, the sentence is composed of clauses, but that rhetorically and orthographically it need not be. Both in conversation and in texts that simulate the spoken mode, we can find orthographic units that are **clausal** and others that are **non-clausal**. The difference is one of degree, however, rather than absolute. In context, ellipted material can often be recovered, as we saw in section 29.5. With other units, such as *fax*[5] in the advertisement, it is not possible to recover any material with certainty. Consequently this unit cannot in this context be considered clausal.

31.3 DEGREES OF DEPENDENCY BETWEEN CLAUSES

We adopt the view that dependency is not an absolute property, but rather a question of degree. It has been suggested that the degree of dependency between two clauses reflects the degree of integration, as perceived or imagined by the speaker or writer, between events. That is, the stronger the semantic or pragmatic connectivity perceived between two events, the stronger will be the syntactic connectivity between the clauses that encode the events.

The tightest integration is that of **embedding** (see 3.7.3), by which one clause functions as the constituent of another clause. In previous chapters we saw that in clause structure embedding occurs at Subject **1**, Object **2**, Complement **3** (Cs), **4** (Co), **5** (obligatory Locative Complement), and A (Adjunct) **6** and **7**. See also 5.1.2F (p. 46). For embedding of units in nominal group structures, see Module 49.

1 *Why he resigned* was never revealed.   (clause embedded at S)
2 She explained *that the machine was out of order.* (clause embedded at Od)
3 The question is *whether we can finish in time.* (clause embedded at Cs)
4 He made the club *what it is today.* (clause embedded at Co)
5 Put the flowers *where we can see them.* (clause embedded at C$_{loc}$)

Among the various types of Adjunct described in section 8.2, circumstantial Adjuncts of time, contingency and manner are those which are most similar to the central clause constituents. They are dependent on the main clause and subordinate to it. Unlike clauses functioning at Object and Complement, they are optional, they are not controlled by the verb and they occur in both initial and final positions.

6 *Although Ed is only seven*, he plays the piano beautifully. (subordinate clause as A)
7 Annie has been saving up *to buy her mother a birthday present.* (subordinate clause as A)

The functionally based reason for analysing such clauses as Adjuncts is the functional parallelism with adjuncts realised as adverbial or prepositional phrases. Compare:

The match was cancelled *because of the rain.*
The match was cancelled *because it started to rain.*

Like Subject and Object, they can usually be made the focus of a cleft:

It was *because of the rain* that the match was cancelled.
It was *because it started to rain* that the match was cancelled.

Circumstantial Adjuncts often appear to be more integrated into the main clause when they occur finally, as in **7**, than when they are initial, where they fulfil a framing function, as in **6**. These differences are explained and illustrated in section 35.5.

More peripheral are the *-en* and *-ing* supplementive clauses (see 8.2.2) illustrated in **8** and **9**, together with the so-called 'sentence relative' clause **10**, also a supplementive. Verbless clauses such as 'if necessary' are likewise peripheral. All are set off from the main clause by a comma and have their own intonation contour. Their function is to provide background information when they are placed initially, and supplementary details when final:

8 *Built of cypress, brick and glass*, the house exhibits many of Wright's significant contributions to architecture. (*-en* participal clause)
9 He sat and looked at her, *not knowing what to say*. (*-ing* participial clause)
[BNC HOF 2512]
10 The door may be locked, *in which case go round to the back*. (sentence relative)

Finally, at the opposite end of the scale of dependency, we have coordinated and appositional clauses in which one clause is not subordinated to another, but has a relationship of equivalence and interdependency based on similarity of function and on relevance of content.

We now discuss the structural relations between combinations of clauses and also the semantic relations which unite them. The latter are essential if we are to say anything of interest about the grammatical structure of any combination of clauses, since a mere enumeration of main and dependent elements reveals at best only the degree of complexity at sentence level, but not the semantic and pragmatic relations between the component clauses.

Relationships between clauses, both semantic and syntactic, are most clear and explicit when a subordinator or coordinator are present. Where these are absent, and especially if the dependent clause is non-finite, the relationship is less explicit. The functional motivation for less explicit meanings is that, at the point at which they occur in discourse, greater explicitness is not necessary, and economy of expression is preferred:

He has a summer job with a travel agency, *guiding parties of tourists.*
It's my new timetable – *to help me finish my thesis.*
They advised me to emigrate – *which is the last thing I'd do.*

TYPES OF RELATIONSHIP BETWEEN CLAUSES

SUMMARY

1 The clauses which comprise a complex sentence are related in two different ways: syntactically and semantically.

2 Syntactic relationships are basically of equivalence, holding between clauses of equal status, or of non-equivalence, holding between clauses of unequal status.

3 The semantic relations are grouped under the notion of expansion, by which one clause expands the meaning of another in some way.

32.1 SYNTACTIC RELATIONSHIPS AND SEMANTIC RELATIONSHIPS

There are two kinds of relationship between clauses that together form a sentence: syntactic and semantic.

The syntactic relationship is one of interdependency. Clauses are related to each other basically in one of two ways: either the relationship is one of **equivalence**, both or all clauses having the same syntactic status, or the relationship is one of **non-equivalence**, the clauses having a different status, one being dependent on another. Coordination and apposition display relationships of equivalence, while dependency and subordination are based on non-equivalence.

The semantic relations are very varied, as they represent the way the speaker or writer conceptualises the connection made between one clause and another, at one point in the discourse. Such connections do not simply link clauses within a sentence, however, but also clauses within a paragraph and paragraphs within discourse. These semantic relations can be grouped together under the heading of **expansion**, by which one clause expands another by clarifying or exemplifying (elaboration); by adding or contrasting some feature (extension), or by providing circumstantial information such as time, cause and condition (enhancement).

Both types of relationship, the syntactic and the semantic, are present in all the clausal relationships described in this chapter.

32.2 SYNTACTIC RELATIONSHIPS OF EQUIVALENCE: COORDINATION AND APPOSITION

Coordination is the syntactic relationship between units of equal status and often of similar form. For this reason, a repeated part may be ellipted, as in **3**. Semantically, the contents of the two clauses have to be seen as relevant to each other in some way.

1 I don't like it *and* I don't want it.
2 You can keep it *or* you can give it away.
3 It's a fine piece of furniture, *but* (it is) too large for this room.

The linking relationship is made explicit by the **coordinating conjunctions** ('**co-ordinators**' for short) ***and***, ***or*** and ***but***. In listing a series of elements, the explicit links may be omitted, although the coordinator is typically retained between the last two items. The coordinator can also be replaced by a comma in short conjoined clauses as in *This one's yours, that one's mine*.

It is not only independent clauses that can be coordinated. Dependent clauses may be coordinated as long as they have the same function:

It's much nicer here *when the rain stops* and (*when*) *the sun comes out.* (finite dependent circumstantial clauses as A)

She *sat* there, *watching television and eating chocolates.* (non-finite *-ing* dependent supplementive clauses as A)

When no explicit formal link is present, but the relationship is one of equivalence, we have **apposition**, as long as a relation of relevance can be inferred. This involves a kind of 'bridging assumption'. For instance, example **1** below relies on the knowledge that a hallmark guarantees authenticity. The term 'apposition' is extended here from its usual application to nominal groups in order to account for this type of relationship between clauses, which is close to coordination, but without an explicit link, as seen by comparing **2** and **3**:

1 It must be genuine; it has the hallmark.   (appositive clauses)
2 Tom is an astrophysicist and works at the CERN in Geneva
      (coordinated clauses)
3 Tom is an astrophysicist; he works at the CERN in Geneva.
      (appositive clauses)

Semantically, as such clauses have equal status, the information presented in one clause is as important as that presented in the other or others. This does not mean that such combinations are necessarily reversible.

Syntactic and pragmatic factors frequently intervene to make reversibility impossible. Three such factors are:

- if the second clause contains a term which refers anaphorically to an antecedent in the first clause, as does *them* in **1** below;
- if the second clause contains an item which makes it cohesive with the first, as does *as a result* in example **2**;
- if the order of the clauses is of pragmatic significance, as shown by **3** and **4**, which suggest different pragmatic interpretations:

    1   I have bought some beautiful tapestries and I think you will like *them*.
    2   There was no moon that night; *as a result*, they took the wrong turning.
    3   She got married and moved to York. (She first married and then moved to York)
    4   She moved to York and got married. (Her move to York resulted in her marrying)

See also section 28.13 for clauses as Themes.

32.3 SYNTACTIC RELATIONSHIPS OF NON-EQUIVALENCE: DEPENDENCY AND SUBORDINATION

When units of unequal status are related, the relationship is one of **dependency**. One clause is dependent on another or on a cluster of clauses, as seen in section 31.1. The relationship between the clauses is therefore not symmetrical, as with coordination and apposition, but hierarchical. Syntactically and semantically, the dependency relationship is most clearly signalled by subordinating conjunctions ('subordinators') such as *because, although, if, as*. However, when no subordinator is present, as often happens with non-finite clauses, as in **Clutching her umbrella**, *she hurried to a bus shelter*, the non-finite form itself indicates dependency. We here use the terms 'dependent' and 'dependency' to include subordination.

32.4 THE SEMANTICS OF CLAUSE COMBINING: TYPES OF EXPANSION

Traditional grammar has no terms for the overall semantic relationships holding between clauses, although (as we shall see) the syntactic relations are traditionally established. Following the classification proposed by M. A. K. Halliday, we shall say that in coordinated and appositive clauses the second clause **expands** the first clause by (a) **elaborating**, (b) **extending** or (c) **enhancing** it. The same semantic relations hold between a main and a dependent subordinate clause, no matter what position the subordinate clause occupies. These combinations are shown below.

Expansion	(i) coordination or apposition	(ii) dependency
(a) elaboration	Tom kept quiet; he said nothing.	Tom kept quiet, which was unusual.
(b) extension	Tom kept quiet but Ed spoke out.	Tom kept quiet, whereas Ed spoke out.
(c) enhancement	Tom was afraid and so he kept quiet.	Tom kept quiet, because he was afraid.

In clause combining by **elaboration**, one clause expands another by elaborating on it in greater detail – by **clarifying** it, in other words, as in (a).

In clause combining by **extension**, one clause expands another by **adding** something new – giving an **alternative** or an **exception**, as in (b).

In clause combining by **enhancement**, clauses of result, reason, and so on, expand the primary clause by contributing these **circumstantial features**, as in (c).

In the following sections we pay particular attention to the semantic features which result from the combination of these two systems, and the connectives which reinforce them.

ELABORATING THE MESSAGE   *MODULE 33*

SUMMARY

1   Elaborating clauses are clauses that clarify or comment on a first clause. These secondary clauses can be finite or non-finite, and occur in a coordinating or a subordinating relationship with the first clause. Connective adjuncts (**connectives**) such as *in other words, for instance, in fact, actually*, can be used to reinforce the semantic relationship.

2   Clauses in an appositional relationship have no coordinator. With finite clauses of equal status, the second clause provides a clarification of the first by restating or exemplifying it. Dependency with elaboration is manifested in non-defining sentential relative clauses which add extra, omissible information to the first clause.

3   As in all clause combining, the semantic relationships are typically much less explicit when realised by non-finite clauses.

33.1 APPOSITION AND ELABORATION IN FINITE CLAUSES

Appositive clauses stand in a syntactic relation of equivalence but have no formal link. The 'clarifying' meaning of elaboration is important in establishing the semantic connection between them, as in *it's no good – it doesn't work*. We interpret them by inferring the semantic connection between them, based on our cultural knowledge. In the spoken language, intonation is a helpful guide, while in writing the symmetry of this type of clause relationship is reflected in punctuation by the use of the semi-colon, colon or dash:

1   It's like going out with a child; she stops dead and refuses to go any further.
2   He had been drinking very hard – only I knew how hard.
3   You must make up a better excuse: no-one will believe that.

Evidently, the content must be appropriate. The secondary clause commonly 'elaborates' the meaning of the primary clause by 'exemplifying' it **1**, or 'clarifying' it – as a whole, or in part **2**. Causal relationships, such as reason **3**, can also be inferred. Ultimately, it is the choice of the speaker or writer to present the relationships as s/he sees them, relying on the hearer's ability to make the connection.

33.1.1 Clarifying connectives: restating, exemplifying and upgrading

Instead of relying on an implicit semantic connection between the clauses in apposition, the type of connection can be made explicit by the use of connectives that provide cohesive, not structural linking. The key concept is **clarification**, which is spelt out by connectives in three ways: restating, exemplifying or upgrading.

A. Restating

Here, the second clause restates the content of the first from another point of view, often making it more specific. Connectives include *in other words, or rather, that is (to say), specifically, namely, as follows* and *i.e.* (used only in writing).

> This picture is not an original; *in other words*, it's a forgery.
> We became tourists; *or rather*, we became tramps.
> There is still another topic to be discussed; *namely*, the re-allocation of space in this building.
> We need someone to fix this machine, *that is to say*, we need a mechanic.
> Alcoholic drinks are sold only to adults, *i.e.* people over 18.
> Several countries have signed the pact; *specifically*, all the EC countries have done so.

B. Exemplifying

In this, the second clause develops the content of the first by means of an example. Typical connectives are *for example* and *for instance*.

> There are lots of things you might do – *for example*, you might learn to play a musical instrument.
> You can't count on the trains being punctual here; *for instance*, the 10.55 left at 11.15 yesterday.

C. Upgrading

In this case, the second clause clarifies the meaning of the first by presenting a stronger argument for the point made, which in the case of *actually* may be contrary to expectations. These connectives can be used to signal discrepant viewpoints in conversation: *in fact, indeed, actually.*

I was completely ignorant of women; *in fact*, I knew none except my own sisters.
I didn't mind their questions – *indeed*, I was glad to be able to answer them.
We should get through this job fairly soon; *actually*, there is very little left to do.

33.2 SENTENCE RELATIVE CLAUSES

The syntax of dependency together with the clarifying meanings of elaboration provide the category of **non-restrictive (or non-defining) sentence relative clauses**. Non-restrictive relative clauses of whatever type are treated as **supplementives** (see Module 49 for defining and supplementive relative clauses in nominal groups).

The sentential relative clause has as its antecedent the whole first clause, or its complement. The relative pronoun is *which*. *Which is what* is also used, especially in spoken English:

> They decided not to go, *which turned out to be a mistake*.
> We promised you the sun would shine, *which it did*.   (tourism ad)
> His new novel is a bestseller, *which is what* everyone had expected.

The sentential relative is characterised by the following features:

- It is only loosely connected to its antecedent clause. Although its subordinate status is signalled by the relativiser *which*, it is a parenthetical supplementive that has considerable semantic independence.
- Semantically, the sentence relative makes an independent statement, which is an extension of the already complete unit. It adds additional, omissible information to something that is already presented as identified.
- These features have much to do with information flow, as explained below.
- Intonationally, the supplementive clause constitutes an independent intonation unit which is signalled by a comma or, more informally, by a dash. It contributes new information to what has already been established or is assumed to be known, for instance, that we promised you the sun would shine.
- The discourse function of non-restrictive clauses (whether sentential or nominal, as in Module 49) is to assert new information without making it the main point of the utterance.

Sentential relative clauses are becoming versatile in English. It is now quite common to find them functioning as freestanding subordinate clauses after a pause. They may be uttered by the same speaker or added by the addressee as a collaborative response, usually of an evaluative nature:

A. Perhaps she thinks it sounds better.   B. *Which it does really*.

[BNC KD8 44 447]

A. He goes out playing squash, then   [B No, I know]
he's not eating his main meal until
eleven o'clock at night.   *Which is stupid*   [KBC 14.505]

Many such clauses can be paraphrased by a coordinated clause (e.g. *and it does*). The relativiser *which* in a supplementive clause marks the closeness of the comment to the previous discourse. *Which* is sometimes considered as a one-word substitute for the coordinated or appositive structure.

33.3 NON-FINITE SUPPLEMENTIVE CLAUSES: SPECIFYING AND COMMENTING

The non-finite participal forms *-ing* and *-en* are used as supplementives to elaborate another clause by specifying or giving an explanatory comment on it, as in **1** and **2**. The non-finite form may have its own explicit subject as in **3** and **4**:

1 At that moment Charles appeared in the hall, *propelling himself in a wheelchair.*
2 The mountains were invisible, *enveloped in a thick mist.*
3 That was the last time I saw him, *his face all covered in bandages.*
4 The soldiers filled the coaches, *the younger ones eating sandwiches and chocolate.*

For thematised supplementive clauses, see Chapter 6.

Some of the elaborating types of clause combining occur in the following extract from an anthropologist's account of life with the Dowayos, a people of Cameroon:

> Faced with the impossibility of eating off the land,[1] I decided to keep my own chickens. This, also, was not a success. Some I bought, some were given to me.[2] Dowayo chickens, on the whole, are scrawny, wretched things; eating them is rather like eating an Airfix model of a Tiger Moth.[3] They responded to treatment, however. I fed them on rice and oatmeal, which Dowayos who never feed them at all found a huge extravagance.[4] One day, they began to lay. I had fantasies of being able to eat an egg every day. As I sat in my hut, gloating over my first day's haul,[5] my assistant appeared in the doorway, an expression of bland self-satisfaction on his face.[6] 'Patron,' he exclaimed, 'I just noticed the chickens were laying eggs so I killed them before they lost all their strength!'
>
> (Nigel Barley, *The Innocent Anthropologist*)

[1]non-finite *-en* supplementive clause; [2]two short coordinated clauses with the coordinator replaced by a comma; [3]two clauses in apposition; in the second, the meaning of 'result' can be inferred; [4]elaborating clause whose antecedent is the whole main clause; a further nondefining relative clause introduced by *who*, without punctuation, has 'Dowayos' as antecedent; [5]explanatory non-finite *-ing* clause elaborating on the previous finite clause; [6]verbless supplementive clause

EXTENDING THE MESSAGE   *MODULE 34*

SUMMARY

1   Extension combines the syntax of coordination with the meanings of addition and contrast. The second clause extends the meaning of the first clause by such meanings as addition, variation, alternation, explanation and exception. As well as the coordinating conjunctions *and, or* and *but* which connect the clauses, cohesive connective adjuncts such as *besides, in fact, actually* and *instead* can be used to reinforce these meanings.

2   Similar meanings of alternation and contrast can be expressed by finite clauses in a relationship of dependency, signalled by the connectives *while, whereas* and *except that*, among others. Non-finite clauses can be introduced by the conjunctive prepositions *besides, without* and *instead of*.

34.1 THE SEMANTICS OF COORDINATION

The combination of equal status and the meaning of extension is encoded as **coordination** between clauses. As we have seen, clauses can be conjoined when they share related meanings and fulfil the same function. Linking is carried out by the coordinators *and, or, nor, but* and *yet*. These have fixed positions at the clause boundary, unlike cohesive **connectives** such as *instead* and *actually*, which are more moveable.

34.1.1 Addition – and, or, nor, but, yet

Two situations are represented as adjoined in a relationship of equality that is positive, negative or adversative. The adversative expresses contrast:

   He doesn't like bacon *and also* he's better without it. (positive)
   I have no intention of going, *nor in fact* did I ever promise to. (negative)
   It's an extremely simple device, *but actually* it's very effective. (adversative)

Additive connectives include *also, furthermore, in addition, besides.*

Upgrading connectives include *in fact, as a matter of fact, actually.* The upgrading connectives that we have seen clarifying appositional clauses are equally appropriate with coordinated clauses, whether additive or adversative, since they add force to the argument. As can be seen from the previous examples, *actually* can indicate surprise; it also signals that what follows may be contrary to expectations. These features makes it especially useful with the adversative conjunction *but,* since contrast and surprise are compatible. *Yet* shares these features of surprise and contrast, and can be used as an alternative to *but* with surprisal and concessive meanings:

A four-year-old child was buried for three days under rubble, *yet* survived.

34.1.2 Variation – but instead; in fact; only

This is replacive coordination, which can occur after a negative or a positive statement. The second clause is presented as replacing the first clause or contrasting with it. Variation **connectives** include *instead, in fact* and *only. In fact* is here not additive but replacive:

He didn't stay even an hour, *but instead* returned to London on the next train.
Peaches are marvellous just now, *only* they are very expensive.
She promised to keep in touch, *but in fact* she never wrote or phoned us.

34.1.3 Alternation – either . . . or(else); neither . . . nor

Alternation is expressed by the coordinator *or.* The meaning can be reinforced by adding *else* (*or else*) and by the **correlative coordinators *either* . . . *or*.** These make explicit the meaning of alternation (*either we stay or we leave now*), which excludes one alternative, while the negative correlates ***neither* . . . *nor*** exclude both:

You should (*either*) accept his offer *or* (*else*) never see him again.
Either we give the tickets back *or* (*else*) we drop everything and go.
You should *neither* ask him for money *nor* accept it if he offers.

Connectives associated with alternation include *alternatively, conversely, on the other hand*:

We can arrange for a hotel room to be booked or, *alternatively*, self-catering facilities are available.
You can add the wine to the water, or *conversely*, you can add the water to the wine.

34.1.4 Explanation

The second clause comments on or explains the first clause:

There's one thing you must realise *and that is that I'm leaving.*

The following passage from Evelyn Waugh's *Brideshead Revisited* shows the use that can be made of apposition and coordination to present a situation as being composed of a number of related, though independent situations. It is noticeable that the author makes no use of explicit connectives to reinforce the meaning of the second clause; the semantic connection between the clauses is simply inferred, while the appositional relationships are signalled by means of punctuation:

> **There were few left in the mess now of the batch of volunteers who trained together at the outbreak of war; one way or another they were nearly all gone[1] – some had been invalided out,[1a] some promoted to other battalions,[1b] some had volunteered for special service,[1c] one had got himself killed on the field firing range,[1d] one had been court-martialled[1e] – and their places were taken by conscripts;[2] the wireless played incessantly in the ante-room nowadays[3] and much beer was drunk before dinner;[4] it was not as it had been.[5]**
>
> [1]elaboration (clarifying apposition); [1a–e]elaboration (exemplifying apposition); [2]extension (resultative coordination); [3]elaboration (restating apposition); [4]extension (additive coordination); [5]elaboration (restating apposition)

34.2 CONTRASTIVE DEPENDENCY – *WHILE, WHEREAS, BUT FOR THE FACT THAT*

Meanings similar to those encoded by coordination seen in 34.1 can also be expressed by the combination of dependency and extension. The conjunctions *whereas* and *while* introduce finite subordinate clauses which contrast in some way with the main clause, especially when there is also some point of similarity between the two, as in:

> Jane already speaks two foreign languages, *whereas* her brother hasn't yet learned any.
> Michelle, 24, works in an electronics factory, *while* Colette, 15, is still at school.
> [BNC A7P 409]

Whereas is more formal than *while*. For the temporal meaning of *while*, see section 35.4.1. *Except that, but that* and *but for the fact that* express the meaning of **exception**:

> I would take you to the station, *except that* the car is being repaired.
> It would have been a disaster, *but for the fact that* everyone helped to save the situation.

The forms containing subject–operator inversion (*were it not for the fact that . . . had it not been for the fact that . . .*) can also be used, but are more formal and are stylistically marked forms to express hypothetical situations.

The subordinator which expresses the meaning of **alternation** is *if . . . not*, and corresponds to *either . . . or* in coordinating combinations:

> If your purse isn't here, you must have left it somewhere. (= Either your purse is here, or you must have left it somewhere)

34.3 *BESIDES, INSTEAD OF, WITHOUT* + NON-FINITES

Functioning conjunctively to introduce non-finite *-ing* forms, we have prepositions:

- with an additive meaning: *besides, as well as*
- with replacive, adversative and subtractive meanings: *instead of, without, other than*

An alternative analysis to the conjunctive use of the prepositions is that of a prepositional phrase with a non-finite clause as its complement.

> *Besides/ as well as* caring for her own family, Mary runs a kindergarten. (additive)
> *Instead of* turning down that side road, *you* should have kept straight on. (replacive)
> He has embarked on a huge project, *without* realising what is involved. (adversative)
> You won't get any information from him *other than* by paying him. (subtractive)

34.4 IMPLICIT MEANINGS OF *-ING* SUPPLEMENTIVES

Without a preposition, the *-ing* form is indeterminate in meaning. We find it interpreted as having elaborative, extending and enhancing meanings, and we should not be surprised if in some cases it is difficult to determine the exact semantic nuance expressed. This is not to be considered as some sort of deficiency, but rather as an economical means of expressing relationships which are not required to be further specified, since hearers and readers infer the relevance of the relationship intended by the writer. With the *-ing* form and a main clause with a finite verb, the following implied meanings are typical:

- **an action (main clause) and a mental process (*-ing* clause) occurring simultaneously:**
    > They drove on, *wondering how long their petrol would last.* (additive = and wondered)
- **a mental process, with the *-ing* clause implying an adversative meaning + an action:**
    > *Not realising the danger*, she stumbled towards the edge of the cliff. (adversative = she stumbled . . . but she didn't realise the danger/without realising the danger)
- **two or more actions occurring simultaneously:**
    > The dog leapt forward, *baring its teeth.* (additive)

- **two consecutive actions:**
    Leaving the car unlocked, he walked quickly towards the group of people.
    (additive = He left the car unlocked and walked . . .)
- **the same, but replacive**:
    He barely stayed to express his condolences, *returning to London on the next
    train*. (replacive = instead, he returned . . .)
- **a mental process (-*ing* clause with an explanatory meaning) and an action:**
    Hardly feeling the cold, she removed her coat and gloves. (because she hardly
    felt the cold . . .)

Note that the main-dependent order of the clauses may be reversed (see Chapter 6
for the thematic significance of initial non-finites).

The following extract from David Lodge's *Thinks* . . . illustrates some of these
meanings, as well as coordinated clauses and an -*en* supplementive clause (*supervised
by Carrie*):

My 'lunch' invitation had been stretched inordinately, and in the end we all left the
house together at about seven o'clock. Suddenly the pace of life speeded up.
Everybody bustled about, supervised by Carrie, picking up things and putting them
away, resetting thermostats and turning off lights, drawing curtains and fastening
shutters, making the house secure for another week. It was as if the curtains had
come down on some dreamy pastoral idyll, and the company was suddenly
galvanized into action, shedding their costumes and packing up their props before
moving on to the next venue. We parted in the lane outside the house as we got into
our respective cars. I said goodbye and thanked them sincerely.

ENHANCING THE MESSAGE   *MODULE 35*

SUMMARY

1   We use the term 'enhancing' for those dependent clauses which expand the meaning of the main clause by providing some circumstantial feature: time, place, manner, condition, purpose, cause, concession, etc. They correspond in general to the 'adverbial clauses' of traditional grammar. Their function is to add background information.

2   Not all enhancing clauses are subordinate, however. *So* (of result) *yet* and *then* have a coordinating function when preceded by *and*, making the coordination explicit.

3   A great variety of conjunctions and conjunctive expressions are available to express circumstantial meanings. Non-finite verb forms are also used, of which the *to*-infinitive is the most explicit.

35.1 COORDINATION OR APPOSITION + CIRCUMSTANCE (COORDINATING ENHANCEMENT)

The combination of coordination (or apposition) and circumstantial meaning gives a kind of coordination that is intermediate between that of the 'pure' coordinators – *and, but* and *or* – and subordination. The secondary clause is introduced by one of the following:

•   the connective adverbs *then, so, yet, still* and the conjunction *for*;
•   a conjunctive combination formed by *and* followed by another item: *and then, and here, and this, and so, and yet*;
•   *and* plus a connective such as *at that time, soon afterwards, till then, in that case*.

Some of the circumstantial meanings expressed by these combinations are listed below:

time: *now; then*
> The lights have gone out; *now we won't be able to do any more today.*
> They spread the cloth on the grass *and then began unpacking the picnic things.*

place: *and there*
> She turned the corner, *and there stood Robin waiting for her.*

manner:
either (a) **means** (*and*) (*in*) *that way*
> Put labels on everything, *and* (*in*) *that way you'll know what you've got in the freezer.*

or (b) **comparison**: (*and*) *similarly; in the same way; likewise; and so . . .*
> The Secretary of the Association should be informed of any change of address; *similarly, the Treasurer should be notified of changes regarding the payment of subscriptions.*
> The face of a small baby is different from that of every other baby; *in the same way, the development of each child is different.*
> He likes music, *and so does she.*

cause/effect: *and so*
> We had left the tickets at home, *and so there was nothing to do but go back for them.*

effect/cause: *for* (rather formal)
> We left in silence, *for there was little we could say.*

condition (positive): *and then; (and) in that case*
> You might have an accident, *and in that case who would rescue you?*

condition (negative): *otherwise; or else*
> Replace everything carefully in the drawers; *otherwise something will get mislaid.*

concession: *still; yet*
> My age is against me; *still, there's no harm in trying.*
> He criticises his colleagues, (*and*) *yet relies on them for support.*

consequence: *consequently; as a result*
> He had not taken the precaution of being vaccinated *and as a result he got malaria.*

35.1.1 Inferred meanings of 'and'

Even without the help of connectives, the conjunction *and* is pragmatically interpreted, according to context, as expressing meanings of simultaneity, sequentiality, condition, cause–effect, result and concession:

> I made the sandwiches and Jill made the salad . . . (simultaneity)
> He got dressed quickly and went out. (temporal sequence)
> He was found guilty of harassment and was dismissed from his post. (cause–effect)
> You give me your telephone number and I'll give you mine. (condition)
> She came to my house and I was out. (inclusion: time 'while')

35.1.2 Similar meanings expressed by coordinators and subordinators

Certain meanings such as contrast and concession can be expressed by either coordinators or subordinators:

He was the best of them all *and* (*yet*) didn't come first. (coordinator)
He was the best of them all *but* didn't come first. (coordinator)
Although he was the best of them all, he didn't come first. (subordinator)

35.2 FINITE DEPENDENT CLAUSES OF TIME, CONTINGENCY AND MANNER

Dependency combined with enhancement is encoded as the traditional adverbial clauses of time, condition, purpose, concession, reason and manner. They are either finite or non-finite. When introduced by subordinators they are frequently termed 'subordinate clauses'.

35.2.1 Finite dependent clauses and subordinators

Finite clauses are introduced by a subordinator, which serves to indicate the dependent status of the clause together with its circumstantial meaning. Formally, subordinating conjunctions can be grouped as follows:

- **simple conjunctions:** *when, whenever, where, wherever, because, if, unless, until, while, as, although*
- **conjunctive groups:** *as if, as though, even if, even though, even when, soon after, no sooner*
- **complex conjunctions:** there are three subclasses:
  - (i) derived from verbs, usually from present or past participles, but occasionally from imperatives. All but the adverbial type have optional *that: provided (that), granted (that), considering (that), seeing (that), suppose (that), supposing (that), so (that)*
  - (ii) containing a noun: *in case, in the event that, to the extent that, in spite of the fact that, the day, the way*
  - (iii) adverbial: *so/as long as, as soon as, so/as far as, much as, now (that)*

Some of these conjunctions and the meanings they convey in finite dependent clauses are illustrated below. Certain meanings, such as time, have several subtypes: for instance, 'eventive' refers to an event that really occurs or occurred, whereas 'potential' refers to an event that hasn't yet occurred and perhaps won't occur. Other terms for eventive and potential are 'realis' and 'irrealis', respectively. Most conjunctions of time can be used to introduce either meaning.

Time

As (simultaneous)	The crowd roared *as* the ball went into the net.
After (anteriority) eventive	*Soon after* the war ended, the men returned.
Before (potential event)	He got away *before* they could stop him.
Since (starting point of duration)	I haven't seen him *since* we were at school together.
When (eventive)	*When* he saw me, he waved.
When (potential event)	*When* you reach the station, give me a ring.
Whenever (potential/eventive)	Come round *whenever* you like. He visits *whenever* he can.
While (time – simultaneous)	The burglar broke into the house *while* they were asleep.
Now that (time–reason)	*Now that* the days are longer, it's worth driving up to the Lakes.
As soon as (eventive)	*As soon as she got into bed*, the telephone rang.
The day (eventive)	We first met *the day* we went on a staff excursion.
The moment (potential)	*The moment* you hear the car draw up, give me a shout.
Until (duration + end point)	Stay in bed *until* the pain goes away.

Contingency

As far as (to the extent that . . .)	*As far as* I know, no date has been fixed for the wedding.
In so far as (to the degree that . . .)	*In so far as* their marketing policy is a policy at all, it may reach its targets.
If (open condition)	*If* all goes well, we should finish by tomorrow at the latest.
If (rhetorical condition)	*If* you believe that, you'll believe anything
Unless (negative condition)	You won't be allowed in *unless* you are wearing a tie.
As long as (condition)	Go wherever you like, *as long as* you don't get lost.
Provided that (condition)	*Provided (that)* you give me the order, I will deliver the goods in ten days' time.
Before (implied condition)	Get out *before* I call the police!
Although/though (concession)	He'll probably say no, *though* it's worth trying.
While (concession)	*While* I admire his tenacity, I deplore his ruthlessness.
Much as (concession)	*Much as* I dislike driving in heavy traffic, I've got to put up with it or live somewhere else.
As (reason)	*As* he's an only child, he gets a good deal of attention.

Because (reason)	We had to stay overnight, *because* the car broke down.
Since (reason)	*Since* he won't answer the phone, we'd better leave a note.
So that (purpose)	Fasten the sunshade securely, *so that* it won't blow away.
In order that (purpose)	*In order that* no mistakes should be made, everyone was informed by letter.
So that (result)	The oil tanker ran aground, *so that* the whole coastline was polluted.

Manner

As if / As though	He talks *as if / as though* he owned the place.
The way (manner)	*The way* things are going, there'll be more tourists than residents here.

Note that, when referring to a potential future event or state, the verb in time clauses in English, unlike some languages, does not take *will* or a subjunctive, nor a future perfect form of the verb, but instead a normal present or past form, occasionally *should* + infinitive. This is illustrated by the examples with *the moment* and *until*, and is equally applicable to other time subordinators such as *when* and *as soon as*.

Causal, concessive, conditional and resultative clauses depend on the hearer's knowledge of the world, which provides an inferential link between the content of the main clause and that of the dependent clause. For instance, in the example of the oil tanker, the inferred proposition that links the cause to the effect is suggested as follows:

The oil tanker ran aground	so that the whole coast was polluted.
(inferential link)	
[oil leaks from a damaged vessel]	

35.3 PRAGMATIC CONJUNCTION

Conjunctions express the semantic relationship between the units they connect, reflecting the speaker's view of the connection between states of affairs in the world. Pragmatic conjunction, on the other hand, has more to do with speech acts or with discourse moves than with experiential organisation as described above. Compare:

1   *If* all goes well, we'll reach Dover by four. (experiential)
2   *If* you're looking for Amy, she's left. (pragmatic)

In **1**, reaching Dover by four is conditional on all going well. In **2**, however, it is not possible to interpret the relationship experientially, as in **1**. The fact that Amy has left is not conditioned by the possibility that you may be looking for her. Rather, in **2** the *if*-clause specifies a situation in which the main clause *she's left* would be relevant. In other words, the *if*-speech act indicates the condition under which the following speech act counts. Now compare the following:

> **3** Sam arrived late *because* he missed his train.
> **4** Is there a fire somewhere? *'Cos* I can smell smoke.

In **3** the *because*-clause states the reason Sam arrived late – he missed his train. In **4**, on the other hand, my smelling smoke is not the reason for the fire. Rather, the *because*-clause – here in its abbreviated form *'cos* – gives a reason for the performance of the speech act of enquiring whether there is a fire.

Pragmatic clauses with ***'cos***, as in **4**, have something in common with non-restrictive supplementive clauses: both are semantically and prosodically independent while syntactically marked as dependent (by a conjunction and by a *wh-* relative, respectively). These somewhat conflictive properties lead one to think that both pragmatic conjunctions and the *wh-* non-restrictor are taking on functions in discourse different from the traditional functions ascribed to them.

Both **2** and **4** give reasons or justifications for the speech act expressed in the main clause. In a different sub-type of pragmatic conjunction, the conjunction itself implicitly signals the kind of speech act being performed. In **5** the contrastive meaning of *but* is pragmatic as well as semantic. It signals as inappropriate A's request to know the time, since speaker A has a watch him/herself: the adversative meaning of *but* here takes on the force of a mild protest.

> **5** A. Can you tell me the time?
> B. *But* you're wearing a watch yourself!

Pragmatic conjunctions occur sentence-initially and paragraph-initially, often at the beginning of a speaker's turn in conversation, typically (though not necessarily) in direct relation to what the previous speaker has just said, as in **5** and **6**.

And is the most difficult to characterise. One possibility is that, whereas ordinary *and* connects units which make up a single category of knowledge, pragmatic *and* re-opens a concluded category, making it an explicit point of departure for a new unit, a new direction in spoken and written discourse. It is common at turn boundaries in conversation and also in radio and television presentations (**7**).

So indicates that a conclusion has been drawn, while pragmatic ***or*** introduces a question. Both *so* and *or* elicit a response. ***For*** as a conjunction is always pragmatic, while ***since*** sometimes is – that is, when it gives a reason for the statement made in the main clause (**10, 11**). They are both rather formal.

> **6a** He stopped me *and* said 'Where are you going?' (experiential)
> **6b** *And* I said 'Just down the road to the bank.' (pragmatic)
> **7** *And* now it's nine o'clock and time for the news.
> **8** *So* this is where you live.

9 Can you give me a hand with this? *Or* don't you want to have it fixed?

10 We all fell silent, *for* there was nothing else to say.

11 *Since* you're here, you may as well sit down.

35.4 NON-FINITE CLAUSES EXPRESSING CIRCUMSTANTIAL MEANINGS

35.4.1 Explicit markers of circumstantial meanings

Not all conjunctions and prepositions are able to function as introducers of non-finite dependent clauses. Those that can do so form a subset of the total class of each:

subset of conjunctions

when	Take extra care *when* driving at night.
while (time)	*While* talking, he jotted everything down on a pad.
while (concession)	*While* agreeing basically with your proposal, we would nevertheless suggest certain amendments.
though	*Though* feeling unwell, she made an effort to appear cheerful.
if	*If* travelling abroad, watch out for pickpockets.
rather than/sooner than (with bare infinitive)	Rather/sooner than wait for hours, she returned the following day.

subset of (conjunctive) prepositions

before	Look both ways *before* crossing the road.
after	*After* applying one coat of paint, leave to dry.
since	I have thought about it a great deal *since* receiving your letter.
from	*From* being a junior clerk, he rose to become General Manager.
by	*By* turning this handle, you can make ice-cubes come out.
in	*In* learning a foreign language, several skills are involved.
on	*On* entering the mosque, we were impressed by its spaciousness.
with	*With* redecorating the house, our funds are pretty low.
without (concession)	*Without* wishing to offend our hostess, I should like to leave now.
without (reason)	*Without* having read the book, I can't give an opinion.

35.4.2 VERB FORMS AS CIRCUMSTANTIAL MARKERS

Certain circumstantial meanings of enhancement are frequently expressed by the *to*-infinitive, the *-ing* and the *-en* participle forms alone. Of these, the *to*-infinitive form is the most explicit, since it usually signals purpose. Some examples follow of verb forms used in this way:

to-infinitive clauses:	*To relieve backache*, apply liniment twice daily.
	Don't do it just *to please me*.
-ing clauses:	*Living abroad*, he rarely sees his relatives.
	(= because he lives abroad)
-en clauses:	*Too excited to sleep*, he paced up and down the room.
	(because he was too excited to sleep)

There is one use of the *to*-infinitive in dependent clauses which is extending rather than enhancing in meaning; that is, it seems to replace coordination, as in:

She arrived home *to find the house empty*. (= and found the house empty) (Adjunct of 'outcome')

Conventions of good English require that the implicit subject of a non-finite clause should be identical with the explicit subject of the main clause. Compare the acceptable (i) with the less acceptable (ii), which unintentionally suggests that the jellyfish was bathing in the sea:

(i) Bathing in the sea, I got stung by a jellyfish.
(ii) Bathing in the sea, a jellyfish stung me.

That this norm is not always adhered to is illustrated by the following 'editor's comment' from the BBC series *Yes, Prime Minister*.

[Working funerals are the best sort of summit meeting. *Ostensibly arranged for another purpose, statesmen and diplomats* can mingle informally at receptions, churches and gravesides, and achieve more than at ten 'official' summits for which expectations have been aroused. This is presumably why Hacker immediately agreed to a state funeral for his late and unlamented predecessor – Ed.]
(Jonathan Lynn and Anthony Jay, *The Complete Yes Prime Minister*)

35.5 DISCOURSE CONNECTIVITY AND COHESION: INITIAL VS FINAL CIRCUMSTANTIAL CLAUSES

These clauses are usually placed either before the main clause as in **1**, or after it, as in **2**:

1 *If you have a problem*, call us immediately.
2 Call us any time *if you need advice*.

Position is related to the degree of integration of the two clauses.

Semantically, a circumstantial clause in final position tends to have tight local connections to the main clause, to which it may be linked without a comma in writing or a pause in speech. In such cases it is closely integrated into the semantic structure of the main clause:

3 The problem arises *because there is nothing in our day-to-day life to provide us with sufficient exercise*. [BNC AYK 199]

From a discourse perspective, an initial circumstantial clause tends to have wider textual connections with what preceded it, often reaching back some distance. It also provides a frame for what follows, often for the whole clause or even more, as it can be not only sentence-initial but also paragraph-initial and episode-initial (see Chapter 6). It is likely to be followed by a comma or pause. Consequently an initial circumstantial clause is less integrated into the structure of the main clause. The following example illustrates the greater integration of the final *to*-infinitive clause compared with the framing function of the initial *because* clause. We consider both to have the syntactic status of adjunct, however, as both are embedded.

4 *Because* tranquillisers simply mask symptoms rather than provide a cure, you may need to seek help *to deal with the problem which caused you to need the tablets in the first place*. [BNC AYK 183]

Position is also related to information structure, discussed in Chapter 6. In a complex sentence, the initial clause is likely to contain given information, while the final clause tends to present the new. In **3** the main clause is initial, with 'the problem' referring to preceding discourse, while the clause of reason provides new information. In **4** we have the reverse: the reason clause presents as known the fact that tranquillisers mask symptoms, preparing the way for the main clause and the final purpose clause as new.

An initial dependent clause, often with progressive aspect (see 43.4), can provide a background state or activity for an event in past tense:

While all the other kids were pulling on their coats, the teacher found Harry sitting sobbing in the cloakroom. [BNC CHR 913]

REPORTING SPEECH AND THOUGHT

SUMMARY

1   Speakers report the utterances of other speakers, or their own, in one of two ways: either directly by 'direct reported speech' (also known as 'quoted speech'), or indirectly by 'indirect reported speech'. Thought processes can also be reported. Quoted speech supposedly repeats the exact words spoken, whereas indirect speech reporting gives the content or even only the gist of what was said.

2   Verbs of saying and of thinking are used to introduce direct speech and thought, respectively. Idiomatic uses of the verbs *go* and *be like* are also used by some speakers as alternatives to verbs of saying.

3   Indirect reporting of speech (traditionally known as 'indirect speech') reports the content of statements, questions and directives. A number of formal adjustments are made, referred to as 'backshift', which shift deictic elements away from the speech situation to the reported situation.

4   In fictional dialogue, and to a lesser extent in conversation, a wide variety of reporting verbs occur, many not strictly verbs of speaking, which aim to convey such features as speaker's stance, voice quality and speech-act force.

5   In addition, and in order to give the reader the illusion of entering a character's mind, writers of fiction combine features of quoted and reported speech to produce the varieties known as 'free direct speech' and 'free indirect speech'.

36.1 DIRECT AND INDIRECT REPORTING

There are two main ways of reporting what someone said or what we ourselves said: directly **1**, and indirectly **2**:

1   She said 'I'll wait for you'.
2   She said she would wait for us.

Direct ('quoted') speech reporting supposedly repeats the exact words that someone said or wrote, while **indirect speech** reporting gives the meaning, or the gist of the content. Depending on the verb used, a good deal of further information can also be provided – for instance, the type of speech act being carried out, such as asking, complaining, responding, or the voice quality of the speaker:

> 'I hear you've been having a tough time,' he *responded*.
> 'You haven't sent me the Sunday supplement,' she *complained*.

Between quoted and indirect reported speech, there is a difference of immediacy. In quoting, the quoted clause appears to have independent status; its effect, therefore, is more dramatic and life-like. Tenses, pronouns and other deictic elements are orientated towards the speech situation, while in reported speech they shift away from it. The formal modifications of this shift are explained in section 36.3.

There is also a difference in referring back to something which has been quoted and something which has been reported. To refer to the actual words quoted, a reference word such as *that* is typically used, whereas to refer to an indirect report, a substitute form such as *so* or *not* is used:

> He said, 'I'll pay this time.'   Did he really say that?
> He said he would pay that time.   Did he really say so?

This is because the quoted words refer to a real event that can be referred back to, whereas the reported version is a representation of a representation, that is of what someone said.

36.2 DIRECT REPORTING OF SPEECH AND THOUGHT

Direct ('quoted') speech is a common feature of everyday conversation, of fictional dialogue and, to a lesser extent, news and other genres. In direct speech, the reporting clause contains a verb of saying, while the reported clause contains what is said. The reporting clause may be placed initially, finally or medially. If it is placed medially, the quoted speech is discontinuous as in (**c**).With a proper name, inversion of subject and verb is another option (**d**). However, with a pronoun (*said she*), inversion is archaic.

> (**a**) She said, 'I'm a telly addict and I always have been'.
> (**b**) 'I'm a telly addict and I always have been,' she said.
> (**c**) 'I'm a telly addict', she said, 'and I always have been.'
> (**d**) 'I'm a telly addict', said Danielle, 'and I always have been.'

As there is no linking or subordinating element in (**a**) between the reporting verb and the quoted speech, the structural relationship between them is indeterminate. In (**b**), (**c**) and (**d**) the reporting clause is clearly parenthetical.

In spoken English, the reporting clause receives less prosodic prominence than what is reported, in whatever position it occurs. This reflects the fact that what is said is more important than the introductory clause of saying.

These two features – the mobility of the reporting clause and the importance of what is said – are sometimes interpreted as evidence that *I think, he said*, for example, in whatever position, are not main clauses at all, but are better analysed as epistemic, evidential or evaluative **parentheticals**, while what is traditionally classed as the complement clause is in fact the main proposition.

A further view sees the relationship between the clauses as one of projection: the reporting clause 'projects' the projected clause as either a locution or an idea.

Quoted speech in conversation and written dialogue

Verbs used to introduce quoted speech in conversation and writing are summarised in the table below.

Conversation	Written dialogue
say (and, less commonly, *tell*)	*Say* is the basic verb
go, be like	*Tell, write* (the latter quoting written sources is used only to characterise a type of user)
not normally used	Verbs quoting statements: *announce, explain, observe, point out, remark, report*
ask is used – the others not normally used	Verbs quoting questions: *ask, demand, query, enquire*, and exclamations: *exclaim*
not normally used	Verbs indicating speech act force: *affirm, answer, argue, beg, complain, object, protest, urge, warn,* or verbs which refer to the circumstances of the speech act: *interrupt, reply, respond*
normally only *shout*	Verbs indicating manner of locution: *bark, bleat, chirp, cry, drawl, grumble, hiss, holler, moan, mumble, murmur, mutter, scream, shout, shriek, snap, snarl, stutter, whisper, whine, yell*
not normally used	Non-utterance emotive verbs accompanying speech: Laughter: *chuckle, laugh, smile, grin, giggle, twinkle* Weeping: *sob, moan, wail* Excitement, concern: *breathe, pant* Incredulity: *gasp* Pain, anger: *bellow, choke, flash*

For the difference between **say** and **tell**, see Chapter 3. Basically, *say* is a two-place verb which does not take a core Recipient, not admitting, for example, *say me your name. *Tell* is a three-place verb with a core Recipient (*tell me your name*). Pragmatically, *say* is used to report a locution (what is said), while *tell* typically informs.

Go and **be like** are becoming widely used as **quotative** alternatives to *say*, both in younger speakers' conversation and in the popular media. Like *says* and *said*, *go* and *be like* signal that the speaker is moving into direct speech mode. Normal combinations of tense and aspect occur with *go* and *be like*; however, the present tense appears to predominate even for past time reference (*I'm like, she's like*):

> . . . and I *was going* . . . I'll have to take my stereo home and *he goes* yeah your stereo's quite big isn't it, and *I went* when have you seen my stereo and *he goes* oh I came up the other day to see if you were in. *I went* why why, he *said* I just came round to your room and you weren't there but your music was on.
> [BNC KPH 1361–1362]

> 'It's just happened so fast,' says the former Shanna Jackson. 'Some days people will call me "Paris" and I'm like, "Who?" My mother still refuses to call me Paris.'
> [BNC HSJ 663–664]

The range of verbs used as 'quotatives' is wider in written dialogue than in spoken because writers attempt to heighten interest by conveying not only the words said but also something of voice quality, attitude and manner of speaking of the character, whether fictional or real. All these are perceived by hearers in a speech situation but are absent from basic verbs of saying. Examples 1, 3, 5 are taken from *Lightning in May*, 2 and 4 from *Girls Out Late* and 6 from *The Peacemakers*:

1 'I'll take the cases,' he *whispered*.
2 'I haven't got any money,' I *hiss*.
3 'Come on, lads,' Tommy *yelled*.
4 'You're mad at me, aren't you?' I *mumble*.
5 'I said come in, Mrs. Friar!' John *barked* at her
6 Trumbic *gasped*. "You can't be serious."

Direct reporting of thought

Not only words may be quoted, but also thoughts. The first two examples below are often heard in the spoken language, the third would be typical in fiction:

> I think I'll have a beer.
> I wonder what he's doing.
> 'I'll have to get a new bulb for this lamp,' thought Peter.

Mental process verbs which occur as quotatives are few in number in English, in comparison with the wide variety of verbs used in quoted speech. They include *think*, the basic verb, and other verbs of cognition which express some additional, often aspectual meaning: *muse, ponder, reflect, wonder*.

In representing their characters' thought, writers of fictional narrative often omit the prosodic signals of quoting (inverted commas or dashes), and make the clause of thinking parenthetical. The following extract from Virginia Woolf's *Mrs Dalloway* illustrates this technique:

> He's very well dressed, thought Clarissa, yet he always criticises me.
>
> Here she is mending her dress; mending her dress as usual, he thought; here she's been sitting all the time I've been in India; mending her dress; running to the House and back and all that, he thought, growing more and more irritated, more and more agitated, for there's nothing in the world so bad for some women as marriage, he thought; and politics; and having a Conservative husband, like the admirable Richard. So it is, so it is, he thought, shutting his knife with a snap.

36.3 BACKSHIFT IN INDIRECT SPEECH AND THOUGHT REPORTING

Indirect speech reporting is characterised by a series of formal features that distinguish it from quoted speech reporting. They have the effect of shifting all deictic elements (personal pronouns, demonstratives, tense and adverbs of time and place) away from direct reference to the speech situation, and instead to the reporting situation, as in the following example (we don't give all the possible personal pronoun shifts, which depend on context):

'I want you to drink this juice.'   I/you/he/she said she wanted him/me to drink that juice.

The shifts involved are as follows:

- **Personal pronouns** in the 1st person, which refer to the speaker, are shifted to 2nd or 3rd person, unless the speaker is reporting him/herself, as in **1** below. The 2nd person pronoun, which refers to the listener, is shifted to 1st or 3rd, according to the identity of the listener, again as in **1**.
- **Demonstratives** and **deictic adverbs** which refer to the here and now (*this, these, here, now*) are replaced by more remote forms (*that, those, there, then*) **1** and **4**.
- **Verb tenses** are 'back-shifted' – that is, present forms are replaced by past forms **1**, **2**, **4**, **5**. This shift is not obligatory if the described state still holds, as in **3**.
- **Clause type** is also affected. A quoted interrogative with *say* is replaced by a declarative introduced by *ask* in reported speech **7**. Imperatives and verbless clauses have less clear correspondences, and are discussed later in this and other sections.

Direct (quoted) speech	Indirect speech
1 'I want you to drink this juice.'	I/ you/ he/ she said I/she wanted him/ me to drink that juice.
2 'I won't be long,' she said.	She said she wouldn't be long.
3 He said 'We are naked apes. They are the same as us inside.'	He said that we are/ were naked apes and that they are the same as us inside.
4 'Can you leave this book here?' he said.	He asked if I/ we/ she could leave that book there.
5 'It's good!' Magda says.	Madga said that it was good.
6 'Do it yourselves!' I said.	I told them to do it themselves.
7 'Must you go so soon?' she said.	She asked whether we/ they had to go as soon as that.

Verbs used in indirect statements and questions are essentially the same as those used in quoting. The main exceptions are shown in the table.

Verbs used only in quoting	Verbs used only in indirect reporting
	(a) verbs which express rhetorical processes: *claim, deny, hypothesise, imply, insinuate, maintain, make out, pretend.*
	(b) verbs of cognition, wishing and affection: *believe, feel, hold (=believe), imagine, understand, fear, suspect, think, hope, wish, want, like.*

(c) Non-utterance verbs as in 36.2, such as *laugh, smile, sob, moan, gasp*:
 	
   'Thank you,' she smiled.
   'Yes,' he sighed.
	Occasionally, these verbs are used in indirect reporting, for instance:
	
	   She smiled her thanks.
	   He sighed his consent.

(a) Verbs such as *claim, deny, insinuate* represent an interpretation on the part of the reporter of the speech act force in the original situation, and can indicate a certain stance, for instance of reservation or disbelief:

   She *claims* her mother was related to a Polish aristocrat.
   He *denies* being involved in the incident.
   Are you *insinuating* that he knows something about it?

(b) The combination of mental processes with a reporting clause is the normal way of representing what people think, believe, hope, want and like. These typically occur as reported states of wishing, wanting, and so on, since such mental states are rarely quoted; even the possible form with *let* as in *'Let me be the first to speak to him'*, *Janet wished* is relatively infrequent. Syntactically, they are no different from the complementation patterns described in Chapter 3:

> I hope that no damage has been done
> It is feared that many lives have been lost.
> She wishes she had never met him.

(c) Conversely, verbs which are not intrinsically verbs of saying are not normally used in indirect reporting. These include verbs of laughing, weeping, and the like, as exemplified in section 36.2. A quoted locution such as *'So what?', he sneered* would be difficult to report in a similar form, and even perhaps with a similar meaning. A paraphrase such as *He asked with a sneer what it mattered* might be considered acceptable within a certain context.

36.4 REPORTED OFFERS, SUGGESTIONS AND COMMANDS

So far we have considered quoted or reported statements and questions. We now turn to the reporting of directives – reported offers, suggestions and commands – which typically involves summary and paraphrase. Certain verbs are used in quoted directives but are not used for reporting. Conversely, there are many verbs used in reported directives that are not used in quoting. There is some overlap, however, as may be seen from the table below.

Quoted directives	Reported directives
the general verb *say*	the general verb *tell*
verbs specific to offers, suggestions and commands: *call, suggest, offer, order, request, tell*	some, but not all of those in quoted directives: *suggest, order, command, request, tell*
verbs embodying some circumstantial or other semantic feature: *threaten, vow, promise, agree, beg, insist, plead, urge, warn*	the same as in quoted directives
verbs with a connotative meaning: *bark, bleat, sob, gasp*	not used
not used	verbs expressing a wide range of complex rhetorical processes: *encourage, forbid, persuade, recommend*

36.5 CLAUSE TYPE IN THE REPORTED CLAUSE

When we quote an offer, order or suggestion directly, there is typically an imperative in the quoted clause:

> **1** '*Hurry up!*', she said (to us).
> **2** 'Do eat more slowly', she begged the child.
> **3** '*Come* in and *sit* down', I suggested (to her).

In reported directives, the imperative of the quoted type is replaced by one of four structures. The first two are:

- an Object + *to*-infinitive after verbs such as *tell, order, command, urge, beg* as in **1**, **2**; and
- a *that*-clause after verbs of recommending, insisting, proposing and suggesting as in **3** (see also Chapter 3).

The examples **1–3** of quoted directives would be reported as follows:

> **4** She told/ urged us to hurry up.
> **5** She begged the child to eat more slowly.
> **6** I suggested that she (should) come in and sit down.

Say takes a *that*-clause containing an embedded directive expressed either by the semi-auxiliary *be to* or by a modal of obligation (*should, must, have to*). See also Section 11.2 for the complementation patterns of *say* and *tell*.

Using *say*, example **1** could be reported as follows:

> **7** She *said* (that) we were to hurry up.
> **8** She *said* (that) we should/must hurry up.

Say can also report a *to*-infinitive clause with no subject (**9**). In AmE a subject of the reported clause is here preceded by *for* (**10**). In both cases the use of *say* rather than *tell* suggests that the message is being relayed by a 3rd person. Compare these with **11**:

> **9** She *said* to hurry.
> **10** She *said* for us to hurry.
> **11** She *told* us to hurry.

Of the verbs indicating manner of locution listed on page 301 and used in fictional narrative to introduce quoted speech, only a few can be used in reporting, and require an oblique Object. They are usually verbal processes with an emotive element predominating:

('Turn off the gas!', he yelled.)   He yelled to me to turn off the gas.
('Stay a little longer', he whispered.)   He whispered to her to stay a little longer.

Verbless clauses are quite common in quoted speech, especially in fictional narrative:

'Not a word!', he whispered (to us).   He whispered to us not to say/ breathe a word.

The absence of a verb presents a problem in reporting. Frequently a verb can be provided, although again this involves an interpretation on the part of the reporter. Inevitably, therefore, more than one reported version is possible, some differing considerably from the quoted version:

'This way, please', the usher said.   The usher asked/ invited (us?) to accompany
                                        him.
                                        The usher showed (us?) the way.

As can be seen from these examples, an additional problem in reporting verbless clauses is that not only a verb but also a receiver of the directive must be provided. Presumably, the context or the co-text would enable the Recipient of the offer, order or suggestion to be identified. The verbless clause, itself, however, does not provide this information. In effect, the two versions are different messages.

36.6 FREE DIRECT SPEECH AND FREE INDIRECT SPEECH

We have seen so far that speakers and writers make use of direct speech and indirect speech to report the statements, questions and directives of others. In their attempts to portray the stream of thought of their characters, writers have modified the paradigm of reporting as outlined in the preceding sections in certain ways.

What we call '**free direct speech or thought**' consists in omitting the inverted commas or dashes which conventionally signal quoting, as seen in the extract from *Mrs Dalloway*. More drastically, the reporting clause is omitted altogether. This is called '**free indirect speech**' and also covers cognitive processes. In addition, certain structures of direct speech are retained, such as direct questions and exclamations, vocatives, utterance-time adverbs such as *now* and tag questions. Other features may belong to indirect speech, however: tense back-shift, and the temporal and spatial shifts of deictic words towards remoteness.

Some of these features are present in the following extract from Joyce Carol Oates' story *Happy*, which describes a girl's journey home from the airport with her mother and her mother's new husband.

> They stopped for dinner at a Polynesian restaurant ten miles up the Turnpike, her mother explaining *that there wasn't anything decent to eat at home,*[1] *also it was getting late, wasn't it, tomorrow she'd be making a big dinner,*[2] *That's okay honey isn't it?*[3] She and her new husband quarrelled about getting on the Turnpike then exiting right away, but at dinner they were in high spirits again, laughing a good

deal, holding hands between courses, sipping from each other's tall frosted bright-colored tropical drinks. *Jesus I'm crazy about that woman*,[4] her mother's new husband told the girl when her mother was in the powder room, *Your mother is a high-class lady*, he said.[5] He shifted his cane chair closer, leaned moist and warm, meaty, against her, an arm across her shoulders. *There's nobody in the world precious to me as that lady, I want you to know that*, he said,[6] and the girl said *Yes I know it*,[7] and her mother's new husband said in a fierce voice close to tears, *Damn right, sweetheart, you know it.*[8]

[1]indirect speech; [2]free indirect speech; [3]free direct speech; [4-8]direct speech

A variant of free indirect speech, illustrated in [2]above, is to retain the reporting clause, together with the features enumerated above. Here is an instance from *Mrs Dalloway*:

And she opened her scissors, and said, *did*[1] *he*[2] mind *her*[3] just finishing what *she*[4] *was* doing[5] to *her* dress, for *they*[6] *had*[7] a party *that night?*[8]

[1]direct interrogative + past form; [2-4, 6]pronominal shifts; [5-7]tense shifts; [8]temporal deictic shift

36.7 FREE INDIRECT THOUGHT

In the following passage from *Lightning in May*, John suspects for the first time that his wife may have tuberculosis. His reaction is expressed partly in direct speech introducd by verbs of manner (italicised) and partly in free indirect thought (underlined). By means of the latter, the writer or oral storyteller aims to represent the thoughts of a character. No reporting verb is used; indeed, there is no overt signal that the character's, rather than the author's, view or thought is being portrayed. What alerts us to the change of perspective is some 'perspective-changing' detail in the immediately preceding narrative – in this case 'he opened the handkerchief' and 'he looked at her':

'Ruth,' he *breathed*, 'how long have you had this cough?' He stood up and she followed. He opened the handkerchief again. <u>There was no mistake.</u> Silently he cursed himself. <u>He saw her now in a completely different light.</u> 'How long?' he *demanded*.

He looked at her then held her to him. <u>It became bluntly clear to him now. The pale, tired face that was thinner; the droop of her body. All the symptoms that he had put down to her mental state had matured into a physical one. And now a cough. How could he have been so stupid? Yet he had to make sure.</u>

> 'Ruthy,' he *whispered*. 'Let's get back to the surgery. I want Dr. Jenkins to see you.'
> 'What is it, John?' she *queried*.
>
> (Gordon Parker, *Lightning in May*)

FURTHER READING

Coordination and subordination Quirk et al. (1985), Biber et al. (1999); on expansion, elaboration, extension, enhancement, projection, internal and external conjunction, Halliday (1994); on non-restrictive relative clauses: Huddleston and Pullum (2002), Bache and Jakobsen (1980); on circumstantial (adverbial) clauses, degrees of event integration and dependency, Givón (2001b), Matthiessen and Thompson (1988); on epistemic parentheticals, Thompson (2002), Kärkkäinen (2003); Pragmatic (internal) connectives, van Dijk (1979), Matras (1997), Stenström (1998), Smith and Jucker (2000).

EXERCISES ON CHAPTER 7

Expanding the message: Clause combinations

Modules 31 and 32

1   Gather a number of advertisements, with short texts and a headline or title, and compare them for the amount of clausal and non-clausal material they use. Identify the types of unit used – a single clause, a combination of clauses, a nominal group, a word, etc. – relating them to a picture if there is one. Draw up a chart showing the range of units used and the distribution of these units between the headline and the short text. Next, sort them with regard to the product or service advertised (e.g. automobiles, cosmetics, insurance companies, foodstuffs, holiday packages). Do you find any significant differences according to these or other factors, such as the amount of space the advert covers?

2   †Analyse the following news item in terms of its sequencing of coordination and subordination. Does the sequencing follow the chronological order of the real events?

> After hundreds of shrimps came gushing out of taps in Warrington, Cheshire, yesterday, householders collected teapots full of the creatures and were forced to filter the water before they could drink it.

3   †In each of the following clause combinations, say which consist of clauses in a relationship of equivalence and which hold a relationship of non-equivalence:

(1) To advertise in the Homes and Gardens section, please contact one of our sales teams for further information.

(2) 'Clean your arteries – it could save your life.'

(3) Heart disease is the UK's number one killer – and one of the main causes is clogged arteries.

(4) Scottish children receive the most pocket money in the UK, while those in East Anglia receive the least.

(5) The ginkgo tree once flourished around the world but survived the last Ice Age only in remote eastern China.

Module 33

1 Using (i) punctuation signals and (ii) the clarifying connectives listed in 33.1.1, add further clauses to the following examples so as to make complex sentences which stand in an appositive relationship to each other:

(1) **with restating meanings** (*or rather, that is to say, in other words, namely, i.e.*)
   (a) For ten days she ate nothing but yoghurt
   (b) At three in the morning the party was over
   (c) The bar is open only to members of the club

(2) **with exemplifying meanings** (*for example, for instance*)
   (a) It's not clear how much she understands
   (b) There are a hundred things you could do to get fit
   (c) He's no good at mending things

(3) **with upgrading meanings** (*in fact, indeed, actually*)
   (a) The week started badly
   (b) She looks marvellous in a sari
   (c) I was beginning to feel most embarrassed

2 †Taking the clause as antecedent, add (i) finite and (ii) non-finite, non-restrictive relative clauses to each of the following primary clauses, so as to form complex sentences:

(1) She blamed herself for the accident
(2) Most party members were disheartened by the congress
(3) A high-rise building collapsed in Ankara yesterday
(4) Certain parts of the Pacific are notorious for typhoons
(5) Several hostages were released by the plane hijackers today

Module 34

1 Using the conjunctions and connectives associated with coordination + extension, add a conjoined clause to the following examples:

(1) A man carrying a new strain of AIDS virus has left the country
(2) The job was quite attractive

(3) Adventurous children like sleeping in caravans
(4) Either you buy yourself a mobile phone
(5) The dress suits you very well

2 †We have in this chapter seen three meanings of *but*. One is adversative, in which case it is interchangeable with one use of *yet* as in *It's a very simple device but/ yet it's very effective*. Another is replacive, with the meaning *except for* or *instead* as in *He didn't stay even an hour, but returned to London on the next train*. The third meaning is concessive, corresponding to the subordinator *(al)though* as in *The story is certainly strange, but it's not entirely unbelievable*.

Decide which of these three meanings corresponds to *but* in each of the complex sentences below, and replace it by an appropriate connective, adding a pronoun when necessary:

(1) The city may be prosperous, but to claim that it is a tourist attraction is absurd.
(2) Zoo officials are trying to find new homes for the animals, but it is difficult to re-house orang-utangs.
(3) A degree in engineering should open many doors, but without business expertise many graduate engineers have difficulty in finding a job.
(4) Lorne originally thought of doing social biology and chemistry, but has changed to the new BSc in Industrial and Business Systems.
(5) He almost decided to work on an oil-rig, but turned down the offer at the last minute.

3 Using the conjunctive prepositions *besides, as well as, except that, but for the fact that* and *without*, add clauses to the following examples. Identify the resulting meaning:

(1) Gillian buys all her clothes in boutiques
(2) The trip would have been most enjoyable
(3) The singer has filed a lawsuit against her video company
(4) It might have been a good idea to wait a little while
(5) We sat there in silence

Module 35

1 Discuss the status of the combination of *and* and *or* with circumstantial elements such as *then, there, so, in that way, consequently, as a result, otherwise*. Are they coordinators or subordinators?

2 Using these items, add further clauses to the following examples:

(1) I opened the door
(2) The new law came into force a year later
(3) The milk is sure to have turned sour by now
(4) Don't forget to put a stamp on your letters
(5) We left the casserole too long in the microwave

3 †Say which of the following uses of conjunctions are pragmatic (internal) rather than entirely semantic (external). Give an explanation if pragmatic:

(1) *If* you don't mind my saying so, your hair looks much nicer short than long.
(2) Did you see King Lear when it was on on the television? *'Cos* I taped that as well.
[BNC KDM 3696–3697]
(3) I'll lend it to you *if* you lend me your video of Hamlet.
(4) Many birds lose the power of flight, *for* there are no longer predators to make it worthwhile.
[BNC AMS 1356]
(5) *Since* there is no means of changing the weather, there is no question of protest.
[BNC AN 42791]
(6) I've only seen Shirley once *since* she and her husband went to live in New York.
(7) When you gonna find your way up around my way? *But* you know I've been terribly busy lately! Yeah
[BNC KBO 2468–2470]

4 †Analyse the following paragraph from *Newsweek* from the point of view of coordinating and subordinating enhancement:

> You can blow up a balloon so far, and then it bursts;[1] you can stretch a rubber band so far, and then it snaps;[2] you can bend a stick so far, and then it breaks.[3] How much longer can the human population go on damaging the world's natural systems before they break down altogether?[4]

5 Check the list of subordinators and their meanings in Section 35.2.1. Use as many of these items as possible to add subordinate clauses in either initial or final position, in relation to the main clauses below. Here are a few suggested meanings:

(1) We'll have to leave very early (purpose, open condition, negative condition, time-eventive)
(2) I had to leave what I was doing and rush upstairs (reason, purpose, time-eventive)
(3) I would like to speak to you about the new time-table (time-potential)
(4) The film is certainly watchable (concession, condition-rhetorical)

6 †Analyse the following news item 'A Robot for Granny' from *The Week* in terms of complex sentences. Comment on the relative integration of the subordinate clauses and how their position affects their function:

> The Japanese are too hard-working these days to take care of elderly relatives – and so scientists have invented a robot to do the job for them, we discovered this February.[1] The Wakamaru robot trundles around the house, keeping an electronic 'eye' out for trouble.[2] If the owner falls, it will send an alarm call to a friend or

relative;[3] it can recognise faces and will contact a security firm if a stranger enters the house.[4] It can be programmed to ask: 'Are you all right?'[5] If there is no reply, the robot will take action.[6]

Module 36

1 †Give one or more possible reported forms for each of the following statements and questions taken from *The Complete Yes Prime Minister*. Replace *say* and *ask* by verbs with connotative meanings:

(1) 'I'm sorry to interrupt you in this vital discussion,' said Annie.
(2) 'What exactly is your job?' I said to the EEC official.
(3) 'Minister! You realise the press will be printing something that isn't true?'
     'Really?' I smiled at him. 'How frightful!'
(4) 'But what about Duncan?' Annie asked. 'You'd recommend him?'
     'No.' Desmond was unequivocal.
(5) 'I mean, Prime Minister . . . you . . . you – lied,' said Humphrey.

2 †Give a possible reported form for each of the following quoted directives taken from the same script:

(1) 'Won't you sit down for a minute?' Annie said to the official.
(2) 'Why don't you wear a sports jacket?' Fiona said to Godfrey.
(3) 'Suppose I sort of put on my glasses and take them off while I give my speech,' said the Prime Minister.
(4) 'My God,' croaked Luke, a broken man, 'You can't send me to Israel. What about my career?'
(5) 'Don't be silly,' I replied briskly, 'It's an honour. Promotion.'

4 Using information you have learned throughout this chapter, analyse the following extract from Pat Rushin's story *Speed of Light* from the point of view of clausal and non-clausal material and of complex sentence. Identify types of reporting.

> Things go wrong.
>   Take Constantine Muzhikovsky. He had everything going for him. Good law practice. Nice secluded house on the outskirts. Sweet little vegetable garden out back that brought him no end of pleasure come springtime. Handsome, devoted wife. Kids grown and gone. The way Muzhikovsky saw things, it was time to ease off and enjoy a tranquil, orderly life.
>   Then zap.
>   One night while they lay in bed watching Johnny Carson, Muzhikovsky's wife told him it was over. Johnny's last guest, a religious nut plugging a book, ranted on.

'Did you hear me?' Muzhikovsky's wife said.

'Yes,' Muzhikovsky said. He stared at the glowing TV. 'What,' he said.

A blind man could see it, Johnny's guest assured him. The signs, the portents: all heralding the impending arrival of the blazing glory of our Lord and Saviour, you bet. Johnny nodded sagely; then, when his guest wasn't looking, dropped his jaw, mugged dopey credulity.

The audience roared.

'I said I want a divorce.'

TALKING ABOUT EVENTS   *CHAPTER 8*

The Verbal Group

EXPRESSING OUR EXPERIENCE OF EVENTS

SUMMARY

1   Verbal Groups (VG) encode our experience of events. The term 'event' is used here in representation of all types of process, including events, states and activities.

2   The VG consists of a lexical verb (v), either alone (*takes*) or preceded by one or more auxiliaries (*is taking/has been taken*). The first auxiliary, the operator, has a special status and is distinguished by certain syntactic features.

3   The operator is of the utmost importance in English as it carries the four 'NICE' functions of **N**egation, **I**nversion, **C**ode (substitution) and **E**mphasis. It is realised by various types of auxiliary: primary, modal and lexical auxiliaries, which help to build up the symbolic representation of the event and carry a wide range of modal and aspectual meanings.

4   Certain of the lexical auxiliaries (e.g. *be bound to*) have 'raised' Subjects.

37.1 SYNTACTIC ELEMENTS OF STRUCTURE OF THE VERBAL GROUP

The Verbal Group is the grammatical unit by means of which we most typically express our perception of events. 'Event' will be used in this chapter to cover all types of process, whether events, activities, states or acts of consciousness. These are described from the point of view of their place in the semantics of the clause in Chapter 4.

The VG consists of a lexical verb (e.g. *take*) or a primary verb (a form of *be, have* or *do*) as main verb (**v**), either alone or preceded by one or more grammatical elements – the auxiliaries (**x**) as in *has been* and *has taken*. The lexical and grammatical elements are all integral parts of an analytical form. The first auxiliary has a special status and is usually called the 'operator' (**o**) (see 3.1.1), for reasons which are explained in section 37.5. The constituent elements of the English VG can therefore be represented and exemplified as in the diagram.

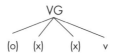

v	waited	I **waited** an hour
o v	is waiting	Everyone **is waiting**
o x v	have been waiting	He **has been waiting** an hour
o x x v	will have been waiting	He **will have been waiting** an hour

37.2 REALISATIONS OF THE ELEMENTS: LEXICAL VERBS AND AUXILIARIES

The elements of the VG are realised by the following classes and forms of verbs:

- lexical verbs: wait, come, rain, bring, etc.
- primary verbs: **be**, am, is, are, was, were, being, been, **have**, has, had, having; **do**, does, did
- modal auxiliaries: shall, should, will, would, can, could, may, might, must, ought to
- semi-modals: need, dare, used to (modals in certain uses)
- lexical auxiliaries:

  (1) be able to, be about to, be apt to, be bound to, be due to, be going to, be liable to, be likely to, be certain to, be sure to, be to, be unlikely to, be supposed to
  (2) have to, have got to
  (3) had better, would rather, would sooner

The primary and modal verbs are limited in number, as this list shows, and form closed sets. Lexical verbs, the **v** or main element, constitute an open set; new ones can be coined and added to the lexicon at any time.

The primary verbs carry grammatical meaning (tense, aspect, person, number), the modal auxiliaries express modal meanings (obligation, possibility, probability, necessity) (see Module 44) rather than lexical or grammatical meaning. On the other hand, the lexical element of the VG expresses both lexical meaning and grammatical meaning.

The primary verbs *be, have, do* can function both as auxiliary and as lexical elements of the VG (with the exception of *doing* and *done*, which function only as lexical elements). The syntactic function determines the type of meaning expressed, whether grammatical or lexical, as shown here.

Functioning as auxiliary	Functioning as lexical (main) verb
Elections *are* approaching.	Elections *are* imminent.
We *didn't* do anything about it.	We *did* everything.
He *has* had nothing to eat.	He *had* nothing to eat.

In addition to its function as a main verb, *be* therefore has three auxiliary functions: as an aspect auxiliary in the progressive: *is taking*; as a passive auxiliary: *is taken* (38.4); and as the basis of the lexical auxiliaries that take *be*.

37.3 TYPES OF LEXICAL AUXILIARY

Lexical auxiliary is the term used for a set of verbs of modal or aspectual meaning which form chain-like structures with the main verb of the VG. The majority are followed by a **V-*to*-inf** form, but a few take the infinitive without *to*. They can be divided into three types according to whether their first word is (1) *be*; (2) *have*; (3) a modal idiom.

As with other *to*-infinitive uses (see 12.2), the lexical auxiliaries tend to point to a future event, though not invariably so. They express subjective estimations by the speaker as to the imminence of the event, the certainty, probability or usualness of the event taking place, or the speaker's duty or ability (based on knowledge or skill) to do something. Some of these auxiliaries have undergone semantic change, so they are not what they seem at first sight. (See 41.6 for more on future time.)

37.3.1 *Be* + Lexical item + *to*-infinitive

	Be + lexical item + V-*to*-inf	**meanings**
be going to	We're *going to* need more staff here.	(prediction based on evidence)
be about to	The plane *is about to* take off.	(imminence of event)
be due to	He's *due to* arrive at any moment.	(expectation of scheduled event)
be to	As a young girl, she little knew she *was to* marry the heir to the throne.	(planned event or destiny)
be bound to	There's *bound to* be some cheese in the fridge.	
be certain to	She *is certain to* resign.	(confident anticipation)
be sure to	He's *sure to* be waiting outside.	
be likely to	They're *likely to* win by several goals.	(probability)
be apt to	He's *apt to* ask awkward questions.	
be liable to	This machine *is liable to* break down.	(tendency or usualness)
be supposed to	We're *not supposed to* smoke in here.	(duty, general belief)
be able to	I *am* not *able to* guarantee the results.	(ability, possibility)

Note that a few of the lexical words in this list can also function as adjectives: an *able* mechanic; an *apt* quotation; a *certain/ sure* winner; the *likely* winner of the elections.

37.3.2 *Have* or *Have got* + *to*-infinitive

	Have and ***have got*** + **V-*to*-inf**	**meanings**
have to	I ***have to*** finish these letters.	(obligation)
	There ***has to*** be a solution.	(necessity)
have got to	***I've got to*** go now. Oh, ***do you have to***?	(obligation)
	There***'s got to*** be a solution.	(necessity)

Like *must*, these combinations have meanings of both obligation and necessity (see 44.5). In type 3, *had better* has the meaning of advisability and *would rather/would sooner* indicate preference.

The Subject-Finite operator inversion characteristic of *be, have* and other auxiliaries in interrogative and negative clauses is explained in Module 23, together with the require-ment of a *do* operator by lexical verbs. As a reminder here, we exemplify *have to* and *have got to* in interrogative clauses, showing that while *have to* can function either as a primary auxiliary or as a lexical verb, *have got to* functions only as an auxiliary:

Have to	**Auxiliary**	**Lexical verb**
Interrogative	Have you to go?	Do you have to go? Don't you have to go?
Negative declarative		You don't have to go.

Have got to	**Auxiliary**
Interrogative	Have you got to go?
	Haven't you got to go?
Negative declarative	You haven't got to go.

Furthermore, *have got* + *to*-infinitive has no non-finite forms and does not combine with modals. None of the following structures are possible, therefore, all being used with *have to*:

*To have got to live there must be dreadful	*To have to* live there . . .
*I don't like *having got to* get up early.	*I don't like having to get up early.*
*We have had got to repaint the kitchen.	We *have had to repaint* . . .
*You will *have got to* watch out for mosquitoes there.	You *will have to watch out for* . . .

37.3.3 Modal idioms: *had better, would rather*

	Modal idioms with *had* and *would* + V-inf	**meanings**
had better	You *had better* come back tomorrow.	(I advise you to . . .)
would rather	I *would rather* stay here with you.	(I would prefer to . . .)
would sooner	I *would sooner* pay in advance.	(I would prefer to . . .)

37.4 'RAISED' SUBJECTS

You may have noticed that in clauses such as *They are likely to win*, the NG at Subject does not appear to be the logical Subject of the Complement *likely to win*. In fact, the likelihood refers not to the subject *they*, but to the situation of winning. Syntactically, then, the NG (*they*) is the logical subject of a clause embedded at subject, as in (a) below (that *they* will win), which is then extraposed, as in (b). Finally the subject of the subordinate clause is raised to become subject of the main clause, as in (c):

> (a) That **they** will win is likely
>> (b) It is likely that **they** will win
>>> (c) **They** are likely to win.

This is known as **subject-to-subject raising** (see also section 30.5.1). *Likely* is used a great deal in this construction, perhaps because its apparent synonym *probable* does not admit raising (**He is probable to win*). Other lexical auxiliaries that are the result of raising are *be certain to, sure to* and *supposed to*.

Object-to-subject raising occurs when a NG Object of a clause embedded at subject (*them* in (a) below) is extraposed as in (b) and then is raised to subject of the main clause, as in (c):

> (a) To find **them** is hard
>> (b) It is hard to find **them**
>>> (c) **They** are hard to find

Raised subjects have the advantage of referring to persons or things by names, nouns or pronouns in a clause that is shorter and simpler than the corresponding *that*-clause or extraposed structures. They also provide a different Theme and Topic (28.4).

37.5 SYNTACTIC FEATURES OF THE OPERATOR ELEMENT

Any of the primary verbs or the modal auxiliaries can stand in initial position and so function as operator in a VG.

The operator element has four major distinctive properties which are not shared by lexical verbs. They carry the 'operations' in what have been called the NICE constructions: **N**egation, **I**nversion, **C**ode and **E**mphasis. Compare:

	operation	operator aux.	lexical vb
1	**Negation**: contraction with neg. particle	I ***don't*** eat meat	**I eatn't . . .*
2	**Inversion** with S in interrogatives	***Will*** you sign?	**Sign you?*
3	**'Code'**, that is, substitute for the Predicator and predicate in a clause (cf. 29.5)	I'll go, if Ed ***will***	I want to go if you ***do*** (if you **want*)
4	**Emphasis** (by tonic stress)	Yes, I ***will*** go	I ***do*** want to go

Four more features also distinguish the operator from a lexical verb:

	operation	*operator aux.*	*lexical vb*
5	Position of frequency adverb: follows operator but precedes lexical verb	I can **always** go	I **always** want to go *I want always to go
6	Postposition of quantifiers *all* and *both*	They **have all/ both** gone	*They went **all/ both** They all/ both went
7	Verbal element in a tag question	You **will** come, **won't** you?	. . . ***comen't you?**
8	Independence of subject	Ed will teach the juniors The juniors will be taught by Ted	Ed expects to teach the juniors The juniors expect to be taught by Ted

With verbs which have the active–passive contrast, operators usually show no change of meaning, whereas with some finite lexical verbs (e.g. *expect*) there is a change of meaning.

BASIC STRUCTURES OF THE VERBAL GROUP

SUMMARY

1   The experiential structure of the VG consists of Finite + Event + auxiliaries. The Finite expresses tense, person, number and modality (the latter when realised by a modal auxiliary). These relate the verbal process to the 'speaker-now' and establish the Verbal Group in relation to the speech exchange. The Event expresses lexical meaning, which provides the representational content. Finite and Event are fused in e.g. *runs, asked; was, has* (as primary auxiliaries).

2   Verbal Groups can be marked for tense or modality but not both.

3   Verbal Group structures can be **simple**, consisting of one element only (*runs, asked*), or **extended**, consisting of one or more auxiliaries + a main verb (*may have been running*).

4   Up to four auxiliaries can occur, or five if a lexical auxiliary is included.

5   The meanings expressed by the auxiliaries are: **modal, perfect, progressive, passive**, in this order. The structures which realise these meanings are telescoped in the VG.

6   The longer combinations are more frequent in spoken than in written English.

7   Non-finite VGs (*having been seen*) can express perfect, progressive and passive meanings, but not tense or modality.

8   Verbal Groups are **discontinuous** in English when the sequence of elements is interrupted by other clause elements or by intensifiers.

38.1 EXPERIENTIAL STRUCTURE OF THE VERBAL GROUP

In finite clauses the experiential structure of the Verbal Group is Finite + Event. The Finite carries tense, number and, to a limited extent, person. A modal auxiliary provides an alternative to a tensed auxiliary, for instance *is going/ may go*. A tensed form and a modal auxiliary do not occur together: *is may go. In one-word VGs, such as *takes, has* (*she **has** long hair*), the finiteness is realised on the lexical verb. In longer sequences the Finite is realised by an operator and may be followed by one or more auxiliaries: *It **has** been snowing all day*.

There is a parallelism between the Nominal Group and the Verbal Group as regards their respective experiential structures. Both begin with an element which relates them to the 'speaker-now' of the speech situation. The NG does this by means of the deictic, or 'pointing' element, such as 'this' in *this house*, the VG by means of the operator, which carries tense, modality and person (*is waiting/**will** wait*), or the lexical verb alone (*waits*). The Verbal Group ends with the Event, which corresponds to the Entity in the Nominal Group, and provides the representational content. Both Event and Entity represent the nucleus of the lexical meaning.

38.2 SIMPLE STRUCTURES OF THE VERBAL GROUP

A simple Verbal Group structure consists of a single element, usually the lexical element, realised by a finite or non-finite form of a lexical verb, for example *drive*:

Finite forms
drive (pres. indic.)	They *drive* on the left in the UK.
drives (pres. indic.)	He *drives* to work every day.
drove (past indic.)	He *drove* out of the garage.

Non-finite forms
(to) drive (inf.)	It's important to *drive* with care.
bare infinitive	They won't let you *drive* without a licence.
driving (pres. part.)	*Driving* to work this morning, I heard the 9 o'clock news.
driven (past part.)	*Driven* away by night, the car was then abandoned.

Simple VG structures are illustrated in the passage below:

> Rivers perhaps *are* the only physical feature of the world that *appear* at their best from the air. Mountain ranges, no longer *seen* in profile, *dwarf* to anthills; seas *lose* their horizons; lakes *have* no longer depth but *look* like bright pennies on the earth's surface; forests *become* a thin impermanent film, a mass on the top of a wet stone, easily *rubbed* off. But rivers, which from the ground one usually *sees* in cross sections, like a small sample of ribbon – rivers *stretch* out serenely ahead as far as the eye *reaches*.
>
> (A. M. Lindbergh, *North to the Orient*)

38.3 EXTENDED STRUCTURES OF THE VERBAL GROUP

An 'extended' Verbal Group structure consists of a lexical verb at the head, preceded by up to four auxiliaries, or five if we include the lexical auxiliaries. The order in which the auxiliaries occur is fixed and depends upon the grammatical meanings they convey. The features of grammatical meaning which can be expressed in an extended VG comprise the following pairs, marked and unmarked, respectively, in 3rd person singular:

		marked	**unmarked**
tense	past, present	*went*	*goes*
finiteness	non-finite, finite	*going*	*goes*
anteriority	perfect, non-perfect	*has gone*	*goes*
aspect	progressive, non-progressive	*is going*	*goes*
modality	modal, non-modal	*will go*	*goes*
polarity	negative, positive	*doesn't go*	*goes*
emphasis	contrastive, non-contrastive	*does go*	*goes*

These major features of grammatical meaning represent sets of options between which speakers choose every time they combine elements to form a Verbal Group. The basic or unmarked options are: the present, finite, non-perfect, non-progressive, non-modal, positive, non-contrastive. Taking a 3rd person form of *go, goes* is the unmarked option in each case.

The auxiliaries serve to build up the meanings expressed by the modal, perfect, progressive and passive combinations, operating not in isolation but each telescoping with the next, as is explained below. The meanings of these and the other pairs are described in this and subsequent chapters. In the following examples, we let *has* and *is* stand for any form of **have** and **be**, *must* for any of the modal auxiliaries and *be about to* for the set of lexical auxiliaries.

38.4 STRUCTURES WITH ONE AUXILIARY: O V

In the finite VG with only one auxiliary, this auxiliary is necessarily the operator and, according to its type, selects a corresponding form of the lexical verb. The o v structure can express the following features of grammatical meaning, in addition to the obligatory choices of tense, finiteness, polarity and contrastiveness:

		features	**realisations**	**example**
A	1	modal	modal aux.+ V-inf	must drive
B	2	perfect	have + V-*en*	has driven
C	3	progressive	be + V-*ing*	is driving
D	4	passive	be + V-*en*	is driven

With a lexical auxiliary:

5   be + about to + V-inf   is about to drive

The four basic combinations also combine with each other to make up more complex Verbal Groups, all of which function as one VG at Finite + Predicator in clause structure. The features **modal, perfect, progressive, passive** occur in ordered combinations, like the letters of the alphabet ABCD. Thus, for instance, B can follow A, or D can follow C, but not vice versa. A certain feature may be omitted, as in ACD, BD. Lexical auxiliaries can occur with any combination, as illustrated in the next section.

The grammatical meanings listed above, which are realised by one auxiliary (the operator) + the lexical verb, are illustrated in the following passage. Forms of *be* occur as main verb, there is one main verb *fell* and also one 'phased' VG (see 39.2.7):

One day, as you *are washing*[1] your hands, you *happen* to glance[2] into the mirror over the basin and a sudden doubt *will flash*[3] across your mind: '*Is*[4] that really me?' 'What *am* I doing[5] here?' 'Who *am*[6] I?' Each one of us *is* so completely *cut off*[7] from everyone else. How *do* you *know*[8] you *are reading*[9] a book? The whole thing *may be*[10] an illusion. How *do* you know[11] that red *is*[12] red? The colour *could appear*[13] blue in everyone else's eyes. A similar doubt, differently expressed, *is*[14] inherent in the well-known question: 'A tree that *has fallen*[15] in the forest, far from the nearest man – when it *fell*,[16] *did it make*[17] any noise?'

(Magnus Pike, *The Boundaries of Science*)

Be as main verb: [4], [6], [12], [14]. *Be* as aux. progressive: [1], [5], [9]. *Be* as aux. passive: [7]. *Have* as aux. perfect: [15]. *Do* as aux. present: [8], [11]. *Do* as aux. past: [17]. Modal aux: [3], [10], [13]. Phased VG with catenative *happen to*: [2].

This text illustrates the options listed as ABCD choices. It must be remembered, however, that **all finite Verbal Groups** also select obligatorily for tense, polarity and contrastiveness. This means that a full description of any one VG realisation would have to specify all these choices, as can be exemplified by [1]*are washing*: finite, present, positive, non-contrastive, non-modal, + progressive, non-perfect, non-passive.

38.5 STRUCTURES WITH TWO GRAMMATICAL AUXILIARIES: O X V

6	modal + perfect	must have driven
7	modal + progressive	must be driving
8	modal + passive	must be driven
9	perfect + progressive	has been driving
10	perfect + passive	has been driven

In combination with a lexical auxiliary:

11	modal + lexical-aux	must be about to drive
12	perfect + lexical-aux	has been about to drive

13 lexical-aux + progressive   is about to be driving
14 lexical-aux + passive   is about to be driven

Structures with two auxiliaries occur widely in both spoken and written English. The following extract is adapted from a report about problems facing language-school students when they come to the UK to study English:

> It *must be realised*[1] that many students *will be going*[2] abroad for the first time and *may* well *be likely to feel*[3] anxious about the kind of reception they *will be given*,[4] about the kind of work they *are about to have to do*[5] or about the host family to which they *happen to have been assigned.*[6] Many of these worries *can* easily *be allayed*[7] by giving them as much information as possible beforehand. In the past, some students *have been apt to complain*[8] that they *have had to face*[9] certain difficulties in the first weeks owing to lack of sufficient information.
>
> [1]modal + passive; [2]modal + progressive; [3]modal + lexical-aux; [4]modal + passive; [5]lexical-aux + lexical-aux; [6]catenative (*happen to*) + perfect + passive; [7]modal + passive; [8]perfect + lexical-aux; [9]perfect + lexical-aux

38.6 STRUCTURES WITH THREE GRAMMATICAL AUXILIARIES: O X X V

15 modal + perfect + progressive   must have been driving
16 modal + perfect + passive   must have been driven
17 modal + progessive + passive   must be being driven
18 perfect + progressive + passive   has been being driven

Verbal groups of three grammatical auxiliaries are more common in speech than in writing. With a modal or a lexical auxiliary, complex forms easily occur in spoken English, as in the following examples:

> . . . and (they) think the killer *could be being protected* locally   [BNC KIE 23370]
> The matter *could and should have been dealt* with as set out above   [BNC FD6 2851]

Groups with the two forms *been being* are uncommon, but they can occur if they are needed.
    With a lexical auxiliary added there are now four auxiliaries:

19 modal + perfect + lexical-aux   must have been about to drive
20 modal + lex.-aux + progressive   must be about to be driving
21 modal + lex.-aux + passive   must be about to be driven
22 perfect + lex.-aux + progressive   has been about to be driving
23 perfect + lex.-aux + passive   has been about to be driven
24 progressive + lex.-aux + passive   is about to be being driven

Then his application *would have to have been made* to the Commission by March.

[BNC FBK 14.655]

We will go no further with the structure of the finite extended VG, as no examples of five auxiliaries have been found in a large corpus. In principle, however, there is no grammatical constraint on their composition and the telescoped order of elements allows for their use if the context requires them.

38.7 TELESCOPED ORDER OF ELEMENTS OF THE VERBAL GROUP

It is important to note that each semantico-syntactic feature of a complex VG (tense and modality, perfect, progressive and passive) is expressed, not by one element only, but by each element telescoping into the following one:

modality:	must + V-inf
perfect:	have + V-en
progressive:	been + V-ing
passive:	being + V-en
main verb:	driven

= Verbal Group: must   have   been   being   driven
(4 grammatical auxiliaries)

With respect to the other auxiliaries, lexical auxiliaries have a relatively free ordering, the basic requirement being that they are followed by an infinitive. This blocks such combinations as **is likely to can drive* and **is bound to must drive*. However the meaning of *must* can be expressed by the lexical auxiliary *have* + *to*-infinitive, and of *can* by *be able to*, giving the acceptable combinations *is likely to be able to drive* and *is bound to have to drive*, as illustrated in the following spoken example:

> If pain and other symptoms were being so badly managed these patients should have been referred promptly to other health care professionals *who might have been able to provide* a better quality of analgesia.   [BNC FT2 31.588]

Note that, as we mentioned in Module 37, forms of *be* participate in extended structures in various ways: as auxiliary of the progressive (*is taking*); as auxiliary of the passive (*is taken*); and in a lexical auxiliary combination (*is bound to*). These can be telescoped successively as in: *is being taken* (prog. + passive), *is bound to be taken* (lex. aux + passive).

38.8 EXTENDED NON-FINITE STRUCTURES

Non-finite VGs do not possess the full set of sequences that we find in finite groups because they do not express the grammatical meanings of tense, mood or modality.

The perfect, progressive and passive meanings can, however, be expressed in the non-finite VG, giving the following possible combinations (the bracketed form is not common):

	Infinitive structures	**Participle structures**
25	to have driven	having driven
26	to have been driving	having been driving
27	to have been driven	having been driven
28	to be driving	(being driving)
29	to be driven	being driven

Lexical auxiliaries can of course also be incorporated into non-finite structures, making for even longer combinations, which can be produced spontaneously when they are needed, as in the example:

Having been about to be operated on more than once, his operation was nevertheless postponed on each occasion.

With an appropriate lexical verb and an appropriate context, such as someone who is teaching needing extended time to complete an essay on a course she is following, the participial sequence of *being* + V-*ing* is acceptable, as in the following example from Michael Halliday:

You might get an extension on the grounds of *being teaching*.

38.9 RELATIVE FREQUENCY OF COMPLEX VERBAL GROUPS

It must be realised that extended VG structures have developed and become acceptable over time, and that this process has not yet been completed. Even short progressive + passive combinations such as *are being killed* were avoided by writers before the second half of the nineteenth century. (Macaulay is said to have written 'Good soldiers are killing . . .' because he could not bring himself to write 'are being killed'.) There is still a similar reluctance to use the longer forms such as *might have been being killed*. The language's resources, nevertheless, can generate them so that they are at the user's disposal when they are needed. The reason that longer VGs occur more frequently in spoken English than in written lies partly in the on-line nature of spontaneous speech and the kind of meanings conveyed by the VG. Such meanings are related not simply to an objective point of time at which an event occurred, but also more subjectively and spontaneously, to evaluations, speculations and predictions made by the speaker as to what may happen in the future or to what could, should or might have happened in the past.

38.10 DISCONTINUOUS VERBAL GROUPS

The sequence of elements in VGs is often interrupted by other clause elements, such as subject, adjunct and intensifiers as in *has not yet been completed*. Such interruptions can be seen in the following exchange, in which A asks B about her father, who is a wine dealer:

A. *Did* he *import*[1] from any particular place in France, or all over?
B. Well, he *used to* sort of *be*[2] forever *going*[3] to Bordeaux, so I assumed from that that that was his main connection.

(adapted from J. Svartvik and R. Quirk, *A Corpus of English Conversation*)

[1]interrupted by Subject; [2]interrupted by intensifier; [3]interrupted by Adjunct

As well as in interrogative structures, separation of the VG by the subject is produced in certain types of thematisation (Only then *did* he *realise* the harm he had done; *Had* we *known* your address, we would have got in touch with you). This is explained in section 28.10.

Discontinuity of the VG is also produced by negative or semi-negative items (I *would* never *have believed* that of him; You *can* hardly *expect* them to wait all day).

ORGANISING OUR EXPERIENCE *MODULE 39*
OF EVENTS

SUMMARY

1 Verbal groups can be linked by coordination to express sequences of related events.

2 VGs in a dependency relationship are described by the semantic notion of **phase**. They form chain-like sequences which symbolise a complex event consisting of two phases (*try to win, end up winning*).

3 The first VG in a phased structure is often a catenative (*start, happen*) and can express the aspectual meanings of initiation, continuation, attempt, manner and usuality.

4 These catenatives are mid-way between lexical verbs and auxiliaries. They are not able to function as operators, and so require the *do*-operator.

5 The second VG is non-finite. The *to*-infinitive points to a beginning or end-point of the second phase, (*start to cry*) while the *-ing* form implies its duration (*start crying*).

We now begin to examine some of the means used in English to express the internal nature or character of the event for which the verb is a linguistic symbol.

39.1 SEQUENCING AND PHASING EVENTS

Verbal groups can be joined, either by coordination or by dependency to express events which occur in sequence, or are 'phased', respectively.

When linked by **coordination**, VGs are **conjoined**. They express two events with the same subject which occur in sequence and are semantically related (*washed and dressed*, but hardly *washed and scolded*). Just as with the conjoining of other types of grammatical unit, the VGs may be linked in three ways: by the linking words *and, or* and *but*; without any linking item; or by a combination of both when more than two events are related:

She *washed and dressed* the child.
Our last typist just *left, disappeared* without saying a word.
He *was born, lived and died* in Bristol.

In section 12.1 we considered verbs which can set up a chain of non-finite complements as catenatives, and the non-finite clauses themselves as catenative complements. Here we look at a largely different set of verbal groups e.g. *happened to see, keep on running*, which can in many cases be interpreted semantically as one complex or phased process, realised by two VGs, the second dependent on the first. The first VG is a catenative, which may be finite (such as *happened*) or non-finite (such as *having kept on*). Unlike the lexical auxiliaries, these verbs cannot themselves be operators. Instead they take the *do* operator, as in *Did he happen to see it?*

The second VG is always non-finite, the form of the verb being controlled by the first. The infinitive form, usually with *to*, as in *it started to rain*, tends to draw attention to the initial or terminative stage of the phased event. The participial *-ing* form, as in *it started raining* tends to suggest the durative nature of the second phase. The *-en* form in the *get*-passive suggests termination, while *get* invokes partial responsibility, or bad luck/ good luck, for the action (see 30.3.5). *Get* can be used in the three types of phase:

Initial:	Let's get moving.
Terminating:	I got to know him well.
Terminating + responsibility/bad luck:	He got run over by a bus.

Verbs which can function as the first verb in the phased verbal groups include the following:

- + *to*-infinitive: appear to, chance to, come to, fail to, get to, happen to, help to, hesitate to, manage to, prove to, regret to, seem to, tend to, try to, turn out to, venture to
- + *-ing*: keep (on), go on, carry on
- + *to*-infinitive or *-ing*: begin, start, get, cease, stop
- get + V-*en* (the *get*-passive)
- help + *to*-infinitive or bare infinitive

The non-finite forms are illustrated as follows:

to-infinitive	He *tried to kill* the snakes.
-ing form	He *went on killing* the snakes.
to-inf./*-ing*	He *began to kill* the snakes.
To-inf./bare inf.	He *helped kill/ to kill* the snakes.
	He *began killing* the snakes.
-en	He *got killed* by a snake.

These verbs have in common with the lexical auxiliaries the ability to form chained sequences of non-finite constructions as in *Those pears don't seem to be getting eaten* and *He always seems to be certain to pass his driving test, but in the end he keeps on managing to fail*. Although they require the *do*-operator, many of them satisfy the 'independence of the subject' criterion which is characteristic of auxiliaries and illustrated below (see also 37.5). When used as catenatives, then, the following verbs are midway between auxiliaries and full lexical verbs:

	appears to	
	happens to	
Phil fails to		recognise the implications.
	tends to	
	ceased to	
	came to	

	appear to	
	happen to	
The implications	fail to	be recognised by Phil.
	tend to	
	ceased to	
	came to	

39.2 TYPES OF PHASE

Verbal Group complexes of this kind are said to be 'phased', because the process expressed by the VGs is interpreted as being realised by a single subject in two or more phases. The types of phase are classified notionally here in terms of the meaning of the first verb.

39.2.1 The phase of initiation

Some verbs admit the aspectual contrast of initial/ terminative as opposed to durative in the second:

It began *to rain.* It began *raining.*
She started *to cry.* She started *crying.*
- - - - - - - - - - - - - Get *moving!*

39.2.2 The phase of continuation

- - - - - - - - - - - - Why do you keep on *complaining?*
He went on *to talk* about his future plans. He went on *talking* for hours.
It continued *to snow* for a week. It continued *snowing* for a week.
- - - - - - - - - - - - Carry on *working*, please!

There is a difference of meaning between *go on* + *to* inf. and *go on* + *-ing*. The infinitive form suggests movement to a different topic or activity, depending on the verb, while the *-ing* form encodes the continuation of the same activity. Compare: *He went on (afterwards) to study Physics*, and *He went on (as usual) studying Physics*.

39.2.3 The phase of termination

I have ceased *to mind* the harsh climate.	I have ceased *minding* the constant noise.
- - - - - - - - - - - -	He will end up *resigning*.
- - - - - - - - - - - -	Have the children finished *eating?*
- - - - - - - - - - - -	Can't you stop *making* such a noise?
I got *to know* him well	I got *working* on the essay and finished it before dinner-time. (phase of initiation)

The use of *stop* with a following *to*-infinitive indicates the end of one process and the beginning of another, rather than one phased process. Syntactically, the *to*-infinitive is analysed as adjunct. Compare:

He stopped *to think*. He stopped *thinking*.

39.2.4 The phase of appearing or becoming real

The sky *seemed to get* darker. The patient *appears to be improving*.
The job *proved to be* quite unsuitable.
The stranger *turned out to be* a neighbour after all.

39.2.5 The phase of attempting, succeeding, failing, helping

The verbs used with these meanings include *try, attempt, manage, be able, fail, neglect, omit, learn*, which are followed by the *to*-infinitive form of the subordinate verb. Again, this form often draws attention to the initiation or completion of the process:

He *tried to learn* Arabic.
We *managed to find* the key.
We had arranged to meet at 9, but he *failed to turn up*.
You must *learn to* relax.
I *attempted to explain* but they wouldn't listen.
She *neglected to turn off* the gas and there was an explosion.
He *helped feed* the baby / This herbal tea *will help you to relax*. (See also section 12.3.)

39.2.6 The phase of manner or attitude

The manner in which a person performs an action or an attitude of mind towards performing it are expressed by verbs such as *regret, hesitate, hasten, pretend, decline, bother*. All are followed by the *to*-infinitive form, except *bother*, which can also take an -*ing* form:

I regret to *inform you* . . .	=	inform with regret
I *hesitate to ask* you this favour.	=	ask reluctantly
They *hastened to* reassure her.	=	reassure immediately
He's only *pretending to* be deaf.	=	acting as if deaf

He *declined to* answer the question. = was not willing to answer
I never *bother to iron/ ironing* sheets. = trouble myself to iron
I *happen to* like her a lot, so shut up. = showing annoyance at something said

39.2.7 The phase of chance and tendency

An element of chance or usualness, in the performance of the action denoted by the second verb, is expressed by certain catenatives. Semantically, these verbs are similar to the lexical auxiliaries described in section 37.3, such as *be apt to, be liable to*, which express usualness.

She *happened to notice* the number-plate. = noticed by chance
I *chanced to overhear* their conversation. = heard by chance
He *tends to be* nervous, doesn't he? = often is

Two phased verbs are illustrated in the following news item from *The Sunday Times of India*:

> **Project to save Pisa tower**
>
> Workers have *started removing* soil from under the base of the leaning tower of Pisa, Italy, the second phase of a project meant to *keep the monument from toppling over*.
> The digging that started on Friday was carried out through 12 tubes, inserted to a depth of six metres to remove some soil. Experts hope the tower will then settle better into the ground and lean less. It now leans 6 degrees, four metres off the perpendicular.

An illustration of the occurrence of complex and phased VGs (together with lexical auxiliaries and phrasal verbs) in spoken English is provided by the following short extract from a recorded conversation:

> Rachel: We *got locked out*[1] of the flat yesterday.
> Harry: How did you *get back*[2] in?
> Rachel: We *had to borrow*[3] a long ladder and *climb up*[4] to the first floor balcony.
> Harry: I thought that with the kind of security lock you've got, you're *not supposed to be able to lock* yourself *out*.[5]
> Rachel: That's true. But if you *happen to bang*[6] the door a bit too hard, it locks itself.
> Harry: It's better *to have to lock*[7] it from the outside.
>
> [1]*get*-passive, phrasal verb; [2]phrasal verb; [3]lexical aux; [4]phrasal verb; [5]lexical aux. + lexical-aux. + phrasal verb; [6]phased VG; [7]lexical-aux

THE SEMANTICS OF PHRASAL VERBS

SUMMARY

1 **Phrasal verbs** consist of a lexical verb + an adverb-like particle (*She walked out*). The syntax of these verbs, as of other multi-word combinations, is described in Chapter 2.

2 The function of many of the particles is to modify the nature of the activity expressed by the verb. The result is an extended meaning which is often quite different from the meaning(s) of the verb when it functions alone.

3 The more transparent combinations combine the meaning of the verb and the particle, and these allow substitution (*go out/run out/hurry out: go away/run away/hurry away.*

4 In a Motion Event analysis the lexical verb in such combinations expresses Motion, while the particle expresses the Path taken by the moving Figure with respect to the Ground.

5 The notions of Manner and also Cause are typically incorporated, together with Motion, in English verbs.

6 Phrasal verb particles can also draw attention to the beginning or end of an activity, to its continuation, slow completion, increased or decreased intensity and many other meanings.

40.1 PHRASAL VERBS

No student of English can fail to notice that phrasal verbs are one of the most distinctive features of present-day informal English, both in their abundance and in their productivity. New combinations are constantly being coined. A phrasal verb is a combination of a lexical verb and an adverb-like particle such as *run in, fly away, get off, walk back, drive past, come over*. The syntactic behaviour of phrasal verbs is compared with that of prepositional verbs in Chapter 2.

In this section we turn our attention to the combinations of meanings provided by the lexical verb together with its particle. We will try to show how the concept of Motion Event offers a cognitive explanation for these combinations in English that should help to dispel the opaqueness often ascribed to phrasal verbs. (We present here only a small part of what is a far-reaching model, which provides a typology of motion events across languages.)

The function of many of the particles is to modify the nature of the activity expressed by the verb. The result is an extended meaning which is often different from the meaning(s) of the verb when it functions alone.

40.1.1 Semantic cohesiveness and idiomaticity

Phrasal verbs are semantically highly cohesive. The verb and particle function as a whole, and the more idiomatic combinations frequently have a unique, idiomatic meaning which is not merely the sum of the two parts.

Other verb + particle combinations, however, present varying degrees of cohesiveness and little or no idiomaticity. For practical purposes, the following three degrees will be recognised: **non-idiomatic, semi-idiomatic** and **fully idiomatic**. We shall deal with each type separately.

40.2 NON-IDIOMATIC PHRASAL VERBS: FREE COMBINATIONS

The lexical verb and the adverbial particle each keep their own meaning, the sum of the meanings being one of **movement + direction**. The particle encodes the direction of the movement, while the lexical verb encodes the movement, as in:

> The children *went down* to the beach

40.2.1 The Motion Event: Figure, Ground, Path and Manner

It is here that the concept of Motion Event is revealing. The components in the Motion Event are Figure, Ground, Motion, and optionally, Path and Manner. **Figure** is the salient moving or stationary object in a motion event (we centre here on moving objects). In our previous example *the children* functions as Figure, while *the beach* serves as a point of reference or **Ground** with respect to which the Figure's Path is conceptualised. **Path** refers to the one or more paths occupied by the Figure. In our example Path is fully expressed by the adverb-like particle *down* plus the preposition *to*. The lexical verb *went* expresses **Motion**.

Figure	Motion	Path	Ground
The children	went	down to	the beach
	ran		
	walked		

In English the notion of Manner is easily incorporated together with Motion in the lexical verb, giving combinations such as *ran down* and *walked down*, which encode the different ways in which the movement is carried out. In this way, the manner of movement is integrated into the verbal group without the need to add an adverbial phrase or clause of manner.

Both Path and Manner are important components of phrasal verbs. In many clauses which express motion in English, the particle expressing Path can stand alone without the preposition, and also without the rest of the Ground, as in *The children went down/ walked down*. When the information in the Ground can be inferred from the context, it is conventionally omitted, as is the bracketed part in **1** and **2**. In **3** the whole of the Ground is retained (*back on the shelf*):

> **1**   The bus stopped and we *got on/got off* (it, the bus).
> **2**   We *turned off* (the main road) down a side-road.
> **3**   *Put* all the books *back* on the shelf.

Non-literal uses of Path combinations may not admit this reduction of the Path component. Compare the literal use of *into* as in *go into* the house with the non-literal use as in *go into* the matter: *They went into the house/They went in. They went into the matter/ *They went in.*

While many adverb-particles have the same form as prepositions (*get on/off the bus – get on/ off*), the two categories are distinguished by certain features:

- A preposition is unstressed or lightly stressed; a particle receives heavy stress, even when they have the same form: compare *come to class* vs *come TO* (= recover consciousness).
- A preposition is followed by a nominal element (noun, pronoun, *-ing* clause), a particle does not need to be followed by anything cf. *climb up the cliff* vs *climb up*.
- The category of particle includes words that don't function as simple prepositions: *apart, together*. Conversely, *from* and *at* are always prepositions, never particles; consequently, *apart from* and *together with* are complex prepositions (see Chapter 12).

English admits multiple expressions of Path, which include both particles and a preposition, as in:

> Paul ran back down into the garage.

In this very ordinary English sentence, a great deal of information has been packed in: that the manner of motion was by running (*ran*); that Paul was returning to the place where he had been before (*back*); that his starting-point was higher than the garage, so that he had to descend (*down*), and that he went inside the garage, which was an enclosed place (*into*). Note that, in a semantic roles analysis, the preposition (*in*)*to* is a marker of Goal, the final location after the movement (see 59.2).

A further (optional) component of the Motion Event is Cause. This is incorporated into English verb roots such as *blow* and *knock*, while the particle encodes Path as usual:

The paper *blew* off the table.	=	The Figure (the paper) moves from the Ground (the table) (due to the air blowing on it)
I *blew* the crumbs *off* the table.	=	The Figure (the crumbs) moves from the Ground (the table) (due to my blowing on it)
He *knocked* the lamp *over*.	=	The Figure (the lamp) moves from a vertical position (on an unspecified Ground) to a horizontal one (due to his giving it a blow)

The causer is not necessarily expressed, and when it is, the cause may be deliberate or accidental.

40.2.2 TRANSLATING MOTION, MANNER AND PATH COMBINATIONS

It is characteristic of everyday colloquial English, and of a number of other languages, to express Path by particles (+ preposition) and to combine Manner with Motion in the verb.

This is not so in the Romance languages, however. Spanish and French, for instance, have a different pattern. Let us take the sentence **Paul ran back up into the attic**. Spanish can combine Motion in the lexical verb with just one of the above components, either Manner alone (*corrió*=ran), or just one of the Path notions (*subir*=go up; *entrar*=go in, *volver*=go back, followed by a participle expressing Manner). The literal equivalents of these are not idiomatic English and should be avoided:

Pablo corrió al ático.	('Paul ran to the attic')
Pablo volvió al ático corriendo.	('Paul went back to the attic running')
Pablo subió al ático corriendo.	('Paul went up to the attic running')
Pablo entró en el ático corriendo.	('Paul went into the attic running')

To attempt to put in more would be awkward and stylistically unacceptable. For this reason, translators working from English to Spanish are obliged to under-translate, usually omitting Path or Manner meanings. Conversely, in translations from Spanish into English over-translation is common through the addition of Path or Manner meanings. In both cases the aim is to provide a natural text in the target language.

English phrasal and prepositional verbs often require to be translated into other languages by transposing the meanings of the verb and particle in the target language. For example, *row across the lake* can be translated into Spanish as *cruzar el lago remando* [literally *cross the lake rowing*]. The English particle *across* is translated as the main verb, *cruzar*, while the verb *row* is translated as a participle, *remando*. This process has been called **cross transposition**. In this case the transposition was complete, since both verb and adverb were translated. In other cases, either the verb or the particle is better not expressed, being inferred, as in: *A bird flew in: Entró un pájaro*. The transposition is then 'incomplete' since the notion of flying has been omitted as not salient.

40.2.3 Substituting Manner and Path elements

The lexical verbs in non-idiomatic combinations are among the most frequently used English verbs, denoting basic movement, either with the whole body (*go, carry, come, walk*, etc.) or, more specifically, with part of the body (*kick, hand, head, elbow*, etc.), whereas others have very general or directional meanings (*get, put, bring, take*).

They combine with a wide variety of adverb-particles. Since they allow substitution, we can start from each lexical verb such as those below and make combinations with various particles. Obviously, other lexical verbs and other particles can be used. Not every lexical verb can combine with every particle. Here is a small selection:

	up		up		up	Take it up
	down		down		down	Take it down
	in		in		in	Take it in
take	out	go	out	carry	out	Take it out
	off		off		off	Take it off
	away		away		away	Take it away
	back		back		back	Take it back

Alternatively, you can replace the basic lexical verb by a more specific verb of movement, while retaining the same adverbial particle. Instead of the basic *go out*, for instance, we can specify the manner of movement more exactly: *walk out, run out, hurry out, rush out*. With the notion of Cause added (= make come out), we have *bring out, print out, squeeze out* (*You squeeze the toothpaste out like this*). Such combinations have frequently developed a non-literal meaning, as in the following business news item:

> More supermarkets opening in-store chemists could *squeeze out* High Street pharmacies.

40.3 BASIC MEANINGS OF A PARTICLE: *BACK*

A great deal of the opaqueness that learners find in phrasal verbs can be dispelled by acquiring a grasp of the basic meaning of each adverb-particle, together with some of the derived meanings. Take *back*, for instance. *Back* has two basic Path meanings.

First, *back* can represent **a circular path in which the Figure ends up where it started**. This is the one expressed by *Come back* tomorrow, *Put the books back on the shelves*. The person or thing comes to be in the place or position where they were before, so that *I'll be back at 4.30* means 'I'll be again in this place where I am now'.

Close to the basic meaning is *give back* and *pay back* as in *I'll give/ pay you back the money tomorrow* (that is, I'll return the money to you tomorrow). By a short extension, we have the meaning of reciprocity 'in return, in reply' as in *I'll ring you back this evening.* A metaphorical extension of *pay back* occurs as a threat in *I'll pay you back for this!*

Second, *back* can have the meaning '**in the opposite direction to the one a person is facing**' as in:

stand back: *Stand back* from the edge of the platform!
keep back: The police kept the crowd *back* as the royal car drew near.

This meaning is given a figurative extension in *His illness has kept him back all this term.* With this second meaning, the end-point is not the same as the initial point.

40.4 SEMI-IDIOMATIC PHRASAL VERBS

In semi-idiomatic combinations the lexical verb, generally speaking, keeps its literal or metaphorical meaning, while the particle is used as an **aspectual marker** of various kinds. By this we refer here to the way a particle with a verb in English can express the completion, beginning-point, end-point or high intensity of an event. Continuation, a kind of non-completion, can also be expressed. These notions are explained and discussed in Chapter 9 under the concepts of perfectivity and imperfectivity, respectively.

Aspect is seen here as the pattern of distribution through time of an action or state, and relates to such questions as its completion, beginning-point, end-point or high intensity, all kinds of perfectivity. Non-completion, which is a type of imperfectivity, can also be expressed.

The following connotations of particles have been suggested:

1 beginning of an activity: *doze off, switch on, start out*

> He sat in an armchair in front of the television and soon *dozed off*.

2 momentary character of an activity: *cry out, sit down, wake up, stand up*

> Everyone *cried out* in fear when the boat capsized.

3 the bringing of an activity to an end or getting to a certain limit: *eat up, catch up, drink up, fill up, heat up, mix up, use up, sweep up; count out, hear out, knock out, sort out, throw out, wear out; break off, call off, cut off, sell off, switch off*

> *Heat up* the milk but don't let it boil over.
> He hit the burglar so hard that he *knocked* him *out*.
> The two countries have *broken off* diplomatic relations.

4 the slow completion of an activity: *melt down, wind down, die away, fade away, melt away, pine away, waste away; chill out, peter out.*

> The sound of thunder gradually *died away/faded away*.
> We are all stressed out. Let's go and have a drink to *wind down/chill out*.

---

5 the completion of an activity from beginning to end: *read through, rush through, think through*

> I don't think they have really *thought* the problem *through.*

6 reach a different, non-integral or denatured state: *break up, burn up, tear up*

> Their marriage *broke up.*
> She *tore up* the letter and threw the bits of paper into the fire.

7 the continuation or resumption of an activity: *carry on, go on, keep on, work on, stay on, walk on.*

> George *carried on* the family business.
> The orchestra *went on/kept on* playing as the Titanic sank.
> We stopped for a ten-minute break and then *worked on* until 7 o'clock.

8 the continuation of an activity with dedication or abandon: *work away, chat away*

> They'll sit *gossiping away/chatting away* happily for hours.

9 end of motion: *settle down*

> Isn't it time he got a job and *settled down?*

10 distribution: *give out, share out*

> What are those leaflets that are being *given out?*

11 decreased intensity: *slow down, die down*

> *Slow down* before you reach the crossing.
> The clamour finally *died down.*

12 mass character of an activity in progressive sequence: *die off, kill off*

> All the rabbits have *died off* in this area. Flies *die off* as soon as winter comes.

13 reciprocity of an activity: *hit back*

> Tom hit Bill and he *hit* him *back.*

In phrasal verbs the notion of completion or bringing to an end is most clear in those cases in which there is a contrast with a single verb, as *in use* vs *use up, eat* vs *eat up, drink* vs *drink up, knock* vs *knock out* and so on. Compare *I've used this detergent* (i.e. some of this detergent) with *I've used up this detergent* (= there is none left); *He knocked the burglar down the stairs* with *He knocked him out* (= left him unconscious).

40.5 FULLY IDIOMATIC PHRASAL VERBS

Fully idiomatic combinations are those in which the meaning of the whole is not easily deduced from the parts, although it may well be deduced from the context:

The conversation *petered out* after about ten mintues. (gradually came to an end)

Someone *tipped off* the police that a robbery was being planned. (warn, give secret information)

The government has decided to *crack down* on antisocial behaviour. (impose sanctions).

The nonsense song *caught on* and was soon being heard everywhere. (become popular)

Please stop *butting in*. We are trying to balance the accounts. (interrupt)

The illustrations given in these sections show that it is by no means easy to establish boundaries between what is idiomatic and what is not. Many verbs, both one-word and multi-word, have a number of related meanings according to their collocation with different nouns and depending on the contexts in which they are used. Particularly characteristic of phrasal verbs are their metaphorical extensions of meaning, from concrete to abstract or abstract to concrete; and from one context to another less typical one. A simple phrasal verb such as *put up* offers the following examples, among others:

The boys have put up the tent. (erect)
They're putting up a new block of flats. (build)
They've put the bus fares up. (raise)
I can put two of you up for a couple of nights. (provide a bed for)
The others will have to put up at a hotel. (lodge)
The project has been approved, but someone will have to put up the necessary
    funds. (provide)
Our neighbours have put their house up for sale. (announce, offer)

FURTHER READING

For structure of the VG and phase, similarity to the NG, Halliday (1994); Multi-word verbs, Quirk et al. (1985); aspectual meanings of phrasal verbs, Slobin (1996); Spasov (1978); Motion Event, Talmy (2002), Goldberg (1995). *Collins Cobuild English Dictionary* (1987); *Cambridge International Dictionary of English* (1995); *Shorter Oxford English Dictionary* (2002).

EXERCISES ON CHAPTER 8

Talking about events: The Verbal Group

Module 37

1   *Discussion*: Discuss the importance of the operator in English by examining its various syntactic features. Taking your own or another language as a basis of comparison, discuss how in that language each of the functions of the English operator would be realised.

2 †Read the following extract and identify the functions of *be*, *have* (*got*) *to* and *get* as primary verb, as part of a lexical auxiliary or as a lexical verb:

> Imagine that you're out,[1] you're in Wolverhampton,[2] and you're about to cross the street,[3] and round the corner comes a big lorry. What happens? Your sense organs have told you there's a big lorry. You've got to deal with it,[4] you can't fight it. You've got to[5] get across that road quickly.[6] All these things happen to you, all those hormones, particularly adrenaline, have got into your bloodstream[7] because you need this sudden burst of energy to get you across the road.[8]
>
> [BNC JJH 8026]

3 †Underline the Verbal Groups in the sentences below and then answer the questions:

(1) A bicycle whizzed past me as I was crossing the road.
(2) It startled me.
(3) It also startled the elderly woman just ahead of me. She was clutching a bag or bundle or something, and almost fell.
(4) 'Can't you be more careful?' I shouted after the cyclist.
(5) He just turned his head a little, but said nothing.
(6) He was pedalling fast and was soon lost in the traffic.
(7) He could have injured us both.
(8) The elderly woman's bundle had fallen open into the middle of the road. A strange collection of objects was rolling everywhere.
(9) 'Are you all right?' I asked, as we scrambled to pick up the things before the lights changed.

In sentences 1–9 above:

1 List the Verbal Groups of one element (v).
2 List the Verbal Groups of two elements (o v)
3 Are there any Verbal Groups of three elements (o x v)?
4 What is the syntactic status of *are* in sentence 9?
5 Write the elderly woman's answer to the question in sentence 9.
6 Continue with another sentence starting: *We might have* . . .
7 Now give the speaker's opinion of the cyclist, starting *He was* . . .
8 Conclude with a general comment starting *People should* . . .

4 †Using the lexical auxiliaries and modal idioms listed in section 37.2, fill in the blanks in the sentences below with a form of *be* or *have* and the lexical auxiliary you consider most appropriate in each case:

(1) Wheat-germ _ _ _ _ _ _ _ _ _ _ _ _ good for you, isn't it?
(2) We _ _ _ _ _ _ _ _ _ _ _ have finished exams by the second week in July.
(3) At what time _ _ _ _ _ _ _ _ _ _ _ the concert _ _ _ _ _ _ _ _ _ _ _ start?
(4) Don't you think we _ _ _ _ _ _ _ _ _ _ _ enquire at the Information desk?

(5) Will you .... pick us up at the station tomorrow evening?

(6) I .... say something tactless, but I stopped myself in time.

(7) The storms are so severe in this part of the world that basements .... flooded after ten minutes' rain.

(8) Do you feel you really .... work in the library on a day like this?

5 Rewrite the following sentences, which contain *that*-clauses, so that they have a raised subject with the same lexical auxiliary:

(1) It's likely that the main markets will be France, Germany and Spain.

(2) It was virtually certain that Diana and Charles would divorce.

(3) It is sure that you will be among the first three.

(4) It is supposed that he is her boyfriend.

(5) It's not likely that you'll get a question like that.

Module 38

1 †What is the function of *be* in the following examples: lexical verb, progressive auxiliary, passive auxiliary or lexical auxiliary?

(1) It's getting late.

(2) I have never been here before.

(3) Has he been invited to the reception?

(4) There is sure to be some delay at airports this summer.

2a †Give the syntactic structure of the Verbal Groups in the sentences below, and analyse them for the tense and ABCD features they contain. Do you see any discontinuous VGs?

(1) Someone *should be telling* the present administration about Kenya.

(2) Kenya *was about to take off* economically.

(3) Our population *has been* greatly *increased*.

(4) That increase *should have been expected*.

(5) It *was realised* that modern medicine *was cutting back* the death rate dramatically.

(6) But numerous mistakes *were being made* in the allocation of scarce national resources.

(7) Our exports *were earning* less in real terms than *they had been earning* a decade ago.

(8) Many developing nations *are* gradually *shifting* their economic policies towards free enterprise.

(9) We feel that the country *has not* yet *been able to achieve* its potential.

(10) But that potential *should* at least *be receiving* recognition.

2b Now, re-write each sentence in 2a with a different combination of features but maintaining the lexical verb. For instance, for 1: *should have told* or *may have told*.

3 †Complete the sentences below (which make up a text) with Verbal Groups containing two, three or four auxiliaries, using the verbs indicated. Example 1 is done for you:

(1) The last photograph _ _ _ _ _ _ _ _ _ _ _ _ (prog. + pass.+ *take*) when I arrived. (was being taken)

(2) Pete _ _ _ _ _ _ _ _ _ _ _ _ (*past* + perf. + prog. + pass.+ *instruct*) on how to use a wide-angle lens.

(3) He _ _ _ _ _ _ _ _ _ _ _ _ (*must* + perf. + prog. + *use*) a filter.

(4) He _ _ _ _ _ _ _ _ _ _ _ _ (*can't* + perf. + prog.+ *use*) a filter.

(5) She _ _ _ _ _ _ _ _ _ _ _ _ (*must* + perf.+ *move*) when the photograph _ _ _ _ _ _ _ _ _ _ _ _ (*take* + prog. + pass.)

(6) The film _ _ _ _ _ _ _ _ _ _ _ _ (*will* + prog. + pass. + *develop*) by my brother.

(7) More colour films _ _ _ _ _ _ _ _ _ _ _ _ (*be likely* + *pass.* + *sell*) than ever this year.

(8) And more cameras _ _ _ _ _ _ _ _ _ _ _ _ (*be sure* + perf. + pass. + *buy*) in the holiday period.

(9) Look! Some kind of television film _ _ _ _ _ _ _ _ _ _ _ _ (prog. + pass. + *shoot*) over there.

(10) I should say it _ _ _ _ _ _ _ _ _ _ _ _ (*shoot* + *must* + perf. + prog. + pass. + *shoot*), rather. They seem to have finished.

Text for modules 37 and 38 combined

5 † Underline the Verbal Groups in the following passage and then answer the questions below:

> A car with a trailer coming our way is passing and having trouble getting back into his lane. I flash my headlight to make sure he sees us. He sees us but he can't get back in. The shoulder is narrow and bumpy. It'll spill us if we take it. I'm braking, honking, flashing. Christ Almighty, he panics and heads for our shoulder! I hold steady to the edge of the road. Here he COMES! At the last moment he goes back and misses us by inches.
>
> **(Robert M. Pirsig, *Zen and the Art of Motorcycle Maintenance*)**

(1) Which are more important to this text – actions or states?

(2) Identify the finite VGs in the text. List separately the VGs in which finiteness is realised on the verb (the Finite is fused with the Event), and those in which the Finite is realised by an operator.

(3) Are there any non-finite Verbal Groups in this extract?

(4) What tense choice has been made in this text?

(5) What aspectual (progressive) choices have been made?

(6) What modality choices have been made?

(7) What positive–negative polarity choices have been made?

(8) What choices of contrastiveness have been made?

(9) Can you explain how the sum of these choices helps to give the impression of movement and excitement and danger in this text?

Module 39

1 †Discuss the different behaviour of the italicised verbs in (a) their use as an ordinary lexical verb and (b) as a catenative in phased verbal groups. Apply constituency tests (2.2), consider 'raised subjects' (37.3), and take into account possible lexical alternatives:

- (1) (a) What has *happened*? I pressed the switch but nothing *happened*.
  - (b) We all *happened* to be away when the burglar broke in.
- (2) (a) A strange figure *appeared* in the doorway.
  - (b) He *appears* to have misunderstood your explanation.
- (3) (a) Pete has *failed* the driving test again.
  - (b) He *fails* to realise how important it is to practise.

2 †Using the VGs listed in 39.2, complete the phased Verbal Groups in the sentences below. The first one is done for you:

- (1) The supposedly quiet fishing village *turned out to be/proved to be quite different from* what the travel agency had led us to expect.
- (2) Did you go all the way to the other side of town to take part in the demonstration? – No, I just _____ there.
- (3) Some years ago we _____ to enquire whether a visa was necessary and were held up at the frontier for two days.
- (4) After _____ unsuccessfully on several occasions to pass the seamanship test, he eventually _____ do so at the fourth attempt.
- (5) Isn't there any washing-up liquid anywhere? – Well, there _____ a little left at the bottom of the container.
- (6) The shop assistant _____ reassure the child that her mother would come soon.
- (7) Even old black-and-white films _____ coloured these days.
- (8) He _____ convince the Customs official that he was not smuggling anything, but it _____ be impossible.

3 Read the following letter, taking note of the variety of Verbal Group structures used. Then write a reply to it, telling your own experiences in any environment you like.

> Dear Angela,
> Sorry I've taken so long to answer your very welcome letter. I meant to do so ages ago but then it got left to the half-term break. I must say, holidays do suit me much better.
>
> School is insane because of the new exam. No-one knows what rules we're supposed to be following for criteria assessment. Someone high-up issues a decree and then disappears while the opposite is decreed. If parents really knew what a mess it was, they'd be frantic. I've stopped worrying about my candidates as I feel it's out of my control. We're also secretly planning another reorganisation in Liverpool. I haven't been hit or sworn at yet.

Philip is doing teaching practice in a hilarious school in Leicester where there is no 'confrontational discipline', i.e. some were arm-wrestling, some talking, some listening to walkmans and some working. I hesitate to think about exam results. They've a 90% attendance record, which implies that our arm-wrestlers are just shoplifting somewhere, so perhaps they've hit on the right idea. They're all on individual programmes. Here am I intending to try *Romeo and Juliet* on my low ability fourth year. I've told them it's not fair to deprive them.

Claire's brother seems to have worked out a good arrangement. He lectures in Manchester, has three months on sabbatical leave and goes digging in Turkey or Greece. Funding doesn't seem to be a problem because the relevant countries or international groups give him grants, because his wife, who's a botanist, also comes up with information about plant types and soil, etc., that have succeeded or failed in the past. They have three children and all go camping, the baby being two weeks old on the last trip.

I have talked about my family all the time. How are all of you? Keep me in the picture.

Much love, Jean

Module 40

1 †Underline the Figure and Path(s) in the following examples. Decide whether the verb expresses (a) just Motion, (b) Motion + Manner or (c) Motion + Cause.

(1) The president and his wife drove in an open carriage through the Place de la Concorde and on up the Champs-Élysées to their residence.
(2) The ship slid out of the New York dock past the Statue of Liberty to the Atlantic.
(3) She accidentally knocked a book off the bedside table.
(4) Several trees were blown down.
(5) He gulped down his beer.
(6) We cycled back home.

2 With the help of a good monolingual dictionary, list the Path meanings of *up* and *out*, with examples.

3 †Suggest an aspectual meaning for the italicised words in each of the following examples:

(1) *Fill up* the tank, please.
(2) He was *kept on* by his firm.
(3) A lot of this scrap metal can be *melted down* and used again.
(4) His vocation *urged* him *on*.
(5) She *woke up* suddenly when the alarm went off.

4 With the help of a good dictionary, try to work out the Path meaning(s) of *over* from the following examples (see also 59.2.3).

(1) The travel agency is just *over the road*.
(2) You can walk *over the cliffs* to Robin Hood's Bay.
(3) Why don't you *come over* for a drink this evening? Fine! We'll *drive over* about seven.
(4) The milk has *boiled over*.
(5) Many smaller firms have been *taken over* by larger ones.

5 †In the passage preceding the one below in the novel, the 'three men in a boat' have tried unavailingly to open a tin of pineapple without a tin-opener (see 6.4.3, p. 63).

> **Then we all got mad. We took the tin out on the bank, and Harris went up into a field and got a big, sharp stone, and I went back into the boat and brought out the mast, and George held the tin and Harris held the sharp end of the stone against the top of it, and I took the mast and poised it high in the air, and gathered up all my strength and brought it down.**
>
> **It was George's straw hat that saved his life that day, while Harris got off with merely a flesh wound.**
>
> **After that I took the tin off by myself, and hammered at it with the mast till I was worn out and sick at heart, whereupon Harris took it in hand.**
>
> **We beat it out flat; we beat it back square; we battered it into every form known to geometry, but we could not make a hole in it . . . Harris rushed at the thing, and caught it up, and flung it far into the middle of the river, and as it sank we hurled out curses at it, and we got into the boat and rowed away from the spot, and never paused till we reached Maidenhead.**
>
> **(Jerome K. Jerome, *Three Men in a Boat*)**

(1) Identify the phrasal verbs in this passage.
(2) Discuss whether the particles in the first paragraph have (a) a Path function, (b) an aspectual function. Suggest a meaning associated with each one.

6 Read again the section on translation at the end of 40.2.2. Then translate the following into your own or another language and indicate whether the translation is complete or incomplete:

(1) He got on his bike and rode off.
(2) The orders were sent out yesterday.
(3) The cracks in the wall have been plastered over.
(4) Now that all the kids have left we end up back where we started – just the two of us.
(5) He was sent out to get some stamps.
(6) He walked on away from the Real Madrid stadium entrance and the crowds towards the bus-stop on the Castellana.

VIEWPOINTS ON EVENTS   *CHAPTER 9*

Tense, aspect and modality

EXPRESSING LOCATION IN TIME THROUGH THE VERB

MODULE 41

Tense

SUMMARY

1 Tense is the grammatical expression of the location of events in time. It anchors an event to the speaker's experience of the world by relating the event time to a point of reference. The universal, unmarked reference point is the moment of speaking – speech time. In narrative, a point in past time is usually taken as the reference point.

2 English has two tenses, the present and the past, the past being the marked form, both morphologically and semantically.

3 The basic meaning of the present tense is to locate a situation holding at the present moment. This may be an instantaneous event (*I promise to wait*), a state which holds over time (*Jupiter is the largest planet*), or a habitual occurrence (*He works in an office*). Secondary meanings of the Present include reference to past and future events, 'historic present' (*This man comes up to me . . .*) and the quotative (*and she goes/she's like 'I don't believe it'*).

4 The past tense primarily refers to a definite event or state that is prior to utterance time. Its secondary uses refer to a present event or state as hypothetical (*If I were you*).

5 English has no verbal inflection to mark a future tense. Instead, English makes use of a number of forms to refer to future events.
   Finite clauses in English can be marked for either tense or modality but not both. Verbs marked for tense are said to be 'tensed'. Non-finite clauses are not tensed.

41.1 THE MEANING OF TENSE

Tense is the grammatical expression of the location of events in time. It anchors (or 'grounds') an event to the speaker's experience of the world by relating the **event time**

to a point of reference. The normal, universal and therefore unmarked point of reference is the moment of speaking – **speech time**, what has been called 'the inescapable and constantly changing **now** in which all verbal interaction takes place'. Past events take place before the 'now', while future events are thought of as taking place after it.

The location of the speaker, the moment of speaking and the speaker her/himself make up 'the *I*, the *here* and the *now*'- the '**deictic centre**' – which serves as the point of reference for definiteness and proximity (see Chapter 10). Tense, therefore, has a deictic function; it distinguishes a 'proximal' event expressed by the present tense from a 'distal' event expressed by the Past tense. The 'now' can be diagrammed as shown.

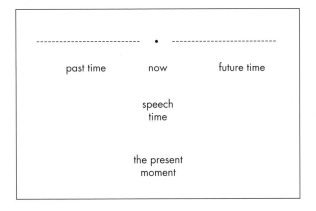

41.1.1 Present tense, Past tense and future time

Tense is a grammatical category that is realised in English morphologically on the verb. In accordance with this criterion, English has just two tenses: the Present and the Past, as in *goes/ went*, respectively. English has no verbal inflection to mark a future tense. The forms *shall* and *will* are not verbal inflections but modal auxiliaries which, when reduced, are attached to pronouns, not to the verb root (*I'll wait outside*). Also important are the form–meaning relationships. *Shall* and *will* belong to a set of modal auxiliaries and can express meanings other than reference to future time, as we shall see later in this chapter (see 44.1). Instead of a future tense, English makes use of a number of combinations such as *be going to* to refer to future events (see 41.6) Compare:

> They *do* the shopping on Saturdays. (present tense)
> They *did* the shopping on Saturday. (past tense)
> They *are going* to do/ *will* do the shopping on Saturday. (lexical auxiliary/ modal)

In general, as these examples illustrate, past and present events are taken to have the status of real events, while references to the future are to potential, that is unreal, events.

In English, therefore, the three-term semantic distinction into past, present and future time is grammaticalised as a two-term tense distinction between Past tense and Present tense.

Besides tensed forms of verbs, other linguistic forms, particularly adverbs of time such as *now, then, tomorrow*, PPs such as *in 1066* and lexico-grammatical expressions such as *ten minutes after the plane took off* can make reference to time. English, in fact, relies to a considerable extent on such units to make the temporal reference clear.

The **Past tense** in English is the marked form. Cognitively, the situations conceptualised by the speaker as past have the status of known, but not immediate, reality; they are not currently observed. Morphologically, the vast majority of verbs in English have a distinctive past form, (*played, saw*) and, semantically, the past tense basically refers to a situation that is prior to the present, as in *Yesterday was fine*. (See 41.5 for secondary meanings.)

The **Present tense** is the unmarked tense. Cognitively, it expresses situations which have immediate reality, that is, what is currently observed. Morphologically, it is marked only on the 3rd person singular (with the exception of *be*, which has three forms (*am, are* and *is*). Semantically, it covers a wider range of temporal references than the Past tense, including reference to future time (*Tomorrow is a holiday*).

Even in our everyday use, 'at present' and 'at the present time' have a wider application than simply to the present moment of speech time. Thus, *Birds have wings* represents a situation which holds not only at the present time but has also held in the past, and will conceivably continue to hold in the future. It can be diagrammed as shown here.

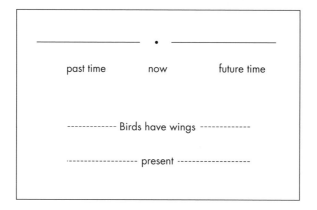

41.1.2 Stative and dynamic uses of verbs

The meaning expressed by a verb in present or past tense depends to a great extent on whether the verb refers to a single constant state, as in *I know her address*, or to a dynamic occurrence, as in *He goes to work by train*.

More exactly, the meaning depends on whether the verb is being used statively or dynamically, since many verbs lend themselves to both interpretations. 'Have' usually refers to a state, as in *birds have wings*, but it also has dynamic uses as in *have breakfast*.

In general, dynamic but not stative senses can occur with the imperative and progressive, and after *do* in *wh*-cleft sentences:

Have breakfast!   We are having breakfast.   What we did was have breakfast.
*Have wings!   *Birds are having wings.   *What birds do is have wings.

It is important to realise that, in the following sections, the Present tense is what is sometimes referred to as the 'simple' Present, more exactly as the 'non-progressive Present'. The Progressive, consisting of a form of *be + -ing*, is a verbal aspect which combines with tense. It is discussed in Module 43 as encoding a single event observed in the process of happening. There is a meaningful distinction – and an obligatory choice in English – between expressing a situation by means of the Present tense alone and expressing it by the Present Progressive. Compare:

> The sun *doesn't shine* everyday in Brussels, (non-Progressive Present)
> but *it is shining* today. (Progessive Present)

41.2 BASIC MEANINGS OF THE PRESENT TENSE

The basic meaning of the Present tense is to locate a situation holding at the present moment. The tense itself does not say whether that same situation continues beyond the present moment and whether it also held in the past. These are implications which we derive from our knowledge of the world and from the type of situation encoded in the clause.

In fact it is relatively rare for a situation to coincide exactly with the present moment, that is, to occupy a single point in time, literally or conceptually. Situations of this nature do occur, however and can be classed together as types of the Instantaneous Present.

41.2.1 The Instantaneous Present

These are events which coincide, or are presented as coinciding, with speech time and have no duration beyond speech time:

> Performatives: I *promise* I'll be careful. (see 25.1)
> Exclamations with initial directional adverb: Off they *go*! (at the start of a race)
> In you *get*! (helping someone to get in a car, etc.)
> Commentaries: Jones *passes* and Raul *kicks* the ball into the net.
> Demonstrations: I *place* the fruit in the blender, *press* gently, and then *pour* out the liquid.

More characteristically, the Present is used to refer to situations which occupy a longer period of time than the moment of speaking, but which nonetheless include speech time. Traditionally these situations are classed according to the verb as stative uses and habitual uses of the Present.

41.2.2 The State Present

Used with stative verb senses, the Present refers to a single uninterrupted state, which began before the moment of speaking and may well continue after it. They include **timeless statements**, that is, statements which apply to all time, including speech time:

> Jupiter *is* the largest planet in the solar system.

They also include states whose time span is not endless, e.g. *know, think, believe, belong, stand for.* They are nevertheless states in which no change or limitation into the past or future is implied. Here too the temporal reference includes speech time.

> I *think* you are right.
> MP *stands for* Member of Parliament.

41.2.3 The Habitual Present

This is used with dynamic verbs to encode situations that occur habitually over time, even if the action is not being carried out at the moment of speaking. For instance, referring to the following examples, Tim may not actually be working, nor the leaves falling at the moment of speaking. Nevertheless, the recurrent situation holds as the normal course of things and is appropriately referred to by the Present tense.

> Tim *works* in an insurance company.
> Many trees *lose* their leaves in autumn.

Again, it must be pointed out that the plain Present tense used for habitual and other meanings contrasts with the Present Progressive, which encodes an actual occurrence of a dynamic action observed in the process of happening, as in *Tim is working late today, The trees are already losing their leaves* (see 43.4–43.7).

41.3 SECONDARY MEANINGS OF THE PRESENT TENSE: REFERENCE TO PAST EVENTS

The Present can be used to refer to past events in certain limited ways.

In newspaper headlines and captions to photographs

> Thousands *flee* persecution.
> Demonstrators *clash* with armed police as violence *increases*.

In relating incidents in informal, casual speech: the historic present and the quotative

> He was only an average athlete, and then suddenly he *wins* two Olympic medals.
> I had just left the bank when *this* guy *comes* up to me and *asks* for money.

The Present tense in headlines and the sudden switch from Past to Present in speech have the effect of dramatising the event, bringing it before the reader's eyes as if it were an instance of the instantaneous Present. However, the headline stands apart from the text, while the '**historic present**' switch occurs within the discourse at a key point in the narrative, and is frequently paralleled by a switch to a proximal demonstrative (*this*), as in the example: *this guy comes up*.

Go and *be like* are used by young speakers talking among themselves, as **quotative** verbs like *say*, to introduce direct speech as in: 'and she *goes* "What's he like?" and I'*m like* "Gorgeous".' They usually occur in the Present tense. These verbs are not used in this way by all speakers.

In reporting information

With verbs of communicating (*say, tell*) and of perception (*see, hear, understand*) the use of the Present implies that the reported information is still valid, even though the communicative process took place in the past. With a Past tense, the validity is not implied:

> The weather forecast *says* that rain is on the way.
> I *understand* that you would like to move to London.

Some of the uses of the Present tense are illustrated in this feature article from *The Week*:

Pete earns his living by breaking into other people's homes. He rises early, dresses smartly – 'jeans, loafers, shirt, good coat; everthing ironed and clean' – and tucks surgical gloves (his anti-fingerprint protection) up his sleeves. He picks 'nice' – by which he means moderately affluent – houses within five minutes of an underground or railway station in case he needs an emergency getaway. He targets houses screened from the street by a hedge or fence, and rings the bell. 'If someone comes, I've got a set of car keys in my hand. "Minicab? No? Oh, sorry. Wrong house, Third time that's happened this week".'

Once he's certain no one's at home, he goes down the side of the house, vaulting gates. 'Boof – over the top. I'm only ten stone and I'm fit. I've gone up plastic drainpipes and got through toilet windows this size,' he indicates a tiny square with his hands. He either forces or smashes a small window, leans in and breaks the main window locks. 'They do feel solid, but you can snap 'em.' His aim is to be in and out in three minutes. He double locks the front door to forestall unwelcome interruption. – 'I'm on my toes now . . . running for the stairs . . . I'm doing like four steps at a time' – and identifies the master bedroom. 'Your jewellery is either on your bedside chest, or in the top two drawers. Not there? Your wardrobe or the drawers in your bed – I've got it.' He leaps up and claps his hands, reliving the adrenaline rush. 'I pull your pillow out – everything goes wrapped up in a pillowcase, then inside my jacket and boof! – I'm off. I don't bother with the other rooms.' He leaves by the front door or through a neighbouring garden. If he's spotted he brazens it out. 'I walk past 'em. All right mate?' I do six, seven, maybe ten burglaries in a day's work" (Pete uses the words 'work' and 'earning' without irony.) He steals only jewellery, netting thousands of pounds. But the money – spent on drugs, clubbing, clothes, his daughters – slips through his hands like wet soap.

41.4 BASIC MEANINGS OF THE PAST TENSE

We have seen that the basic meaning of the Past tense in English is to locate an event or state in the past. It situates the event at a 'temporal distance' from the moment of speaking, whether in time, towards the past, or with regard to potential or hypothetical events which have not yet occurred in the present or the future.

When used to refer to a definite past event or state, the Past in English contains two semantic features:

- The speaker conceptualises the event as having occurred at some specific time in the past.
- The event is presented as wholly located in the past, in a time-frame that is separated from the present.

These features are illustrated in the following examples:

> James Joyce *was born* in Dublin in 1882.
> He *lived* in Ireland until 1904 and *spent* the rest of his life abroad.

The Past tense in English says nothing about whether the event occupied a point in time or a longer extent. These additional meanings are understood from the lexical verb used and from the whole situation represented by the clause. In the examples above referring to one single person, *was born* is interpreted as referring to a point in time, while *lived* and *spent* are interpreted as being of longer duration. With a plural subject, the Past tense *were born* is interpreted here as referring not to one single point in time but to many:

> Generations of writers *were born* who imitated Joyce's style of writing.

In using the Past tense, speakers do not need to specify a past occurrence by means of an Adjunct, however. As long as the speaker has a specific time in mind and can assume that the hearer infers this from the situational context, the Past tense is used, as in:

> *Did you see* that flash of lightning?
> [Who *said* that?] It *wasn't* me.
> I *spoke* to a dancer from the Bolshoi ballet.

41.5 SECONDARY MEANINGS OF THE PAST TENSE: PRESENT AND FUTURE REFERENCE

The Past tense can refer to time-frames other than the past in the following three ways:

- **In 'closed conditionals' and other hypothetical subordinate clauses** which express a counterfactual belief or presupposition on the part of the speaker. The reference is to present time. The past in such expressions was originally a subjunctive whose only relic remains in the form *were* for all persons of *be*.

If we *had* enough time . . .   presupposes we haven't enough time
He talks as if he *owned* the place.   presupposes he doesn't own the place
I often wish I *were* somewhere else.   presupposes I am not somewhere else

- **In reported speech or thought:** after a reporting verb in the Past tense, the reported verbs in the dependent clauses are also in the Past. This phenomenon is known as 'backshift' (see 36.3). Present tense forms are optional, as in *She said she prefers/ preferred vanilla ice cream*, as long as the situation is still valid.
- **In polite requests and enquiries**, the past form 'distances' the proposed action, so making the imposition on the hearer less direct:

Did you want to speak to me now?
I *wondered* whether you needed anything.

41.6 REFERRING TO FUTURE EVENTS

We cannot refer to future events as facts, as we can to past and present situations, since future events are not open to observation or memory. We can predict with more or less confidence what will happen, we can plan for events to take place, express our intentions and promises with regard to future events. These are modalised rather than factual statements, and are treated in 44.3. Here we simply outline the main syntactic means of referring to future events as seen from the standpoint of present time.

41.6.1 'Safe' predictions

These are predictions which do not involve the subject's volition, and include cyclical events and general truths. *Will* + infinitive is used, *shall* by some speakers for 'I' and 'we':

Susie *will be* nineteen tomorrow.
You'*ll find* petrol more expensive in France.

Will/shall + progressive combine the meaning of futurity with that of focusing on the internal process, in this way avoiding the implication of promise associated with *will* when the subject is 'I' or 'we'. Compare:

I *will (I'll) speak to him about your application tomorrow.*
We *shall (we'll) be studying* your application shortly.

41.6.2 Programmed events

Future events seen as certain because they are unalterable **1** or programmed **2, 3** and **4** can be expressed by the Present tense + time adjunct, by ***will*** or by the lexical auxiliaries ***be due to*** + *infinitive* and ***be to*** (simple forms only):

1   The sun *sets* at 20.15 hours tomorrow.
2   Next year's conference *will* be held in Milan.

3 He *is due to retire* in two months' time.
4 She *is to* marry the future heir to the throne.

41.6.3 Intended events

Intended events can be expressed by *be + going to + infinitive* **1** and by the Progressive (*be + -ing*) **2**. These forms can be marked for tense. The past forms refer to an event intended at some time in the past to occur in some future time **3**. As with all intended events, they may or may not actually take place. (See also modal *will*, 44.6.)

1 I am *going to try to get* more information about this.
2 Pete *is thinking of changing* his job.
3 I *was going to leave* a note but there was no-one at Reception.   [BNC BMR 625]

41.6.4 Imminent events

An event seen as occurring in the immediate future is expressed by *be + going to* or by combinations such as: *be about to + infinitive, be on the point of/ be on the verge of + -ing*. There is usually some external or internal sign of the imminence of the happening.

It looks as if there's *going to be* a storm.
This company is *about to be/ on the verge of being taken over* by a multinational.

An expectation orientated to past time is expressed by the corresponding forms in the past:

It's not what I *thought* it was *going to be*.
. . . the territory which *was* later *to be* part of Lithuania.

41.6.5 Future anterior events

A future event anterior to another event is expressed by the **Future Perfect**:

The programme will *have ended* long before we get back.
By the time he is twenty-two, he'*ll have taken* his degree.

Otherwise, the Future Perfect expresses the duration or repetition of an event in the future. The addition of the Progressive emphasises the incompletion of the sequence (see 43.4):

We'*ll have lived* here for ten years by next July.
We'*ll have been living* here for ten years by next July.

PAST EVENTS AND PRESENT TIME CONNECTED

MODULE 42

Present Perfect and Past Perfect

SUMMARY

1 Both tense and aspect have to do with time relations expressed by the verb, but from different perspectives. While tense basically situates an event or state in present or past time, aspect is concerned with such notions as duration and completion or incompletion of the process expressed by the verb. English has two aspects, the Perfect and the Progressive. We first consider **the Perfect aspect**, noticing how it differs from the simple tenses. In Module 43, we go on to consider the **Progressive aspect**.

2 The **Present Perfect** is a retrospective aspect which views a state or event as occurring at some indefinite time within a time-frame that leads up to speech time.

3 The event is viewed as psychologically relevant to the present. By contrast, an event encoded in the Past tense is viewed as disconnected from the present.

4 Consequently, the Perfect is not normally interchangeable in English with the Past tense. For the same reason, the time adjuncts accompanying them are normally different.

5 Implications of recency, completion and result, derived from the combination of Present Perfect and verb type, are all manifestations of **current relevance**.

6 The Past Perfect is used to refer to events previous to those expressed by a past tense or by a Present Perfect.

42.1 PRESENT PERFECT ASPECT AND PAST TENSE COMPARED: ANTERIORITY VS DEFINITE TIME

The Perfect construction in English relates a state or event to a relevance time (R). This is speech time for the Present Perfect, some point in time prior to speech time for the Past Perfect and some point in time after speech time for the Future Perfect.

The Present Perfect is a subtle retrospective aspect which views states or events as occurring in a time-frame leading up to speech time. Expressed by *have* + past participle, the *have* element is present, the participle is past. The event is psychologically connected to the present as in the following example, which is diagrammed to show relevance time:

```
--------------------------------------------------------------------------------- R
```

His marriage *has broken down* and he *has gone* to live in another part of England   speech
                                                                                              time

These and other features contrast with those of the Past tense:

	Present Perfect	**Past Tense**
a.	Its time-frame is the extended **now**, a period of time which extends up to speech time.	Its time-frame is the **past**, which is viewed as a separate time-frame from that of the present.
b.	The event occurs at some **indefinite** and **unspecified time** within the extended now. The Perfect is **non-deictic** – it doesn't 'point' to a specific time but relates to a relevant time.	The event is located at a **specific and definite time** in the past. The Past tense is **deictic** – it points to a specific time in the past.
c.	The event has '**current relevance**', that is, it is viewed as **psychologically connected** to the moment of speaking.	The event is seen as **psychologically disconnected** from the moment of speaking.

Within the extended now, the Present Perfect is used in English when the speaker does not wish to refer to a definite moment of occurence of the event, but simply to the **anteriority** of the event. This is in marked contrast with the definite time use of the Past tense. Compare:

They *have left* for New York.
They *left* for New York an hour ago.

Similarly, the Present Perfect is not normally used in main clauses with interrogative adverbs, which imply definite time and require the Past tense.

We can say	Have they started?	Have they finished? (Present Perfect)
Or	When did they start?	At what time did they finish? (Past tense)
But not	*When have they started?*	*At what time have they finished?*

When a definite time is not implied by the verb the Present Perfect is possible:

Where have you most enjoyed working? [BNC BNA 28496]

In subordinate clauses, with future reference, the Present Perfect can follow *when*, since this use refers to an unspecified time: *When I have finished, I'll call you.*

Furthermore, the Present Perfect operates in a time-frame that is still open, blocking examples such as **1a** and **2a**. By contrast the **b** examples are grammatical, as are **3** and **4**:

1a *James Joyce *has been born* in Dublin.   **1b** James Joyce *was born* in Dublin.
2a *He *has lived* in Ireland until 1904.   **2b** He *lived* in Ireland until 1904.
3   Michael *has lived* in Ireland all his life (implying that he still lives there).
4   Generations of writers have been influenced by Joyce (and are still influenced).

In **1a** and **2a** the Perfect is blocked because Joyce's life-span is over. In **3** this is not the case. In **4** the plural subject 'generations of writers' allows for a time-frame that is open.

The perspective of the 'extended now' time-frame in contrast with that of the Past tense is illustrated in this passage from Penelope Lively's *Moon Tiger*:

> *I've grown old* with the century; there's not much left of either of us. The century of war. All history, of course, is the history of wars, but this hundred years *has excelled itself*. How many million shot, maimed, burned, frozen, starved, drowned? God only knows. I trust He does; He should have kept a record, if only for His own purposes. *I've been* on the fringes of two wars; I shan't see the next. The first *preoccupied* me not at all; this thing called War *summoned* Father and *took* him *away* for ever. *I saw* it as some inevitable climactic effect: thunderstorm or blizzard. The second *lapped* me up but *spat* me *out* intact. Technically intact. *I have seen* war; in that sense *I have been present* at wars, *I have heard* bombs and guns and *observed* their effects.

42.2 TIME ADJUNCTS AND THE PRESENT PERFECT ASPECT

The Present Perfect aspect is frequently accompanied by time Adjuncts that refer to a period of time that is still open at the moment of speaking, e.g. *this week, this month, this year*, etc. Adjuncts which refer to a period of past time that is now over (e.g. *last month, last year, yesterday*) are incompatible with the Perfect. Compare:

Have you seen any good films *this month?*   **Have you seen* any good films last month*

A period of time expressed by an adjunct such as *in July* is either open or closed depending on the speaker's vantage-point. If closed, the verb is in the Past tense:

Temperatures *have reached* an all-time high *in July*. (July is not yet over)
Temperatures *reached* an all-time high *in July*. (July is over)

Adjuncts of indefinite or unspecified time used with the Perfect, such as:	Adjuncts of definite or specific time used with past tense, such as:
sometimes, often, always, never, at times	yesterday
twice, three times	last week, last year, last month
in the last ten years	an hour ago, two years ago
lately, recently, now	last June, in 1066
	at 4 o'clock, at Christmas, at Easter

42.3 CURRENT RELEVANCE

By 'current relevance' we mean that the event referred to by means of the Present Perfect is psychologically connected to speech time, and has some (implicit) relevance to it.

This meaning is quoted in all accounts of the present perfect and is considered by some to be the main one. It is undoubtedly of the utmost importance. Nevertheless, we prefer to consider current relevance as a pragmatic implication deriving from the combination of time-frame, perfect aspect and verb type. This will become clear as we turn to the interpretations of the perfect in discourse.

At this point we simply illustrate the notion of current relevance as follows: *They have been out* implies that they have now come back, whereas *They went out* has no such implication. It would not be normal to say **They have been out a moment ago* (since an adjunct such as 'a moment ago' visualises a definite time in the past, no matter how recent).

Occasional occurrences in spoken English of forms which appear to combine the two can be explained as mental switches from an indefinite to a definite time-frame produced as speakers modify their messages as they go along. Regional variation may also be a factor.

42.4 FUNCTIONS AND DISCOURSE INTERPRETATIONS OF THE PRESENT PERFECT

Interpretations of the functions of the Perfect are described under certain well-known labels, as follows.

42.4.1 The experiential Perfect

This refers to the fact that there have been one or more experiences of the event in the recent history **1** and **2**, or in the life-span **3** of a certain person **up to the present time**, as in:

1 I've been ill.
2 We've been away.
3 You've lived in Brighton, and you've lived in Kingston and now you live in Lewes. [BNC KRG 1188]

Included in this type is the **first-time experience** use, as in *It's the first time I've been here*, for which certain languages use a Present tense.

Another is the contrast between the one-way **have gone to** and the cyclic **have been to**, as in:

Peter's gone to England = he's still there
Peter's been to England = he has returned after a visit to England

This explains the anomalous *I've gone to England, and the fact that *I've been to England several times* is normal, whereas *I've gone to England several times* is odd.

42.4.2 The continuous Perfect

This is a state, duration or repeated occurrence of a process such as *walk*, lasting up to speech time. An adjunct of extent is virtually necessary to complete the meaning.

I *have known* Bill since we were at school together. (i.e. and I still know him)
We *have walked* for hours. (up to the present moment)
For the last ten years he *has lived* and *worked* in Brussels. (i.e. He still does)
Over the last three years the pressure group *has staged* a number of hunger strikes.

For and *over* + a unit of time (*for hours, over the last three years*) express the duration of the event from the vantage point of speech time, and this form is retrospective. *Since* + a point of time expresses extent viewed from the initiation of the event, and is prospective.

42.4.3 Implied meanings of the Present Perfect

Deriving from the features and main uses of the present perfect, certain implications are associated with it, especially in BrE. These are **recency**, **completion** and **resulting state**.

Recency

The Present Perfect lends itself to a '**hot news**' interpretation, which can be reinforced by *just*. In AmE, at least with some verbs, the Past + *just* is used.

The Prime Minister *has resigned*.
He's *done* it! (played the winning ball in a golf tournament) (sports commentary)
We've *just eaten*/had lunch. (BrE)   We *just ate*. (AmE)

Completion

This is the pragmatic implication arising from the combination of the Perfect with processes having an end-point (see 43.2), as in *grow up, tape something*:

> Hundreds of people *have been evacuated* from their homes, which *have been burnt to rubble*. (news)
> His brothers *have grown up* and have left home.
>   You can listen to what you*'ve taped*. Oh yeah, you can play it back. [BNC KCL7]

Resulting state

Such situations with the Perfect are in many cases interpreted as having a visible result as in:

> *You've squashed my shoe!*   [BNC KPO 838]
> (The shoe is in a squashed state)
> *I've baked a cake.* (the cake is visibly made)

The result may be resulting knowledge or know-how, as implied in *He has learned to drive*. These are all forms of current relevance.

In certain types of discourse such as news items a topic is presented as 'hot news' by a clause with the Present Perfect and an indefinite NG. Once the topic has been introduced, the narrative continues in the Past tense, and the NGs are treated as definite, as in the following short news item from *The Week*.

> *A polar bear has become the star attraction at a zoo in Argentina.* But the extraordinary spectacle only happened by accident. When Pelarus, a 14-year-old bear, developed a stubborn case of dermatitis, zookeepers at Mendoza zoo tried every medicine under the sun, but to no avail. As a last resort, they gave the bear an experimental medication which had a bizarre side effect – it turned Pelarus purple. Officials aren't complaining: not only is the bear on the road to recovery, but visitor numbers are up by 50%.

42.5 EXPRESSING MORE DISTANCED EVENTS: THE PAST PERFECT

To refer to an event that is previous to another event in the past, the Past Perfect is used (*had* + past participle). It can represent a distanced event of three different types:

(a) the past of the Past tense as in the **1a** examples. When the time relation is unambiguous, the past tense can replace the Past Perfect in English as in **1b**:

> **1a** We *had heard* nothing from Tony before he returned.
>   She didn't mention that she *had seen* you at the match.

1b We *heard* nothing from Tony before he returned.
   She didn't mention that she *saw* you at the match.

(b) the past of the Present Perfect:
   She *had lived* in the north since she changed her job.

corresponding to:

   She *has lived* in the north since she changed her job.

(c) the 'unreal' past in counterfactual conditions:
   If I *had known* he was in trouble, I would have helped him.

As the Past Perfect refers to a time previous to a time signalled somewhere else in the context, it is not always easy to determine its time reference. For this reason, the Past Perfect often occurs in subordinate clauses accompanied by time Adjuncts, both of which help to establish the temporal links between events. Furthermore, as English has only this one tense to refer to any time previous to the past, it is used to express a series of events each preceding the other.

The role of the Past Perfect in orientating the reader in tracking events is illustrated in this extract from William Boyd's *The New Confessions*. The Past tense *described* marks a switch from one space-time unit to another in the story:

> Duric Ludokian *was*[1] a huge wealthy Armenian who *had fled*[2] from his native country to Russia in 1896 shortly after the first Turkish massacres and pogroms against the Armenian people *had begun*.[3] He *had fled*[4] again in 1918 after the Russian Revolution and was among the first of the thousands of Russian emigrés who *found*[5] sanctuary in Berlin. Ludokian *had made*[6] his fortune in nuts. He described himself as a 'nut importer'.

The sequence of events in time would be as follows, reading from right to left:

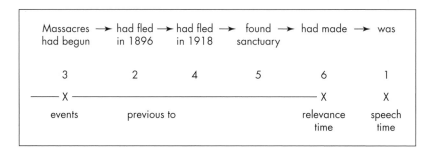

42.6 NON-FINITE PERFECT FORMS

The time-frame of the Perfect is also reflected in non-finite Perfect forms *to have* + participle and *having* + participle:

To have made such a statement in public was rather unwise.
Having satisfied himself that everything was in order, he locked the safe.

SITUATION TYPES AND THE PROGRESSIVE ASPECT

MODULE 43

SUMMARY

1 Important aspectual contrasts include **perfectivity** (viewing the event as a whole) vs **imperfectivity** (viewing the event as incomplete). These distinctions remain indeterminate in English in the simple Past and Present tense forms. Perfectivity then must be interpreted from the whole clause.

2 The only grammaticalised aspectual contrasts in English are the Progressive vs non-progressive and the Perfect vs non-perfect. (The Perfect is not identical to perfectivity!)

3 Progressiveness is a type of imperfectivity which focuses on the continuousness of the internal part of the event. Another type, that of past habituality, is expressed by the lexical auxiliary *used to* + inf.

4 Situations (and verbs) can be classed according to their inherent aspectual meaning as states (with no internal change: *It's hot*), as punctual occurrences (*the cable snapped*), as durative occurrences without an end-point: *we walked along* (activities) and as durative with an end-point: *we walked home* (accomplishments).

5 The Progressive and Perfect aspects add their communicative perspectives to the inherent aspectual meaning of the verb. Other factors to be taken into account, in order to understand the aspectuality of a particular verbalised situation, are the single or multiple nature of the subject and object, and the presence of Adjuncts.

43.1 THE MEANING OF ASPECT

While tense is used to locate events in time, aspect is concerned with the way in which the event is viewed with regard to such considerations as duration and completion when encoded by a verb. This is sometimes defined as the internal temporal contour of the event. Compare, for instance, the following representations of a situation:

1a He *locked* the safe. **1b** He *was locking* the safe.

As regards tense, both are the same – the Past. They both locate the situation in past time. The difference is one of aspect, expressed by the verbal form *was locking* as opposed to the ordinary past *locked*. What we have is a difference of **viewpoint** and of **focus of attention**.

A basic aspectual distinction is that of **perfectivity vs imperfectivity**:

- Perfective: the situation is presented as a complete whole, as if viewed externally, with sharp boundaries, as in **1a**. (Note that perfectivity is not the Perfect aspect!)
- Imperfective: the situation is viewed as an internal stage, without boundaries and is conceptualised as ongoing and incomplete; the beginning and end aren't included in this viewpoint – we see only the internal part, as in **1b**. The Progressive is thus a kind of imperfectivity.

In many languages the perfective/ imperfective pairs are related morphologically. Having fewer aspectual inflections, English has fewer grammaticalised aspectual choices than some languages. Take for instance the following examples containing the verb *speak*, together with their Spanish counterparts:

2a He stopped and *spoke* to me in English.   (Spanish *habló*)
2b He *spoke* English with a Welsh accent.   (Spanish *hablaba*)

The Past tense in English does not distinguish formally between the single event represented in **2a**, whose counterpart in Spanish is marked as perfective (*habló*), and the habitual event represented in **2b**, which is marked as imperfective in Spanish (*hablaba*).

In other words, the Past tense in English is indeterminate between a perfective and an imperfective interpretation. This distinction is captured inferentially by speakers according to the relevance of one meaning or other within a context, but is not grammaticalised.

43.2 LEXICAL ASPECT OF ENGLISH VERBS

Before examining the second grammatical aspect available to speakers of English, the Progressive, we turn for a moment to lexical aspect. All verbs (and predicates) have an inherent lexical aspect. We have touched on this concept in outlining the stative vs dynamic distinction, phased verbal groups and the behaviour of particles in phrasal verbs.

Lexical aspect proves to be an invaluable tool for understanding the functioning of the Progressive and the Perfect aspects. In fact, it is not easy to grasp the contribution made by the grammatical aspects without realising how they interact with the lexical aspect of the verb. In taking a little further the stative–dynamic distinction, we will now be considering whole situations to which the verb brings its own inherent aspectuality, in terms of two factors:

* temporal boundaries: whether the situation is bounded (i.e. has an end-point) or unbounded (has no end-point)
* duration or non-duration (through time)

The diagram illustrates the main situation types.

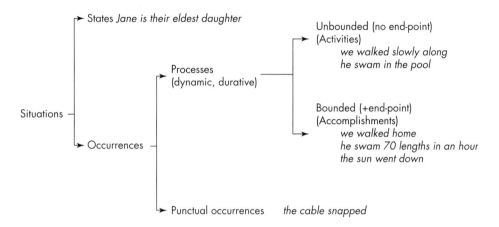

Reading from left to right in the diagram, situations can be classified as follows:

1 **States vs Occurrences**. States have relatively long duration but do not have boundaries: they are unbounded, as with verbs such as *be, stand* (The house *stands* on a hill). Occurrences are dynamic and more complex. They are subdivided according to duration into:
2 **Processes vs punctual occurrences**. Processes are durative, they last through time, while punctual occurrences occupy little or no appreciable time and have sharp boundaries, e.g. *the cable snapped*. (Note that 'process' is used here differently from its use as a general term for the semantic structure of clauses, as discussed in Chapter 5.)
3 **Durative processes** are divided into those that have **no end-point** (unbounded Activities), as in *He walked slowly along*, and those that have **a sharp end-point** (bounded Accomplishments), as in *he walked home*. The latter consist of two phases, a durative phase, the walking, and a terminative phase, the arrival home. The durative phase is usually not in focus unless combined with progressiveness (see 43.5.4).

Note that although the traditional terms, Activities and Accomplishments, suggest human agency, it is not the case that all processes are agentive. *It rained heavily*, for instance, is a non-agentive activity. The key concept here is boundedness, that is, whether or not there is an end-point.

The way in which a situation is viewed can be modified in various ways:

- By adding an adjunct or an adverbial particle such as *up*, which establishes an end-point: In this way an unbounded situation can be made bounded. Compare:

unbounded process	**bounded process**
It rained heavily.	It rained heavily *until six o'clock*.
The children have grown in your absence.	The children have *grown up* in your absence.
He read the book for an hour.	He read the book *in an hour*.

- By including a multiple subject or object instead of a single element, a situation is presented as repeated or 'serial'. This effect can also be achieved by adjuncts.

  He rang his agent last week.   They rang their agents every day last week.

- By grammatical aspect, which we deal with next.

  Verbs corresponding to each of the four groups include:

  1   **Stative verbs**: be, belong, seem, stand, lie, have, want, know, understand, see, hear, feel, like, dislike, hate, love.
  2   **Punctual or momentary verbs**: cough, blink, flash, hit, tap, slam, slap, kick, shoot.
  3a   **Unbounded-process verbs**: bend, dance, drive, read, sleep, write, walk, work.
  3d   **Bounded-completion verbs**: be born, die, fall, drop, arrive, sit down, stand up.

43.3 GRAMMATICAL ASPECTS IN ENGLISH

English has two clearly grammaticalised aspectual distinctions: the **Progressive**, as in *was locking* vs the non-progressive in *locked*; and the **Perfect**, as in *has locked* vs the non-perfect *locked*. We have seen that the Perfect is a subtle aspect which is not to be confused with perfectivity. Perfect and Progressive may combine in one VG and are marked for present or past tense:

Present + progressive	is locking
Past + progressive	was locking
Present perfect	has locked
Past perfect	had locked
Present perfect + progressive	has been locking
Past perfect + progressive	had been locking

As we saw in Chapter 8, progressive and perfect aspects also combine with modals, lexical auxiliaries and the passive.

43.4 THE MEANING OF THE PROGRESSIVE

The basic function of the English progressive aspect is to indicate a dynamic action in the process of happening. Attention is focused on some internal stage of the process, which cognitively, is viewed as something directly observed, unfolding before our eyes. English makes a grammatical contrast between the progressive and the non-progressive. That is to say, there is an obligatory choice between viewing the situation as in the process of happening and viewing it as a complete whole:

What was he doing? What did he do?
(Past + progressive) (Past, non-progressive)

There is more to grammatical aspect than obligatory choice, however. The best way to understand grammatical aspect is to see it working in conjunction with the lexical aspect of verbs. The Progressive (and, in a different way, the Perfect) add a communicative perspective to events and states that is different from their lexical aspect.

43.5 LEXICAL ASPECT AND THE PROGRESSIVE

As the Progressive is essentially dynamic in character, it lends a dynamic interpretation to whatever verbal action it is applied to. For this reason, not all types of verbal situation admit the Progressive, as in **1a**, and those that do admit it are affected in different ways.

43.5.1 States and the Progressive

Most stative situations are in general incompatible with the progressive. Permanent qualities such as *be tall, be red* and relations expressed by such verbs as *own, belong, seem* are conceptualised in English as invariable and therefore non-dynamic. When normally stative verbs are used with the Progressive the situation is viewed as a temporary state, often with the implication of a type of behaviour or stance, as in **1b**. Compare:

1a *You *are being tall*, George.   **1b** You *are being far too optimistic*, George.

The stative meanings of verbs such as *see, hear* (involuntary perception), *like, love, hate* (affection) and *know, believe, understand, wonder* (cognition) are in general incompatible with the progressive. However, many such verbs have taken on dynamic uses and these admit the progressive, as in the following examples:

I'm *seeing* the doctor tomorrow. (= consulting) (programmed event)
Janet is *seeing* her friends *off*. (= taking leave of)
They *were seeing* so much of each other, he was almost one of the family.
How *are you liking* your visit to Disneyland? (= enjoying)
Pat: Oh, *I'm just loving it./ I'm enjoying* it. Ben: Frankly, I'*m hating* it.

43.5.2 Punctual occurrences and the Progressive

With punctual verbs such as *tap*, *kick*, *fire*, *sneeze*, *bounce*, *flash*, *hit* and the progressive, the situation is interpreted as iterative, that is, repeated:

> Someone *is tapping* on the wall next door.
> The rain *is hitting* the windows harder now.   [BNC FP6 296]

These categories are approximate, rather than absolute. Some processes appear to be more punctual than others. Some end-points appear to be more final than others. It would, for instance, be unusual to hear *He's slamming the door* for it is not possible to keep on slamming the same door unless you keep on opening it. *He kept slamming the door* would imply this process, but would nonetheless be unusual. A multiple situation in which several doors slammed can be expressed by the Past tense, as in the following:

> Behind the swing door, cupboards opened and slammed shut. Pots cracked against work tops.

Punctual verbs are frequently used metaphorically with the progressive, in which case the resulting situation may perhaps be considered durative:

> The recession *is hitting* the stores hard. (=affecting adversely)   [BNC ABE 1784]

43.5.3 Verbs with no end-point and the Progressive

With those durative verbs that have no end-point (*play, sing, work, talk, dance, rain, snow,* etc.), including verbs of bodily sensation (*ache, hurt, itch, feel cold*), the Progressive has the effect of **perspectivising** the process as seen in progress by an observer (the speaker when the reference point is speech time, the relevant participant when it is in the past):

> Something very strange *is going on* here.
> That's what we *were talking* about.

The contrast between the temporary, ongoing nature of the progressive as seen by an observer and unbounded duration expressed by the simple Past or Present is noticeable:

Observed ongoing process	**Unbounded duration**
Lamps were glowing in the dark.	Lamps glowed in the dark.
Snow was falling gently.	Snow fell gently.
My back is aching.	My back aches.

Similarly, **habitual events**, when combined with the progressive, have limited duration. The use of the progressive implies a temporary situation, whereas the ordinary Present tense suggests greater permanence. Compare:

She is running a fringe theatre group (over the summer holidays).
She runs a fringe theatre group (as her permanent job).

43.5.4 End-point-completion verbs and the Progressive

With these bounded processes (e.g. *die, heat up, recover*) the effect of the progressive is to bring into our focus of attention the durative phase of the process before the end-point:

He is *dying* from AIDS. [BNC AH2 12366]
The atmosphere *is heating up* and the seas are rising. [BNC CER 55]
Last night the 53-year-old father-of-two *was recovering* in intensive care.
[BNC CH2 9805]

Plurality can lead to an interpretation of multiple accomplishments. *Arrive*, with a singular subject, will be interpreted as a single event, the Progressive stretching the stage previous to the endpoint, as in *Hurry! The taxi is arriving*. With a plural subject and the progressive, *arrive* will be interpreted as a series of arrivals: *The guests are arriving*.

This effect is illustrated in the following passage about an autumn game of rugby:

> Autumn has come early in the north. The leaves *are turning*,[1] the nights *are drawing in*[2] and the lustre has faded from the lakeside boathouses. On the playing-fields, smallish boys in red shirts *are bending and hooking*[3] in a scrum, before straightening up again to run, pass and tackle, try and kick, urged on by men with large knees and piercing whistles. Rain is *starting to fall*[4] as the last whistle of the day shrills out over the darkening field.
>
> [1]stretching out the process before the end-point (multiple Activities); [2]serial Accomplishments; [3]serial Activities; [4]stretching the phase of initiation of an Activity (this is a phased verbal group (see 39.2.1) in which *start to* marks ingressive aspect)

43.6 THE DISCOURSE FUNCTIONS OF THE PROGRESSIVE

The Progressive presents an ongoing event as something directly observed **in relation to** some point in time. This is either explicitly mentioned, as in **1** and **2** or else inferred as coinciding with speech time, **3**:

1 By the end of January 1919 the main outlines of the peace settlement *were emerging*. (*The Peacemakers*)
2 At half-past five, crowds *were pouring* into the subways.
3 What *are you doing?* I'*m switching on* the answer-phone (coincides with speech time)

Progressive aspect provides a frame within which another event takes place. That is to say, the time-frame of the progressive event includes the bounded event:

We finally *reach* the supermarket and they *are* just *closing* the doors.
What *was* she *wearing* when she *came* to your house for her music lesson? (temporary state framing bounded event in simple past 'came')
She *was wearing* her school uniform. She always *wore* it. (Elizabeth George) (temporary behavioural state contrasted with habitual ('wore')

Two simple forms, by contrast, are normally interpreted as a sequence:

We finally *reach* the supermarket and they *close* the doors.
Crowds *poured* into the subways and *boarded* the trains.

In the following text about a boat trip down the River Amazon, the Progressive is used to provide a frame for the details of the party related in the non-progressive past form.

> On the first evening of a 7-day-trip, I *was sitting* in the bow *enjoying* the cooling breeze and *watching* the sun go down. Soon a small crowd of Peruvian and Brazilian passengers and crew *gathered*, and a rum bottle and a guitar *appeared*. Within minutes we *had* a first-rate party going with singing, dancing, hand-clapping and an incredible impromptu orchestra. One of the crew *bent* a metal rod into a rough triangle which he *pounded* rhythmically, someone else *threw* a handful of beans into a can and *started shaking*, a couple of pieces of polished wood *were clapped* together to interweave yet another rhythm, a mouth harp *was produced*, I *blew* bass notes across the top of my beer bottle and everyone *had* a great time. A couple of hours of rhythmic music as the sun went down *became* a standard part of the ship's routine and *gave* me some of my most unforgettable moments of South American travel.
>
> (Rob Rachowiecki, *Peru: A travel survival kit*)

43.7 PRESENT PERFECT AND PROGRESSIVE ASPECTS COMBINED

When these two aspects combine in one VG, the progressive brings into focus the continuous nature of the situation, whereas the Perfect leads the situation from an indefinite time in the past up to the present, usually to speech time. The possible situations include:

a. **continuous state lasting up to the present**
   I *have been wanting* to meet him for ages.
   He *has been hearing* better since he got the hearing-aid.

b. continuous habitual process

> The government has been spending beyond its means. [BNC AAK 416]
> She has been going to therapy since she was about two. [BNC CAS 1200]

c. iterative ocurrence lasting up to the present

> *You have been coughing* since you got up.

d. unbounded situations lasting up to the present

> We *have been waiting here* for some time.

e. normally bounded situations become unbounded

> *I have been fixing* the lamp.
> So people *have been taping* this talk?

The non-progressive forms would remain bounded: I *have fixed* the lamp, So people *have taped* this talk?

The Past Perfect Progressive combines the anteriority of the Past Perfect with the features of the Progressive:

> He *had been seeing* her quite a lot at that time.

The unbounded result does not necessarily mean that the event was not completed; simply that the Perfect Progressive concentrates on the internal phase of the process.

43.8 HABITUALITY: PAST HABIT OR STATE

Progressiveness is considered here as a type of imperfectivity, or incompletion. Other types of imperfectivity include habituality and iterativity. **Habituality** is, as we have seen, expressed by both present and past tenses in English. Present tense uses are almost invariably imperfective, the only perfective uses being performatives (e.g. *I promise not to be late*) and the others classed as 'instantaneous present'. **Past habit or state** is expressed by the lexical auxiliary *used to + infinitive* as in the following examples. There is a strong pragmatic implication that the state or event no longer holds:

> He knew he *used to speak* too fast.
> We *used to see* each other quite often.
> There *used to be* trees all round this square.

Used to avoids the temporal indeterminacy of the past tense (e.g. *visited* = on one occasion or on many occasions) by making clear the habitual. Compare:

> She visited us. (perfective or imperfective)
> She used to visit us. (imperfective only)

Furthermore, although a time expression such as *not any longer* may be added, the implicit meaning of discontinued habit is so strong that an additional expression is unnecessary.

Used to + infinitive is not to be confused with *be used to + -ing* 'be accustomed to' + *-ing* as in: He *is* not *used* to working late hours.

Iterativity is interpreted from the progressive with punctual verbs, and also from *keep on/ continue+ -ing* (*kept on shouting*) and from the phrasal verb particle *away* (*he hammered away*, As regards perfectivity, ingressive aspect focuses on the initial point of a situation and egressive aspect on the end-point. These are not expressed by inflections in English, but by combinations such as phased VGs (*start to rain/raining*) and phrasal verb particles (e.g. *She came to, We ended up exhausted*).

Summary of certain aspectual distinctions realised in English in the lexico-grammar

Prospective: I am going to write a note
Immediate prospective: I am about to write a note
Ingressive: I started to write a note
Progressive: I am/was writing a note
Iterative: I kept writing notes
Habitual in the past: I used to write notes
Egressive: Finish writing the note
Retrospective, Recent Perfect: I have just written a note
Retrospective, Perfect: I have written a note

EXPRESSING ATTITUDES TOWARDS THE EVENT

Modality

SUMMARY

1 Modality is the semantic category by which speakers express two different kinds of attitude towards the event.

2 One attitude is that of assessing the truth of the proposition or the potential occurrence of the event in terms of modal certainty, probability or possibility. This is epistemic (or extrinsic) modality as in *The key must be here somewhere. It may be in your pocket.*

3 A different kind of attitude is expressed when speakers intervene in the speech event, by laying down obligations or giving permission. This is deontic (or intrinsic) modality as in *You must go now; the others may stay.*

4 The modal auxiliaries (except *can*) in English express both types of modal meanings, which have in common the fact that they express the speaker's attitude to a potential event. Closely related to these meanings are those of ability and intrinsic possibility as in *We can take the early train.* This is known as dynamic modality. In addition, a number of other forms are available for the expression of particular modal meanings.

5 All modal expressions are less categorical than a plain declarative. For this reason modality is said to express a **relation** to reality, whereas an unmodalised declarative treats the process **as** reality.

44.1 THE MEANING AND FUNCTIONS OF MODALITY

From a semantic point of view, in making an assertion such as *It's raining*, speakers express a proposition and at the same time commit themselves to the factuality of that proposition. In ordinary subjective terms, we should say that speakers **know** that their assertion is a fact.

If, on the other hand, speakers say *It must be raining*, or *It may be raining*, they are not making a categorical assertion, but are rather modifying their commitment in some degree by expressing certainty or possibility based on evidence or inference. It is paradoxical that as speakers we only express certainty when we are not sure about something. Compare:

> That's the First Lady over there. (categorical assertion)
> That *must/may/can't be* the First Lady over there. (modalised assertion)

A different kind of modification is made when the speaker intervenes directly in the speech event itself, by saying, for example, *I must leave now. You'd better come too. The rest of you may/ can stay*. Here the issue is not about factuality but has to do with the actualising of a potential event. The speaker brings about an action, using modal expressions to lay down an obligation or give permission regarding the event. Basically, both types of modality are subjective: the speaker is involved. And by means of modality speakers are enabled to carry out two important communicative functions:

• to comment on and evaluate an interpretation of reality;
• to intervene in, and bring about changes in events.

Modality is to be understood as a semantic category which covers such notions as possibility, probability, necessity, volition, obligation and permission. These are the basic modalities. Certain other types of modality, not all speaker-based, will be mentioned in the following sections. In very general terms, modality may be taken to express a *relation* with reality, while a non-modal utterance treats the process *as* reality.

44.2 REALISATIONS OF MODAL MEANINGS

Modality covers a broad semantic area and can be expressed by many forms. In English the syntactic class of **modal auxiliaries** (37.2) is the most central, and these will be our main concern in this chapter. Other modal realisations include the following:

• Other verbs expressing modal meanings:

  (a) The lexical-modal auxiliaries listed in 37.3 composed of *be* or *have*, usually another element + infinitive (*have got to, be bound to, be likely to*, etc.).
  (b) The semi-modals *need* and *dare*.
  (c) Lexical verbs such as *allow, beg, command, forbid, guarantee, guess, promise, suggest, warn* (discussed in 25.1 as performatives).
  (d) The verbs *wonder* and *wish*, which relate to non-factual meanings.

• Other means of expressing modality:

  (e) Modal adverbs such as *probably, possibly, certainly, hopefully, thankfully, obviously.*
  (f) Modal adjectives such as *possible, probable, likely*, used in impersonal constructions such as *He is likely to win* or as part of a nominal group, as in *a likely winner of this afternoon's race* or *the most probable outcome of this trial.*

(g) Modal nouns such as *possibility, probability, chance, likelihood*, as in *There's just a chance that he may win*.

(h) The use of the past tense to indicate remoteness from reality, as in *I thought I'd go along with you*, if you don't mind. Similarly, the past form in the closed conditional, as in 'If you *went*, I would go too.'

(i) Parentheticals such as *I think, I guess*.

These other diverse forms and uses serve to provide a contextual frame for the more central meanings and exponents of modality. Here we take modality to be basically the expression of possibilities, probabilities, certainty, obligations and permission, as expressed by modal auxiliaries. These, together with the lexical-modal auxiliaries, are the most basic exponents of modality in English.

The other modal elements tend to reinforce the modal meaning, as in the example: *I'm sure she couldn't possibly have said that*. This is called **modal harmony** and illustrates the way in which modality can be expressed not simply at one point in an utterance, by a modal auxiliary, but at different points right throughout the clause.

Modal harmony is exemplified in this short extract from a novel by Richard Gordon, in which George expresses his doubts about his future as a doctor.

'Dad –' George shifted his feet. 'I *wonder*[1] if I'm really *suited*[2] for medicine.' 'Of course you are,' his father told him briefly. 'We've had medical men in this family since the days of Gladstone bags and leeches. I *wish you'd*[3] follow the example of your sister. She *will*[4] *certainly* be[5] studying upstairs with her usual diligence. And what, *might*[6] I ask, *would*[7] you *intend*[8] to do instead?'

'I've thought of the – er, drama.'

[1]lexical modal verb; [2]conditional clause expressing doubt; [3]lexical modal verb + hypothetical *would*; [4]*will* of prediction; [5]modal adverb, [6]ironical use of *might* = requesting permission; [7]hypothetical *would*; [8]lexical verb of intention

---

44.3 EXTRINSIC MODALITY: MODAL CERTAINTY, PROBABILITY AND POSSIBILITY

These three options represent the three degrees of confidence, or lack of it, that the speaker feels towards the factuality of the proposition expressed.

44.3.1 Modal certainty: *will, must, be bound to*

What we call modal certainty is not the hundred per cent certainty of a categorical assertion. An unmodalised declarative constitutes a stronger statement of fact than any additional expression of certainty can. If, for instance, George's father had said 'Your sister is studying upstairs', this is a stronger statement of fact than 'Your sister will certainly be studying upstairs', in which he expresses a strong assumption, reinforced by *certainly*.

Modal certainty is, therefore, diminished certainty, chosen either because the speaker's state of knowledge has not permitted a plain assertion or because the speaker does not want to express strong commitment at a given moment in a particular interpersonal interaction, perhaps for reasons of politeness (see Chapter 5).

With modal certainty expressed by **will** and **must**, the speaker does not accept any possibility of the proposition not being true. For this reason adding *but it may not be* to **1** and **2** would result in a contradiction.

1   The concert will *be* over by now.
2   The concert must *be* over.

Assumption or prediction: will

Will expresses a confident assumption by the speaker as observer, based on experience, known facts or what is usually the case. It can be glossed by 'I assume that . . .', as in **3**.

3   Her mother *will* know her age. (I assume that her mother knows her age.)

When the orientation frame is past time, as in a narrative, *would* is used, as in **4**. It is not limited to future occurrences, but can refer to present time.

4   He *would* be about sixty when I first met him. (I assume that he was about sixty)

Will can also be used to refer to future time, expressing a modal judgement or prediction, as in **5** and **6**. (See also 27.5 and 44.7 for *will* and *must* as committing the speaker to a future action. See 41.6 for other means of referring to future events.)

Predictive *shall* is much less common than *will*. It is used by some speakers for the 1st person singular and plural, as in **7**, and is usually contracted to *'ll* (*I'll, we'll*), negative *shan't* in spoken English:

5   It won't work. (I predict that it *won't* work)
6   Scotland *will* be dry tomorrow with a fair amount of cloud.
7   I must have an early night, otherwise I *shall* (I*'ll*) be worn out tomorrow.

Logical necessity: must

The second type of modal certainty is that of 'logical necessity' meaning 'it is necessarily the case that x is true'. **Must** is the modal most used in BrE and is usually subjective, expressing strong conviction based on deduction or inference from evidence, which may or may not be stated. *The concert must be over* might be said, for instance, if the speaker sees that the lights are off or the concert hall is closed. The lexical-modal *have to* **2** is relatively uncommon in BrE with the epistemic meaning of logical necessity, but it is now used by some speakers as an alterntive to epistemic *must* **1**. In AmE, *have to* or *have got to* is generally preferred to *must* in the meaning of logical necessity. A strict meaning of logical necessity ('this is the only possibility there is') is objective in **4**. There is little difference in meaning between the modal and the non-modalised declarative in **4**, while this is not the case in the subjective uses.

1   The key *must* be in your pocket.
2   The key *has to* be in your pocket.
3   The key is *bound to be/is sure to be* in your pocket.
4   If Jane is Pat's sister and Jill is Jane's daughter, Pat must be Jill's aunt.

44.3.2 Probability or 'reasonable inference': *should, ought*

A medium degree of conviction is expressed by *should* and the less common *ought*. A driver might say, studying a map 'It should be easy to reach York from here', glossed as 'I assume it is easy' or 'it is probably easy'. Here we have the notion of probability, or what is reasonable to expect, based on deduction from facts known to the speaker.

The main semantic feature distinguishing these modals from *must* is that they implicitly admit non-fulfilment of the predicated event, whereas *must* and *will* do not. We can say *It should be easy to reach York, but of course it may not be*, but not **It must be easy to reach York, but of course it may not be*. *Should* and *ought* are said to be 'non-factive', that is not binding, as opposed to *will* and *must* which are 'factive' or binding. They can be illustrated as follows:

Dinner *should* be ready. *You must* be hungry after such a long journey.

Similarly, with past time reference, made by *have + -en*, *should* and *ought* imply probability, but can be contradicted. *Will* and *must*, because of their strong epistemic commitment, do not make this implication and can't be contradicted by the speaker. Compare:

He *should have reached* York by now (but Pat has rung to say he hasn't).
He *will/ must have reached* York by now (*but Pat has rung to say he hasn't).

The probability meaning of *should* and *ought* is often merged with that of non-binding obligation (see 44.5.4), as in *The hotel should be good for this price*, i.e. one would expect it to be good/it has the obligation to be good. *Likely* and *likelihood*, with the corresponding negative forms *unlikely* and *unlikelihood*, unambiguously express probability:

All flights *are likely to be* delayed.
There's no *likelihood* of frost tonight.

44.3.3 Extrinsic possibility: *may, might, could*

Weaker conviction is expressed as the possibility of an event occurring or being true. English speakers make use of the modal auxiliaries *may, might* and *could*, the latter particularly in the media. These are all stressed and can be glossed by 'it is possible that x':

> They *may* be real pearls, you know.
> They *might* be real pearls, you know.
> They *could* be real pearls, you know.

All three expressions mean 'It is possible that they are real pearls'. We can see that *might* and *could*, although historically past forms, don't in such cases refer to past time, but to present states of affairs. They can also be used to refer to future events:

> It *may/ might/ could* snow tonight. (= it is possible that it will snow tonight)

Can is not used in positive declarative clauses that express extrinsic ('epistemic') possibility. We do not say **They can be real pearls *It can snow tonight.*

Degrees of confidence

It is not easy to claim with certainty that *may, might* and *could* represent points on a scale of confidence or, in other words, that one or other of these modals expresses either a stronger or a more remote possibility. They can all be intensified by (*very*) *well*, which heightens the possibility, and by *just*, which lowers it:

> They *may/ might/ could very well* be real pearls.
> They *just may/ might/ could* be real pearls.

The following examples, **1** from spoken English, **2** from written, illustrate how the three can be used in one utterance:

> **1** I *may* be a few minutes late; it *might* be seven o'clock before I can get away; it could even be half-past.
> **2** The provision *might* be deleted altogether; it *may* remain as it stands; or it *could* emerge considerably strengthened and broadened.

In these examples the three modals are interchangeable, with little difference to the message. Factors such as speakers' age and social dialect, and the degree of formality or informality of the situation, undoubtedly influence the choice of modal. We suggest that *may* is more formal and indicates reserve, *might* being now the more neutral form, especially with younger speakers, while *could* expresses tentative possibility.

44.4 STRUCTURAL FEATURES OF EXTRINSIC MODALITY

Modal auxiliaries expressing extrinsic meanings correlate with the following features:

existential Subject	There may be trouble ahead
be + -*ing*	She might be waiting
stative main verb	It might be cold
dynamic main verb	I might leave early
lexical auxiliary	It might have to be abandoned
past reference by have + -*en*	He might have left by now

When we refer to past events by the extrinsic modals, the modal meaning of prediction, certainty, possibility or probability is not itself past; the speaker carries out the act of predicting, or whatever in present time. Pastness is realised by the *have + -en* perfect form attached to the main verb, as in *I may have made a mistake. It must have got lost. They will have finished.*

44.4.1 Summary of extrinsic modal and lexical-modal auxiliaries and their meanings

He will be there by now.	(assumption/prediction based on experience or common sense)
I shall probably be back before you	(prediction)
He must be there by now.	(logical necessity, deduction based on evidence)
He can't be there yet.	(logical necessity negated) (see 44.5.3)
He's bound to be there.	(modal certainty + inevitability)
He has to be there by now.	(logical necessity, objective)
He's likely to be there by now.	(probability)
He should be there by now.	(reasonable inference based on deduction)
He could be there by now.	(tentative possibility)
He might be there by now.	(neutral possibility)
He may be there by now.	(weak possibility)
He may be intelligent, but he's a bit of a prat.	(concessive meaning of *may*)

For lexical auxiliaries, modal idioms and modal auxiliaries in VG sequences, see Chapter 8. For backshifted modals in reported speech, see 36.3.

44.5 FEATURES OF INTRINSIC MODALITY: VOLITION, OBLIGATION, NECESSITY, PERMISSION

Functionally, these modal meanings are used to establish and maintain social relations and interaction. Through them, speakers influence and control others, and commit themselves to certain courses of action. They may bring about changes in their surroundings by obligations which are met, permissions given, promises kept and so on.

Semantically, the modal utterance forms part of the linguistic event, and the speaker intervenes in the action.

Syntactically, we find the following correlates:

(a) Unstressed 'there' is rare as Subject, which is typically a human Agent controlling the main verb.
(b) The main verb is usually dynamic.
(c) With past time reference, **must** and **may** express obligation/ permission that took place in past time and is expressed, not by *have + -en*, but by forms of other verbs.

Present	**Past**
I *must go.*	I *had to* go.
They *may* go.	They *were allowed* to go.

44.5.1 Volition: willingness and intention *will, shall, 'll*

The concept of volition covers the meanings of **willingness** as in *Will you sign this for me?* and **intention** as in *I'll bring it back tomorrow.* The negative form is ***will not/won't***.

Willingness

This can be paraphrased by *be willing to.* The action predicated by the main verb can coincide with speech time, or refer to repeated or future events:

Will you give a donation to the Wildlife Society? – Yes, I will.
The key *won't* go in the lock. (speaker attributes unwillingness to an inanimate thing)

As in these examples, *will* is used for all persons. The reduced form *'ll* occurs in the affirmative, except when stressed to express insistence, which requires the full form, as in I WILL do it.

The meaning of willingness, realised by *will*, readily lends itself to various pragmatic uses. For instance, *will* would be interpreted as a directive in *Will you listen to me and stop interrupting?* and as a polite offer in *Will you have another slice of melon?* (See Chapter 5.)

In interrogatives *shall is* used with a 1st person subject to consult the addressee's wishes or ask for advice. This is the most widespread use of *shall* in present-day English.

Shall we go back home now? (= Do you want us to . . .?)

Intention

This can be glossed by *intend to.* When a speaker expresses an intention, the intention is, naturally, coincident with speech time, but the intended action is in the future:

I'*ll* ring you sometime next week.
I think I'*ll* just tape this bit of opera.

Will is used for all persons, *shall* by some speakers for the 1st person singular and plural.

The speaker's commitment in using these modals is as strong as in the extrinsic meanings. For this reason the *will* of intention can have the force of either a promise or a threat, according to whether the intended action is beneficial to the addressee or otherwise. These interpretations are reinforced by the addition of such verbs as *promise* and *warn*:

I'*ll* bring you something back from Paris, I promise.
I warn you that if you keep talking this way I *shall* hang up.

The full form *shall* is also used with a 2nd or 3rd person subject with the meaning of speaker's guarantee, as in *you/they shall be paid tomorrow*.

44.5.2 Inescapable obligation: *must, have to, have got to/ gotta, shall*

In English, obligation and necessity can be thought of as an inescapable duty or requirement, realised by *must, have (got) to* and, in a lesser degree, by *shall*; or else, simply as an advisable course of action, realised by *should* and *ought*. *Must* can have the force of a command.

Must as a modal of obligation

When realised by **must**, obligation can have the force of a direct command, as in **1** and **2**, although modal lexical verbs are more explicit. Compare *You must go* with *I order you to go, I urge you to go*.

   1   *You must try* harder.
   2   *You must copy* this out again.

This force derives from the fact that (a) in certain cultural contexts such as school, family, the Armed Forces, the speaker has authority over the addressee, who is the subject 'you'; (b) the speaker takes the responsibility for the action being carried out; and (c) the verb is agentive and in active voice.

The force of *must* is diminished if one or more of these factors is modified, providing useful strategies to mitigate the directness of the obligation, although not its inescapability:

I must catch the last bus without fail. (subject is *I*, the obligation is internal)
Drug-traffickers must be punished. (3rd person subject; authority does not reside
   in the speaker; passive voice)
Applications *must be* in by May 1st. (non-agentive verb; passive; 3rd person subject)

When no human control is implied, the meaning is that of intrinsic necessity, as in:

> Lizards *must* hibernate if they are to survive the winter. (= it is necessarily the case that.)

The following news item 'Killing with a Kiss' from *The Sunday Times of India* illustrates the inescapable obligation of intrinsic *must*:

> **Medics were on standby as 53 couples locked their lips on Saturday at the start of a bid to set a new world record for the longest kiss.**
>
> **The couples will need to kiss non-stop for more than 29 hours and 57 minutes to make it into the Guinness Book of Records. The Valentine weekend attempt was organised by a local radio station, which advertised for participants to take part in the competition at Newcastle, Sydney.**
>
> **To break the record, participants must follow strict rules, station spokeswoman Tricia Morris said. "Their lips *must* be touching at all times, they *must* be standing, they *must* not fall asleep, *must not* leave the venue, *mustn't* wear any incontinence pads or adult nappies and there are no toilet breaks," Morris said.**

Shall, have to, have got to, gotta as modals of obligation

Of all the modals of obligation ***shall*** is the most imperious, direct and subjective, and for this reason is little used in the spoken language. It occurs in legal language and other formal contexts, as in the regulations of the Olympic Games **1**.

Of the lexical-modals, ***have to*** is objective (the obligation is external) and ***have got to*/gotta** subjective (the obligation is internal). Compare **2** and **3**.

Syntactically, *have to*, unlike *must* and *have got to*, has non-finite forms *having to, to have to*. Both *have to* and *have got to* have a past form *had (got) to*. Only *have to* can combine with the modal auxiliaries (*may have to*, *may have got to).

Must has no past form as it is, historically, itself a past form. Forms of *have to* are therefore brought in to express past and future obligation **4**.

1 All competitors in the Games *shall wear* a number.
2 I've *got to* go now. (I *gotta* go now) (the obligation is internal)
3 I have *to* go and see the Dean. (the obligation is external)
4 We *had to* pay in advance. We*'ll have to* pay in advance. (external)

44.5.3 Negation of the modals *must* and *may*

Negation of the modal verbs *must* and *may* is complex because either the modal concept (in the 'a' examples) or the lexical concept (in the 'b' examples) can be negated.

1. obligation and permission (intrinsic meanings)

positive	negative		meaning
You **must** go now	a_1	You **needn't** go now	= you are not obliged to go
	a_2	You **don't have to** go now	= you are not obliged to go
	b	You **must** not (mustn't) go	= you are obliged not to go
You **may** go now	a	You **may** not/ **can't** go	= you have not permission to go
	b	You **may**/ **can** not go	= you have permission not to go

2. necessity and possibility (extrinsic meanings)

positive	negative		meaning
It **must** be true	a	It **can't** be true	= It is not possible that it is true
	b_1	It **needn't** be true	= It is not necessarily true
	b_2	It **doesn't have to** be true	= It's not necessarily true
It **may** be true	(a)	It **can't** be true	= It is not possible that it is true
	(b)	It **may** not be true	= It is possible that it is not true

When *might* and *could* express possibility, they negate in the same way as *may*, with replacement by *can't* for modal negation and *not* to negate the lexical verb.

Need not (needn't) is often replaced by the objective form *doesn't/ don't have to* in both kinds of modal meaning, the extrinsic and the intrinsic. *Have to* is also used by many speakers in the interrogative: *Do you have to go now?* for *Need you go now?*, especially in the meaning of obligation. Questioning is less common with meanings of possibility and necessity, for example: *Does it have to be true?*

Mustn't is usually reserved for the obligation meaning of *must*, for example, We *mustn't* forget to ask Sue to water the plants (= obligation not to forget).

May in its meaning of permission does not have a full set of unambiguous forms: *you may not go* serves for both modal and lexical negation. The meaning 'you have permission not to go' can be conveyed by stressing the negative particle *not* – *You may **not** go, if you like.*

Can and *can't* have replaced *may/ may not* in the expression of permission except in the most formal contexts.

Can't, needn't and *don't have to* negate and question the modal concept. When the lexical concept is negated, this is achieved by *not*, which can be attached as *n't* to *must* (*mayn't* is not normally used).

Can't is the usual form used to negate *must* (necessity) and *may* (possibility).

44.5.4 Non-binding obligation: *should, ought*

Should and *ought* express a medium obligation, which is not binding and may be unfulfilled:

> People *should* drive more carefully.
> You really *ought* to cut down on smoking.

These modals are used instead of the stronger *must* when the speaker lacks authority to impose the obligation. Tact, politeness or a lack of conviction of the absolute necessity of the predicated action are further motivations. The following invented advertisement clearly distinguishes the necessary from the merely desirable:

> Candidates *must* be university graduates.
> Candidates *must* be between 21 and 35.
> Candidates *should have* a knowledge of two foreign languages.
> Candidates *should have* at least three years' experience.

Referring to a past event, with *should* and *ought* + *have* + *-en*, the speaker implies that the obligation was not fulfilled. *Ought* is less common than *should* nowadays. *Be supposed to* is similar to *should* and *ought* in being contrary to fact:

> He *ought to* have been more careful.
> The Government *should have taken* a decision earlier.
> They *were supposed* to be here by eight, but most people turned up at half-past.

44.6 DYNAMIC MODALITY: POSSIBILITY, ABILITY, PERMISSION, PROPENSITY *CAN, BE ABLE, COULD, WILL, WOULD, MAY*

A. Can, could

Dynamic modality expresses properties or dispositions of the subject referent. The three related meanings are expressed by ***can***, negative ***cannot, can't***:

This paint can be applied with a spray.	(= It is possible to apply this paint . . ./for this paint to be applied . . .) (dynamic possibility)
Can you reach the top shelf?	(= Are you able to reach . . .?) (ability)
You can't park here	(= You are not allowed to park here) (intrinsic permission)

It is important to distinguish dynamic possibility, which is expressed by *can* and is paraphrased by 'It is possible to . . .'or 'It is possible for . . . to . . ., from extrinsic possibility, which is expressed by *may, might* or *could*, and is paraphrased by 'It is possible *that* . . .'. Compare:

| I can be there by 10 o'clock. | (= It is possible *for* me *to* be there by 10 o'clock) |
| I may/might be there by 10 o'clock. | (= It is possible *that* I'll be there by 10 o'clock) |

B. Will and would: propensity

This is a dynamic meaning which involves a property or a propensity of the subject referent. From our knowledge of how the world is structured, we are able to predict not only single instances (see p. 382) but regular occurrences, using *will*. *Would* is used in a past time-frame:

Ice *will* melt at room temperature.	(Ice has the property to melt . . .)
They'*ll* gossip for hours.	(They have a tendency to gossip for hours)
They *would* gossip for hours, sitting in the park.	(They tended to gossip . . .)

Heavy stress on *will* and *would* is emotive and can suggest that the propensity is not welcome to the speaker:

He WILL ring up late at night asking silly questions.

Dynamic *would* in narrative is illustrated in the following passage by James Thurber: With the lexical-modal *be apt to*, propensity shades into usuality, since it is based on the natural habits or tendency of the subject. It refers to repeated states or happenings, as in *He's apt to turn up for dinner without warning*.

> When Grandpa got to his office, he *would* put his hat on his desk. . . . It was a device of his to get away from bores or talkative friends. As the door opened, he *would* automatically reach for his derby, and if it was somebody he didn't want to see, he *would* rise and say, 'I'm sorry, but I was just about to leave.' He *would* then walk to the street with his visitor, find out which way the man was going, and set off in the opposite direction, walking around the block and entering the store by the back door.

C. The core meaning of can – *You can't do that*

The meanings expressed by *can* all correspond to a basic pattern, which in its positive form can be expressed as 'nothing prevents x from occurring' and in its negative form as 'something prevents x from occurring'. That 'something' in each case represents a set of laws, whether natural laws, moral laws, laws of physics, of good manners, and perhaps many more. For this reason, an utterance such as *You can't do that* will be interpreted in different ways according to the context in which it occurs, and depending on which set of laws applies in a particular case:

You can't do that	=	It's not possible for you to do that, e.g. walk from Genoa to Tangier.
You can't do that	=	You are not able to do that, e.g. lift such a heavy box.
You can't do that	=	You are not allowed to do that, e.g. park your car in the square.
You can't do that	=	social norms prevail against doing that, e.g. infringe local customs.

As the possibility and ability to carry out an action is a necessary requirement for a person to perform that action, *can* lends itself to various pragmatic interpretations by implication:

willingness	I *can* get the copies for you, if you like.
command	If you won't keep quiet, you *can* get out.
request	*Can* you help me lift this sofa?
existential	It *can* be very cold in Edinburgh in winter.

D. May (negative may not) – You may go now

May is a more formal alternative to *can* in the meanings of permission and dynamic possibility, and is extended to such meanings as polite offer.

May I come in? Yes, you *may*. (request for permission and giving permission)
In spring, wild orchids *may* be found in the woods. (possibility = it is possible to find . . .)
May I help you with the luggage? (polite offer)

Might is sometimes used for an indirect request:

You might fetch me a bottle of tonic water and a bag of crisps.

E. The past of can is could or was/were able + to-infinitive

depending on whether an imperfective or perfective meaning is intended. With *be able* a single, predicated action is achieved, that is to say, it is seen as holistic, perfective; with *could*, the action is viewed as extended in the past, that is, as imperfective:

From the top of the hill we *could* see for miles.
He *was able* to escape in time. (not *He *could* escape in time)

This distinction is obligatory only in the affirmative and the interrogative. In the negative, *could* and *be able to* are interpreted as having the same result and are therefore interchangeable:

He *wasn't able* to escape. He *couldn't* escape.

44.7 HYPOTHETICAL USES OF THE MODALS

Apart from their other meanings, the past tense modals *could, might, would* can be used in a 'remote' or hypothetical sense in both main and subordinate clauses. Compare:

I *will* help you if I can.   **I *would* help you if *I could*.**
She *may* pass if she works hard.   She ***might*** pass if she worked harder.

To refer to a past event *have* + *-en* is used. The event is understood to be contrary to fact:

I *would have helped you* if I had been able to.
She *would/ might have passed* if she had worked harder.

Should is also used, especially in BrE, as the replacement of a subjunctive in referring to states of affairs that may exist or come into existence (see also Chapter 3):

It is only natural that they *should* want a holiday.
I am amazed that he *should* think it's worth trying.

44.7.1 Summary of intrinsic modals and modal meanings

Will you sign here?   (willingness)
Shall we go to the theatre?   (suggestion/consulting addressee)
I'll let you know tomorrow   (intention)
You must try harder   (inescapable obligation, subjective)
You have to try harder   (inescapable obligation, objective)
We must go; we've got to/ gotta go   (inescapable obligation, self-imposed)
You needn't go; you don't have to go   (absence of obligation)
All competitors shall wear a number   (inescapable obligation, formal)
You should drive more carefully   (medium obligation, not necessarily fulfilled)
You can do it   (ability, possibility, or informal permission)
It can be cold in Edinburgh   (existential)
You may go now   (permission, formal)
You can go now   (permission, informal)
I would help you if I could   (hypothetical)

The following extract from a novel by David Lodge illustrates some of the realisations of modal meanings in English. It is noticeable that the dialogue, in which members of a family debate possible courses of action, contains more modals than the narrative part:

> Their Dad *would be coming*[1] home the next day and they *would*[2] have to[3] look after him until he was too ill to stay out of hospital. The question was, *should*[4] he be told? 'How long . . .?' somebody *wondered*.[5] The doctor hadn't been specific. A matter

of months rather than weeks. One *could*[6] never be sure. 'Who *would*[7] tell him?' 'I *couldn't. I* just *couldn't,'*[8] said their mother and wept. 'I *would,*[9] said Angela, 'if we agreed that was the right thing to do.' 'Why tell him?' said the youngest sister. 'It *would*[10] just be cruel.' 'But if he asks . . .' said another. '*Are you going to*[11] lie to your own Dad?'

Tom lit a cigarette and blew smoke from his nostrils. A grey haze from previous cigarettes hung in the air. All the men in the family were heavy smokers, perhaps because cigarettes had always been readily available. No reference was made by anyone to this as the *likely*[12] cause of their father's disease.

'I see no reason to tell Dad yet,' Tom said at length. 'We *should*[13] try to keep him as cheerful as possible.'

Their mother looked at Tom gratefully, but fearfully. 'But he *must*[14] have time to . . . receive the last . . . sacraments and everything,' she faltered.

'Of course, Mum, but there's *no need*[15] to rush these things. Let's make him as happy as we can for the rest of his days.'

[1]past time prediction; [2]past time prediction; [3]obligation; [4]advisability; [5]doubt; [6]intrinsic possibility; [7]willingness; [8]incapability; [9]willingness; [10]hypothetical; [11]intention; [12]probability; [13]advisability; [14]inescapable obligation; [15]lack of necessity/ obligation

FURTHER READING

On tense Brazil (1995), Comrie (1985); and aspect Comrie (1976), Givón (2001a), Kravchenko (2002), Langacker (1991); on situation types Huddleston and Pullum (2002), Mourelatos (1981); on Perfect aspect McCoard (1978); Stoevsky (2000); on modality Coates (1983); Palmer (1988); Huddleston and Pullum (2002).

EXERCISES ON CHAPTER 9

Viewpoints on events: Tense, aspect and modality
Module 41

1   Discussion: To what extent do the Present and Past tenses of English correspond to present and past time?

2   †Identify the Present tense verb in each sentence as a state or an event. If an event, is it instantaneous, habitual, 'historic', past referring, reporting or quotative?

(1)   They cycle to work on a tandem most days.
(2)   Ignorance is bliss.
(3)   I had just got off the bus when up comes this guy and asks me for a light.

(4) And he's like 'But she looks just like a little kid.'
(5) Finally, I plug in and press the button.
(6) Wounded tell of terror march.
(7) Many believe that violence on television is partly the cause of violence in real life.
(8) Clinical tests prove conclusively that untreated gum disease leads to tooth loss.

3 Turn to the article on Pete the burglar on p. 357. Discuss the function type of the Present tense in: (a) the writer's narrative and (b) Pete's quoted words.

4 Write a description, using the Present tense, of some piece of equipment that you find useful, for instance an answer-phone, a mobile phone, or a personal computer.

5 †Decide which is more meaningful, the Past or the Perfect, in the sentences below and write the correct form of the verb (given in brackets) below. Give reasons for your choice:

(1) We . . . . (set off) early and . . . . (leave) the car by the bridge.
(2) 'I . . . . (get) it,' he shouted, 'I think I really . . . . (get) it.'
(3) During his short lifetime, he . . . . (compose) some of the most beautiful organ music of his time.
(4) How many plays . . . . Shakespeare (write)?
(5) I (wake up) late this morning and . . . . (have) any breakfast yet.
(6) What . . . . you (say) your name . . . . (be)?
(7) . . . . you (come) for a work permit, or for something else?
(8) When . . . . your son (qualify) as a doctor?
(9) . . . . the children (like) the circus?
(10) I'm afraid there . . . . (be) a mistake. You . . . . (put, passive) in the wrong group.

Module 42

1 Discussion: Compare the uses and implications of the Present Perfect in English with those of its counterpart in any other language you know.

2 †Discuss the difference in meaning between the use of Past tense and Perfect aspect in the following sentences. What pragmatic inferences would be made to establish the psychological link between past and present time in the case of the Perfect uses?

(1) (a) His last film set a new standard in horror and violence.
    (b) His latest film has set a new standard in horror and violence.
(2) (a) I was a colleague of hers, working in the same Department, for several years.
    (b) I have been a colleague of hers, working in the same Department, for several years.
(3) (a) How far did you get?
    (b) How far have you got?
(4) (a) Where did you go?
    (b) Where have you been?

(5) (a) What did you do?
   (b) What have you done?
(6) (a) She made a fool of herself in public.
   (b) She has made a fool of herself in public.
(7) (a) Mobile phones suddenly became popular.
   (b) Mobile phones have suddenly become popular.
(8) (a) That report that I gave you has a couple of serious errors.
   (b) That report that I've just given you has a couple of serious errors.

3 †Turn to the William Boyd text on p. 367. You will see that the dates make explicit the exact relationships in some cases of the Past Perfect. Change the first *was* to *is* and examine carefully the effect on the rest of the verb forms. Justify your decision to make or not to make changes in the verb forms.

4 †In each numbered section from the following short news item from *The Week*, identify the verb forms as Past, Present or Present Perfect (there is also one modal). Do you find any of the following types or uses: habitual, reported, quotative?

> **Padma Lakshmi feels she is famous for all the wrong things[1] . . . She has always wanted to be an actress[2] but she gets distracted by alternative careers: first as a model, then as a presenter on Italian television and next as a celebrity chef in America.[3] In Britain, she's most famous as the girlfriend of novelist Salman Rushdie.[4] This, in particular, drives her mad.[5] "I would like to be known for myself," she says.[6] "Like today, in the paper I read something that said, 'Rushdie's girlfriend Padma Lakshmi,'[7] and I thought[8] 'Oh, when is this going to end?'[9] It's terrible because, of course, I love him, so of course I'm proud of him,[10] and he's achieved so much[11] and blah, blah, blah, but I'm like,[12] 'When is it my turn?'[13]**

Module 43

1 †Discussion: Comment on the aspectual meaning of the past tense in: *His rubber-soled shoes squeaked on the vinyl floor.* Does it refer to one occurrence or more?

2 †Decide whether the situation expressed in each sentence below is bounded (with an end-point) or unbounded (without an end-point).

(1) They dumped their bags on the floor.
(2) They are negotiating with the Chinese to buy a panda.
(3) The west wind blows constantly across the beaches of Almería.
(4) The cat pounced on the unwary mouse.
(5) Snow fell gently on the city streets.
(6) He dragged himself along the road.
(7) A man in a pin-striped suit stepped off the bus.
(8) He slipped the pen into his pocket.

(9) The sofa cast a shadow on the wall.

(10) She handed me the paper bag containing the mushrooms.

3 †Put the main verb in each of the sentences below into the Progressive, and say what kind of meaning ensues:

(1) Paul drove us home.

(2) Sue crossed the street when she saw us.

(3) The children jumped up and down with excitement.

(4) I have tried to trace an old friend who lives in an unfamiliar town.

(5) Peter sees the Health Officer tomorrow.

(6) A big fire crackled in the grate.

(7) They photographed the trail of footprints around the pool.

(8) I shiver and cough.

(9) The police car pulled up in front of the hotel.

(10) The doctor bent over the man who lay on the ground.

Module 44

1 Discussion: Modals in context: Do the modals in the following three short texts have intrinsic or extrinsic meanings? Give a gloss of each to help you decide.

(a) 'He surrounds himself with people that want to win. He taught me to win at all costs. Quite simple. *Must* win. No secret to it. But you *have to* manage your way because if you fail, it's you that's done it.' [*He* refers to Sir Alex Ferguson, the manager of Manchester United]

(b) Motorists who use their mobile phones at the wheel *are to* face fines of up to a thousand pounds from this December. But the real question *may* be whether these fines *can* or *could* be enforced.

(c) You *could* be exceptionally bright and super-competent so far as brain work and the thought processes are concerned. The trouble *could* be that you put all this mental efficiency into unimportant, instead of worthwhile, issues. (Horoscope)

2 †Supply the modal verb which corresponds to the paraphrase in each case. In some cases more than one form is acceptable:

(1) I _____ let you know as soon as 1 have any news. (intention, promise)

(2) We _____ get away until the end of August. (It will not be possible for us to get away.)

(3) There _____ be something burning. I can smell it. (It is necessarily the case that . . .)

(4) The banks _____ be closed at this time of day. (prediction)

(5) You _____ have forgotten your house keys! (It's not possible that you have forgotten.)

(6) This 12-can pack of beer _____ be enough. (probability, reasonable inference)

(7) Because of his wide experience, he .... to find an acceptable solution. (ability, past)

(8) That young man .... be our next Prime Minister. (It is possible that . . .)

(9) You .... not feed the animals at the zoo. (You are under the obligation not to . . .)

(10) You .... (not) tip the waiter. (It is not necessary that you tip the waiter.)

3 †Change the modalised verb form in each sentence below to the past. Make any adjustments necessary to tenses or adverbs, for instance, in the rest of the sentence.

(1) They *will not wait* for us more than ten minutes.

(2) He *must be mistaken* about his daughter's age.

(3) You *can't be listening* to what *I'm saying*.

(4) Ben *should take* two tablets every day this week.

(5) Lying in our tent, we *can hear* the wind howling down from the heights.

(6) With their fast patrol-boats, the police *can capture* drug-traffickers operating in the Strait.

(7) There *may be* a hold-up on the motorway this afternoon.

(8) I *must have* the baby *vaccinated*.

(9) He will *telephone us* immediately if he *can*.

(10) They *oughtn't to be talking* while the pianist *is* playing.

4 Study the following extract from an article by Angela Carter in *Nothing Sacred*, about her memories of her parents. The occasion is a visit to her father's new home, after her mother's death:

> **My father had lined the walls of his new home with pictures of my mother when she was young and beautiful; and beautiful she certainly was, with a broad, Slavonic jaw and high cheekbones like Anna Karenina, she took a striking photograph and had the talent for histrionics her pictures imply. They used to row dreadfully and pelt one another with household utensils, whilst shrieking with rage. Then my mother would finally break down and cry, possibly tears of sheer frustration that he was bigger than she, and my father, in an ecstasy of remorse – we've always been very good at remorse and its manifestations in action, emotional blackmail and irrational guilt – my father would go out and buy her chocolates.**

Analyse the tenses and aspects used by the writer in this lively evocation of her parents. For instance, which tense does the author use to describe her mother? Do the verbs in this part of the article refer to states, repeated actions or events in the past?

Which forms does the writer make use of to describe her parents' life together? With which tense-aspect form does the author establish a psychological link between past and present time, with regard to certain family characteristics?

TALKING ABOUT PEOPLE AND THINGS

CHAPTER 10

The Nominal Group

EXPRESSING OUR EXPERIENCE OF PEOPLE AND THINGS   *MODULE 45*

SUMMARY

1 **Nouns refer to classes of entities**: persons, objects, places, institutions, actions, abstract ideas, qualities, phenomena, emotions, etc.

2 **How we experience entities**: experiential features: countability, definiteness, quantity, description, classification, identification.

3 **Structural elements that realise experiential features**: the head, the determiner, the pre-modifier, the post-modifier.

4 **Noun heads**

   1. Common nouns. Countability. The notion of 'count' and 'non-count' (or 'mass').

   2. Proper nouns.

   3. Pronouns. Personal pronouns: *I, we, he/she it, one*. Demonstrative pronouns: *this, that, these, those*. Interrogative pronouns: *who, which, what*. Substitute words: *one/ones*.

45.1 CLASSES OF ENTITIES

Nominal Groups refer semantically to those aspects of our experience that we perceive as entities. The term 'entity' refers here not only to concrete entities such as persons, objects, places, institutions and other 'collectives', but also to the names of actions (*swimming, laughter*), abstractions (*thought, experience*), qualities (*beauty, speed*), emotions (*anger, excitement*) and phenomena (*thunder, success*), among others. Prototypical entities are those which are concrete, with well-defined outlines and relatively stable in time ('person', rather than 'weather'). The following description of the sale of the painting known as *L'Absinthe* includes a number of nominal groups, which represent several classes of entities. (The article appeared under the ironic title 'Fairy Liquid' in *The Times* Weekend Review).

When we name an entity, we usually add some information about it which shows how we 'experience' or perceive it. In expressing this 'experiential' information about an entity, some of it is placed before the noun and some after it, as we can see in some of the groups contained in the example text:

	Pre-head		Head	Post-head
1	one	Saturday	morning	in February 1893
2	a		sale	
3	the	smart new	rooms	of a London art dealer
4	a		street	leading to the flower market in Covent Garden
5		smartly dressed wealthy art	lovers	
6			pictures	from the estate of Henry Hill
7			lot 209	showing a man and a woman in a Paris café
8			staff	
9		quiet	appraisal	
10	a		hush	
11	the		gallery	
		low	groans	of disgust
12	the	sibilant	sounds	of hissing anger
13	a		group	of well-off English art lovers
14	a		painting	by the acknowledged master Edgar Dégas

In this text, we see that the post-head information, given on the right about the head nouns in the middle column, also contains nouns with their own pre-head and post-head information.

45.2 OVERVIEW: THE STRUCTURE OF THE NOMINAL GROUP

The nominal group has four primary elements or structural functions: the **head**, which is the central element, the **determiner** and the **pre-modifier functions** in the pre-head position, and the **post-modifier** function in post-head position. Of all these elements, the pre- and post-modifiers can usually be omitted, while the head together with the determiner, when present, may realise the NG (*a sale, staff*), as illustrated in the following examples:

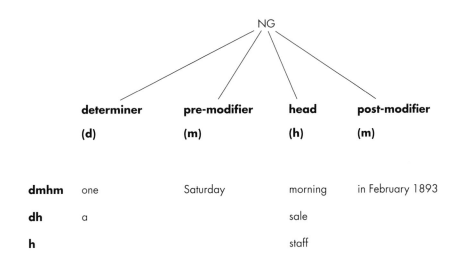

dmhm	one	Saturday	morning	in February 1893
dh	a		sale	
h			staff	

The head

The head is typically realised by a noun or pronoun (*book, it*). Instead of a noun we may find a **substitute head**, realised most commonly by *one/ ones* (a good *one/* good *ones*). Adjectival heads are limited in English, for example: *the poor, the unemployed, the supernatural.*

The determiner

The determiner function particularises the noun referent in different ways: by establishing its reference as definite or indefinite, by means of the **articles** (*a book, an actor, the actor/ the book*), or relating the entity to the context by means of the **demonstratives** *this, that, these, those* (which are **deictics** or 'pointing words'), signalling that the referent is near or not near the speaker in space or time (*this book, that occasion*). The **possessives** signal the person to whom the referent belongs (*my book, the Minister's reasons*) and are sometimes reinforced by *own* (*my own book*).

Other particularising words are the ***wh*-words** (*which* book? *whatever* reason) and the **distributives** (*each, every, all, either, neither*). **Quantifiers** are also included in the determiner function. Quantification may be exact (*one, seven, a hundred, the first, the next*) or inexact (*many, a lot, a few, some*). All these classes of item that realise the determiner function are called **determinatives**.

With regard to their position in the NG, determinatives fall into three broad groups:

- **central determinatives:** the articles, the demonstratives, the possessives, including the 's possessive, the quantifiers *each, every, either, neither, some, any, enough, no*.
- **pre-determinatives:** *all, both, half* and *once, twice, double, three times, such, what*.
- **post-determinatives:** the ordinal numerals (*first, second*, etc.) and the semi-determinatives *same, other, former, latter, last, next, certain, own*.

The central determinatives are mutually exclusive, that is, each NG has only one. They can combine with the pre- and post-determinatives, however, as we shall see shortly.

The pre-head modifier

After the defining, particularising and quantifying items of information, which select the noun referent from others in the surrounding context, the **pre-head modifier** function (**pre-modifier** for short) describes or classifies the referent. Within this function, the **epithet** characterises the referent by attributing qualities to it, realised by adjectives (*smart, new* rooms, a *young* man). The **classifier** restricts the referent to a sub-class (*art* lovers) and is realised by nouns (one *Saturday* morning, *art* lovers, *top* ten) or certain types of adjectives and participles (a *political* broadcast, *general* elections, *leading* articles).

The post-head modifier (post-modifier for short)

includes all the experiential post-head items that are placed after the head noun and which, like the pre-head items, help to define and identify the noun referent still further. The **post-modifier**, for which one can also use the term **qualifier**, is realised by finite and non-finite clauses, (the film *we saw*, a man *reading a newspaper*), PPs (*in February 1893*) and, to a lesser extent, by other groups: NGs (shoes *that size*) and adverbial groups (the car *outside*).

Supplementive (or 'non-defining') post-head elements are parentheticals. They don't define the noun referent, which is already defined, but instead contribute additional information. Compare the integrated relative clause which helps to define the noun referent **1** with the supplementive **2**:

    1   I picked up the umbrella that was lying on the floor. (= the one on the floor)
    2   I picked up the umbrella, which was lying on the floor. (= the only umbrella)

Different from the post-modifier is the **complement**, realised for instance by content clauses (*the fact that he left, the belief that peace is round the corner . . .*).

Nominal groups can also function in apposition to the head noun (*the acknowledged master Edgar Dégas*).

As we have seen in chapters 2, 3 and 4, nominal groups function in clause structure as Subject, Object and Complement, realising the principal participants in the situation described by the clause: Agent, Affected and Recipient in material processes, and the corresponding participants in mental and relational processes. To a lesser extent the nominal group occurs as Adjunct (They left *last Saturday*). The NG also functions as complement of a preposition (*in progress*).

45.3 THE HEAD ELEMENT 1: COMMON NOUNS

Nominal heads fall into three main categories: **common nouns, proper nouns** and **pronouns**. **Common nouns** are characterised by having number contrast (i.e. having both singular and plural forms) and by being countable or non-countable, as described shortly.

45.4 REGULAR AND IRREGULAR PLURALS

Regular plurals are formed by the addition of a suffix:/iz/ after a sibilant, as in *kiss – kisses, church – churches* (with the spelling *-es*); /s/ after a voiceless consonant as in *books, cakes*; or /z/ after a voiced consonant, as in *pole – poles, streams – streams*, or a vowel *eye – eyes, cry – cries* (the spelling is *-s*, with y becoming i after a consonant, but not after a vowel: *day – days*). A number of words of classical origin retain their original plurals, for example: *phenomenon – phenomena; criterion – criteria*.

Most common **irregular plurals** are formed by a change of vowel (or of two vowels): *woman – women, man – men, tooth – teeth. Child – children* has developed a 'double' plural, having both a vowel change and a suffix. Another group marks the plural by a consonant change: *half – halves; calf – calves; loaf – loaves*. A third group of nouns have the same form for both singular and plural. This is known as **'zero plural'**: *trout, salmon, sheep, deer, series, species, aircraft*.

45.5 COUNTABILITY: COUNT AND NON-COUNT NOUNS

English obliges us to make a distinction with regard to how a referent is cognitively perceived: whether as a discrete, countable entity, such as *cow*, or as an indivisible, non-countable 'mass' entity, such as *beef*. This difference constitutes a feature which is salient in speakers' experience of 'things'.

Other languages make a count–mass distinction, but we must never assume that particular items are conceptualised and lexicalised in the same way in different languages. *News*, for instance, is a singular mass noun in English (*the news is good*); *one news*, *a news*, *many news* are ungrammatical. In Spanish, by contrast, *noticia* is a normal count noun: *una noticia, dos noticias, muchas noticias* (=one/a, two, many news, respectively).

Note that we use the terms 'non-count' and 'mass' without distinction, as both are in common use.

A **count noun** is basically one whose referent can be counted, as in *one cow, two cows*, but not *one beef*, *two beefs*. The referents of these nouns are viewed as individuated things or persons. The following count nouns include both regular plurals in *-s* and invariable or 'zero' plurals:

ten cyclists	two trout	a dozen eggs	three new television series
five minutes	five salmon	one grapefruit	four crossroads
two and a half kilos	a hundred sheep	two US aircraft	two spacecraft

A **non-count noun** is one whose referent is cognitively perceived as not countable. We don't say, for example *three furnitures, *one luggage. Both *furniture* and *luggage*, as well as *news* can be individuated by a preceding 'counter' – 'a piece of' – as explained shortly.

45.5.1 Grammatical features of countability

Although individuation by cardinal numerals is a useful guide to countability, to get a more accurate description we have to consider the range of determiners that a noun admits.

Grammatical features of count nouns

- the cardinal numerals *one, two, three*, etc. (*four* miles)
- other quantifiers which imply numerals: *both, a dozen*, etc. (*both* hands, *a dozen* eggs)
- the article *a(n)* taking a singular form:

    I'm looking for *a new job.*

- the determiners *each, every, either, neither*, which precede singular heads.

    Each day is different. We go there *every year.*

- the plural (including 'zero') form of the noun preceded by a plural determiner: *many, several, few, these, those.*

    many choices, few opportunities; these aircraft, those sheep, several series.

- the plural with number contrast marked on the noun: *lion/lions; child/children; mouse/mice; stimulus/stimuli.*
- plural number concord with verb or pronoun: *People want* to be happy, don't *they?*

Grammatical features of non-count (mass) nouns

The following grammatical forms and structures mark a NG typically as 'mass':

- the singular form of the noun with zero determiner:

    Water is necessary for animal and plant life.

- the singular form of the noun preceded by *all*:

    I say this in *all sincerity. All equipment* must be regularly inspected.

- the singular form of the noun, quantified by *much, little, a little*:

> There *isn't much room* in our apartment so we have *little furniture*.

Nominal Groups that are not marked for countability

The determiners *the, this, that, my, your, his, her, its, our, their* are neutral to the mass–count distinction and can be used with both types of reference: *this house, this bread; our friend, our friendship*.

45.5.2 Selected classes of non-count nouns

As non-count nouns are usually the most problematic for students of English, we group them into various types, starting with singular only or plural only. The selection of items is not intended to be exhaustive.

1. *Non-count singular nouns – The news is good*

(a) Nouns which end in *-ics* and appear to be plural, but are in fact singular:

> linguistics logistics aerobics athletics mathematics
> ethics statistics phonetics physics politics

These are areas of study or activities. They take all the grammatical markers of mass nouns. *Ethic* and *statistic* are sometimes used as count nouns: *an ethic, a statistic*.

(b) Nouns which refer to a number of items conceptualised as an aggregate:

> baggage luggage cutlery crockery jewellery furniture

The referents of these nouns consist of different objects: cutlery includes knives, forks and spoons, among other items. We can add or remove an item without affecting the concept expressed by the noun. They take all the grammatical markers of mass nouns.

(c) Names of certain illnesses, diseases and of certain games:

> measles mumps rickets AIDS draughts darts skittles

Darts and skittles take their names from the objects used, which are count nouns: one dart, two skittles.

(d) Substances: natural phenomena, food

> rain snow hail sand water soil
> bread butter coffee meat fruit spaghetti

The notion of substance is useful and may be extended to oxygen, heat, light and so on.

(e) Abstractions

sleep	luck	advice	anger	disgust	love	fun
peace	magic	silence	information	courage	justice	time
safety	knowledge	health	music	childhood	youth	age

(f) Activities

research   work   homework   housework   travel

(g) Miscellaneous

money   progress   environment   weather   electricity   machinery

Researches and *works* in *works of art* occur as plural, but *homework* and *housework* do not pluralise. *Travel* can be compared with the count noun *journey*. *Travel* is used for generic reference (see 46.6): *air travel, sea travel* in the singular, and in expressions such as *on your travels* in the plural. *Journey* is a regular count noun. Compare:

*We went on a *travel*.   We went on a *journey*.
Travel broadens the mind.   *Journey broadens the mind.

2. Non-count plural nouns – *pyjamas and shorts*

These nouns have a plural morpheme but do not combine with numerals. They have no singular form. These 'things' may be lexicalised in other languages as regular count nouns, (for example *un pantalón, un pijama* in Spanish: 'a pair of trousers/pyjamas'). In English such items consisting of two equal parts are individuated by *a pair of* (a pair of trousers, shorts, etc.) to refer to one item of clothing.

1   trousers   shorts   pyjamas   scissors   specs   sunglasses
    binoculars
2   manners   thanks   belongings   surroundings   means   clothes
    goods

More problematic are the nouns *people, police* and *cattle*. All three are singular in form but plural in meaning, taking plural concord with verbs. In other ways, however, they differ from each other. *People* and *police* can be enumerated (*two or three people, six police*). *People* generally replaces the use of *persons* with definite reference. *Police* is a collective (*the police, police*) and can be individuated by a noun compound (*policeman/ policewoman/police officer/police constable*), all count nouns. *Cattle* is individuated by 'head' (*a/two head of cattle*), used in specific registers.

These nouns are only partially count in that they are not compatible with all the markers of countability. They take plural concord on the verb. Typical collocations with neutral quantifiers (*a lot of, lots of*) and plural quantifiers *many, few, several* are as follows:

A lot of police/people/cattle/clothes.
Lots of police/people/cattle/clothes.

(Not) many/ few police officers/ people/ cattle/ clothes.
Several policewomen/ police constables.

3. Nouns with count and non-count uses – *(some) coffee; two coffees*

Many mass nouns can be interpreted as count when they refer to instances of the mass referent, conceptualised as conventional quantities of food or drink. Compare:

Mass: Coffee and tea help to keep you awake.
Count: Two coffees, please, and three teas.

In the context of restaurants or in-flight meals, even nouns such as *beef* and *chicken* may be interpreted as portions or choices, and countabilised: *One beef and two chickens, please.* In other cases the shape matters. Eatable entities visualised as having a definite shape are count (a cheese, a ham, a cake, a potato, an egg, a chicken, a fish) while the substance or flesh is conceptualised as mass: *(some) cheese, (some) ham, (some) cake, (some) tomato, (some) mashed potato, (some) egg, (some) chicken, (some) fish*.

You've got egg on your tie.
Susie prefers chicken to veal.

The same happens with edible fishes. The animal itself is count, the flesh mass: *He caught a salmon. We had salmon for dinner. Shellfish*, however, is always non-count. The non-count is lexicalised differently in pairs such as *cow* (count) versus *beef* (mass), *pig – pork*, *sheep – mutton*, *calf – veal*, *deer – venison*.

4. Abstract nouns – *health, wealth and love*

Many, but not all, abstract nouns can be re-conceptualised as concrete instances of the mass meaning. Some, but by no means all, can be pluralised:

Everyone needs sleep. | She fell into a deep sleep.
Silence in court! | His remark was followed by a long silence.

They're making a lot of noise. | I hear many strange noises at night.
Time is on your side. | How many times have you seen that film?
Business is improving. | His several businesses are doing well.
One can never be sure of success. | As an actor, he had more successes than failures.

Health is more important than wealth. | *Healths are more important than *wealths.

45.5.3 Countability markers of non-count referents

There are a number of nouns which evoke smallness or shape and which are used to suggest a minimal quantity of a substance or of something not concrete. They are followed by *of* and the non-count word, and tend to have particular collocations. Here are some of the most common ones, preceded by the indefinite article:

A bit of	paper, cheese, ham, cloth, wood, information, fun, advice, news
A piece of	paper, cheese, meat, chocolate, bread, toast, wood, advice, news
A clove of	garlic (vs a head of garlic)
A drop of	milk, whisk(e)y, sherry, water, blood
A game of	cards, tennis, monopoly, golf
A loaf of	bread
A pinch of	salt
A ray of	sunshine, light, hope
A scrap of	paper, cloth, evidence
A slice of	bread, ham, cheese, turkey
A speck of	dust, dirt (often used in the negative *not a speck of dust/dirt*, etc.)
A spoonful	of sugar

Note that *toast* meaning 'toasted bread' is always non-count and requires 'a piece of' in order to refer to an individuated piece (*a piece, two pieces of toast*). The count use as in *a toast* is only found in the sense of 'act of proposing a celebratory drink to someone'. Let's drink *a toast* to the happy pair'. *A piece/a bit of news* can be contrasted with *a news item*, used in the media.

As well as these, various types of **container** are used to quantify both mass and count referents:

A bottle of	wine, beer, whisk(e)y, water
A cup/ mug of	tea, coffee
A can of	beer, petrol
A carton of	yogurt, cream, custard
A pack of	cards, milk, fruit juice, yoghurts
A packet of	detergent, tea, coffee, cigarettes, biscuits
A tablet of	soap, chocolate
A tin of	tomatoes, soup, sardines, biscuits

45.6 THE HEAD ELEMENT 2: PROPER NOUNS

Traditionally a distinction is made between **proper nouns** and **proper names**. Proper nouns such as *Hilary*, *Madrid* are nouns that have no definable meaning in the language. They are arbitrary. That is, we can't specify characteristics of entities called *Hilary* or *Madrid* as we can for the entities referred to by the common noun *horse*. Proper names potentially have a more complex structure. They may consist of a proper noun such as *Coca-Cola* or include a proper noun as in *Real Madrid*, the *University of Oxford*. This is not necessarily the case, however, as can be seen from the titles of films and TV comedies with names such as *The Office, Sex and the City, The Golden Globe*. These and others, such as the names of universities, hospitals and other institutions, are – or started out as – descriptive labels.

All are definite (see 46.1) and many contain a definite article as part of the name. Proper nouns such as *Washington, Moscow, Brussels* are used metonymically to stand for the administrative centre of the state or entity of which they are the capital.

Artefacts such as cars, designer clothes and paintings are commonly referred to by their owners by proper nouns functioning as common nouns: a *Volvo*, an early *Picasso*, your *Reeboks*.

45.7 THE HEAD ELEMENT 3: PRONOUNS

45.7.1 Personal pronouns and reflexive pronouns

The personal prounons *I, we* (1st person), *you* (2nd singular and plural), *he, she, it* and *they* (3rd person) derive their functions directly from their relation to the speaker in the speech event They are therefore a type of 'pointing' element in that some of their meaning is derived from the context. (Other deictics include the demonstrative and possessive pronouns and determiners, which we deal with later on in this chapter).

I and *you* refer directly to the participants engaged in the discourse exchange. *I* is the current speaker and *you* the addressee(s). The 3rd person pronouns *he, she, it* and *they* refer to persons and things who are not, at the moment of speaking, addressees. They may be either physically present or completely outside the discourse event.

One is an impersonal singular pronoun which is sometimes used in formal styles to make general statements, often of (the speaker's own) opinion, or simply to avoid using *I*, as in examples **1** and **2**, quoting the actor Edward Fox in *The Times*.

The pronoun *you*, as in **3**, can refer informally to people in general to describe a common kind of happening or experience. These are non-deictic (non-pointing) uses:

1 '*One* thinks about life a lot more as time goes by.'
2 'My two years there [at RADA, the Royal Academy of Dramatic Art] were an utter waste of time but I did meet *one's* first wife and had *one's* first child.'
3 It's embarrassing when *you* can't remember someone's name.

I and we

Whereas *I* refers to the current speaker, *we* is not the plural of *I*, but rather *I* plus one or more other persons. The pronouns *we/us* either include or exclude the addressee:

inclusive *we*:	Shall *we* sit together over there?
inclusive *us*:	Let's go! Let us pray. (formal)
exclusive *we*	*We* wanted to ask you a favour.
exclusive *us*:	Let *us* go! (see 24.2.3)

Strong stress (marking information focus) on *we* can disambiguate a potentially ambiguous reference. Otherwise, the addressee has to work out the meaning from the context:

A. How are we going to get there?   (ambiguous: speaker's intended meaning
                                                      was probably inclusive)
B. Well, *WE*'re going in Tom's car.   (exclusive)

We/ us can refer to 'everybody in general':

We don't seem to be near world peace yet.

   The following letter, which appeared as a question (Q) in the Dear Doctor section of
the *Guardian*, illustrates how context enables us to identify the referents of personal
pronouns. For instance, who is the referent of the pronoun 'I' (in Q) and 'you' (in the
answer A)? And of 'he/she' in Q, and 'they', 'themselves' in A? Are the references to
'we' and 'our' inclusive or exclusive?

> **Q.** I live on the outskirts of London and have noticed a very tame fox that seems to
> be getting increasingly bold and is coming near the house. Last week, he (she?)
> even stuck his nose into the kitchen and we spotted him playing on the kids'
> swings and eating leftovers on the picnic table in the garden. He looks wary
> when he sees us but doesn't exactly run away. My wife is concerned about the
> potential health risk to us and to our young children. Should we get rid of him,
> and if so, how?
>
> **A.** He's not a health risk unless you're a hen or a rabbit, in which case you're in
> mortal danger. Urban foxes never attack humans unless they're cornered and
> under attack themselves. Rabid foxes sometimes do, but there is officially no
> rabies in the UK. Apparently, at this time of year, parent foxes turf out their
> young to fend for themselves, which is why they can be spotted wandering
> disconsolately round the garden, playing on swings and scavenging for food.

He, she and they as gender-neutral pronouns

Until fairly recently the pronouns *he* and *his* (in both pronominal and determiner
function) were regularly used, not only to refer to a male referent, but also as a
supposedly gender-neutral pronoun to include a female referent, as in **1** below. Such a
discriminatory use in favour of males has become increasingly unacceptable to many
speakers, particularly with reference to occupations, jobs and roles. One alternative, to
use *she* as the unmarked form, has not caught on extensively, presumably because it
discriminates in favour of females, as in **2**, so it does not solve the problem, which is
essentially the fact that English does not have a sex-neutral 3rd person singular pronoun.
   In writing, the combination *s/he* is becoming common, but it is not transferable to
the spoken language. The disjunctive *he or she* becomes cumbersome if repeated too
often. A further alternative, the use of *they* with both singular and plural verb forms, is
becoming more extensive as in **2**:

1   Every human being of adult years and sound mind has a right to determine
    what shall be done with *his* own body.   [BNC ASK 1476]

2   . . . the non-distressed parent may choose to make explicit to the friend *her* own
    thinking, such as 'well, the children do usually obey us and every parent gets
    wound up from time to time with *their* child.'   [BNC ALN 778]

The pronoun *it*

The pronoun *it*, besides referring to specific objects and animals, can refer to a situation
1 or a fact **2**. It is also used to refer to babies and infants, especially if the sex is
undetermined by the speaker **3** or the reference is generic **4**. In addition, *it* is often non-
referring as in **3**, its presence responding to the need, in English, for an overt syntactic
subject (except in the imperative) (see 24.2).

1   They were all shouting and fighting; *it* was terrible.
2   She was very scared, but she tried not to show *it*.
3   Olga's baby is due in October. – Oh, is *it* a boy or a girl?
4   After the child is born, *it* needs constant care.
5   *It* won't be easy to pass the driving test first time.

The pronouns *he* and *she* are often used to refer to animals, especially when they are in
contact with humans. Otherwise they are referred to as *it*.

The reflexive pronouns

These pronouns – *myself, yourself, himself, herself, itself, ourselves, yourselves, themselves* –
have three functions: co-reference with the subject **1**; an emphatic use, in which the
pronoun is either appositive to the subject or postponed **2**; and where they are required
by the verb **3**:

1   *They* learned to take care of *themselves*.
2   *Susan herself* told me so. *Susan* told me so *herself*.
3   She knows how to fend for *herself*. *One* should avail *oneself* of such opportunities.

Interrogative and indefinite pronouns

The **interrogative pronouns** – *who, whose, which, what* – are described and illustrated
in their pronominal and determinative functions in Chapter 5, devoted to interpersonal
meaning.
      Rather different are the **indefinite pronouns** compounded from *some, any, no* and
every

somebody, someone, something	anybody, anyone, anything
everybody, everyone, everything	nobody, no-one, nothing

These pronouns refer directly to an indefinite person or thing, or a broad class or persons
or things, not to a referent already present in the discourse. In this respect they behave

more like nouns than like pronouns, and are often post-modified, as in *nothing new, someone like you.*

45.7.2 The pronouns *this* and *that*

The deictics *this* and *that* can function as NG heads to refer to a whole proposition or situation or something inferred from it, a use which we classify here as pronominal. (For their function as determiners, see 47.2). These pronominal references may be anaphoric (to a previous part of the discourse), cataphoric (to a later part of the discourse) or exophoric (to something outside the discourse):

Anaphoric reference: Hilda was making a Dutch Delft cake at the oven. *This* was her speciality and she made it on every occasion.

[BNC ATE 1180–1181]

Cataphoric reference: *This* is a security announcement: Would those passengers who have left bags on their seats please remove them.

Exophoric reference: I never thought things would come to *this.* (= to this extreme)

We can see that all the referents in these examples are inanimate and general, and some of them refer to pieces of extended discourse.

Reference to persons by the pronouns *this* and *that* is limited in English to the following uses:

1. **This is** (+ *one's own name*) for identifying oneself in a non-face-to-face situation, illustrated by **1a**; as compared with self-introduction when face-to-face **1b**, where we can use *I am/I'm* (+ one's own name).
2. **This is . . .** for introducing one person to another **2** (less formal than *May I introduce you to X?*).
3. **That . . .** for asking or giving the identification of a more distant 3rd person, using *that* **3**.

1a *This* is Sally Jones speaking (non-face-to-face self-identification,
(not *I am Sally Jones*)   for instance, on the telephone)
1b *I* am Sally Jones (not *This is* (face-to-face self-identification)
Sally Jones)
2 *This* is my friend June. (introducing one person to another)
3 Who is *that*? *That*'s my friend (identification of a 3rd person
June.   at some distance away from the speaker,
or looking at a photograph)

So far we have seen *this* indicating proximity to the speaker and *that* distance. However, these terms are often interpreted subjectively. For instance, an event distant in time may be referred to as *this* if it has just been mentioned:

Columbus discovered the Bahamas in 1492 and *this* changed the course of history.

Conversely, events near in time may be referred to by *that* when an effect of psychological distancing is required. In many cases, however, the choice is open:

If the Opposition wins the motion of 'No Confidence' today, *that/ this* will mean the end of the present government.

45.7.3 The discourse function of pronouns

The principal function of personal pronouns is to help establish major referents in the discourse by setting up **referential** (or identity) **chains** by means of anaphora (Chapter 6). This is an important part of **referential coherence**, of making important referents continuous and salient enough to be perceived and remembered by listeners and readers. In conversation, interlocutors participate in the joint construction of referential chains, as can be seen in our next illustration.

A new referent is likely to be introduced first by a proper noun such as *Vera* or *Mother*, when the speaker expects the addressee to be able to identify the referent. Otherwise, a full nominal group containing descriptive information is used (*a/ the girl* I met this morning at the Post Office). Subsequent mentions can be carried out by pronouns, which are 'lighter' than nouns and much lighter than extended nominal groups. Finally, zero anaphora (*She came in and* (0) *sat down*) is even lighter than the pronoun. From time to time, especially if ambiguity might arise through two referents having the same gender ('Vera' and 'Mother', *she . . . she*), the pronoun is replaced by the proper noun. Anaphoric reference has also been described as a device of **cohesion**.

In the following extract from *Just Between Ourselves*, by Alan Ayckbourn, Dennis is telling his friend Neil about the bad relations that exist between his mother and his wife Vera. The italicised pronouns function in referential chains:

Neil: Vera's looking better.
Dennis: Oh, *she* is. *She*'s a lot better. *She*'s getting better every day. Once *she* and mother can bury the hatchet, we'll be laughing.
Neil: Are *they* still . . .?
Dennis: Not talking at all.
Neil: Really.
Dennis: Well, actually, it's Vera *who*'s not talking to mother. Mother comes in one door, Vera goes out the other. Ridiculous. Been going on for weeks. I said to *them* – look, girls, just sit down and have a laugh about *it*. There's only one life, you know. *That*'s all you've got. One life. Laugh and enjoy *it* while you can. We'll probably all be dead tomorrow so what's the difference? Do *they* listen to *me*? Do *they* hell!

When two referents share identifying properties, naming may not be sufficient to avoid ambiguity in the use of a pronoun. In the following example, inference based on the interpretation of concession in 'though', and of reason in 'because' enables the hearer or reader to correctly assign the reference of *he* in the subordinate clauses:

> Tom jumped in the river to save Bill *though he* couldn't swim. (*he* = Tom)
> Tom jumped in the river to save Bill *because he* couldn't swim. (*he* = Bill)

45.7.4 Substitute *one/ ones*

An object that has already been mentioned or is visible in the discourse can be referred to by the head-word *one*, plural *ones*. These words have no semantic identity of their own, but only the grammatical function of substituting for a noun or NG in order to avoid repetition. When used in this way, these items are classed as 'substitute heads', to distinguish them from the classes of 'pronominal heads' of NGs.

It is important to note that *one/ ones* can replace either a whole antecedent NG or only part of it. Compare **1** and **2** with **3**. In **4**, the elliptical plural *some*, not *ones* is the plural of *one*:

> **1**   I knew Mavis wanted *a* blue scarf, so I bought her *one*. (*one* = whole NG *a blue scarf*)
> **2**   I knew Mavis wanted a blue scarf, so I bought her a lovely *one*. (= *blue scarf*).
> **3**   I couldn't find a blue scarf for Mavis, so I bought her a green *one*. (= *scarf*)
> **4**   I know Mavis likes scarves, so I bought her *some* lovely ones. (= scarves)

The substitute item *one/ ones* may be accompanied by a determiner, a pre-modifier or a post-modifer, thus producing NGs of varying structures:

> **dh:**   this one, each one, either one, which ones, any ones.
> **dmh:**   that big one, a small red one, a few ripe ones.
> **dhm:**   that one over there, any one you like.
> **dmhm:** some fresh ones from the country.

Possessive determinatives are rarely used before *one/ ones* in standard English. Possible uses are *?my one, Peter's one, my friend's ones*, although *those ones* is becoming standard. For other comments on substitution and ellipsis in the NG, see also 29.6.

REFERRING TO PEOPLE AND THINGS AS DEFINITE, INDEFINITE, GENERIC

SUMMARY

1   Definiteness is marked by the definite article *the* and by the determinatives *this, that, these, those* or by the possessives *my, your,* etc. + noun.

2   Indefiniteness is marked by *a(n), some, any* and *zero*. Indefinite nouns are specific or non-specific.

3   Generic reference by zero (+ singular mass, plural count nouns); by *a(n)* and by *the*.

46.1 DEFINITE AND INDEFINITE REFERENCE

In English, the grammar obliges us to refer to people and things as definite, indefinite, or generic. This is done syntactically by the use of determinatives, and among these, in particular, by the **definite**, **indefinite** and **zero articles**, which are traditionally treated separately as a subsystem of the system of determination.

Definite reference is made by *the* or a deictic determinative (*this, that, these, those*) or a possessive (*my, your,* etc.). Indefinite reference is made by *a(n)*, unstressed *some, any* or the absence of a marker, which, since its absence is grammatically significant, is called the 'zero article'. 'Zero' doesn't mean that an article has been omitted, as may occur in a newspaper headline, such as *Plane crashes on village*, but is a category in its own right.

The three articles are distributed as follows with mass and count nouns:

	Mass	**Singular count**	**Plural count**
definite	the butter	the woman	the women
indefinite	– (zero) butter	a woman	– (zero) women
	(unstressed) some butter	–	(unstressed) some women

An entity is considered as 'indefinite' if there is nothing in the discourse or the situation or our general knowledge of the world that identifies it for us. This is the case with *a tiger, a child of six, a show* and *a school* in the news item from *The Sunday Times* below.

> **A *tiger* attacked *a child of six* during *a show* at *a school* in California after *its handler*
> lost control of *the 200lb animal*. *The head teacher* wrestled the boy from *the animal's*
> *jaws* and he was flown to hospital.**

Once the entity has already been mentioned it can be considered as 'definite': *the 200lb animal, the boy, the animal's jaws*. Definiteness is inferred if there is sufficient information to identify it, either in the text (*its handler, the head teacher*) or in the non-linguistic situation (Don't forget to lock *the door*) or in general knowledge (*The Olympic Games*). Note that neither the handler nor the head teacher in this text had been previously mentioned. We identify them in relation to 'tiger' and 'school', respectively through general knowledge and inference: animals on show have a handler and schools have a head teacher. This is known as **indirect anaphoric reference**.

46.2 INDEFINITE REFERENCE: SPECIFIC AND NON-SPECIFIC

Although the term 'indefinite' might appear to be synonymous with 'non-specific', it can in fact be applied to both non-specific and specific entities, whether these are count or mass:

singular:	I've bought *a new car*.	(indef. specific)
	I need *a new car*.	(indef. non-specific)
plural:	I've got *some friends* in London.	(indef. specific)
	I've got *friends* in London.	(indef. non-specific)
mass:	I managed to find *some work*.	(indef. specific)
	I managed to find *work*.	(indef. non-specific)

The examples show that with singular count nouns (*a car*), the article *a(n)* refers to both specific and non-specific entities, the different interpretations being deduced pragmatically from shared knowledge and also from the different predicates. When we need a car, it is obviously not yet specific, but potentially any car. When we have bought a car, it is obviously a specific one. The article *a(n)* can be indeterminate, however, between specific and non-specific interpretations:

Ted wants to buy *a house in Sussex*.   (= any house, as long as it's in Sussex)
Ted wants to buy *a house in Sussex*.
   It's number 2, Farm Road, Brighton. (= a specific house)

As an indefinite determinative, *some* (unstressed) is used mainly with mass and plural count nouns, but the stressed form is sometimes used with mass or count nouns with the meaning of indefinite specific as in: *There is still some hope of recovery*, or non-specific as in *I'll need some book or other to read on the beach*. Either would be meaningful here.

46.3 INDEFINITE PROPER NOUNS

Since proper nouns (Albert Einstein, William Shakespeare) refer to unique entities, they are already definite and cannot logically be conceived of as indefinite. On the other hand, since it is often possible for several entities to be denoted by the same name, such as persons or days of the week, they can be treated sometimes as classes composed of individual members. This allows expressions such as the following:

Is there *a John Smith* in this class?	(indef. specific)
It would be better to meet on *a Monday*.	(indef. non-specific)
We had *a very hot June* last year.	(indef. specific)

Indefinite reference can be made to proper nouns used as common nouns:

I'd like a Martini.

46.4 DEFINITE REFERENCE

The definiteness of a common noun is indicated by the article *the*. This does not by itself identify the referent, but indicates that it can be identified within the text, or outside the text in the situation or from general knowledge. Within the text, the reference may be anaphoric (backwards) or cataphoric (forwards). The anaphor often expresses the antecedent in different words, as in the following news item:

> Ten lionesses at the city zoo are to be put on a contraceptive pill to prevent a population explosion. For 20 years **the lions**[1] have prided themselves on their breeding capabilities. Now, **the treatment**[2] will make them infertile for 3 years and so stop **the increase**.[3]
>
> [1]= ten lionesses; [2]= a contraceptive *pill*; [3]= a population explosion

The referent of a definite head noun can be identified cataphorically by the information contained in the post-modifer, as in: *the bus coming now, the journey home, the Ministry of Health*; or by a determiner or pre-modifier: *this bus, the first bus, the red bus*.

Reference to shared knowledge immediately identifies the referent of, for example, *the sun, the sky, the rain, the government, the political situation, the television*.

Clearly dependent upon inference for their interpretation, but totally normal in certain professional registers of English are metonymic uses, where the thing stands for the person, as in the following examples:

The ham sandwich has left without paying.
The kidney transplant in 104 is asking for a glass of water.

When a personal noun, such as *secretary*, *queen*, *director*, *head*, functions as Subject Complement in a clause and refers to a unique social role, definiteness can be marked either by *the* or by *zero*, with certain lexico-grammatical constraints:

He soon became *director/ the director* of the firm.

When the noun functions as Complement in a verbless clause introduced by *when, while, if, although*, definiteness can be marked by zero:

While Minister of Health, he introduced many reforms.
Although not party leader, he greatly influenced the party's policies.

46.5 DISCOURSE FUNCTIONS OF DEFINITE AND INDEFINITE NOMINAL GROUPS

The semantic function of the articles is to present the referents of NG heads as definite, indefinite or generic.

The first two meanings are basically discourse functions, associated with the information packaging of the content of a clause, sentence or extended discourse into **Given** and **New** information; that is, what is taken by the speaker as known to the hearer, and what is taken as not known, respectively (see Chapter 6). The following paragraph, also from Alan Ayckbourn, giving the stage directions for the play, illustrates these functions. 'New' is marked by *a/ an* or *zero*, and 'Given' by *the*:

> February. *A* garage attached to *a* medium price executive house on *a* private estate belonging to DENNIS and VERA. Down one wall of *the* garage *a* workbench littered untidily with tools, etc. In fact *the* whole place is filled with *the* usual garage junk, boxes, coils of rope, garden chairs, etc. In *the* midst of this, *a* small popular car, at least seven years old, stands neglected. Over *the* work bench *a* grimy window which looks out over *a* small paved 'sitting area'. On *the* other wall *a* door, leading across *a* small dustbin yard to *the* backdoor of *the* house. There is also *a* paved walkway round *the* side of *the* garage, nearest *us*, leading to *the* 'sitting area'.

The text begins naturally with New items (*a garage, a house* and *a private estate*); followed by a second mention of *the garage*, which is now known or 'Given'; then a 'New' item, *a workbench*, with indefinite 'New' *tools*, and a second mention, by inference, to *the whole place*. The text continues to build up a description of the stage cohesively, bit by bit, in a straightforward, coherent way. This is a normal way of introducing Given and New information in a text of this kind.

Quite commonly in fiction, however, a writer introduces a new referent at the beginning of a story as if it were already known. This happens in the novel *Watership Down*, where the first sentence is 'The primroses were over'. The use of the definite article here perspectivises the story from a particular viewpoint: that of the rabbits, the protagonists of the story, as readers soon discover.

46.6 GENERIC REFERENCE

Each of the articles can also be used when we wish to refer to a whole class of entities, usually with regard to their typical characteristics or habitual activities:

the + *singular* count noun:	They say *the elephant* never forgets.
a(n) + *singular* count noun:	They say *an elephant* never forgets.
zero + *plural* count noun:	They say *elephants* never forget.
zero + *mass* noun:	They say *exercise* keeps you healthy.

In the everyday use of English, the zero form with plural count nouns (elephants) is most applicable, while with mass nouns (e.g. *love*) the zero form is obligatory. The three articles express genericity from different points of view, which we will gloss as follows:

- *the* represents the referent of the noun as a single undifferentiated whole class of entities;
- *a(n)* represents any individual member of a class of entity as typical of the whole class;
- zero implies that all or most members of the class of entity possess the characteristic that is predicated of it.

The four structures mentioned above are not freely interchangeable in all generic statements. The generic use of *a(n)* is restricted, in that it can't be used in attributing properties which belong to the class as a whole. For example, *the* but not *a* is acceptable in the following, since an individual kangaroo does not constitute a species, whether near extinction or not, whereas the class as a whole, represented by *the*, does:

The kangaroo is far from being extinct.
*A kangaroo is far from being extinct.

Both *the* and *a(n)* are acceptable with a characterising predicate, as in our next example, since carrying its young in a pouch is characteristic of each and every female kangaroo:

The female kangaroo carries its young in its pouch.
A female kangaroo carries its young in its pouch.

The article *the* tends to generalise more readily than *a(n)*, which refers essentially to a singular indefinite member as representative of its class. *The* + singular count noun may have a generalising value, even when not used in a generic statement:

> Do you play *the piano?*
> Some people sit for hours in front of *the television*.

The definite article is also used:

* with certain adjectival or participial heads of NGs referring to abstract qualities (*the unknown*);
* for groups of people named by a nominalised Attribute, *the underprivileged, the vulnerable*;
* with nouns derived from PPs (*the under-fives, the over-forties*);
* for nationalities (the *Dutch*, the *Swiss*).

All but abstract qualities have plural concord with the verb:

> Science proceeds from the *known* to the *unknown*.
> Nursery schools for *the under-fives* are desperately needed in this area.

Not all adjectives and PPs can function in these ways and the non-native speaker should be cautious in choosing them.

The loosest and therefore most frequent type of generic statement is that expressed by the zero article with plural count nouns or with mass nouns:

> *Kangaroos* are common in Australia.
> *Wine* is one of this country's major exports.

Zero article with plural count nouns may have generic or indefinite reference according to the predication:

> *Frogs* have long hind legs.   (generic = all frogs)
> He catches *frogs*.   (indefinite = an indefinite number of frogs)

A mass noun with zero article can be considered generic even if it is modified: *Colombian coffee is said to be the best*. It is definite, however, if preceded by *the*. Contrast, for example:

> **generic:** *Nitrogen* forms 78% of the earth's atmosphere.
> **definite:** *The nitrogen* in the earth's atmosphere is circulated by living organisms.

SELECTING AND PARTICULARISING THE REFERENT

The determiner

SUMMARY

1 **The determiner**

The first element of the nominal group, the determiner, particularises by 'selection'. Four main types of selection: demonstrative and possessive, quantification and distribution.

2 **Demonstrative and possessive determinatives**

Demonstrative: this week, that day, these events, those ideas
Possessive: my coat, Tom's house, their university, our bus, the moon's orbit . . .

3 *Wh-* **determinatives**: which, what, whose, whichever, etc.

4 **Quantifying determinatives**

Exact quantifiers (numeratives): cardinal and ordinal numerals
Non-exact: some, any, no, much, many, little, few, several

5 **Distributors**: all, both, each, every, either, neither,

6 The semi-determinatives: such, same, certain, another, other, former, latter, last, next

7 Summary of determinative elements

8 Multiple realisations of the determiner

47.1 THE DETERMINER FUNCTION

Common nouns in the dictionary refer to classes of things, but when they are used in discourse they need to be particularised. This is done by the first element of the nominal group, called the **determiner**. The basic function of this element is to particularise and so help to identify the NG referent in the context of the speech situation.

As in other areas of the grammar, we distinguish between a function, in this case the determiner, and the classes of units, here called **determinatives**, which realise the function. The determiner is an element in the syntactic or 'logical'structure of the NG. (Module 50); the various classes of determinatives contribute to the 'experiential structure' of the NG (see 45.2); that is, their functions are semantic, and express the different features the speaker chooses in order to select and particularise the noun referent within the context of discourse.

Determiners identify a nominal group referent by telling us which or what or whose it is, how much, how many, what part or degree of it we are referring to, how big or frequent it is, how it is distributed in space or time. In the following short passage about the problem of waste disposal, the writer refers to the entities: *rubbish, day, year, goods, amount, plants, factories, fuel, snags, risk, damage, degrees centigrade*, and specifies them in respect to the questions given below:

Three quarters of the rubbish[1] we generate *every*[2] *day* could be recycled, and *more of it*[3] could be, if the production of biodegradable goods were encouraged. At present *the same*[4] *amount* is wasted *every*[5] day because of the notorious lack of incineration plants. *Such*[6] plants could be installed in *all*[7] factories so that *each*[8] company could burn *its own*[9] rubbish and save *a great deal of*[10] fuel. The *only*[11] snag about waste burners is that they emit *certain*[12] kinds of highly contaminating gases, but it is calculated that in *a few*[13] years rubbish will be burned without causing *any*[14] damage to the environment. A further argument is that, although nuclear fusion has *none of*[15] the risk of fission, so far, *no*[16] scientist has yet found a system which can function at temperatures lower than *millions of*[17] degrees centigrade.

(*Speak Up*, no. 66)

[1]how much? [2]how often? [3]how much? [4]which amount? [5]how often? [6]which kind? [7]which ones? [8]how many? or which? [9]whose? [10]how much? [11]which? [12]which? [13]how many? [14]how much? [15]how much? [16]which? [17]how many?

47.2 DEMONSTRATIVE AND POSSESSIVE DETERMINATIVES

Demonstratives: this, that, these, those

These items particularise the NG referent by indicating whether it is near (*this, these*) or not near (*that, those*) the speaker, in space or time or psychologically, as explained in 45.7.2 for demonstrative pronouns. They can refer to both human and non-human entities in both singular and plural (*this century, these girls, that cat, those brakes*).

Like the demonstrative pronouns, the determinatives are used with anaphoric, cataphoric and situational reference (see 45.7.2).

The determinatives *this* and *these* are also used to introduce a new topic entity into the discourse. This use is particularly common in anecdotes, stories and jokes:

I'm walking along the street when *this man* comes up to me and says . . .

Possessive determinatives

These include not just the possessive determinatives *my, your, his, her, its, our, your, their,* but also the inflected *'s* genitive form.

The *'s* determinative must be understood in a broader sense than that of the traditional term 'possessive'. The following selection, each with a corresponding paraphrase does not pretend to be exhaustive:

Example	Paraphrase	Function
My daughter's car	My daughter has a car	possessive
Napoleon's army	N. commanded the army.	subjective
Napoleon's mistake	N. made a mistake.	subjective
Napoleon's defeat	N. was defeated by X.	objective
Europe's chief cities	The chief cities in Europe.	locative
Today's paper	The paper published today.	temporal
A month's holiday	The holiday lasted a month.	extent
The dog's tail	The dog has a tail.	metonymy (part–whole relation)
The car's brakes	The car has brakes	metonymy
The sun's rays	The rays come from the sun.	source

These varied functional relationships also exist between a noun head and the determinatives *my, your, his, her, its, our, their, someone's, everyone's, nobody's* and the like:

His mistake	He made a mistake.	subjective
Our friendship	We became friends.	reciprocal
Their love	They love each other.	reciprocal
Its collapse	It collapsed.	subjective

The *'s* determinative is formally a NG plus an inflected genitive morpheme. By convention, the apostrophe is placed before the *s* with a singular noun, but after it with a regular plural noun in *s*. Compare: *the boy's bicycle, the boys' bicycles*. With a name of three syllables or more ending in *-s*, the apostrophe tends to be placed after the *s*: *Socrates' wisdom*. With a name of two syllables, the placement of the *s* is optional: *Dr. Davies' surgery, Dr. Davies's surgery*, the latter case reflecting the additional syllable in speech/deivisiz/.

The inflection is added not merely to the head noun but to the group as a whole:

> *My supervisor's* advice; *my mother and father's* wishes.
> I liked *those other children's* paintings very much.
> *That young Japanese pianist's* performance was wonderful.

47.2.1 Functions of the *'s* phrase

The examples seen so far have all illustrated the central function of the *'s* phrase: to **specify** the nominal group referent, as in *that girl's name*.

Some *'s* NGs may also function as **classifiers**, as in *girls' names*. With the article *a(n)* the NG may have two interpretations. The NG *a lady's bicycle* may refer to the bicycle of a particular lady, or to the class of bicycle designed for ladies, not for men. The context of discourse normally clarifies the interpretation. Other examples of this type include: *a lion's mane, a bird's nest, a child's toothbrush*, and also:

> I need *a specialist's* opinion, not *a journalist's*.

Classifying genitives are typically used with plural personal nouns: *children's clothing, a men's club, boys' names*.

47.2.2 Possessives as nominal group heads

The possessive pronouns *mine, yours, his, hers, (its), ours, theirs* function not as determinatives but as pronominal heads. (*Its* is not used to realise this function.)

> This suitcase is *yours*. Where is *mine*? It's over there with *Tom's*.

The *'s* phrase stands alone as an elliptical head of the NG when the noun head is recoverable, either because it has already been mentioned, or by convention. In the latter case the *'s* element often refers to people's homes or establishments such as restaurants and shops, as well as to individuals:

> Let's have dinner at Archy's.   These gloves aren't mine, they're Daniel's.
> I have to go to *the cleaner's* (dry cleaner's), *the butcher's, the florist's*.

A friend of mine, a friend of my sister's

The post-modifying possessive phrase *of mine, of yours* etc. is equivalent to the 'double possessive' as in *a friend of my sister's*. They have the meaning of 'one among several' as opposed to the more exclusive meaning of 'my friend', 'my sister's friend'. An exclusive meaning, which may also express an attitude on the part of the speaker, is found, however, when the phrase occurs together with another determinative (*this, that, a, the, other*, etc.), a combination that is not possible otherwise:

> That motorcycle of your brother's

47.3 *WH- DETERMINATIVES: WHICH, WHOSE, WHAT*

Which, whose express specific selection among a known number; *what* asks about the identity or kind of thing something is. *Whatever, whichever* express non-specific selection, meaning 'it doesn't matter what', 'it doesn't matter which', respectively, when the speaker is not able to specify a particular type. *What* can also be used as an equivalent to *whatever* or stressed *any* (see 47.4.1):

Which bus do you take?
Whose car did you come in?
What plans have they made for the summer?
You'll have to rely on *whatever transport* is available.
You'll find plenty of traffic *whichever road* you take.
What hopes we had are now fading. (= *whatever hopes, any hopes*)

47.4 QUANTIFIERS

A speaker may select or particularise a referent by referring to its quantity, which may be exact (*three friends*), non-exact (*many friends*), ordinal (*the first friend*), or partitive (*three of my friends*).

Exact numeratives

These include the **cardinal numerals** one, two, three . . . twenty-one, twenty-two . . . a hundred and five . . . one thousand, two hundred and ten, and so on. These function directly as determinatives.

The **ordinal numbers** – first, second, third, fourth, fifth . . . twenty-first . . . hundredth . . . hundred and fifth and so on – specify the noun referent in terms of order. They follow a determinative, as in: *the first time, a second attempt, every fifth step*, and in this respect are more like the semi-determinatives, including *the next, the last*.

Non-exact quantifiers

The two types select referents by referring to:

*   their indefiniteness: *some, any, no, much, many, little, few   (a(n)* is treated in 46.1).
*   their distribution: *all, both, either, neither, each, every, another, other*.

47.4.1 Indefinite quantifiers

Some, any, no, (none)

Some specifies a quantity (with mass nouns) or a number above two (with count nouns) as in *some money, some time, some friends, some details*. Other quantifiers are used to express very small or very large amounts. The word *some* is pronounced in two ways, according to its function. It has a weak form when used non-selectively as an indefinite determiner (see 46.1), but it is strong when used as a selective quantifier:

non-selective	/səm/	We're spending some days by the sea.
selective	/sʌm/	Some days it's hot, other days it's cold.

Stressed *some* can also be used with various types of evaluative force:

quantifying:	I haven't seen you for some time.	(= a long time)
appreciative:	That really was some meal!	(= a wonderful meal)

Any has two meanings, as illustrated in the following examples (see also 3.3):

1   Have you *any* money/*any* coins? I haven't *any* money/*any* coins.
2   *Any* information would be useful.

In **1**, *any* specifies an indeterminate amount or number of something. It occurs in non-affirmative clauses, that is, in negative and interrogative clauses mainly (see non-assertion, 3.4). It is typically unstressed.

In **2**, *any* is equivalent to 'no matter which or what'. It occurs typically in affirmative clauses and is stressed. Compare this use of *any* with *anything* and *either.*

You can choose *any* of the main courses on the menu.	(it doesn't matter which)
You can choose *anything* on the menu.	(it doesn't matter what)
You can choose *either* meat or fish.	(one or the other, not both)

The negative determinative *no* has mass, count, singular and plural references: *no time, no change, no changes.*

There is *no* need to worry. *No* changes will be made. *None* (pronoun) will be made.

Some and *any* – but not *no* – can function as elliptical heads of the NG. Instead of *no*, the pronoun **none** is used, as in the previous example, and also for the partitive ('none of the men').

Have you any change?	Yes, I have *some*. No, I haven't *any*.	I have *none*.
Did you have any *problem* in parking?	No, *none*. (= no problem)	
Did you have any difficulties with your papers?	No, *none*. (= *no difficulties*)	

Note that *not* is a negative particle, and does not function as a determinative or a pronoun. It can precede the quantifiers *much* and *many* in elliptical responses.

Isn't there anything to eat?	*Not* much.
Haven't you any *friends*?	*Not* many.

Much, little, a little, many, few, a few

These quantifiers are used with both indefinite and definite NGs. With definite reference they are followed by *of* and have **partitive** reference: they represent a sub-set of an already selected class.

Indefinite reference – non-partitive		*Definite reference – partitive*
much time, much food	(+ mass n.)	Much of the time, much of the food
little time, little food	(+ mass n.)	little of the time, little of the food
many pubs, many people	(+ count n.)	many of the pubs, many of the people
few seats, few people	(+ count n.)	few of the seats, few of the people
a few seats, a few people	(+ count n.)	a few of the seats, a few of the people

These quantifiers can function as ellipted heads. *Much* and *many* are used mainly in negative and interrogative clauses. *Much* and *little* are commonly modified by *very* or replaced by *a lot, not very much*, respectively.

> Is there much food? There's very little. There's a lot. *There's much. There isn't much. There aren't (very) many people.

A lot of, lots of, plenty of, a great deal of, a number of a lot of/lots of

These quantifiers are determinatives with noun heads followed by a PP complement. They range from the informal (*a lot/ lots of*) to the formal (*a great deal/ number of*). Some of them admit both mass and count nouns, others do not:

Singular mass and plural count:	a lot of, lots of, plenty of	a lot of/lots of/ plenty of money
		a lot of/lots of/plenty of friends
Singular mass only	a great deal of	a great deal of money
Plural count only:	a number of	a number of policemen

More informal combinations of this type which function like *a lot/ lots of* include *loads of, heaps of, masses of*.

These phrasal quantifiers are not partitives even though they contain the preposition *of*. Partitives have definite reference and represent subsets from already selected sets. Here is a selection of examples of non-partitive quantifiers, as well as cardinal and ordinal numbers, together with their partitive counterparts:

Non-partitive quantifiers	Partitive quantifiers
A lot of money was wasted	A lot of the money was wasted
No money was wasted	None of the money was wasted
They spent a great deal of time in pubs	They spent a great deal of the time in pubs
Some books were damaged in the fire	Some of the books were damaged in the fire
Few seats were vacant	A few of the seats were vacant
Three people were injured	Three of the people were injured
Their first child was born in Wales	The first of their children was born in Wales

47.4.2 Distributors: *All, both, either, neither, each, every*

Of the distributive determinatives, *all* refers to a totality; it can be used with mass nouns (*all power* corrupts), plural nouns in a generic sense (*all men are mortal*) and certain temporal and locative nouns (*all day, all night, all America*). When the reference is not generic, *all* is optionally followed by *of* + noun (*all the pie/ all of the pie; all the pages/ all of the pages*).

Both refers to two entities together. *Either* and the negative form *neither* refer to two entities as alternatives. *Each* and *every* refer to one of a group or series, but while *each* emphasises the separateness of the entity, *every* highlights the individual within the group. *Each* can refer to two entities separately (*each hand, each foot*) but *every* is applicable only to groups of three or more. *Both, either, neither* and *each* (but not *every*) can take optional *of* before the noun (the partitive use). Here are some examples:

> *All* birds have feathers, but *not all* birds can fly. (generic)
> *All* the bedrooms/*All* of the bedrooms have a balcony and telephone, and *some* take a third and fourth bed.   [BNC AMD 1724]
> Keep hold of the wheel with *both hands*.
> *Both children/both the children/both of the children* had measles at the same time.
> He can write with *either* hand/with *either of* his hands.
> *Neither* twin/*neither of the* twins is very good at maths.
> *Each* player/*Each of* the players was given a premium.
> This applies to *each of* us – men as well as women.   [BNC AT9 192]
> Two out of *every* five people catch more than one cold a year.
> *Every* known criminal of New York was there.   [BNC ATE 1753]
> They went to visit her, as they did nearly *every* Sunday.

All, both and each following pronouns

These distributors can follow pronouns, whether subjective or objective, for emphasis:

> They all/both/each carried backpacks.
> We've bought them all/both bicycles. We've bought them each a bicycle.
> All of them have bicycles. Both of them have bicycles. Each of them has a bicycle.

All, everything, everyone/everybody

All is marginally used in formal styles as an alternative to *everything* to refer to a situation, ideas, objects, actions in general terms.

> *All* went well. *Everything* went well.
> *All* is ready. *Everything* is ready.

All is much less common than *everything* and *everyone* in everyday English, however. Furthermore, it is not used as an elliptical head in Object and Complement functions, where it can be used with a pronoun. Compare:

> *I liked all. I liked everything. I liked it all.

Everyone and *everybody* refer to all the people in a particular group. The notion of generality can be extended to wider groups and even everyone everywhere:

> *Everyone* enjoyed the show.
> He poured drinks for *everybody*.

Everyone condemned the terrorist attack.
Everyone has their own opinion.

All is not normally used in this way, without a head or modifier. Compare:

*All enjoyed the show.	All those present enjoyed the show.
*He poured drinks for all.	He poured drinks for all present/ for us all/ for them all

All people is not an acceptable alternative to *everyone/ everybody*. *All the people there* would refer to definite people on a specific occasion, rather than the more general meaning of totality expressed by *everyone*.

The following horoscope illustrates some of these quantifiers:

Libra (Sep 24 – Oct 23)

None of it matters quite as much as we think. *All* of it is a journey, a dream. Of course, it seems real. Dreams always do while we are dreaming them. This does not make life any the less precious. To the contrary. We should treasure *every* moment because we never know *how many more moments* we will have left. Yet sometimes, we cannot properly treasure *each* moment because we are too worried about making the most of *our every* moment. This weekend brings magic. Enjoy it.

47.5 THE SEMI-DETERMINATIVES: *SUCH, WHAT, CERTAIN, SAME, (AN)OTHER, FORMER, LATTER*

These words (except *such*) are sometimes classed as adjectives. However, they do not describe the referent and appear to have a specifying function. They precede either a definite or an indefinite determiner.

Such and exclamatory *what* are among the few elements of this kind which precede the indefinite article. They require *a(n)* before a singular count noun, zero before non-count and plural nouns.

Such classifies an entity by kind or intensifies it by degree. It usually relates to something already mentioned in the discourse.

Classifying: (= of that kind)
    I've never heard of *such an animal*.
    Such cruelty is incomprehensible.
    Such people are dangerous

Intensifying:
    Don't be *such a fool*!   They are *such idiots*!   (= of that degree)

Certain, by contrast, follows *a(n)* or is followed by zero. It helps to pick out a specific, but as yet not identified, person or thing:

> There is a *certain* opposition to the Government's proposals.
> A *certain* person in this room might disagree with you.

Same indicates that the person or thing referred to is exactly like one previously mentioned.

> He always asks *the same* two questions.

Another (+ singular count noun) has two meanings: it indicates that the entity referred to is different from one already mentioned; and it refers to a subsequent entity of the same kind as the one already mentioned in the discourse. The indefinite plural **other** (+ plural count noun) is used mainly in the first sense.

> Couldn't you choose *another* title? (= a different title)
> Would you like *another* beer? (= of the same kind, not of a different kind)
> I saw him *the other* day. We talked about *other* things.

Former and ***latter*** refer back to the first and the second respectively of two entities already mentioned. They are preceded by the definite article and can occur together with the *'s* possessive determinative.

> Bill and Steve both made proposals. The *former's* was rejected, the *latter's* approved.

Former is also used adjectivally with the meaning of 'previous' when referring to jobs, positions or roles. In this function it may be preceded by a possessive determinative such as *my, your*.

> A *former* President *of the Royal Society*.
> *His former* partner has set up business on his own.

Note that *such* and *the same* can function as substitute heads (see 45.7.4), as in:

> Is this a dangerous area?   I wouldn't consider it as *such* (= a dangerous area)
> Alice had a cola and Sue had *the same* (= a cola)

In Spanish, for instance, instead of *el mismo* ('the same'), the pronoun *otro* ('another') is used.

47.6 SUMMARY OF DETERMINATIVE FEATURES

The following table summarises the four broad experiential types of determination by which referent things can be particularised in English, together with their subtypes and principal exponent.

1 Defining and Particularising	2 Quantifying and Distributing	3 Numbering and Ordering	4 Semi-determinatives
Definite the	**Fractional** (± of) half, (a) quarter, two-thirds, four-fifths, etc. a dozen, a thousand	**Cardinal** one, two, ten, two hundred, etc.	such, certain, former, latter; same, other, last, next, own
Indefinite a(n), some zero (0)	**Multiplying** (*of) double, treble, twice, hundreds of, thousands of, millions of	three times,	
Demonstrative This, that, these, those			
Possessive my, your, his, her, their Sam's, my friend's etc.	**Non-exact** some, any, no much, (a) little, (a) few, many, several, enough	**Ordinal** first, second, third . . .	
Interrogative/ relative what, whose, which, whichever	**Other quantifiers** A lot of, lots of, plenty of, a great deal of, a number of		
Exclamative what (a) . . .			
	Distributives all, both, either, neither, each, every, none (of)		

47.7 ORDERING OF DETERMINATIVES

The governing principle of placement of multiple determinatives is the same as that of a whole NG, that is, a gradual process of dependency selection from right to left, as in:

Pre-determinatives and partitives	Central determinatives	Post-determinatives		HEAD
half	his	last	sixty	dollars
a few of	my	many	other	friends
some of	the doctor's	former		patients
none of	those	several		options
such	an			experience
	their	own		house
	the	same		day
	that	certain		feeling
What	an			idea!

Here, from all *dollars*, we first select *sixty*; these are particularised as his *last sixty dollars* and of these we select *half* and say: 'He paid only *half his last sixty dollars* for his seat'.

DESCRIBING AND CLASSIFYING THE REFERENT   *MODULE 48*

The pre-modifier

SUMMARY

1   The **epithet** and the **classifier** functions, realised by descriptors and classifiers, respectively.

2   The epithet function is realised by adjectives and participles whose reference may be: **descriptive:** a *popular* disco, a *sunny* day, a *galloping* horse, an *abandoned* car

> **evaluative:** a *princely* meal, *a vile* crime
> **either of the above:** *absolute* zero, *absolute* rubbish

3   The classifier function limits the entity to a subclass in relation to:

> **affiliations:** *Indian* art, *French* window, a *Buddhist* monk
> **quality:** a *poisonous* snake, a *non-alcoholic* drink
> **norms:**   *average* age, *standard* size, *top* ten
> **process:** the *rising* tide, a *growing* population
> **society and institutions:** *metropolitan* police, a *football* club; *social* status
> **technology:** a *nuclear* power-station, *electric* light, *solar* energy

4   Some words can function as either epithets or classifiers: *civil*: a *civil* manner (epithet); *civil* rights (classifier).

5   The elements of a NG are organised in a relationship of successive dependency and selection, from the head leftwards to the classifier, the epithet and the determiner, and rightwards to the postmodifier, as indicated by the arrows in the following example:

d←	e←	clas.	←h→	fin. cl.
that	short	summer	course	we attended

6   The order of epithets is semantic and partly conventional, rather than grammatical.

48.1 THE PRE-MODIFIER FUNCTIONS: EPITHET AND CLASSIFIER

The pre-modifier (experientially the **epithet** and the **classifier**) is different from the determiner in certain ways. While the determiner function is realised by closed class items which define and select the referent, the pre-modifier function describes or classifies the referent by means of open-class items, mainly adjectives and nouns. Unlike the determiner, these are optional. Furthermore, and again unlike determinatives, there is no grammatical constraint on the number of modifiers placed before a noun. The main types of structural element that either describe or classify are illustrated by examples from the art sale text ('Fairy Liquid') in Section 45.1, among others:

Descriptor and classifier elements

(a) adjectives	*smart* rooms, *low* groans, a *tall* building, *good* weather (epithet); *new* rooms, *digital* camera (classifier)
(b) *en*-participle	*well-dressed* art-lovers (epithet), the *acknowledged* master, *worn-out* machinery, *fallen* leaves (classifiers)
(c) *ing*-participle	a *disappointing* exam result/ finish (to a match), *breathtaking* speed (epithet); *running* water, a *leading* article, *coming* events (classifier)
(d) noun	the *flower* market, a *Paris* café (classifier)

In addition, the following are also used, though less commonly, as modifiers:

(e) nominal group	a *no-frills* airline
(f) adverb	the *then* President
(g) coordinated clauses	a *take-it-or-leave-it* attitude

The true *-en* participial epithet derived from a verb, such as *broken* in *a broken cup*, must be distinguished from **'pseudo-participials'**, which are derived from nouns, as in:

A dark-green, *big-leaved, long-stemmed* plant with orange flowers.

Such pseudo-participials are often modified, as the modification represents some non-essential feature. We don't say *a *leaved* plant, *a *haired* girl, because plants normally have leaves and girls have hair. Not all leaves are big and not all girls' hair is dark, however, allowing the formation of *big-leaved* and dark-*haired: a dark-haired girl*. In *a camera'ed bystander*, by contrast, no modifier is needed because carrying a camera is not an essential feature of a bystander.

48.2 ADJECTIVES AS EPITHET: DESCRIPTORS AND ATTITUDINAL USES

In the epithet function the adjective is used to ascribe a quality (*big, old, red*, etc.) to the referent. This may be an objective quality (e.g. a *square* box, a *round* table, *a blue* truck, *old* magazines) while others are subjective and represent the speaker's or writer's attitude towards the referent (*good, bad, nice, stupid, lovely, horrible*, etc.).

The subjective–objective distinction is not as clear as we might think, however. The act of appreciation is bound to be subjective, because the quality is inevitably presented through the eyes of the speaker, and yet the appreciation is objectivised because it is related to some cultural norm. Some 'objective' qualities are culture-specific. What counts as a tall man or a narrow street in one culture may not appear to be so to members of another.

Adjectival epithets expressing objective qualities may simply 'describe' an entity (*I bought a small bottle*) or 'define' it (*I bought the small bottle*). The meaning in both is clearly 'experiential' in that it denotes a quality experienced by everyone in the culture and denoted by the word 'small'. The two semantic functions of describing and defining are reflected in the grammar by the *a/ the* contrast. That is to say, the terms 'descriptive' and 'defining' don't refer to two subclasses of adjectives, but to two potential functions of most objective adjectives.

The defining function of an epithet is different from the classifying function, as illustrated in the following extract from Paul Gallico's *The Silent Hostages*:

> The car carrying the two *escaped*[1] killers, Rickman and Hoser, nosed carefully into the *unidentified*[2] desert town. It was that *darkest*[3] hour before dawn of a *moonless*,[4] *starlit*[5] night. Rickman, the more *vicious*[6] man, driving, with *cold*,[7] *snake-like*[8] eyes and *bloodless*[9] mouth.
>
> Since they had murdered their three hostages, they had been attempting to find their way towards the *Mexican*[10] border, driving without lights on back roads and wagon trails.
>
> [1-3]defining; [4-5]descriptive; [6]defining; [7-9]descriptive; [10]classifying

The **attitudinal** epithet expresses the speaker's or writer's subjective evaluation of the referent, and is interpersonal, rather than experiential. There are two broad kinds of evaluation:

appreciative: good, wonderful, heavenly (a *good* film, an *intelligent* remark)
pejorative: bad, idiotic, monstrous, appalling (a *horrible* film, a *foolish* remark)

Certain adjectives can be used both to describe objectively and to express attitude:

Descriptive	Attitudinal
a poor part of the city	Poor you! Poor little boy!
a *huge* piece of machinery	The show was a *huge* success.

Epithets used attitudinally don't usually have the potential to define the referent of the noun, as is usual with the objective use of adjectives. The superlative preceded by *the*, with attitudinal adjectives, for instance, simply intensifies the effect but does not define. Compare: *We saw the sweetest little girl/ the most horrible film* (attitudinal) with *we saw the poorest part of the city* (objective).

Attitudinal adjectives are usually placed before descriptive ones: *a marvellous sunny day*; a *sickly greenish yellow*. They also tend to be preceded or followed by others which express similar or related meanings and so reinforce or intensify the attitude or emotion in question:

a lumbering great lorry	a whopping big lie
that splendid, delicious meal	a sweet little girl

So although these two uses of certain adjectives have different communicative effects, they are not always easy to distinguish, and we should not think of epithets as divided into two rigid sets called 'descriptive' and 'attitudinal'.

We will use the symbol **e** for both attitudinal and descriptive uses, distinguishing these from the **classifier** (**clas**).

If we divide the determinative features of a referent entity into the two broad types – defining/ deictic (**d^d**) and numerative/quantifying (**d^q**) – we can now give some idea, in the following tree, of the experiential structure of the NG as we have described it so far, and without including the post-modifier described in Module 49:

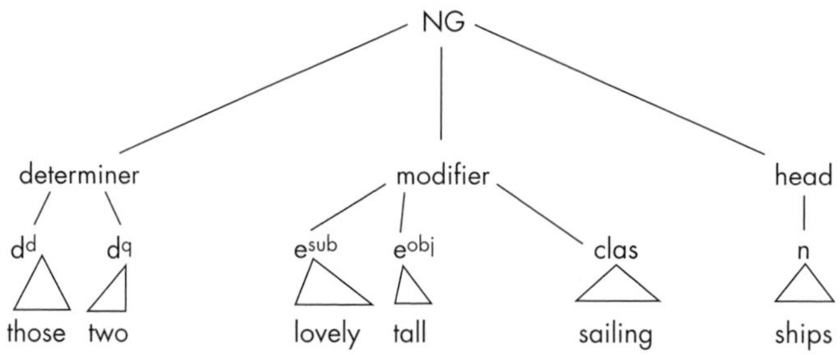

Strictly speaking, it is not an adjective but an adjectival group that can modify the head noun. This will be considered again in Chapter 11. For the present we simply point out that many adjectives can be pre-modified by an intensifier, as in a *very tall* building, and post-modified, as in *a very exciting thing to do*.

Multiple epithets

Sequences of two epithets (mainly adjectives and participles) are found in many types of speech and writing. Strings of three, four or five epithets can have a rather marked effect. They are common in certain genres, such as advertisements, especially personal classified ads, as the second and fourth below, from *The Times* [square brackets enclose other elements]:

Two items:	long, winding roads; hard, stale cheese
Three items:	exotic, exciting, focused female [seeks professional male, 38+, to live life to the max with]
Four items:	[what an] absurd, cruel, strange, mad thing [to do]
Five items:	educated, kind, slightly mad, solvent, good-looking gent, [53, seeks partner for long-term relationship]

Adjectives functioning as multiple epithets may be **coordinated** or **subordinated**.

Coordinated epithets (without a coordinator) were illustrated in the previous examples. Below are examples of coordinated adjectives (with a coordinator: *and, or, either . . . or, but, yet*) and subordinated ones:

Co-ordinated:	*and*	good *and* bad camping-sites
	or	hot *or* cold meals
	either . . . or	*either* white *or* light blue shirts
	but	a long *but* interesting trip
	yet	a strange *yet* friendly person
Subordinated:		an enlightening *if* heated discussion
		a disappointing *though* not unexpected result

Epithets, like classifiers, can be sub-modified: *slightly* mad, *very* good-looking.

48.3 ORDERING OF MULTIPLE EPITHETS

Epithets are not necessarily ordered in a relation of dependency, as classifiers are (see 48.5). Nevertheless, their order of occurrence is not totally free, and various suggestions have been offered of preferred orderings:

- attributes of **size**, **age**, **shape** and **colour** usually occur in that order: *a large, rectangular, black box.*
- **de-verbal adjectives** (i.e. derived from verbs) before **denominal** ones (derived from nouns; see 51.2), as in: *an attractive, ambitious woman.*
- **short adjectives** before **long** ones, as in: *a small, pretty, well-kept garden.*
- **well-known words** before **less common ones**: *a strange, antediluvian monster.*
- the **most forceful or 'dynamic' adjective** tends to be placed at the end: *a sudden, loud, ear-splitting crash*; such sequences are also felt to be more satisfying rhythmically, compared with *an ear-splitting, loud, sudden crash.*

We shall return to the ordering of pre-modifiers in the following section, since many sequences are mixed, consisting of both epithets and classifiers.

48.4 FUNCTIONS AND PROPERTIES OF THE CLASSIFIER

The function of the classifier is to sub-classify the noun referent; for instance, *dental treatment* is a subclassification of *medical treatment, dental* contrasting with other sub-domains of medicine. Although certain words can function as both epithets and classifiers, these functions can normally be distinguished by the following criteria:

(a) Classifiers are **not gradable**, as descriptive adjectives are; that is, they don't admit degrees of comparison or intensity; we can't say *more dental* treatment', *very dental* treatment, as we can with descriptors: *more effective* treatment, *very effective* treatment.

(b) Classifiers tend to be organised into mutually exclusive sets, as in *presidential election, the presidential airplane* (AmE), which contrast with other elections and airplanes (BrE aircraft) not relative to a president or a presidency. Another set in a different domain, that of ways of cooking eggs, includes *fried, boiled, poached, scrambled* [eggs].

(c) The classifier function is realised by adjectives, nouns, participles, ordinal numbers and, to a lesser extent, adverbs, phrases and clauses. We shall illustrate these in turn.

48.5 ADJECTIVES, PARTICIPLES AND NOUNS AS CLASSIFIERS

Adjectives as classifiers are frequently derived from nouns and restrict the noun head in relation to another referent. There is a wide variety of relations expressed, including:

(a) *affiliations to national, political or religious groups*, such as: African, American, British, Buddhist, Canadian, Chinese, Christian, Conservative, Dutch, French, German, Indian, Liberal, Muslim, Norwegian, Russian, Socialist, Swiss (all written with a capital letter);

(b) *related to norms, sequences, sizes, ratings, scales*, for example: average, chief, main, standard, regular, top; previous, following, initial, final; personal, particular, external, internal;

(c) *related to areas of study, art, science and institutions*, as in the following examples:

affiliations:	African politics, Swedish voters, the Conservative party;
norms, ratings:	average age, regular doctor, standard size, top ten, main road, personal contribution, particular occasion;
time, place:	former boss; old friend; previous page; left leg; right hand;
periods:	prehistoric remains, modern times, classical music;
institutions:	municipal authorities, industrial unrest, metropolitan police;
professions:	medical student, social worker, agricultural expert;
devices:	atomic energy, digital watch, mobile phone (BrE)/ (AmE cell phone).
processes:	Both -*ing* and -*en* participles classify an entity by a process: *coming* events, *sun-dried* tomatoes

Here too, a participle + noun may be a compound: *guided missile, leading article.* The *-ing* classifiers mentioned here are different from de-verbal nouns such as *boxing* as in *boxing-gloves, snorkling gear, reading materials,* which belong to the noun class.

When the adjective and noun are written as one word, as in *software, hardware,* they are compounds, referring to a single class referent, not to a subtype of a class. The same may happen with separate or hyphenated words: *fancy dress, fast-food, first-aid.*

A noun as classifier functions in a similar way to an adjective, delimiting the referent according to membership of a mutually exclusive set (e.g. *ham sandwich, bacon sandwich*).

Types of noun classifier
simple (*apple* blossom)
genitive (a *girls'* school)
compound (*farmyard* animals)
short NGs (*Social Security* contributions)

The classifying function of a genitive noun or NG, as in *The Minister gave a typical Minister of Labour's reply,* must be distinguished from its determiner function as in *the Minister of Labour's reply.*

Nouns as classifiers are not usually pluralised: **trouser** *belt,* **car** *production,* **rebel** *forces,* but certain plural nouns are regularly used, including **women** *drivers;* **sales** *campaign.* Plural forms are also used when the referent of the classifier has come to be regarded as a collective noun, as in *arms race, sports field, Olympic Games medal, the Arts Council.*

When the semantic relation between a classifier and a noun is very cohesive, they frequently become fused as a **noun compound** denoting a single referent, rather than a subclass of a larger class of referents. The dividing line between a noun modifier + noun and a noun compound is not entirely clear. Punctuation, as we have seen, provides only a rough guideline to the degree of integration achieved by the two nouns.

When the combination is written as separate words, it is likely to be a noun with a noun modifier (*head waiter*); if written as a single word it is more likely to be a noun compound (*headache, headrest*). Hyphenation signals those elements which form a compound (*walkie-talkie*) and which otherwise would appear to be separate pre-modifiers. This is a useful guide with units occurring within a larger unit (*high-rise block, high-speed bullet train*).

Stress-patterning is not always reliable. Compounds are said to have the tonic stress on the first noun. However, many compounds do not follow this pattern (*cotton wool, zebra crossing*), while some classifiers do (*steam vehicles, rose-bush*).

The factor that best distinguishes noun classifiers from noun compounds is that classifiers can enter into relations of coordination and modification. Compare:

Coordinated classifiers	Modified classifier
new and second-hand stereos	brand-new stereos
European and local councils	various agricultural colleges
Lunch and dinner menus	early Chinese pottery
plane or coach trips	modern sculpture techniques

silk and cotton shirt	pure silk shirt
bus and coach stations	inter-city coach station

Compound nouns do not admit coordination or modification of their component elements:

*soft and hardware	*extremely software
*pain and insect killers	*persistent painkiller
*silk and earth worms	*pure silkworm

Classification by other classes of units

Certain institutionalised word, group and clausal expressions are sometimes used:

morpheme:	pro- and anti-abortionists
adverb:	an only child, an away match
PP:	over-the-counter sales, on-line editing
NG:	a New Year's Eve party
VG:	a stop-and-go policy, a live-and-let-live philosophy
AdjG:	a bored-with-life attitude
clause:	a couldn't-care-less attitude.

Phrasal modifiers are used daily in many practical registers of English. The following short example occurred in the report of a meeting called to prepare an English language examination of the Royal Society of Arts:

> It was decided that section 1 of the examination would involve *no-choice short-answer* questions, and section 2 an *essay-style* question on language systems. The group felt that the candidates should also be required to submit *six non-exam-type* pieces of work done at home.

48.6 WORDS FUNCTIONING AS BOTH EPITHET AND CLASSIFIER

Many words can function as both epithets and classifiers. Some classifiers can be modified and then lose their classifier function: a *very French* lady.

Epithet	Classifier
fresh bread (= freshly made)	*fresh* water (i.e. not salty, not sea-water)
a *sick* person	*sick* pay, *sick* leave
new houses (= recently built)	*new* rooms (new to the occupier)
to do that would be *criminal*	the *criminal* court
a *medieval* state of sanitation	a *medieval* castle
a *provincial* attitude	a *provincial* town

48.7 MULTIPLE CLASSIFIERS

Classifiers are related by coordination or dependency. A lot is left implicit in classifier + noun combinations, and with more than two elements the complexity increases.

Related by coordination

The History and Geography Faculty	Apple and blackberry tart
The Management and Finance Committee	A plane and coach trip

The singular head noun indicates that there is only one Faculty, committee, tart and trip, each of a dual kind. Ambiguity may arise if the head noun is plural. For example, plane and coach trips could refer to several trips of a plane + coach type, or to plane trips separate from coach trips, analysed as : [[plane and coach] trips] or [[plane] and [coach] trips]], respectively.

Related by dependency

Sequences of two classifiers can occur before a noun head, as in the following:

chrome bathroom fittings
Madrid terrorist bombings

In these examples the semantic relations can be inferred directly as increasing dependency from the head noun towards the left. That is, *chrome* modifies *bathroom fittings*, not *bathroom*, and *Madrid*, in the actual sense used, modified the *terrorist bombings*. This combination is ambiguous, however, as another reading could be 'bombings by Madrid terrorists'.

It is common, then, to find combinations in which either the classifier or the head is itself sub-modified, or rather, sub-classified, as in the following examples:

Sub-modified classifier	*Sub-modified head*
dining-car service	pocket address book
state school pupils	*The Observer* book reviews
two-litre plastic jug	Italian graduate students
hard-boiled eggs	Australian ostrich eggs

In fact, both head and classifier may be sub-modified: Human Rights Select Committee; two hard-boiled Australian ostrich eggs.

Such combinations reflect cultural realities. In everyday contexts as well as in more specialised areas of knowledge and activity, there is a tendency in English to 'encapsulate' experiences, devices and phenomena of all kinds into short but complex NGs. The 'telescoped' effect of such ordered sequences means that, on a first encounter, not only non-native speakers but also natives sometimes have to put in some inferencing to work out the semantic relations.

In medical, political and other institutionalised contexts, the NG is often represented as an acronym, that is, initial letters which themselves are pronounced as a word, or, if that is not possible, as initials:

NATO: North Atlantic Treaty Organisation
AIDS: Acquired Immune Deficiency Syndrome
TEFL   Teaching English as a Foreign Language
VIP: Very Important Person

Note that with reference to the AIDS sequence, 'Acquired' does not modify 'Immune' but 'Immune Deficiency'.

48.8 MIXED PRE-MODIFIERS AND THEIR ORDERING

Between the head of a NG and the other elements, there is one basic logical relationship, that of successive dependency: leftwards from the head to the pre-head elements and rightwards in the case of the post-head elements, as indicated by the arrows in the following example:

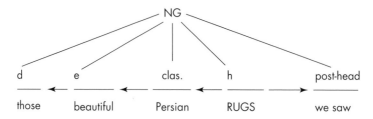

Within this logical framework, speakers seem to use semantic criteria, based on degrees of permanence and objectivity, to decide the order of pre-modifiers. Those properties perceived as permanent, intrinsic and undisputed are placed nearest the head of the nominal group. Those that are more variable, subjective or attitudinal are placed further from the head.

Immediately to the left of the head is the classifier, since this is the closest relationship, as in *Persian* rugs, *radio* programme, *park* entrance, *leather* suitcases.

Where there is more than one classifier, affiliation precedes substance as in *German leather* suitcases, *Indian lamb* curry. If there is no affiliation, substance precedes other classifiers (*steel medical* instrument, *cotton gardening* gloves).

The next place, moving to the left, is occupied by colour adjectives, and before them come any participial modifiers (*battered brown* German leather suitcases, *stained blue* plumbers' overalls). Preceding these are the most central adjectives, such as *tall, young, long, hot* (for ordering of these, see 48.3). At the start of the list are the attitudinal adjectives – such as *beautiful, ugly, marvellous, horrible, nice, nasty* – after any determinatives. This is the unmarked order, which causes us to say:

a large oil tanker   and not *an oil large tanker
increased income tax rebates and not *income increased tax rebates

| a beautiful blue silk scarf | and not *a silk beautiful blue scarf |
| a nice hot Indian curry | and not *a hot Indian nice curry |

Participial modifiers can occupy various positions. Those that are verbal nouns, such as *gardening* in *gardening gloves*, always stay close to the head noun, whereas those that have become gradable adjectives, such as *interested*, *bored*, *exciting*, may occur nearer the determinative, if there is one. If the participial seems to have an evaluative tinge, it is even more likely to precede other adjectives:

interested foreign spectators
an exciting new adventure story
a battered old leather suitcase

IDENTIFYING AND ELABORATING THE REFERENT

MODULE 49

The post-modifier

SUMMARY

1   The post-modifier elements of the nominal group either provide information that helps to identify the referent of the nominal group, or else they add supplementary information not essential for identifying it.

2   Most of the units (clauses, phrases, groups) which occur in post-head position of the NG can be either **restrictive** (integrated) or **non-restrictive** (supplementive). Restrictive post-modifier units are embedded in the structure of the NG and have the function of helping to identify the referent of the NG among other possible referents. Non-restrictive units are not embedded in the NG structure. Their function is to add supplementary information to a referent which is already defined. These units are classed as **supplementives**.

3   The post-modifier is realised by a wide variety of units, including the following, which are here used restrictively:

PPs	the house *on the corner*, a new album *by a top musician*
finite relative clauses	the man *who is standing in the corridor*
non-finite relative clauses	the man *standing in the corridor* (-*ing* cl.) the man *to consult* is Jones (*to*-inf. cl.) the fax *sent this morning* (-*en* cl.)
adj or adjG	a room *full of furniture*; the *best* hotel *available*
adverb	the flat *upstairs*
apposition NG	my friend *the doctor*
reflexive pronoun	the doctor *himself*

4   Complements of nouns are a different type of post-modifier element.

49.1 COMMUNICATIVE FUNCTIONS OF THE POST-MODIFIER ELEMENTS

The post-modifier elements have two basic communicative functions:

(a) to supply information enabling the hearer/reader to specify and identify the person or thing referred to by the NG, as in:

    1   This is the house *where the Prime Minister lives.*

(b) to add supplementary information about the referent when it has already been identified, as in:

    2   This is Number 10 Downing Street, *where the Prime Minister lives.*

These two roles or functions are encoded as restrictive (or defining) and non-restrictive (or non-defining) units, respectively. In **1**, the restrictive type, the clause *where the Prime Minister lives* is integrated (embedded) within the nominal group structure. Its function is to identify the house where the Prime Minister lives from all other possible houses.

When the referent is already identified or assumed to be known, as in **2**, the non-restrictive unit is subordinate but not embedded. Its function is to add descriptive, supplementary information. Thus the same clause *where the Prime Minister lives* does not identify the house where the Prime Minister lives in **2**, because Number 10, Downing Street is already identified or assumed to be known. Rather, it makes a linked, but separate assertion and has the status of a supplementive.

The difference between the two types of unit is marked both prosodically and in writing. Restrictive units such as **1** are not separated from their antecedent by either pauses or punctuation. By contrast, non-restrictive units are usually written between commas, dashes or brackets and pronounced between short pauses as separate information units (33.2). Punctuation is not a hundred per cent reliable, however and it is possible that prosodic features such as pauses are not generalised either. We shall see further distinguishing characteristics in the section on relative clauses (49.3)

49.2 RESTRICTIVE AND NON-RESTRICTIVE REALISATIONS OF THE POST-MODIFIER

Most of the various units that occur as post-modifiers or as complements of the noun (see p. 348 and Module 50) can be either restrictive or non-restrictive. We shall look at each type in turn, starting with the restrictive.

Restrictive (embedded) realisations of the post-modifier

The post-modifier is realised by a wide range of units, including clauses, phrases and groups.

Type of unit	Example
1 finite relative clause	Perhaps the people *who were waiting* are still there.

2 non-finite clauses

    to-infinitive clauses   It's time *to say good night*; there's nothing *to eat*

    -ing clause   an envelope *containing a white powdery substance*

    -en clause   spring water *bottled in the Malvern hills*

3 prepositional phrase   a policeman *on a motor-cycle*; a new album *by a top musician*

4 adjectival group   a box *full of screwdrivers and spanners*

5 adverbial group   the Prime Minister's speech *yesterday*

6 appositive NG   our son *Barney*; the explorer *Marco Polo*

7 reflexive pronoun   the Americans *themselves*

8 noun complement clause   expectations *that we'll win the Cup*; their plans *to go on strike*

9 PP complement   reliance on public transport; a threat to our security

Non-restrictive (supplementive) realisations of the post-head element

1 finite relative clause   A meeting was arranged with the gypsies, *who were allowed to stay until the 24th of July*

                                                      [BNC BPK 1301]

2 non-finite clauses

    -ing clause   . . . and the taps, *gleaming as gold*, were surrounded by a platoon of little bottles and cases, *all matching*   [BNC ECU 2433]

    -en clause   the enormous volume, *dedicated to his wife*, lay on the desk

3 prepositional phrase   The departure time, *at 5 a.m.*, was uncomfortably early.

4 adjectival group   and he opened out the big, blue toolbox, *full of screwdrivers and spanners*

5 circumstantial clause   We were all just trying to get through high school so we could hurry up and get to college, *where, we'd heard, things were better*

                                                   (*All American Girl*)

6 appositive NG   our youngest son, *Barney*; Marco Polo, *the explorer*

7 verbless clause   and the Minister, *himself a Quaker*, made no objection

8 complement clause   her life-long wish, *to own a horse*, was at last fulfilled

Complements of nouns, whether restrictive or non-restrictive, differ from post-modifiers in being controlled by the noun and are dealt with separately in Module 50.

49.3 FINITE RELATIVE CLAUSES AS POST-MODIFIERS

49.3.1 The relativisers

Finite relative clauses are introduced by a relative pronoun or adverb (called a **relativiser**). English uses several different relativisers: *who, whom, whose, which, that, where, when, why* and zero (0). The relativiser refers back to the head of the nominal group, which is termed the **antecedent**, for example, 'people' in *the people who were waiting*.

Who (objective ***whom***) is used after an animate, particularly a human, head noun. The relativiser *who* is not omitted when it functions as subject in the relative clause:

> Perhaps the people *who were waiting* are still there. (perhaps **the people were waiting are still there*)

The only exceptions are introduced by unstressed *there* or by a cleft. They are on the borderline between dialectal and very colloquial speech, and are not obligatory uses:

> There's a man outside (0) wants to speak to you.
> It was John (0) told me about you.

Whom is always used when it directly precedes a preposition, as in **1**. This is a formal use. In less formal speech and writing *whom* is commonly avoided by 'stranding' the preposition (see 6.3.3) and replacing *whom* by *who*, *that* or *zero*, as in **2**. Compare:

> **1**   the students *with whom I share a flat*.
> **2**   the students *who I share a flat with/ that I share a flat with/ (0) I share a flat with*

Which is used with inanimate heads in both subject and object functions in the relative clause, and before a preposition. The same alternatives are open for *which* as for *whom*:

> the matter *which concerns us at present* (subject)
> there is one matter *which I must bring up* (object)
> Their life was one *for which she was unprepared*. (following a preposition)
> Their life was one *that/ which/ (0) she was unprepared for*.

That is used in both subject and object functions and for both animate and inanimate heads in integrated relative clauses. It is a useful alternative to *who(m)* and *which* when the speaker prefers to avoid the animate–inanimate distinction:

> The large Alsatian *that* lives next door is rather fierce.

However, *that* is not normally used after a personal proper name, as such a use is typically non-restrictive (see below). Neither is *that* used following a preposition.

As a relative pronoun, *that* is more common than *which* in spoken and in much written English, but *which* is said to be more common than *that* in academic writing. When the antecedent is a demonstrative pronoun, *that* tends to be avoided (*What's that* [that] *you have there?*), zero being preferred over both *that* and *which* (*What's that* [0] *you have there?*). When the antecedent is an indefinite pronoun, *that* is more common than *which* in subject function (*Anything that might happen . . .*) whereas zero is common in object function (*Everything* [0] *we know . . .*).

Zero (that is, the non-use of the relative pronouns *whom, which* or *that*) is common practice when these pronouns function as object in the relative clause. Compare the various options, ranging from most formal to informal, in the following example:

the girl *to whom I lent my coat*
the girl *whom I lent my coat to*
the girl *that I lent my coat to*
the girl (0) *I lent my coat to*

When and **where** as relativisers introduce circumstantial information, of time and place respectively: the place *where he was born*; the time *when he's sure to be at home*.

Why occurs as a relative only after the noun 'reason' and the like – cause, explanation, excuse: There's no reason *why we shouldn't be friends*.

Whose is the possessive form and is used not only to refer to animate head nouns but also to inanimates, as a shorter alternative to *of which* + *determiner*.

children *whose parents both go out to work*
the houses *whose roofs were in need of repair*.

49.3.2 Features of the restrictive relative clause

The restrictive relative integrates with the head noun together with its pre-modifiers to form a larger unit, syntactically, prosodically and semantically.

- Syntactically it is embedded in the NG matrix structure.
- Prosodically, it shares the intonation contour of its antecedent, as the two together constitute one information unit:
  They admitted the immigrants *who had their papers in order*. (= only the immigrants who had their papers in order)
- Semantically, the restrictive relative is an integral part of the meaning of the whole nominal group. It helps to establish what (or whom) the speaker is talking about. It picks out the referent(s) from other possible referents by some distinguishing property; in this case, that only the immigrants who had their papers in order were admitted.
- The larger NG unit with its relative clause can be expanded by a further relative clause:

  The umbrella[1] *we bought*[2] *that has a duck's head handle* made a good present.

Restrictive relatives are not common after proper names, as their referents are normally already identified. However, they can serve to distinguish between two referents with the same name (by treating them as common nouns), as in:

Do you mean the Toledo *which is in Spain* or *the Toledo in the United States?*

49.3.3 Features of the non-restrictive relative clause

Unlike restrictive (integrated) relative clauses, non-restrictive relative clauses are not embedded in the matrix nominal group. Although they are marked as subordinate by a relativiser, they are parentheticals which have considerable semantic independence.

Prosodically, they don't share the intonation contour of the matrix clause. Instead, they have their own intonation contour, which constitutes an independent information unit:

> They admitted the immigrants, *who had their papers in order.*

They don't identify one referent from other possible referents. The antecedent is already restricted and the clause is complete. *The immigrants* is a delimited subset of immigrants.

Consequently, unlike integrated relatives, non-restrictive relatives can have as antecedent a proper noun or name which identifies a particular person or persons, object(s) or institution(s). The pronouns used are *who, whom, whose* and *which*, rarely *that*:

> I'll give the CD to Ben, *who* likes music. (*that likes music)
> The injured child was taken to Alderhey Children's Hospital, *which* is in Wavertree.

Semantically, the non-restrictive clause is not an integral part of the NG. As the antecedent is already defined, the supplementive provides additional new information which is not essential, but may explain or elaborate on the content of the previous clause.

When placed medially, the non-restrictive relative is enclosed:

> Plans for the new airport, *which will cope with ten times the present air traffic*, are now under way.
> You would think that my dad, *who is an international economist with the World Bank*, would understand this. (*All American Girl*)

It makes an independent statement, which is an extension of the already complete unit. As such, non-restrictive relatives are increasingly found functioning as freestanding subordinate clauses, which may initiate a new paragraph in written discourse. (See also 33.2 for spoken examples of 'sentential' relatives, whose antecedent is the whole clause.)

> And into the room walked David, the President's son.
> *Who also happened to be David from my drawing class with Susan Boone.*
> (*All American Girl*)

49.4 NON-FINITE RELATIVE CLAUSES AS POST-MODIFIERS

-ing clauses and -en clauses

> He wrote a book *containing his reminiscences of five U.S. Presidents.*
> The book also described his own life as a press officer *serving them in the White House.* (*Libra*, journal of Foyle's Ltd)

The value of these restrictive *-ing* clauses is similar to that of a finite relative clause: *a book that contained . . . a press officer who had served them.* However, in such cases, the participle is not to be interpreted as an abbreviated progressive, as is proved by the fact that *contain* is a state verb and does not combine with the progressive: **the book was containing.* As we saw in Chapter 7, the *-ing* form is, in many constructions, an economical resource for expressing relationships where tense or aspect do not need to be further specified.

This property of the *-ing*, as also the *-en* clauses, which are always passive, is particularly evident in their non-restrictive function as supplementives.

-ing clauses	He was sent several letters, *all containing a white, powdery substance.*
	The stained-glass windows, *illustrating biblical scenes*, are splendid.
-ed-clauses	The enormous volume, *dedicated to his wife*, lay on the desk.

to-infinitive clauses – nothing to fear

As post-modifiers, *to*-infinitive clauses can correspond to full relative clauses in which the relative pronoun is S, Od or C:

S   The next train *to arrive at Platform 5* is the express train to York
   (= the train *which/that will arrive*)

Od   They have nothing to eat. (= nothing *which* they can eat)
   The man *to consult* is Jones. (= the man *whom/that* you should consult is Jones)

C   The commonest kind of worker *to become nowadays* is an unemployed one.
   (= The commonest kind of worker *that one can become*)

49.5 OTHER TYPES OF UNIT AS POST-MODIFIERS

49.5.1 Prepositional phrases

This is by far the commonest class of circumstantial post-modifier used in English NGs. It is also the most economical. The listed examples are all restrictive, except the last, which is non-restrictive (supplementive):

the concert on Monday   a clown with a red nose
the plane from Oslo   a job for the experts
a ticket to Paris   the man in the dark suit
the end of the story   the back wheels of the car
The departure time, *at 5 o'clock in the morning*, was uncomfortably early for most
    passengers. (non-restrictive)

Multiple PP post-modifiers can be either coordinated or embedded:
The path over the cliffs and down to the beach. (coordinated)
Those books [on the top shelf [of the bookcase [in my bedroom]]]. (embedded)

49.5.2 Adjectival groups

Single adjectives are rarely used as post-modifiers and are limited to the following types:

- a small number of fixed expressions, the relic of a French structure: a court *martial*,
  the devil *incarnate*, from time *immemorial*;
- after certain pronominal heads: those *present*, something *nice*, nobody *interesting*;
- adjectives placed after a modified noun head, but which modify the modifier, not
  the head: *the worst time possible* = the worst possible, not *the time possible. The
  close relationship between *worst* and *possible* is shown by the possibility of placing
  them together as an epithet: *the worst possible time.*

Adjectival group post-modifiers usually contain their own modifier elements:

We chose the solution *most likely to succeed*.
He always wore socks *full of holes*.

In supplementive verbless clauses, coordinated or post-modified adjectives are said
to be more acceptable than single ones. Thus, the single adjective in **1** is less likely than
the longer, coordinated structure in **2**:

1   The other candidates, *confident*, all passed the test.
2   The other candidates, *confident and well-prepared*, all passed the test.

But see the following extract from an article by Jeremy Clarkson in *The Sunday
Times*, which illustrates the use of various supplementive units. Adjectival groups are
underlined:

> **Here's a game you might like to try next time you're in America. Go into a Denny's
> restaurant and see if you can order breakfast in such a way that the waitress can
> ask no supplementary questions.**
>   **It's very hard. Denny's offers a vast range of everything, *all of which can be
> cooked in ways you haven't even dreamed of*. Take eggs: they can be soft-boiled,**

> hard-boiled, scrambled, sunny-side up, sunny-side down, easy over, over easy, easy easy, over there or poached. So you have to be specific.
>
> 'Hello, I'd like a table, <u>wooden preferably</u>, *for two*, *in the smoking section*, and I would like to eat four rashers of bacon, <u>crispy</u>, two eggs, *sunny-side up*, rye bread, sausages, no grits, no water, no hash browns, and coffee, *with milk*, <u>semi-skimmed</u>, and two level teaspoons of sugar, *not sweetener*.'
>
> You'll sit back, <u>confident that</u> <u>you've covered all the bases</u>. But you haven't, have you? You didn't say whether you wanted sausage links or sausage patties, and the waitress is going to pounce on that. So you lose.

49.5.3 Adverbial groups

Adverbial group heads used to post-modify nouns express notions such as space, time and reason. In many cases they may be analysed as ellipted adverbial groups or clauses:

place:	Is this the way *out?*
time:	He came, and left the week *after.*
reason:	She fell out with her sister, but I never knew the reason *why.*

Relative adverbial clauses as post-modifiers

The relative adverbs *where, when* and *why* introduce clauses which post-modify nouns denoting places, times or reasons. *Where* and *when* have corresponding supplementive uses. The examples with *why*, however, do not correspond in function. In **3b** *why* is a supplementive headless relative in apposition with 'the mystery'.

Restrictive	**Supplementive**
1a She took her degree at the university *where she was studying.*	1b She took her degree at London University, *where she was studying.*
2a The week *when the exams take place*, I intend to be ill.	2b The week after, *when the exams took place*, I was ill.
3a The reason *why I ask* is very simple.	3b And the mystery, *why the numbers were changed*, was never solved.

The relative adverbs *when* and *why*, but rarely *where*, can be replaced by *that* or *zero* in restrictive clauses:

> In the week (*that*) the exams take place . . .
> The reason (*that*) I ask you . . .
> The town where I was born but not *The town that I was born.

Zero is also common after the head noun *way*: That's not the way (0) we do it here.

49.5.4 Appositive nominal groups

The closest post-modifying relationship is that between the head of a NG and an appositive unit, that is, a nominal unit that has the same referent. The relation between them and the head noun may be integrated (*my friend the doctor* . . .) or supplementive (*my friend, the doctor I told you about* . . .).

The following are some of the appositive relationships these may express:

definition:	My friend the doctor.
naming:	The explorer Marco Polo.
role:	Thierry Henry, Arsenal's leading goal-scorer.
description:	Chivalry, the dominant idea of the medieval ruling classes, was symbolised by the Round Table, nature's perfect shape.
particularisation:	The members voted for a change in the statutes: *the election of the chairman by popular vote.*
identity:	We British; Me Tarzan, you Jane.

49.6 MIXED REALISATIONS OF THE POST-MODIFIER

Post-modification of the noun head can be realised by a wide variety of units, including clauses. Futhermore, the units can freely expanded. When units of different types are used, a common-sense criterion is to avoid ambiguous or incongruent sequences.

The following is an example of a pronominal head ('something') which has as post-modifier a single finite relative clause, some of whose elements are realised more than once. Embedding is indicated here by a bracket, and coordination by '+':

The other night, on television, I saw SOMETHING [which reminded me of the Spaniards [going into South America + and advancing over the mountains + and terrifying the population with terrible new weapons, + cannon + and the horse [which nobody [in their world] had ever seen]]].

A different organisation of successive post-modification is used in the following sentence which describes a system of grants which, sadly, no longer holds in the UK. In the sentence each of the two NGs, EVERY STUDENT and A GRANT, is post-modified by three coordinated units: AdjG + PP + non-restrictive relative clause in the case of the first, and PP + two relative clauses in the case of the second. Three of these six modifiers contain embedded units of their own:

Virtually every STUDENT
    [normally resident in England or Wales],
    [with specified minimum qualifications],
    [who is admitted to a full-time degree, [at a university [in the UK]]]
is entitled to a GRANT
    [from his/ her Local Education Authority],
    [which is intended to cover his/ her TUITION FEES AND MAINTENANCE
      [for the duration [of the course]
    [and which also includes AN ELEMENT [towards his/ her vacation maintenance.]]

Ambiguity

The relation between two post-modifying units may be potentially ambiguous in NGs such as *Those books on the table which you bought*, which can represent two different structures:

coordinated   Those books [on the table] [which you bought.]
embedded   Those books on the table [which you bought].

In reverse order – Those *books which you bought on the table* – the meaning can only be guessed.

In writing, the solution is to punctuate the parenthesis:

Those books, that you bought, on the table . . .

In spoken English, the most likely form is:

Those BOOKS you bought | on the table | . . .

This would be understood as

[Those books [that] you bought, [the ones] on the table, . . .

NOUN COMPLEMENT CLAUSES   *MODULE 50*

SUMMARY

1   A different type of post-head element is the complement clause, which is controlled by head nouns.

2   The two main types of noun complement clause are *that*-clauses and *to*-infinitive clauses. Less common types are *of* + *-ing* clauses and *wh*- complement clauses. Adjectives which control clausal and prepositional complements are dealt with in Module 53.

50.1 FEATURES OF THE *THAT*-COMPLEMENT CLAUSE

Although they look superficially similar to relative clauses, they are in fact quite different. The *that*-clause which complements the noun is a **content clause**, not a relative clause.

That is not normally omitted from complement clauses. Compare:

> The news *(that) we received* was worse than expected. (relative clause, admits zero)
> The news *that the President had fled the country* was expected. (complement clause)
> ?The news (0) the President had fled the country was expected. (zero not common)

While relative clauses can modify all types of nouns, complement clauses are dependent on a relatively small number of abstract nouns, such as *fact, belief, suggestion, hope, idea, expectation, wish*. These can take a content clause as dependent, whereas general nouns such as *house, bicycle, institution* take only relative clauses.

The content clause expresses the whole content of the head noun, as in: the news *that the President had fled the country*, his belief *that he was always right*.

The nominal groups taking noun complements tend to be definite and singular, as illustrated in the present examples.

Head nouns that take complement clauses are mainly nominalisations which have corresponding verbs or adjectives, though a few are simple. Here is a sample:

with a corresponding verb:	knowledge, belief, assumption, claim, thought, report, hope, reply, wish, proof, guess, expectation, suggestion, intuition, hypothesis
with a corresponding adjective:	awareness, confidence, probability, eagerness, possibility, likelihood
simple:	fact, story, idea, news, message, rumour

The fact *that inflation is going down* is a sign *that our economy is improving*.
The possibility *that they might be beaten* never crossed their minds.
His *suggestion* that the meeting be postponed was accepted. (cf. He suggested that . . .)

The function of the *that*-complement clause is to report a proposition (*that inflation is going down, that they might be beaten*) derived from the previous discourse. The head noun represents the proposition in a particular light, which conveys different types of stance, depending on the noun used: nouns of cognition and reasoning: *knowledge, belief, idea, assumption, hypothesis, conclusion*; speech-act nouns, such as *suggestion, proposal, claim*; personal assessment: *possibility, doubt, fact, fear, hope, chance*, or the source of knowledge (*evidence, rumour*) (see 8.2.5 for epistemic, evidential and evaluative stance).

Stance in complement clauses is much less direct than in *that*-clauses following a verb, such as 'he believes that . . . etc.' (see 11.1). Furthermore, as the head noun often takes the form of a nominalisation and is typically definite, it presents the following proposition as Given information and therefore beyond dispute. These factors make the complement clause a useful tool in argumentation.

Noun complement clauses occur mainly in formal written and spoken English. They are not at all common in conversation.

The following lines from *The Sunday Times* about social systems in the Pacific Islands illustrate this type of complement:

> **No culture has failed to seize upon the conspicuous facts of sex and age in some way, whether it be *the convention* of one Philippine tribe *that no man can keep a secret*, the Manus' *assumption* that only men enjoy playing with babies, or the Toda *belief* that almost all domestic work is too sacred for women.**

Noun complement clauses can also be used non-restrictively following a relative clause that post-modifies the same noun:

The rumour *that was circulating, that the Chancellor was about to resign*, proved to be false.

50.2 *TO*-INFINITIVE COMPLEMENT CLAUSES

Head nouns which take *to*-infinitive complement clauses are likewise often related to a verb or an adjective and include the following:

de-verbal:	attempt, decision, desire, failure, plan, tendency, permission
de-adjectival:	ability, inability, right, capacity
simple:	chance, effort, opportunity

The function of *to*-infinitive complements is to point to human acts or goals, as in:

attempts to trump up facts and evidence
failure to warn the students in advance
plans to build a new underpass

To-infinitive complements must be distinguished from PP complements with the preposition *to*. The following quotation illustrates the difference:

The global threat *to our security* was clear.   (PP complement = x threatened our security)
So was our duty *to act* to eliminate it. (*to*-infinitive complement)
                        (PM Tony Blair's speech on the threat of international terrorism,
                                                              5 March 2004)

50.3 *OF* + *-ING* COMPLEMENT CLAUSES

Head nouns which take *-ing* followed by *of* complement clauses include: *thought, habit, importance, way, effect, danger, risk*

There is overlap with the *to*-infinitive construction in that some nouns (*idea, way, possibility, thought, hope*) can take either of these constructions as complement, besides taking a relative clause with *that* as post-modifier:

The risk *of losing* your way in the forest/*that* you might lose your way. (comp.)
The possibility *of not being rescued*/*that* you might not be rescued. (comp.)
The risk/possibility *that* you told us about was very real. (restrictive relative clause)

50.4 *WH*-COMPLEMENT CLAUSES

A further type of post-head complement is the *wh*-clause. It is most common when following the preposition *of* or *about*. Both finite clauses and non-finite *to*-infinitive clauses can occur:

The question (of) *how much we should spend on our holidays* . . .
He has strong doubts (about) *whether he should accept the post.*

The question (of) *how much to spend on our holidays* . . .
He has strong doubts (about) *whether to accept the post.*

50.5 PREPOSITIONAL COMPLEMENTS OF NOUNS

These are typically controlled by nouns which have corresponding verbs:

A desire *for* fame	x desires fame
Reliance *on* public transport	x relies on public transport
A lack *of* knowledge	x lacks knowledge

The preposition *of*, however, is controlled by many nouns which are not related to verbs: *advantage, danger, effect, importance, means, method, problem, purpose, task, way.*

The following extract from David Lodge's novel *The British Museum is Falling Down* illustrates the use of certain types of post-modifier and complement:

> . . . the Department did not have the resources *to mount a proper graduate programme,*[1] and in any case espoused the traditional belief *that research was a lonely and eremitic occupation,*[2] a test *of*[3] character rather than learning, which might be vitiated by excessive human contact.[4] As if they sensed this, the new postgraduates, *particularly those from overseas,*[5] roamed the floor accosting the senior guests. As he left the bar with his first sherry, Adam was snapped up by a cruising Indian:
> 'How do you do', said Mr Alibai.
> 'How do you do', said Adam, *who knew what was expected of him.*[6]
>
> [1]inf. cl. modifier; [2]*that*-cl. complement; [3]prep *of* complement; [4]non-restrictive relative clause; [5]supp. appositive, narrowing down the referent to a smaller group; [6]non-restrictive relative clause

50.6 FUNCTIONS OF THE NOMINAL GROUP

In clauses, NGs can realise any structural element except the Predicator. At group rank they can be embedded in PPs as complements of the preposition and in NGs as pre- or post-modifiers, or as supplementives, of the head element. Here are examples of the functions that can be realised by a simple NG such as *the best player available.*

NGs as clause elements

The best player available was a Brazilian.   **S**

The committee engaged *the best player available.*   **Od**

They offered *the best player available* a high salary.   **Oi**
Ronaldo seemed to be *the best player available*.   **Cs**
Everybody considered him *the best player available*.   **Co**
He signed the contract *last week*.   **A**

NGs as group elements

They paid a high price for *the best player available*.   **c**
The best player-available topic was not discussed   **pre-modifier**
Ronaldo, *the best player available*, earns a high salary.   **Appos. sup.**

50.7 NOMINALISATION

In many professional registers, above all in written genres, the use of **nominalisation** has become extremely common. Superficially, it consists of the use of a nominal form, such as 'starvation' in the following text, instead of the corresponding verb 'starve', from which the nominal is derived. Other examples from the text are:

accuracy   derived from the adjective 'accurate'
explanation   derived from 'explain'
increase   has the same form as the verb 'increase'
speed   has the same form as the verb 'speed'

It has been known for nearly a century that *starvation for about two weeks*[1] increases *the speed and accuracy of mental processes*,[2] *especially mental arithmetic*.[3] This is probably *the explanation of the huge increase in self-starvation among young women doing academic work*.[4] *An extreme form of this condition known as 'anorexia nervosa'*[5] is now common and *our studies*[6] have shown that in *75% of cases*[7] they start *crash-dieting*[8] in *the year in which they are working for a major examination*.[9]

It is clear that nominalisation is no mere substitute for a verb or adjective, however. Instead, the use of a nominalised expression requires an entirely different organisation of the whole sentence, and indeed a completely different semantic conceptualisation. (This is discussed in Chapter 5.) In this way, a great deal of information, which would otherwise be expressed as verbs, adjectives and PPs, is packed into the nominal groups. The result is very long, dense NGs, which tend to be abstractions, instead of referring to concrete persons who act as Agents. In fact, personal participant subjects in heavily nominalised styles tend to be no longer the head of the NG.

A non-nominalised equivalent of the first four NGs in the extract above might look something like this:

> 1 If you/people starve for about two weeks, 2 you/they think faster and more accurately, 3 especially when doing arithmetic; 4 This probably explains why young women who are doing academic work starve themselves.

One reason for the use of nominalisation is that it is shorter than the non-nominalised form. More important, the nominalised form encapsulates a whole situation in one word, such as 'self-starvation', 'crash-dieting'. Because density and brevity prevail over clarity, heavy nominalisation can become difficult to understand in unfamiliar contexts. For those familiar with the subject-matter, on the other hand, nominalisation provides them with a kind of shorthand by which complex concepts and processes are easily handled without further explanation. All adult speakers of English handle at least some specialised registers such as education, business, football, etc. and pick up nominalised expressions such as 'infant primary schools' or 'mixed comprehensive schools'. Such expressions become relatively fixed until new cultural developments give rise to new combinations – something which is happening in all areas of life.

FURTHER READING

Some of the ideas presented in the revised version of this chapter are indebted to the following publications: for ordering of pre-modifiers, Quirk et al. (1985); for supplementive units and noun clause complements, Biber et al. (1999), Huddleston and Pullum (2000); for experiential and interpersonal meanings, subjective and objective epithet, Halliday (1994); for frequencies of occurrence, see Biber et al. (1999).

EXERCISES ON CHAPTER 10

Talking about people and things: The Nominal Group

Module 45

1   †Identify all the nominal groups in the following examples. Remember that NGs may have other units embedded in their structure, especially in post-head position. Identify the head of each NG:

(1)   Everyone in the library was concentrating on what they were doing.
(2)   There were old men reading newspapers and there were high-school boys and girls doing research.
(3)   The outcome of the current crisis would determine the pattern of international relations for the next generation.
(4)   Someone here once told me a story about the most notorious of the dictators who ruled this country at the turn of the century.   [BNC BMR 1298]

(5)   The seat on my left was occupied by a fat lady who was busy peeling an orange. On my right was a thin-faced man with a moustache and a blotchy skin. He was the one who gave a friendly smile and a cheery 'Good evening!' I nodded amiably

[BNC BN3 1700–1703]

(6)   The violent attacks on the police by the counter-demonstrators who used bottles, bricks, and other assorted missiles resulted in a large number of casualties.

[BNC BNE 191]

2   †Underline the nominal groups marked in the following text based on an advert, and then write each one out in three parts as for the description of the art sale in 45.1:

Fit, fun, funky, single parent seeks gorgeous, good-humoured, intelligent, London-based man interested in a loving and lasting relationship

3   Complete the following advertisement for an 'au pair' in the country where you live, using NGs different from those in task 2:

Young married couple need _ _ _ _ _ _ _ _ _ _ _ _ _ with _ _ _ _ _ _ _ _ _ _ _ _ _ and _ _ _ _ _ _ _ _ _ _ _ _ _ Applicant must have _ _ _ _ _ _ _ _ _ _ _ _ _ as well as _ _ _ _ _ _ _ _ _ _ _ _ The family consists of _ _ _ _ _ _ _ _ _ _ _ _ _.

4   In the form of full NGs, write the continuation of this advertisement for your college notice board beginning as follows: Penniless student offers the following articles for urgent sale:

_ _ _ _ _ _ _ _ _ _ _ _ _

5   †In the following conversation, Neil is telling his friend Dennis about the bad relations existing between him and his wife Pamela. Dennis is having some difficulty in following him. After reading the passage, answer the questions on the numbered pronouns:

NEIL: . . . You see, my trouble – Pam's trouble – is *this.*[1] I think *we*[2] both expect things from *each other.*[3] Things that *the other one*[4] is not prepared to give – to *the other one.*[4] Do you get me?

DENNIS: Uh – huh.

NEIL: I suppose *it's*[5] nature really, isn't it?

DENNIS: Ah.

NEIL: *You*[6] have your opposites – like *this*[7] (he holds up his hands). *This*[8] is *me*[9] – *that's*[10] *her.*[11] And *they*[12] attract – like a magnet. Only with people, as opposed to magnets, the trouble is with people – *they*[13] get demagnetised after a bit. I honestly think Pam and *me*[14] have reached the end of the road.

(1)   Explain the type of reference carried out by each of the numbered pronouns.
(2)   Comment on the use of the objective pronouns *me,*[9] *her*[11] and *me.*[14]

6   †Read the following news item and then answer the questions:

> Health workers in two Birmingham hospitals went on strike yesterday after one of their members had been dismissed. About 300 laundry staff and kitchen staff walked out, and within a few hours, their colleagues at the city's main maternity and children's units had stopped work in sympathy. *This* has caused disruption to all areas of health care and forced the cancellation of operations.

  (1)   If somebody asked you: *This what?* what would you answer?
  (2)   How would you analyse *This?*

Module 46

1a   †Are the NGs in the following examples interpreted as mass or count?

  (1)   I haven't time[1] to go to the gym[2] these days. But I'm really keen on gym.[3]
  (2)   The only things my sister likes are fashion[4] and shopping.[5]
  (3)   I'll see you in class[6] on Tuesday – unless, of course, I'm moved to a different class.[7]
  (4)   My agent will be handling my appearance[8] in the show next week.
  (5)   Cynthia and I are going over to Jean's this evening to do our homework[9] together.
  (6)   My sister's boy-friend is really good at football.[10]

1b   †Say which of these NGs (apart from those in sentences 2 and 3 could be used in the other sense. Make sentences to illustrate your answer.

2   †Read the following passage by Valentina Tereshkova, the first woman in space, and say whether you interpret each NG as count or mass:

> It is deep in *one's nature* to expect or not to expect *material comfort* and it starts as a *habit* in *childhood*. That is why I did not find *the cosmonaut's denial* of *terrestrial comforts* difficult.
>   The space flight was like being born again – not only the *satisfaction* of *the scientific achievement*, but also *the impact* of seeing how fragile *our planet looks* from *outer space*. It is so beautiful. I wish I could be a *painter*. *The sight* convinced me that we must treat it kindly and that *humanity* must have *the common sense* never to let *atomic flames* engulf it. All *cosmonauts* feel like *members* of *one family* but *my space experience* inspired me to see *the people who live on our planet* also as one family.

3   †The article *the* indicates that the referent of a noun is being presented as definite, and can be identified either somewhere in the text or from our general knowledge. Read the following short paragraph from Mario Puzzi's *The Godfather* and then do the exercise given below.

> The Don was a real man at the age of twelve. Short, dark, slender, living in the strange Moorish-looking village of Corleone in Sicily, he had been born Vito Andolini, but when strange men came to kill the son of the man they had murdered, his mother sent the young boy to America to stay with friends. And in the new land he changed his name to Corleone to preserve some tie with his native village. It was one of the few gestures of sentiment he was ever to make.

(1) Write out the definite nouns in the text and say how each one is identified, within the text or outside it.

(2) Write out the indefinite nouns in the text, and say how their indefiniteness is marked,

e.g. *The Don*: The article forms part of a proper noun and proper nouns are inherently definite.
the age: Identified by the qualifying information *of twelve*.
a real man: Marked by *a* as an indefinite-specific count noun.

4 †In this first paragraph of a short story by Philip Smith, *The Wedding Jug*, all the 'things' mentioned are presented as definite. How does the reader identify them?

> I stood at *the* backdoor and looked up at *the* moon. Its brightness from over *the* dark hump of *the* hillside made clear *the* pale drifting smoke from somebody's garden. *The* wood-smoke and *the* moon made me restless, eager to be moving in *the* sharp October night.

Read the paragraph aloud, replacing *the* and *its* by *a*. Is it possible to do so? If so, how does it change our interpretation of the scene?

5 †The following are generic statements in which the first noun is preceded by a definite or indefinite or zero article. Test each noun for its use with the other two articles, and say whether either of them can also be used to express generic reference.

(1) *A liquid* has no shape.
(2) *Gases* have no mass.
(3) *A human being* needs the company of others.
(4) *War is* politics carried out by violent means.
(5) *Animals* that live in captivity play with their food as if it were a living animal.
(6) *Television is* a mixed blessing.
(7) *The bicycle is* a cheap form of private transport.
(8) *The computer* has revolutionised business methods.

6 †Which of the following statements do you interpret as indefinite and which as generic, according to the definition of genericity given in 46.6?

(1)   *Bicycles* are very useful during a holiday.
(2)   We always hire *bicycles* during our holidays.
(3)   I have *official information* for you.
(4)   *Official information is* usually difficult to obtain.

7 †What are the two possible interpretations of the final noun in the following sentence?

My sister wants to marry *a Frenchman.*

Module 47

1 †What type of semantic function is realised by the 's phrase in each of the following expressions (see 47.2.1)?

(1)   the firm's success
(2)   our team's defeat (by our rivals)
(3)   America's film industry
(4)   today's news
(5)   a stone's throw
(6)   the BBC's director
(7)   the director's orders
(8)   nobody's responsibility
(9)   my bus
(10) cow's milk

2 †Express the following sentences differently, using 's determinatives if you think this structure is acceptable:

(1)   I should like the opinion of another doctor.
(2)   Have you read the report of the chairman of the examination committee?
(3)   The failure of the Regional Training Scheme was inevitable.
(4)   The dog belonging to my next-door neighbour barks all night.
(5)   The grandmother of one of the girls in my class has died.
(6)   Here's the address of the only person I know in London.

3 †Complete each sentence with a suitable determinative of the class indicated on the left:

(1)   (Non-specific): _ _ _ _ _ _ _ _ _ _ _ _ _ – member of our family has a car.
(2)   (Non-exact cardinal): _ _ _ _ _ _ _ _ _ _ _ _ _ My young brother has collected – of butterflies.
(3)   (Non-specific): _ _ _ _ _ _ _ _ _ _ _ _ _ I had – very good news today.
(4)   (Specific) (indef): _ _ _ _ _ _ _ _ _ _ _ _ _ – people wouldn't agree with that opinion.
(5)   (Partitive): _ _ _ _ _ _ _ _ _ _ _ _ _ – of the people in this office have a car.

(6) (Negative): _ _ _ _ _ _ _ _ _ _ _ _ _ – of this work will be wasted.

(7) (Specific comparative): _ _ _ _ _ _ _ _ _ _ _ _ _ You will never have – opportunity again.

(8) (Fractional): _ _ _ _ _ _ _ _ _ _ _ _ my friends have given up smoking.

4 †Complete the following sentences with one of the following: *each, every, both, either, neither, all, any, none, no* (In some cases more than one determinative is possible):

(1) She tells me she plays golf almost _ _ _ _ _ _ _ _ _ _ _ _ weekend.

(2) _ _ _ _ _ _ _ _ _ _ _ _ _ of the brothers applied for the job but _ _ _ _ _ _ _ _ _ _ _ _ was successful.

(3) Draw a line between _ _ _ _ _ _ _ _ _ _ _ _ item and the next.

(4) _ _ _ _ _ _ _ _ _ _ _ _ child should spend some of its leisure time with _ _ _ _ _ _ _ _ _ _ _ _ parent.

(5) There are two good films on the television this evening, but I have seen them _ _ _ _ _ _ _ _ _ _ _ _ _

(6) Ah, in fact there are three and I haven't seen _ _ _ _ _ _ _ _ _ _ _ _ of them/ I have seen _ _ _ _ _ _ _ _ _ _ _ _ _

(7) He has passed _ _ _ _ _ _ _ _ _ _ _ _ exam so far.

(8) _ _ _ _ _ _ _ _ _ _ _ _ type of coffee except the soluble kind will do.

5 †Complete the following sentences with either *all* or *everything*:

(1) If that happened, she would lose her job. It would be the end of _ _ _ _ _ _ _ _ _ _ _ _ _

(2) You need a sports bag to carry _ _ _ _ _ _ _ _ _ _ _ _ _ your things in.

(3) But how much would _ _ _ _ _ _ _ _ _ _ _ _ this cost?

(4) My father paid for _ _ _ _ _ _ _ _ _ _ _ _

(5) They did _ _ _ _ _ _ _ _ _ _ _ _ together and people thought they were twins.

Module 48

1 †Read the following passage from *The Sunday Times* and discuss with another student which NG heads are modified by epithets and which by classifiers. Is any of the post-head information of a classifying type? Test this by the effect on the meaning when the information is omitted.

> **MORE THAN 200 young *Europeans* will assemble in Lisbon's national assembly *building* this weekend to debate *issues* ranging from the need for a common defence *policy* to nuclear *power* and pollution.**
>
> **The *students*, aged between 17 and 19 and chosen after competitions between *schools* throughout the Community, make up the European Youth *Parliament*. How they vote over the coming *week* of activities will reveal much about young people's *attitudes* to major European *questions*.**

2 †The following newspaper advertisement of a job vacancy consists of twelve NGs, in which each head noun is modified by an epithet or a classifier. Identify these and comment on their distribution between the 'essential qualifications' and the 'outstanding benefits'. Can you explain the difference which you will observe?

Essential qualifications
(1) A good examination record at school
(2) Effective self-presentation
(3) Persuasive rapport with others
(4) An optimistic commitment to hard work
(5) Sound judgement
(6) Mental agility

Outstanding benefits offered
(7) A competitive salary
(8) Excellent leave entitlement
(9) Non-contributory pension scheme
(10) Personal home loans
(11) A company car
(12) Career development and training

---

3 Write a letter to a business firm or a public organisation in which you would like to work. Present it in two parts, describing, in the form of Nominal Groups, (a) your qualifications for the job and (b) the working conditions and benefits you would like to receive. Do not use the phrases contained in the example.

4 Choose some of the following nouns and mention three or four subclasses of each general class. Use any form of classifier you wish.

train	machine	department	officer	tree
club	shop	affairs	problems	life

e.g. passenger train, goods train, express train, etc.

5 †Which of the adjectives in the following NGs function as epithets and which as classifiers? Remember that classifiers are non-gradable.

(1) cultural activities   popular activities
(2) a professional attitude   a professional opinion
(3) medical treatment   a medical student
(4) a mechanical engineer   a clever engineer
(5) quick agreement   international agreement
(6) efficient workers   mining workers
(7) electric light   bright light

6 †Consider the order of the epithets and classifiers in the following sentences. Change the order if you think it is necessary, and say why. Insert a coordinator or subordinator where you think it is required, and insert commas where needed (see 48.1).

(1) It was an *unforgettable, heart-breaking sad* sight.
(2) We heard a *tinkling, mysterious, faint* sound.
(3) Her *artistic, slender, long* hands fluttered in the air.
(4) She had a pair of *designer, exotic-looking, smart* sunglasses.
(5) The lavatory was a *wooden, brown, smallish* box inserted in the floor.
(6) We drove through the *granite, wooded, threatening, dark* mountains.

Module 49

1 †In the following sentences. Which NG post-modifiers are integrated (restrictive) and which are supplementive (non-restrictive)?

(1) The morning we were supposed to leave my car broke down.
(2) I didn't like certain strange noises coming from the engine.
(3) These noises, which I had never heard before, worried me.
(4) We went to Greece, a country which I didn't know.
(5) An archaeologist, an American from Yale, was in the party.
(6) Excursions with a well-informed guide are more interesting.
(7) I finally achieved my ambition, to see the Parthenon.
(8) It was the main reason we went to Greece.
(9) The narrow streets, full of chaotic traffic, made progress slow.
(10) We gazed up at the night sky, studded with stars.

2 †Identify the type of post-modifier in the following sentences:

(1) My sister Jessica lives in Milan.
(2) The new Youth Training Scheme, a failure by any standard, has been abandoned.
(3) Inflation, the curse of twentieth-century democracy, is once again out of control.

3 Complete the following sentences with the classes of NG post-modifier given on the left:

(1) **PP:** There should be a law _ _ _ _ _ _ _ _ _ _ _
(2) **PP:** The countryside _ _ _ _ _ _ _ _ _ _ _ is lovely.
(3) **PP:** Have you any experience _ _ _ _ _ _ _ _ _ _ _
(4) ***That*-clause:** The discovery _ _ _ _ _ _ _ _ _ _ _ was fundamental for scientific advance.
(5) ***Wh*-adv clause:** The day _ _ _ _ _ _ _ _ _ _ _ has not arrived yet.
(6) **Rel. clause:** She had a voice _ _ _ _ _ _ _ _ _ _ _
(7) ***V-ing* clause:** We went up a rickety old staircase _ _ _ _ _ _ _ _ _ _ _
(8) ***V-en* clause:** All my postcards _ _ _ _ _ _ _ _ _ _ _ got lost in the post.
(9) **V. Inf clause:** Have you got a licence _ _ _ _ _ _ _ _ _ _ _
(10) **AdjG:** I would like something _ _ _ _ _ _ _ _ _ _ _

4 †Give the symbol for each element of the following NGs, repeating the symbol if an element is realised more than once, e.g. (2) **eeh**.

(1) university students
(2) clear, cool water
(3) our first day in London
(4) that new colour magazine about photography that I bought
(5) six beautiful old Chinese Ming vases
(6) somebody more knowledgeable with teaching experience

5a Give a paraphrase of the following NGs.

(1) television aerial repair service
(2) Manchester University Research Fellowship Appointments
(3) daytime telephone calls price reduction
(4) adult education reform proposals alarm
(5) university athletics teams gold medals award

5b †Express the following as single NGs.

(1) missiles based on land and carrying multiple warheads
(2) weapons of a nuclear type having an intermediate range
(3) an exhibition of robots designed for use in the home and now available all over Europe
(4) a lady's suit for wearing in the evening made of velvet and having the blue colour of the night in a classic style
(5) a farmhouse made of stone having the colour of honey and built two years ago in Malta

6 †In the following sentence from a novel we have changed the positions of four post-modifying units. Can you say why these positions are not appropriate and how they should be rearranged?

> **A clear fire burned in a tall fireplace and an elderly man with a chain round his neck in evening dress and standing with his back to it, glanced up from the newspaper he was holding before his calm and severe face spread out in both hands.**

7 Each of the following NGs is post-modified by two units of different classes. Decide whether it is possible to re-order each sequence without resulting in a change of meaning, incongruity or ambiguity.

1 *to*-inf. cl. + relative cl: (I have) something//to tell you//that you won't like//
2 Relative cl. + *to*-inf. cl: the decision//(which) *they* took//to organise a *demo*//
3 AdjG + relative cl: something/very odd//that may surprise you//

4	PP + relative cl:	the woman/in hospital//whose life you saved//
5	AdjG + AdvG:	nobody/intelligent/there (would believe that)
6	AdvG + relative cl:	the journey/back//which was quite short// . . .
7	Relative cl. + -en cl:	the officer//that came,//sent by the general//

8 Write a short description of one of the following groups of persons or things. Include a sufficient number of epithets, classifiers and post-modifiers to make the description interesting. Write it in the form of a letter to a friend:

(1) the members of your family
(2) columns of people you have seen on television, fleeing from a war zone
(3) people and things at the scene of an earthquake (seen on TV)
(4) some new clothes that you have seen in shops and which you would like to buy

Module 50

1 Identify the extent of the NGs in the following sentence from *The Times*. Then consider whether the numbered sections have a post-modifier or complement function. Give evidence for your decision.

> **The annual celebration of a pagan Spanish ritual[1] honouring the coming of spring[2] is always an expression of unity and fun.[3]**

2 †Read the following short paragraph and identify the extent of each numbered NG; then indicate the syntactic function of each one in a clause or group:

> **In describing his taste in women,[1] the famous baby doctor,[2] Benjamin Spock[3] said: 'I have always been fascinated by rather severe[4] women, women I then could charm despite their severity.[5] The model for these women[6] – as Dr. Spock was well aware – was his own mother.[7] And if, in his early eighties,[8] he is indeed a most exceptionally charming man,[9] the wish to win over his mother[10] may help explain why.**

3 Rewrite the following sentence from *The Guardian* in simpler, less abstract terms. Instead of de-verbal nouns like *introduction, approach, increase, insistence*, and the de-adjectival noun *truth* use the corresponding verbs: *introduce, insist*, etc. and adjectives *true* and *independent*. Even better, use some simpler English verbs such as *grow* and *use* instead of the more formal words. Avoid other abstractions.

Begin: If we introduced classes of no more than 15 children in infant primary schools, this would allow . . .

> The introduction of a maximum class size of 15 in infant primary schools, combined with a child-centred approach, would permit the increase of class sizes as children progress, utilising their learning skills and expanding their independence. We already acknowledge the underlying truth of this approach in nursery education by insistence on low teacher–children ratios which increase dramatically and illogically in the first year of compulsory education.

4 Rewrite the following sentence in a more abstract way, by nominalising some of the verbal predications:

> Most archaeologists think that men and women began to become civilised in the Middle East, where natural conditions helped them to change the way they lived from constantly moving around and hunting animals to settling down in one place and cultivating the land.

DESCRIBING PERSONS, THINGS AND CIRCUMSTANCES

Adjectival and Adverbial Groups

ADJECTIVES AND THE ADJECTIVAL GROUP

SUMMARY

1   AdjGs and typical AdvGs have potentially the same structure: head (*clear*, *clearly*), pre-modifier (**very** *clear*, **very** *clearly*) and post-modifier (*very clear* **indeed**, *very clearly* **indeed**).

2   Both AdjGs and AdvGs are frequently realised by the head element alone (a *fast* train; drive *fast*).

3   Their main functions and uses, however, are different. The AdjG typically provides information about people, places and things, while the adverb typically characterises the process expressed by the verb. For this reason we deal first with adjectives and the adjectival group, and later with adverbs and the adverbial group.

4   Formally, adjectives may be simple (*tall, brilliant*), prefixed (*un-, im-, dis-, ab-*), suffixed (*-ful, -able, -ous, -ive*), participial (*-ing, -en*) or compound (*home-made, duty-free, sunburnt*).

5   Syntactically, AdjGs typically function attributively as pre-modifier (in NG) (*hot water*) and predicatively as Complement of the Subject in clauses (*the water is hot*). In addition they can function as Complement of the Object (*I like it hot*) in clauses, and less commonly, in various other functions in groups and clauses.

6   Semantically, AdjGs can express a state (*lonely*), a quality (*narrow*), a sub-class (*northern*) or a property (*creative*). They can indicate an attitude (*lovely, odious*) or a judgement (*true*).

7   Many adjectives may take a complement in post-head position which completes their meaning (good *at chess*, glad (*that*) *you came*).

51.1 STRUCTURE AND CHARACTERISTIC USES OF THE ADJECTIVAL GROUP

The adjectival group is composed potentially of three structural elements: a head (**h**), a modifier (**m**) and a post-head element, which will be either a modifier (**m**) or a complement (**c**). Post-modifier and complement can occur together in the same AdjG. The basic structures are as follows:

		m	h	m	c
1	**h**		good		
2	**hc**		good		at chess
3	**mh**	very	good		
4	**mhm**	very	good	indeed	
5	**mhmc**	very	good	indeed	at chess

Other examples of full AdjG structures are:

extremely	hot	for this time of the year (mhm)
very	glad	that you won the match (mhc)
quite	fond	of music (mhc)

The difference between a post-modifier and a complement is that the complement is controlled by the adjectival head (*good at . . ., fond of . . ., glad that . . ., glad to . . .* etc.), whereas the post-modifier is not.

The head of an AdjG is always realised by an adjective, which may function alone in representation of a whole AdjG. The following sentence contains four coordinated AdjGs:

> You couldn't call it a bang or a roar or a smash; it was a *fearful, tearing, shattering, enormous* sound like the end of the world.
>
> (G. B. Shaw, *The Emperor and the Little Girl*)

In the following blurb of a novel from *The Review*, four of the adjectives are modified (5, 8, 10, 17) and one has a complement (14). The rest are single (1, 2, 3, 4) or coordinated (6–7–8, 11–12–13, and 14–15).

Ben and Olly are ten. For as long as they can remember they have been *best*[1] friends and *close*[2] neighbours in a *quiet*[3] Northern suburb. Then Carl moves into their street, Carl is *bad.*[4] Carl is *very bad.*[5] His games are *rough,*[6] *dangerous*[7] and *strangely exciting.*[8] But soon Ben begins to wonder where their *new*[9] friend is leading them. Why is Carl so *fearless?*[10] Why are they never allowed into his house? And why is it that Carl seems to want Olly all to himself? In a *funny,*[11] *heartfelt*[12] and ultimately *shocking*[13] story, Sutcliffe reveals how childhood friendships can be as *consuming*[14] and *intense*[15] as any love affair, and how, when jilted, children are *capable*[16] of taking the *most extraordinary*[17] steps.

These short examples illustrate the **descriptive** use of adjectives: they characterise NG referents in evaluative and emotive terms. By contrast, the **classifying** use is illustrated in *Northern* suburb and *best friends*. Classifying adjectives are more commonly found in the media and academic prose.

51.2 SIMPLE, DERIVED AND COMPOUND ADJECTIVES

The most frequently used adjectives in English are monosyllabic or bisyllabic words of native origin such as *good, bad, big, small, little, tall, short, black, white, easy, hard* which have no distinctive form to mark them as adjectives.

Many adjectives are derived from nouns, other adjectives and verbs by the addition of certain characteristic suffixes. Some of these are of native origin, as in green*ish*, hope*ful*, hand*some*, hand*y*, fore*most*, while others are formed on Greek or Latin bases, as in centr*al*, second*ary*, appar*ent*, civ*ic*, creat*ive*, and yet others via French such as marvell*ous* and read*able*.

Most adjectival prefixes are added to words which are already adjectives: *unhappy, insecure, discourteous, abnormal, irrelevant*. Some adjectives are formed by adding the prefix *a-* to a verb or adjective (*asleep, awake, ablaze, alone*).

Many adjectives have compound forms composed of various classes of words, for example:

noun + adjective:	tax-free (goods)
determinative + noun:	all-American (girl)
number + noun	four-wheel (drive)
adverb + participle	well-balanced (character)
adverb + adverb	well-off (people)

Adjectives in English are invariable in form. They are not marked for gender or number.

A fair-haired girl – fair-haired girls; a tough character – tough characters

51.3 PARTICIPLES AND PARTICIPIAL ADJECTIVES

Many present and past participles of verbs perform grammatical functions which are typical of those realised by adjectives, and for this reason are recognised as adjectives having the same form as participles, or as being derived from participles. We indicate them here by the symbols *-ing* and *-en*, and recognise the following classes:

Participial adjectives seldom used in VGs

This is a small set of forms which are never or very rarely used as part of a Verbal Group, but only as modifiers in NGs or as Complements (Cs and Co) in a clause, for example:

-ing: interesting, amazing, charming, disappointing, pleasing
-en: animated, ashamed, assorted, sophisticated

Pseudo-participial adjectives

An increasing number of adjectives are coined by adding *-ing* or *-ed* not to verbs but to nouns. These are termed pseudo-participial adjectives, such as:

-ing: enterprising, neighbouring, appetising
-en: talented, skilled, gifted, bearded, detailed

Participial adjectives commonly used as VGs

A large number of participial adjectives derived from transitive verbs can be used as modifiers in a NG and as Complements in a clause, while also retaining their ability to function as part of a VG: A *confusing* remark (m); That is *confusing* (Cs); You are *confusing* me (part of VG). Forms which can carry out these functions include the following:

-ing: annoying, exciting, frightening, surprising, boring, distressing, satisfying, tiring
-en: annoyed, excited, frightened, surprised, bored, distressed, satisfied, tired

In both their attributive and predicative functions, these participial adjectives can be graded and intensified (see 52.1 and 52.2):

	Attributive	**Predicative**
-ing:	*very* distressing news	the news is *most* distressing
-en:	*rather* frightened tourists	the tourists seemed *quite* frightened

Participial modifiers

To distinguish the *-ing* adjectives from participial modifiers such as *rising prices* (48.5), we shall adopt the following criterion: if the *-ing* form cannot be graded, or intensified by *very*, as in **1**, we shall consider it to be a participial modifier. If it can be graded, or intensified by *very*, we consider it an adjective. Compare *a sleeping child* with *a horrifying story*:

1   (participial modifier)   *a more/very* sleeping child   *the child is *more/very* sleeping

2   (adjective)   a *more/very* horrifying story   the story is *more/very* horrifying

Furthermore, *is sleeping* in *the child is sleeping* will be interpreted as a verb, the predicative adjective being *asleep*. In examples such as *sleeping bag, sleeping pill*, the word *sleeping* is neither adjective nor verb, but a noun modifier (a bag/ pill for sleeping), the combination now having the status of a count noun.

Past participles may often have either an adjectival or a verbal interpretation. In *The flat was furnished*, the participle may be understood either as part of a passive verb form or as the adjectival Cs of the copula *was*.

Compound forms

Many participial forms are compounded with a noun, an adjective or an adverbial prefix, whose syntactic relationship with the verbal participle may be Subject, Object or Adjunct:

> *-ing*:   heart-breaking news; good-looking girl; fast-selling magazines
> *-en*:   well-paid workers; sun-tanned legs; well-known brands

Compound forms are extremely common in English, where new ones are freely coined every day, many of them being nonce formations,such as *ankle-twisting* and *toil-broken* coined by G. B. Shaw in the following paragraph from *A Sunday on the Surrey Hills*. The relative absence of morphological markers in English adjectives can be observed in the following text, where some are marked (e.g. poison*ous*), others are not (e.g. *dull*), and two are compounds:

> As I am not a *born*[1] cockney I have no illusions on the subject of the country. The *uneven*[2] *ankle-twisting*[3] roads; the *dusty*[4] hedges; the ditch with its *dead*[5] dogs, *rank*[6] weeds and swarms of *poisonous*[7] flies; the groups of children torturing something; the *dull*,[8] *toil-broken*,[9] prematurely *old*,[10] *agricultural*[11] labourer; the *savage*[12] tramp; the manure heaps with their *horrible*[13] odour; the chain of milestones, from inn to inn, from cemetery to cemetery: all these I pass heavily by until a *distant*[14] telegraph pole or signal post tells me that the *blessed*,[15] rescuing train is at hand.
>
> [1]participle; [2]prefixed; [3]compound; [4]suffixed; [5]participial; [6]unmarked; [7]suffixed; [8]unmarked; [9]compound; [10]unmarked; [11]suffixed; [12]unmarked; [13]suffixed; [14]unmarked; [15]participial

51.4 SEMANTIC CLASSES OF ADJECTIVES

As we saw in Module 48, when discussing modifiers of nouns, adjectives in use fall into two broad groups: those that describe the referent (descriptors) and those that sub-classify it (classifiers). Here we simply provide some further subtypes and examples of each, with the reminder that many adjectives have both uses. Furthermore, there are words outside these two groups that can function as pre-modifiers (see 51.4.4).

51.4.1 Descriptors

Such adjectives express the following types of meaning:

- **size, weight, extent**: (note that these are often paired as opposites): big/ little, large/small, heavy/light, long/short, tall/short, wide/narrow, deep/shallow
- **colour**: black, white, red, blue, green, yellow
- **meanings related to time**: young, old, new, recent, early, late, weekly, daily
- **evaluative**: pretty, beautiful, good, bad, nice, awful, dreadful, shocking
- **an active or passive process** (participial adjectives): frightening, surprising, soothing, tired, exhausted, refreshed
- **general qualities**: hot, cold, full, empty, sweet, sour, hard, soft, strong, weak, bright, dull
- **a temporary state**: asleep, alone, awake, ajar (with predicative function only)

51.4.2 Classifiers

These are of three types:

- **restrictive**: they restrict the referent of a noun in relation to another referent: average, additional, chief, complete, entire, final, following, initial, main, only, particular, primary, public, single, standard.

  – A sub-type relates the noun referent to time or place: old, new, previous, former, right, left;

- **relating to groups** such as nationalities, religions, politics: Brazilian, Christian, Muslim;
- **category-specific meanings** associated with culture, technology, science, and so on.

All these are listed more extensively according to topic in 48.5.

> **restrictive:** an *only* child, the *standard* size, the *main* reason, the *entire* novel, the *previous* page, his *former* boss, my *old* school, her *current* boyfriend, your *left* leg, my *right* hand
> **relating to groups:** *Greek* sculpture, the *Western* powers, *African* music
> **category-specific meanings:** a *nuclear* plant, a *medical* student, *parliamentary* debates

51.4.3 Degree emphasisers

In addition to these two main types, certain adjectives can function as degree empha-sisers with a strongly emotive tinge. Of these *mere* and *utter* have no other meaning as adjectives; the others can be used as descriptors (a *sheer* cliff, a *true* story, *pure* water):

> *sheer* nonsense; *mere* repetition; *utter* rubbish; a *real* mess; a *true* genius; *absolute* folly; a *perfect* fool; *pure* ignorance

The words *sheer, mere, utter, only, previous, main, chief, sole* cannot function as predicative Complements. The words *real, true, absolute, perfect, pure* can be used predicatively when they have qualitative (not emphatic or restrictive) meaning, as in *pure water – this water is pure*.

51.4.4 Non-adjectival words used as modifiers

Although it is mainly the semantic feature of attribution that induces us to classify a word as an adjective, this is not an infallible criterion for classification, any more than the morphological one. For example, in the expressions *the then president, velvet curtains, rising prices*, the words *then, velvet, rising* are normally classed as adverb, noun and verb, respectively and there is no need to reclassify them as adjectives simply because the temporal circumstance, the substance and the active process which they denote function as premodifiers of nouns. There is no grammatical problem in saying that an adverb or noun or verb functions as an epithet or a classifier in a NG or (with the exception of verbs) as Subject Complement in a clause. That is, we distinguish the premodifier function from the class of item that realises it. Compare:

1 *velvet* curtains, a *stone* path
2 *velvety* fur, a *stony* path

In **1**, *velvet* and *stone* are nouns which classify the head noun. In **2**, *velvety* and *stony* are adjectives which modify the head noun.

51.5 SYNTACTIC FUNCTIONS OF THE ADJECTIVAL GROUP

AdjGs can realise functions in both group and clause structures, as follows:

AdjGs in groups:
- (pre-)modifier in a NG: a *very good* actor, *heavy* rain, an *old friend*
- (post-)modifier in a NG   something *cheap*, the person *responsible*
- head of a NG: the *French*, the *sick*, the *most expensive*
- complement of a preposition: at *last*, for *good*, in *short*
- modifier in an AdjG: *bright* red, *pale* blue, *red* hot

AdjGs in clauses:
- Subject Complement: The acting was *brilliant.*
- Object Complement: I consider that *offensive.*

Peripheral AdjGs
- Stance Adjunct: *Strange*, I never suspected him.
- Detached predicative supplement: *Angry and tearful*, Susan walked out.
- Exclamation: *Fine! Great! Right! Fantastic!*

Among adjectives as modifiers, the type 'a *good* actor' constitutes a special use of certain adjectives, as in a *slow* reader, a *hard* worker, a *big* eater. This is sometimes called the **process-oriented** use, as the adjective doesn't modify the noun directly, but rather the manner of performing the action. However, the manner of performing the action may become a characteristic feature of the entity: *I'm a sound sleeper* means, in effect, 'I always sleep soundly'.

Stance Adjuncts make an evaluative comment on the content of the whole clause. In common use in this function are: *odd, strange* (*Odd*, I never noticed). Others such as *More important still* can also function as **connectives** between clauses.

Detached predicatives such as *angry and tearful* are a type of supplementive unit, that is, a unit used non-restrictively (see 49.2) and are illustrated in the text in that section. Syntactically, they are not integrated into the unit which they modify. They are thus free as regards position, though in practice they are usually found in initial rather than final or medial positions. They provide an economical means of adding contextual information which fills out the reader's perception of the person or thing referred to. They are common in certain written genres and generally absent from conversation.

Adjectives as exclamations as in *Great!* can be considered as ellipted copula clauses: *That's great!* In addition, adjectives function in the exclamative structure initiated by how: *How dreadful it was!* This too can be ellipted to *How dreadful!* (see 24.1).

51.6 CENTRAL AND PERIPHERAL ADJECTIVES

Of these functions the most central are the **attributive** function, as modifier in the NG, and the **predicative** function, as Subject Complement in the clause. It is normal to classify as **central** those adjectives which fulfil these two functions, and as **peripheral** those which realise other functions, or only one, or neither of these central functions.

Interestingly, central adjectives are also descriptors. They add information as part of the nominal group or as subject complement, which fills out and enlivens the description of people, places and things. Central adjectives also play an important role as evaluators, expressing the subjective or objective evaluation of the speaker.

With the exception of the adjectives of temporary state beginning *a-*, all the adjectives discussed in 51.4.1 are central and are different types of descriptor. By contrast, the classifiers, degree emphasisers and process-oriented adjectives are all peripheral.

Summarising, then, we have:

1 **Central adjectives**:   descriptors
2 **Predicative adjs only**: *afraid, asleep, ablaze, afloat, alive, alone, alike, aware,*
                                 averse

3   **Attributive adjs only**:   these can be grouped into the following types:

- restrictive classifiers: the *chief/ main* reason; *sole* responsibility; an *only* child
- time/ space: the *previous* page; my *old* school; a *new* baby; your *left* leg
- associative classifiers: an *agricultural* college, *foreign* affairs, a *nuclear* weapon
- degree emphasisers: *sheer* nonsense; *utter* rubbish; an *outright* lie
- process-oriented: a *big* eater; a *hard* worker, a *light* sleeper, a *slow* reader

Most peripheral adjectives have a further restriction in that they cannot be graded or intensified: **very main*, **extremely chief*, **more utter*. This also applies to adjectives functioning as classifiers: **a very nuclear weapon*, **a rather Egyptian mummy*, **fairly prehistoric remains* (see Module 52). However, as is explained in Chapter 10, a number of classifying adjectives can also be used as descriptors and graded, some more easily than others: *British* exports (classifier), a very *British* attitude (descriptor).

The following book blurb from *The Review* illustrates several of the grammatical functions that can be realised by adjectives and AdjGs.

Advertising director Charles Schine is just another New York commuter, regularly catching the 8.43 to work. But the day he misses his train is the day that changes his life. Charles has never cheated on his wife in eighteen years of marriage. But then Charles has never met anyone like Lucinda Harris before. And though Lucinda is *married*[1] too, it is *immediately apparent*[2] that the feeling is *mutual*.[3] Suddenly their temptation turns *horrifically sour*,[4] and their *illicit*[5] liaison becomes caught up in something *bigger*,[6] *more dangerous*,[7] *more brutally violent*.[8] *Unable to talk to his partner or the police*,[9] Charles finds himself trapped in a world of *dark*[10] conspiracy and *psychological*[11] games. Somehow he's got to find a way to fight back, or his *entire*[12] life will be spectacularly derailed for *good*.[13]

[1-4]predicative Complement; [5]m in NG; [6-8]post-modifier in NG; [9]detached predicative; [10]m in NG; [11]m (classifier) in NG; [12]m (classifier) in NG; [13]complement of preposition

---

DEGREES OF COMPARISON AND INTENSIFICATION

SUMMARY

1 **Comparative and superlative** forms in -er, -est and *more, most,* respectively. Irregular forms: *better, best; worse, worst; farther/ further, farthest/ furthest.* Comparative constructions with *the* + adjective. Structures of sufficiency (*enough*) and excess (*too*).

2 **Intensification**: high: *very, most, extremely, extra, seriously* (stupid); medium: *quite, rather, pretty, fairly* (cool).

3 **Attenuation**: *slightly* (better), *a little* (different), *a bit* salty; *not very* (good), *hardly* (likely).

4 **Quantification**: exact: *one-mile; a mile (long); 2-foot-thick; 2 feet thick; 3-year-old; 3 years old;* non-exact: *not that long; this big.*

5 **Description**: by adjs: *pale* green, *dark* blue, *deep* red; by advs: *strangely* silent, *cheerfully* confident; by nouns: *pitch* black, *paper*-thin, *world*-wide.

6 **Submodification**: *just as* easy, *really quite* angry, *far too* expensive, *quite old enough.*

An important feature of central adjectives is that they are **gradable**, that is, the quality they express can be held in differing degrees. We can question and express the degree by a degree adverb *How important is it? It is **extremely** important.* Many descriptive adjectives are gradable, classifiers in general are not.

52.1 COMPARATIVE AND SUPERLATIVE DEGREES

When we want to express the notion that a person, thing or situation has more or less of a quality, we can mark a gradable adjective for **comparative** or **superlative** degree.

This is done grammatically in one of two ways: by inflection, adding *-er* and *-est* to the base form, or analytically by the adverbs *more* and *most*:

Base form	Comparative	Superlative	
big	bigger	biggest	(inflectional)
comfortable	more comfortable	most comfortable	(analytic)

Inflected forms are used with:
- Short adjectives of one syllable, and two-syllable adjectives ending in *-y* (*hot–hotter–hottest; easy–easier–easiest*). Exceptions are *right, wrong* and *real*.
- Disyllabic adjectives in *-ow* (*narrow, shallow, hollow, mellow*) can be inflected, as can other short adjectives ending in weak syllables such as *-le* (*simple, able, noble*).

Analytic forms are used with:
- adjectives of more than two syllables (e.g. *encouraging*); and
- adjectives which are already inflected (e.g. *lovable, famous, greenish, pleased*).

However, ease of pronunciation and smoothness of sound are important factors, and speakers sometimes improvise if the result sounds acceptable. Lewis Carroll, the creator of *Alice in Wonderland*, is said to have introduced 'curiouser and curiouser', which is still used, though jocularly, by some speakers.

Adjectives in *-y* which commonly take *-er* and *-est* include: happy, lazy, cosy, crazy, dirty, empty, lucky, nasty, pretty, silly, sexy, tidy, tricky.

The following adjectives have suppletive forms for grades 1 and 2:

good, better, best   far, farther, farthest
bad, worse, worst   far, further, furthest

The word *further* can also be used with the sense of 'other', 'later', 'additional':

There will be a *further* meeting next week.
The theatre is closed until *further* notice.

The adjectives *elder, eldest* (alternative to *older, oldest*) refer only to persons.

my elder son; our eldest daughter; an elder brother or sister;
John is the elder of the two. I was the second eldest.   [BNC FY1 45]

The adjective *elderly* is not comparative, but refers euphemistically to a person approaching old age. The comparative degree of certain other adjectives has the value of a classifier:

junior rank (= low)   inferior quality (= bad)   major error (= great)
senior rank (= high)   superior quality (= good)   minor error (= small)

your upper/ lower jaw   my inner life   the outer walls (of the city)

There are no inflections of lower and lowest degree corresponding to -er and -est. For this meaning *less* and *least* are used as modifiers. The following table summarises the grading options in English:

The scale of degree	Inflectional	Analytic
1 Comparative superiority	easier	more difficult
2 Superlative superiority	the easiest	the most difficult
3 Equality		as easy, as difficult
4 Comparative inferiority		less easy, less difficult
5 Superlative inferiority		the least easy, the least difficult
6 Sufficiency		easy enough, difficult enough

Adjectives and adverbs whose meanings are inherently superlative such as *unique* and *perfect* are prescriptively banned from comparative and superlative marking. They are sometimes heard in conversation however, intensified by the 'absolute' *most*: a **most perfect** example.

52.1.1 Functions of comparatives and superlatives

Adjectives graded for comparative and superlative degree can function both as modifiers of a noun and as Complements in a clause. Most descriptive adjectives are gradable:

As modifiers of a noun

> Have you got a *larger* size?
>
> I think you need a *more up-to-date* stereo.
>
> What's the *funniest* joke you've heard recently?
>
> It wasn't *the most exciting* match of the season.
>
> The *cleverest* animals, as well as the *better-looking, better-humoured* and *more classy*, are not the ones holding the leads.   (Philip Howard in *The Times*)

As Cs in clauses

> This house is *smaller*, but it's *nicer*, and it's got a *bigger* garden.
>
> We need something *more central*.
>
> We went into several pubs, but this one was undoubtedly *the best*.
>
> Really, they should appoint Jones. He's the *most experienced*.

The analytic forms of the comparative and the superlative are illustrated in this short description from an in-flight magazine:

The miles of clean, pristine sandy beaches look especially inviting to the tourist. They are safe for *even the most daring* swimmers. *The more adventurous* may avail themselves of scuba diving training at beginner, intermediate and advanced levels from the Professional Association of Diving Instructors. From May to October the water is so warm that no wet-suits are needed. Light 3mm suits are comfortable for the rest of the year. Submerged wrecks and coral reefs that attract an array of vivid tropical fish contribute to a fascinating diving experience.

For the complementation of graded adjectives by *than*-clauses, *that*-clauses and PPs, see Module 53.

When a comparative adjective is not followed by a complement, the other entity in the comparison should be inferrable, as happens in the previous text. We understand that *the more adventurous* implicitly compares with other swimmers who are less adventurous. In fact, it is normal in everyday communication, especially in conversation, to use graded adjectives without mentioning the other entity in the comparison.

52.1.2 The *-er* and *-er* construction

The repeated comparatives joined by *and* are used to express a gradually increasing degree of the quality denoted by the adjective (or adverb; see 56.1). Verbs of becoming such as *become, get* and *grow* are commonly used with adjectives. *More and more* occurs with adjectives which don't admit the comparative inflection.

It's growing *darker and darker.*
This crossword is getting *more and more* difficult.
They became *wearier and wearier* as time went on.

52.1.3 The *nice and* construction

Nice and is often used in informal speech to intensify a second adjective: *nice and hot, nice and cold, nice and dirty. Good and* is also used in the same way.

52.1.4 The degree of sufficiency

This comprises three terms: 'excess', 'sufficiency', 'insufficiency', realised by the adverbs *too, enough, not enough*, respectively. When functioning predicatively, that is at **Cs**, the AdjG structure is as follows:

excess:	This knife is *too sharp.*
sufficiency:	Is this knife *sharp enough?*
insufficiency:	This knife is *not sharp enough.*

When the AdjG modifies a noun, the NG structures are as follows:

excess:	This is *too sharp a knife.*
sufficiency:	This is *a sharp enough knife.*
insufficiency:	This is *not a sharp enough knife.*

If the noun is uncountable or plural (e.g. *weather, knives*), only the predicative structure is used for the expression of 'excess':

excess:	The weather was *too* wet.	*It was *too wet weather.*
	These knives are *too* sharp.	*These are *too sharp knives.*

The degree of excess can be expressed by the lexical item *over* (AmE *overly*) used as a compound adjective: Don't be *over-anxious* about the future.

52.2 INTENSIFYING THE ATTRIBUTE

Intensification is a kind of grading and will be described here in terms of three degrees: 'high', 'medium' and 'attenuated'. They constitute a cline rather than a scale of fixed points, since they are realised exclusively by lexical items rather than by varied structures. In spoken English, the intended degree of intensification can be reinforced by stress and intonation patterns.

52.2.1 High intensification

This is expressed by adverbs, adjectives and, exceptionally, nouns. The following examples show them in AdjGs in both of the central adjectival functions:

very:	the *very* latest techniques	That's *very* kind of you
really:	a *really* good film	It was *really* good
awfully:	an *awfully* nice man	He looked *awfully* tired
most:	a *most* extraordinary performance	His ideas are *most* odd
way:	I am *way* concerned about the environment (AmE) (Cs only)	

Some intensifiers, such as *very* and *extremely*, can intensify almost any adjective. Others are more limited to specific types of adjectives or to individual ones. Notice that the original meaning of some high intensifiers has undergone semantic change. For example, *terrifically* indicates approval, *awfully* and *terribly* can intensify both good and bad qualities, while *dreadfully* and *horribly* are used only with bad ones. The following are common collocations:

dripping wet; boiling hot; freezing cold; blind drunk; dead straight; wide awake; fast asleep; frozen stiff; extra special; stinking rich; fully aware; raving mad; highly controversial; radically opposed; eminently suitable; deeply moving; seriously stupid; hugely successful; supremely confident; terrifically good-looking; horribly disfigured.

Quite, which normally expresses a medium degree of intensification, can express a high degree in the sense of indicating a complete degree or extent to which something is the case: *I stood quite still*. To convey this meaning, *quite* is spoken with higher pitch and emphasis. *Quite* always takes on a high degree when it modifies an emotive adjective as in *quite amazing, quite incredible, quite disastrous*.

> He looks *quite* different in his everyday clothes.
> You are *quite* right.

52.2.2 Medium intensification

A medium degree of intensification is expressed by the four adverbs *quite, pretty, rather, fairly*. Within the medium degree, we can recognise four sub-degrees in order of descending intensification:

> It's *quite* cold here in the winter.
> It's *rather* cold here in the winter.
> It's *pretty* cold here in the winter. (informal, spoken style)
> It's *fairly* mild here in the winter.

Quite denotes moderate but unequivocal intensification of the adjective, whether this is appreciative as in *quite pleased, quite satisfactory, quite nice*, unappreciative as in *quite dangerous, quite pessimistic, quite nasty*, or neutral as in *quite tall, quite cheap/expensive, quite short/long*.

> She felt there was something not *quite* right about the room.

Politeness or lack of certainty are often the motivations of the use of *quite*, as in *I'm not quite sure*. *Quite* is used to modify not only adjectives but also verbs and adverbs: *I don't quite know, I didn't quite understand*.

Rather can lower the force of a statement by indicating a certain limited degree, as in *it looks rather difficult*. It becomes related to indirectness (see Chapter 5) when used in situations which warrant a stronger word such as *very* or *extremely*. Politeness is sometimes the motivation for the use of *rather*, for example, to avoid direct criticism of others, *I'm rather worried about your exam results*, or to mitigate the expression of the speaker's own emotions, as in *I was rather pleased at winning the lottery*. At the same time it implies that a larger degree or extent is to be understood, for instance *very worried*, *very pleased*. This ability to say one thing while implying another makes *rather* a subtle tool in interpersonal interaction. *Rather* is a word that has contributed greatly to the notion of 'English understatement', as in:

> Buying that second-hand car may turn out to be a *rather* costly mistake.

Pretty expresses the notion of *quite but not completely*. It is used with all types of gradable adjective, but has an approximative value characteristic of informal speech; e.g. *She's pretty good-looking, I feel pretty tired after that long walk, That film was pretty awful, don't* *you think?* Like *rather*, it can also imply a stronger degree, especially when expressing a negative evaluation: *That paper of his was a pretty poor effort* (= *very poor*). The idiomatic combinations *pretty well, pretty much* can modify certain adjectives and determinatives, for instance, *pretty well impossible, pretty much the same.*

> He's going to have a *pretty* bad headache for a while, and the cut is *pretty* deep, so it's bound to be sore . . .   [BNC JXU 32349]

Fairly as a modifier indicates an almost large or reasonable degree of a quality (*fairly accurate, fairly well-off*). It can be used more easily with favourable and neutral adjectives than with strongly unfavourable ones, as with *fairly honest, fairly intelligent, fairly reasonable*, but not *?fairly dishonest, ?fairly foolish, ?fairly unreasonable:*

> He seems to have a *fairly* good idea of what he wants to do.

The above glosses represent only the typical semantic orientation of these four intensifiers. At the same time, their references are all slightly indeterminate, rather than fixed points on the scale. The attitudes they express can be varied in speech by intonation.

Other adverbs which suggest that something is very close to having the quality named are: *almost, nearly, roughly, approximately, partly, largely.*

The following ironical report from the economics section of a newspaper illustrates a normal everyday use of intensified adjectives in English:

> A remarkable *entirely new* economic cure-all has just emerged from *widely extensive* tests. The miracle drug, called taxcuts, is the *most versatile* drug since penicillin. The manufacturers say that if applied in *sufficiently liberal* doses, it will make people *more hardworking* and *less preoccupied* with their own financial problems.

52.2.3 Attenuation

Attenuation refers to a slight degree of the quality or its entire absence, and is expressed as follows:

slightly better	*a little* disappointing	*a bit* salty
kind of weird	*sort of* greyish hair	*somewhat* odd (formal)

Sort of and *kind of* are used, in very informal English, when the speaker is uncertain how to express the exact quality of something.

At all can be used as an attenuator in *yes/no* interrogative, negative and conditional clauses, as a politeness strategy in the case of conditionals. It is placed before or after the adjective:

> Are you *at all* worried? Are you worried *at all?*
> We'd like to stay another week, if it's *at all* possible (*or* if it's possible *at all*).

Slight attenuation or reservation can be expressed by negating a high degree:

> *not very* likely   *not quite* sure of her name
> *not entirely* true   *not particularly fond* of insects

The following modifiers express in **1** a minimal degree of attribution and often imply a certain degree of the opposite quality; in **2** they express absence or denial of the quality named:

1   *hardly* likely, *barely* necessary, *scarcely* believable, *none too* happy
2   *I'm not at all* surprised at the result, or, I'm *not* surprised *at all* at the result

52.3 QUANTIFYING MODIFIERS

Exact quantification

If we ask the questions *How old is she? How long was the queue? How high is Everest? How bad was the traffic-jam?* the depth, length, height and age can be measured or quantified by saying:

> She is *20 years old*.   The queue was *100 yards long*.
> Everest is *8,708 metres high*.   The cars were *four* deep on the motorway.

These AdjGs can be lexicalised as *compound adjectives* to modify nouns:

> *a twenty-year-old* girl   *a hundred-yard-long* queue
> an *8,708-metre-high* mountain   a *four-deep* traffic-jam on the motorway

Non-exact quantification

With predicative function, non-measurable quantification is expressed by the determinatives *the, that, this, any, all, little* and *no*, as in:

> Things are not getting *any* better. Well, as long as they're not getting *any* worse . . .
> The situation is *no* worse than it was before.
> The trip wasn't *that* interesting after all.
> We need a box *this* big.
> She looked *all* upset.

That + adjective can be used to modify a singular noun, but not a plural or non-count noun:

> It wasn't *that interesting a trip* after all.
> The trips were not *that* long.   *They were not that long trips.
> The thunder was not *that* loud.   *It was not that loud thunder.

52.4 DESCRIPTIVE MODIFIERS

If adjectives serve to describe nouns, they themselves can also be described, by reference to (a) a quality or (b) a specific context:

(a) Qualitative modification of adjectives is realised by the following classes of units:

-ly adverbs:	strangely attractive; deathly pale; reasonably friendly
adjectives:	light brown; deep red; dark blue; vivid green; bright yellow
nouns:	pitch black; emerald green; blood red; rose pink; paper-thin; feather-light; day-long; world-wide

Note that an expression like *a strangely attractive city* does not mean '*a strange and attractive city*' but '*a city which is attractive in a strange way*'; it is the adjective (*attractive*) which is modified, not the noun (*city*). The structure 'adj + adj' (e.g. *light brown*) is used especially with colour adjectives. When it modifies a noun, ambiguity may occur: *The deep blue sea* (a sea of *deep blue*? or a *deep sea* which is blue?)

(b) Relational (or contextual) modification indicates the sense in which the adjective is to be understood. It is realised by:

-ly adverbs:	socially acceptable; economically difficult; technologically impressive; financially independent; physically handicapped
nouns:	music-mad; girl-crazy; foot-weary; duty-free

The following short paragraph exemplifies the use of modified AdjGs:

> He is one of *the most compellingly*[1] *watchable* comic talents I have seen for a long time; a *slightly*[2] comic nose, a *retiringly*[3] *unassertive* chin and a wide *loosely*[4] *shaped* mouth contribute a *totally convincing*[5] performance as the court jester. He obviously has a *cheerfully perceptive*[6] gift for comedy.
>
> [1]intensification; [2]attenuation; [3]description; [4]description; [5]intensification; [6]description

52.5 SUBMODIFYING THE ADJECTIVE

Modifiers of degree (e.g. *less* in *less interesting*) are often themselves graded or intensified by a submodifier (**sm**) placed before them, e.g. *rather less* interesting. The following are examples of this **smmh** structure which occur in both spoken and written discourse.

sm	m	h	sm	m	h
not	quite	right	only	too	pleased
much	more	productive	not	nearly as	nice
far	too	expensive	just	as	complicated

This type of AdjG structure reflects two converse types of intensification which are characteristic of many English speakers: (a) That of **attenuating the negative value** of an Attribute, as in **1**, and (b) that of **reinforcing a positive value**, as in **2**:

1   This time the results are *not quite so* clear-cut.   [BNC KRL 96478]
2   We would be *only too pleased* to provide information on the Association.

[BNC GX9 13997]

The submodifier of the modifier *enough* is placed immediately before the adjective:

hardly good enough; *not nearly* clever *enough*; *quite* old *enough*

COMPLEMENTATION OF THE ADJECTIVE

SUMMARY

1   When an adjective (e.g. *happy*) functions in a clause, as Complement of the Subject (e.g. *I am happy*) or of the Object, it is often followed by a complement relating it to a fact (e.g. *that you are here*), a process (e.g. *to see you*), or a circumstance (e.g. *about your success*). This information indicates the way in which the adjective is to be understood and is expressed mainly by finite and non-finite clauses, and by prepositional phrases (PPs).

2   When the complement is a PP, the preposition is determined by the adjective and the context: *dependent on, clever at, clever with, fond of* (see also Chapter 12).

3   When the adjective is modified (graded, intensified, etc.), the modifier partly determines the type of complement or post-modifier: *too cold for us, too cold to swim, too cold for us to swim, too cold for swimming in the sea.*

4   When the adjective modifies a NG, it is separated from its complement: *too difficult* a problem *to solve.*

53.1 ADJECTIVAL COMPLEMENTS

Adjectival heads can take as post-head complements finite and non-finite clauses, or prepositional phrases which relate the Attribute to a fact, a situation, a process or a circumstance and so tell us how the Attribute is to be understood.

All adjectives which can take complements indicate the speaker's or writer's stance with respect to the proposition stated in the complement. They comprise three semantic types: epistemic (*sure, certain*, etc.), affective (*glad, sorry*, etc.) and evaluative (*right, wrong*, etc.).

53.1.1 Complementation by finite clauses

Adjectives which take embedded *that*-complement clauses indicate the speaker's or writer's stance with respect to what is expressed in the complement. Semantically, they fall into two main types:

1 **degrees of certainty**, such as: *sure, certain, positive, convinced*
2 **affective meanings**, such as: *glad, sorry, happy, sad, afraid, grateful, pleased, amazed, annoyed*

This structure relates the adjectival quality to a factual complement and is realised by a finite clause introduced optionally by *that*:

We are sure (that) he is innocent.
We are proud (that) you are so successful.

After some adjectives of emotive or modal meaning, such as *anxious, willing, eager, insistent, determined, essential*, the non-factual auxiliary *should* (in Br E), or the subjunctive (especially in Am E), can be used in the *that*-clause to suggest a present or future action. An indicative is used by some speakers, as in **3** (see 11.1).

1 The public is anxious that the truth (*should*) *be known*.
2 We are not willing that justice (*should*) *be forgotten*.
3 Bill's wife is *insistent that he give/* gives up smoking.

The complement can also be realised by a *wh*-clause. I am not quite *clear what you mean*.

Extraposed clausal subject

In the following type of sentence, the second clause does not function as a complement of the preceding adjective, but as extraposed subject, replaced by *it* in the main clause (see 5.1.2). Compare the extraposed with the non-extraposed clauses.

I just think *it's* unfortunate *that all these rumours have circulated.*   [BNC KRT 91068]
That all these rumours have circulated is unfortunate. (non-extraposed *that*-clause)
It is not clear *why she left.*
Why she left is not clear. (non-extraposed *wh-clause*)

The adjective in this construction expresses an evaluative attitude, (usually the speaker's) towards the content of the following clause. But because the construction has anticipatory *it* as subject, the stance or attitude is not directly attributed to the speaker or some other person, as occurs with complement clauses, whose subjects are referential pronouns or NGs.

Adjectives which occur in structures with anticipatory *it* tend to be more impersonal than those taking a complement clause. They include:

advisable, evident, (im)possible, (un) likely, noticable, (un)typical, important, obligatory, curious, obvious, shocking, surprising, true, vital

Certain adjectives can occur in both constructions, however: *clear, certain, sure.*

53.1.2 Complementation by non-finite clauses

This AdjG structure is used to describe the relation between an Attribute and a process or situation. The Attribute and process/situation both refer to the same Subject in examples (a–g) below:

(a) The adjective evaluates the process performed by the subject:

>   You are *kind to visit me.*
>   She must be *clever to have won the first prize.*

(b) The adjective describes the manner of performing the process:

>   The Minister was *quick to reject the accusation.*
>   You are *very slow to give your opinion, aren't you*?

(c) The adjective expresses an emotion caused by the process. The subject of the main clause is also the implied subject of the *to*-clause:

>   Everyone was *sorry to hear about the accident.*
>   We were all *delighted to receive your invitation.*

(d) The adjective expresses an attitude or state concerning the process:

>   I am not *willing to believe that story.*
>   The police are *powerless to take action in this matter.*

(e) The adjective expresses a property of the subject:

>   Mountain water is not always *safe to drink.*
>   Are these pamphlets *free to take away* (or *to be taken away*)?

(f) The adjective forms part of a lexical auxiliary (*be sure to, be likely to be bound to*) in a VG (see 37.3). It denotes a degree of certainty or the tendency of the process to occur. The subject is a 'raised subject' (see 37.4):

>   He is *sure to arrive late.*   It is *bound to rain.*
>   She is *likely to get angry.*   I am *apt to forget details.*

(g) The adjective evaluates the process realised by an *-ing* clause or a *to*-inf:

>   You were *foolish going out/ to go out without an overcoat.*
>   He must have been *crazy driving/ to drive as fast as that.*

The above examples refer to processes performed by the Subject of the clause, that is, the Carrier of the Attribute. The following ones refer to processes not performed by the Subject:

(h) The adjective does not refer to the Subject:

> Smoking is *hard/ difficult to give up.*

This sentence does not mean that smoking is difficult, but that to give up smoking is difficult. Structurally, it is a 'raised object', that is, the implied object of the *to*-clause *to give up smoking* is raised to subject (see 37.4).

(i) In other cases, the Subject may possess the Attribute and at the same time be the prepositional Object of the *to*-infinitive verb:

> This paper is *thin to write on.*   The Atlantic is *cold to swim in.*

53.1.3 Prepositional phrase complements

Prepositional phrase complements are not usually obligatory (though a few are), but they are all controlled by particular adjectives. The complement completes the meaning with respect to the adjective. Especially in conversation, where speakers can assume a knowledge of what has been said, it is frequently unnecessary to add a complement. We can say *I was angry, we were anxious, everyone was delighted* without specifying the reason. In writing, however, we often need to make the motivation more specific. A number of adjectives, including *accustomed* (to), *conscious* (of) and *prone* (to) (with the appropriate senses) require a complement. Several adjectives control more than one preposition, for instance *good at maths, good for your health, good with children; similar to mine, similar in shape.*

We here offer a small representative selection of everyday examples. These are grouped according to the preposition and the types of meaning conveyed by the adjective.

1 adjective + ***about*** or + ***at*** is used for emotional reaction to something:

> *angry about* what I said;   *annoyed about* the delay
> *mad about* music   *concerned about* his safety

2 adjective + ***at*** has two meanings: (a) emotional reaction to something or someone, and (b) an ability:

> (a) *happy at* the prospect   *alarmed at* the news
>   *mad at* my sister   *indignant at* the accusation

> (b) *clever at* getting what he wants   *bad at* letter-writing
>   *good at* mathematics   *hopeless at* remembering names

Other adjectives used with *at*: (a) pleased, annoyed (b) brilliant, terrible, adept, skilled, marvellous

3 adjective + ***by*** (with adjectives derived from past participles and passive in meaning):

> *amused by* the anecdote   *puzzled by* the question
> *hurt by* her remarks   *worried by* their failure to return

4 adjective + *for* means the value the adjective has for something or someone:

    anxious for success   *hopeful for* the future
    good for the health   *responsible for* their welfare

5 adjective + **from** has two meanings: (a) separation and distancing; (b) effect–cause:

    (a) *remote from* civilisation   *different from* everyone else
    (b) *sleepless from* anxiety   *tired from* overworking

6 adjective + *in* is used for an existing or resulting state:

    dressed in white   *slow in* reacting
    deep in a book   *lost in* thought

7 adjective + *of* is used for (a) mental state in terms of the antagonist or process; (b) mental state in terms of the protagonist; (c) containment:

    (a) *afraid of* wild animals   *capable of* great concentration
    (b) *kind of* you   *stupid of* him
    (c) *full of* enthusiasm   *sick of* it all

The (b) sequence occurs in clauses beginning *It is* + adjective + extraposed subject:

    It is *kind of you* to take such trouble.   It was *stupid of him* to lose the keys.

8 adjective + *on* is used for dedication, dependence or aim:

    keen on sport   *intent on* divorce
    dependent on other people   *set on* studying abroad

9 adjective + *to* means (a) mental state or attitude related to a phenomenon; (b) equivalence, similarity or comparison:

    (a) *opposed to* innovation   *kind to* old people; *accustomed to* hardship
    (b) *similar to* the others   *equal to* half a kilo

10 adjective + **with** can be (a) emotional reaction or physical state due to a cause, or (b) property or ability:

    (a) *fed up with* the weather   *pale with* fear
    (b) *skilful with* his hands   *good with* children

Note that 2(b) describes ability in relation to the task; 10(b) describes ability in relation to the tools or raw material.

11 adjective + *beyond* means to an extreme degree (with non-count nouns):

    cruel beyond endurance   *injured beyond* recovery

The fact that a PP occurs after an adjective does not necessarily mean that it complements the adjective; it may be functioning as a clausal or stance Adjunct:

    Complement: He is *brilliant at maths.*
    Clausal Adjunct: He is brilliant *in many respects.*
    Stance Adjunct: *In my opinion*, he's a brilliant mathematician.

The following extract from Roald Dahl's *Boy* illustrates the use of adjectives and their grading and complementation:

> It was always a surprise to me that I was good at games. It was an even greater surprise that I was exceptionally good at two of them. One of these was called fives, the other was squash-raquets.
>
> Fives, which many of you will know nothing about, was taken seriously at Repton and we had a dozen massive, glass-roofed fives courts kept always in perfect condition.
>
> We played the game of *Eton*-fives, which is always played by four people, two on each side, and basically it consists of hitting a small, hard, white, leather-covered ball with your gloved hands. The Americans have something like it which they call handball, but Eton-fives is far more complicated because the court has all manner of ledges and buttresses built into it which help to make it a subtle and crafty game.
>
> Fives is possibly the fastest ball-game on earth, far faster than squash, and the little ball ricochets around the court at such a speed that sometimes you can hardly see it. You need a swift eye, strong wrists and a very quick pair of hands to play fives well, and it was a game I took to from the beginning. You may find it hard to believe, but I became so good at it that I won both the junior and the senior school fives in the same year when I was fifteen. (see exercise 3 on p. 524).

53.2 DEGREE COMPLEMENTS

When the adjective is graded, the complement is dependent, not on the adjective directly, but on the grading element (*-er, more, less, as,* etc.), and is realised according to the type and structure of the grading element. The following examples serve as a brief summary of this area of English grammar.

Comparative degree

This takes one of two forms: either adjective + *-er* + *than*, or *more/ less* + adjective + *than*, plus a word, phrase or clause:

Adj + *-er* + *than* + PP	It was coole*r than in Russia*
Adj + *-er* + *than* + clause	It was bett*er than we expected*
more + adj + *than* + AdvG	It was *more* comfortable *than usual*
less + adj + *than* + clause	It was *less* complicated *than any of us expected*
more + adj. + *-ing* clause	It was *more* enjoyable *than travelling by air*

Superlative degree

Adj + *-est* + PP (*in*)	It is *the* long*est in the world*
most + adj + PP (*of*)	It is *the most* famous *of all his plays*
least + adj + *that*-clause	It is *the least* interesting novel (that) *I have ever read*

Degree of equality

as + adj + *as* +AdvG	It was *as* lovely *as ever*
neg + *as* + adj + *as* + clause	It was not *as* easy *as most of us expected*
so + adj + *as* + *to*-clause	It was *so* difficult *as to be impossible*

If the comparison is between two adjectives, the complement of equality is realised by a finite clause:

She is as good-looking *as she is intelligent.*
*She is as good-looking as intelligent.

If the comparison is negative, the modifier *not as* may be replaced by *not so*, though *so* suggests intensification besides equality: In winter, London is *not as/ so cold as* New York.

*Degree of sufficiency (*enough*) and excess (*too*)*

Heads modified by postposed *enough* and preposed by *too* are qualified by similar units to the above:

Sufficiency:	**Adj + *enough* + PP**	Is the water *hot enough for you?*
	Adj + *enough* + *to*-cl	Is the water *hot enough to take a shower?*
	Adj + *enough* + PP + *to*-cl	Is the water *hot enough for you to take a shower?*
Excess:	***Too* + adj + PP**	This coffee is *too hot for me.*
	***Too* + adj + *to*-cl**	This coffee is *too hot to drink.* (not *to drink it)
	***Too* + adj + PP + *to*-cl**	This coffee is *too hot for me to drink.* (not *for me to drink it)

If the *to*-infinitive verb is prepositional (e.g. *think about*), the preposition is stranded (see 6.3.3):

To-inf cl + prep.	Your project is too expensive to think about. (*about it)
	This knife is too blunt to cut with. (*with it)

Notice the emotive use of *too* in expressions such as: The film was *too* awful for words! and its equivalence to *very* in: I shall be *only too pleased* to help you (= very pleased).

53.2.1 Discontinuous degree complements

A degree complement is separated from its adjective when the AdjG premodifies a noun. The AdjG is said to be **discontinuous**, as in examples **1** and **2** below.

If we want to put the notion of **equality** before the noun, the adjective functions as a pre-determinative (preceding the article a/ an), with the *as*-clause following the noun:

1   It was *the most comfortable* journey *(that) we have ever made.*
2   It's *as nice* a country garden *as you could ever find.*

When an adjective is graded by a modifier, e.g. *more convinced*, one complement may relate to the modifier as in *more (convinced) than I was*, and a second one to the head, as in *(more) convinced of the man's guilt*. They may be placed in either order, the emphasis normally being on the second one:

The judge seemed more convinced than I was *of the man's guilt.*
The judge seemed more convinced of the man's guilt *than I was.*

If one complement is notably longer than the other(s), it is usually placed at the end:

The judge seemed more convinced than I was *of the evidence that had been given by one of the witnesses.*
*The judge seemed more convinced of the man's guilt after listening to the evidence given by one of the witnesses than I was.

When complements are coordinated by *and, but, or*, they are often of the same class form:

PP: He's fond *of teaching* and *good with children.*
***to*-inf cl:**   The programme was delightful *to watch and to listen to.*

ADVERBS AND THE ADVERBIAL GROUP   *MODULE 54*

SUMMARY

1   **AdvGs** have certain general characteristics similar to those of AdjGs:

- Potentially three structural forms: a **head**, a **modifier**, and a **post-head** element, which may be a post-modifier or a complement.
- They are frequently represented by the head element alone.
- Morphologically, the adverbial head may be simple, derived or compound.
- Semantically, many adverbs express qualities of processes and situations, just as adjectives express qualities of people and things.
- Not all adjectives and adverbs have the potential of heading a group structure: e.g. *mere, merely; sole, solely.*

2   In other respects, AdvGs are different from AdjGs:

Adverbs are a more heterogeneous word class, and can be roughly grouped into three main semantic sets:

- circumstantial: place, time, manner
- degree or focus
- connective: addition, reinforcement, result, concession, and the like

Many adverbs fulfil several functions, however, and their meanings may change according to the function.

54.1 STRUCTURE AND GENERAL CHARACTERISTICS OF THE ADVERBIAL GROUP

The structure of the adverbial group is similar to that of the adjectival group; that is, it is composed potentially of three elements: the head **h**, the modifier **m** and the post-head element, either **m** (post-modifier) or **c** (complement). These elements combine to form the following four basic structures:

	AdvG			
1	**h**		yesterday	
2a	**h**		early	
2b	**hm**		early	in the morning
3	**mh**	very	early	
4	**mhm**	very	early	in the morning

Other examples of full AdvG structures are:

mhc	more	slowly	than necessary
mhc	far	away	from civilisation
mhc	so	fast	(that) I couldn't catch him
mhc	quite	clearly	enough

The head element is always realised by an adverb (see 54.3). The modifier (see 56.1–2) is realised typically by grading and intensifying adverbs, as in these examples, and less typically by quantifiers (*ten miles across*). The complement (see 56.3) expresses a different type of meaning from that of the modifier, as it does in AdjGs. It expresses the scope or context of the meaning expressed by the head (e.g. luckily *for us*); alternatively, it can serve to define the modifier more explicitly (e.g. *more correctly than before*). It is for this reason that complements of adjectives and adverbs are mostly realised by PPs and clauses, whereas pre-modifiers are usually realised by words. However, we shall see that few adverbs take prepositional complements.

General characteristics of adverbs and adverbial groups

1. Whereas adjectives modify nouns as one of their main functions, adverbs modify verbs, clauses, adjectives and other adverbs.
2. Adverbs and AdvGs function typically in the clause as Adjunct or Complement, and in group structures as pre-modifier and post-modifier. In addition, they marginally realise subject and object functions in clauses. Many adverbs of directional meaning function as particles (*up*, *down*, *in*, *out*, etc.) in phrasal verbs (Complement or Adjunct in clauses.)
3. They express a wide variety of types and subtypes of meaning (see 54.3).
4. They perform a wide variety of syntactic functions (see 55.1).
5. They can occupy different positions in clause structure, when functioning as manner, evidential, stance and connective adjuncts (see 55.2; see also Chapter 2).
6. They are very frequently optional, in the sense that they can be omitted without the clause becoming ungrammatical.

54.2 FORMS OF ADVERBS

Morphologically, English adverbs are either **simple**, **derived** or **compound**.

Simple forms

These are words of one or two syllables, usually of native origin, that are not compounded and do not have derivational affixes. Examples: *now, then, here, there, far, near, soon, as, such, pretty, quite, rather, else, well, even, ever, ago.*

Many adverbial forms also function as prepositions (see p. 543, 'homograph'). However, prepositions are best contrasted with **adverbial particles**: *up, down, in, out, on, off, over, away, back,* and so on. These are a sub-set of short forms with meanings of direction and 'path', among others, which are used with verbs to form **phrasal verbs**: *walk down the street – walk down; get off the bus – get off* (see 40.2). Adverbs are also used to form **complex prepositions**, such as *far from, as well as, instead of.*

Certain simple adverbs have the same form as the corresponding adjective:

A *hard* worker – he works *hard*   a *fast* car – she drives *fast*
An *early* arrival – we arrived *early*   a *late* performance – we left *late*

Derived forms

- Those formed from adjectives by the addition of the suffix -*ly* include: *badly, happily, fairly, freely, slowly, proudly, honestly, cheerfully, sadly, warmly.*
- Some adjectives already have the -*ly* suffix (*friendly, princely, daily, weekly, monthly,* etc.), and this form is also that of the adverb. That is to say, another -*ly* suffix is not added: we don't say **monthlily.*
- Some adjective–adverb pairs have quite unrelated meanings: *hard–hardly; bare–barely; scarce–scarcely; present–presently; late–lately; short–shortly.*
- A few adverbs in -*ly* are not derived from adjectives: *accordingly, namely, jokingly,* among others.
- Certain very common adjectives expressing very basic meanings don't lend themselves to adverb formation: *big, small, young, old, tall, tiny, fat,* among others.
- Those formed from nouns, by the addition of -*wise,* -*ways,* -*ward(s),* include: *clockwise, moneywise; sideways, lengthways; backward(s), forward(s).*
- A small group of adverbs beginning *a-* indicate mainly position or direction: *about, above, across, again, ahead, along, aloud, apart, around, aside, away.*
- Another small set of adverbs has *be-* as first syllable, also indicating position or direction: *before, behind, below, beneath, besides, between, beyond.* These can also function as prepositions: I've been here *before* (adv.); It was *before* the war (prep.).

Compound forms

There are two types:

- shortened forms of what were originally PPs: *downhill, indoors, inside, outside, downstairs, overhead, overall, overnight,* and others.
- combinations with other classes of word: *somewhere, anywhere, nowhere, everywhere; however, moreover, nevertheless; anyway, anyhow.*

Phrasal adverbs are those which do not form compounds, but consist of more than one word: *of course; at all; kind of, sort of; in fact; as well*.

A representative number of adverbs appear in the following passage adapted from Joyce Cary's novel *The Horse's Mouth*, which tells how he finds his studio on his release from prison:

> I could see my studio from *where* I stood, an old boathouse *down* by the water-wall. A bit rotten in places, but I had been glad to get it . . . When I had my canvas *up* it was two feet off the ground, which *just* suited me. I like to keep my pictures above dog level.
>
> "*Well*", I thought, "the walls and roof are *there*. They haven't got blown *away*, *yet*. No-one has leaned *up* against them." I was pleased, but I didn't go *along* in a hurry. One thing at a time. Last time I was locked *up*, I left a regular establishment *behind*. Nice little wife, two kids, flat and a studio with a tin roof. Water-tight *all round* . . . When I came *back*, there was nothing. Wife and kids had gone *back* to her mama. Flat let to people who didn't *even* know my name. My cartoons, drawings, ladders, they'd *just* melted. I hadn't expected to see the fryingpan and kettle *again*. You can't leave things like that *about* for a month in a friendly neighbourhood and expect to find them in the same place. When I came *back* from gaol, *even* the smell had gone.

54.3 TYPES OF MEANINGS EXPRESSED BY ADVERBIAL GROUPS

Adverbs express five broad types of meaning in clauses and groups: circumstantial, stance, degree, focusing, connective. As with many adjectives and other word classes, however, the meaning of a particular adverb must be seen together with its function in context. The literal meaning of many adverbs can become figurative, or completely different, when used as an intensifier. So, although *far* is listed in section A (below) as meaning distance, *Don't go too far*, it expresses degree in *Prices won't go down very far*. When it functions as an intensifier it takes on a meaning similar to *much: far too short, a far nicer place*, while *so far* expresses time, similar to *up to now*.

A Circumstantial adverbs: where, when and how things happen

Space

Position:	Put the chairs *here/outside/upstairs*. An *away* match.
Direction:	Push it *inwards/down/through/out/away*. The trip *back*.
Distance:	Don't go too *far/near/close*.

Time

Moment:	They will be coming *tomorrow/sometime/then/soon/later*.
Frequency:	The doctor came *once/daily/frequently/now and again*.
Duration:	We didn't stay *long*. We spoke *briefly*.

Relation: The train will arrive *soon*. It has*n't* arrived *yet*.
Sequence: *first, second, next, then, last, finally*.

Manner Hold it *carefully*.

Domain The concert was a success *artistically* but not *financially*.

B Stance: expressing a personal angle

Certainty, doubt: You are *certainly right. Perhaps* I'm wrong.
Evidential: *Apparently*, they emigrated to Australia.
Viewpoint: We are in good shape *financially*, and *healthwise*, too.
Emphasis: He is *plainly just* a creep. *Indeed* he is.
Judgement: The Minister has *wisely* resigned.
Attitude: *Thankfully*, it didn't rain. *Hopefully*, it will be fine tomorrow.

C Degree adverbs: comparing, intensifying

Comparison: This is the *most/*the *least* efficient scanner we've had so far.
Intensification: He lives *all* alone but seems *quite/fairly/pretty* happy.
Attenuation: It was *kind of* strange to see her again.
Approximation: There were *about/roughly/more or less* 20 people there.
Sufficiency: Is the water hot *enough*?
Excess: Well, actually, it's *too* hot.

D Focusing adverbs: restricting the scope

Restriction: That is *merely* a detail. He is *just* interested in money.
 He *hardly* ate anything, *only* a yoghurt.
Reinforcement: The hotel had everything, *even* a fitness centre.

Even is a scalar adverb which carries an implication that the unit modified by *even* is either high or low on a scale of expectedness, in the context. In the example, a fitness centre is higher than expected, as not all hotels have a fitness centre. In *he wouldn't stay even for one day*, it is implied that *one day* is a shorter stay than had been expected. Both are interpreted as slightly surprising.

E Connective adverbs: logical connection

Sequence: *First*, we have no money, and *second*, we have no time.
Reinforcement: The house is small and *furthermore* has no garden.
Conclusion: It was a tiring trip, but *altogether* very interesting.
Restating: We've got two pets, *namely* a rabbit and a canary.
Reason: I couldn't find you, *so* I left.
Condition: Take an umbrella; *otherwise* you'll get wet.
Clarification: He wants to live abroad, *or rather* anywhere away from home.

Contrast:	They accept his invitations, *yet* they run him down.
Alternation:	There's no tea. Would you like a cup of coffee *instead*?
Concession:	What you said was true; *still* it was unkind.
Attention-seeking:	*Now*, you listen to me! *Now then*, what's all this about?

Technical description often makes use of adverbs of degree and quantity as in the following extracts from an elementary textbook on *Metals* by H. Moore.

> Of the ninety or *so*[1] *naturally*[2] occurring elements, about seventy are metals. Of these, *over*[3] half are put to practical use, although many of them *only*[4] in small amounts. In every household there are dozens of metal implements . . . from water-tanks to tea-spoons. Industrial machinery is made *almost entirely*[5] of metals. If man had not learnt to use metals, we would *still*[6] be living in the Stone Age. Some metals are used in a *relatively*[7] pure state, for example aluminium, whose lightness and corrosion-resistance make it *especially*[8] useful. But metals are used *mostly*[9] with other elements to form alloys and *so*[10] in this way their properties can be improved and their range of uses *widely*[11] extended.
>
> [1]quantity; [2]classification; [3]quantity; [4]restriction; [5]restriction; [6]duration; [7]degree; [8]degree; [9]intensification; [10]degree; [11]consequence (connective); [12]degree

SYNTACTIC FUNCTIONS OF ADVERBS AND ADVERBIAL GROUPS

MODULE 55

SUMMARY

1   Just as adverbs express many meanings, they also realise many kinds of syntactic functions:

   • potentially as head of an adverbial group;
   • as Adjunct, Complement and, marginally, as Subject and Object in clauses;
   • as modifiers, and complements in AdjGs, AdvGs, NGs, VGs and PPs;
   • as stance adjuncts associated with whole clauses;
   • as connectives between clauses.

2   Some adverbs have fixed position; others are mobile between initial, middle and end positions.

3   Some adverbs vary their meaning according to their functional role, so *just* may denote an event near to speech time, *We've just finished*, or be used to intensify, as in *That's just fine*.

55.1   SUMMARY OF THE SYNTACTIC FUNCTIONS OF ADVERBS AND ADVERBIAL GROUPS

Adverbs have three main functions:

•   as Adjunct in clause structures;
•   as modifier in group structures; and
•   as connectives between clauses.

Less typically, adverbs and AdvGs can realise the integrated clause functions of Complement, Object and Subject.

In clause structures

1	Adjunct:	I knew her *pretty well.*
2	Stance adjunct:	*Fortunately*, it didn't rain.
3	Inferential connective	*So* you don't want to come, *then.*
4	Subject Complement:	That's *quite all right.*
5	Directional Complement:	Everyone rushed *out.*
6	Direct Object:	I don't know *when.* They didn't tell me *why.*
7	Subject (marginally):	*Today* is the last Friday in the month.

In group structures

8	modifier in AdjGs:	*all* wet; *quite* nice; *too* long; *completely* new.
9	modifier in AdvGs	*nearly* there; *more* easily; *very* often.
10	modifier in NGs:	the *then* Minister of Health; a *nearby* hotel; *quite* a success.
11	modifier of determiners:	*about* double; *roughly* half; *almost* all.
12	modifier in PPs:	*right* out of sight; *just* down the road.
13	submodifier in AdjGs:	*much* too short; *rather* more interesting.
14	submodifier in AdvGs:	*(not) all* that easily; *far* too often.
15	post-modifier in AdjGs:	quick *enough*; very beautiful *indeed.*
16	post-modifier in AdvGs:	quickly *enough*; beautifully *indeed; never again.*
17	post-modifier in NGs:	the journey *back*; the way *ahead.*
18	complement of determinative:	any (interest) *at all*; somewhere *else.*
19	complement in PPs:	over *here*; through *there*; from *inside*; till *now.*
20	particle in VGs:	pick *up*; put *on*; take *out*; pull *off*; go *in.*

Note that 6 and 7 are realised only marginally by adverbs and AdvGs. As Direct Object, *when* and *why* can be used elliptically to stand for a whole clause: *There's to be another meeting soon, but I don't know when/ why* [there's to be another meeting].

Since Adjuncts of various kinds are syntactic elements that can be realised not only by adverbs and AdvGs but also by PPs and finite or non-finite clauses, some grammars group all these classes of realisations under the general name of 'adverbial'. In this book, we reserve the term 'adverbial' strictly for a class of unit, the Adverbial Group, not to be confused with a type of function.

55.2 POSITIONS OF ADVERBS IN THE CLAUSE: INITIAL, MIDDLE AND FINAL

In their function as modifier in group structure, adverbs occupy fixed positions. As adjuncts, however, they are more mobile, occupying initial, middle or end positions, as the following examples show:

1	***Really***, I don't like driving.
2	I ***really*** don't like driving.

3 I don't ***really*** like driving.
4 I don't like driving, ***really***.

Not all adjunctive adverbs are equally mobile. The choice of position is determined by its type (circumstantial, modal, degree, etc.), the scope of its meaning (whole clause or part of a clause), the degree of emphasis the speaker wishes to give to it, and the general information structure of the clause (see Chapter 6).

55.2.1 Adverbs in initial position

When an adverb is placed in initial position as adjunct, its scope extends to the whole clause. In this position, the meaning may be one of two broad kinds:

- It may be thematised (see 28.8), functioning as what is traditionally called a 'sentence adjunct', having the same status as the other clause elements, though referring to them all together, as in:

    Slowly, the rising sun appeared over the distant horizon.

- It may function as a stance adjunct **1**, expressing the speaker's attitude to the content of the clause or comment on its truth value **2**. Stance adjuncts stand outside the clause structure (see Chapter 2).

    1 *Hopefully*, the new plan will lead to some improvements.
    2 *Undoubtedly*, the success is due to your efforts.

Hopefully, and other similar adverbs such as *seriously, frankly*, may also function as adjuncts of manner, within the clause:

    She underwent the operation *hopefully*. (i.e. full of hope)

55.2.2 Scope of reference of adverbs as adjuncts

The different positions an adverb may occupy determine the **scope** of its reference. Compare the examples at the start of Section 55.2, all containing the adverb *really*. In **1** the scope of the adverb comprises the whole sentence, the subject and the predicate. In **2** the scope covers the predicate, without the subject, but including the negation and auxiliary (*don't*). In **3** the scope comprises the predicator and its complement (*driving*). In **4**, as in **1**, the adverb is parenthetical, separated from the clause. Both function as stance adverbs whose scope comprises the whole clause, the first strongly, the second weakly, as if it were an afterthought.

In **2** and **3** the adverb focuses mainly on the predicator and its complement and is placed before or after the auxiliary, which in this case carries negation. In **2** *really* emphasises the negation more strongly than in **3**. Other elements are sometimes focused, for example by restrictive adverbs: *He alone, only for them.*

55.2.3 Adverbs of place, time and manner

Adverbs referring to the **place**, **time** and **manner** of an event are placed most naturally in final position. This is equivalent to 'immediately after the verb', as long as there is no direct object, as in **1** with the intransitive verb *arrive*. When there is a direct object, however, the adverb must be placed after the object, as in **2**. Compare:

1   We arrived *early*.
2   We caught the bus *easily*.   Not *We caught *easily* the bus.

This is because in English, unlike some languages, an object is not separated from the verb which selects it, even by adjuncts of degree:

I like apples *very much*.   Not *I like *very much* apples.

The only exception to this is when the direct object is exceptionally long and so requires end-focus.

Indefinite time adverbs such as *sometimes, eventually, immediately, finally, recently, previously*, can be placed in final, pre-verbal or initial position. Again separation of verb–object is excluded:

(a)   He stopped the machine *immediately*.
(b)   He *immediately* stopped the machine.
(c)   *Immediately* he stopped the machine.
(d)   *He stopped *immediately* the machine.

Of these, (a) is the normal unmarked position, (b) focuses on the process *stop*, and (c) on the whole of the clause. By contrast, (d) is unacceptable.

Certain adverbs of **frequency** – *always, never, seldom, hardly ever, often, rarely, sometimes, usually* – tend to occur in mid-position, between Subject and Predicator or between operator and main verb. The word *often* may also focus on the whole clause, in initial position:

(e)   We *always* spend our holidays abroad. (*Always we spend . . .)
(f)   We have *never* been to Africa. (*Never, we have . . .)
(g)   Lawyers *often* love to tell you about how good they are. (Often lawyers love
        to . . .)   [BNC J75 3288]

The adverbs of **negative import** – *never, seldom, rarely, hardly ever* – are occasionally fronted and followed by Subject–operator inversion for purposes of emphasis, though this structure is formal in style (see also 28.10.1):

Rarely does one find such kindness nowadays.
Never in my life have I heard such crazy ideas!

The adverbs ***still, yet, already*** express certain time relationships which are described briefly and illustrated in the table on p. 513 in question-and-answer structures which show their contrasting meanings.

The examples given of these three adverbs show that their scope of meaning extends to the process or the whole predicate, and for this reason they normally occur in mid- or end-position.

Finally we may observe the similarity of meaning of *still* and *yet* in a *be* + *to*-infinitive structure, and as concessive connectives:

He'll make a champion of you *yet/ still*.
A cure for chronic bronchitis is *still/ yet* to be found.
It was a hard climb. *Still*, it was worth it. (concessive)
He's rather uncommunicative, *yet* everyone seems to like him. (concessive)

Spatial adverbs such as *abroad, across, back, everywhere, downstairs, inside, uphill, forwards, sideways*, expressing position and direction, are normally placed after the Predicator or in end-position: *Push it forwards; turn it sideways*.

Adverbs of manner

The unmarked position for adverbs of manner is at the end of the clause, as in *He speaks English fluently*, not **He speaks fluently English*. If the Object is long, and the adverb is a single word, the Od may be placed at the end, as in *He speaks fluently several European and oriental languages*. If the adverb is modified or complemented as a group, it may still occupy end-position, according to the principles of end-focus and end-weight (30.3.2) even if the Od is also long:

He speaks English *fluently*.
He speaks several European and oriental languages as well as Arabic *very fluently indeed*.

Adverbs in *-ly* include many of manner: *carefully, easily, correctly, cheaply, politely, peacefully, urgently*, and also some emotive ones: *angrily, gladly, desperately*. Both can also occur as adjuncts in mid-position, before the lexical verb. Together such combinations constitute a useful pattern, as they lend force to what immediately follows:

We *sincerely* hope you enjoyed your stay with us.
I have been *seriously* thinking of changing my job.
I will *gladly* help you if you need me.

55.2.4 Adverbs of modality, evidence and degree

The tendency to occupy mid-position extends also to these semantic types:

They're *probably* still partying. (modal)   [BNC JY7 9563]
She is *supposedly* a rich woman. (hearsay evidential)
I *totally* disagree with you. (degree)

The adverbs *still, yet, already*

These three adverbs express, in broad terms, the following time relationships:

Still refers to processes or states which continue to occur or not occur up to the present.
Yet refers to processes or states which may occur in the future or have not occurred up to the present moment.
Already refers to processes or states which occurred before the present moment.

The following table shows their interrelated uses in questions and answers, as in interpersonal communication. In negative replies, there is sometimes an equivalence between the *not yet* and the *still not* constructions. When used in monologues or continuous prose, these adverbs may be found in other syntactic frames, but mostly in the same basic placements as those shown in the table.

Question	Affirmative answer	Negative answer
1 Does Tom *still* visit you?	Yes, he *still* visits us. Yes, he *still* does.	No, he doesn't visit us *any more.* No, he doesn't visit us *any longer.* No, he *no longer* visits us.
2 Is Tom *still* working?	Yes, he is *still* working. Yes, he *still* is.	No, he isn't working *any more.* No, he isn't *any more.* No, he isn't working *any longer.* No, he is *no longer working.*
3 Is Tom working *yet*?	Yes, he is *already* working. Yes, he *already* is.	No, he isn't working *yet.* No, he *still* isn't working.
4 Has Tom arrived *yet*?	Yes, he has arrived *already.* Yes, he has *already* arrived. Yes, he *already* has.	No, he hasn't arrived *yet.* No, he *still* hasn't arrived. No, he hasn't *yet.*
5 Has Tom *already* gone? Has Tom gone *already*?	Yes, he has *already* gone. Yes, he has gone *already.* Yes, he *already* has.	No, he hasn't gone *yet.* No, he is *still* here.
6 Does Tom know *yet*?	Yes, he *already* knows. Yes, he knows *already.* Yes, he *already* does.	No, he doesn't know *yet.* No, he *still* doesn't know. No, he doesn't *yet.*

55.2.5 Function and type

Since there is rarely a one-to-one relationship between function and type, many words can realise more than one syntactic function, with the position of the adverb varying according to its function. This is illustrated by the adverbs 'altogether' and 'later':

Altogether: He owes me a hundred dollars *altogether* (adjunct)
I think you are *altogether* wrong (modifier of adj.)
There were a lot of interesting people there, so *altogether* we had a very good time. (connective)

Later: There will be another performance *later*. (adjunct)
The *later* performance will be at midnight. (modifier of noun)
The performance *later* will be a better one. (post-modifier of noun)

In conversation, adverbs sometimes occur alone, as responses to something said by the previous speaker. In such cases the adverb can carry out such discourse functions as agreeing emphatically, expressing mild interest, asserting strongly or granting permission in particular contexts:

Maybe that's a way to do it. [BNC F7C 26–27]
Absolutely   (emphatic agreement)

Now that's what I call a first-class meal!
Definitely!   (emphatic agreement)

Did you enjoy the outing?
Tremendously, yes!   (emphatic assertion)

Can I have a look at the contract?
Certainly.   (granting permission)

MODIFICATION AND COMPLEMENTATION IN THE ADVERBIAL GROUP

SUMMARY

1 Adverbs are graded in the same way as adjectives by *more, less, as* and so on, and the same suppletive forms are used for *well* and *badly* as for *good* and *bad*.

2 Similarly, intensification is carried out by *very, quite, rather, pretty, fairly*, among others.

3 Adverbs of space or time are frequently modified by other adverbs of space or time (*out there, back home*). Adverbs of manner are not normally used to modify other adverbs of manner, except when expressing modal attitudes.

4 Few adverbs take direct complements with prepositions or clauses (Luckily *for us, long to wait*). Indirect complements of graded forms function in the same way as with adjectives.

56.1 COMPARATIVE AND SUPERLATIVE USES

Adverbs are graded by the same words as adjectives:

> *more* often, *most* often, *less* often, *least* often, *as* often, often *enough*, *too* often.

Although the adverb *enough* is placed after the head adverb, we shall consider it as a modifier as we do with adjectives, since it can itself be submodified by an adverb placed before the head: *not quite often enough* (**not quite enough often*).

The following suppletive forms are used as comparative and superlative forms of the adjectives *good, bad* and *far*, and the adverbs *well, badly and far*. Good/well: *better, best*; bad/badly: *worse, worst*; far: *further, furthest*.

> Tomorrow morning would suit me *best*, for the meeting.
> It was the driver who came off *worst* in the accident.

The forms shared by adverbs and adjectives *early, late, quick, fast, long, soon* take *-est* and *-er* in grades 1 and 2.

> His speech was long*er* than mine. He spoke long*er* than I did.
> I arrived lat*er* than Monica, because I came by a lat*er* train.
> Please come the *earliest* you possibly can. Take the *earliest* train.

Correlative forms

The constructions formed by *the more . . . the more* (or *-er . . . -er*), *the less . . . the less, the more . . . the less* can be used correlatively to indicate a progressive increase, or decrease, of the quality or process described. Both adjectives and adverbs can occur in this construction:

> *The bigger* they are, *the harder* they fall, don't they? (adj–adv)   [BNC KBB 4742]
> *The sooner you* forget the whole incident, *the better.* (adv–adv)
> It's funny, *the more* painting you do, *the more* you realise you don't know.
> [BNC CCO 344]
> The *more closely* I look at the problem, the *less clearly* I see a solution. (adv–adv)

This construction is illustrated in the following extract from an in-flight magazine:

> **Don't eat a large high-fat meal if you want to be mentally sharp afterwards. Too much food brings on lethargy. Fat stays in the digestive tract longer, prolonging tiredness. *The fattier and heavier* the meal, *the longer* it takes you to recover mental alertness and energy.**

56.2 INTENSIFYING THE ADVERBIAL MEANING

As with adjectives, intensification may be (a) high, or (b) medium.

> (a) *very* soon   *quite* recently   *right* now   *high* up
>   *just* then   *far* back   *soon* after   *close* by
> (b) *fairly* well *pretty* easily   *rather* badly

We saw in 52.1.2 that coordinated comparative adjectives indicate a progressively high degree of the quality expressed: it's getting *colder and colder*. Adverbial heads also participate in this structure, with the adverb as head or as modifier:

> He drove *faster and faster* along the motorway.
> Her paintings are selling *more and more successfully* every day.

Reduplicative adverbs have an intensifying effect:

very very fast	much much better	never ever	through and through
over and over	up and up	again and again	round and round

Attenuation

a bit harshly	*kind of* hesitantly	*almost* never
somewhat casually	*sort of* sarcastically	*hardly* ever

Quantification

As with adjectives, this refers mainly to circumstantial adverbs of space and time and may be either exact, or non-measurable:

Exact: Our houses are *only two streets* apart.
I saw her *a moment* ago.

Non-measurable: quantity is expressed by modifiers such as: *soon* after, *long* before, *quite* near, *shortly* afterwards.

These circumstantial adverbs can be questioned by *how* + adj/adv:

How long have you been waiting? Not long.
How far is it to the railway station? Not far.

The focusing modifier: only

Only is a restrictive focusing adverb which can modify different units:

I wanted *only* one piece of toast.
We go there *only* once a year.

There is a tendency in spoken English to front the adverb to a position before the verb:

I *only* wanted one piece of toast.
We *only* go there once a year.

Description

Adverbs of space or time are often preceded by other adverbs of space or time which reinforce or describe them more explicitly:

straight ahead	*back* home	*up* above	*early* today
out there	*late* yesterday	*down* below	*in* here

As with adjectives, we may note the **emotive modification** of adverbs by swear words such as *damn(ed)*, as in *You behaved damn foolishly*, and other less polite ones.

Though less common in adverbial groups than in adjectival groups, modifiers can be found **submodified**, or even **sub-submodified**, especially in spoken English:

rather	less	fluently	
very	much	more	profitably

The following adapted extract from a conversation illustrates a rather British use of intensifiers:

J.W. What in fact do we think of when we think of a camel?

A.R. *Well*,[1] . . .

J.W. Is it a pleasant animal or . . .

A.R. An unpleasant animal? . . . Obtuseness I should say *generally*,[2] the whole attitude of a camel seems to be, er, obtuse. It has this, er, *rather*[3] supercilious look on its face . . . for example . . . and they have, I'm told, I've *never*[4] experienced this I'm happy to say, but they have this magnificent facility for spitting *quite*[5] a considerable distance with great accuracy, er . . .

J.W. I don't know that spitting shows obtuseness. I should have thought it *probably*[6] shows perspicacity . . .

G.T. I think he's *slightly*[7] ridiculous, the camel, isn't he? The, er, weird expression he has on his face is *rather*[8] like the ostrich, but the ostrich carries it off. The ostrich looks marvellous, where, whereas the camel *just*[9] doesn't bring it off at all.

K.B. Camels *always*[10] strike me as *rather*[11] mean, they're ready to do you down at the slightest opportunity.

(L. Dickinson and R. Mackin, *Varieties of Spoken English*)

[1]hesitation; [2]frequency; [3]medium intensification; [4]frequency; [5]high intensification; [6]modality; [7]attenuation; [8]medium intensification; [9]emphasis; [10]frequency; [11]intensification (= very)

56.3 COMPLEMENTATION OF ADVERBS

The *wh*-items *when, where, why, how* and their compounds (*somewhere, anywhere*, etc.) have nominal as well as circumstantial value, as is shown in their post-modification by AdjGs (*somewhere more exotic*), PPs (*everywhere in the world*), non-fin cl (*nowhere to sleep*) and the adverb *else*:

where else?	=	in what other place?
when else?	=	at what other time?
how else?	=	in what other way?
why else?	=	for what other reason?

The forms *somewhere, anywhere, nowhere* are often replaced in informal AmE by *someplace, anyplace, no place*, though not in *wh*-questions, e.g. *someplace else, anyplace else, no place else* Circumstantial adverbs are sometimes qualified by others of a similar type, so that it is not always clear which is the head and which the modifier:

> We'll be meeting them *sometime soon*.
> I need a drink. There must be a pub *somewhere near*.

In clauses like the following, the AdvG realising the Adjunct is composed of two apposed adverbs: We'll meet *tomorrow Sunday*. In informal speech, intensification and reinforcement of circumstantial adverbs may be expressed by post-modifiers, such as the following:

> The train will be arriving *now any minute / any minute now*.
> It always arrives *punctually on the dot* (= on time).

Stance adverbs are sometimes modified by *enough*, in the sense of intensification rather than sufficiency:

> *Curiously enough*, he doesn't seem to mind criticism.
> The police never found out, *oddly enough*, who stole the jewels.

56.3.1 Complements of comparison and excess

Complements of adverbs are almost exclusively of one type, namely grading. As with adjectives, many adverbial heads admit indirect complements, which depend, not on the adverb itself, but on the degree modifier.

More, less . . . than	Bill speaks Spanish *much more* fluently *than his sister*.
	It rains *less often* here *than in some other countries*.
-er . . . than	Our coach left earlier *than it should have done*.
as . . . as	I don't translate *as* accurately *as a professional*.
too . . . to-inf	We reached the station *too* late *to catch the train*.
not adv enough . . . to-inf	We did*n't* leave *early enough to get there in time*.

Such structures may be considered (as with AdjGs) as discontinuous complementation, though the two parts of the structure, before and after the head, differ in position and content. The modifiers *more* (*-er*) and *less* do not necessarily require the *than*-complement; on the other hand, complements introduced by *than* cannot be used without a previous modifier which controls this construction.

If a comparison of equality (*as . . . as . . .*) is established between two adverbs of manner (such as *elegantly, amusingly*) the second *as* must be followed by a finite clause with a form of *be, do,* or *have* substituting for the predicator:

> Jane Austen wrote as elegantly as *she did* amusingly. (and not **as elegantly as amusingly*)

Adverbs modified quantitatively by *so* and *that* are also complemented in the same way as adjectives. The sequence of the clauses can be inverted, the second one then becoming an explanatory comment on the first:

> He explained the problem *so clearly* (*that*) everybody understood.
> Everybody understood the problem, he explained it *so clearly*.

56.3.2 Adverbs taking direct complements

Whereas a good number of adjectives take prepositional and clausal complements, only a few adverbs, all ending in *-ly*, take direct complements in this way. The preposition or clausal complement associated with an adjective is in most cases not extended to the adverb: Compare *mad about music, safe to drink*, but not **madly about music* or **safely to drink*. Only a few prepositions complementing adjectives are also found with an adverb. These include: *similarly to, independently of, separately from* and *differently from*. Apart from these, *luckily, fortunately*, when used as stance adjuncts, can be complemented by *for* + *NG*, while the adverbs *long* (= a long time) and *far* (=a great distance), take a *to*-infinitive and tend to occur in non-assertive contexts (p. 24), e.g. negative, interrogative:

> *Luckily/ fortunately for us* another coach came along shortly afterwards.
> We didn't have *long to wait*.
> Do you have *far to go*?

The following recorded conversation is characterised by a variety of very commonly used adverbs in various syntactic and discourse functions:

A. So what's new, Ann?
C. *Well* I *don't* know if anything's *terribly*[1] new *at all*[2] *really*[3] or is it all *much*[4] the same?
B. You *still*[5] living with Deb?
C. No, she moved *out*[6] at the end of April.
B. Oh.
A. *So*,[7] you know, *well*,[8] we'd been *scarcely*[9] speaking for almost a year *really*,[10] *so*[11] it was *a bit of a*[12] heavy atmosphere it didn't *really*[13] bother me in fact
   . . .
B. m
C. In fact we just[14] sort of[15] lived entirely[16] separate lives. I used only[17] to see her when she came through the kitchen her nose in the air sort of thing. *Anyway*,[18] *really*,[19] I think, the kitchen . . .
B. A *bit*[12] awkward, that, I should think you would think a door could be pushed *through*,[21] through where you've got that little room with the cupboard in it.
C. I suppose *so*,[22] you see, I mean, *even*[23] if it were a couple living *together*,[24] it

would be *just*[25] ideal, that sort of thing wouldn't matter, but it isn't *really*[26] suited to people who are living separate lives *really*.[27] *So*[28] at any rate, she moved out.[29] I *never*[30] heard from her *since*.[31]

B. You haven't, not a word?

C. No, I haven't heard from her *at all*[32] and I haven't contacted her, and she hasn't contacted me. I haven't *really*[33] felt I wanted to, cos it was a *little*[34] *sort of*[35] *rather*[36] unpleasant in the end.

(Adapted from Jan Svartvik and Randolph Quirk (eds),
A Corpus of English Conversation)

FURTHER READING

Some of the ideas presented in the revised version of this chapter are indebted to the following publications: Biber et al. (1999); Halliday (1994); Huddleston and Pullum (2002); Quirk et al. (1985).

EXERCISES ON CHAPTER 11

Describing persons, things and circumstances

1 ADJECTIVES AND THE ADJECTIVAL GROUP

Module 51

1 After reading the two book blurbs (pp. 477 and 483), use some of the structures to write a description of any person you know or have seen, or any novel you have read.

2 †Express the following sentences differently using a pseudo-participial adjective in *-ing* or *-en* formed from the noun shown in italics. The first is done for you:

(1) Lots of people drink spring water *sold in bottles*. Lots of people drink *bottled* spring water.

(2) You have shown great *enterprise* in setting up this firm.

(3) The newspapers reported all the *details* of the case.

(4) Conflicts often arise between countries that are *neighbours*.

(5) We live in an ancient town with a great *wall* round it.

(6) There are often better opportunities for workers who have *skills* than for those who *have not*.

3 †Turn to the passage about Ben and Olly on p. 477. State (a) the function of each numbered adjective or AdjG, for example: 1 modifier in NG; (b) Which are classifiers and which descriptors; (c) How would you analyse 'ten' in 'Ben and Olly are ten'?

4 †Say whether the *-ing* forms derived from transitive and intransitive verbs in the following phrases are participial adjectives or participial modifiers. Give a grammatical reason to support your analysis:

> transitive: an *alarming* inflation rate; *disturbing* rumours; a *relaxing* drink.
> intransitive: a *ticking* clock; *fading* hopes; a *growing* debt.

5 Write very short sentences using the following formal types of compound adjectives. If you are not sure of the meaning, consult a good dictionary:

(1) **Adj + V-*ing***:   nice-looking, good-looking, easy-going, hard-wearing.
(2) **Adj + V-*en***:   deep-frozen, big-headed, sharp-eyed.
(3) **Noun + Adj**:   world-famous, water-tight, self-confident.

6 Suggest appropriate nouns or adjectives to form compounds with the following adjectives, e.g. sea-green.

> -blue, -green, -pink, -red, -cold, -hot, -black, -sweet, -white.

7 †Express the following NGs differently, using a compound adjective as modifier of the head noun. The first is done for you:

(1)   a story so scarifying that it raises the hair on your head = a *hair-raising* story
(2)   an activity that consumes too much of your time
(3)   cakes that have been made at home
(4)   a speed that takes your breath away
(5)   troops that are borne (= transported) by air
(6)   a plain that has been swept by the wind
(7)   the performance that won an award
(8)   a device that saves a great deal of labour

Module 52

1a †Say which of the following adjectives take the inflected forms (*-er, -est*) for grading and which the analytical (*more, most*): risky, real, varied, blue, typical, mistaken, friendly, user-friendly, small, tight, generous, bitter.

1b Say which of the adjectives as used in the following phrases can be graded:

> (1) *shallow* water; (2) the *closing* date; (3) a *daily* newspaper; (4) a *small* size; (5) the *probable* outcome; (6) the *main* reason; (7) a *fast* driver; (8) the *political* consequences.

2 In the course of a conversation, a friend makes the following remarks to you. Disagree with your friend emphatically using highly intensified adjectives and, where possible, an emotive adjective. Use a different intensifier each time, chosen from the following: *very, extremely, absolutely, really, thoroughly, terrifically, most, exceedingly, completely, highly, utterly, perfectly, awfully, hopelessly, dreadfully.*

(1) I don't think much of these paintings, do you?
(2) The food in the students' canteen is pretty awful.
(3) Have you seen Ross's new car? It's a real beauty!
(4) Apparently, two members of the team have been involved in some kind of scandal.
(5) You don't seem to know what's going on.
(6) I don't think she's the right girl for him.
(7) Did you see that lousy match on the telly last night?
(8) You're looking very energetic and happy today.

3   On this occasion, your friend will ask you for your opinion, and you will answer using adjectives that are moderately intensified by *quite, pretty, rather, fairly, reasonably* or attenuated by expressions such as: *a bit, a little, slightly, not particularly, not very, not really, to some extent, in some respects, kind of, sort of, not at all.*

(1) Did you have an interesting time in Egypt?
(2) Was it very hot there at that time of the year?
(3) Were you in a very large group?
(4) What were the hotels like?
(5) Did you find it difficult to communicate with people?
(6) Were the guides well informed?
(7) Was the trip expensive?
(8) Didn't you find all that travelling tiring?
(9) I expect you were glad to get home, weren't you?

4   Working in pairs, ask and answer questions using how? and the following measurable adjectives:

How long is . . . ?   How old . . .?   How deep . . .?   How thick . . .?
How high is/are . . . ?   How tall . . .?   How wide . . .?

4b   Ask each other questions with How? and non-measurable adjectives, and use any types of intensifier you wish in the answers, for instance: not nearly tall enough to play in a basketball team.

How important . . .?   How clever . . .?   How hungry . . .?   How difficult . . .?

5   †Add qualitative modifiers to the adjectives in these sentences, choosing them from the following list: *essentially, genuinely, imaginatively, pleasantly, ferociously, radically, ideally.*

(1) The new cultural centre is a(n) _ _ _ _ _ _ _ _ _ _ international project.
(2) It will be in a style _ _ _ _ _ _ _ _ _ _ different from the usual urban architecture.
(3) It will be _ _ _ _ _ _ _ _ _ _ placed outside the city, and _ _ _ _ _ _ _ _ _ _
(4) _ _ _ _ _ _ _ _ _ _ surrounded by fields and trees.
(5) Some traditionalists have been _ _ _ _ _ _ _ _ _ _ critical of the design.
(6) The architect has said: 'We have tried to combine the _ _ _ _ _ _ _ _ _ _ old with the _ _ _ _ _ _ _ _ _ _ new'.

6 †Express these sentences differently by using a 'relational modifier + adjective' unit, as in the following example:

> From a scientific point of view that opinion is not based on facts or evidence.
> *That opinion is scientifically unfounded.*

(1) Drugs are necessary for medical purposes, but if abused they may be dangerous from a social point of view.
(2) The new oral examinations are very good in theory but have proved somewhat time-consuming to administer.
(3) Countries which are advanced in technological matters should help those in which science is under-developed.

Module 53

1 Complement the adjectives in the following clauses with a finite or non-finite clause. The first is done for you:

(1) Jasmine and Nick are *keen* **to take up golf**.
(2) I am *sorry* _ _ _ _ _ _ _ _ _ _ _ _ _ _ _ _ _ _ _ _ _ _
(3) My girl-friend is *insistent* _ _ _ _ _ _ _ _ _ _ _ _ _ _ _ _ _ _ _ _ _
(4) You are *right* _ _ _ _ _ _ _ _ _ _ _ _ _ _ _ _ _ _ _ _ _
(5) This extraordinarily violent film on the passion of Christ is *likely* _ _ _ _ _ _ _ _ _ _ _ _ _ _
_ _ _ _ _ _ _ _
(6) We are *convinced* _ _ _ _ _ _ _ _ _ _ _ _ _ _ _ _ _ _ _ _ _
(7) The Olympic team's trainer feels *confident* _ _ _ _ _ _ _ _ _ _ _ _ _ _ _ _ _ _ _ _ _
(8) You must be *crazy* _ _ _ _ _ _ _ _ _ _ _ _ _ _ _ _ _ _ _ _ _
(9) I am *happy* _ _ _ _ _ _ _ _ _ _ _ _ _ _ _ _ _ _ _ _ _
(10) Is she *glad* _ _ _ _ _ _ _ _ _ _ _ _ _ _ _ _ _ _ _ _?

2 †Complement the following adjectives with PPs expressing the types of information mentioned on the left. The first one is done for you.

(1) a cause: I'm angry *about what you said yesterday* _ _ _ _ _ _ _ _ _ _ _ _ _ _ _ _ _ _
(2) a cause: I was *delighted* _ _ _ _ _ _ _ _ _ _ _ _ _ _ _ _ _ _ _ _ _
(3) a process: Not all the students are *satisfied* _ _ _ _ _ _ _ _ _ _ _ _ _ _ _ _ _ _ _ _ _
(4) a phenomenon: Many of them are *opposed* _ _ _ _ _ _ _ _ _ _ _ _ _ _ _ _ _ _ _ _ _
(5) an emotion: He went *white* _ _ _ _ _ _ _ _ _ _ _ _ _ _ _ _ _ _ _ _ _
(6) an activity: He is really *expert* _ _ _ _ _ _ _ _ _ _ _ _ _ _ _ _ _ _ _ _ _
(7) an activity: Aren't you *tired* _ _ _ _ _ _ _ _ _ _ _ _ _ _ _ _ _ _ _ _?
(8) a subject: I'm very *keen* _ _ _ _ _ _ _ _ _ _ _ _ _ _ _ _ _ _ _ _ _

3 Turn to the extract from Roald Dahl's *Boy* on p. 499. Then (a) Underline all the adjective and AdjGs and state their function; (b) Discuss the parallel aspects of 'complement' in both nominal groups and adjectival groups, as illustrated in this passage. (NG complements are discussed in Chapter 10.)

4 The following extract comes from the *Time* discussion transcript archive. The topic was the cloning of humans. Read the passage, underlining whole groups containing adjectives and adverbs. Use these in sentences of your own on the same topic:

> **Timehost presents question:** I would like for you to clearly define why you think it is morally wrong to clone a human being. So far that has been totally unclear.
>
> **Thomas Murray says:** 'I think the reasons have been made abundantly clear in much of the conversation that has taken place since June. The immediate and most compelling reason is that cloning, from all the evidence, appears to be an extremely unsafe activity right now. The US, and other nations as well, have very strong traditions of protecting the human subjects of research. At this time, and for the foreseeable future, trying to clone a human being would be clearly unethical experimentation.'

Another question:

> **Timehost presents question:** What are your views on the possibility of a 'master race' possibly being created, where 'perfect' children are bought and sold on the black markets around the world?
>
> **Thomas Murray says:** 'Well, probably the most fortunate thing about that scenario is that at this point it's really science fiction. I wish I could assure everybody that there's not some crazy person someplace who wouldn't find a scenario like that attractive.'

Later, the final question . . .

> **Timehost presents question:** If this is a fertility treatment, what about custody? Wouldn't a parent that provided the DNA for the cloned child be predisposed to custody?
>
> **Thomas Murray:** 'Well, it would be a brand new problem for the law to decide. An easy way to dismiss cloning is to raise a variety of legal complexes that it would create. And it would create lots of them. I don't in the end think that's the most useful way to think about what's good and bad about cloning. I'm more concerned about the precise control over the characteristics of offspring that people think, almost certainly erroneously, that cloning might provide.'

Module 54

1 †Read again the passage by Joyce Cary on p. 505 and identify the type of meaning expressed by each adverb or AdvG printed in italics. Are any types used more frequently than others? Do you think there is any reason for this?

2 †Do the same with the following passage, and say whether the relative frequency of the types of meanings is the same as in the previous text:

> Is there life *elsewhere* in the cosmos? One view is that life on earth, *especially* intelligent life, is the result of an *incredibly* unlikely set of circumstances, and that there is no intelligent life *anywhere* else in our Galaxy, *perhaps* none in the entire Universe. The opposing argument is that there are so many stars and planets in the Galaxy that, provided there is *even* a small chance of intelligence developing on one planet, it has *probably* happened on many others, *too*. Observations show that *about* 10% of all bright stars are *roughly* similar to the sun. In our Milky Way Galaxy *alone* that means *approximately 40* billion stars of the right type. This number is great *enough* to suggest that the odds are quite high.
>
> James Jeans, *The Universe Around Us*

3 †Insert in the following sets of sentences, in appropriate places, suitable adverbs chosen from the list of examples suggested for each set.

(a) **Stance adverbs**: certainly, reportedly, obviously, allegedly, admittedly, undeniably, actually, clearly, undoubtedly, eminently.

(1) This novel is well suited to the cinema.
(2) The film is brilliant and moving, though it might have been even more so.
(3) A visit to the National Theatre is an educational experience for anyone interested in twentieth-century architecture.
(4) The President has not decided yet on seeking a second term.
(5) The collection includes a poem written by Hitler.
(6) It was not a well-planned 'coup', because it failed so quickly.
(7) He became a star during the revolt, which allowed him to turn it into a political asset.
(8) Their popularity is rising, judging by the number of fans at their concerts here.

(b) **Adverbs of respect**: historically, stylistically, politically, socially, racially, ideologically, morally, constitutionally, clinically, formally.

(1) Though not 'true enemies', they are unyielding.
(2) He is well connected.
(3) The sentences are too long and complex.

(4) The British are mixed.
(5) The higher ranks were responsible for the harsh treatment of the prisoners.
(6) The costumes designed for the play are accurate in every detail.

(c) **Restriction and reinforcement**: merely, hardly, solely, alone, exclusively, simply; just, even; also, too, again, as well, similarly.

(1) The doctor who begins by searching for a heart-beat on the right-hand side will convince the patient that he will be able to help him.
(2) These taxis are always there when you need one, in the rain.
(3) To put it in a few words, we do not know the answer.
(4) The emphasis in language study was for a while on formal grammar.
(5) Harry said that the river would suit him perfectly, and I said so.
(6) What has happened explains many problems of the past and will help us avoid future ones.

(d) **Process adverbs of manner**: cautiously, soundly, surreptitiously, heavily, momentarily, secretly, endlessly, rigorously, slowly, mechanically.

(1) Yusuf was sleeping on his back.
(2) Apparently, the man was suspected of carrying diamonds and should be searched.
(3) Behind the barrier, Wilson worked at his code books.
(4) He went on speaking, choosing his words.
(5) It was said that he drank.
(6) The rain had stopped.

Module 55

1 Revise briefly the list given in 55.1 of the syntactic functions which can be realised by AdvGs in groups and clauses. Then make a list of the functions realised by all of those used in the text on metals on p. 507. Write out the list and comment on the relative frequency of each function.

2 †Revise the table of uses of *still, yet, already* given on p. 513. Then answer the following questions, (a) affirmatively, and (b) negatively. Give two or three answers to each question.

(1) Is it time to go yet? -
(2) Have you had your lunch yet? -
(3) Do you still love me? -
(4) Are you still studying Russian? -
(5) Is it ten o'clock already? -
(6) Have you already been to Venice? -

3 †In the following sentences, insert the adverb given on the left in its appropriate position, Indicate alternative positions where they are acceptable, and say whether this affects the meaning in any way:
(1) *sometimes:* We take long holidays in mountainous areas.

(2) *often:* Journalists working in war zones are in danger.
(3) *abroad:* She gets on well with people.
(4) *yesterday:* They gave a concert.
(5) *longingly:* The cat gazed at the brightly coloured fish in the aquarium.
(6) *perhaps:* You'd better take an overcoat with you.
(7) *probably:* We shall leave tomorrow.
(8) *hopefully:* They have arrived at their destination.

4 We have included the word *today* in the category of adverb, functioning marginally as subject in clause structure and more centrally as adjunct. In one of the grammars mentioned in the 'Further Reading', *today* and *tomorrow* are classed as deictic pronouns, not adverbs. Another grammar treats these words as nouns. Discuss these proposals, providing criteria and evidence for the different views. Does *yesterday* fulfil the same conditions as *today* and *tomorrow*?

Similarly, *ago* is sometimes analysed as a preposition with a postposed complement. Discuss.

Module 56

1 Modify the adverbs marked in the following sentences, in the senses indicated on the left:

(1) **Intensification:** She answered *automatically*, without thinking.
(2) **Medium intensification:** He recovered *quickly* after the operation.
(3) **Description:** The book is selling *well*.
(4) **Attenuation:** The look on his face was weird.
(5) **Quantification:** He had a few drinks and *later* was involved in an accident.
(6) **Description:** The winner of the car rally drove *fast*.
(7) **Intensification:** Our team didn't play *well* on that occasion.

2 Add a post-modifier or complement to the AdvG in the following sentences:

(1) It's hotter in the Sahara than *anywhere* _____
(2) When we came out of the Pyramids, I said to myself: 'Never' _____
(3) I can't find my glasses. They must be *somewhere* _____
(4) *Curiously* _____ he used exactly the same word as I did.
(5) She doesn't dance as *beautifully* _____
(6) Do your friends live *far* _____?

3 †Read the conversation on pages 520–1, nd identify the syntactic function of each numbered adverb and the semantic type to which it belongs.

SPATIAL, TEMPORAL AND OTHER RELATIONSHIPS

CHAPTER 12

The Prepositional Phrase

PREPOSITIONS AND THE PREPOSITIONAL PHRASE (PP)

SUMMARY

1 Prepositions have a relating function: they establish relations between nominal units, mainly nouns and nominal groups, and other units in the surrounding discourse. The prepositional phrase consists of a preposition together with its complement, typically a nominal group as in *under the chair*.

2 Prepositions may consist of one word (*from*), two words (*because of*) or three (*in contact with*) and occasionally four (*with the exception of*). All are single prepositions.

3 The sequence **preposition + nominal complement**, with optional **modifier**, can function as a clause element (It fell *right into the water*) or a group element (the house *on the corner*). Unlike nouns, adjectives and adverbs, which can function alone as head of their respective groups, the preposition cannot stand alone, without its complement (**it fell right into*, **the house on*). In other words, the combination of preposition + complement is not reducible to a single element and for this reason is classified as a 'phrase'.

4 The complement may be realised by a nominal group represented by a noun (in *town*), a pronoun (after *me*), a full NG (for *a long time*), an adjective (in *full*), an adverb (for *now*), a PP (except *at work*), a *wh*-clause (because of *what happened*), a non-finite *-ing* clause (by *concentrating hard*).

5 When modified, the preposition, or sometimes the whole PP, may be graded (*more* like a canary), intensified (*right* through the wall), quantified (*a mile* down the road) or described (*wonderfully* on form).

INTRODUCTION

A notable feature of the English language is the extremely wide lexico-grammatical use it makes of prepositions. And where there is a preposition there is a PP, since prepositions cannot normally stand alone, although they can be separated from their complement by 'stranding' (see 6.3.3; 60.1).

57.1 INTERNAL STRUCTURE OF THE PREPOSITIONAL PHRASE

Nouns, adjectives and adverbs each function as head of their respective groups. In AdjGs, AdvGs and NGs, the 'head' is the main element, to which the other elements, when present, are subordinate. For this reason, the head element – a noun, an adjective or an adverb – can be used alone, without other elements, potentially in representation of the whole group. Structures of this kind centre on the head.

In a prepositional phrase (PP), the relation between the preposition and the nominal unit that follows it (e.g. under *the bed*, from *home*) does not centre on a head. A preposition cannot normally occur without a nominal unit, and a nominal unit is not part of a PP if there is no preposition. Both are equally necessary to form the phrase; both have equal grammatical status. For this reason we refer to the unit consisting of a preposition, its complement and an optional modifier as a 'prepositional phrase' (PP).

The internal structure of PPs consists of a preposition and its complement, both of which are obligatory, and an optional modifier. It can be represented as follows:

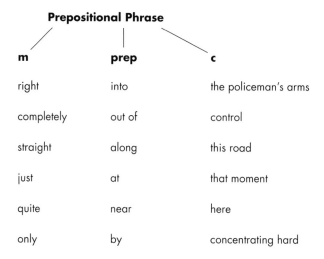

Prepositional Phrase		
m	prep	c
right	into	the policeman's arms
completely	out of	control
straight	along	this road
just	at	that moment
quite	near	here
only	by	concentrating hard

Not all PPs contain a modifier but all of them contain a preposition and a complement. The modifier typically intensifies the preposition by adding something semantically specific to the sense of the preposition, such as exactness and immediacy in the case of *right*, together with completion (*right into* the policeman's arms) or exclusiveness (*only by concentrating hard*).

Here is a recorded conversation between three students and a teacher (T), which illustrates the abundant use of prepositional phrases in English. Examples are numbered for future reference and explanation:

T:	What's this *about?*[1]
B:	Oh, animals.
T:	Oh, yes. People are obsessed *in this country*[2] *with being kind*[3] *to animals,*[4] aren't they?
A:	Alison and her cat . . .!
B:	Don't talk *to us*[5] *about Alison's cat!*[6]
C:	That cat is definitely not popular *in our house!*[7]
B:	That cat moults constantly *all over our carpet and sofa!*[8]
T:	But is it true, though? See what I mean? She hates cats!
A:	*Just for that silly reason?*[9]
T:	No, but there seem to be more cases *of animal cruelty*[10] going on here *than anywhere else.*[11]
A:	Yeah. I get the impression *from the little I know*[12] they're *just as crazy about dogs*[13] *in Belgium and Holland and France and Italy*[14] as they are *over here.*[15]
T:	Is it just one of those myths that we perpetuate *regarding the British character?*[16] Is it true?
A:	I think it probably is a myth.

(recorded conversation)

57.2 FEATURES OF THE PREPOSITIONAL PHRASE

The prepositional phrase normally functions as:

- an element of clause structure, for example as Adjunct (e.g. I decided to become a writer *precisely for that reason*); or
- as a unit embedded in classes of groups, for example as post-modifier of a noun (e.g. the girl *at the cash desk*) or as complement of an adjective (e.g. delighted *at your success*) as explained in 58.2.

PPs are frequently embedded in other structures, including other PPs:

On top of [the cupboard [[*in* your office]]]
In [an envelope [*under* the letters [*in* the drawer]]]
Obsessed [*with* being kind [*to* animals]]

The sequence **prep + NG + prep + NG** may sometimes be structurally ambiguous. For instance, '*near* the bar *on* the corner' can represent the following two structures which express different meanings:

1 a simple preposition + complement, which contains another PP as post-modifier:

near [the bar on the corner] (*on the corner* is m in the NG headed by '*bar*')

2 two independent PPs, functioning as two adjuncts, which might be reversed in order:

> near [the bar] + [on the corner]
> on [the corner] + near [the bar]

The preposition is often stranded to the end of a clause and is separated from the nominal. Stranding is typical of spoken English, while the non-stranded counterparts are very formal:

> *What's* this *about?* ('*What*' functions as complement of *about: about what?*)
> *Which book* are you referring *to?* (*To which book* are you referring?)

The meanings of prepositions are either **lexical** and 'free', or **grammaticised** and 'bound'. Grammaticised uses of prepositions are those which are controlled by a verb, adjective or noun, as happens in *obsessed **with**, talk **to** us, kind **to** animals, cases **of** cruelty*. Lexical prepositional meanings are those freely chosen according to the speaker's communicative intention (*in this country, all over our carpet and sofa*). Both are discussed in Module 59.

57.3 ONE-WORD, TWO-WORD AND MULTI-WORD PREPOSITIONS

Prepositions may be 'simple' (consisting of a single word) or 'complex' (consisting of two words or three).

One-word prepositions

The short, simple forms are by far the commonest, such as:

> *about, across, after, around, as, at, by, down, for, from, in, like, near, of, off, on, round, to, towards, with, without*

Other one-word prepositions include:

> *above, against, beneath, besides, below; during, inside, throughout; considering, regarding; given, granted; opposite; despite; than*

Two-word prepositions

These consist of a preposition (e.g. *except*), an adjective (e.g. *contrary*), an adverb (e.g. *instead*) or a conjunction (e.g. *because*), followed by one of the prepositions *for, from, of, to, with*:

> **+ for**:   *as for, except for, but for*
> **+ from**:   *apart from, away from, as from*

+ of:	*ahead of, because of, inclusive of, instead of, regardless of, out of*
+ to:	*according to, as to, close to, contrary to, due to, next to, on to, near to; on to, owing to, thanks to, up to*
+ with:	*together with, along with*

In most two-word prepositions, the meaning is expressed by the first word, the second serving to link it to the complement:

> *according to* my information; *because of* what I said

The forms *into* and *onto* can be considered as merged forms, consisting of an adverb (*in, on*) merged with a preposition *to*. Some other one-word prepositions were once two words: *upon, without, throughout* among others.

Three-word prepositions

These usually have the form **prep + noun + prep** (e.g. *in conflict with*), with the noun sometimes being determined by *the* (e.g. *in the hands of*). The first preposition is virtually limited to *in, on, by, at, for, with*, and the second to *of, with, for* and *to*. Two other combinations in common use have an adverb between two occurrences of *as*: *as **far** as, as **well** as*.

> *as far as, as well as, by means of, by way of, in aid of, in charge of, in view of, in return for, in exchange for, in spite of, in contact with, on top of, on the part of, at the hands of, with regard to, with reference to*

Four-word prepositions

All these have the form **prep + a/ the + noun + of** (e.g. *as a result of, at the expense of, on the part of, with the exception of*).

Sometimes the noun of a complex preposition may be modified by an adjective, as in *with the **surprising** exception of Tom; in **close** contact with you*.

PPs with the possessive

A small number of PPs containing complex prepositions ending in *of* have an alternative structure in *'s*, no doubt because the complex preposition could also be analysed as a simple preposition with a NG complement: *for + the sake of the children; on + behalf of the committee*:

> **for the sake of** the children;   **on behalf of** the committee;
> for the children's sake;   on the committee's behalf.

However, non-personal reference is not always used with the genitive form: compare *for heaven's sake*, but not **for peace and quiet's sake*.

57.4 REALISATIONS OF THE COMPLEMENT ELEMENT

The complement element of a PP is most typically realised by a nominal group, but it may also be realised by the classes of groups and clauses shown below. Simple nouns and pronouns, adjectives and adverbs are treated as 'groups' represented by the head:

NGs:	at *home*	after *which*	on account of *his age*
AdjGs:	in *private*	at *last*	for *good*
AdvGs:	for *ever*	since *when*	until *quite recently*
PPs:	except *in here*		from *out of the forest*
fin. *wh*-cl:	Have you decided about *when you're leaving?*		
***wh* + *to*-inf. cl:**	Have you any problems apart from *where to stay?*		
-*ing* cl:	The miners charge the employers with *ignoring their claims.*		

The following restrictions exist on the realisation of complements:

Adjectival and adverbial groups

Nouns, pronouns and NGs are by far the most common realisation of the prepositional complement. By contrast, the use of AdjGs and AdvGs as complements is infrequent and limited to certain set expressions such as *at last, for good, for ever*, as in:

At last I'm free! [BNC GWH 1268]

. . . the family left Ireland *for good* and made its future in England.

[BNC EDA 313]

I could stay here *for ever*, it's so beautiful.

Wh-clauses

English prepositions are not followed by *that*-clauses (see 11.1.2, p. 104). The only type of finite clause admissible is the *wh*-clause, and the only non-finite type the -*ing* clause. *To*-infinitive clauses are not admissible either, except when introduced by a *wh*-item. Combinations **1a** and **2a** (below), therefore, are not acceptable. An -*ing* clause can often provide an acceptable alternative, as in **1b** and **2b**:

1a *I was pleased about (that) Pat won the prize.
1b I was pleased *about Pat winning* the prize.
2a *We were annoyed at not to get any news from you.
2b We were annoyed *at not getting* any news from you.

One must be careful to distinguish *to*-infinitive clauses from the preposition *to*, which can take an *-ing* clause, as in the first example below. Most other prepositions likewise take the *-ing* form, as this is the most nominal among clauses:

> He devoted his career *to helping* needy and deprived children.
> The intruder escaped *by clambering* over a back fence.

The following continuation of the recorded student–teacher conversation shows that the largest number of complements are realised by nouns, pronouns and full NGs, with a sprinkling of finite and non-finite clauses (see exercise on p. 559).

The 'Green' Party

A: It's really making a come-back *all of a sudden*.[1]

B: Seems to come *in and out of fashion*.[2]

A: Yeah.

B: We had elections *at school*[3] and the 'Green' party did win, actually.

A: So did we. It was a big surprise *to everyone*,[4] so many anti-establishment adherents *amongst us*.[5]

T: I get the impression that it's a non-vote, just a comfortable way *of not having to take a decision*.[6]

B: Yeah, a pressure vote, so that you don't have to vote either *for the Conservatives*[7] or *for the Labour Party*.[8] People just can't be bothered *with comparing programmes and thinking*[9] about *who to vote for*.[10]

T: And you think this has a significant impact *on the way the other parties have formed their policies*?[11]

B: Yeah, but it's . . . it's just waffle, just an excuse *for getting votes*.[12]

T: Do you feel very cynical *about them*,[13] then?

B: Suppose I do, a bit.

T: One of the things people say *about, well, at least some of the younger generation*,[14] not all of *them*,[15] but *on the whole*[16] is, there's no radicalism *among people* today[17] who are *in their late teens and twenties*.[18] It's what the forty-year-olds say *about the twenty-year-olds*.[19] They think back *to when they were young*[20] and *what they were like then*[21] and say that the younger generation don't have any radical or controversial views any more.

A: I don't think radicalism has disappeared. Maybe it has been channelled *into that 'green' area*.[22]

B: Yeah. A lot of former ideas have been ditched in favour *of moving towards a position much closer to the centre than before*.[23]

57.5 REALISATIONS OF THE MODIFIER ELEMENT

Like nouns, adjectives and adverbs, prepositions can also be modified. As already stated, the modifier tends to modify the preposition, though, as we have mentioned, it sometimes appears to modify the relationship expressed by the *preposition + complement*, for instance, in the case of directional modifiers. The modification usually takes the form of intensification, direction, attenuation, quantification, description (as with adjectives and adverbs) or simply of focusing and reinforcement. Grading by comparative or superlative appears to be more restricted. Not all prepositions admit modifiers. The following are attested examples.

Grading modifiers – more, less, far more, much less, the most, the least, in the least

It was a wonderful day. A day that seemed **more** like a dream than real life.

[BNC FRY 494]

Later, the two houses **nearer** the church were made into one.   [BNC B13 600]

He says he does**n't** want to sound **in the least** like our noisy neighbours.

Intensifying modifiers – completely, directly, right, well, all, absolutely, greatly, straight, badly, much

The ball went **right** *through* the window.

Today I'm feeling **absolutely** *on top of* the world.

Sit down, Paul, and I'll tell you **all** *about* it.

The walls are **badly** *in need of* a coat of paint.

Directional modifiers – up, down, out, over

I'll meet you **down** by the river.

The balloons floated **up** over the houses.

The race-course is **over/out** on the other side of Madrid.

Attenuating modifiers – partly, scarcely, not fully, to some extent, slightly, a little, a bit, hardly, not at all, not altogether, somewhat

I think you're **slightly/a bit** *out of* touch with reality.

It's **hardly** thanks to Mr Payne's advice that the deal was concluded successfully.

Quantifying modifiers – a long time, not that much, miles, two hours, way back, light years, streets; nearly, almost

She was **streets** *ahead of* her rivals.

That all happened **way** *back* in history.

Almost *at the same moment*, they realised they were lost.

Descriptive or attitudinal modifiers – *surprisingly, hopelessly, dangerously, unexpectedly*

> We were ***dangerously*** *close to* having an accident.
> He is ***hopelessly*** *in love with* a girl who ignores him.

Focusing or reinforcing modifiers – *precisely, mainly, just, principally, chiefly, merely, only*

> Emil told him that alcohol was available ***only*** *after* departure   [BNC BP9 317]
> You say that ***just*** *for the sake of* arguing.

In many of these examples – just as with prepositions that have adverbs of the same form, such as *near, after, before, in, above* – it is the preposition rather than the prep + complement that is being modified:

> We live ***quite*** *near* the main square.
> We arrived ***just*** *before* midnight.

On the other hand, certain modifiers seem to relate semantically, though not syntactically, more closely to the complement, as is sometimes seen in the possibility of using an alternative construction, where the adjective or adverb do modify the head syntactically:

> I obtained my first job ***purely*** *by accident.*
> We worked ***almost*** *until midnight*
> The firm is ***badly*** *in debt.*

> I obtained my first job *by* ***pure*** *accident.*
> We worked *until* ***almost*** *midnight.*
> The firm has some ***bad*** *debts.*

SYNTACTIC FUNCTIONS OF THE PREPOSITIONAL PHRASE

SUMMARY

1 The basic grammatical role of a preposition is to establish a functional relationship between its complement and another syntactic element in a nearby structure, whether a clause or a group.

2 In doing this, the whole PP itself functions as an element of the clause (e.g. as adjunct in: He works *at Heathrow Airport*) or group (e.g. complement in: angry *at his refusal*).

3 PPs can realise up to six syntactic functions in groups and eight in clauses. Some of these are frequent and others infrequent.

4 Some words can be used not only as prepositions but also as adverbs (e.g. *about*) or conjunctions (e.g. *until*) or verbs (*considering*), or adverbial particles (*up*). It is important to recognise their different class and functions.

5 The two-word and three-word prepositions tend to have a 'core' or 'prototype' meaning. The one-word items cover a more varied range of case meanings.

58.1 THE GRAMMATICAL ROLE OF PREPOSITIONS

The grammatical role of prepositions is to express a variety of syntactic and semantic relationships between nominal entities and

- other nominals (*the bridge over the river*),
- verbs (*he ran into the room*),
- clauses (*support for raising the subscription*),
- adjectives (*angry at his refusal*),
- adverbs (*up to the top*).

When a preposition links its complement to another element of a clause or a group, the whole PP itself becomes a functional element of the clause or group.

58.2 SYNTACTIC FUNCTIONS OF PREPOSITIONAL PHRASES

PPs can realise up to fourteen syntactic functions as constituents of groups, of clauses or outside clauses. They share the functions with other classes of unit and are therefore mentioned again in the sections below.

58.2.1 PPs embedded as elements of groups

1	(Post-)modifier in NG	A bridge *over the river*, apricots *on the tree*.
2	Complement in NG	He is a teacher *of French literature*.
3	(Pre-)modifier in NG	*Off-the-record* comments should not be printed in a newspaper.
4	Complement in AdjG	My son is brilliant *at mathematics*.
5	Complement in AdvG	They don't live far *from here*.
6	Complement in PP	I'm free all day *except on Mondays*.

An important feature of PPs is their ability to be embedded recursively in other PPs or in groups. In other words, one unit is embedded in another, which is embedded in another, and so on (see 3.6.3), as in:

7 A car accident [on the motorway [to Yorkshire]].

58.2.2 PPs as elements of clauses

Prepositional phrases can realise every element of clause structure except the predicator. However, their use in the central functions of subject and object is marginal, and is normally restricted to expressions of place or time.

8	Subject	*After dark* is the only good time for fireworks.
9	Direct Object	I don't consider *next to a railway line* a good place to live.

Some verbs are closely related to a specific preposition and take a prepositional object (see also 6.3.1):

10 Prepositional Object   Someone has been tampering *with the scanner*.

Prepositional phrases are used freely as Complements of the subject or the object to express temporary states, where they are often interchangeable with adjectives. Even more commonly, they occur after verbs of position or movement to specify place or direction (Locative/ Goal Complement):

11 Subject Complement   Monica must be *out of her mind* to reject such an
interesting offer. (Monica must be *mad*.)

12 Object Complement His illness left him *without a job*. (His illness left him *jobless*.)

13 Locative/Goal Complement   The train to London is now standing *at the platform* and the high-speed train from York is drawing *into the station*.

Prepositional phrases are also commonly used to realise the three main types of adjunct: circumstantial, stance and connective.

As circumstantial adjuncts

In this function they typically occur in either final or initial position:

14 final position   All this happened *long before the war*.

15 initial position   *Behind us*, we saw that the queue on the motorway stretched for miles.

As stance adjuncts

Like some other classes of units – mainly adverbs, AdvGs and clauses – certain PPs can function syntactically as Stance Adjuncts (see 8.2.5), that is to say outside clause structures, to express a comment on–or an attitude to–the form or content of a whole clause. They then have the status of supplementives (see 2.4.1):

16 *In all honesty*, I don't believe a word he said.

17 *By all means*, do whatever you think best.

Although we regard Stance Adjuncts here as syntactically outside clause structure, from a semantic and psychological point of view they are part of the thematic organisation of the discourse surrounding the clause. In other words, the clause itself is not the domain of Theme, but rather the clause plus any supplementive attached to it. For this reason, we include them in Chapter 6 as a type of non-experiential Theme (see 28.12).

As connective adjuncts

Prepositional phrases can also be used as connective Adjuncts to link clauses, or groups and words within clauses:

18 A. I'm leaving now.   B. *In that case*, I'll go too.

Of these syntactic functions, by far the commonest are adjuncts of various kinds and Locative/Goal Complements in clauses, together with modifiers in group structures, especially NGs.

58.3 CLASSES OF WORDS WITH THE SAME FORM AS PREPOSITIONS

Some of the one-word prepositions included in 57.3 can also realise functions characteristic of verbs, conjunctions, adverbs and adjectives. Such items are considered here as words having the same form (homographs), but fulfilling different functions as a result of diachronic extension.

58.3.1 Prepositions and verbs

The following participial forms can function either as prepositions or as verbs: *barring, considering, excepting, excluding, following, including, regarding, given, granted*. For example,

prep:	No-one ***barring*** a lunatic would start a nuclear war.
verb:	There are restrictions *barring* the employment of children under sixteen.
prep:	There are always problems ***regarding*** punctuality.
verb:	Up to now I have been *regarding* you as a friend.
prep:	We open seven days a week ***excluding*** Christmas Day.
verb:	I'm not *excluding* the possibility of an agreement.
prep:	These prices refer to a double room, ***including*** breakfast.
verb:	We are *including* two new colleagues in the research group.

58.3.2 Prepositions and conjunctions

It was mentioned in Section 57.4 that prepositions may be followed by finite *wh*-clauses and by non-finite clauses in *-ing*, since these have nominal reference. A small number of items referring to moments of time can, however, be used to introduce declarative finite clauses, and are then usually considered as having a conjunctive function (35.2.1):

prep:	***after*** his accident; after having an accident.
conj:	*after* he had his accident.
prep:	***before*** your arrival; *before* arriving.
conj:	*before* you arrived.
prep:	***since*** our meeting; since *meeting you*.
conj:	*since* we met.
prep:	***until*** my visit to Paris; *until going* to Paris.
conj:	*until* I went *to* Paris.

Three of the participial items mentioned in Section 57.3, *considering, given, granted*, enter into construction with finite *that*-clauses and so can be classed as conjunctious having the same form as the corresponding prepositions:

prep:	***Considering*** *his age*, he did very well in the competition.
conj:	*Considering* that he is so young, he did very well.

	prep:	**Given** *your interest in painting*, you'll enjoy living *in Florence*.
conj:	*Given* that you are so interested in painting, you'll enjoy your stay in Florence.
prep:	**Granted** *the changes nuclear energy will bring about*, it will still need to be carefully controlled.
conj:	*Granted* (that) nuclear energy will bring about many changes, it will still need to be carefully controlled.

58.3.3 Prepositions and adverbs

Both prepositions and adverbs express, typically, circumstantial meanings, especially those of space and time. It is not surprising, therefore, that some words can realise functions of both classes. The following are examples: *aboard, about, above, across, after, along, around, behind, below, beneath, between, beyond, down, in, inside, near, off, on, opposite, outside, through, throughout, under, underneath, up*.

Here are some structural criteria for distinguishing prepositions from adverbs:

- A preposition – but not an adverb – requires a nominal complement, and when this is a pronoun, the preposition governs its case (*for him, to them*).
- In paired examples such as *We went **into** the café – we went **in***, what was a preposition in the first version is replaced by an adverb in the second.
- the adverb is heavily stressed, whereas the preposition is normally unstressed, or only lightly stressed (*lower down the scale vs lower DOWN; we walked past the café – we walked PAST*); see Section 6.4.2.

In certain positions prepositions are stressed; for instance, when stranded at the end of a *wh*-question: *What is it FOR? Where is it FROM?* The preposition *with* is stressed in the expression '*with it*' (= trendy), and also in one adjunctive use *I'll take it WITH me*, but not in *to start with* (= (at) first). *Without* is similarly stressed in *I can't do WITHOUT it, WITHOUT you*. In the combinations *do without* and *go without* (*food*), the word *without* functions as an adverb particle: There's no milk left, so we'll just have to *do without*.

In the following examples, both the adverb and the PP are functioning as Adjuncts or Locative Complements:

	Adverb	Preposition
There are always two pilots	aboard	aboard the plane.
All the children were running	around	around the playground.
The last time I met Monica was in September, but I haven't seen her	since	since then. (cohesive with September)
The rule is that workmen must go	outside	outside the factory if they want to smoke during the morning break.

However, not all prepositions have adverbial counterparts: the forms *at, from* and *towards* function as prepositions, but not as adverbs. Conversely, the forms *together, apart* and *forth* function singly as adverbs but not as prepositions. When combined with a preposition, however, *together with* and *apart from* function as complex prepositions.

Furthermore, even when a form serves both functions, the sense may be different in each case. *To* as a preposition is different from its adverbial function in *The unconscious boy came TO* (= recovered consciousness) in both stress and meaning.

In the following examples, the words in italics function as part of a PP (in the left column) and as modifier of a NG head (in the right):

PP	m in NG
near the town centre	*near* neighbours of mine
outside the gates	an *outside* broadcast
inside the museum	some *inside* information
tears rolled *down* her cheeks	a *down* payment

SEMANTIC FEATURES OF THE PREPOSITIONAL PHRASE   *MODULE 59*

SUMMARY

1   The choice of preposition in a PP may be (a) governed by the particular noun, verb or adjective that precedes it (a *threat to, depend on, bored with*), or (b) chosen freely from a set of prepositions expressing different relationships (*under, over, between, across, along*, etc.), as in *Let's place the lamp in the corner/ on the desk/ by the armchair*). The former type is said to be 'grammaticised' or 'bound'. The latter type is 'lexical' or 'free'.

2   Location in space and change of location are the most basic types of prepositional relations. When speakers use *in* or *on* or *under* in English, for example, they make use of cognitive patterns or mental image schemas of each relationship, in accordance with the way each relation is perceived in the culture.

3   The concepts of Figure and Ground (or, more specifically, Trajector and Landmark) are used to refer to the salient object, whether moving or stationary, and the point of reference, respectively, in a spatial event. The preposition expresses the relation between the two – such as 'containment' (*in*), or 'support' (*on*) – in the most basic use. Further uses can then be explained as modifications of the basic image schema, as these mental pictures are perceived and derived from our experience of the world.

4   Many basic patterns of spatial location are carried over to time relations, e.g. *in the house, in November, in 1492*, and to ordinary metaphorical uses which form part of our daily interaction (*in love, in time, in pain*).

59.1 TWO TYPES OF PREPOSITIONAL MEANINGS

Prepositional meanings can be divided into two broad types:

- those in which the choice of preposition is determined by the verb, noun or adjective preceding it; and
- those in which a preposition is chosen freely in accordance with the speaker's intentions.

We say that the first type has become 'grammaticised' or 'bound', while the second type is more 'lexical' and 'free':

grammaticised	I agree *with* you; I have confidence *in* you; fruit is good *for* you.
lexical	We flew */in/into/out of/through/above/below/close to/ near/a long way from* the clouds.

In previous sections we have discussed those prepositions which are determined by nouns (50.5), adjectives (53.1.3) and verbs (6.3.1; 10.5) (e.g. *look after, rely on, put up with*). These are all grammaticised; that is to say, in such cases the preposition does not have its full lexical meaning and is not in open choice with other prepositions. We noticed that nouns which take prepositional complements are related to cognate verbs or adjectives that take the same prepositional complement, as in the following examples:

nouns:	compatibility *with*, reliance *on*, damage *to*, a liking *for*, an attack *on*, a quarrel *with*
adjs:	compatible *with*, opposed *to*, free *of/from*, lacking *in*
verbs:	to rely *on*, to dispose *of*, to amount *to*, to hope *for*, to quarrel *with*, give it *to me* (with the Recipient encoded as a prepositional phrase)

But notice that, when the noun or adjective takes *of*, the verb (if it exists) does not necessarily take the same, as with 'hope(ful) *of* success' but 'hope *to* succeed'.

59.2 LEXICAL PREPOSITIONAL MEANINGS

59.2.1 Location in space

The most basic prepositional meanings have to do with location in space. When we express spatial relationships we use a mental picture or image schema for each type of relationship, in which a salient Figure, typically a person or thing, is located – or moves – with relation to a reference point or Ground (usually another entity). It is the principle of salience or prominence which enables us to explain why it is more natural to say 'the book is on the table' than 'the table is under the book'. In Chapter 8, we encountered Figure and Ground, together with Path and Manner, when describing a Motion Event, with the example: *The children went down to the beach*, in which the Figure is 'the children' and the Ground is 'the beach'.

In **1** (below), the Figure (the boy) is stationary with respect to the Ground (the water), while in **2** the Figure (the boy) is moving with respect to the Ground:

1   The boy is *in* the water.   **2**   The boy is going *into* the water.

As we examine the different spatial relationships expressed by prepositions, we see that the nominal group or clause following the preposition represents the Ground, while the Figure is a nearby entity in the clause, like *the boy*. (Other, more specific terms which have been widely adopted in the analysis of prepositions are 'Trajector' and 'Landmark' for Figure and Ground, respectively.)

We now turn to the main types of meaning expressed by spatial prepositions in English, in terms of Figure and Ground:

At:	point in space:	Tim is at home, at the football match, at the cinema, at the supermarket, at work
On:	in contact with a surface:	on the floor/wall/ceiling; on the corner of Bond Street; on a bicycle; on the train/bus/ on board ship; on the map; a wasp on my hand
In:	containment:	in the universe, in the world, in France, in the garden; in the corner, in the car, in a boat, the coin in my hand

The preposition **at** is used when attendance at the typical function of the premises is implied (e.g. *at the cinema* in order to see a film; *at church* to attend a religious service), all when the speaker is not at the same location as the Figure. In visualising Tim's location at the cinema, the speaker is deliberately vague about exactly where at the cinema Tim is. Tim may in fact be in the queue outside the cinema, or inside, seeing the film. If the speaker were already outside the cinema and asks where Tim is, the answer would be specific: *He's in the cinema, he's inside.*

On prototypically has the Figure in contact with and supported by a surface (the Ground), whether horizontal (*there's a pen on the floor*) or vertical (*there's a fly on the wall*). The Ground includes vehicles and animals on which one rides (*on a bicycle/motorcycle/ horse*), and larger vehicles in transit which have a walkway (*on the bus/train, plane, on board a ship*), whereas *in* is used where no such walkway exists (*in a boat, in a car, in a helicopter*). However, referring to a train, we say *in the dining-car, in the first-class compartment*, which are conceptualised as containers. When the vehicle is not in active use, it is conceived as a container and *in* may be used (*The children were playing in the abandoned bus*).

In implies containment: *There are strong security forces in the stadium.* Containment may be complete (*the coins in my purse*) or in part (*Put the flowers in water, a man in a blue shirt and jeans*). The difference between *in the corner* (of a room) and *on the corner* (of the street) is one of perspective, whether the right-angle is perceived as containing or projecting.

59.2.2 Change of location

Change of location implies motion. Source (see 8.2.3) represents the initial location, and is typically marked by the preposition **from**, while Goal represents the final location and is most often marked by **to**, or by *to* in combination with *on* for a surface (**onto**) or *in* for a container (**into**). 'Home' in *go home* is an exception in not expressing the notion of final location (Goal) explicitly. (Note the explicit encoding of location in BrE 'stay **at** home' against the inexplicit AmE 'stay home').

From (source) . . . **to** (goal)	*From* the bus-stop *to* the stadium.
Off . . . (source) . . . **onto** (goal)	The vase fell *off* the table *onto* the floor.
Off . . . (source) . . . **into** (goal)	The boy fell *off* the cliff *into* the sea.
Out of (source)	I took the money *out of* my purse. He ran *out of* the house.
Across, along (path)	We went *from* the bus-stop, *along* the street *to* the stadium.
Through (passage)	We went *through* the tunnel.

Out of is visualised as exit from a container. Note that the adverb *out* + the preposition *of* provides the converse meaning with respect to *into*: *into the water/ out of the water*, while **away + from** indicates greater distancing: *away from the water*. Similarly, *off* is the converse of **on** and **onto** (*off the table onto the floor*).

As we saw in 40.2.2, embeddings of prepositional phrases within adverbial groups express complex spatial meanings which are difficult to translate, for example: *back from the front line, in from the fields, over to the left, up from below*.

Across, *along* express **Path**. The difference is that *along* simply follows a horizontal axis, (We walked *along the river bank*, Cars were parked *along the street*), while *across* involves crossing the axis, or an open space, at an angle, from one side to another (She walked across the *street/ the field*).

Through prototypically has the meaning of **Passage** (motion into a point and then out of it (He hurried *through* the doorway). The Ground can also be two-dimensional (You could go *through the park, through a maze of streets*) or three-dimensional, with volume (We drove *through the tunnel*).

Past is similar to *along*, but with respect to some fixed point: Go *past the stadium* and you'll come to a supermarket.

59.2.3 Other spatial prepositions

Other basic spatial prepositions include **over**, **under**, **up** and **down**. **Over** is used in several ways:

(a) A picture hangs *over the fireplace*.
(b) A helicopter flew *over our heads*.
(c) They live *over a sweet-shop*.
(d) He wore a raincoat *over his suit*.
(e) The lake is *just over the hill*.

(f) They sprayed paint *all over the wall*.
(g) The horse jumped *over the fence*.
(h) I fell *over a stone* and broke my leg.

In (a) and (b), one entity is higher than the other, with a space between, the difference being that (a) is static location (b) involves motion. The notion of 'higher' is still clear in (c) but less clear in (d) where, in addition, 'space' is reduced to the meaning of 'on top of'. In (e), *over* implies location at the end of a path. One has to go over the hill to reach the lake. In (f) *all over* is 'pervasive' or 'covering', whereas (g) signals a movement of going up higher than an obstacle and down again on the other side, and (h) moving from an upright to a non-upright position. (Compare *fall over* as an intransitive phrasal verb with an adverbial particle: The lamp *fell over* and broke.)

Under, meaning vertically below, but with some intervening space, is the converse of *over*. It can function with verbs of location and motion, and the distance may be greatly reduced:

There's a rug *under the table*; a bench *under the tree*. (i.e. under the branches of the tree!)
I pushed the letter *under the door*.
He's wearing a T-shirt *under his sweater*. (conversely, a sweater *over his T-shirt*)

Above and **below** are similar to *over* and *under*, but absolute verticality is not a requirement:

The castle stands *above the town*; *below the castle* there is a river.

Up and **down** indicate a higher or lower position respectively, as in (a), or motion towards that position, as (b). Like *under*, they can imply the path taken to the higher or lower location, as with (b):

(a) There's a pub *just up/ down the road*.
(b) We had to walk *up/ down* three flights of stairs.

Up and *down* are, however, more commonly used as adverb particles in phrasal and phrasal-prepositional verbs, such as *If you **take** it **up***, *I'll **bring** it **down*** (see 6.4).

Round/ around express circular movement along a path in *She danced around me*, but circular position on a path in *The children sat round the teacher* (though probably the circle was not a full one). In the sentence *They drove furiously round the race track*, the track was probably irregularly curved, not circular. Sometimes the meaning is indeterminate movement in different directions within an area, as in *We walked for hours round the streets looking for a cheap hotel*. At other times, the movement may be neither circular nor along a clear path, but varied and indeterminate in a volume of space (e.g. *The bees swarmed around us*.) These differences may be regarded as different senses of the general meaning of 'circularity'.

By, **beside**, **at my side**, **next to**, **in front of**, **behind** (AmE **in back of**), **on the left**, **on the right**, **facing**, all express degrees of proximity. They correspond to the physical orientation of our bodies, and are extended to certain objects such as cars and houses which have a front, a back and sides.

By has also the meanings of agency (*a novel by Tolstoy*) and means (*by train, by bus, by air*).

Between and ***among*** express relative position, referring to two entities, or more than two, respectively.

59.2.4 Non-locative meanings

For has been explained in chapters 2 and 3 as the Beneficiary meaning, that is, intended Recipient. It also expresses purpose and intended destination (I've brought it *for you*; an extra-fast machine *for copying*; they're *making for the coast*).

Like expresses similarity of features or character (She looks *rather like* Lady Macbeth, *What* is she *like* as a person?) It can also introduce a simile (*The lake shone like a mirror*) and draw on a more vague similarity of situations (Let's not quarrel over a silly thing *like this*). *Like* is related to the predicative adjective *alike* (The brothers look *alike*) and to the adverb *alike* (The change in climate affects young and old *alike*).

As is used when referring to roles, jobs or functions (He made his name *as a pop singer*, Have you ever worked *as a shop assistant*?). *As* is grammaticised in comparisons (*as* clear *as* crystal) and is related to the conjunction *as* (*As I was saying, . . .*).

With and ***without*** can signal (a) accompaniment and lack of it, respectively (I'll go *with you*; she turned up at the gala dinner *without her husband*); (b) possession (a girl *with red hair*, a street *without a name*) or a part–whole relationship (a cup *without a handle*); or (c) instrument (he broke the lock *with a hammer*, she pushed her hair back *with her hand*).

59.3 TIME RELATIONS

Certain prepositions expressing location in space are also used to express location in time. Other prepositions – such as *during, until* and *since* – are not used with spatial meanings.

	examples	**usage**
At:	*at one o'clock*; *at Christmas*; *at midday*	point in time: clock time, fixed holidays
On:	*on Friday, on June 2nd*	for specific days and dates regarding the occurrence of events
In:	*in May, in the year 1888, in the evening*	months, years, times of day, seasons, centuries and other periods of time, all conceptualised as containers; note however, ***in** the morning/ afternoon/ evening*, but ***at** night*

Over:	We stayed with them *over the weekend, over Christmas*	periods of short duration
During:	*during the war, during my stay in Rome*	experiential periods of time
For:	We read *for hours* (cf spatially, We walked *for miles*); We are camping here *for the summer, for a long time, for good* (= 'for ever')	duration of time
	for the third time	frequency
Since:	I've been here *since 10 a.m.*	retrospective, referring to the initiation of the duration
Until:	We'll wait *until 4 o'clock*; *until the plane takes off*; We didn't eat *until four o'clock*; *from morning till night; up till now*	typically marks end-point of duration, but marks a starting-point with negative sentences; *till* and *up till* are informal variants, but *till* is not used to start a sentence
Before and after:	*before the Flood; the week after next*	almost always express time meanings, but note the formal spatial expression 'He appeared *before the judge*'
By:	(a) Essays must be handed in *by Friday*	(a) a time deadline
	(b) *By the summer*, she was feeling stronger	(b) before a certain time

59.4 METAPHORICAL AND ABSTRACT USES

Many spatial prepositions are used in abstract or metaphorical expressions. For example, ***about*** in *walk about the house* expresses 'indeterminate spatial movement', whereas in *talk about the house* it expresses the notion of 'reference'.

Although many abstract and metaphorical uses of prepositions (and adverbs) may at first sight appear arbitrary, metaphor and metonymy can provide enlightening explanations. For instance, the expressions *in love, in pain, in anger* construe these emotions as containers, yet this construal is not applicable to happiness and hate (*in happiness, *in hate.) For these, *full of happiness/joy/hate* and also *anger* are normal uses, with the body in this case construed as the container. The field of vision as well as the mind are also seen as containers, as in the expressions '*in* full view', '*out of* sight, *out of* mind'.

Between, meaning relative position, is extended to both temporal and abstract meanings: *Between six and seven* this evening; the discussion *between them* turned into a quarrel.

Into, used metaphorically, indicates active participation in something, as in *he's into rugby these days*.

Over and **under** have non-spatial meanings as in: it weighs *over a kilo*, it cost *under ten euros*, while in the verbs *overact*, *overcharge*, *under-estimate*, *undernourished* the meaning is 'excess' and insufficiency', respectively. A different extension of meaning, something like 'subordination' or 'subjection to' is illustrated in: *under the influence* of drugs; *under his leadership*; *under the threat* of expulsion; *under control*; *under the circumstances*; *under contract* for a year.

With *over*, the meaning of 'surmounting an obstacle' is extended to that of illness and difficulties – *get over an operation* has the sense of recovering from its effects – while *control over/power over* someone, or something, is an extension of the basic higher-vs-lower spatial meaning, as is also the use of *over* in 'let's discuss it *over a cup of coffee*'. Here the mental image is of persons leaning slightly foward, engaged in talk, with the coffee on the table between them.

Out of as 'exit from a container' is extended to expressions such as *out of* petrol, *out of* sugar, *out of* work (=jobless), *out of* date (=obsolete). *Out* also responds to the 'emergence metaphor' as in *He did it out of despair, out of love for his family,* and to the 'object comes out of a substance' metaphor, as in *Mammals developed out of reptiles.* The opposite is the 'substance goes into the object' metaphor, as in *I made a sheet of newspaper into a plane.*

Off and **on** have converse meanings in relation to the notion of support as the Ground: the pen fell *off* the table *onto* the floor. They are used colloquially as converses in expressions such as *he's off alcohol, he's on drugs*.

Up and **down** are often metaphorically construed as converses, with positive and negative connotations respectively, in expressions such as as *coming up in the world, going down in the world, look up to someone* and *look down on someone. Up north* and *down south* reflect geographical orientation, whereas *up to London, down to the country* reflects the status of the capital.

Through can have the meaning of completion and result: He went *through* a fortune in a year; I finally got *through* that long novel.

With can metaphorically signal the manner of doing something (*Say it with a smile* = smiling; *With a wave of his hand, he left*) or result, in *black with the smoke*, together with increasing or decreasing value (*This wine has improved with age*).

The following descriptive-narrative paragraphs from Graham Greene's novel *The Heart of the Matter* illustrate a variety of meanings expressed by PPs:

Wilson stood gloomily *by his bed*[1] *in the Bedford Hotel*[2] and contemplated his sash, which lay uncoiled and ruffled *like an angry snake;*[3] the small hotel room was hot *with the conflict*[4] *between them.*[5] *Through the wall*[6] he could bear Harris cleaning his teeth *for the fifth time*[7] that day. Harris believed *in dental hygiene.*[8] 'It's cleaning my teeth *before and after every meal*[9] that's kept me so well *in this climate*,[10] he would say, raising his pale exhausted face *over an orange squash*.[11] (*now* he was gargling: it sounded *like a noise*[12] *in the pipes*.)[13]

Wilson sat down *on the edge*[14] of *his bed*[15] and rested. He had left his door open *for coolness*[16] and *across the passage*[17] he could see *into the bathroom*.[18] The Indian *with the turban*[19] was sitting *on the side*[20] of *the bath*[21] fully dressed: he stared inscrutably back *at Wilson*[22] and bowed. 'Just a moment, sir,' he called. 'If you would care to step *in here*'.[23] Wilson angrily shut the door.

[1]proximity; [2]containment; [3]similarity; [4]result; [5]abstract, derived from relative position; [6]transversality; [7]frequency; [8]grammaticised prep.; [9]time relative to point; [10]containment (metaphorical); [11]verticality + activity; [12]similarity; [13]containment; [14]support ; [15]part–whole; [16]purpose; [17]path; [18]goal; [19]possession; [20]support; [21]part–whole; [22]grammaticised prep. (direction); [23]direction–container

59.5 GRAMMATICISED PREPOSITIONS

Outlined next are some of the most common grammaticised prepositions, functioning mainly as complements of verbs.

At is the preposition controlled by certain verbs such as *laugh*, verbs of looking – *look, glance, gaze, stare* – and verbs of aiming: *aim, shoot at* someone or something. The latter implies that the attempt failed, whereas transitive shoot + Od is effective: The terrorist *shot* two policemen dead (i.e. killed them; the addition of the Object Complement *dead* clarifies the difference between a fatal shooting and an injury); he *shot at* the escaping criminal, but missed.

In is used with the verbs *believe, confide, trust, engage, interest* and *succeed* (I tried to *engage her in conversation, to interest them in world affairs, to get them interested in politics*).

On is the preposition selected by *agree, rely, count, concentrate, depend*, and by the ditransitive verbs *feed* and *spend* (spend a lot *on entertainment*; feed them *on cereals*).

By has so many meanings in addition to those already mentioned that it appears not to call up one basic mental image. Here are just a few:

Agency:	The goal was scored *by Evans.*
Means:	They travelled *by bus, by air, by plane.*
Extent:	The envelopes measure 9cm *by 6 cm.*
Time during:	Travel *by day or by night.*

By is also used with intransitive or transitive phrasal verbs: *stand by, get by, pass by; Don't let the opportunity **pass** you **by***.

For is used with the verbs *allow* (*allow for delay*), ask (*ask for help*), (exchange) *exchange one coin for another*, (hope) *hope for the best*, (wait) *I'm waiting for you*.

From is used with verbs of preventing (*keep, discourage, exclude, exempt, prevent, restrain* someone from doing something), among other meanings.

Of is also highly grammaticised, and occurs after verbs (*think, hear, approve, convince someone, die*), adjectives (*full, tired*) and nouns (*a bottle of wine, the home of a former PM*). These and other prepositions are discussed and illustrated in the chapters referred to above.

STRANDED PREPOSITIONS;   *MODULE 60*
DISCONTINUOUS PREPOSITIONAL
PHRASES

SUMMARY

There are five clause structures in which the preposition is normally or optionally separated from its complement and placed after the verb. The prepositional phrase is then discontinuous. Inversion permits different constituents to be fronted as marked theme and so emphasised (see 28.8). In some fixed expressions discontinuity is not possible.

60.1 STRUCTURES WHICH INVOLVE STRANDING A PREPOSITION

The normal order of the elements, **preposition + complement**, is frequently inverted, as in *Who is the play by?* The nominal complement is fronted to initial position in the clause, and the preposition is placed at the end, the prepositional phrase being consequently discontinuous. This is called **stranding**. It occurs frequently in English, particularly in the five types of sequence illustrated below. Although grammatically it is a marked form, it has become the normal, unmarked form used in conversation. It has the effect of giving prominence to certain parts of the message. The examples on the left illustrate its use, in contrast with the non-stranded order on the right, which in the bracketed examples sounds stilted or, if marked by an asterisk, ungrammatical. The other examples are all grammatical and normal.

In cleft clauses

It is *your health I* am worried *about.*	[It is your health *about which* I am worried.]
What I am worried *about is* your health.	[**About what* I am worried is your health.]

In clauses with restrictive meaning

> The *only thing* he thinks *about* is his work.

> [The only thing *about which* he thinks is his work.]

In passive clauses

With many prepositional verbs (see 6.3), stranding of the preposition is the only way a passive can be formed:

> *My opinion is* never asked *for.*   Nobody ever asks for *my opinion.*
> I don't like *being shouted at.*   I don't like people shouting *at me.*

In active clauses with a 'raised object' equivalent to sequences introduced by anticipatory it

> *That firm* is wonderful to work for.   It is wonderful to work for that firm.
> *My boss is* easy to get on with.   It is easy to get on with my boss.

In each of these examples, the two different forms have different 'theme' and 'focus'. For instance, in the last example, one structure has *my boss* as Theme and focuses on *easy to get on with*, while the other has the evaluative word *easy* in the Theme, and focuses on *my boss* (see 30.5.1).

With wh-complements in interrogative and relative clauses

When the complement of a preposition is realised by an interrogative or a relative pronoun, the discontinuous structure is normal in familiar styles of expression, while the continuous (preposition + complement) order is distinctly more formal:

Familiar style

Who can we rely *on?*

The person we can rely *on* is Tom.

Formal style

On whom can we rely?

The person *on* whom we can rely is Tom.

Some wh-questions admit only the discontinuous structure

> What's the weather *like?*   [*Like* what is the weather?]
> What have you come *for?*   [*For what have you come?]
> *Where do* we leave *from?*   [*From *where do* we leave?]

Short questions in response to statements or directives are very common in English:

> We are leaving tomorrow.   *Where from*?
> I have to speak to your headmaster.   *What about*?
> We had better leave now.   *What for*?

What for? as an independent question is used as an informal alternative to *why?* to ask the reason for the previous statement. Discontinuous *What . . . for?* asks about the purpose of something, as in *What is that tool for?*

Certain PPs which constitute fixed phrases are very rarely discontinuous

To what *extent do* they disagree?   [*What extent do they disagree to?]
In which respect do you think I am   [*Which respect do you think I am wrong
   wrong?   in?]

Finally it may be mentioned that PPs containing complex (two-word or three-word) prepositions can also be discontinuous, though perhaps less often than those based on simple prepositions:

His death was *due to natural causes.*   *What* was his death *due to?*
There are certain regulations which   There are *certain regulations* that these
   are *in conflict with* these proposals.   proposals are *in conflict with.*

The following extracts are from an interview in *Play* in which Iain Banks talks about things he dislikes. They illustrate in context some of the prepositions and adverb particles that we have examined in these sections (see exercise 2 for module 60):

Pet hates

For me,[1] the theatre is *a bit like porridge.*[2] I don't like porridge very much, but I force myself to eat it every now and again because, damn it, I am a Scotsman and I should like it. But even if I *dress those rubbery oats up*[3] *with strawberry jam or salt,*[4] I can't *get over the impression*[5] that I am eating wallpaper paste.

Theatre is just the same. I just don't have the taste *for it.*[6] I go to see things *at the Edinburgh Festival*[7] now and again, but I usually find myself staring *at my watch*[8] and wondering what time the pub shuts.

I avoid opera *like the plague.*[9] There are two reasons *for this.*[10] Firstly, the plot *of your average opera*[11] is just nonsensical. Secondly, I detest vibrato singing. I used to think that opera singers were unfortunate people who couldn't hit a note *without warbling,*[12] until my wife told me that they are trained to sound *like that.*[13] I was shocked. You mean they actually choose to sing *in that ridiculous manner?*[14]

That said, I have been *to a few operas*[15] *in my time.*[16] I normally just *settle down*[17] *in my seat*[18] and ask *whoever I am with*[19] to wake me up when it is all over, or when the world ends, whichever comes first.

FURTHER READING

For the structure of the prepositional phrase, Halliday (1994); for the semantics of prepositional phrases in terms of Figure, Ground, Path, Talmy (1986); in terms of Trajector, Path and Landmark, Langacker (1987); for the container schema and other metaphors, Lakoff and Johnson (1980), Lakoff (1987); for an introduction to these concepts Ungerer and Schmid (1997); for grammaticised vs lexical prepositions, Huddleston and Pullum (2002); prepositions as bound vs free, Biber et al. (1999).

EXERCISES ON CHAPTER 12

Spatial, temporal and other relationships: The Prepositional Phrase

Module 57

1   Complete the PPs in these sentences with units of the classes indicated on the left:

(1)   NG: We were woken up by a sound like _____
(2)   AdjG: The couple left Scotland for _____ and settled in Brussels.
(3)   AdvG: I was sitting in the back row and couldn't hear the speaker from
                      _____
(4)   PP.   The shops are open every day except _____
(5)   fin. *wh*-cl: Can you see the sea from _____ ?
(6)   *wh* + *to*-inf. cl: Have the judges decided on _____ ?
(7)   *-ing* cl: Are you worried about _____ ?

2   †Read again the conversation on 'The Green Party' on p. 537. Write a list of the complements of the PPs used, and say what classes of unit they belong to. Compare the relative frequency of the classes. Which classes are not represented in this text?

3   Insert suitable modifiers of the types indicated, before the PPs marked in the following sentences. Refresh your memory first by re-reading the examples in Section 57.5:

Grading

(1)   His proposals for changes in the public transport system are _____ *in* line with the opposition party
(2)   However, they also go _____ *against* public opinion.

Intensification

(3)   Many villages isolated by the snow were left _____ *without* electricity for several days.
(4)   Our plane flew _____ *over* the North Pole.

Attenuation

(5)   I am _ _ _ _ _ _ _ _ _ _ _ _ _ _ *in* agreement with you.

(6)   We moved to this area for financial reasons, but also _ _ _ _ _ _ _ _ _ _ _ _ _ *on account* of my health.

Quantification

(7)   Archaeologists found prehistoric remains _ _ _ _ _ _ _ _ _ _ _ _ _ *below* the surface.

(8)   You would have to travel _ _ _ _ _ _ _ _ _ _ _ _ _ *into* space to find another planet like the earth.

Description or viewpoint

(9)   As a journalist, he is _ _ _ _ _ _ _ _ _ _ _ _ _ *out of touch with* what's going on in the developing countries.

(10) Certain industries that have not been modernised are now finding themselves _ _ _ _ _ _ _ _ _ _ _ _ _ _ *without* resources to be competitive.

Focus or reinforcement

(11) The barmen told the boys that alcohol was served _ _ _ _ _ _ _ _ _ _ _ _ _ *to* persons over eighteen.

(12) She got the job _ _ _ _ _ _ _ _ _ _ _ _ _ *because of* her knowledge of Arabic.

Module 58

1   †To illustrate the syntactic potential of PPs in English, re-read the conversation about animals on p. 533 and identify the syntactic function of each PP.

2   †In the following sentences, classify the italicised words as prepositions or adverbs. Can you spot the one which is neither a preposition nor an adverb?

(1)   The children had left their toys lying *about* all over the floor.
(2)   Our friends live just *across* the road from us.
(3)   It's cold on deck. Why don't you go *below* to your cabin?
(4)   Some people have the telly *on* all day.
(5)   Keep *on* walking.
(6)   Keep *on* the right side.
(7)   We usually go to a little pub *up* the street.
(8)   Come on, drink *up* your beer.
(9)   Tell me all *about* what happened.
(10) I'll run *off* enough copies for all the students.
(11) Everything is going to change in the *near* future.
(12) In debates he puts his ideas *across* very well.
(13) Some plants can live at temperatures *below* freezing.
(14) The picture is not finished yet, but I'll paint *in* the sky later.
(15) There were just a few light clouds high up *in* the sky.
(16) We're a long way *off* understanding the real causes of this situation.

Module 59

1 †Identify the different contextual meanings of the preposition *over* in the following

   (1)   They built a bridge *over the river*.
   (2)   We live *over the road*.
   (3)   I weigh *over 80 kilos*.
   (4)   He looked at the blue sky *over his head*.
   (5)   We had to climb *over the wall*.
   (6)   She laid a blanket *over his bed*.
   (7)   The baby fell *over a toy*.
   (8)   The thief knocked me *over the head*.

2 Work in pairs or small groups, as follows:

   (1)   Choose one of the simple, frequently used prepositions, e.g. *for, at, from, with, through, on*, etc.
   (2)   Collect a good number of examples of the use of the chosen preposition, by consulting various dictionaries, periodicals, books or spoken sources.
   (3)   Arrange the examples in groups that have a common and reasonably definable meaning.
   (4)   Study the groups and observe how close the meanings are: (a) within each group; (b) between the groups.
   (5)   In the light of your observations, try to formulate a core meaning, either for the general meaning of the preposition or for the meaning of each group.

3 Work in pairs or small groups as before:

   (1)   Choose one of the following sets of spatial prepositions: (a) *by, beside, close to, near to, next to* or (b) *under, underneath, beneath, below*.
   (2)   Collect examples of their use in their ordinary spatial senses.
   (3)   Test the prepositions for substitutability one for another, and try to explain in what ways and to what extent they differ in meaning and use.

4 †There are many fixed PPs in common usage. Can you formulate for each of the following four sets a basic meaning relating the preposition to the five complements?

at once	**on** duty	**out of** work	**in** a hurry	**under** stress
at times	on purpose	out of practice	in full view	under control
at sea	on business	out of fashion	in luck	under-privileged
at work	on time	out of sight	in labour	under the tyrant's thumb
at war	on holiday	out of breath	in charge	under-weight

5 †The following sentences all express processes taking place in a period of time. Can you explain the different semantic relations between process and period which motivate the choice of a different preposition in each sentence?

(1)   I have worked here *for* two years.
(2)   I have been happy here *over* the two years.
(3)   We have had problems *during* the two years.
(4)   We have lived *through* two years of problems.
(5)   There has been steady progress *throughout* the two years.
(6)   The building will be finished *in* two years.
(7)   The building will be finished *within* two years.

6   †The following incident from the autobiography of Shirley MacLaine, *Don't Fall Off the Mountain*, includes many examples of location and change of location. Suggest a semantic function such as Source, Path, Location, Goal for each numbered phrase:

> **Late one evening on our way home[1] *from the studio*,[2] we pulled up *at a red light*.[3] As we chatted quietly *about the day's work*,[4] something suddenly kicked us *in the rear*[5] and my feet went *over my head*.[6] I reached out *for Steve*,[7] screaming. I didn't know where down was, and my head wouldn't move *on my neck*.[8] The car came *to a halt*.[9] We had been knocked sixty feet *to the opposite side*[10] of the highway[11] *into the path*[12] of oncoming traffic.[13] Our trunk was *in the front seat*[14] and Steve was pinned *under it*.[15] 'Are you all right?' he called *to me*.[16] He was twisted *out of shape*[17] on the floor,[18] with one arm tangled *in the steering wheel*.[19]**

7   Use the following in sentences to show the difference in meaning between the two members of each pair:

in view of	in search of	in contact with
in the view of	in the search for	in our contact with

8   Many verbs and adjectives allow only one or two specific prepositions. Try testing your knowledge of the prepositions selected by the following items:

Verbs		**Adjectives**		**Nouns**
ask	plot	bored	aware	answer
agree	hope	tired	surprised	damage
amount	pay	delighted	prone	desire
appeal	suffer	anxious	related	search
depend	complain	sorry	fraught	anger
point	insist	suspicious	lacking	effect

9   Words related in meaning though of different class usually occur with the same preposition, though not always. Illustrate this by composing sentences with the following related words:

to rely	reliant	reliance
to care	careful	care
to boast	boastful	boast
	grateful	gratitude
	furious	fury

Module 60

1 †Rewrite these sentences with a stranded preposition, beginning each one as indicated.

(1) I am most interested in the ecological consequences of this project. – *It is the* _ _ _ _ _ _ _ _ _ _ _ _

(2) You must be particularly careful about your money when walking in the streets. – *What you must be* _ _ _ _ _ _ _ _ _ _ _ _

(3) I haven't yet paid for the meals. – What _ _ _ _ _ _ _ _ _ _ _ _ *the meals.*

(4) I find it difficult to talk to my parents. – *I find my* _ _ _ _ _ _ _ _ _ _ _

(5) In what do you believe then? *What* _ _ _ _ _ _ _ _ _ _ _

(6) On which flight did you say we are booked? *Which flight* _ _ _ _ _ _ _ _ _ _ _ ?

(7) We are collecting this money in aid of the refugees. *Who are you* _ _ _ _ _ _ _ _ _ _ _ ?

(8) Caracas is the capital of Venezuela. *Which country* _ _ _ _ _ _ _ _ _ _ _ ?

(9) The caretaker said that you can't park in this parking place. *Which parking-place did the caretaker* _ _ _ _ _ _ _ _ _ _ _ ?

2 †Read again the extract 'Pet Hates' at the end of Module 60 (p. 558). Comment on the numbered items in ways relevant to the contents of this chapter.

ANSWER KEY

CHAPTER 1

Module 1

1 (1) participant; (2) participant; (3) circumstance; (4) circumstance; (5) participant.

2 (1) Adjunct; (2) Subject; (3) Direct Object; (4) Subject; (5) Adjunct.

Module 2

3 (1a) No; (1b) Yes; (1c) No; (1d) No; (2a) No; (2b) No; (2c) Yes; (2d) No.

4 (1) independent; (2) verbless (3) dependent non-finite (as in *Not being a tele viewer myself, 1 have no preferences as regards programmes*; it could also be embedded, as in *Not being a televiewer myself does not worry me*); (4) dependent finite; (5) independent; (6) abbreviated; (7) verbless; (8) dependent finite; (9) dependent finite; (10) independent.

5 (1) NG; (2) AdjG; (3) PP; (4) AdvG; (5) VG; (6) AdjG; (7) NG; (8) PP.

Module 3

6 (1a) finite independent are 3, 4, 5, 6, 10; (1b) finite embedded are 7, 8; (1c) abbreviated are 1, 2; (1d) verbless is 9; (2) 1 and 2; 4 and 5; 7 and 8; (3) 1, 2, 5, 8, 9; (4) All the coordinated elements are recursive. These include, as well as the clauses: coordinated colour nouns as c in PP (of *reds and blues, golds and silvers, greens and purples*); adjectives as modifiers in NG (*louder and louder* yes; *bold, exotic and decidedly unnatural* colors); mixed modifiers in NG (*inexpensive, temporary, hair-coloring products;* shocking British and American punk emblem); nonfinite -*ing* forms in VG (*streaking, squiggling and dotting*).

Possibly, the use of elements of equal syntactic status in this text provides, first, an element of suspense by means of the conjoined abbreviated interrogative clauses, and then a cumulative effect of movement and colour, which mirrors the notions expressed and is therefore to some extent iconic.

7 **(1a)** It won't be difficult . . . **(1b)** Won't it be difficult . . . **(2a)** Sheila hasn't anything/ has nothing to tell you. **(2b)** Hasn't Sheila anything/ Has Sheila nothing to tell you. **(3a)** No-one has left a bag on a seat in the park, **(3b)** Hasn't anyone/ Has no-one left a bag. . . . **(4a)** He doesn't know anyone/ He knows no-one who lives in Glasgow; Doesn't he know anyone . . ./ Does he know no-one . . . **(5a)** It isn't worth going/ It's not worth going to see any of those pictures. Isn't it worth going to see any of those pictures?

8 **(1)** any (in an interrogative clause); **(2)** ever . . . anything (*hardly* is a semi-negative word) **(3)** anywhere/ anything/ any place (in an embedded clause after negative *don't think*); **(4)** anyone/ anybody (in an embedded clause after negative *don't remember*).

9 **(1)** The alternative negative forms *never* in **(a)** and *not . . . ever* in **(b)** establish negative clauses and within this scope are followed by non-assertive items such as *any*. **(1c)** by contrast contains *ever*, which is not a negative word, but a non-assertive word. The clause is therefore not negative as it would be with *never*, but neither is it correctly positive.

(2) Similarly, *no*-negation and *not*-negation are used correctly in **(a)** and **(b)** respectively. In **(c)** as *anybody* is non-assertive but not negative, it can't make a clause negative.

CHAPTER 2

Module 4

1 **(1)** (since my father's day); **(2)** (briefly) (to Mrs Davies); **(3)** (at the time); **(4)** none; **(5)** none; **(6)** (in the park); **(7)** (before the fall of the Berlin Wall) (practically); **(8)** (just); **(9)** (insistently) (at six o'clock in the morning) (on a cold November day); **(10)** (for the fifth time) (on Monday). Note that although 10 is grammatically complete, the use of the past tense 'became' creates expectations of at least an adjunct expressing a point in time (see Chapter 7). With a present perfect 'has become' this would not be the case.

Module 5

1 Position in relation to the verb in a declarative clause (All except **(1)** and **(8)**; Position in interrogative clauses **(1)** and **(8)**. Ellipted in conjoined clauses with same subject **(3)**. Concord with verb (all except **(7)** which lacks number agreement.) Realisations: pronouns, subjective forms (all, note 'which' in **(6)**) *there* **(6)**; dummy *it* **(4)**. The criterion not represented is the question tag.

2 **(1)** the use of caves for smuggling; **(2)** there (Subject place-holder), half a dozen men (notional Subject); **(3)** the light of a torch; **(4)** what the critics failed to understand; **(5)** the list of people who she says helped her; **(6)** it (anticipatory) to meet him before he died (extraposed Subject); **(7)** Run like mad; **(8)** it (anticipatory) to tell the neighbours you are going away on holiday (extraposed Subject); **(9)** it (anticipatory) that there is no real progress (extraposed Subject); **(10)** reading in a poor light.

3   **(1)** It surprised us that Pam is seeking a divorce. **(2)** It was bad manners, really, to leave without saying goodbye. **(3)** It doesn't interest me who she goes out with. **(4)** It requires a lot of nerve for such a man to succeed in the world of politics. **(5)** It is obvious that recognising syntactic categories at first sight is not easy.

4   **(1)** lies, finite; **(2)** is, finite; **(3)** called, non-finite; **(4)** is, finite; **(5)** quarried, finite; **(6)** and **(7)** decorating, filling, non-finite; **(8)** laid, finite; **(9)** surrounded, finite; **(10)** making, non-finite. Note that *dried up, mummified* and *bejewelled* do not realise clause constituents but are participial modifiers in nominal groups.

Module 6

1a   **(1)** most of my life (NG); **(2)** the door (NG); **(3)** that foreign doctors were not allowed to practise in that country (finite *that* clause); **(4)** very little (AdvG as quantifier); **(5)** discretion (NG); **(6)** what they believe to be sunken treasure (nominal relative cl.); **(7)** Anticipatory *it* as place-holder; that the money will be refunded as extraposed object. **(8)** that many will survive the long trek over the mountains (finite *that*-clause); **(9)** what is the use of all this (*wh*-interrogative clause); **(10)** a ton of gravel (NG).

1b   All the NGs are prototypical, except **(5)** discretion, which is non-prototypical. The verb 'lack' does not passivise. However, in other respects, 'discretion fulfills the criteria for Od. **(4)** 'very little' might be considered as an ellipted NG, but in this case the ellipted part is not as easily recoverable as it is in 'we ate very little' i.e. (food). The *that*-clauses are less prototypical realisations, as are the *wh*-clauses, but are nevertheless perfectly normal. Anticipatory *it* is not prototypical, but is a requirement in extraposition.

2a   **(1)** S and Od NGs; **(2)** S-NG. Od *that*-cl; **(3)** Od-NG; **(4)** S-NG, Od-NG; **(5)** S-ellipted (they), Od-*that*-cl.; **(6)** S-NG and name in apposition, Od-NG; **(7)** S-NG; **(8)** S-pron; **(9)** S-pron; **(10)** S-*there*.

2b   Realisations of Subject: there are 3 long and heavy ones, the rest short and one ellipted. Object: the opposite occurs: All are long and heavy, carrying a lot of information. Heavy S and Od occur in 'reported speech', the short subjects occur in 'direct speech'. The heaviness is a direct result of the amount of information conveyed. The subject in **(5)** is the same as that of **(4)**, ellipted in coordinated clauses. The subject in **(8)** refers to the whole of **(7)**.

3   **(1)** Recipient; **(2)** Beneficiary; **(3)** Beneficiary; **(4)** Recipient; **(5)** Recipient; **(6)** Beneficiary; **(7)** Recipient; **(8)** Beneficiary.

4   **(1)** put off (phrasal, trans.;) stare + prep at; **(2)** approve + prep of; **(3)** get back (intrans phrasal); **(4)** break into (prepositional); **(5)** turn up (intrans phrasal); **(6)** get at (prepositional); **(7)** come up to (phrasal prepositional; **(8)** intrans phrasal (ellipted version of prepositional get off (the bus/train).

5a **(a)** Prepositional Object; **(b)** Adjunct; **(c)** Adjunct; **(d)** Prepositional Object. Sentences **(a)** and **(d)** can be passivised, and the verb + preposition have lexical equivalents (rehearse and be wise to, respectively). Sentences **(b)** and **(c)** don't have these possibilities. In **(b)** *through the streets* can be fronted, but **(c)** *through the trees* can't, presumably because *see* is not a verb of movement.

5b In *run up large bills, run up* is a transitive phrasal verb, with *large bills* its Od. *Run up* can be discontinuous, as in *she ran large bills up*. But *up large bills* is not a constituent, and consequently can't be fronted. Furthermore, only directional/locative adverbs in phrasal verbs can be fronted. *Up* in *Run up bills* is not directional/locative, whereas in *run up the stairs* it is.

5c In one meaning *on the bus* is a locative Adjunct; in another, *on the bus* is a Prepositional Object, equivalent to *she opted for the bus.*

5d He rode out; we swam across; they jumped over; get in, all of you!

Module 7

1 **(1)** not very hard Cs (AdjG) to be able to laugh and to cry Cs (conjoined *to*-inf clauses; **(2)** fit for the task Co (AdjG); **(3)** a multi-million pound industry Cs (NG); **(4)** what Co (pronominal head of NG); **(5)** a series of accidents Cs (NG), what he thinks Cs (finite nominal clause); **(6)** accessible to a wide public Co (AdjG); **(7)** unexpectedly cold (AdjG); **(8)** happy Co (AdjG); **(9)** utterly miserable Cs (AdjG); **(10)** illegal Co (AdjG).

2a **(1)** healthy; **(2)** smart; **(3)** one of the most efficient ways of getting about; **(4)** so versatile as transport or for simple pleasure; **(5)** to work **(6)** fit; **(7)** effective exercise. All are Subject Complements except **(5)** Locative/ Goal and **(6)** Object Complement. The particles of phrasal verbs in **(3)** *about* and in sitting *down*, because predicted by the verb, can be considered circumstantial Complements.

Module 8

1 **(1)** *for five years*, circ.; **(2)** *first, then, after that*, connectives; **(3)** *allegedly*, hearsay evidential; *under the barbed wire*, circ. directional/locative Complement; *to reach the arms depot*, circ. purpose; **(4)** *hopefully*, stance, attitudinal; **(5)** *shaped like a spiral staircase*, supplementive.

2 **(1)** *the gang's hideout* is Direct Object, *without* much *difficulty* is Adjunct; **(2)** *the* gang's *hideout* is Direct Object, *more elaborately equipped with technology than they had expected* is Object Complement.

3 The sun | never | sets | on the tourist empire. | | But

S	A	P	A	(conj.)
NG	Adv.	VG	PP	

travel pictures, business contracts and sports programmes|

S				
NG	+	NG	(conj.) +	NG

don't tell | the full story: || getting there | may be | no fun at all.
    P   Od   S   P   Cs
  VG   NG   *-ing* cl.   VG   NG
                            (appositive clause.........................)

|| Aircraft | perform | flawlessly, || but what|
   S   P   A   (conj) S
  NG   VG   Adv   WH

happens | to passengers, flight crews and cabin staff? | |
  P   Ob
  VG   PrepG + (ellipted prep. + 2 NGs)

Jet lag. | | A mass phenomenon, almost as universal as the common cold. | |
Verbless cl.   verbless cl.
  NG   NG   Supplementive

CHAPTER 3

Module 9

1 Exclusively intransitive **(a)**: 2, 4 and 8. Those that can function either as intransitives or transitives: **(b)** 1, 3, 5, 6, 7, 9 and 10.

2 **(a)** Objects unexpressed by social convention 1, 3, 7, 9, 10. **(b)** With implied reflexive meaning 6 (adapt himself). **(c)** With reciprocal meaning 2 (collided with each other).

3 A valency of 4: for example, I, [PAY] Tom, a lot of money, for his mountain bike

Module 10

1 **(1)** *reason with: Cecil can't be reasoned with*; **(2)** *dispose of: Old, broken furniture is not easily disposed of,* **(3)** *call on*: The *Minister of Defence will be called on . . .*; **(4)** *aim at: The target that is being aimed at . . .*; **(5)** *keep to: Your schedule should be kept to . . .*

Module 11

1 **(2)** I doubt whether we have enough petrol to reach Barcelona. **(3)** Who knows whether/ if there is an emergency kit in the building. **(4)** I asked where the nearest Metro station was. **(5)** We have all agreed (on it) that you keep/should keep the keys. **(6)** The Under-Secretary can't account for the fact that some of the documents are missing. **(7)** I suggest he look/should look/looks in the safe. **(8)** The spokesman confirmed what we had just heard. **(9)** We must allow for the fact that he has been under great strain lately. **(10)** Will you see to it that these letters are posted today, please?

2 **(1)** clause containing NG placed between main clause and *that*-clause favours retention of *that*, despite co-referential pronoun in *that*-cl.; **(2)***think* in previous cl., followed by pronoun in *that*-cl. favours omission of *that*. **(3)** *Say* + co-referential pronoun in that-clause. *Think* followed by pronoun in *that*-clause.

3 **(a)** noun head (proper name) in the *that*-clause favours retaining *that*; **(b)** verbs *say* and *think* followed by pronouns in *that*-clauses favour omission.

4 1st *that*-cl. as Od complement of *says*: he's really sorry he said he'd take someone else to the dance.

2nd *that*-cl as complement of *sorry*: he said he'd take someone else to the dance.

3rd *that*-cl as complement of *said*: he'd take someone else to the dance.

5 **(1)** indirect interrogative; **(2)** nominal relative; **(3)** embedded exclamative/ indirect interrogative; **(4)** indirect interrogative; **(5)** embedded exclamative **(6)** nominal relative nominal relative.

6a *Suggest* does not take *to*-infinitive complements. (It takes non-finite *-ing*-complements when only the same subject is involved, and finite *that*-clause complements when a different subject is involved.)

6b *Explain* does not allow an Indirect Object (*me*). But it does allow a prepositional Object (*to me*). Otherwise just the *that*-clause Object.

Module 12

4 **(1)** He never *allowed*/Thomas/to drive the jeep in his absence./ V+NG+*to*-inf cl.
  (2) The shopkeeper *asked*/me/what I wanted./ V+NG+*wh*-interrog cl.
  (3) His powerful imagination *makes*/ him/quite different from the others./ V+NG+AdjG
  (4) *Keep*/ your shoulders/straight./ V+NG+AdjG
  (5) He *left*/her/sitting on the bridge./ V+NG+ *-ing* cl.
  (6) They *like*/their next-door neighbours to come in for a drink occasionally./ V+*to*-inf cl. with overt subject
  (7) I would *prefer*/Mike to drive you to the station./ V+*to*-inf with overt subject

5 (all patterns) [1]V+NG+ *wh*-cl. (*if* =*whether*); [2]V+NG+*to*-inf. cl., [3]V+*that*-cl. with v in subjunctive mood; [4]and [5]V+NG+Adjunct; [6]V+PP; [7]V+NG+*that*-cl.+ *to*-inf. cl. as adjunct, [8]V+NG+*that*-cl., [9]V+NG+*wh*-(*if* =*whether*)cl.; [10]V+NG+*that*-cl.; [11]V+*that*-cl., indicative; [12]V+NG+*to*-inf.cl.

CHAPTER 4

Modules 13 and 14

1 **(1)** material; **(2)** mental; **(3)** relational; **(4)** mental; **(5)** material; **(6)** relational.

2 **(1a)** *Teach* has a semantic valency of 3: it is trivalent. In 1a all the participants are actualised. In 1b they are reduced to 2, and in 1c they are reduced to 1.**(2)** *Bite* has a semantic valency of 2. In this example only one is actualised, the valency is reduced to 1. **(3)** *Purr* has a valency of 1, as in this example.

3 **(1)** Subject-filler; **(2)** participant (the sum of ten pounds; **(3)** participant (the baby); **(4)** participant (the bicycle); **(5)** Subject-filler.

4 Suggested participants might be: **(1)** a strong wind; **(2)** waves; **(3)** tide; **(4)** river; **(5)** landslide.

6 **(1)** Agent; **(2)** Affected; **(3)** Agent; **(4)** Affected; **(5)** Affected.

Module 15

1 **(1)** Yes; *Most Prime Ministers age prematurely*; **(2)** No; **(3)** Yes; *The sky darkened*; **(4)** No; **(5)** Yes; *His brow wrinkled*; **(6)** Yes; *The camera clicked*; **(7)** Yes; *The load of sand tipped onto the road*; **(8)** Yes; *The company's sales have doubled*.

2 **(1, 6** and **7)** the facility to undergo the action expressed; **(2)** acted upon; **(3)** acted upon; **(4)** acting Agent; **(5)** acting Agent.

3 **(a)** is transitive-causative: Sarah causes the rice to cook; **(b)** is transitive with an unactualised Affected participant; **(c)** is anti-causative. It forms an ergative alternation with (a); **(d)** *cook* is basically a bivalent process, but in this case its valency is reduced to 1 (the same applies to (b); **(e)** is a pseudo-intransitive involving the facility of rice to undergo cooking; **(f)** Do you often hear of persons being cooked?

4 All the italicised verbs are used causatively in this extract. (*Wither* = make x shrivel and dry up; *stale* = make x stale; *cloy*= make x sick with sweetness; *satisfy* = make x satisfied). The Affected participant is different in each case and only the first two refer to Cleopatra.

Module 16

1 **(1)** Recipient; **(2)** Recipient; **(3)** Beneficiary; **(4)** Beneficiary; **(5)** Recipient.

Module 17

1 **1)** cognition, Ph=entity; **(2)** perception, Ph=entity; **(3)** cognition, Ph=fact; **(4)** affectivity, Ph=situation; **(5)** behavioural, Ph=entity, or rather, an event, **(6)** cognition, doubt; **(7)** cognition, fact; **(8)** perception (sense of taste), Ph=entity.

2 **(1)** The members of the commission were not pleased by/with either of the proposals. **(2)** We were amazed at/by his presence of mind. **(3)** The government is alarmed at/by the dramatic increase of crime in the cities. **(4)** She is worried by the fact that she seems unable to lose weight. **(5)** Will your wife be annoyed by the fact that you forgot to phone?

Module 18

1a **(1)** instantation of a type, attributive, Carrier-Attribute; **(2)** the same as 1; **(3)** identifying, Identified-Identifier; **(4)**attributive, Carrier-Attribute; **(5)**possessive, Possessor-Possessed; **(6)** circumstantial; Carrier-(intensive)-circumstance; **(7)** identifying, Identified-Identifier; **(8)** identifying, Identified-Identifier.

1b **(7)** Food (Identified/Token) is the supreme symbol (Identifier/Value).

(8) What we call civilisation or culture (Identified/Value) represents only a fraction of human history (Identifier/Token).

2 **(1)** e.g. exhausted, resulting; **(2)** e.g. safe,current; **(3)** e.g. risky, profitable etc, resulting; **(4)** e.g. still, current; **(5)** free, current.

Module 19

1 **(1)** reported directive, with *to*-infinitive cl., **(2)** reported quote, as in 'No smoking' or reported statement, with *that*-cl.; **(3)** reported statement, with *that*-cl.; **(4)** reported question, with *wh*-cl.; **(5)** either a reported question (expressed by a *wh*-clause) or a reported directive (expressed by a *to*-infinitive clause); **(6)** either a reported statement (expressed by a *that*-clause) or a reported directive (expressed by a *to*-infinitive clause); **(7)** reported statement or (if suitably modalised) a reported directive, e.g. that passengers should proceed to Gate number 2; **(8)** reported statement, with *that*-cl.

2b *There* could be omitted from **(4)** and **(5)** since each has a 'presentative' locative Adjunct in initial position.

3 This explanation applies equally well to the instances of *there* omission in *The Lost Girl*.

Modules 20 and 21

1 **(1)** time (distribution); time (location); **(2)** manner (means); **(3)** contingency (concession); **(4)** contingency (cause); **(5)** goal/destination in time; **(6)** contingency (reason); **(7)** role (capacity); **(8)** matter.

2 **(1)** Instrument; **(2)** Range; **(3)** Range; **(4)** Instrument; **(5)** Range.

Module 21

1 **(1)** *We chatted* for *a long time*; process is realised as entity (*chat*), circumstance (for *a long time*) as part of entity. **(2)** *X continued to drop bombs (on Y) throughout the night*; process as entity (*bombing*). **(3)** *An election campaign that would last* for *50 days was launched in Canada last weekend*; circumstance of place (locative) as entity (*Canada*), process as entity (*launch*), new process *see*, circumstance (extent in time) as part of entity (*50-day*). **(4)** *Because he (Franz Josef Strauss) was obviously intelligent and spoke exceptionally well in public, Konrad Adenauer appointed him minister without portfolio in his cabinet in 1951*; Attribute as entity (*his obvious intelligence*), circumstance (reason) as entity (*exceptional oratory*), both of these being causative Agents in the metaphorical version *won him a place*. **(5)** X *was released after people in Washington had been increasingly expecting throughout the day that the hostage who would be released would be Professor Steen, aged 48*; processes as entity (*release* and *expectations*), circumstance as part of entity (*rising*).

3   We have seen that nominalisation and grammatical metaphor tend to reorganise an experience in terms of abstractions rather than persons as Agents. This in itself results in lower transitivity than when the sentence contains an Agent. Verbs tend to be relational (*be, have*) or if they are material (*won*) or mental (*see*) they do not have their basic meaning, although they can occasionally have endpoints. Objects are rarely Affected.

CHAPTER 5

Module 22

1   Except for the first line and the last, each line of the text consists of one positive declarative clause, with Subject-Finite structure. There are primary auxiliaries as operators (*is, are,*) the modal auxiliary *may*, and the rest are finite lexical verbs. They all make statements, whose purpose is to persuade the reader that software is better than paper. Punctuation could be by semi-colon or comma. The first line is a PP functioning as an Adjunct and does not require punctuation. The last is an imperative, exhorting the reader to opt for the better choice, and could be followed by an exclamation mark.

Module 23

1   **(1)** positive declarative; Yes; **(2)** exclamative; Yes; **(3)** and **(6)** imperative; No, they introduce an illustration; **(4)** and **(7)** modalised declaratives, giving an opinion; **(5)** *wh*-interrogative + intensifier, rhetorical question; **(8)** *whenever* is an adverb of frequency, and does not introduce a *wh*-question.

2   **(1)** I am not going . . ./ Aren't you going . . .? **(2)** Nadine's Mum didn't buy . . ./ Didn't Nadine's Mum buy . . .? **(3)** He doesn't tell/ Doesn't he tell . . .? **(4)** Sheila didn't know . . ./ Didn't Sheila know . . .? **(5)** Bill didn't take on . . ./ Didn't Bill take on . . .?

3   **(1)** What's your name?; **(2)** What is your address? **(3)** Where were you born? **(4)** Are you using eye drops? **(5)** Do your eyes smart? **(6)** Do you take any medicines? **(7)** Do you wear spectacles/glasses? **(8)** How long have you been wearing them? **(9)** Are you allergic to anything? **(10)** When did you start to have visual problems?

4   Abbreviated clauses have the same polarity as the previous utterance, and are typically said by a partner in the conversation. Question-tags usually have reversed polarity, and are typically said by the speaker making the previous utterance.

5   **(a)** *wh*-type; **(b)** Why Ellie has gone pink, i.e. is blushing; **(c)** No, 2 and 4 are not answers; **(d)** In 2: exclamation and question tag. In 4: ellipted clause.

6 **(1)** Yes it does, No it doesn't; **(2)** Yes, I have, No, I haven't; **(3)** Yes, I will/shall, No, I won't/shan't; **(4)** O.K. All right/Let's; Oh no, let's not sit down.

7 **(1)** isn't it? **(2)** haven't you?/have you? **(3)** doesn't she? **(4)** will you? **(5)** won't/can't you? **(6)** didn't he?/did he? **((7)** don't they? **(8)** did he?

Module 24

1 **(1)** vocative, **(2)** *Somebody*: subject-vocative; *dear*: endearment, vocative; *you*: subject, contrastive; **(3)** *Everybody* (initial), subject-vocative, (final) vocative; **(4)** vocative; **(5)** subject; **(6)** subject-vocative.

2 **(1)** pragmatic particle introducing a wish (optative mood); **(2)** 2nd person imperative (= 'allow'); **(3)** optative. Type c, suggesting a joint action, is not represented, no doubt because Gore did not win the election and so was not in a position to invite the American people to collaborate in joint action with him.

Module 25

1 **(1)** Yes; **(2)** Yes; **(3)** Yes; **(4)** No; **(5)** Modalised performatives are less explicit, but yes, it counts; yes; **(6)** Yes; **(7)** No, the speaker is assuring, not promising; **(8)** Yes; **(9)** No, it means 'I suppose'; **(10)** Yes, this really was a wager. The *'ll* form is conventionally used with 'I bet'.

Module 26

1 **(1)** *yes/no* ('polar' is also used) interrog., query; **(2)** verbless clause; offer; **(3)** modalised *yes/ no* interrog., polite request; **(4)** *wh*-interrog., rhetorical question; **(5)** declarative, leading question (with marker); **(6)** polar interrog., exclamation; **(7)** *wh*-interrog., rhetorical question; **(8)** polar interrog. as preliminary to request; **(9)** declarative as leading question (with marker); **(10)** the same, but negative.

2 **(1)** any; **(2)** some; **(3a)** anything; **(3b)** nothing; **(4)** anyone/ anybody; **(5)** anywhere; **(6)** some.

Module 27

2 **(a)** Uncooperative: Yes, I would mind (without signing). Cooperative: No, I wouldn't mind/ Not at all (signing); **(b)** Yes, without explaining, or No; Yes (explaining); **(c)** The butler is reacting to the pragmatic meaning of an order, and says 'yes' in compliance; **(d)** He might say 'Not at all, sir'.

4a **(1)** declarative, explicit performative; **(2)** negative imperative; **(3)** declarative, modalised performative; **(4)** nominal group; **(5)** passive declarative; **(6)** modalised polar interrog.; **(7)** passive declarative, performative; **(8)** declarative, explicit performative of thanking (although the thanking is given beforehand!).

4b 1–5 are orders (4 and 5 are more specifically prohibitions), 6–8 are requests, 8 is an indirect request.

5 **(1)** *Wh*-interrogative, question, but also disapproval, as is clear from **(8)**; **(2)** answer, statement; **(3)** declarative, statement (+ aggrieved protest); **(4)** declarative, apology; **(5)** declarative, explanation/excuse in answer to **(3)**; **(6)** declarative, explanation of **(5)**; **(7)** acceptance of explanation; **(8)** declarative, statement + disapproval; **(9)** invitation/polite order.

6 **(1)** reprimand; **(2)** request; **(3)** request; **(4)** offer; **(5)** permission; **(6)** suggestion.

8 **(1)** indirect request following reason for request; **(2)** ignoring the reason and refusing the request; **(3)** and **(4)** further reasons for request; **(5)** suggestion; **(6)** challenge; **(7)** provocation; **(8)** suggestion; **(9)** explanation; **(10)** order; **(11)** provocation; **(12)** provocation; **(13)** warning; **(14)** threat; **(15)** threat; **(16)** self-identification/ implied warning; **(17)** request; **(18)** apology; **(19)** excuse.

CHAPTER 6

Module 28

1 **(1)** *Paul*, unmarked; **(2)** *Abruptly*, marked, Adjunct; **(3)** *Is he*, unmarked; **(4)** *Celebrating her victory today*, marked, non-finite Predicator + operator *is*; **(5)** *freezing cold*, marked, Subject Complement; **(6)** *meet*, unmarked; **(7)** *In the American soft-drink industry*, marked, Adjunct; **(8)** *For months*, marked, Adjunct; **(9)** *crazy*, marked, object complement; **(10)** *Never again*, marked, negative Adjunct.

2 **(1)** *all of these* I bought him; **(2)** *fun* you call it; **(3)** *most of it* we already knew; **(4)** *Government spokesman* he is; **(5)** *get there* I did.

3 **(1)** The two topic entities in the paragraph are Mrs Mooney and Mr Mooney. Mrs Mooney is introduced as primary topic referent at subject in an intransitive (copular) clause. Mr Mooney is first introduced as 'her father's foreman', as object of the verb *marry*. He is later identified as Mr Mooney, as subject of an intransitive verb *go* (*to the devil*). The topical referent chains are maintained mainly by means of anaphoric reference realised by personal pronouns. One chain is initiated by *Mrs Mooney*, and continues with *she . . . herself . . . she . . .* (zero). Another chain is initiated by *Mr Mooney* and continues with *he . . .* (zero) *. . . him . . . he*. In the last four lines the two topic referents appear together with Mr Mooney as primary topic referent, at subject, and Mrs Mooney as second topic referent at object (*he . . . his wife*). The last line has both of them together (*they*) as subject. *That* refers to the events related in the previous sentence *One night he went for his wife*, etc. until the end of the sentence.

Module 29

2 **(1)** SAY; KNOW; HEAR; ANYthing; TOLD; ROOM; CARE; DO; TALK; ALways; **(2)** marked focuses are CARE, DO and ALways.

4 The intonation nuclei could be assigned as follows: EGG; YOU; YOU; YOU'RE; I; NO; ARE; COOKing; yourSELF; THAT; I'LL; I'LL; DO; NO; DON'T; YOU; EAT.

5 **(1)** can; **(2)** have/'ve done so; or did/did so; **(3)** haven't/haven't done so; **(4)** would/would like to; **(5)** how/how to; **(6)** didn't/didn't want to; **(7)** did/did so; **(8)** so/it was.

Module 30

1 The thematic progression type between 1, 2 and 3 is Type 2, constant theme (*Vincent van Gogh* – (zero) – *he*, with the subject in 2 being implicit. Between 3 and 4 we have Type 1, simple linear (his mother's keeping – his mother). Between clauses 4, 5 and 6 the progression type is constant theme (*his mother – she – she*). From 6 to 7 we have Type 1, simple linear, (*with a family friend – the friend*) and from 7 to 8 constant theme with zero anaphora after *and*.

2 **(1)** It is on the recycling of plastic that experts are working; The ones who are working on . . . are experts; What experts are working on is . . .; **(2)** It is fatal diseases that smoking can cause; what smoking can cause are fatal diseases; what can cause fatal diseases is smoking; **(3)** It's by reading and listening to the radio that I unwind last thing at night; how I unwind . . . is . . .; when I unwind by reading . . . is . . .; **(4)** It's against viruses that the computer industry is fighting; it's the computer industry that is fighting . . .; what the computer industry is fighting against are viruses; **(5)** It was shortly after I got home that I realised that . . .; what I realised shortly after I got home was that . . .; when I realised that I had lost my purse was . . .

3 **(1)** Sentence 5; then. **(2)** Its discourse function is to signal an upcoming shift in the story.

4 **(1)** a + c; **(2)** a + c; or **a** + **b**, as Edith is higher on the empathy hierachy, and so a better topic, than the cake; **(3)** **a** + **c**; **(4)** **a** + **b**.

5a Suggested preferences for active and passive: **(1)** passive, because *the first kindergarten in the United States* announces the main topical referent, whereas *they* refers to people in general; **(2)** either: active makes for topic continuity with 1, while passive achieves topic continuity with 3; **(3)** better active; **(4)** active effectively gets *the unthinkable* in apposition with its explanation, while passive would separate these; **(5)** either is possible, but when the passive does not fulfil a specific purpose, it is wise to opt for the simpler active form; **(6)** the passive effectively brings *the choices* in topic continuity with *the dilemma*, leaving *budget* in final position, where **(7)** active maintains topic continuity with *budget*.

CHAPTER 7

Modules 31 and 32

2 The sequencing of the clauses is as follows: Finite subordinated circumstantial clause (*After–yesterday*), two coordinated finite clauses (*householders–water*), finite subordinated circumstantial clause (*before–it*). Chronological sequencing is maintained.

3 **(1)** non-equivalence (subordinate clause of purpose + imperative clause); **(2)** syntactic equivalence (two clauses in an appositional relationship), semantically there is an implied cause–effect relationship; **(3)** equivalence (two clauses in an appositional relationship, the second with pragmatic *and*); **(4)** non-equivalence (contrastive dependency); **(5)** equivalence (contrastive coordination).

Module 33

2 Suggested completions: **(1)** which she needn't have done/ causing herself much remorse; **(2)** which was totally to be expected/ resulting in many absences in the following weeks; **(3)** which has happened several times before/ causing many injured; **(4)** which makes them dangerous areas/ causing merchant vessels to avoid them; **(5)** which is good news/ ending their families' distress.

Module 34

2 **(1)** adversative (*yet*); **(2)** concessive (*although*); **(3)** adversative (*yet*); **(4)** replacive (*but instead*); **(5)** replacive (*but instead*).

Module 35

3 **(1)** pragmatic; **(2)** pragmatic) **(3)** semantic; **(4)** pragmatic; **(5)** pragmatic; **(6)** semantic; **(7)** pragmatic. The pragmatic uses give a reason or justification for the speech act expressed in the main clause.

4 **(1)**, **(2)** and **(3)** are instances of coordinating enhancement, the combination that is intermediate between coordination and dependency; in each case, there is a finite secondary clause conjoined to the primary clause by the conjunctive combination *and + then*. The circumstantial meaning expressed is that of time, but also, implicitly, one of cause and effect. **(4)** is an instance of subordinating enhancement, in which the primary clause is followed by a finite dependent clause introduced by the conjunction *before*. Again, the circumstantial meaning is that of time, together with implicit cause and effect. The parallel or similar organisation of these clause complexes, together with the same explicit and implicit meanings in each, contribute considerably to the force of the argument expressed.

6 **(1)** The independent clause *The Japanese . . . relatives* is followed by a coordinated enhancement clause introduced by and so. This whole complex is dependent on the parenthetical *We discovered this February*. **(2)** The independent clause *The Wakamaru . . . house* is followed by a non-finite clause, with an implicit meaning of simultaneity and could be replaced by a coordinated clause *and keeps*; **(3)** There are two complex sentences joined by a semi-colon, indicating an appositional relationship. In the first, the subordinate *if*-clause frames the independent clause by a condition which points to the result in the main clause. The second appositional combination is similar to the first, except that the main clause precedes the conditional clause; **(4)** A main clause is followed by direct reported speech in the second clause; **(5)** A subordinate conditional clause followed by a main clause.

Module 36

1 **(1)** Annie said she was sorry/Annie apologised for interrupting us/ them in that vital discussion. **(2)** I asked the EEC official what exactly his job was. **(3)** X demanded whether I realised that the press would be printing something that wasn't true. I agreed with a smile that indeed it would be frightful. **(4)** Annie inquired about Duncan and asked whether he would be recommended/Annie asked Desmond whether he would recommend Duncan. Desmond said he wouldn't/flatly refused to do so. **(5)** Humphrey stammeringly/in a stammering voice accused the Prime Minister of lying.

2 **(1)** Annie invited the official to sit down for a minute. **(2)** Fiona suggested to Godfrey that he (should) wear a sports jacket. **(3)** The Prime Minister suggested that he could sort of put on his glasses and take them off while he gave his speech. **(4)** Luke exclaimed in horror and begged/pleaded not to be sent to Israel, claiming that his career would be at stake. **(5)** I told him briskly not to be silly, and pointed out that it was an honour and could be considered as promotion.

CHAPTER 8

Module 37

2 **(1)** primary verb; **(2)** primary verb; **(3)** part of lexical aux. *be about* + *to*-inf; **(4)** lexical aux. *have got* + *to*-inf); **(5)** same as 4; **(6)** lexical verb *get*; **(7)** lexical verb *get*; **(8)** lexical verb *get* (causative).

3 **(1)** one-element VGs: *whizzed, startled, fell, shouted, turned, said, are, asked, scrambled, pick, changed*; **(2)** two-element VGs: *was crossing, was clutching, can't . . . be, was pedalling, was lost, had fallen, was rolling*; **(3)** three-element VG: *could have injured*; **(7)** *are* in **(9)** functions as a main verb.

4 suggested combinations are as follows: **(1)** is supposed to be; **(2)** are (un)likely/ bound/sure to; **(3)** is . . . due to; **(4)** had better; **(5)** be able to; **(6)** was about to; **(7)** are apt/liable to be; **(8)** have to/would rather/sooner.

5 **(1)** The main markets are likely to be France, Germany and Spain. **(2)** Diana and Charles were virtually certain to divorce. **(3)** You are sure to be among the first three. **(4)** He is supposed to be her boy-friend. **(5)** You are not likely to get a question like that.

Module 38

1 **(1)** as aux in progressive; **(2)** as lexical verb; **(3)** as aux in passive; **(4)** lexical aux (*is sure to*) and lexical verb (be).

2a **(1)** oxv, present, modal, progressive; **(2)** oxv, past, lexical-modal; **(3)** oxv, present, perfect, passive; **(4)** oxxv, modal, perfect, passive; **(5)** ov, past, passive; oxv, past, progressive; **(6)** oxv, past, progressive, passive; **(7)** ov, past, progressive; oxv, past, perfect, progressive; **(8)** ov, present, progressive; **(9)** oxv, present, perfect, lexical-modal; **(10)** oxv, present, modal, progressive.

3 **(1)** was being taken; **(2)** had been being instructed; **(3)** must have been using; **(4)** can't have been using; **(5)** must have moved; was being taken; **(6)** will be being developed; **(7)** are likely to be sold; **(8)** are sure to have been bought; **(9)** is being shot; **(10)** must have been being shot.

Modules 37 and 38

1 **(1)** There are only three occurrences of states: the stative verbs (*is, sees, sees*); all the rest are dynamic, showing actions; **(2)** Finiteness is realised on the lexical verb (i.e. Finite is fused with Event) in *flash, sees, is, take, panics, heads, hold, comes, goes, misses*; Finite is realised by an operator in *is passing, (is) having, can't get, (wi)ll'spill, 'm braking, honking, flashing*; **(3)** Yes: *coming, getting, to make* (sure); **(4)** Present; **(5)** five progressive choices, the rest non-progressive; **(6)** One instance of *can't* meaning inability or impossibility, one instance of *will* with a predictive meaning (see Chapter 9; **(7)** One instance of negative polarity, the rest positive; **(8)** One instance of emphasis (*COMES*); **(9)** Briefly, the non-progressive forms are used to express a series of actions presented as complete and, in this text, sudden and for this reason alarming. The sense of imminent danger is heightened by the use of emphasis (*COMES*) and by modalising the declarative in two cases. The interjection (*Christ Almighty*) and exclamative force of the following clause, indicated by punctuation, also contribute. The progressive forms at the beginning of the extract plunge the reader into the scene by presenting an action in the process of happening, not yet completed (the car with a trailer *is passing* and *having trouble* getting back in lane); a later sequence of progressives (*I'm braking, honking, flashing*) represents iterative actions (see Module 42, here conveying an impression of urgency. The overall use of positive polarity, with one exception, together with the use of Present rather than Past tense in the narrative effectively convey the impression of a series of events which happened, rather than, for instance, a speculation on events which didn't happen or might have happened.

Module 39

1 Clues for the discussion: The italicised verbs in the (a) sentences are lexical verbs; in the (b) sentences they are catenatives. The subjects of 1b and 2b are 'raised' from being subjects in *that*-clauses to subjects in the sentence: 'It happened that we were away' to 'We happened to be away'; 'It appears that he has misunderstood your explanation' to 'He appears to have misunderstood your explanation.'

2 **(2)** happened to be/chanced to be; **(3)** neglected to/failed to; **(4)** trying . . . managed to do so; **(5)** seems to be; **(6)** hastened to; **(7)** tend to be/ tend to be being; **(8)** tried to; proved to be.

Module 40

1 **(1)** Figure: the president and his wife; Path: *through* and *on up*; Verb: Motion + manner; **(2)** Figure: The ship; Path: *out of* . . . past. Verb: Motion + Manner; **(3)** Figure: She; Path: *off.* Verb: Motion + Manner + cause; **(4)** Figure: several trees; Path: *down*; Verb: motion + Manner + Cause; **(5)** Figure: he; Path: *down*; Verb: motion + Manner; **(6)** Figure: we; Path: *back*; Verb: motion + Manner. The preposition *to* + a nominal group, as in **(1)** and **(2)** can be analysed as marking Goal, i.e. as end of Path.

3 **(1)** bring activity to end by reaching a certain limit (a form of completion); **(2)** continuation of an activity; **(3)** slow completion of an activity; **(4)** continuation of an activity; **(5)** momentary character of an activity.

5 **(1)** Particles with Path meanings: (*took*) . . . *out on*, (*went*) *up into*, (*went*) *back into*, *brought* . . . *out*, *brought* . . . *down*; (*take*) . . . *off*, (*rowed*) *away from*; Both *off* and *away* indicate distancing from a point.
(2) Particles with aspectual meanings: (*gathered*) *up* (bringing to a certain limit – intensifying function; (*worn*) *out* (bringing to a certain limit) – Intensifying function; (*caught*) . . . *up*.

CHAPTER 9

Module 41

2 **(1)** event, habitual; **(2)** state; **(3)** comes . . . and asks, both events, historic present; **(4)** events, quotative; **(5)** instantaneous events (a demonstration); **(6)** events, referring to past (in press headline); **(7)** states; **(8)** 'prove' reporting an event that is still valid, 'leads' habitual.

5 **(1)** Past, Past. *Early* suggests that the speaker is visualising the event as occurring at some specific time in the past. The coordinated sequence of events suggests Past in both, although in the second the Perfect is marginally possible (*have left*), in which case the car is still by the bridge; **(2)** Perfect in both: *Get* here could mean 'grasp' in either its literal sense or its figurative senses of 'understand' or 'discover'; in either case continuation of what has been grasped is more likely than definite possession (*got*) followed by a gap in time; **(3)** Past, necessarily, since the referent of 'he' is obviously now dead; **(4)** Past, for the same reason as in 3; **(5)** *woke up* (Past), since the waking is clearly over, with a gap in time between the waking and speech time; *haven't had* (Perfect) since no gap is established; **(6)** Past (*did you say*), since the action of saying is seen as occurring at some specific time in the past; Past (*was*) with back-shift, or Present (*is*), since 'your name' is presumably still the same; **(7)** Perfect because no specific time is implied, and there is no disconnectedness, the addressee still being present; **(8)** Past, a specific point in time being implied; **(9)** Past, a specific event being visualised; **(10)** better Perfect in both, since the interpretation of connectedness is the more likely: 'you are still in the wrong group'. The Past in both would imply that the situation described no longer holds.

Module 42

2 **(1)** In **(b)** the standard set-up still prevails, whereas in **(a)** this is not necessarily the case. **(2)** The implication in **(a)** is that I am no longer a colleague of his, nor in the same department, whereas in **(b)** the situation still holds. **(3)** **(a)** asks about the point at which you stopped some time in the past; **(b)** asks about the point at which you are now. **(4)** **(a)** asks about a destination in the past unrelated to the present, whereas **(b)** connects the destination to present time, with the inference that the hearer has (recently) been somewhere and has now returned. **(5)** In **(a)** the action is over, in **(b)** it is recent and its effects are probably still felt or visible. **(6)** is similar to 5. **(7)** In **(b)** mobile phones are still popular, whereas no such implication exists in **(a)**. **(8)** In **(b)** the action of giving is recent, in **(a)** there is no such implication.

3 **(1)** *is*; **(2)** *fled*, because located at a definite time, in 1896; **(3)** *had begun*, because previous to 'fled'; **(4)** *fled*, for the same reason as in 2 – definite time; **(5)** *found* or *has found*, the latter if he still lives in Berlin; **(6)** *has made* because relevant to present time.

4 **(1)** *feels*, *is*, Present; **(2)** *has wanted*, Present Perfect; **(3)** *gets distracted* Present habitual; **(4)** *is*, Present state; **(5)** *drives*, Present habitual; **(6)** *says*, Present reporting **(7)** *read*, Past said Past, reporting; **(8)** *thought*, reporting, Past; **(9)** Present + progressive, *is it going to end*, reference to future time; **(10)** Present states *is*, *love*, *am*; **(11)** *he's achieved*, Present Perfect; **(12)** *I'm like*, quotative; **(13)** *is*, Present with future reference.

Module 43

1 The Past form 'squeaked' is indeterminate between an imperfective (repeated) and a perfective (single) occurrence. As 'squeak' is a punctual verb whose subject is 'shoes', it makes more sense to interpret it as repeated (iterative).

2 **(1)** bounded **(2)** unbounded **(3)** unbounded **(4)** bounded or punctual, depending on how you visualise the pouncing **(5)** unbounded **(6)** unbounded **(7)** bounded, comprising the stepping and the landing phases **(8)** bounded **(9)** unbounded **(10)** bounded.

3 **(1)** *was driving*, focuses on the internal phase of the process before the end-point *home*; **(2)** *was crossing*, extended internal phase of the process. Provides a frame for *when she saw us*; **(3)** *were jumping*, iterative; **(4)** *have been trying*, continuous phase anterior to speech time; **(5)** *is seeing*, dynamic use of a normally stative verb, *see* (='visit'). Both *sees* and *is seeing* have future reference, but *sees* emphasises the scheduled nature of the visit; **(6)** *was crackling*, ongoing event of temporary duration as seen by an observer; **(7)** *were photographing*, as in 6, and indeterminate (as is *photographed*) as to whether a single (perfective) or several (serial, imperfective) photographs were taken; **(8)** *am shivering and coughing*, iterative, speaker observing the process at speech time; **(9)** *was pulling up*, focuses on the internal phase of the process before the end-point expressed by '*up*'; **(10)** *was bending*, ongoing event of temporary duration as seen by an observer. In all but 4 and 8 the point of time or past event to which these ongoing events relate is not made explicit. In 4 and 8 the progressive relates the event to speech time.

Module 44

2 **(1)** will/'ll/shall; **(2)** can't/won't be able to; **(3)** must; **(4)** will; **(5)** can't; **(6)** should; **(7)** was able to **(8)** might, could; **(9)** must; **(10)** needn't/don't have to.

3 **(1)** ambiguous: with volitional meaning, wouldn't wait; with predictive meaning, won't have waited; **(2)** must have been mistaken; **(3)** can't have been listening . . . was saying; **(4)** should have taken; **(5)** could hear; **(6)** were able to capture; **(7)** may have been; **(8)** had to have . . . vaccinated; **(9)** would have telephoned, had been able; **(10)** oughtn't to have been talking/shouldn't have been talking, was playing.

CHAPTER 10

Module 45

1 **(1)** [*The head is underlined*] <u>Everyone</u> in the library; **(2a)** old <u>men</u> reading newspapers; **(2b)** high-school <u>boys and girls</u> doing research; **(3a)** the <u>outcome</u> of the current crisis; **(3b)** the <u>pattern</u> of international relations; **(4a)** <u>Someone</u> here; **(4b)** a <u>story</u>, etc. (to end of sentence), the most <u>notorious</u> of the dictators . . . to end; this <u>country</u>; (at) the <u>turn</u> of the century **(5a)** the <u>seat</u> on my left; **(5b)** a fat <u>lady</u> who, etc. (to end of sentence); an <u>orange</u>; **(5c)** my <u>right</u>; a thin-faced <u>man</u> etc. (to end of sentence); a <u>moustache</u>; a blotchy <u>skin</u>; **(5d)** He was <u>the one</u> who . . . etc. (to end); a friendly <u>smile</u>; a cheery '<u>Good evening</u>'; **(6a)** The violent <u>attacks</u> . . . missiles; the <u>police</u>; <u>bottles, bricks</u> and other assorted <u>missiles</u>; **(6b)** a large number of <u>casualties</u>.

2

pre-head	head	post-head
(1) fit, fun, funky, single	parent	
(2) gorgeous, good-humoured, intelligent, London based	man	interested in a loving and lasting relationship
(3) a loving and lasting	relationship	

5 *Questions* 1 and 3: **(1)** cataphoric reference to the next clause; **(2)** exclusive *we*: speaker and another, not the addressee; **(3)** reciprocal; **(4)** reference to speaker or *Pam*; **(5)** ambiguous: either anaphoric reference to the mentioned situation or relationship, or cataphoric reference to the Complement *nature* as the cause of the relationship (impersonal use of *it*); **(6)** impersonal use of *you*; **(7)** exophoric (ostensive) reference to speaker's gesture; **(8)** exophoric (ostensive) reference to speaker's hand; **(9)** exophoric reference to speaker; **(10)** exophoric (ostensive) reference to speaker's other hand; **(11)** anaphoric reference to *Pam*; **(12)** anaphoric reference to *this* and *that*; **(13)** anaphoric reference to *people*; **(14)** exophoric reference to speaker.

Question 2: (9) normal use of objective form of pronoun at Cs under prosodic stress of end-focus; (11) the same as 9 for *her*; (14) ungrammatical use of objective form of pronoun instead of subjective form.

6 (1) Ambiguous: either *this whole sequence of events*, or *this last event* (i.e. 'the stopping of work at the city's maternity and children's units'); (2) Analyse as pronoun.

Module 46

1a 1 mass; 2 count [= gymnasium]; 3 mass [= gymnastics]; 4 and 5 mass; 6 mass; 7 count; 8 ambiguous: appearance[1] = looks, mass; appearance[2] = performance, count; 9 mass; 10: mass.

1b *Fashion* and *football* can be used as count nouns (*new fashions; a new white football*); *shopping* and *homework* can't be used as count nouns.

2 The following are used in the text as: (1) mass NGs: *one's nature, material comfort, childhood, outer space, humanity, the common sense*; (2) count NGs: *a habit, the cosmonaut's denial, terrestrial comforts, the satisfaction, the scientific achievement, the impact, our planet, a painter, the sight, atomic flames, all cosmonauts, members, one family, my space experience, the people who live on our planet.*

3 (1) definite nouns: *The Don* (proper noun); *the age* (identified by its post-modifier); *the village* (identified by its post-modifier); *the son* (identified by its post-modifier); *the man* (identified by its post-modifier); *the young boy* (identified anaphorically by inference from 'the son' and 'the age of twelve'); *the new land* (identified anaphorically by inference from 'America'); *the few gestures* (identified by its post-modifier); (2) indefinite nouns: *a real man* (marked by *a* as indefinite-specific); *strange men and friends* (marked by zero article as indefinite-non-specific); *some tie* (marked by *some* as indefinite-specific).

4 *the backdoor* by inference that it is the backdoor of the speaker's house, or of a house which will be identified later in the text; *the moon*, exophoric reference to the earth's only moon; the *dark* hump of the *hillside*, identified by inference, as what the speaker saw from 'the backdoor'; the smoke, the *moon*, the *night*, *identified* by inference as the view from 'the backdoor' and 'the moon', which shines at 'night'.

5 Genericity could also be expressed by the following forms: (1) Liquids have no shape, (2) A gas has no shape. (3) Human beings need the company of others. (4) A war is politics carried out by violent means. (5) An animal that lives in captivity plays with its food . . . (6) A television (set) is a mixed blessing. (7) A bicycle is a cheap form of transport. Bicycles are a cheap form of transport. (8) Computers have revolutionised business methods.

6 (1) generic; (2) indefinite; (3) indefinite; (4) generic.

7 Either an indefinite but specific Frenchman; or, any man who is French (indefinite-non-specific).

Module 47

1 **(1)** subjective; **(2)** objective; **(3)** locative; **(4)** temporal; **(5)** extent; **(6)** objective; **(7)** subjective; **(8)** subjective; **(9)** subjective; **(10)** source.

2 **(1)** I should like *another doctor's* opinion. **(2)** Have you read the chairman of the *examination committee's report?* **(3)** The Regional Training *Scheme's* failure was inevitable. **(4)** My next door *neighbour's dog* barks all night. **(5)** No change, in order to avoid *in my class's grandmother.* **(6)** Preferably no change, for similar reasons to 5.

3 **(1)** Every member . . . ; **(2)** . . . hundreds of butterflies; **(3)** . . . some/ sǝm/ very good news; **(4)** Some/s ʌ m/ people . . . ; **(5)** Most of the people in this office have a car. . . . ; **(6)** *None* of this work . . . ; **(7)** . . . such *an* opportunity; **(8)** *Half* my friends.

4 **(1)** every; **(2)** both . . . neither; or, all . . . none; **(3)** each; **(4)** every . . . each; **(5)** both; **(6)** any/ none; **(7)** every; **(8)** any (= it doesn't matter which) or, no (= only the soluble kind will do).

5 **(1)** everything; **(2)** all; **(3)** all; **(4)** everything; **(5)** everything.

Module 48

1 modified by epithets: *Europeans*; modified by classifiers: *building, policy, power, Parliament, week, questions.* The post-modifiers of *students* and *attitudes* are of a classifying type.

2 The adjectives *good, effective, persuasive, optimistic* and *sound* are evaluative epithets, all of an appreciative kind, which describe the ideal person for the job. In the context of essential qualifications, however, *good* at least takes on a classifying besides a descriptive value. ('*Good*' is a grade in many academic institutions.) *Mental* is clearly classifying. The outstanding benefits *non-contributory* (pension), *personal* (loan), *company* (car), *career* (development), are classified administratively, except for the epithet *excellent.*

5
(1)	classifier	ambiguous
(2)	ambiguous	classifier
(3)	classifier	classifier
(4)	classifier	epithet
(5)	epithet	classifier
(6)	epithet	classifier
(7)	classifier	epithet

6 **(1)** Place first the shortest, and last the one which you prefer to emphasise; separate them by commas. **(2)** Most speakers would say: *We heard a mysterious, faint tinkling sound*; that is: subjective + short objective + participial epithets. **(3)** Place shortest first, longest last; also in order of ascending 'dynamism': *her long, slender, artistic hands.* **(4)** Shortest first, then submodified *-ing* epithet, then classifier (a) *She had a pair of smart, exotic-looking designer* sunglasses **(5)** The most natural order is: size + colour + material: *The toilet was a smallish, brown, wooden box.* Place *wooden* last as classifier. **(6)** The most likely order is: two subjective + two objective epithets. Classifier *granite* nearest the noun: We drove through the *dark threatening, wooded, granite mountains.* No comma after *dark* (threatening because dark).

Module 49

1 **(1)** integrated; **(2)** integrated; **(3)** supplementive; **(4)** a country which I didn't know, supplementive; which I didn't know, integrated; **(5)** supplementive; **(6)** integrated; **(7)** supplementive; **(8)** integrated; **(9)** supplementive; **(10)** supplementive.

2 **(1)** *Jessica*: appositive integrated. **(2)** *a failure by any standard* and **(3)** *the curse of twentieth-century democracy* appositive, supplementive NGs.

4 **(1)** clas. h; **(2)** eeh; **(3)** ddhm; **(4)** de clas. hmm; **(5)** dee clas. clas. h; **(6)** hmm.

5a **(1)** service for the repair of television aerials; **(2)** Appointments of Research Fellows at the University of Manchester; **(3)** reduction of the prices of telephone calls made during the daytime; **(4)** alarm about the proposals for the reform of adult education; **(5)** awards of gold medals made to the athletics teams of universities.

5b **(1)** land-based multiple-warhead missiles; **(2)** intermediate-range nuclear-type weapons; **(3)** an all-European home-robots exhibition; **(4)** a classic midnight-blue lady's velvet evening suit; **(5)** a two-year-old Maltese honey-coloured stone farmhouse.

6 **(a)** If there is no comma after neck it seems that it is his neck that is in evening dress; moreover one would normally perceive the whole evening dress before the chain round the neck. **(b)** 'it' is here placed too far from its presupposed NG *a clear fire,* and appears to say that he is 'standing with his back to his own evening dress'. **(c)** It also appears that 'his face is spread out in both hands'. Rearrange the sentence as follows: *A clear fire burned in a tall fireplace, and an elderly man, standing with his back to it in evening dress and with a chain round his neck, glanced up from the newspaper he was holding spread out in both hands before his calm and severe face.*

Module 50

1 First NG *The . . . ritual*; second NG *the coming of spring*: third NG *an expression of unity and fun*. **(1)** complement, **(2)** complement, **(3)** complement. All take prepositional complements, as the nouns *celebration, coming* and *expression* are derived from verbs.

2 **(1)** *his taste in women*: **Od** of *describing*; **(2)** *the famous baby doctor, Benjamin Spock*: **S** of *said*; **(3)** *Benjamin Spock*: supplementive appositive of *doctor*, **(4)** *rather severe women*: complement **(c)** of the preposition *by*; **(5)** *their severity*: **c** of the preposition *despite*; **(6)** *The model for these women*: **S** of *was*; **(7)** *his own mother.* **Cs** after the copular verb *was*; **(8)** his early *eighties*: **c** of the preposition *in*; **(9)** *a most exceptionally charming man*: **Cs** after the copular verb *is*; **(10)** *the wish to win over his mother.* **S** of *may help.*

CHAPTER 11

Describing persons, things and circumstances

1 ADJECTIVES AND THE ADJECTIVAL GROUP

Module 51

2   **(2)** You have been *very enterprising* in setting up this firm. **(3)** The newspapers have published/ given *detailed reports* of the case. Newspaper reports *of the case were very detailed.* **(4)** Conflicts often arise between *neighbouring countries.* **(5)** We live *in an* ancient *walled town.* **(6)** There are often better opportunities for *skilled workers than for unskilled* (ones).

3   **(a)** Pre-modifiers in NG: 1, 2, 3 (also *Northern*); 9, 11, 12, 13, 17. As predicative Cs in clause: 4–8, 10, 14–16. **(b)** classifiers: 1 and 9, the rest are descriptors. **(c)** Possibly as an ellipted AdjG: ten years old.

4   The transitive ones are participial adjectives; they can be graded by *more, most* and intensified by *very.* They can also function as Complements of the Subject and of the Object. The intransitive ones do not fulfil these criteria. *Ticking, fading* and *growing* are participial modifiers of the head noun. (Notice that, in 'the clock is ticking', *is ticking, are fading*, etc. are verbs.)

6   *navy/ sky/ royal blue; grass/ olive green; shocking pink; brick-red; ice-cold; boiling hot; pitch black; bitter-sweet; snow-white.*

7   The compound adjectives are: **(2)** *time-consuming;* **(3)** *home-made;* **(4)** *breath-taking;* **(5)** *airborne;* **(6)** *wind-swept;* **(7)** *award-winning;* **(8)** *labour-saving.*

Module 52

1a   Inflected for grading: *risky, blue, friendly, small, tight.* (*Bitterest* is normal but *more bitter* is probably preferred to *bitterer*). The remaining adjectives take analytic forms.

1b   Gradable are: *shallow* (*er/ more*), *small, probable* and *fast.* The rest are not gradable.

5   Suggested correspondences: **(1)** *essentially;* **(2)** *radically;* **(3)** *ideally* placed and **(4)** *pleasantly* surrounded; **(5)** *ferociously;* **(6)** *genuinely* old, *imaginatively* new.

6   **(1)** *medically necessary, socially dangerous.* **(2)** *theoretically very good/ very good theoretically;* **(3)** Countries which are *technologically advanced* . . . those which are *scientifically under-developed.*

   The remaining exercises in this module invite free answers; they require only reference to the text book or to a good dictionary for some items, and then the free composition of examples. For these reasons, no key is offered.

Module 53

2 Introduce your PPs with the following prepositions: **(2)** (*delighted*) at; **(3)** (*satisfied*) with; **(4)** (*opposed*) to; **(5)** (*white*) with; **(6)** (*expert*) at; **(7)** (*tired*) of; **(8)** (*keen*) on.

3 **(a)** The adjectives and AdjGs in the extract from *Boy* are: (i) functioning at Cs in clause: *good at games; exceptionally good at two of them*); *far more complicated; far faster than squash; so good at it that I won . . .* (to end of clause); (ii) functioning as m in NG: *glass-roofed; perfect; small, hard, white, leather-covered; gloved; subtle and crafty; fastest . . . on earth* (m and c); *swift, strong, very quick*; and (iii) functioning as Object Complement in clause: *hard to believe*.

2 ADVERBS AND THE ADVERBIAL GROUP

Module 54

1 *where* (space, position); *down* (space, position); *up* (space, position); *just* (degree, intensification); *well* (discourse marker, attitude of acceptance); *there* (space, position); *away* (space, direction); *yet* (time, relation); *up* (degree, intensification); *along* (space, direction); *up* (degree, intensification); *behind* (space, position); *all round* (degree, intensification); back (space, direction); *back* (space, direction); *even* (scalar, not knowing a neighbour's name is less than expected); *just* (focusing by reinforcement); *again* (time, frequency); *about* (space, indeterminate position); *back* (space, direction); *even* (focusing by reinforcement). Comment: the preponderance of circumstantial (space and time) adverbs, together with focusing adverbs, is in accordance with the topic and the subjective stance manifested in this personal account.

2 In this passage, the adverbs are distributed as follows: circumstantial: *elsewhere, anywhere*; modal: *incredibly, perhaps, probably*; focusing: *especially, even, too* (= also), *alone*; degree: *roughly, about, approximately, enough, quite, so*. Comment: the passage contains argumentation about space rather than its description, and therefore contains only two 'spatial' adverbs. No subjective attitude is expressed; the adverb *incredibly* is not emotive in this context, where it means little more than *very*. The modal, focusing and grading meanings of the other 13 adverbs express, not personal feelings, but a cautious assessment of the arguments concerning a relatively undocumented scientific matter. The observation of this one linguistic feature (use of adverbs) in two different kinds of text (personal experience and objective exposition) shows how subject matter and its mode of treatment by an author always affects the choices of language forms in which a text is written or spoken.

3a **(1)** *eminently* well suited; **(2)** *certainly* brilliant and moving, though *admittedly* it might; **(3)** an *undeniably* educational experience; **(4)** *Reportedly*, the President; **(5)** a poem *allegedly* written by Hitler; **(6)** it was *obviously/ clearly*; **(7)** He *actually* became a star . . . which *clearly* allowed him to; **(8)** Their popularity is *undoubtedly* rising.

3b **(1)** *ideologically* unyielding; **(2)** *socially* well-connected; **(3)** *stylistically* too long and complicated; **(4)** *racially* mixed; **(5)** *morally* responsible; **(6)** *historically* accurate.

3c (1) *hardly* convince; (2) *even* in the rain; (3) we *simply* do not know; (4) *solely/exclusively* on formal grammar; (5) and I said so *too/also*; (6) and will *similarly* help us.

3d (1) sleeping *soundly*; (2) *surreptitiously* carrying diamonds; (3) Wilson worked *endlessly*; (4) speaking *slowly, carefully* choosing; (5) he drank *heavily*; (6) *momentarily* stopped.

Module 55

2 (a) Affirmative answers: (1) Yes, it's *already* time. (2) Yes, I've *already* had it. Yes, I've had it *already*. (3) Yes, I *still* love you. Yes, I *still* do. Yes, I love you *still*. (4) Yes, I'm *still* studying it. Yes, I *still* am. (5) Yes, it's *already* ten. Yes, it's ten *already*. (6) Yes, I've *already* been there. Yes, I've been there *already*. Yes, I *already* have.
(b) Negative answers: (1) No, it *isn't* time to go yet. It *isn't* yet time to go. (2) No, I haven*'t* had it yet. I haven*'t* yet had lunch. (3) No, I don't love you any *more/ any* longer. I no *longer* love you. (4) No, I'm *not* studying it *any more/ any longer*. No, I'm no *longer* studying it. (5) No, it's *not* ten o'clock yet. No, it's *not* yet ten o'clock. (6) No, I haven*'t* been there yet. No, I haven*'t* yet been there.

3 Possible positions are indicated by #. The adverb is given in the unmarked, preferred position. (1) #We *sometimes* take long holidays# in mountainous areas#. (2) #Journalists #working in war zones are *often* in danger. (3) #She gets on well with people *abroad*. (4) #They gave a concert *yesterday*. (5) #The cat gazed *longingly* at the brightly coloured fish in the aquarium#. (6) *Perhaps* you'd better take an overcoat with you#. (7) #We shall *probably* leave tomorrow#. (8) Hopefully, they have arrived at their destination. They have arrived *hopefully* at their destination. Comments: Remember that the different positions an adverb may occupy determine the scope of its reference. When the adverb is in initial position, the whole clause is in its scope, and may express either stance or judgement. Within the clause, it focuses mainly on the predicator and so is placed closely before, after or within the Predicator: *sometimes take, are often, gaze longingly, shall probably leave*. Other elements are sometimes focused, for example by restrictive adverbs: *He alone, only for them*. In end-position, the adverb is either in focus, or else is almost parenthetical, as in: *We shall leave tomorrow, probably*.

Module 56

3

	Adverb	Function	Semantic type
(1)	*terribly*	modifier of *new*	intensification
(2)	*at all*	postmod. of *anything*	attenuation
(3)	*really*	Adjunct	modal, judgement
(4)	*much*	modifier of *the same*	intensification
(5)	*still*	Adjunct	time relation
(6)	*out*	Adjunct	spatial direction
(7)	*so*	connective	result

(8)	*well*	connective	concession
(9)	*scarcely*	Adjunct	attenuation
(10)	*really*	Adjunct	modal, judgement
(11)	*so*	connective	result
(12)	*a bit of*	modifier of NG	attenuation
(13)	*really*	Adjunct	modal, judgement
(14)	*just*	Adjunct	restriction
(15)	*sort of*	Adjunct	attenuation
(16)	*entirely*	modifier of *separate*	intensification
(17)	*only*	Adjunct	restriction
(18)	*anyway*	connective	concession
(19)	*really*	Adjunct	modal, judgement
(20)	*a bit*	modifier of *awkward*	attenuation
(21)	*through*	Adjunct	spatial direction
(22)	*so*	substitute	clausal
(23)	*even if*	concessive-conditional	focus on *if*
(24)	*together*	Adjunct	manner
(25)	*just*	modifier of *ideal*	intensification
(26)	*really*	Adjunct	modal, judgement
(27)	*really*	Adjunct	modal, judgement
(28)	*so*	connective	result
(29)	*out*	Adjunct	spatial direction
(30)	*never*	Adjunct	time, frequency
(31)	*since*	Adjunct	time, relation
(32)	*at all*	modifier of *not*	intensification
(33)	*really*	Adjunct	modal, emphasis
(34)	*a little*	modifier of *unpleasant*	attenuation
(35)	*sort of*	modifier of *unpleasant*	attenuation
(36)	*rather*	modifier of *unpleasant*	intensification

Comment: some common adverbs may be interpreted semantically in more than one way. For example, 13 (*really*) may be considered as an Adjunct having intensifying force instead of as an Adjunct expressing a judgement of the truth value of the statement. Similarly 14 (*just*) may be interpreted as expressing attenuation rather than restriction. Discussion of the other adverbs in this exercise may well reveal further examples of this semantico-syntactic fluidity.

CHAPTER 12

Module 57

2 **(1)** *a sudden*: The determiner *a* gives the impression that we have here a NG. However, the whole phrase is an invariable idiom, which functions as Adjunct NG; **(2)** *fashion*: noun; **(3)** *school*: noun; **(4)** *everyone*: pronoun; **(5)** *us*: pronoun; **(6)** *not having to take a decision*: -*ing* cl; **(7)** *the Conservatives*: NG; **(8)** *the Labour Party*: NG;

(9) *comparing programmes and thinking*: -*ing* cl; **(10)** *who to vote for*: PP; **(11)** *the way* etc: NG; **(12)** *getting votes*: -*ing* cl; **(13)** *them*: pronoun; **(14)** *at least some of the younger generation*: NG; **(15)** *them*: pronoun; **(16)** *the whole*: NG; **(17)** *people*: NG; **(18)** *their late teens and twenties*: NG; **(19)** *the twenty-year-olds*: NG; **(20)** *when they were young*: fin. cl; **(21)** *what they were like*: PP with *wh*- complement; **(22)** *that 'green' area*: NG; **(23)** *moving towards a position etc*: -*ing* cl.

Comments: **(a)** distribution of these complement forms is as follows: NG **(12)**, noun **(2)**, pronoun **(4)**, -*ing* cl **(4)**, *wh*-cl **(2)**; **(b)** AdjG, AdvG, PP (0). **(9)** consists of two coordinated non-finite -*ing* clauses, the second containing a PP whose complement is another PP *who to vote for*, with stranded preposition. **(13)** is a NG containing a finite relative clause post-modifier, *people say*. **(14)** itself contains a PP, *about . . .*, whose complement is a NG containing another PP, *of . . .* whose complement is a NG **(14)**. **(17)** is a NG, *people today*, whose post-modifier contains a finite relative clause, itself containing a PP, *in . . .* with a NG as complement **(18)**. Nos. **(20)** and **(21)** are coordinated finite clauses, functioning together as a complex complement of the preposition *to*. *Of* in **(13)**, **(14)** and **(15)** is a grammaticised preposition functioning as part of a quantitative modifier (see 47.4). AdjGs and AdvGs are not represented; they are in fact very restricted in this function.

Module 58

1 **(1)** Cs (with stranded preposition) in clause; **(2)** A in clause; **(3)** c of *obsessed*; **(4)** c of AdjG *kind*; **(5)** Ob in clause; **(6)** A in clause; **(7)** A in clause; **(8)** A in clause; **(9)** A in clause (of previous speaker); **(10)** m in NG; **(11)** m in NG. Graded pre- and post-modifier (*more cases of . . . than . . .*) form one discontinuous unit; **(12)** A in clause; **(13)** m in AdjG; **(14)** A in clause; **(15)** A in clause; **(16)** in NG headed by *myths* post-modifier.

2 **(1)** adverb, **(2)** prep; **(3)** adverb; **(4)** adverb; **(5)** adverb; **(6)** prep; **(7)** prep; **(8)** adverb; **(9)** prep; **(10)** adverb; **(11)** neither adverb nor preposition, but an adjective; **(12)** adverb; **(13)** prep; **(14)** adverb; **(15)** prep; **(16)** prep.

Module 59

1 **(1)** static, extending from one side to the other, space below; contact only at each end; **(2)** path leading to position; on the other side; contact with surface; **(3)** non-locational; more than a mentioned quantity; **(4)** position; higher than; without contact; **(5)** movement up one side and down the other; with contact; **(6)** extent; covering a horizontal surface; with contact; **(7)** movement downwards from an upright position; caused by an obstacle; making contact with the obstacle; **(8)** indeterminate position of a blow on an object. Comment: some different semantic features can be expressed by the preposition *over* in other contexts; e.g. *to fall over a cliff; to be over an operation; to be over the worst; all over the world; conversation over lunch; over the telephone; to take a long time over something; to have difficulties over something.*

4 *At*: related to points in space (*sea*), time (*once, times*), and engagement in an activity (*work, war*). *On*: related to a state or activity. *Out of*: related to a lack of, or absence of something, derived from the basic meaning of exit from a container; *out of sight*, not within the field of vision. *In*: related to a state, or field of vision (*in full view*) abstracted from the container metaphor. *Under*: in a disadvantaged state, abstracted from the basic meaning of 'in a lower position' relative to something else.

5 **(1)** *for* is the preposition most often used for the simple expression of the extent of a period; **(2)** *over*, metaphorical use, spanning the period as a whole; **(3)** *during* refers to points or short periods at different times during the whole period; **(4)** *through*, metaphorical use, treating the years of problems as having volume, like a forest or a tunnel; **(5)** *throughout* intensifies the notion of 'the entire period' and 'constant activity'; **(6)** *in* means 'at the end of the next two years'; **(7)** *within* means during the next two years or a period not longer than two years.

6 **(1)** Path; **(2)** Source; **(3)** Location (point) in space; **(4)** reference; **(5)** Location in space; **(6)** movement of going up higher than something and down again; **(7)** purpose; **(8)** Location; **(9)** Goal; **(10)** Goal; **(11)** part–whole; **(12)** Goal; **(13)** part–whole; **(14)** Location (partly contained); **(15)** Location; **(16)** Recipient; **(17)** metaphorical; **(18)** Location; **(19)** Location.

Module 60

1 **(1)** It is *the ecological consequences of this project* that I am most interested *in*. **(2)** *What you* must be particularly careful *about* when walking in the streets is your money. **(3)** *What I* haven't paid *for* yet are the meals. *The meals* haven't been paid *for* yet. **(4)** I find *my parents* difficult to talk *to*. **(5)** *What* do you believe *in*, then? **(6)** *Which flight* did you say we are *booked on*? **(7)** *Who* are we collecting this money *for*? **(8)** *Which country* is Caracas the capital *of*? **(9)** *Which parking-place* did the caretaker say we can't park *in*?

2 **(1)** *for*, abstract, orientation, functioning as a stance adjunct; **(2)** *like*, similarity, modified by *a bit*; **(3)** *dress . . . up*, discontinuous transitive verb + adv. particle; **(4)** *with*, means; **(5)** *get over*, prep. verb, metaphorical, 'overcome'; **(6)** *for*, selected by the noun, *taste*; **(7)** *at* the Edinburgh Festival, location viewed as point, function; **(8)** *at*, selected by the verb stare; **(9)** *like*, similarity; **(10)** *for*, selected by the noun *reasons*; **(11)** *of*, grammaticised, part–whole; **(12)** *without*, conjunctive preposition; **(13)** *like*, similarity, selected by verbs such as *look* and *sound*; **(14)** *in that . . . manner*, abstract; **(15)** *to*, direction, grammaticised; **(16)** *in*, container metaphor of time; **(17)** *settle down*, v + adv. particle; **(18)** *in*, container metaphor, a theatre seat has arms and is comfortable; **(19)** *with*, stranded preposition in *wh*-relative clause (*with whoever* I am).

SELECT BIBLIOGRAPHY

Austin, L.J. (1962) *How to do Things with Words*. Oxford: Oxford University Press.

Bache, C. and L.K. Jakobsen (1980) 'On the distinction between restrictive and non-restrictive relative clauses in modern English'. *Lingua* 52 (1980): 243–267.

Biber, D., S. Johansson, G. Leech, S. Conrad, S. and E. Finegan (1999) *Longman Grammar of Spoken and Written English*. London: Longman.

Bloor, T. and M. Bloor, (1995, 2nd edition 2004). *The Functional Analysis of English. A Hallidayan Approach*. London: Edward Arnold.

Bolinger, D. (1977) *Meaning and Form*. London: Longman.

Brazil, D. (1995) *A Grammar of Speech*. Oxford: Oxford University Press.

Brown, E.K. and J.E. Miller (1980) *Syntax: A Linguistic Introduction to Sentence Structure*. London: Hutchinson.

Brown, P. and S. Levinson (1987) *Politeness. Some universals in language usage*. Studies in International Sociolinguistics 4. Cambridge: Cambridge University Press.

Butler, C.S. (1985) *Systemic Linguistics, Theory and Practice*. London: Batsford.

Butler, C.S. (2003) *Structure and Function. A Guide to Three Major Functional Theories. Part I. Approaches to the simplex clause* and *Part II. From clause to discourse and beyond*. Amsterdam and Philadelphia: Benjamins.

Chafe, W. (1976) 'Givenness, contrastiveness, definiteness, subjects, topics and points of view'. In Li, C. (ed.) *Subject and Topic*. New York: Academic Press: 22–55.

Chafe, W. (1994) *Discourse, Consciousness and Time*. Chicago: Chicago University Press.

Chafe, W. and J.A. Nichols (1986) *Evidentiality: The Linguistic Coding of Epistemology*. Advances in Discourse Processes XX. Norwood, N.JH: Ablex.

Coates, J. (1983) *The Semantics of the Modal Auxiliaries*. London: Croom Helm.

Collins Cobuild English Dictionary (1987) London: Collins.

Cole, P. and J. Morgan (eds) (1975) *Syntax and Semantics 3: Speech Acts*. New York: Academic Press.

Cole, P. and J.M. Sadock (eds) (1977) *Syntax and Semantics 8: Grammatical Relations*. New York: Academic Press.

Collins, P. (1991) 'Pseudocleft and cleft constructions: a thematic and informational interpretation'. *Linguistics* 29 (1991): 481–519.

Collins, P. (1995) 'The indirect object construction in English: an informational approach'. *Linguistics* 33 (1995): 35–49.

Comrie, B. (1977) *Aspect*. Cambridge: Cambridge University Press.

Comrie, B. (1985) *Tense*. Cambridge: Cambridge University Press.

Connolly, J., R. Vismans, C.S. Butler and R. A. Gatward (1997) *Discourse and Pragmatics in Functional Grammar*, Functional Grammar 18. Berlin and New York: Mouton de Gruyter.

Daneš, F. (1974) *Functional sentence perspective and the organization of the text*. Prague: Academia.

Davidse, K. (1992) 'A semiotic approach to relational clauses'. *Occasional Papers in Systemic Linguistics*, vol. 6: 99–132.

Davidse, K. (1996) 'Ditransitivity and possession', in R. Hasan, C. Cloran and D. Butt (eds) *Functional Descriptions. Theory in Practice*. Amsterdam and Philadelphia: John Benjamins: 85–144.

Davidse, K. (2000) 'Semiotic and possessive models in relational clauses: Thinking with grammar about grammar'. *Revista Canaria de Estudios Ingleses*, 40 (2000): 13–35.

De Clerck, B. 'On the pragmatic functions of *let's* utterances in the ICE-GB', in K. Aijmer and B. Altenberg (eds), *Working with new corpora. Papers from the 23rd International Conference of English Language Research on Computerized Corpora (ICAME 21)*, Göteborg, 2002. Amsterdam and Atlanta: Rodopi: 213–233.

Dik, S.C. (1997) *The Theory of Functional Grammar*, 2 vols., 2nd revised edn, ed. Kees Hengeveld. Berlin: Mouton de Gruyter.

Dirven, R. and M. Verspoor (1998) *Cognitive Exploration of Language and Linguistics*. Amsterdam and Philadelphia: John Benjamins.

Downing, A. (1991) 'An alternative approach to Theme: a systemic-functional perspective'. *WORD*, vol. 42, no. 2 (August 1991): 119–141.

Downing, A. (1996) 'The semantics of *get*-passives' in R. Hasan, C. Cloran and D. Butt (eds) *Functional Descriptions. Theory in Practice*. Amsterdam Studies in the Theory and History of Linguistic Science: Series IV – Current Issues in Linguistic Theory. Amsterdam and Philadelphia: Benjamins: 179–206.

Downing, A. (2000). 'Nominalisation and topic management in leads and headlines', in E. Ventola, (ed.), *Discourse and Community. Doing Functional Linguistics*: 355–378.

Downing, A. (2001) '"Surely you knew!" Surely as a marker of evidentiality and stance'. *Functions of Language*, vol. 8, no. 2: 253–286.

Downing, A. (2002) 'Negotiating topic coherence through talk-in-action', in J. Hladky (ed.), *Language and Function: To the memory of Jan Firbas*. Amsterdam and Philadelphia: John Benjamins: 111–126.

Downing, A. (2004) 'Achieving coherence: Topicality, conceptualisations and action sequences in negotiating conflicting goals'. *Revista Canaria de Estudios Ingleses* 49: 13–28.

Downing, A. (2005) 'The English pragmatic marker *surely* and the functional counterparts in Spanish', in K. Aijmer and A.-M. Simon-Vandenbergen (eds) *Pragmatic Markers in Contrast* [Studies in Pragmatics]. Oxford: Elsevier: 39–58.

Duffley, Patrick J. (1992) *The English Infinitive*. London and New York: Longman.

Eggins, S. (1994) *An Introduction to Systemic Functional Linguistics*, London: Pinter.

Fawcett, R. (2000) *A Theory of Syntax for Systemic Functional Linguistics*. Amsterdam and Philadelphia: John Benjamins.

Fillmore, C.J. (1977) 'The case for case reopened', in Cole and Sadock (1977): 59–81.

Fillmore, C.J. (1982) 'Frame semantics', in The Linguistic Society of Korea (ed.), *Linguistics in the Morning Calm*. Seoul: Hanshin Publishing: 110–137.

Firbas, J. (1992) *Functional Sentence Perspective in Written and Spoken Communication*. Cambridge: Cambridge University Press.

Fraser, B. (1975) 'Hedged performatives', in Cole and Morgan (eds): 137–210.

Fries, P. (1981) 'On the status of Theme in English: Arguments from discourse'. *Forum Linguisticum*, vol. 6, no. 1: 1–38.

Geluykens, R. (1987) 'Intonation of speech act types: an experimental approach to rising intonation in queclaratives'. *Journal of Pragmatics* 11: 483–494.

Givón, T. (1993) *English Grammar. A Function-Based Introduction* (vols. I and II). Amsterdam and Philadelphia: John Benjamins.

Givón, T. (1995) *Functionalism and Grammar*. Amsterdam and Philadelphia: John Benjamins.

Givón, T. (2001a) *Syntax: An Introduction, Vol. I*. Amsterdam and Philadelphia: John Benjamins.

Givón, T. (2001b) *Syntax: An Introduction, Vol. II*. Amsterdam and Philadelphia: John Benjamins.

Givón, T. (2005) *Context as Other Minds. The Pragmatics of Sociality, Cognition and Communication*. Amsterdam and Philadelphia: John Benjamins.

Goldberg, A.E. (1995) *A Construction Grammar Approach to Argument Structure*. Chicago and London: University of Chicago Press.

Gómez-González, M.A. (2001) *The Theme-Topic Interface. Evidence from English*. Amsterdam and Philadelphia: John Benjamins.

Goutsos, D. (1996) *Modelling Discourse Topic: Sequential Relations and Strategies in Expository Text* Advances in Discourse Processes LIX. Norwood, NJ: Ablex.

Greenbaum, S. and R. Quirk (1990) *A Student's Grammar of the English Language*. London: Longman.

Grice, H.P. (1975) 'Logic and conversation', in Cole and Morgan: 41–58.

Grundy, P. (1995) *Doing Pragmatics*. London: Edward Arnold.

Gumperz, J.J. (1982) *Discourse Strategies*. Cambridge: Cambridge University Press.

Halliday, M.A.K. (1994) *An Introduction to Functional Grammar*. London: Edward Arnold.

Halliday, M.A.K. (2004) *An Introduction to Functional Grammar*. 3rd edn, revised by Christian M.I.M. Matthiessen. London: Arnold.

Halliday, M.A.K. and R. Hasan (1976) *Cohesion in English*. London: Longman.

Hidalgo-Downing, L. (2000) *Negation, Text Worlds and Discourse. The Pragmatics of Fiction*. Advances in Discourse Processes LXVI. Stamford, CT: Ablex.

Hopper, P.J. and S.A.Thompson (1980) 'Transitivity in grammar and discourse', *Language* 56: 251–99.

Huddleston, R. (1984) *Introduction to the Grammar of English*. Cambridge: Cambridge University Press.

Huddleston, R. and G.K. Pullum. (2002) *The Cambridge Grammar of the English Language*. Cambridge: Cambridge University Press.

Jiménez Juliá, T. (2000) '*Tema* en español y en inglés: dos conceptos enfrentados', *British Hispanic Society*, LXXVII: 162.

Jucker, A. and Y. Ziv (eds) (1998) *Discourse Markers: Descriptions and Theory*. Amsterdam and Philadelphia: John Benjamins: 127–146.

Kärkkäinen, E. (2003) *Epistemic Stance in English Conversation*. Amsterdam and Philadelphia: John Benjamins.

Kilby, D. (1984) *Descriptive Syntax and the English Verb*. London and Sydney: Croom Helm.

Kravchenko, A.K. (2002) 'A cognitive account of tense and aspect. Resurrecting "dead" metaphors'. *Anglophonia. French Journal of English Studies* 12 (2002): 99–112.

Lakoff, G. (1987) *Women, Fire and Dangerous Things. What Categories Reveal about the Mind*. Chicago and London: University of Chicago Press.

Lakoff, G. and M. Johnson (1980) *Metaphors We Live By*. Chicago and London: University of Chicago Press.

Lambrecht, K. (1994) *Information Structure and Sentence Form*. Cambridge: Cambridge University Press.

Langacker, R.W. (1987) *Foundations of Cognitive Grammar, vol. 1: Theoretical Prerequisites*. Stanford: Stanford University Press.

Langacker, R.W. (1991) *Foundations of Cognitive Grammar, vol. 2: Descriptive Application*. Stanford: Stanford University Press.

Leech, G. (1983) *Principles of Pragmatics*. London and New York: Longman.

Levin, B. (1993) *English Verb Classes and Alternations. A preliminary investigation*. Chicago and London: University of Chicago Press.

Lyons, J. (1977) *Semantics*, 2 vols. London: Cambridge University Press.

Martínez Vázquez, M. (1998) *La Diátesis. Alternancias oracionales en la lengua inglesa*. Universidad de Huelva: Publicaciones.

Matthiessen, C.M.I.M. (1995) *Lexicogrammatical Cartography*. Tokyo: International Language Sciences Publishers.

Matthiessen, C.M.I.M. and S.A. Thompson (1988) 'The structure of discourse and "subordination"', in J. Haiman and S.A. Thompson (eds), *Clause Combining in Grammar and Discourse*. Amsterdam and Philadelphia: John Benjamins: 275–329.

Matras, Y. (1997) 'The function and typology of coordinating conjunctions: evidence from discourse and language-contact situations', in J. Connolly et al.: 177–191.

McCoard, R.W. (1978) *The English Perfect: Tense-Choice and Pragmatic Inferences*. Amsterdam, New York and Oxford: North-Holland.

Mourelatos, A.P. (1981) 'Events, processes and states', in Philip J. Tedeschi and Annie Zaenen (eds), *Syntax and Semantics, vol. 14: Tense and Aspect*. New York: Academic Press: 191–212.

Palmer, F.R. (1986, repr. 1988) *Mood and Modality*. Cambridge: Cambridge University Press.

Panther, K.-U. and L. Thornburg (1998) 'A cognitive approach for inferencing in conversation'. *Journal of Pragmatics* 30: 755–769.

Payne, T. (1997) *Describing Morphosyntax: A Guide for Field Linguists*. Cambridge: Cambridge University Press.

Pérez Hernández, L. and F-J. Ruiz de Mendoza (2002) 'Grounding, semantic motivation, and conceptual interaction in indirect directive speech acts'. *Journal of Pragmatics* 34 (2002): 259–284.

Prince, E.F. (1981) 'Toward a taxonomy of Given-New information', in P. Cole (ed.) *Radical Pragmatics*. New York: Academic Press: 225–255.

Quirk, R., S. Greenbaum, J. Svartvik and G. Leech (1985) *A Comprehensive Grammar of the English Language*. London: Longman.

Round, A. (1998) 'Grammatical constructions and prototype effects in a group of "analytic" phrases'. *CLS 34: The Main Session* (1998). Chicago Linguistics Society: 335–345.

Schriffrin, D. (1987) *Discourse Markers*. Cambridge: Cambridge University Press.

Searle, J. (1975) 'Indirect speech acts', in P. Cole and J. Morgan (eds): 59–82.

Shopen, T. (ed.) (1985, repr. 1995) *Language Typology and Syntactic Description. Grammatical Categories and the Lexicon*. Cambridge: Cambridge University Press.

Slobin, D.I. (1996) 'From "thought and language" to "thinking for speaking"', in J. Gumperz and S. Levinson (eds), *Rethinking Linguistic Relativity*, Cambridge: Cambridge University Press: 70–96.

Smith, S.W. and A.H. Jucker (2000) '*Actually* and other markers of an apparent discrepancy between propositional attitudes of conversational partners', in G. Andersen and T. Fretheim (eds) *Pragmatic Markers and Propositional Attitude*. Amsterdam: John Benjamins: 207–238.

Spasov, D. (1978) *The Verb in the Structure of English*. Sofia: Naouka I Izkoustvo.

Sperber, D. and D. Wilson (1986) *Relevance: Communication and Cognition*. Oxford: Basil Blackwell.

Stenström, A-B. (1998) 'From sentence to discourse: *Cos (because)* in teenage talk', in A.H. Jucker and Y. Ziv (eds) *Discourse Markers. Descriptions and Theory*. Amsterdam: John Benjamins: 127–146.

Stoevsky, A.Y. (1992) 'Tense meaning and pragmatics', in M. Stamenov (ed.) *Current Advances in Semantic Theory*. Vol. 73 of Current Issues in Linguistic Theory. Amsterdam: John Benjamins: 399–416.

Stoevsky, A.Y. (2000) 'The perfect, perfectivity, iterativity and identity', in Z. Catalan, C. Stamenov and E. Pancheva (eds), *Seventy Years of English and American Studies in Bulgaria. Papers of the International Conference, Sofia, 1–3 October 1998*. Sofia: St Kliment Ohridski University Press.

Talmy, L. (1985, 1995, 2002) 'Lexicalisation patterns: semantic structure in lexical form', in T. Shopen (ed.): 57–149.

Talmy, L. (2000) *Toward a Cognitive Semantics*, Cambridge, MA: MIT Press.

Taylor, J. (1989) *Linguistic Categorization*. Oxford: Clarendon Press.

Thomas, J. (1995) *Meaning in Interaction*. London and New York: Longman.

Thompson, G. (1996; 2nd edition 2003) *Introducing Functional Grammar*. London: Edward Arnold.

Thompson, S.A. (1985) 'Grammar and written discourse: initial v. final purpose clauses in English'. *Text* 5: 55–84.

Thompson, S.A. (2002) '"Object complements" and conversation towards a realistic account'. *Studies in Language*, 26–1 (2002): 125–164.

Thompson, S.A. and A. Mulac (1991) 'The discourse conditions for the use of the complementizer *that* in conversational English'. *Journal of Pragmatics* 15: 237–251.

Toolan, M. (1992) 'Token and value: a discussion', *Occasional Papers in Systemic Linguistics*, vol. 6: 85–98.

Ungerer, F. and H-J. Schmid (1997) *An Introduction to Cognitive Linguistics*. London: Longman.

Van Dijk, T. (1979) 'Pragmatic conjunction'. *Journal of Pragmatics* 3: 447–456.

Ventola, E. (ed.) (2000) *Discourse and Community. Doing Functional Linguistics*, Language in Performance 21. Tübingen: Gunter Narr Verlag.

Weber, Elizabeth (1993) *Varieties of Questions in English Conversation*. Amsterdam and Philadelphia: John Benjamins.

Widdowson, Henry G. (1997) 'The use of grammar, the grammar of use', in *Functions of Language*, 4.2 (1997): 145–168.

INDEX

Terms in brackets are (explanation or equivalent) or [category]; a stroke means either/or. Page numbers in italics show diagrams.

Index written by
Angela Downing and Gerard M-F. Hill 2005

SERIES FROM ROUTLEDGE

Routledge Applied Linguistics

Series Editors: Chris Candlin & Ronald Carter

Routledge Applied Linguistics is a series of comprehensive resource books, providing students and researchers with the support they need for advanced study in the core areas of English language and Applied Linguistics.

Each book in the series guides readers through three main sections, introductions, influential readings and tasks and research exercises. Throughout the books, topics are revisited, extended, interwoven and deconstructed, with the reader's understanding strengthened by tasks and follow-up questions.

Titles in the series so far include:
Intercultural Communication by Holliday, Hyde & Kullman
Translation by Hatim & Munday
Grammar and Context by Hewings & Hewings
Second Language Acquisition by de Bot, Lowie & Verspoor
Corpus-Based Language Studies by McEnery, Xiao & Tono

For further information, please visit
www.routledge.com/linguistics

SERIES FROM ROUTLEDGE

Routledge English Language Introductions

Series Editor: Peter Stockwell   Series Consultant: Ronald Carter

Routledge English Language Introductions cover core areas of language study and are one-stop resources for students. Assuming no prior knowledge, books in the series offer an accessible overview of the subject, with activities, study questions, sample analyses, commentaries and key readings.

Titles in the series so far include:
Sociolinguistics by Peter Stockwell
Pragmatics and Discourse by Joan Cutting
Grammar and Vocabulary by Howard Jackson
Psycholinguistics by John Field
World Englishes by Jennifer Jenkins
Practical Phonetics and Phonology by Beverley Collins & Inger Mees
Stylistics by Paul Simpson
Language in Theory by Mark Robson & Peter Stockwell
Child Language by Jean Stilwell Peccei

For further information, please visit
www.routledge.com/linguistics